Expression	Name	Description
$n!$	factorial	product of first n integers, $\prod_{i=1}^{n} i$, $n \geq 1$; $0! = 1$
$\binom{n}{j}$	combinations	$\dfrac{n!}{j!(n-j)!}$; the number of combinations of n things taken j at a time
$\begin{cases} f, \text{ if } p \\ g, \text{ if } q \\ \cdots \\ h, \text{ otherwise} \end{cases}$	conditional	At most one of the boolean expressions is true. The value is: **if** p **then** f **else if** q **then** g ... **else** h.
$\lvert f \rvert$	absolute value	$\lvert f \rvert =$ **if** $f < 0$ **then** $-f$ **else** f
$\lvert S \rvert$	set size	the number of elements in the set S
$f \approx g$	approximately	f is roughly equal to g
$f \ll g$	much less	f is very small compared to g
$f \gg g$	much greater	f is very large compared to g
$\log_b f$	logarithm	x such that $f = b^x$; $\log_b f = (\log_b c) \times \log_c f$
$\lg f, \log f, \ln f$	logarithms	logarithms to the base $b = 2$, 10, and e, resp.
e	2.718281828 . . .	base of the "natural logarithms"
$\infty, -\infty$	infinity	values larger and smaller than any others, resp.
$\lfloor f \rfloor$	floor	the largest integer not larger than f
$\lceil f \rceil$	ceiling	the smallest integer not less than f
F_i	Fibonacci series	$F_0 = 0, F_1 = 1, F_i = F_{i-1} + F_{i-2}$ for $i > 1$
H_n	harmonic series	$H_n = \sum_{i=1}^{n} \dfrac{1}{i} \approx \ln n$
H	entropy	A measure of information content. For a set of probabilities p_i, the entropy is $H = -\Sigma_i p_i \lg p_i$. (p. 83)
$\Pr(p)$	probability	Probability that p is true. $\Pr(p \text{ and } q) = \Pr(p) \times \Pr(q)$. $\Pr(p \text{ or } q) = \Pr(p) + \Pr(q) - \Pr(p \text{ and } q)$.
$A[l..h]$	subsequence	$A[l]$, $A[l+1]$, ..., $A[h]$ (p. 21)
ddd_{16}	hexadecimal	digit string ddd is an integer in base 16 (p. 42)
ddd_2	binary	digit string ddd is an integer is base 2 (p. 54)
$\text{loc}(v)$	location	the address where variable v is stored (p. 112)
ε	empty string	a string of length zero (p. 139)
$\text{level}(t)$	node level	Where t is a node in a tree: The level of the root node is zero; all other nodes have level one greater than their parent (p. 218).
$\text{height}(T)$	tree height	Where T is a tree: An empty tree has undefined height; the height of a nonempty tree is the largest level number for any of its nodes
$f(n) = O(g(n))$	"big-oh"	As n increases, $f(n)$ grows no faster than $g(n)$ (p. 309).
$f(n) = o(g(n))$	"little-oh"	As n increases, $f(n)$ grows more slowly than $g(n)$ (p. 309).

Data Structures
in Pascal

Little, Brown Computer Systems Series

Data Structures in Pascal

Edward M. Reingold
University of Illinois at Urbana-Champaign

Wilfred J. Hansen
Carnegie-Mellon University

Little, Brown and Company

Boston   Toronto

Library of Congress Cataloging-in-Publication Data

Reingold, Edward M., 1945–
    Data structures in Pascal.

    (Little, Brown computer systems series)
    Includes index.
    1. Data structures (Computer science) 2. PASCAL
(Computer program language) I. Hansen, Wilfred J.
II. Title. III. Series.
QA76.9.D35R443   1986   005.7'3   85-19874
ISBN 0-316-73931-6

Library of Congress Catalog Card No. 85-19874

ISBN 0-316-73931-6

9 8 7 6 5 4 3 2 1

ALP

Published simultaneously in Canada
by Little, Brown & Company (Canada) Limited

Printed in the United States of America

The cover is a reproduction of the first panel of the triptych *Three Trees* by Karel
Appel, reproduced by permission of Karel Appel.

Acknowledgment

Figures 8.1–8.13, 8.15: From Reingold/Nievergelt/Deo, *Combinatorial Algorithms: Theory and Practice,* © 1977, pp. 280, 282, 284, 285, 291, 292, 293,
296, 300, 304, 306, and 315. Reprinted by permission of Prentice-Hall, Inc.,
Englewood Cliffs, New Jersey.

To our parents, without whom
this book (and we) would not have been

Preface

I had as soon it said that I used words employed before.

Pensees 22, Pascal

Pascal's remark above seems fitting as we finish revising our earlier work, *Data Structures* (1982), into Pascal, the language most widely used for teaching data structures. Aside from this translation from a ''generic'' programming language to Pascal, and major improvements in Chapters 1, 2, 3, and 6, we have made few changes. We have added, however, a new section in Chapter 7 and an Appendix that lists the Pascal functions and mathematical notations used in the book. With these revisions, the first three sections of Chapter 2 may still be subsumed in some curricula by an assembler language course, but Section 2.4 should be covered in a data structures course.

Many exercises have been added and revised, especially in Chapter 6. The more than 600 exercises are an integral part of the book: Many offer important details, extensions, and alternatives; *all* offer opportunities to absorb the techniques of design and analysis necessary for the more difficult problems that arise in practice. Readers are strongly urged to read and attempt all exercises referred to in the text.

We have used some functions that are not in standard Pascal and have also extended Pascal by replacing the occasional unenlightening detail with a descriptive phrase in quotation marks. We have chosen traditional mathematical typography for programs rather than the limited character set presently available on most computers. All Pascal code was checked for syntactic accuracy with the *pc* Pascal compiler on UNIX* 4.2BSD as distributed by SUN Microsystems.

This edition is the first publication effort to take advantage of the Andrew

---

*UNIX is a trademark of AT&T Bell Laboratories.

system, an advanced workstation environment for programming and publishing developed by the Information Technology Center, a group jointly sponsored by Carnegie-Mellon University and the IBM Corporation. Andrew's capabilities let the principal reviser (WJH) work far more quickly than with older technologies. We are indebted to the sponsors and developers of Andrew for their support.

We gratefully acknowledge the comments and contributions of reviewers and instructors across the country who shared with us their reactions and those of their students to the original version of this text. We also want to thank Ruth N. Reingold for translating and updating the solutions manual.

W.J.H., E.M.R.
May 28, 1985

Preface to
the Original Edition

I saw, when at his word the formless mass,
This world's material mould, came to a heap:
Confusion heard his voice, and wild uproar
Stood ruled, stood vast infinitude confin'd;
Till at his second bidding darkness fled,
Light shone, and order from disorder sprung.

Paradise Lost,   John Milton

All information processed by a computer is ultimately encoded as a sequence of bits; the specialized field of data structures considers how to impose order and structure on those bits so that the encoded information is readily available and easy to manipulate. This field thus includes the design, implementation, and analysis of structures and techniques for information processing at all levels of complexity—from individual bits, characters, and words to aggregates such as records and files, and from abstract structures such as stacks, trees, and graphs to algorithms for searching, sorting, and storage management.

Data structures are central to computer science in general and to the discipline of programming in particular. In the more analytic areas of computer science, appropriate data structures have often been the key to significant advances in the design of algorithms. Their role in programming is no less profound: in most cases, once the appropriate data structures are carefully defined, all that remains to be done is routine coding. A comprehensive understanding of data structure techniques is thus essential in the design of algorithms and programs for all but the simplest applications.

Where there is such practical importance, college courses and textbooks are sure to follow. Since the publication of *Curriculum 68* by the Association for Computing Machinery in 1968, a course in data structures has become a core requirement in virtually every undergraduate and graduate program in computer science. A number of texts have appeared, which by now seem outdated or inadequate. Moreover, in our teaching we have adopted a number of approaches as preferable to those in most texts. In the present text, we have assembled a core of material that is unlikely to be supplanted or revised by further research.

Organization. The chapters are organized in increasing degree of complexity and abstraction, so each can be based on earlier ones. Throughout the book, for each abstract structure we emphasize its conceptual identity as a set of operations and its possible implementations in terms of the lower level structures already discussed.

Chapter 1 introduces the algorithmic and mathematical notations we employ throughout the book by discussing a sample table search problem. This discussion also serves to show the reader the scope of the techniques presented in later chapters. Chapter 2 discusses elementary data objects at the machine level—integers, characters, and so on—and how they are represented in bits (in some curricula this material is covered in a different course; if so, it can be freely omitted without interfering with later chapters). Chapter 3 then considers primitive data structures composed of aggregates of primitive objects. It shows how structures such as arrays, records, and pointers are represented in machines and in typical high-level programming languages.

Building on this basis, Chapter 4 presents material on lists, their various implementations, and their applications to, for example, stacks and queues, sparse matrix representation, and graph representation. Chapter 5 discusses trees in similar fashion: implementations and applications. These two chapters form the core of the course, presenting between them the most important tools in the design of data structures.

The next three chapters cover various more specialized problems that have wide applicability. Chapter 6 examines the techniques used to allocate and deallocate storage, Chapter 7 examines the organization of data for efficient search, and Chapter 8 examines techniques for sorting.

The material in this book is more than sufficient for a one-semester course in data structures; we have provided enough to fill a two quarter course. By choosing only the first five chapters and selected material from the rest, the instructor could cover most important topics in a single quarter, while a semester would allow the inclusion of important additional topics. A two-semester course might include discussion of the more important exercises as well as outside reading to supplement their exposition.

Presentation. Our presentation is unique in several ways. We present only a carefully chosen fraction of the material available but supplement it with a wide variety of exercises, many of which lead the student to discover interesting alternatives. The more complex exercises and those requiring advanced techniques are marked with a ★.

No single book or course can successfully discuss all known data structures and algorithms; far too many minor variants have been devised for special purposes. Rather than an encyclopedic catalog, we present the *art* of designing data structures to prepare students to devise their own special-purpose structures for problems they will encounter.

Examples illustrating the techniques presented have been selected from many different application areas, in order to indicate the importance and ubiquity of data structures. In selecting examples and applications for presentation, we have taken care to keep the presentations self-contained and to avoid undue digressions.

Our presentation is machine and programming language independent. We use **if-then-else, while-do, repeat-until,** and **case** for flow of control, and we have chosen a functional notation for reference to the fields of a record. In this way our notation is readily understood and unambiguous, but unencumbered by the syntax of any specific language.

The presentation has been organized to be clear and interesting to both undergraduate and graduate students. The material covered is accessible to students who have completed an introductory programming course.

We recognize that the student must eventually be able to choose among implementations on the basis of the analyses of the behavior of the corresponding algorithms, but it is beyond the scope of this book to teach any but a few of the basic mathematical techniques of algorithm analysis. We have skirted this issue in part by giving brief sketches of the methods of analysis for certain key algorithms, but mainly by just summarizing the results of analysis for most algorithms. Where mathematical arguments have been unavoidable, we have emphasized the intuition behind the argument.

We have not cluttered the presentation with involved discussion of the origins of the various techniques, except where such discussions are necessary to put the material in proper perspective. The annotated bibliography that concludes each chapter provides sources for students interested in deeper treatments of the topics.

ACKNOWLEDGMENTS

No good textbook can be written in a vacuum. Without the comments and suggestions of critical readers, the authors' impatience would introduce many errors and careless presentations.

We are fortunate to have had the benefit of comments from a number of critical readers, some voluntary (colleagues and reviewers) and some involuntary (students). All added immeasurably to this book, but it is with special gratitude that we thank Amitava Bagchi, Marcia Brown, and Nachum Dershowitz for the time they spent in looking at the manuscript and making comments about it.

A very special acknowledgment is due John S. Tilford who, in writing the very complete solution manual available for this text, suggested innumerable improvements in the presentation.

E.M.R.
W.J.H.

TO THE READER

Si qua videbuntur chartis tibi, lector, in istis
    sive obscura nimis sive Latina parum,
non meus est error: nocuit librarius illis
    dum properat versus adnumerare tibi.
quod si non illum sed me peccasse putabis,
    tunc ego te credam cordis habere nihil.
"Ista tamen mala sunt." quasi nos manifesta negemus!
    haec mala sunt, sed tu non meliora facis.

Epigrams, II, viii, Martial

Contents

xiii

Data Structures
in Pascal

Chapter 1

Concepts
and Examples

So she went on, wondering more and more at every
step, as everything turned into a tree the moment
she came up to it.

Through the Looking Glass, Lewis Carroll

D*ata, data structures,* and *data bases* must certainly be related since all refer to "data." Distinguishing between these terms will be useful as we start an exploration of the field of data structures. We will see that one oversimplified relationship is that *data structures organize data for use in data bases.*

What is *data*? The answer "numbers and words" is not enough; data values must be organized and have context. Dizzy Dean loved to visit radio shows and volunteer to give the baseball scores. The host generally agreed eagerly, but would be surprised to hear only: "3 to 5, 4 to 1, and an exciting 7 to 6." These values are organized and have context as scores, but still fall short of being data. Although Dean's listeners might have been content to know the teams, we today would remain unenlightened unless we also know the date of the games.

Often we can organize data values and give them context in terms of a table of *attributes* for *objects.* Table 1.1 shows four such tables for an imaginary corporation. By themselves the values 4750 and 7000 are not data, but in the context of the Budget they are the proposed expenditures for the Sort Package and Visitor Log, respectively. Other attributes for the Sort Package include its budget line number, the responsible department, and the percent increase from last year's budget.

We can ask questions—or *queries*—of organized data. Questions like: How much is budgeted for the Visitor Log? What is the total budget of the department responsible for the Sort Package? Which department has the highest average salary? The answering of such questions is crucial to conduct of business. Mundane matters of paying the right people the right amount and complex decisions about what product lines to pursue for the next decade all depend on the ability to get good answers.

1

Departments

No.	Name	Supervisor	Personnel
37	Information Systems	(R. S. Teague)	(P. Larson,...)
52	Executive Suite	(H. R. Ahner)	(R. Stocks,...)

Budget

No.	Name	Dept.	Amount	Increase (%)
37–291.5	Sort Package	(37)	4750	4
52–153	Visitor Log	(52)	7000	15

Employees

No.	Name	Dept.	Salary	Hire Date
1728	H. R. Ahner	(52)	65,200	5/28/79
1967	R. S. Teague	(37)	54,360	4/11/67
2053	P. Larson	(37)	13,200	10/30/81
2271	R. Stocks	(52)	25,600	1/1/82

Visitor Log

Date	Time	Min.	Visited	Visitor	Budget Item	Topic
4/1/84	11:30	13	(Ahner)	W. Clout	(37-291.5)	Better sort
4/1/84	11:55	86	(Ahner)	A. Bennet	(52-153)	Improved log

Table 1.1

Extract from a data base for a corporation. Values in parentheses are references from one table to another; data structure techniques implement such references. (See Exercise 5 for an introduction to the issues involved.)

A data base is a collection of sets of data organized *logically* and *physically* so they can be searched to respond to queries. The logical organization describes what objects are represented in the various tables and what attributes are stored for each. Relationships among the tables are carefully determined so values such as department numbers have the same definition in different tables. One way to sketch these relationships is illustrated in Figure 1.1. When the logical organization is properly done, a data base remains adaptable to the solution of a wide range of queries, including those not originally anticipated. Correct logical organization also simplifies the maintenance problem so data is consistent and timely. We will, however, have nothing to say in this text about logical organization of data bases.

The physical organization of a data base is the choice of data structures to store the data and provide references from each item to related items. Data bases are usually stored on disks or other memory external to the computer itself. Some of the techniques in later chapters are applicable to external storage, but most are for directly addressable, internal memory. As such they are important in many of the algorithms for dealing with data from data bases, after the data have been read in from secondary storage.

Data structures are of crucial importance, not only in data base implementation,

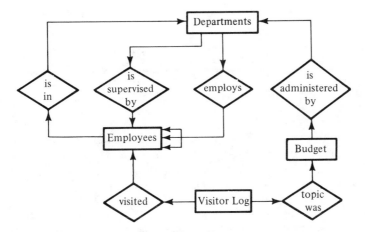

Figure 1.1
Relationships within the data base of a corporation. Each rectangle is a type of object for which attributes are stored; diamonds are references from one object to another. The object at the tail of the arrow has references to objects of the type at the head.

but also in most other programs. The correct choice of data structure for a problem can make a difference of hours or days in the running time of a program. Even when computer time is cheap, a slow response can be frustrating and costly for those awaiting it.

The two most basic data structures are lists and trees, the topics of Chapters 4 and 5. A list is a sequentially organized collection of items; in processing it we progress from one item to the next. A tree is a collection organized hierarchically like an organization chart or a genealogy.

What are some typical applications of data structures? Consider the following examples, all of which occur in later chapters.

A telephone directory is a quintessential data base: the objects are telephone lines and their attributes are name, number, and address. The directory appears on paper as a list in order by a *key*, the name attribute. People do not scan it sequentially and computer programs cannot either if they are to respond to queries quickly.

A coding scheme like the Dewey decimal system or Morse code can be represented as a tree. As we read a symbol written in the code each character distinguishes among a number of alternatives. If a Morse symbol starts with dot and dash, it is either an A (• —) or it branches between two subtrees, one containing R (• — •) and the other containing W (• — —), P (• — — •), and J (• — — —).

Many numerical applications require enormous matrices most of whose entries are zero. To allocate space for the whole matrix would be costly in any system, and time-consuming as well in a virtual memory environment. Instead, a data structure is chosen where the objects are the nonzero elements and their attributes are value and location. For manipulation each element is placed on two lists: one of all elements in the same row and one of all elements in the same column.

Compilers transform arithmetic expressions into a tree form with each operator having its operands as subtrees. Then code can be compiled recursively for the subtrees before generating code for the operator and the precise implementation of the operator can depend on the nature of the operands.

Operands in the compiler tree are represented by references to objects. One attribute of each identifier object is the address of the location (or "variable") that will hold the value for the identifier during program execution.

To store the identifiers of a program, compilers use *hash tables* rather than either lists or trees. In a hash table data structure, each identifier string is arithmetically transformed to produce an address in the hash table. The correct entry can then be found by scanning through a small subset of the identifiers.

Graphic imagery is vital to presenting information comprehensibly. Lists are a key tool in representing graphs (networks): one list element for each point or line and sublists for subgraphs. In an engineering drawing a subgraph may be a wheel, a switch, or a transistor. In a book layout a subgraph may be a section, a paragraph, a figure, or an equation.

An operating system uses lists to manage its resources: memory, processes, tape units, disk files, and so on. When a resource is allocated from the unused pool to a particular job, an attribute block for it is moved from one list to another.

Common to most data structure problems is the notion of search. After all, simply recording a piece of data and parroting it back requires little structure. The examples above show just some of the variety of searches: look up a phone number, find the letter for a Morse code sequence, find a sparse matrix element, find the attributes of an identifier, find resources to meet a request. So important is the problem that we devote all of Chapter 7 to it and much of the remainder of this chapter.

Exercises

1. Typical weather forecasting systems subdivide a region into sectors with the assumption that the weather is uniform throughout each sector and can be described by a set of attributes. What attributes would you choose? What is a reasonable

sector size? With these choices, how many data values must be stored to represent the 10^8 square miles of the earth's surface? Discuss the advantages and disadvantages of allowing the sectors within a region to have different sizes.

2. Sometimes it is difficult to distinguish an object from its representations. A computer program, for instance, can have many different physical representations. List five. Define "computer program."

3. The United States Internal Revenue Service has proposed to give auditors on-line access to the past three year's tax returns for each individual they deal with. Estimate the average number of data values in a tax return. How many disk drives of five billion bytes each would be required to keep three tax returns for each of the ten million people most likely to be audited? At one hundred thousand dollars per disk drive, what is the average storage cost for each audit if half the candidates are audited?

4. Consider a query to the data base of Table 1.1 to find the department with the most budget requests that were above average in percentage increase from the prior year. Which subtables and attributes would be examined to satisfy this query? In what order?

5. The visitor log data base in Table 1.1 contains a reference to the budget item discussed. This can be implemented as the item number or as a reference to the cabinet, drawer, folder, and page where details are recorded. What are the advantages and disadvantages of each, considering space, ease of access to the data, and keeping it up-to-date.

6. What data bases might a college or university implement? List the data bases you would scan and the queries you would want to make to work on each of these problems:

   (a) How can we give raises when total income has not grown?

   (b) Should we limit the number of faculty given tenure?

   (c) Have academic standards changed? Is there grade inflation or deflation or has the quality of students changed?

   (d) Shall we build a new building for the Computer Science Department?

1.1 DATA STRUCTURES

What do we mean by the term *data structure*? In this section we first give a formal definition and two examples, then show how data structure concepts help avoid errors, and finally show that the definition implies a hierarchy that leads to an organization for the remainder of the book.

A data structure is an *encapsulation* of a set of operations that the remainder of the program calls on to manipulate some portion of its data. Therefore we describe the external appearance of a particular data structure by saying what operations, or functions, the other parts of the program can ask it to perform. With the data structure of integers the operations are familiar: addition, subtraction, multiplication, division, comparison, assignment. When the data structure is an entire data base, the operations refer to objects: create a new object, change the attribute values of an object, search for an object with given values for its attributes.

Internally a data structure manipulates data in the form of more primitive data objects. For example, an integer value is a collection of bits and a data base object is a collection of the values of its attributes. These more primitive objects are managed in a lower level data structure, which, to avoid confusion, we call a *storage structure*. We thus define a data structure as having these three components:

A set of *function definitions*: each function is an operation defined on values in the data structure.

A *storage structure*: a representation of values in the data structure. It is an organization of values implemented in one or more lower level data structures, as specified by *relations* among those values.

A set of *algorithms*, one for each function: each algorithm describes how to examine and modify the storage structure to achieve the result defined for its function.

The function definitions encapsulate the data structure; they isolate implementation of the data structure from construction of the rest of the program. Together, the function definitions define the externally observable behavior of the data structure, while the storage structure and algorithms are the internal details. The latter can be changed without modifying routines that call upon the functions. Figure 1.2 presents a schematic representation of this definition.

To illustrate our definition of a data structure, consider a very simple example we can call *Array20*. The data structure will store twenty *real* values under subscripts 1 to 20. If we define the data type *range20*

> **type**
> > *range20* = 1..20;

then the two functions of *Array20* are

> **procedure** *storeArray20*(*value*: *real*; *subscript*: *range20*);
> > {Associates value *value* with subscript number *subscript*.}
> > *forward*;
> **function** *retrieveArray20*(*subscript*: *range20*): *real*;
> > {Returns the value most recently associated with *subscript*.}
> > *forward*;

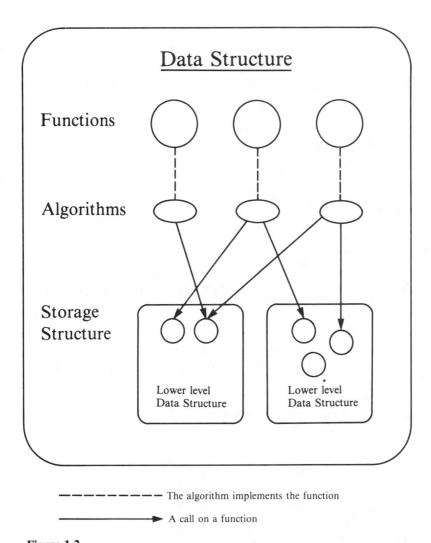

Figure 1.2
The components of a data structure. Algorithms in higher data structures call the functions encapsulated in this data structure just as the algorithms here call functions encapsulated within the lower data structures chosen to implement the storage structure. No details are shown for the lower data structures because their functions are the only parts visible externally.

Since we are using Pascal notation for algorithms, we specify functions by writing a header for a Pascal function or procedure together with a comment describing the behavior of the function. Note that in Pascal some "functions" are implemented as procedures. This is because the term "function" in the definition of data structures refers to a mathematical object, a general mechanism for operating on a specified set of operands to produce a value. (In the case of a procedure, the empty value is "produced.") We have tried to make it clear from context below which definition of "function" is meant by each use of the term.

Storage structures are specified as Pascal declarations with comments. For the storage structure of *Array20*, we make the unusual choice of twenty *real* variables. (Chapter 3 will present the usual storage structure for arrays.)

> **var**
> > {Storage for *Array20*: location *A1* contains the value associated with subscript value 1, *A2* contains the value for 2, ... , *A20* contains the value for 20}
> > > *A1, A2, A3, A4, A5, A6, A7, A8, A9, A10, A11,*
> > > *A12, A13, A14, A15, A16, A17, A18, A19, A20: real*;

Algorithms are described by writing procedure or function bodies to fit the headers that specify the function definitions. With *A1... A20* as a storage structure the algorithms for the two *Array20* functions are straightforward, but rather tedious:

> **procedure** *storeArray20*{(*value: real*; *subscript: range20*)};
> > {Associates value *value* with subscript number *subscript*.}
> **begin**
> > **if** *subscript* = 1 **then** *A1* := *value*
> > **else if** *subscript* = 2 **then** *A2* := *value*
> >
> > > . . .
> >
> > **else if** *subscript* = 20 **then** *A20* := *value*
> > **else** *Error*
> **end**;

> **function** *retrieveArray20*{(*subscript: range20*): *real*};
> > {Returns the value most recently associated with *subscript*.}
> **begin**
> > **if** *subscript* = 1 **then** *retrieveArray20* := *A1*
> > **else if** *subscript* = 2 **then** *retrieveArray20* := A2
> >
> > > . . .
> >
> > **else if** *subscript* = 20 **then** *retrieveArray20* := *A20*
> > **else** *Error*
> **end**

where *Error* performs some appropriate action. These routines exemplify encapsulation: *Array20*, *storeArray20*, and *retrieveArray20* can be changed without affecting the program utilizing the data structure (Exercise 3).

Notice a distinction between the integer data structure and *Array20*. A program may contain many different *integer* variables but can have only one *Array20* because there is only one set of *A1... A20*. We call the integer data structure "multiple-use" while *Array20* is "single-instance." The choice between these must be made in any data structure design. Multiple-use data structures are somewhat more complex but can have as many instances as desired in any given application program.

It is usually possible to generalize a single-instance data structure into multiple-use. If a program wanted multiple *Array20*'s, a type declaration could be arranged (probably with records, as described in Chapter 3):

type
      MuArray = "some suitable storage structure";

We need not know the details of the *MuArray* data type because values of this type are created, accessed, and destroyed solely by the functions of the data structure. As a further extension, we arrange that the creation of a *MuArray* be able to specify the size of the desired array. (Chapter 6 will consider how this might be implemented.)

function *createMuArray*(*size*: *integer*): *MuArray*;
        {Create an instance of the storage structure for a new *MuArray* with
        size elements of type *real*.}
    forward;

procedure *releaseMuArray*(**var** *A*: *MuArray*);
        {Discard a particular instance of *MuArray*. Variable *A* is set to in-
        dicate it no longer refers to a *MuArray* value.}
    forward;

procedure *storeMuArray*(**var** *A*: *MuArray*; *value*: *real*; *subscript*: *range20*);
        {Associates *value* with subscript number *subscript* in *A*.}
    forward;

function *retrieveMuArray*(*A*: *MuArray*; *subscript*: *range20*): *real*;
        {Return the value most recently associated in *A* with *subscript*.}
    forward;

In a program where these declarations are in force, variables can be declared of type *MuArray*. Thereafter the above functions are utilized to create *MuArray* values, use them for storing *real* values, and ultimately discarding the *MuArray* value.

Even with such simple examples as *Array20* and *MuArray* we can discuss how data structure encapsulation avoids the problems that cause incorrect programs. The first problem is that programs can become large, and if a program's size increases without careful planning, interactions between remote pieces develop. One routine may set a variable used by another or a collection of seemingly unrelated routines will have dependencies that require that they be called in some specific sequence. This might happen in *Array20* if the application needed a special test to prevent assigning values that are too small. If *storeArray20* were modified to make the test, the data structure would be specific to that application and revisions to it or the application would have a higher chance of error. Data structure design reduces the complexity of sheer size by shaping the program as a collection of small data structures, each small enough to be maintained without fear of error.

One way dependencies develop between routines is for one routine to have a *side effect*, that is, to assign a value to a variable that is not part of the storage structure for its data structure. If some routine outside *Array20* modified *A2*, it would be hard to revise *Array20* to utilize some other storage structure, say values of larger precision. When data structures are carefully designed, there is less tendency for side effects to arise in the first place; and when they do their presence is made explicit in the description of the functions and relations among values.

Relationships also help avoid errors from *redundant values*. Such redundancies arise in storage structure designs where more than one value refers to a given object. Redundancy can arise from attempts at efficiency, such as storing a list of the employees in each department and also storing the number of employees. If the list is updated without modifying the number, incorrect results may follow. When the redundant values refer to created data values like *MuArray*, the outcome can be even worse. Suppose a higher data structure executes

$$A := createMuArray\ (30);$$
$$B := A$$

What does the second assignment mean? If *B* is a copy of the entire array then changes to *A* will not affect *B*; but if it means that both *A* and *B* refer to the same copy of a *MuArray*, then any changes to either will affect both. For each instance, only one of these interpretations is correct, but if the choice is hidden within the algorithms of the *MuArray* data structure, the higher data structure will suddenly be incorrect when *MuArray* is changed. This problem is minimized by careful definition of data structures and careful specification of the relations within data structures. By adopting the practice of always specifying redundancies clearly, you will be less likely to introduce them in the first place and more likely to build and maintain them without error where they are needed.

A final source of errors will become more apparent after Chapter 6 where we discuss releasing the storage for objects. If the storage for an object is released, it is an error to refer to that object. After setting *A* and *B* as above, *releaseMuArray(A)* modifies *A* to indicate it no longer refers to a valid *MuArray* when there is just one *MuArray*, but *B* may be unmodified. A subsequent call *storeMuArray(B, 3, 5.0)* would be erroneous because *B* would no longer refer to a *MuArray*. This form of error can only be dealt with by careful attention to temporal relationships. For instance, a data structure utilizing *MuArray* could choose to call *createMuArray* only at its start and *releaseMuArray* only at its end, so no value would ever become invalid.

In all the above ways, and more, the notions of encapsulated data structures aid in construction of correct programs.

Data structure notions also imply a hierarchy that lends an organization to this book. This hierarchy arises because the storage structure component of a data structure is described in terms of another, more primitive, data structure. For instance, bits are the storage structure for the word data structure; words are the storage structure for the array and record data structures; arrays and records serve in turn as the storage structures for numerous other data structures; and so on and on. This hierarchy allows us to describe our book concisely as progressing from the most primitive data structures to higher levels. As we progress upward, however, the exposition will turn increasingly from the notion of data structures as storage structures to the use of data structures in algorithms for important problems.

We begin in Chapter 2 with a study of the encoding of individual data items within the bits, bytes, and words offered by computer hardware. A word itself is a data structure based on the bit as a storage structure and words in turn are the basis for a number of data structures, each with its own set of operations: integers, reals, booleans, characters, and strings.

Chapter 3 explores arrays, records, and pointers—mechanisms offered by programming languages to organize groups of words. These constructs differ in that array elements are selected by numeric subscript while record elements are selected by name. Pointers indicate the locations of records. Most of the remainder of the text will depend heavily on records and pointers.

Chapters 4 and 5, the heart of the book, describe lists and trees, the two most common data structures and the foundations for all others. Data elements can be located in a list by advancing from one element to the next. In trees, each data element offers a choice of alternate paths to get to a next element. As we will see, this choice—if we can choose correctly—will access elements in a small fraction of the time for sequential access through a list.

All data structures occupy memory, which is consequently a resource that must be managed; techniques to do so are covered in Chapter 6. List and tree manipulations are important tools in the effort to keep track of which memory is occupied with accessible data and which is not.

Trees are even more vital to the search problem in Chapter 7. Here we will be primarily showing how to find a single key by exact match in a table. The use of trees is that they can reduce the number of operations from a linear dependence on the number of keys to a logarithmic dependence. This improvement in efficiency can make feasible some computations that would otherwise be impossible.

One technique for searching is to have the table in order by the value of the keys. This can be accomplished by the sorting techniques discussed in Chapter 8. Here we will find some very clever approaches to the problem, and again tree notions will reduce the linear to the logarithmic.

Exercises

1. Specify a set of data types and functions that might be provided by a data structure for calendar dates. Include functions to compute elapsed time, compute a date at a given distance in the future, and convert between different formats. What storage structure would you use?

2. Define a data structure for dollar amounts. The data type should exclude the possibility of fractions of a cent. Include a function that divides one dollar amount by another and specify a data type for the value it returns.

3. To evaluate *storeArray20*(x, 20), twenty **if** tests are made. Rewrite the algorithm so no more than five tests are made for any subscript value. What changes would be needed in the rest of the program?

4. Addition of *integer* values returns an *integer* result in most programming languages. However, it is possible to define a set of functions for *integer* values such that rather than returning a result one of the operands is modified (just as is done in the hardware). Define such a set of functions, and use your functions to write a procedure that computes the average of the values in an array.

5. Compilers and assemblers store the identifiers they encounter in a *symbol table* as they process a program. List some attributes a symbol might have. What functions should this data structure support? Can you suggest a storage structure?

6. Suppose that integer operations were defined such that an arithmetic operation would return not an integer value but an indication of where that value was stored. How does this data structure permit two interpretations of an assignment statement? For each, show the final result of executing the assignments $b := 6$; $a := b$; $b := 5$; $c := a$.

1.2   A *TABLE* DATA STRUCTURE

To illustrate further our definition of a data structure, to show some of the programming considerations of data structures, to introduce the problem of *search,* and to provide an example for the rest of this chapter, we now describe a *table* data structure. The table will store a number of elements, each having a *key* attribute and possibly additional attributes. Although this is much like our description of a data base, our implementation will be limited: we make no consideration for storing the data outside main memory or searching for other than a match on the single key.

What functions should a table data structure provide? We must be able to put elements into the table and find out if they are there. Once an element is found, we need some way to access its attributes. Thus the set of functions will have to include:

type

>   *ElementLocation* = "an indication of the location of an element";
>> {See the discussion of *ElementLocation* in the text below.}
>   *KeyType* = "type for key attribute";
>   *AttributeName* = ("a list of names of attributes");
>   *AttributeValue* = "type for an attribute value";
>> {There will usually be more than one *AttributeValue* type}

procedure *InitTable*;
>> {Initialize table to have no elements.}
>   *forward*;

function *FindElement*(*Key*: *KeyType*): *ElementLocation*;
>> {Search table to find the element having key value *Key*}
>   *forward*;

function *EnterElement*(*Key*: *KeyType*): *ElementLocation*;
>> {Create a location in the table to store the element having key value *Key*, and initialize its key to have value *Key*}
>   *forward*;

procedure *StoreAttribute*(*xLoc*: *ElementLocation*; *Attr*: *AttributeName*;
>>   *Val*: *AttributeValue*);
>> {Store *Val* as value for attribute *Attr* for element at location given by *xLoc*}
>   *forward*;

function *RetrieveAttribute*(*xLoc*: *ElementLocation*; *Attr*: *AttributeName*):
>>   *AttributeValue*;
>> {Retrieve the value of the attribute named *Attr* from element at location *xLoc*}
>   *forward*;

Although we show *StoreAttribute* and *RetrieveAttribute* as **procedure** and **function**, our implementation below will instead be code to be inserted in-line where one of these operations is needed to store and retrieve element attributes other than the key.

Three important observations about this set of functions will apply to most other data structures. First, note that we have a function to initialize the data structure. Most data structures have some internal control variables that need to be initialized before its other functions will perform properly. Second, note that the table is not an explicit parameter to these functions. For simplicity we have chosen a single-instance set of functions rather than a multiple-use organization. In particular, the storage for the data structure is in global variables and not passed as a parameter to the function.

The third observation is that specialized data types have been introduced. *KeyType*, *AttributeName*, and *AttributeValue* are merely conveniences; by their use we avoid the need to talk about particular key and attribute types or the complexity of multi-word values or strings. (For the latter, assignment and comparison may be more involved than a single statement.) An *ElementLocation* value, however, is an entirely new kind of information; it is not itself a data value but indicates the location of data values. As an example, consider an application program that is processing a data base transaction to find the element with key value z and set its *Sum* attribute to the sum of its U and V attributes. We declare a variable to store the result of *FindElement*:

> *xLoc: ElementLocation*;

and then perform the operation with

> *xLoc* := *FindElement*(z);
> *StoreAttribute*(*xLoc*, *Sum*,
>   *RetrieveAttribute*(*xLoc*, *U*) + *RetrieveAttribute*(*xLoc*, *V*))

Variable *xLoc* retains the result of the search so *StoreAttribute* and *RetrieveAttribute* can do their work with no more than a few assignment statements.

Without *ElementLocation* values the operations of storing and retrieving attribute values could still be implemented, but less efficiently. We would not even need *FindElement* but would pass the key z itself as the first argument to *StoreAttribute* or *RetrieveAttribute*. The code fragment above would then have only the second statement; but the search for z in the table would have to be done three times, once by each attribute access routine. As we will see, a search requires a possibly lengthy loop, so it is preferable to avoid searches.

Declarations. Finding a representation for the specialized type *ElementLocation* in Pascal is part of defining the entire storage structure for *table*. To specify a storage structure we

> choose a Pascal type for each specialized type;

> define **const, type,** and **var** entries to create the variables of the storage structure; and

specify relationships that are to hold between the values of variables during execution.

In the *Array20* example the Pascal type for data values was *real*, the variables declared were *A1...A20*, and the most important relationships were that variable *A1* held the value associated with subscript value 1, *A2* held the value for subscript 2, ..., and *A20* held the value for subscript 20.

For the *table* data structure, the simplest storage structure is an array, *Table*, with one element for each key. As elements are entered, they are placed in the next available array location. To do a search, we just examine each array location in turn. Will this give a reasonable interpretation for *ElementLocation*, *StoreAttribute*, and *RetrieveAttribute*? If we choose *i* as the *ElementLocation* value for item *Table[i]*, how can that value lead us to its attribute values? The trick is to implement attributes as "parallel arrays" as shown in Figure 1.3. Here the first attribute is *Context* and its value for *Table[i]* is in *Context[i]*. Other attributes would be implemented similarly, as shown by the array for *Attribute2*. In general for this storage structure, an attribute named *Attr* is implemented as an array of that same name. So *StoreAttribute(xLoc, Attr, Val)* is written as *Attr[xLoc] := Val* and *RetrieveAttribute(xLoc, Attr)* is just *Attr[xLoc]*.

One disadvantage of using arrays for a storage structure is that we must specify a maximum size for the array before the program knows how many elements will be in the array. For this we can declare a **const** *MaxElements* with a value large enough for whatever application we have in mind. (It may have to be changed as we tailor the *table* data structure to a specific application.)

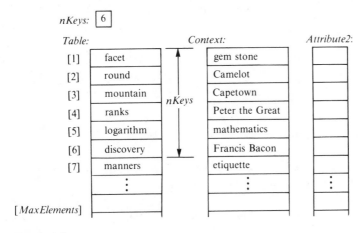

Figure 1.3
Storage Structure for *table* data structure. The string "manners" is in the array, but is not in the table because its location is outside the range 1..*nKeys*.

In addition to the maximum number of elements the array can have, there must be a way to keep track of how many elements are in the *table* at any given time. For this we declare a variable called *nKeys* and make a note that *InitTable* will have to initialize *nKeys*:

$$nKeys := 0$$

to indicate that the table starts with no elements.

Before giving the declarations for *table*, we must consider a data structure design factor that is frequently neglected with unpleasant consequences: error conditions. By their nature errors seldom occur so the fact that a program neglects them may go unnoticed for some time, perhaps even until the program is being employed on a critical task. Good data structure design and good testing procedures help protect against ignoring potential errors.

Examining the three functions for *table*, we can foresee no errors from *Init-Table*; *EnterElement* might discover that the key to be entered was already there or that there was no room in the array; and *FindElement* could easily discover that the element had not been entered. We choose to represent these errors as *Element-Location* values, since that is what is returned by the two functions. We will declare values for the identifiers *DuplicateKey*, *TableFull*, and *KeyAbsent*; to avoid conflict with legitimate values, these will be small negative integers.

The above paragraphs have now introduced all the items we need to declare for the *table* data structure; they appear as Declarations 1.1. In an application written in Pascal, these declarations would be interspersed with declarations for other data

const

    MaxElements = "a suitable maximum number of elements";
        {The following constants define error values that may be returned
        by routines.}
      TableFull = -1;   {from *EnterElement*}
    DuplicateKey = -2;   {from *EnterElement*}
      KeyAbsent = -3;   {from *FindElement*}

type

    KeyType = "data type of each key";
    ElementLocation = *KeyAbsent..MaxElements*;

var

    nKeys: *0..MaxElements*; {number of elements currently entered in table}
    Table: **array** [*1..MaxElements*] **of** *KeyType*;
    Context: **array** [*1..MaxElements*] **of packed array** [*1..40*] **of** *char*;
    Attribute2: **array** [*1..MaxElements*] **of** "data type of this attribute";

Declarations 1.1
Declarations for the *table* data structure.

structures and the main program. (A number of crucial comments are omitted here because they are included in the text above.)

Relationships. Careful identification of the relationships among the variables of a program are important to building a correct program. They aid in setting initial conditions, constructing conditional tests, ensuring that all appropriate variables have been modified in a routine, and proving the correctness of tricky pieces of code.

A fundamental relationship in any array is that values are not stored outside the allocated space. For *Table*, this relationship amounts to

$$0 \leq nKeys \leq MaxElements \tag{1.1}$$

which also states that *nKeys* will not be negative. *ElementLocation* values are constrained either to point to a valid element or to be an error indication. The precise condition on *e* when it is an *ElementLocation* value is

$$
\begin{aligned}
&1 \leq e \leq nKeys \\
&\text{or } e = TableFull \text{ or } e = DuplicateKey \text{ or } e = KeyAbsent
\end{aligned} \tag{1.2}
$$

Relationships specify "invariant conditions"—conditions that are to hold at all times during execution, except temporarily in the midst of a sequence of instructions that modify the variables involved. These conditions are important in verifying properties of programs, as we will do in the next section. They also provide a checklist when modifying values. The condition on *ElementLocation* indicates, for example, that *nKeys* must be incremented *before* storing a new key in the table, because the unincremented value is a valid *ElementLocation* value for some key already in the table.

Algorithms. The term *algorithm* usually refers to the abstract technique used to manipulate the storage structure, rather than to any specific implementation of that technique. In an actual implementation of a data structure, its associated algorithms must be expressed in some programming language. In this book we use Pascal, extending it with the operators and standard functions shown in the Appendix. Occasionally a piece of code will be more appropriately expressed in prose; we surround such text with quotation marks as we have already done in various declarations.

An algorithm may be written in a program either as a separate subroutine—**procedure** or **function**—or as a sequence of statements to be incorporated directly into the program wherever the specific data structure function is required. The three functions for *table* illustrate these three options. *InitTable* is most easily implemented as code to be directly incorporated in-line. From the storage structure design we know that its sole contents are to initialize *nKeys* to zero. Note from relationship (1.2) that as long as *nKeys* remains zero there are no valid, nonerror *ElementLocation* values. *EnterElement* and *FindElement* will be **procedure** and **function,** respectively, since only the latter returns a value.

Both *EnterElement* and *FindElement* need to determine if and where a given key might be in the table. Rather than write this code twice, we extract it to a separate function, *SearchTable*, which will be internal to the *table* data structure implementation, and whose definition we defer to the next section:

> **function** *SearchTable*(*z*: *KeyType*; **var** *zLoc*: *ElementLocation*): *boolean*;
> {Searches *Table* for the element with key *z*. If absent the
> value **false** is returned; otherwise *zloc* is set to the location
> of the element and the value **true** is returned}
> *forward*;

The routine *FindElement* is now rather straightforward; it need only check the return value from *SearchTable* to determine whether to return the element location or the error flag *KeyAbsent*:

> **function** *FindElement*(*z*: *KeyType*): *ElementLocation*;
> **var**
>   *where*: *ElementLocation*;
> **begin**
>   **if** *SearchTable*(*z*, *where*) **then**   {Is *z* in *Table*?}
>   *FindElement* := *where*   {Yes, return its location}
>   **else**
>   *FindElement* := *KeyAbsent*   {No, return error value}
> **end**

The temporary variable *where* saves the location value from *SearchTable* in case it must be returned as the value from *FindElement*. A similar variable appears in *EnterElement*, Algorithm 1.1, but solely because we must pass a parameter to *SearchTable*; its value is thereafter ignored.

A final note will illustrate the interdependence of the declarations, relationships, and algorithms we have written to implement the functions of the *table* data structure. Declared variable *nKeys* delimits the execution-time contents of *Table*, as indicated by both relationships above. We need to demonstrate that the algorithms we have written preserve the relationships: (a) *nKeys* satisfies (1.1), and (b) all *ElementLocation* values satisfy (1.2). The assignment to *nKeys* in *InitTable* gives *nKeys* a valid value. The assignment in *EnterElement* will not be executed unless *nKeys* < *MaxElements*, so incrementing it by one will also preserve (1.1). The *ElementLocation* value from *FindElement* depends on the value returned by *Search-Table*, so we must here rely on the correctness of that routine. *EnterElement*, however, can only return an error value or *nKeys*, both of which explicitly satisfy (1.2). These arguments give confidence in the correctness of the *table* data structure.

function *EnterElement(z: KeyType): ElementLocation*;
        {Store *z* in *Table* after checking for errors.}
var
     where: *ElementLocation*;   {value is ignored}
begin
    if *SearchTable(z, where)* **then**
        EnterElement := *DuplicateKey*   {found *z*, error}
    else if *nKeys* ⩾ *MaxElements* **then**
        EnterElement := *TableFull*   {no more room, error}
    else begin   {enter *z* in *Table*}
        nKeys := *nKeys* + 1;   {note new table size}
        Table[nKeys] := *z*;   {store new key}
        EnterElement := *nKeys*   {return location of new key}
    end
end

Algorithm 1.1
Implementation of the *EnterElement* function for the table data structure

Exercises

1. Suppose the keys for the table are strings. Show the contents of the storage structure variables after execution of the following calls:

        nKeys := 0;   *{InitTable}*
        e := *EnterElement*('Mother');
        e := *EnterElement*('Apple')

   What value will be returned by *FindElement*('Mother')? By *FindElement*('Pie')?

2. The error message *DuplicateKey* may be unnecessary. *EnterElement* could be defined to ensure that the element is in the table, either by finding an existing one or entering a new one. Revise the declarations and algorithms to define this alternative data structure.

3. Revise the definition of the table data structure so that instead of the variable *nKeys* there is a variable that has the subscript of the location in which to store the next entered element. What should its initial value be? Show the complete revised declarations, comments, and relationships. Show a diagram to correspond to Figure 1.3.

4. For this problem you are to define further functions for the *table* data structure. For each give the procedure or function heading and a comment describing the behavior of the function as observable by external routines.

   (a) Define a function to delete an element from the table.

   (b) Define a function that will apply some procedure to all elements in the table.

   (c) Define a pair of functions that *traverse* the table. One returns a "first" element from the table and its *ElementLocation*; the other returns the "next" element and location after a given *ElementLocation* value. What special case must be handled?

   (d) Explain why *FindElement* is unnecessary if the traverse functions (c) are provided. Why is *FindElement* preferable?

5. Define a function to note the table contents and another to restore it to a noted state. There may be *EnterElement* calls between these, but there are to be no deletions. Specify a storage structure for values used to record the state. Consider (a) the case where any prior contents can be restored at any time, and (b) the alternate case where a state can be restored only if no earlier noted state has already been restored.

6. In the *table* data structure error conditions are indicated by special *Element-Location* values. Alternatively, each function could return both the location and a status value encoding either success or one of the error conditions.

   (a) Define data types and functions for a version of *table* with status values.

   (b) Write algorithms for the functions defined in (a).

1.3 SEARCH

> Seek and ye shall find.
>
> *Matthew 7,7*

The *search* problem is to examine a collection of data elements and find one or more satisfying some criteria. We might search the phone book for a name or search a data base for all employees with more than two weeks accrued vacation. Search will be covered thoroughly in Chapter 7, but we give a brief introduction by continuing the *table* data structure example from the preceding section. There the search was to be performed by *SearchTable*, one implementation of which we give here as Algorithm 1.2. The loop in this algorithm checks each element of *Table* in turn until z is found or element *Table*[*nKeys*] is passed.

At the start of the loop body is an Assert comment:

$$1 \leq i \leq nKeys \text{ and } z \text{ is not in } Table[1 \ldots i-1] \qquad (1.3)$$

function *SearchTable*(*z*: *KeyType*; **var** *zLoc*: *ElementLocation*): *Boolean*;
        {Search for key *z* in *Table*. If found, return **true** and set *zLoc* to its
        location. Otherwise, return **false.**}
var
    i: *integer*;
    found: *boolean*;
begin
    i := 1;
    found := **false**;
    while not *found* **and** ($i \leq nKeys$) **do**
        {Assert $1 \leq i \leq nKeys$ and *z* is not in *Table*[1 ... $i-1$]}
        if *Table*[*i*] = *z* **then**
            found := **true**
        else *i* := *i* + 1;   {examine next element in *Table*}
    if *found* **then** *zLoc* := *i*;
    SearchTable := *found*
end

        Algorithm 1.2
        Search algorithm for the *Table* data structure of Section 1.2

Such a comment gives a condition that is true each time execution reaches that particular point in the program. In (1.3) we have extended Pascal's "`..`" notation to give a simple expression for a subsequence of the elements of an array. Thus the second clause of (1.3) means that *z* is not in *Table*[1], *z* is not in *Table*[2], ..., *z* is not in *Table*[$i - 1$]. Assert comments appear in most of the loops throughout this book, although not all are complete. In particular, they sometimes omit the behavior at the beginning or end of the loop.

Carefully chosen assertions can clarify the intent of programs for future readers and ease the task of making the program correct. A good assertion specifies relations among the variables being modified within the loop and their relations to other values outside the loop. The assertion states a condition has been achieved without saying how it has been achieved.

One important application of Assert comments is in proofs that programs have some desirable behavior. As an example of the technique, we can prove that *SearchTable* sets *zLoc* correctly to the location of *z* if it is in the table. Algorithm 1.2 may seem obvious to some readers; if it does to you, the following proof will seem superfluous and indeed it is only important so we can introduce the method without other complexities. However, to emphasize the importance of such proofs, we confess that developing this proof revealed two bugs in a former Pascal version of *SearchTable*.

We build the proof outward from assertion (1.3). It is true at the start of the first execution of the loop body because i is 1 and the range $1..0$ is to be understood to include no elements. [If $nKeys$ is zero, (1.3) is false, but the loop body is not executed.] If the invariant is still true for the final execution of the loop body, it is not hard to show that the algorithm sets $zLoc$ properly: If the loop exits with *found* being **true** then $Table[i] = z$ by the test preceding the setting of *found* and $zLoc$ is set to i. If *found* is **false,** the value of $zLoc$ is immaterial, but now we must show that z is not in the table. In this case, the loop can only have exited because $i > nKeys$; but the loop only increments i by one so its value at the start of the final execution of the body must have been $nKeys$. (This is also true if $nKeys = 0$ and the loop body was not executed.) When $i = nKeys$ the second clause of (1.3) becomes

$$z \text{ is not in } Table[1 \; .. \; nKeys - 1] \qquad (1.4)$$

Since *found* is **false** the **if** test must have failed on the last iteration of the loop, so we know z is not in $Table[nKeys]$. Together with (1.4) this gives us that z is not in $Table[1..nKeys]$. By condition (1.2) the only keys in the table are in $Table[1..nKeys]$, so z's absence means it is not in the table, and *SearchTable* has not failed to set $zLoc$ when it should have.

The crucial step of the proof is to show that the truth of the loop invariant is unchanged by an iteration of the loop body. (It will in fact be temporarily false at one stage of the iteration, but will be true again when the point of the Assert comment is re-encountered.) We begin by assuming that the invariant is true at the start of the body and show that it must still be true after executing the body, retesting the **while** condition and returning the next time to the assertion. To prove that the first clause of (1.3) is true the next time around note the **while** condition: the next iteration will not occr unless $i \leq nKeys$, so the upper bound on i will be met. The lower bound will continue to be met because the loop does not decrease the value of i. To prove the second clause of (1.3), observe that at the start of the body we know from (1.3) itself that z is not in $Table[1 \; .. \; i-1]$. If the **if** test succeeds, i is unchanged and so is the truth of the second clause of the invariant. The only remaining case is when the **if** test fails; but then z is not in $Table[i]$ which combines with the invariant on entry to give

$$z \text{ is not in } Table[1..i] \qquad (1.5)$$

The **else** clause increments i, and when (1.5) is restated in terms of the new value of i, it gives precisely the second clause of the invariant, which is now shown to be entirely true after an iteration through the **while** loop body.

In Algorithm 1.2, *SearchTable* examines each key in turn, a scheme that is far more time-consuming than necessary. We can reduce the time if the keys are in ascending order in the array. Then a check of the middle element of the array quickly eliminates all elements above or below the middle. Here is a sketch of the technique, which is called *binary search*:

```
function SearchSketch(z: KeyType): ElementLocation;
var
        middle: KeyType;
begin
        SearchSketch := KeyAbsent;
        "Consider entire array as the current subtable";
        while "current subtable is not empty" do begin
                middle := "key in middle of current subtable";
                if middle < z then
                        "reduce current subtable to the half above middle"
                else if middle > z then
                        "reduce current subtable to the half below middle"
                else begin {z = middle}
                        "reduce current subtable to no elements";
                        SearchSketch := "location of middle"
                end
        end
end
```

Note that each of the first two cases eliminates half the current subtable. This is considerably better than Algorithm 1.2, which eliminates only one key with each iteration. The half eliminated cannot contain z because of the ascending order of the elements in the table. When *middle* $< z$, all keys below the middle are also less than z; and similarly for ">".

Using binary search, the body of Algorithm 1.2 can be replaced with Algorithm 1.3. The Assert comment in this Algorithm extends the ".." slightly farther than before; a statement like $z < Table[x..y]$ is shorthand for asserting the truth of the sequence of statements $z < Table[x]$, $z < Table[x+1]$, ... , $z < Table[y]$.

This algorithm offers a chance for a somewhat less obvious proof than that of Algorithm 1.2. To be brief we will show here only that the assertion is still true after the branch that sets $h := m-1$. The smallest value m can have is l, which occurs when $h = l + 1$ or $h = l$. With this value of m, h is set to $l-1$ so the loop exits with *found* still **false,** so we must show that z is not in the array. But z could only have been in $Table[l..h]$ and the **if** test showed that $z < Table[m] = Table[l]$. Since the elements of *Table* are in ascending order, z is not in the table when $m = l$. Alternatively, m will have a larger value when $h-l > 2$. In this case we know from the **if** test that $Table[m]$ is greater than z and so all *Table* entries for larger subscripts must also be larger than z. Thus even for the new value assigned to h we

function *SearchTableBinary*(*z*: *KeyType*; **var** *zLoc*: *ElementLocation*):
            Boolean;
            {This function has the same description as Algorithm 1.2, but does
            its work internally with binary search.}
var
        l, h, m: integer; {0 .. *nKeys* + 1}
        found: boolean;
begin
        l := 1;
        h := *nKeys*;
        found := **false**;
        while not *found* **and** (*l* ⩽ *h*) **do begin**
                {Assert: 1 ⩽ *l* ⩽ *h* ⩽ *nKeys*, *z* > *Table*[1 .. *l* − 1], and *z* <
                Table[*h* + 1.. *nKeys*]. Thus if *z* is in *Table*, it is in *Table*[*l*..*h*].}
                m := (*l* + *h*) **div** 2;
                if *z* < *Table*[*m*] **then** *h* := *m* − 1
                else if *z* > *Table*[*m*] **then** *l* := *m* + 1
                else *found* := **true**
        end;
        if *found* **then** *zLoc* := *m*
        else *zLoc* := *l*;   {(Exercise 4)}
        SearchTableBinary := *found*
end

Algorithm 1.3
Binary search to locate a key in *Table*. Replaces Algorithm 1.2. Note that none
of the elements between *l* and *h*, inclusive, have been compared to *z*; therefore
the loop repeats even when *l* = *h*.

have *z* < *Table*[*h* + 1 .. *nKeys*], which is exactly the desired third clause of the assertion. This branch of the **if** affects neither *z* nor *l*, so it cannot affect the truth of the second clause, and the first clause is left to the reader.

The external description of Algorithm 1.3, *SearchTableBinary*, is the same as that of Algorithm 1.2, *SearchTable*, with one important addition. Because binary search requires the keys in *Table* to be in order, the insertion algorithm must ensure that they stay that way. To aid this reordering, Algorithm 1.3 is extended to return the location where a key belongs, even if not found in the array. Then Algorithm 1.4 (on page 26) is used for *EnterElement* instead of Algorithm 1.1. Before inserting the key, all larger keys are moved one position further away from the beginning of the array.

nKeys: [6]

Table:		AttributesLoc:		Context:		Attribute2:
[1]	discovery	6	[1]	gem stone		(for facet)
[2]	facet	1	[2]	Camelot		(for round)
[3]	logarithm	5	[3]	Capetown		(for mountain)
[4]	ranks	4	[4]	Peter the Great		(for ranks)
[5]	round	2	[5]	mathematics		(for logarithm)
[6]	mountain	3	[6]	Francis Bacon		(for discovery)

Figure 1.4
Storage Structure for *table* data structure with ordered key values. The *ElementLocation* value for the *i*th key is in *AttributesLoc*[*i*]; that is, the context for "discovery" is in *Context*[*AttributesLoc*[1]] = *Context*[6] = "Francis Bacon". The *AttributesLoc* values show that the keys were passed to *EnterElement* in the same order as those in Figure 1.3.

The movement of keys in Algorithm 1.4 poses a problem for implementation of *StoreAttribute* and *RetrieveAttribute*. Previously the *ElementLocation* value for the element with key z was just the index of z in the table; but when keys are moved their indexes change. It is possible to move corresponding values in *Context*, *Attribute2*, and the other attribute arrays to keep the attributes of the element with key z at the same index as z. However, this is time consuming and requires that *EnterElement* have statements to deal with all the attribute arrays. Even worse, any previously saved *ElementLocation* value is no longer valid. To solve these problems we assign an *ElementLocation* value to each element only once, when it is entered. We record this value in a subsidiary array *AttributesLoc* as shown in Figure 1.4. When keys are moved by *EnterElement*, the values in *AttributesLoc* must also be moved, as happens in Algorithm 1.4, but all other attributes can remain unmoved. The other attributes can be found because their location is recorded in the *AttributesLoc* array entry corresponding to their key.

With this storage structure, *InitTable* and the attribute scheme given for Algorithm 1.2 are unchanged. Only one line of *FindElement* must be changed; instead of returning *where*, the return value must be set by

$$FindElement := AttributesLoc[where]$$

thus getting the appropriate *ElementLocation* value for the new key.

function *EnterElementBinary*(*z*: *KeyType*): *ElementLocation*;
    {Store *z* in *Table* after checking for errors.}
var
    zLoc: *ElementLocation*;   {where *z* should go}
    i: *ElementLocation*;   {**for** loop index}
begin
    if *SearchTableBinary*(*z*, *zLoc*) **then** {already in *Table*}
        EnterElementBinary : = *DuplicateKey*
    else if *nKeys* $\geq$ *MaxElements* **then** {no more room}
        EnterElementBinary : = *TableFull*
    else begin {move upward the keys larger than *z*}
        nKeys : = *nKeys* + 1;   {new table size}
        for *i* : = *nKeys* − 1 **downto** *zLoc* **do begin**
            Table[*i* + 1] : = *Table*[*i*];
            AttributesLoc[*i* + 1] : = *AttributesLoc*[*i*]
        end;
        Table[*zLoc*] : = *z*;   {store new key}
        AttributesLoc[*zLoc*] : = *nKeys*;   {where to put attributes for *z*}
        EnterElementBinary : = *nKeys*   {return attributes location
                                          for new key}
    end
end

Algorithm 1.4
Enter a key in table organized for binary search. Replaces Algorithm 1.1. Note that it does *not* return the *zLoc* value that it receives from *SearchTableBinary*.

Before leaving binary search, we can use it as an example of one of the more useful programming techniques for data structures: recursion. The trick to writing a recursive procedure is to describe its function carefully; then we can ignore the fact of the recursion and concentrate on the function. As we will see, this trick is surprisingly similar to the technique of proving program properties by invariant expressions.

Consider Algorithm 1.5, a recursive version of the binary search in Algorithm 1.3. The inner function *RecursiveSearch* is the one that is recursive; it calls itself from two different places. Note carefully the comment describing *RecursiveSearch*. The function performed is to scan an interval of *Table*. When the **if** tests have narrowed the search to a smaller range of *Table* we can simply call *RecursiveSearch* to scan that region. This works, but there can be two problems.

The first problem to avoid here (and in any recursive routine) is an infinite loop. This is done in *RecursiveSearch* by testing first if the interval has size one or more and by ensuring that whenever a recursive call is made the size of the interval is smaller. The other problem is to ensure that all requirements are met by each call to the routine. There are two requirements here: (a) return a *boolean* value indicating

function *SearchUsingRecursion(z: KeyType;* **var** *zLoc: ElementLocation):*
Boolean;
        {This function has the same description as Algorithm 1.3,
        but does its binary search recursively.}
  function *RecursiveSearch(l, h: integer): boolean;*
           {Search for *z* in *Table* between *l* and *h*, inclusive.
           Return **true** if and only if *z* is found. Set *zLoc* to the location
           where *z* is or should go.}
           {Assert: $1 \leq l \leq h \leq nKeys$ and if *z* is in *Table*, then it is in
           Table[l..h]}
  var
      m: 1..*nKeys*;
  begin
      if $l > h$ **then begin**
            {The interval has no elements. Fail, but note where
            z belongs in *Table*.}
        zLoc := *l*;
        RecursiveSearch := **false**
     end
     else begin
        m := $(l + h)$ **div** 2;   {find middle of interval}
        if $z < Table[m]$ **then**   {search lower half of table}
           RecursiveSearch := *RecursiveSearch(l, m* $-$ 1)
        else if $z > Table[m]$ **then**{search upper half of table}
           RecursiveSearch := *RecursiveSearch(m* $+$ 1, *h*)
        else begin   {succeed and note location of key}
          zLoc := *m*;
          RecursiveSearch := **true**
        end
     end
  end;   {*RecursiveSearch*}
begin
    SearchUsingRecursion := *RecursiveSearch*(1, *nKeys*)
end   {*SearchUsingRecursion*}

Algorithm 1.5
Recursive binary search procedure

if *z* is in the table; (b) set *zLoc* to indicate where *z* is or should be. To demonstrate
that these requirements are met by every call to *RecursiveSearch*, observe that there
are four paths through the routine. The first and last of these set *zLoc* and return
appropriate values. The other two meet the requirements because they call

RecursiveSearch, which we already know to meet its requirements by any other way it can exit.

What we have just gone through in demonstrating a recursive routine should be compared with the process of proving the correctness of Algorithm 1.2. In both cases we made an invariant statement about the behavior of the program and were careful to ensure that the program preserved the truth of that invariant no matter which execution path was taken.

Is recursion worthwhile? Its use in Algorithm 1.5 can only be justified as an illustration; the function is neither simpler nor faster than the iterative version, Algorithm 1.3. Moreover, Algorithm 1.5 is an instance of *tail recursion*: the function that makes the recursive call does nothing to the value returned except return it one level higher. It is always easy to convert tail recursion to a more efficient iterative algorithm. In many cases, however, recursion can produce clearer and simpler algorithms as examples in Chapters 4 through 8 will show.

A final example of search techniques is the use of indexes to permit a space-time trade-off for data base design. Suppose we wish to be able to find names from telephone numbers, but have only an alphabetical phone directory file. We have three choices: scan the existing file with sequential search, copy and sort the file for a binary search, or create an index to the existing file. The sequential search would require a considerable amount of computing but little additional space. The copy of the file would double the space requirements but would provide fast answers. A good compromise is an index like that shown in Figure 1.5; each entry in the index contains only the telephone number and the location of the corresponding element in the main file. To find a name, the search routine first finds the telephone number in the index and utilizes the corresponding *file location* to access the entry in the main directory file. This scheme is slightly slower than using a copy of the file, but it can require considerably less space. Indeed, indexes are frequently used in data bases where elements have so many attributes that multiple copies would be impossible; in such cases it is not uncommon for a file to have indexes for numerous attributes. With this approach, however, changes to the main file must be carefully reflected in the indexes.

Exercises

1. Prove that the **while** loop in Algorithm 1.2 will always exit after a finite number of executions of the body.

2. Revise the table algorithms to eliminate "**not** *found* **and**" from the **while** loop of *SearchTable* (Algorithm 1.2). Do this by first storing the value z as a dummy key at the end of the table. Note that one location of the table must never be filled. Describe a simplification of *EnterElement* that becomes possible.

Phone Directory File

file location	name	address	number
[1]	Anderson	13 Main	977–4231
[2]	Black	27 Second Ave	964–3210
[3]	Carson	42 Elm	967–8901
[4]	Green	135 Hill	321–4567
[5]	van der Mer	3 Easy	455–1000

Index File

number	file location
321–4567	4
455–1000	5
964–3210	2
967–8901	3
977–4231	1

Figure 1.5
Example of an index for a data base.

3. The **if-then-else** of Algorithm 1.3 tests $<$ first, but could test $>$ or $=$ instead. Which of these three choices is less efficient and results in performing almost twice as many tests?

4. Suppose Algorithm 1.3 has proceeded to the point where $l = h - 1$; that is, there are just two possible elements that might be equal to z. When we consider that either of these elements might be equal to, less than, or greater than z, we have a maximum of nine possible continuations for the algorithm.

   (a) Show that four of the nine possibilities are excluded by the storage structure definition.

   (b) For each of the other five cases show the outcome of further execution. How many more times is the loop executed? To what values are l and h set in each case? What value is returned? Is $zLoc$ properly set to indicate the location where z should be?

5. The **div** in Algorithm 1.3 implies a *floor* operation in that the remainder is discarded. Suppose the statement were revised to $m := ceiling((l + h)/2)$. What changes to the remainder of the algorithm would be needed?

6. Prove that if $l > 1$ in Algorithm 1.3, then all elements with subscripts 1 through $l - 1$ are less than z.

7. It is not necessary to move the keys in Algorithm 1.4. They can be treated as any other attribute and accessed via *AttributesLoc*. In this scheme the smallest key is in *Table*[*AttributesLoc*[1]] rather than in *Table*[1]. Revise Algorithms 1.3 and 1.4 for this scheme.

8. Rewrite Algorithm 1.2 to use recursion instead of a **while** loop.

1.4   EFFICIENCY

Had we but world enough and time.

To His Coy Mistress,   A. Marvell

So far in this chapter we have shown how to define, implement, and prove correct a typical data structure. To these steps we need add one vital factor to get a clear understanding of data structures. That factor is *analysis*.

Analysis of data structure algorithms is mathematical evaluation to determine how much resource—execution time and memory space—the program can be expected to occupy. Typically, the result of the analysis depends on the amount of data; the size of *Table* depends on the maximum number of keys allowed, and the time for a search depends on how many keys are already in the table. We seek, through analysis, to understand the relation between the amount of data and the resource utilization. Do a few more data values mean only a little more cost or do they portend a cost explosion, as happens in some combinatoric algorithms? Analysis will tell us.

Practical results are not the only reason for analyzing algorithms. The work itself is intrinsically interesting, involving a wide variety of mathematical topics. Analyzing an algorithm is a way to understand that algorithm more fully and to capture its essence so as to apply the same principles to the design of other algorithms.

We consider here three tools for analyzing algorithms: expected value, operator counts, and space-time analysis.

1.4.1   Expected Value and Worst Case

A friend offers to sell you a lottery ticket that will pay you $600 if the three-digit number on it is equal to the one drawn at random next Thursday. If neither you nor your friend is to make a profit on the transaction, what price should you pay for the ticket? This sort of question launched the development of probability theory and can be answered by computing the *expected value* of the ticket. In this case, there is one chance in a thousand the ticket will pay off. This probability multiplied by the size of the payoff gives the expected value: 60 cents. Of course, no individual lottery ticket will win exactly 60 cents. This value is merely the average value of all tickets *before* the drawing and is thus the "fair market value" of a ticket. (If you can't in fact get tickets at that price, *someone* is making a profit!)

The general formula for computing an expected value depends on dissecting a situation into a number of mutually exclusive cases—say n of them—each with an individual value v_i and a probability p_i, where the sum of the probabilities is one. The expected value is then

$$\text{expected value} = p_1 v_1 + p_2 v_2 + p_3 v_3 + \cdots + p_n v_n$$
$$= \sum_{i=1}^{n} p_i v_i. \tag{1.6}$$

(Exercise 1 shows that this formula can be derived from the formula for an average.) For the lottery-ticket problem there are two cases: payoff = 600 and payoff = zilch. The probability of any particular three-digit number is $1/1000$, so the expected-value formula gives

$$\text{ticket value} = 0.999 \times 0 + 0.001 \times 600 = 0.60$$

Among the algorithms we have studied only the searches require more than a constant time for each invocation. Let us, then, compute the expected cost of a successful application of the sequential search in Algorithm 1.2. The major cost of this algorithm is the execution time for the **while** loop. (When the number of elements in the table is large enough so that the total cost is significant, the relative cost of the statements outside the loop is negligible.) The **while** loop consumes time in proportion to the number of evaluations of its boolean expression: there is one evaluation if the desired key is first, two if it is second, and so on up to *nKeys* tests for the last key in the table. Thus the cost c_i to find the ith key is proportional to i. In the absence of better information, we assume that each key in the table is equally likely, so all have probability p_i equal to $1/nKeys$. Thus writing n for *nKeys* the expected cost to find a key in the table is proportional to

$$\text{expected number of boolean evaluations}$$
$$= \sum_{i=1}^{n} p_i c_i = \sum_{i=1}^{n} \frac{1}{n} i = \frac{1}{n} \sum_{i=1}^{n} i$$
$$= \frac{n+1}{2}.$$

(See Exercise 2.) Note that the expected cost of $(n + 1)/2$ for linear search is proportional to n itself.

The expected cost of an algorithm is not the only measure of its efficiency, nor is it always the best. In many situations it is necessary to use the *worst-case* cost for an algorithm. In parallel with our discussion of the expected cost above, we have

$$\text{worst case cost} = \max_{1 \leq i \leq n} \{v_i\}.$$

For the sequential search of Algorithm 1.2, the worst-case cost is proportional to

$$\text{worst-case number of boolean evaluations} = \max_{1 \leq i \leq n} \{c_i\} = \max_{1 \leq i \leq n} \{i\} = n.$$

For the binary search of Algorithm 1.3, the cost depends on the expected number of loop executions, as shown in Section 5.3. To demonstrate the efficiency of binary search, however, it is enough to show an upper bound for the worst-case number of loop executions, because this bound is itself considerably less than the cost for sequential search. The upper bound can be derived by observing that each execution of the loop cuts the size of the current section of the array in half. Thus we have

> number of loop executions
> $\leq$ number of times n can be divided in half with a result $\geq 1/2$
> $=$ number of times to double one to reach a value greater than n
> $= l$, where l is such that $2^{l-1} \leq n < 2^l$.

But by the definition of logarithms, when $2^x = n$ we have $x = \lg n$ (where $\lg n$ is the base 2 logarithm of n). Thus

$$\text{number of loop executions} \leq \lceil \lg n \rceil$$

and the cost of binary search is at worst proportional to $\lg n$.

The above discussions have shown these proportional costs:*

> Sequential search n
> Binary search $\lg n$

For all positive values of n, $\lg n$ is smaller than n and, as Table 1.2 shows, the difference is startling for large n. Nevertheless, the cost of binary search could exceed sequential search on small tables if the cost for each loop iteration were large.

---

*As a shorthand expression the proportional cost of an algorithm is sometimes called its "order," as in "Binary search is an order $\lg n$ algorithm." We discuss this in more depth at the beginning of Chapter 7.

nKeys	n	10	20	100	200	1,000	1,000,000
Sequential search	$n/2$	5	10	50	100	500	500,000
Binary search	$\lg n$	4	5	7	8	10	20

Table 1.2
Comparison of number of loop executions for each of two search techniques when
the table size is n

Evaluation of this factor requires the operator-count techniques below (see Exercise
11 of Section 1.4.3). In practice, however, binary search has been found preferable
for twenty or more elements and not too far off for fewer elements. For under twenty
elements, though, neither approach costs enough to affect the total cost of the program.

Analysis of computer algorithms usually finds that their cost is proportional to
one of the few expressions graphed in Figure 1.6. For large n, these expressions
have the relationship

$$1 < \lg \lg n < \lg n < n < n \lg n < n^2 < n^3 < 2^n.$$

Algorithms are generally practical if their cost is proportional to any but the last of
these expressions. Costs proportional to 2^n are disastrously expensive for even moderate n.

Among the possible cost expressions listed above is the constant 1. Algorithms
with cost proportional to a constant exhibit no growth in cost no matter how the
parameter changes. One curious example of such an algorithm is a table search that
can find an alphabetic key in a fixed amount of time. Suppose keys are one letter in
length. Then the table can be an array of 26 integer values, each giving the *Element-
Location* value for one key. When keys are allowed to have two letters, the table
must have $26^2 = 676$ entries, and so on for larger maximum lengths. A table per-
mitting keys of m letters occupies space proportional to 26^m, even though the time is
still constant. Since this table consumes extra space and binary search consumes extra
time, these methods can be sensibly compared only by the space-time method presented below (see Exercise 14 of Section 1.4.3). In practice, however, both methods
are usually inferior to the hashing methods presented in Chapter 7, which have reasonable costs for both space and time.

1.4.2 Operator Counts

In some situations two alternate algorithms both have execution times with the
same proportional costs, so we must analyze their details to judge their relative merits. One suitable measure for the cost of execution is the expected number of "operators" each executes in performing its task. However, the count must include a

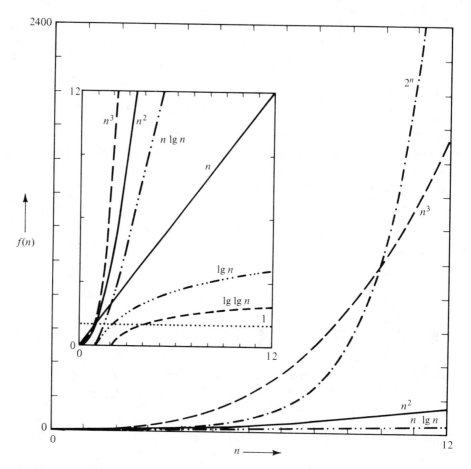

Figure 1.6
Common patterns of growth. Each line is labeled with the function that produces it.

variety of items beyond the ordinary arithmetic operations, as shown in Table 1.3. On this basis, there are ten operators in

$$\textbf{while not } found \textbf{ and } (i \leqslant nKeys) \textbf{ do}$$

$$\quad \textbf{if } Table\,[i] = z \textbf{ then } found := \textbf{true}$$

$$\quad \textbf{else } i := i + 1 \qquad\qquad (1.7)$$

The operators are: **while, not, and,** $\leqslant$, **if,** [ ], $=$, $:=$, $:=$, $+$. The assumption that all operations take the same amount of time is an approximation suitable to the op-

---

data-manipulation operators
    $+$, $<$, **and,** $\ldots$
flow-of-control operators
    if, case
    while, for, to, until   (Count once each time around loop)
miscellaneous
    $:=$, [ ], $\uparrow$
    procedure or function call
    return from a procedure or function
    each parameter passed or function value returned

Table 1.3
Categories of operators to be counted. Each of these items counts as one operator each time it is encountered during execution of a program. Field selection with $\uparrow$ will be discussed in Section 3.2.

erators we will typically encounter in data structure work: assignment, field selection, boolean expressions, and addition and subtraction. The operations of subscription, multiplication, division, and procedure call generally take longer. However, if the choice between two algorithms depends on the duration of specific operations, the analyst will probably spend more in analysis than will ever be saved during execution of the program.

Computation of the number of operator executions must consider the number of times each expression is evaluated. In a **while** loop or other loop where the body is usually executed more than once, the execution count can be a variable introduced as a parameter of the analysis. For a successful search with (1.7) the loop is executed k times, where $Table[k] = z$. Note that the loop control expression of a **while** is actually executed one more time than the body of the loop. Thus the total cost of the fragment is

$$3(k + 1) + 5(k - 1) + 4 = 8k + 2.$$

The alternate version using a dummy key in Exercise 2 of Section 1.3 uses only the operations **while**, [ ], $\neq$, $:=$, and $+$, so it would have a cost of execution of $5k - 2$, which is a 38 percent improvement.

When an algorithm includes an **if**, the statements under **then** are not executed every time the **if** is. Instead, they are executed with probability p, where p is the probability that the **if** test is **true**. Similarly the **else** statements, if any, are executed with probability $1 - p$. For example, consider the **if-then-else** of Algorithm 1.3:

$$\textbf{if } z < Table[m] \textbf{ then } h := m - 1$$
$$\textbf{else if } z > Table[m] \textbf{ then } l := m + 1$$
$$\textbf{else } found := \textbf{true} \tag{1.8}$$

where the eleven operators are **if**, $<$, [ ], $:=$, $-$, **if**, $>$, [ ], $:=$, $+$, and $:=$. If we denote by p the probability of $<$ and by q the probability of $>$, then the expected operator execution count is

$$3 + 3(1 - p) + 2p + 2q + 1(1 - p - q) = 7 - 2p + q$$

The first two terms are for the **if** tests; the last three are for the assignment statements. If another **if** were nested after one of the **then**'s, the probabilities would be reduced by multiplying them (see Exercise 10 of Section 1.4.3).

In a similar vein, we can analyze the worst-case operator count of fragment (1.8): the number of operators performed is five, eight, and seven for the cases $<$, $>$, and $=$, respectively. The worst case is thus eight operator executions.

We can compare the cost of fragment (1.8) with an alternative that is often used unthinkingly (Exercise 3 of Section 1.3):

> **if** $z = Table[m]$ **then** *found* $:=$ **true**
> **else if** $z < Table[m]$ **then** $h := m - 1$
> **else** $l := m + 1$

The primary difference is that equality is tested first. This alternative has the same worst-case cost as (1.8), but an expected cost of

$$3 + 3(p + q) + 1(1 - p - q) + 2p + 2q = 4 + 4p + 4q$$

Usually the probability of equality is low so we can take p and q as being about 0.5. Then the cost of (1.8) is 6.5 while that of the alternative with "$=$" first is 8. The excess cost brings no benefit; it is waste that can be avoided with a little thought.

1.4.3 Space-Time Analysis

Although previous sections have compared algorithms by studying their execution time, the choice is often a *space-time* trade-off: one algorithm will use more space and the other will use more time. Such algorithms are compared by a space-time integral. This value is the product of the program size and its execution time. If the program changes size during execution, the product must be computed for each size. A program that occupies 70 space units for its first 10 seconds and 100 units for another 20 seconds will have a space-time integral of

$$70 \times 10 + 100 \times 20 = 2700 \text{ unit-seconds.}$$

It is convenient to view this integral as a diagram with time on the x axis and space on the y axis. In these terms the example program uses resources in this manner:

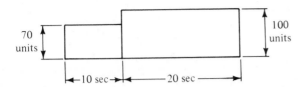

At many computer installations a charge c_t is made for the total execution time of the program in addition to a charge c_s for the space-time integral. The time charge is incorporated in the analysis by converting it to a space overhead of c_t/c_s space units. (It is a good exercise to derive this expression for yourself.) This charge is shown as additional space at the bottom of a diagram:

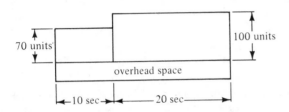

(Typical university computer centers charge a space overhead in the neighborhood of 10,000 to 200,000 words.)

Space-time analysis permits a complete comparison of the search methods in Algorithms 1.2 and 1.3. Our version of sequential search is slower but avoids the use of the *AttributesLoc* array, so the situation can be shown by these two diagrams:

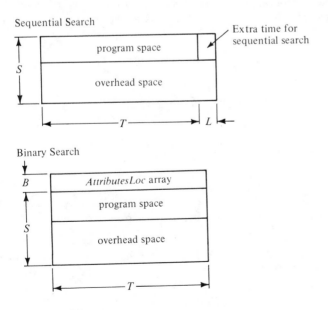

Number of Elements	Sequential Search	Binary Search
10	98	98
100	103	100
1,000	158	116
10,000	1,088	273

Table 1.4

Relative cost of sequential and binary search versions of a typical program. The costs are based on treating binary search with 100 elements as having a cost of exactly one hundred. Because there is considerable processing other than searching, the cost is not much lower when there are only ten elements. Note that with more elements the cost rises much more rapidly for sequential search.

From the areas of the rectangles, it is clear binary search will be superior if

$$(B + S)T < (T + L)S.$$

For a reasonable set of assumptions about an imaginary program, Table 1.4 shows the relative space-time costs for these search methods when different numbers of items are stored in the table (see Exercise 13). The two schemes are close when there are not many items, but binary search is increasingly superior for larger table sizes.

Space-time analysis is also the best method to compare the constant-time search method suggested at the end of Section 1.4.1 with other search techniques. When the space of possible keys is small, say one or two letters, the constant-time approach is feasible. When there are four or more letters per key, however, the table space is considerably more expensive than any possible savings in execution time (see Exercise 14).

Exercises

1. Derive Equation (1.6) from the equation for averages:

$$\bar{x} = \frac{1}{m} \sum_{j=1}^{m} x_j,$$

   where the x_j are the observed values for each of m cases. [*Hint*: Assume that m is some sufficiently large fixed value and use p_i to determine how many x_j should have each value v_i.]

2. Show by induction that $\sum_{i=1}^{n} i = n(n + 1)/2$. Prove that $n(n + 1)$ is divisible by two for all integer values of n.

3. The analysis of sequential search in Section 1.4.1 assumes that every search finds a key in the table. Extend the analysis by assuming that the search is successful only for fraction s of all attempts.

4. Suppose the entries in *Table* are sorted as for binary search, but a sequential search is chosen instead.

   (a) Show a revised version of Algorithm 1.2 that takes advantage of the array order to reduce the cost of searches when the element is not found.

   (b) Compute the expected number of times the **while** condition is tested in your solution to (a).

   (c) Rewrite your solution to (a) to also use a dummy key as in Exercise 2 of Section 1.3.

5. The computation of the number of loop executions for binary search given in the text was only an upper bound. Suppose the table has 100 elements; compute exactly the worst-case and average-case number of loop executions for a search that succeeds. Assume each key is equally likely to be the search target.

6. (a) Evaluate the eight expressions in Figure 1.5 for $n = 10$.

   (b) For what value of n is $2^n = n^2$? $2^n = n^3$?

   (c) For each expression compute the value of n for which the expression has the value 1000.

7.   As I was going to St. Ives, I met a man with seven wives. Each wife
           had seven sacks, each sack had seven cats, and each cat had seven
           kits. Kits, cats, sacks, and wives, how many were going to St. Ives?
   Rather than how many were going to St. Ives, let us consider how many I met. Suppose we have m levels of objects where each possesses seven of the next higher level. (In the riddle, m is 5 and the objects are man, wife, sack, cat, and kit.) Show that the total number of objects is proportional to 7^m.

In the next two exercises the phrase "What is the order of" means "To what expression is the cost proportional?"

8. (a) What is the order of the usual algorithm to add two $n \times n$ matrices?

   (b) What is the order of the usual algorithm to multiply two $n \times n$ matrices?

9. One way to sort n keys is to insert each in turn in a table using Algorithm 1.4.

   (a) What is the order of the number of binary search loop executions required for this sort?

   (b) What is the order of the number of times a key must be moved from one position in the array to another?

10. Suppose the statement **if** B **then** S is executed with the probability p and suppose that B has probability q of being **true**; then S will be executed with probability pq. In general, the probability of execution of a statement is the product of the probabilities along the path to the statement. Compute the expected number of operators executed for the binary search in Algorithm 1.3. Use w to denote the number of executions of the statements within the **while** and t, u, and v to denote the probabilities of $<$, $>$, and $=$, respectively ($t + u + v = 1$).

11. Compare sequential and binary search.

   (a) Compute the expected number of operators executed for the sequential search in Algorithm 1.2.

   (b) Compare the results of (a) with those of Exercise 10. (Assume the number of binary search loop executions is lg n.) For what values of $nKeys$ is binary search preferable?

12. The text compares two **if-then-else** implementations of the binary search loop body by assuming that each comparison requires an operator execution. Suppose that the result of the first comparison can be saved, so the second comparison is never made. What then are the relative costs of the two implementations?

13. Develop the formulas used to generate the data of Table 1.4. The following assumptions were used:

   There are n elements in the table.

   Each element occupies 0.02 space units.

   The program other than the table occupies 30 space units and the overhead charge (c_t/c_s) is 200 units.

   Each execution of the loop in sequential search takes one time unit.

   Each execution of the binary search loop takes two time units.

   After each search, the program spends 1000 time units on other processing.

   Reproduce the values found in Table 1.4. What would the results have been if the program spent only 100 time units on other processing after each search?

14. Extend the analysis of the previous exercise to the constant-time search sketched at the end of Section 1.4.1. The appropriate parameter for analysis is the number of letters per key rather than the number of keys in the table.

1.5 REMARKS AND REFERENCES

Both logical and physical organization of data bases are covered in

Ullmann, J. D., *Principles of Data Base Systems*, second edition. Rockville, MD: Computer Science Press, 1982.

Date, C. J., *An Introduction to Data Base Systems*, Vol. I, fourth edition. Reading, MA: Addison-Wesley, 1985.

For a detailed discussion of the definition of a data structure in Section 1.2 see

Hansen, Wilfred J., "The Structure of 'Data Structures'," *ACM '81 Conference Proceedings*, New York: ACM (1981) 89–95.

Chapter 2

Elementary
Data Objects

Parvis e glandibus quercus.
[Tall oaks from little acorns grow.]

Latin motto

Bits are the indivisible basis of all information storage; they are so primitive that only two values—1 and 0—are possible for each bit. Nonetheless, bits form a data structure, which will be the topic of the next section. The remainder of the chapter will be devoted to applications of the *word* data structure, which uses bits as its storage structure.

A *word* is a sequence of bits, say sixteen or thirty-two in a row. Those at the left are called the *high-order* bits, those at the right, *low-order*. We can picture a word as a row of boxes, one for each bit:

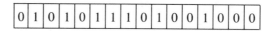

For convenience we normally omit the boxes and write only the bit values:

0101011101001000

Long bit strings are unwieldy, so we write word values in *hexadecimal* notation (base 16). Each group of four bits is replaced by a single symbol, as shown in Table 2.1. With this notation the string above becomes

$$5748_{16}$$

where the subscript "16" indicates the value is in hexadecimal. (If the length is not a multiple of four bits, extra zeroes are added at the high-order end.)

The words above have sixteen bits, which is their *word size* or *word length*.

Bit String Block	Hexadecimal Representation
0000	0
0001	1
0010	2
0011	3
0100	4
0101	5
0110	6
0111	7
1000	8
1001	9
1010	A
1011	B
1100	C
1101	D
1110	E
1111	F

Table 2.1
Hexadecimal representation. In a bit string each block of four bits is represented
by the corresponding symbol from the right-hand column.

Another typical word length is thirty-two bits; we will use both lengths in this chapter, but the remainder of the book is independent of word length. Character values
each occupy an eight-bit *byte*, so we will have two or four bytes per word.

Despite its elementary nature, a word is indeed a data structure:

- There are several sets of functions on words, treating them as logical
  values, integers, reals, and so on.
- Words are defined in terms of a more primitive storage structure, the
  single bit.
- The functions on words are implemented by algorithms that operate
  on bits.

In the case of words, the algorithms are implemented by the hardware; for most
operations—for example, adding two integers—there is a single hardware instruction.
Four interpretations of words are common:

Logical. The value is a string of bits, each of which may be interpreted inde-
    pendently of others. (Section 2.1.)

Integer. The values are treated according to the rules of the arithmetic opera-
    tions—addition, subtraction, multiplication, and division. (Section 2.2.)

Floating Point. As with integers, the operations are those of arithmetic, but a
    portion of each word indicates the location of the decimal point. (Section
    2.3.2.)

Logical

| 0 | 1 | 0 | 1 | 0 | 1 | 1 | 1 | 0 | 1 | 0 | 0 | 1 | 0 | 0 | 0 |

5748_{16}

Integer

| 0 | 0 | 0 | 1 | 0 | 1 | 1 | 0 | 0 | 1 | 1 | 1 | 0 | 1 | 0 | 0 |

5748

| 0 | 1 | 0 | 1 | 0 | 1 | 1 | 1 | 0 | 1 | 0 | 0 | 1 | 0 | 0 | 0 |

22344

Floating point

| 0 | 0 | 1 | 1 | 0 | 1 | 1 | 0 | 1 | 1 | 0 | 0 | 1 | 1 | 1 | 0 |

$.5744 \times 10^4 \quad = .701172 \times 2^{13}$

| 0 | 1 | 0 | 1 | 0 | 1 | 1 | 1 | 0 | 1 | 0 | 0 | 1 | 0 | 0 | 0 |

$.4004 \times 10^{-3} = .820313 \times 2^{-11}$

Character string

| 0 | 0 | 1 | 1 | 0 | 1 | 0 | 1 | 0 | 0 | 1 | 1 | 0 | 1 | 1 | 1 |

"57"

| 0 | 1 | 0 | 1 | 0 | 1 | 1 | 1 | 0 | 1 | 0 | 0 | 1 | 0 | 0 | 0 |

"WH"

Figure 2.1
Alternative interpretations of words. The first word in each pair is a value whose
name, shown at the right, is close to 5748. The second word in each pair is
5748_{16}, but the name at the right shows its interpretation as an integer, floating
point number, or character string.

> *Character.* There is a translation between eight-bit bytes and printed graphic
> characters. This translation is implemented in the hardware of peripheral
> devices, such as terminals and printers. (Section 2.2.3.)

For examples of words with each of these interpretations, see Figure 2.1.

This chapter will first explore these four interpretations of words. Logical values are discussed at length to show some of the ramifications of the operations available on bits. Then integers and conversion to decimal are shown to be related to the
representation of "enumerated" types and characters. A section on "packed" words
demonstrates that values in words are sometimes composed of several integer-like
fields. All of these are discussions of the general concept of *representation:* the use
of one value to record another. The final section of the chapter discusses two important mathematical aspects of representations: reliability and efficiency.

Exercises

1. Bits in main memory are stored in integrated circuit chips, the largest of which—
   at this writing—hold 2^{20} bits (a "mega-bit"). If the chip is two-tenths of an inch
   by five-tenths, how much area is devoted to each bit? Five-inch diameter disks
   currently contain up to a thousand tracks per inch with ten thousand bits per inch
   on each track. What is the surface area devoted to each bit? Can you suggest any
   reasons why bits are bigger on one of these media?

2. Complete the following chart of equivalences between logical and hexadecimal values.

Logical	Hexadecimal
1100000011011110	$CODE_{16}$
10110	16_{16}
1011101010111110	
111111101101	
1111000111010000	
1110011101101	
110000001101	
	$B4_{16}$
	$COFFEE_{16}$

3. Programming languages have diverse notations for distinguishing hexadecimal from decimal values. Find three and invent one of your own. What are their advantages and disadvantages with respect to ease of interpretation by both human and computer?

4. Get a list of the instruction mnemonics and their meanings for some computer. Classify each instruction as to whether it deals with bits, integers, floating-point numbers, characters, or none of these.

2.1 BOOLEAN OPERATIONS AND LOGICAL VALUES

Bits and the operators on them have many important applications including program flow of control, proof of correctness, and computer hardware design. The study of bits is the realm of *boolean algebra*, where the operations are **and, or, not, xor,** and twelve others (see Exercise 6). Expressions and variables over bits are called *boolean expressions* and *boolean variables*, respectively. In this Section we use p, q, and r as boolean variables.

Although boolean variables are conceptually single bits, their values are referred to as **true** and **false** instead of 1 and 0. This is especially appropriate when the boolean expression is part of the condition in an **if** or **while** statement. Since boolean variables have two possible values, there are exactly four possibilities for the input of a boolean function of two arguments:

First argument	Second argument
true	true
true	false
false	true
false	false

p	q	p **and** q	p **or** q	p **xor** q	**not** p
true	true	true	true	false	false
true	false	false	true	true	false
false	true	false	true	true	true
false	false	false	false	false	true

Table 2.2
Truth-table definitions of the four most common boolean operators. The columns labeled p and q specify the values used for each of the other four columns. For example, the third line says that when p is **false** and q is **true** then p **and** q is **false** but the other three operators produce **true**.

To define a boolean operator, then, it is sufficient to specify its output for each of the four possible input states; such a table is called a *truth table*.

In Table 2.2 a truth table defines the four most common boolean operators: **and**, **or**, **not**, and **xor**. When expressed in terms of **true** and **false**, these definitions are more or less obvious: **and** returns **true** when its first *and* second arguments are **true**. The operator **or** returns **true** when either its first *or* second argument or both are **true**. The operator **xor** is an abbreviation for "exclusive or;" it is **true** only when *exactly* one of the arguments is **true**. And **not** is a function of one argument; in the table its output depends on the value of p, but not q. The function **not** is **true** when its argument is **false** and vice versa.

Truth tables are one tool for analyzing boolean expressions. For instance, Table 2.3 shows an analysis of (p **and** q) **or** **not** r. Development of the table begins by listing the variables and writing beneath them one row of the table for each combination of their values; if there are m variables, the table will have 2^m rows. Next a column is written for each subexpression, deriving the values by applying the rules of Table 2.2 to the operands of the subexpression. Finally, the subexpressions are combining to produce values for the expression. In the example, the values in the last column are the **or** of the values in the two subexpression columns.

p	q	r	(p **and** q)	**not** r	(p **and** q) **or** **not** r
true	true	true	true	false	true
true	true	false	true	true	true
true	false	true	false	false	false
true	false	false	false	true	true
false	true	true	false	false	false
false	true	false	false	true	true
false	false	true	false	false	false
false	false	false	false	true	true

Table 2.3
Truth-table evaluation of the expression (p **and** q) **or** **not** r. The left three columns list all possible values for p, q, and r.

Commutativity	(1)	p **and** q = q **and** p
	(2)	p **or** q = q **or** p
Associativity	(3)	p **and** (q **and** r) = (p **and** q) **and** r
	(4)	p **or** (q **or** r) = (p **or** q) **or** r
Distributivity	(5)	p **and** (q **or** r) = (p **and** q) **or** (p **and** r)
	(6)	p **or** (q **and** r) = (p **or** q) **and** (p **or** r)
Absorption	(7)	p **and** (p **or** q) = p
	(8)	p **or** (p **and** q) = p
	(9)	p **and** p = p
	(10)	p **or** p = p
Zero and identity	(11)	p **and true** = p
	(12)	p **and false** = **false**
	(13)	p **or true** = **true**
	(14)	p **or false** = p
	(15)	p **and not** p = **false**
	(16)	p **or not** p = **true**
Double negative	(17)	**not not** p = p
DeMorgan's laws	(18)	**not** (p **and** q) = **not** p **or not** q
	(19)	**not** (p **or** q) = **not** p **and not** q

Table 2.4
Rules for boolean algebra. These rules are similar to those of arithmetic and can be similarly used. When these rules are applied, the letters p, q, and r can be replaced with constant values, other variables, or entire expressions.

Truth tables require enumeration of all possible input states; if there are many variables, it is easier to manipulate the boolean expression according to the rules of boolean algebra. These rules are similar to—and in some cases simpler than—the rules of arithmetic; see Table 2.4. The most complex and counterintuitive—DeMorgan's laws—are also among the most important, so we use them in Tables 2.5 and 2.6 to illustrate proof by truth table and proof by algebraic manipulation.

Input Values		*Expression 1*		*Expression 2*		
p	q	p **and** q	**not** (p **and** q)	**not** p	**not** q	**not** p **or not** q
true	true	true	false	false	false	false
true	false	false	true	false	true	true
false	true	false	true	true	false	true
false	false	false	true	true	true	true

Table 2.5
Proof of equivalence by truth tables. By writing truth tables for two expressions we can determine if they are equivalent. In this example the two expressions are the two sides of DeMorgan's law (rule 18). Since the values of both expressions (boxed) are the same, the two expressions are equivalent.

not(p **or** q)	
= **not**(**not not** p **or not not** q)	rule 17 (twice)
= **not**(**not**(**not** p **and not** q))	rule 18
= **not** p **and not** q	rule 17

Table 2.6
Proof by transformation. Rules (and other theorems) can be proved by transformations applying other rules. In this example, one DeMorgan's law (rule 19) is proved by application of the other DeMorgan's law (rule 18 with p replaced by **not** p and q replaced by **not** q).

Logical Variables. Each boolean operator produces a one-bit result from one-bit arguments. These operators can be extended to operate on entire words by specifying that each bit position is treated separately; the result in position i depends only on the values in position i of the operands. Values and expressions of this sort are called *logical*. Some examples are given in Table 2.7.

In addition to the boolean operators **and, or, not,** and **xor,** several other functions are useful for logical variables:

shift_left(*logical_word*, *shift_count*). The *logical_word* is shifted left the number of places indicated by *shift_count*. The leftmost bits of *logical_word* are lost and the rightmost bits are set to zero. For example:

shift_left(1011011000101101,4) $\Rightarrow$ 0110001011010000.

If *shift_count* < 0, the shift is to the right.

(a)	**and**	first operand	0110100011101000
		second operand	1000110111001101
	result =	first **and** second	0000100011001000
(b)	**or**	first operand	0110100011101000
		second operand	1000110111001101
	result =	first **or** second	1110110111101101
(c)	**xor**	first operand	0110100011101000
		second operand	1000110111001101
	result =	first **xor** second	1110010100100101
(d)	**not**	operand	0110100011101000
	result =	**not** operand	1001011100010111

Table 2.7
The extension of boolean operations to entire words. The bit values 1 and 0 are used for the boolean values **true** and **false,** respectively. Note that the result in any given output position depends only on the operand bits in that same position. Thus for **and** the result has ones only in positions where both operands have ones.

ord(logical_word). This function does nothing to *logical_word*. Its purpose is to allow use of *logical_word* in contexts where an integer is necessary. The integer value derived is the one with the same hexadecimal representation as the value of *logical_word*:

$$ord(1011011) \Rightarrow 91_{10}.$$

logical(integer_value). This function is the inverse of the *ord* function above. It converts its argument so it can be used in contexts demanding logical values:

$$logical(91) \Rightarrow 1011011_2.$$

The functions *shift_left* and *logical* are not in standard Pascal, but we can illustrate how they should work by considering as an example multiplication by a power of two. Successive bit positions correspond to consecutive powers of two, so a left shift of one position multiplies the value by two. Since eight is 2^3, we can multiply k by eight with shifting alone:

$$ord(shift\_left(logical(k), 3))$$

This technique can be a useful optimization, because shifts are faster than multiplication.

Exercises

1. Find an expression for p **xor** q in terms of **and, or,** and **not**. Demonstrate the equivalence with a truth table.

2. What is the value of p **xor** q **xor** p? Prove it with a truth table. Suppose your computer has an instruction "$t := t$ **xor** v" which forms the **xor** of t and v and stores the result in t. Show how to interchange the values of two variables using only this instruction and no temporary variables.

3. Find rules for **xor** like those for **and** and **or** in Table 2.4. Prove the commutativity of **xor** by application of the equivalence between **xor** and the other operators. Prove a distributive rule by a truth table.

4. What is the analog for **xor** of DeMorgan's laws? Prove it with a truth table. Prove it again by application of the equivalence with **and, or,** and **not**.

5. An important technique for devising boolean expressions is to work backward from the truth table. For example, we may want an expression for the truth table shown in Table 2.8. One possible such expression is the *disjunctive normal*

Inputs			Output
p	*q*	*r*	
true	true	true	false
true	true	false	false
true	false	true	true
true	false	false	true
false	true	true	false
false	true	false	false
false	false	true	true
false	false	false	false

Table 2.8
Exercise 5

form; the expression is written as the **or** of a number of terms, each of which corresponds to a row of the table that produces a **true** output. In the example, the term corresponding to the third row would be

$$p \text{ and } (\text{not } q) \text{ and } r;$$

that is, it contains "variable" for **true** inputs and "**not** variable" for **false** inputs.

(a) Give the disjunctive normal form for Table 2.8.

(b) Find a much simpler expression for the table.

(c) Prove by truth tables that your answers to (a) and (b) are correct.

(d) Prove by transformations that your answers to (a) and (b) are equivalent expressions.

6. There are sixteen boolean functions of two boolean variables—one corresponding to each of the sixteen possible combinations of values in the result column of a truth table. For some entries in Table 2.9 we have given the result column; for others we have given an expression equivalent to the result column in terms of **not** and **and**. Fill in the blank entries of the table. (Can any pair of operators other than **not** and **and** be used to express all sixteen functions?)

7. A FORTRAN identifier must begin with a letter and contain no more than six letters and digits. Algorithm 2.1 is the part of a compiler that recognizes an identifier. That is, it returns **true** if the next characters in the input stream constitute an identifier. It also extracts the identifier for further processing by calling *Store* for each of its characters. The input stream is represented by the function *GetCharacter,* successive calls of which return successive input characters. The assumption is that *RecognizeIdentifier* and all other recognizer procedures expect an initial value in *currch* and leave the character following the recognized item in *currch* when they finish.

Function name	Value of function when p and q have these values:				An equivalent expression written with only **not** and **and**
	p: **true**	**true**	**false**	**false**	
	q: **true**	**false**	**true**	**false**	
false	false	false	false	false	p **and not** p
not(p **or** q)	false	false	false	true	(see Exercise 8)
not(q **implies** p)	false	false	true	false	q **and not** p
not p					**not** p
not(p **implies** q)					
not q					**not** q
p **xor** q	false	true	true	false	(see Exercise 1)
not(p **and** q)					**not**(p **and** q)
p **and** q					p **and** q
p **equiv** q	true	false	false	true	
q					q
p **implies** q	true	false	true	true	
p					p
q **implies** p					
p **or** q					
true					

Table 2.9
Exercise 6

```
function RecognizeIdentifier: boolean;
var
        count: integer;  {the number of valid characters so far}
        letdig: boolean; {true if currch is a letter or digit}
begin
        count := 0;
        if (currch < 'A') "(a) _____" (currch > 'Z') then
            RecognizeIdentifier := "(b) _____"
        else begin
            repeat
                Store(currch);
                count := count + 1;
                {Assert: count letters and digits have been Store'd.}
                currch := GetCharacter;
                letdig := "(c) _____"
            until (count "(d) _____" 6) or not letdig;
            RecognizeIdentifier := "(e) _____"

        end
end
```

Algorithm 2.1
Exercise 7

Fill in the blanks so that Algorithm 2.1 fulfills its intention.

(a) a boolean operator

(b) a boolean value

(c) a boolean expression testing *currch*

(d) an integer comparison operator

(e) a boolean expression

Under what circumstances will *currch* contain a letter or digit after Algorithm 2.1 exits?

8. Computer logic circuits represent **true** and **false** as distinct voltages. Signals on two or more wires are combined by logic gates that perform boolean operations. For instance, the sign of a product is the **xor** of the signs of the operands. For electrical reasons primitive logic gates negate their result value. Thus one available gate is **nor**, where *p* **nor** *q* = **not** (*p* **or** *q*). In circuit diagrams this is drawn as

All sixteen functions in Table 2.9 can be built from **nor.** We could build *p* **and** *q* thus

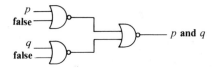

although in practice the input circuits producing *p* and *q* would be rearranged to instead produce **not** *p* and **not** *q*, respectively.

(a) Draw a circuit using **nor** gates to derive *p* **or** *q* **or** *r* from *p*, *q*, and *r*.

(b) Draw a simple circuit for (*p* **or** *q*) **and not** *r*. Use **nor** gates.

9. Write boolean expressions for *c* and *s* in terms of *p*, *q*, and *r* as specified by Table 2.10. (*Note*: If **true** is one and **false** is zero, *c* and *s* are the carry and sum from adding the binary values of *p*, *q*, and *r*. Consequently your expressions for *c* and *s* specify logic circuits for addition.)

10. Imagine a computer with sixteen-bit words and the logical operations on them of **and**, **or**, and **xor**. Write a single statement with one operator that will set the third bit from the left in the logical variable *ioflag* to 1. Write another statement to set it to 0 and a third to invert the value of the bit.

p	q	r	c	s
true	true	true	true	true
true	true	false	true	false
true	false	true	true	false
true	false	false	false	true
false	true	true	true	false
false	true	false	false	true
false	false	true	false	true
false	false	false	false	false

Table 2.10
Exercise 9

11. Suppose c is a character variable. For what values of c will this program print "digit"?

$$\textbf{if } (c \leqslant \text{'9'}) \textbf{ or } (c \geqslant \text{'0'}) \textbf{ then}$$
$$writeln(\text{'digit'})$$
$$\textbf{else } writeln(\text{'not digit'})$$

12. Write a function called *CountOnes* that has a logical value as its argument and returns an integer giving the number of one bits in the argument. (This is an excellent problem for assembly language experimentation. What is the smallest number of instruction executions required in your machine? The least amount of memory?)

2.2 INTEGERS

What is "00010011"?

It might represent a string of bits; but it might equally well represent a binary number with the decimal value of nineteen, as we will see below. The integer corresponding to a bit string is that string's *natural interpretation* as a binary number. This interpretation is precisely how computers compute.

Like logical values, integers are data structures using bit strings as their storage structure. The functions are those of arithmetic: addition, subtraction, multiplication, division. Unlike other algorithms we will study, the functions for integer arithmetic are implemented by single instructions that rely on hardware logic circuits (see Exercises 8 and 9, Section 2.1). Like other algorithms, but unlike mathematics, addition and subtraction can produce errors. Results are limited to the word size, so "overflow" occurs when too large a result would be produced.

In the latter part of this section we will consider how enumerated types and characters are implemented from integers. Before that, we show how to translate values from one base to another; say from binary 00010011 to decimal 19.

2.2.1 Conversion of Integers From One Base to Another

A *positional* number system expresses a number in terms of a *base* or *radix* and a set of *digit symbols*. For a given base b the digit symbols are an ordered set representing the values 0, 1, 2, ..., $b-1$. In the decimal system the base is ten and the digit symbols are 0, 1, 2, 3, 4, 5, 6, 7, 8, and 9, which have their usual values. A number n is represented in base b by writing a string of digit symbols, $a_{k-1}a_{k-2}$ $\cdots a_2a_1a_0$, and is interpreted by multiplying the value of each digit by a corresponding power of the base:

$$n = a_{k-1}b^{k-1} + a_{k-2}b^{k-2} + \cdots + a_1b^1 + a_0b^0$$

$$= \sum_{i=0}^{k-1} a_ib^i. \tag{2.1}$$

In computing, four bases are common: binary (base 2), octal (base 8), decimal (base 10), and hexadecimal (base 16). The digit symbols are the same as the decimal system with the addition of six more for base 16, as shown in Table 2.1. When a value is not decimal and the base is not clear from context, the base is written as a subscript to the value.

In Equation (2.1) the coefficients a_i and the powers of b can be expressed in any base, as long as the arithmetic is carried out using the rules for that base. This fact leads directly to a technique for transformation from one base to another, as illustrated by these three examples:

Example 1.

What is the decimal equivalent of 10011_2? If we do the calculations and representation in decimal, the result will be the required value:

$$
\begin{aligned}
10011_2 & \\
= 1 \quad\quad 0 \quad\quad 0 \quad\quad 1 \quad\quad 1 \quad\quad & \text{(base 2)} \\
= 1 \times 2^4 + 0 \times 2^3 + 0 \times 2^2 + 1 \times 2^1 + 1 \times 2^0 & \\
= 1 \times 16 + 0 \quad\quad + 0 \quad\quad + 1 \times 2 + 1 \times 1 & \quad \text{(base 10)} \\
= 16 + 2 + 1 & \\
= 19 &
\end{aligned}
$$

Example 2.

What is the decimal equivalent of 10011_{10}? We will do the calculation in the decimal system to derive a decimal result.

10011_{10}
$$
\begin{aligned}
&= 1 \qquad\qquad 0 \qquad\quad 0 \qquad\quad 1 \qquad\quad 1 \\
&= 1 \times 10^4 \quad + 0 \times 10^3 + 0 \times 10^2 + 1 \times 10^1 + 1 \times 10^0 \\
&= 1 \times 10000 \; + 0 \qquad\; + 0 \qquad\; + 1 \times 10 + 1 \times 1 \\
&= 10000 + 10 + 1 \\
&= 10011 \qquad \text{(no surprise)}
\end{aligned}
$$
(base 10)

Example 3.

What is the binary equivalent of 10011_{10}? This time we will do the calculation in binary to produce a binary result. Note that 10_{10} is 1010_2.

10011_{10}
$$
\begin{aligned}
&= 1 \qquad\qquad\qquad\qquad 0 \qquad\qquad 0 \qquad\qquad 1 \qquad\qquad 1 \\
&= 1 \times 1010^{100} \qquad\quad + 0 \times 1010^{11} + 0 \times 1010^{10} + 1 \times 1010^1 + 1 \times 1010^0 \\
&= 1 \times 10011100010000 \;\; + 0 \qquad\qquad + 0 \qquad\qquad + 1 \times 1010 \; + 1 \times 1 \\
&= 10011100010000 + 1010 + 1 \\
&= 10011100011011
\end{aligned}
$$
(base 2)

Equation (2.1) is inconvenient for computer calculations because it requires computing large powers of the base. To avoid this, the equation can be rewritten as

$$
n = (((\cdots ((a_{k-1}b + a_{k-2})b + a_{k-3})b + \cdots \\
+ a_3)b + a_2)b + a_1)b + a_0. \qquad (2.2)
$$

At each step of this computation, called *Horner's method*, the present value of the result is multiplied by the base and the next digit is added. Like Equation (2.1), Equation (2.2) lends itself to conversions in both directions between binary and decimal. We will leave most of these to the exercises but will illustrate Equation (2.2) at the end of section 2.2.3.

Exercises

1. What is the largest integer that can be represented in a 32-bit word?

2. Prove that

$$
2^k - 1 = \sum_{i=0}^{k-1} 2^i.
$$

(In other words, prove that the binary representation consisting of k ones has the value $2^k - 1$ and is thus one less than the smallest value that requires $k + 1$ bits for its representation.)

3. How many distinct values can be represented by k bits? Is it possible to partition these values into positive, negative, and zero while having exactly as many positive as negative? How? Or why not?

4. Show how to use successive decimal divisions by the base to convert a number from decimal to some other base. Illustrate this process by converting 497 to base 7.

5. Suppose that your computer has 32-bit words and that eight four-bit quantities have been read into word v. Each quantity represents a decimal digit by the natural interpretation. Show how to write a *loop-free* program using only one temporary location to convert v to binary. [*Hint*: Since the binary for 10 is 1010_2, you can multiply by ten using only shifting and adding.]

The next three exercises explore computer techniques for conversion from binary to decimal.

6. Assume your computer permits representation of decimal values as an array of bytes, with each byte containing a value between 0 and 9. Under this assumption, suppose there is an instruction to add one such array to another. Using this instruction and a table of arrays giving the values of the powers of two, write a program to implement Equation (2.1) for conversion from binary to decimal.

7. What will be the remainder if the quantity n in Equation (2.2) is divided by the base b? What will be the quotient? Use these facts as the basis for a program to convert from binary to decimal by successive divisions.

8. Since multiplication is usually faster than division, write a version of the program in the previous exercise that uses multiplication by $1/b$ instead of division by b.

9. It is not necessary that the positions in an integer representation have the values of powers of some base. For example, in the Fibonacci number system the successive positions have the values: 1, 2, 3, 5, 8, 13, 21, 34, 55, 89, 144, ... (each is the sum of the preceding two). In this system 19 can be represented as 101001 (13 + 5 + 1). Derive a rule so that the representation of every integer is unique, using only zeroes and ones as digits. Show how to add two integers represented in the Fibonacci number system.

10. The product of two integer values in Pascal may exceed *maxint*, the largest permissable value. Write a sequence of statements to multiply the values in a and b and store the high- and low-order portions of the result in *rhi* and *rlo*,

respectively. Assume that a and b are each positive and less than 10^8 and that the true result is given by $rhi \times 10^8 + rlo$. Use only the operations of addition, subtraction, multiplication, and integer division. Assume that multiplication yields only the low-order end of the product. [*Hint*: Split a and b into two parts and perform four multiplications.]

11. There are four missing terms in the sequence below; what are they?

10000, —, —, —, —, 22, 20, 17, *16*, 15, 14, 13, 12, 11, 10, G, G, ...

[*Hint*: Why is sixteen italicized?]

2.2.2 Enumerated Types

When a variable will take on only a small number of values, it is useful to give each value a name: for a sex variable, *Male* and *Female*; for the account type field in a bank's data base, *Savings, Checking, Business, Mortgage*, ... The type of such a variable is an *enumerated type*. In Pascal we first declare the type itself:

type
        AccountType = (*Savings, Checking, Business, Mortgage, Trust*);

Later a variable of this type would be declared by writing:

        CustAcct: AccountType;

The result of these declarations is that a variable has been created and names have been defined for its five possible values. These names can be used in assignment:

        CustAcct : = *Business*

or they can be used for comparison:

        if *CustAcct* = *Trust* **then** ...

The Pascal successor function, *succ*, returns the next value from the enumerated list. When *CustAcct* has value *Business,* the value of

        succ(CustAcct)

is *Mortgage*. The last element in the list has no successor so *succ(Trust)* is undefined. Similarly *pred* returns the predecessor.

Variables of enumerated type are implemented directly as integers: the names in the list are assigned successively higher integers starting with zero. Statements referring to these named constants are translated into operations referring to the appropriate integers. Thus the assignment above would assign the integer value two to *CustAcct* and the **if** predicate would test for value four.

Exercises

1. Write a declaration for a variable *day*, the values of which are to be the days of the week. Write an **if-then-else** statement to advance *day* to the next day of the week.

2. As part of a program to create new bank accounts, there is a routine to read in information about the new account. Some Pascal implementations permit

   read(CustAcct)

   to retrieve an *AccountType* value from the input. The corresponding value in the input stream would be one of the value names: "Savings", "Checking", ...; these would be converted to integers by the input routines. This conversion requires a symbol table during program execution to find the appropriate values for names. What attributes should be defined for each entry in this symbol table?

2.2.3 Character Representations

An important enumerated type is the representation of characters: letters, digits, punctuation, and special characters. The desired characters are listed in a sequence, and the code value for each is its location in the sequence; examples are shown in Tables 2.11 and 2.12. In these tables, the column and row indexes taken together form the hexadecimal value corresponding to the location of the character in the sequence. Thus the top left character has the code 00 and the eighth down has code 07. In ASCII the latter corresponds to the control character BEL, which sounds the bell if transmitted to a user workstation. In EBCDIC this same control character has code 2F, while code 07 corresponds to DEL, which is ignored.

Other than assignment and input/output, the principal operation on characters is to compare two characters to test for equality or relative position in the sequence. When writing programs with such comparisons, it is useful to have some notion of the order in the sequence. For ASCII, the order is

   controls < space < special characters < digits < upper case < lower case.

EBCDIC interchanges the digits and lower case letters:

   controls < space < special characters < lower case < upper case < digits.

In both cases these relationships omit a few special characters that are inserted at other points in the sequence.

	0_	1_	2_	3_	4_	5_	6_	7_
_0	NUL	DLE	space	0	@	P		p
_1	SOH	DC1	!	1	A	Q	a	q
_2	STX	DC2	"	2	B	R	b	r
_3	ETX	DC3	#	3	C	S	c	s
_4	EOT	DC4	$	4	D	T	d	t
_5	ENQ	NAK	%	5	E	U	e	u
_6	ACK	SYN	&	6	F	V	f	v
_7	BEL	ETB	'	7	G	W	g	w
_8	BS	CAN	(	8	H	X	h	x
_9	HT	EM	)	9	I	Y	i	y
_A	LF	SUB	*	:	J	Z	j	z
_B	VT	ESC	+	;	K	[	k	{
_C	FF	FS	,	<	L	\	l	|
_D	CR	GS	—	=	M	]	m	}
_E	SO	RS	.	>	N	^	n	~
_F	SI	US	/	?	O	_	o	DEL

Table 2.11
ASCII character code. The code for each entry in the table is the two-digit hexadecimal value formed by taking the digits at the top of the column and the left of the row. The code for 'A' is 41_{16} (that is, 65 decimal). The two- and three-character names are names for control codes used in communication. For example, BEL at 07_{16} rings the bell at a terminal.

	0_	1_	2_	3_	4_	5_	6_	7_	8_	9_	A_	B_	C_	D_	E_	F_
_0	NUL	DLE	DS		space	&	—									0
_1	SOH	DC1	SOS				/		a	j	~		A	J		1
_2	STX	DC2	FS	SYN					b	k	s		B	K	S	2
_3	ETX	TM							c	l	t		C	L	T	3
_4	PF	RES	BYP	PN					d	m	u		D	M	U	4
_5	HT	NL	LF	RS					e	n	v		E	N	V	5
_6	LC	BS	ETB	UC					f	o	w		F	O	W	6
_7	DEL	IL	ESC	EOT					g	p	x		G	P	X	7
_8	GE	CAN							h	q	y		H	Q	Y	8
_9	RLF	EM							i	r	z		I	R	Z	9
_A	SMM	CC	SM		¢	!		:								LVM
_B	VT	CU1	CU2	CU3	.	$	,	#					♩			
_C	FF	IFS		DC4	<	*	%	@							⊣	
_D	CR	IGS	ENQ	NAK	(	)	—	'					Ч			
_E	SO	IRS	ACK		+	;	>	=								
_F	SI	IUS	BEL	SUB	|	¬	?	"								ED

Table 2.12
EBCDIC character code. This chart is read the same way as Table 2.11. The code for 'A' is $C1_{16}$ (that is, 193 decimal).

Because character codes are integers, arithmetic can be done on their values. In Pascal, the *ord* function returns the position of the character in the sequence, which can then be operated on as an integer value. Compilers generate no code to implement *ord*; the integer for the character has the same bits as the character value itself. Thus in ASCII, $ord('A')$ yields $41_{16} = 65$ as an *integer* value. Similarly, to convert from an integer to a character value, use the function *chr*, which performs the inverse of *ord*.

Consider an algorithm to read a string of digit characters and produce the value of the integer they represent. We could write this as a **while** loop, but it serves in Algorithm 2.2 as an example of recursion (see Exercise 2). Like other routines for processing tokens, *ReadInteger* presupposes a global variable *currch* containing the next character to be processed; after the routine finishes, *currch* contains the first encountered nondigit. *GetCharacter* reads the next input character. An initial call to read an integer would be

$$ReadInteger(0, \; currch)$$

Note that $ord('0')$ is both more meaningful and more portable than would be integer values like 48 or 240.

> **function** *ReadInteger(val*: *integer*; *ch*: *char*): *integer*;
> **begin**
>   **if** $(ch \leq '0')$ **and** $(ch \leq '9')$ **then begin**
>   *currch* := *GetCharacter*;
>   *ReadInteger*
>   := *ReadInteger*$(10*val + (ord(ch) - ord('0'), currch)$
>   {see Equation (2.2)}
>   **end**
>   **else** *ReadInteger* := *val*
> **end**

Algorithm 2.2
Read an integer from the input

Exercises

1. Using first ASCII, then EBCDIC, evaluate these expressions: $'A'<'a'$, $'3'<'8'$, $'9'<'a'$, $'\;'<'2'$, $','<'a'$, $3<'A'$, $','<'\#'$, $ord('3')-ord('0')$, $ord('h')-ord('a')$, and $ord('z')-ord('a')$.

2. Write an iterative version of Algorithm 2.2.

3. If the character code is ASCII, we can determine if variable *ch* contains a capital letter by testing $('A' \leq ch)$ **and** $(ch \leq 'Z')$

   (a) Is this correct for EBCDIC?

   (b) Show how to use an array of boolean values to determine if the value in *ch* is a capital letter.

   (c) Describe how to extend the solution of (b) to determine whether *ch* contains a letter and whether it is upper or lower case.

   (d) Write a routine that correctly initializes the array needed for (c).

4. Write an expression such that if *ch* contains a lower-case letter, the value of the expression will be the corresponding capital letter. Your expression should work for both ASCII and EBCDIC and must not reference an array.

5. Write a program that has no input and has as its only output an exact copy of itself. This trick can be performed in all languages but is easier for some. In those like Pascal where string constants must contain a double apostrophe to represent a single apostrophe in the string, the program contains one such constant and prints it or portions twice to get the double apostrophe in the output.

2.3 PACKED WORDS

Data items need not each occupy an entire word. A person's sex can be encoded in a single bit, and his or her age can usually be encoded in fewer than eight bits (why?). When information is encoded with several data items in a single word, that word is said to be *packed*.

The operations of storing and retrieving packed data are called *packing* and *unpacking* and can be done with arithmetic. For instance, age and sex can be stored in a single word using the low-order bit for sex:

$$AgeSex := 2*Age + Sex$$

This assignment results in the packed word:

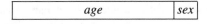

Division can unpack a word to access its components:

$$Age := AgeSex \textbf{ div } 2;$$
$$Sex := AgeSex \textbf{ mod } 2$$

However, integer arithmetic is a poor packing technique because multiplication and division are slower than logical operations.

With logical operations, a field can be extracted from a word by **and**'ing the word with a *mask* and then shifting the field to the low-order end of the result. Suppose *Age*, *Sex*, *NumberOfSiblings*, *NumberOfChildren* are packed in a word called *PersonData* with fields of seven, one, four, and four bits, respectively:

age	sex	# sibs	# kids

Then *NumberOfSiblings* can be extracted by the expression:

$$shift\_left(PersonData \text{ and } 00F0_{16}, -4)$$

The inverse operation of inserting a value for *NumberOfSiblings* is trickier because the values in other fields must be preserved. We first "zero-out" the old value for *NumberOfSiblings* by an **and** with a mask and then **or** the new value in:

$$PersonData := (PersonData \text{ and } FF0F_{16})$$
$$\text{or } (shift\_left(NumberOfSiblings, 4) \text{ and } 00F0_{16}) \qquad (2.3)$$

The final **and** ensures that insertion of the new value does not alter other fields in *PersonData*.

Rather than pack fields separately, we can adopt the strategy of always creating entire values:

$$PersonData :=$$
$$shift\_left(Age, 9)$$
$$\text{or } shift\_left(Sex \text{ and } 1_{16}, 8)$$
$$\text{or } shift\_left(NumberOfSiblings \text{ and } F_{16}, 4)$$
$$\text{or } (NumberOfChildren \text{ and } F_{16})$$

In designing data structures and algorithms the choice of field assignment versus creation of new values leads to very different programs. If a value once created is never modified, there need be no concern as to how many variables refer to a given copy of a value. Indeed, to avoid problems from partial value modification, some theoreticians have recommended total abolition of the assignment statement.

The use of packed data is an excellent example of a space-time trade-off problem. Unpacked data may occupy a large amount of space, but packing and unpacking consume processing time. (See Exercise 3.) Often, hardware provides special conversion operations for a few data representations that are processed by other operations. As discussed in succeeding subsections, these include signed integers, floating-point values, character strings, and decimal digit strings.

Exercises

1. There are two ways to increment the number of siblings for the value in *PersonData*. The first uses the pack and unpack operations shown above, and the second adds a value to *PersonData* directly.

   (a) Show instructions for both methods.

   (b) Show how to extend the second method so the person will not undergo a sex change when there are too many siblings.

2. What error might occur undetected on execution of the second **and** in statement (2.3)? Why is there no need for an **and** with age when creating an entire new value for *PersonData*?

3. Data values may be stored in either packed or unpacked form. The value 250,000,000 (roughly the population of the United States) can be stored in many ways, including one character per word for nine words or as an integer in a 32-bit word.

   (a) Estimate how many operations would be required to convert a nine-digit value to binary using Algorithm 2.2. (See Section 1.4.2.)

   (b) The cost of writing a record to disk can be expressed as $c_1 + nc_2$, where c_1 and c_2 are cost constants and n is the number of words in the record. Roughly speaking, c_1 is at least a thousand operations and c_2 is about one. Assuming one million values of nine digits each are to be written to disk, discuss whether conversion to binary would reduce costs.

2.3.1 Signed Integers

To store a signed integer we must pack together both the sign of the value and its absolute magnitude. There is no natural representation as for positive integers (Section 2.2). Even worse, the choices for signed integers all have various computational drawbacks (see Exercise 1). The four most common encodings of the integers are presented below: two's complement, one's complement, signed magnitude, and offset. To give an intuitive notion of the meaning of these encodings, they will be expressed in terms of the number line—the natural progression of k-bit values shown in Figure 2.2. The first three representations use the second half of the number line, from C to D, to represent the negative values, so in these cases the high-order bit of a negative value is one and of a positive value is zero. Where the discussions include arithmetic expressions, any overflow from the kth to the $(k+1)$st bit is ignored.

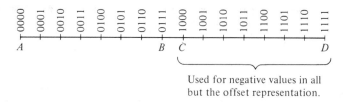

Used for negative values in all but the offset representation.

Figure 2.2
The natural sequence of all four-bit binary values. The letters A, B, C, and D identify points on the line; in succeeding diagrams the letters will appear under the same binary values.

The most common encoding, *two's-complement*, is formed by placing the last half of the number line in front of zero. Thus -1 is represented by the binary value that was last in the natural order; see Figure 2.3. If n is a positive integer of $k - 1$ bits, the k-bit two's-complement representation of $-n$ is given by $2^k - n$. If working by hand, it is simpler to compute the two's complement negative of a value by adding one to its bit-wise complement. For example, with four bits the representation of -2 is given by $0010 \to 1101 \to 1110$, which is indeed the next-to-last value in the natural progression (and is also $2^4 - 2$).

The *one's-complement* encoding also places the last half of the line in front of the positive integers, but the largest number and zero are made to overlap; there are two representations for zero, as shown in Figure 2.4. The k-bit one's-complement representation of $-n$ is given by $2^k - 1 - n$. (This is one smaller than the two's complement.) In one's complement, the negative of a value is simply the bit-wise complement. Thus the four-bit representation of -2 is $0010 \to 1101$ which is $2^4 - 1 - 2$.

The *signed-magnitude* encoding is a packed value; the $k - 1$ bits on the right are used to represent the absolute value of the integer, and the high-order bit is set to one if the value is negative. This corresponds to moving the second half of the number line to the front of zero, but reversing it end for end and overlapping the previously middle value with zero, as depicted in Figure 2.5. As with one's complement, there are two representations for zero. To convert a value to negative, the first

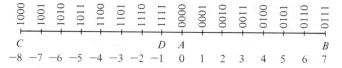

Figure 2.3
The two's complement representation. Note that there are more negative values than positive.

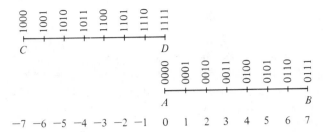

Figure 2.4
One's complement overlaps two values, so there are two representations of zero.

bit is complemented. If n is in signed-magnitude, the representation of $-n$ is given by $2^{k-1} + n$.

The *offset* encoding leaves the number line in its order and the integers in their order as well; however, it abandons the natural representation of the positive integers. The positive integers are represented by the right half of the number line and the negative integers by the left; observe Figure 2.6. The representation of any n is given by $2^{k-1} + n$; for positive values of n this merely means setting the high-order bit to one. The negative, $-n$, of an offset encoded value n is given by $2^k - n$. The offset encoding is often used for the exponent of floating-point values.

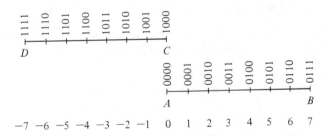

Figure 2.5
Signed magnitude reverses the order of the negative values.

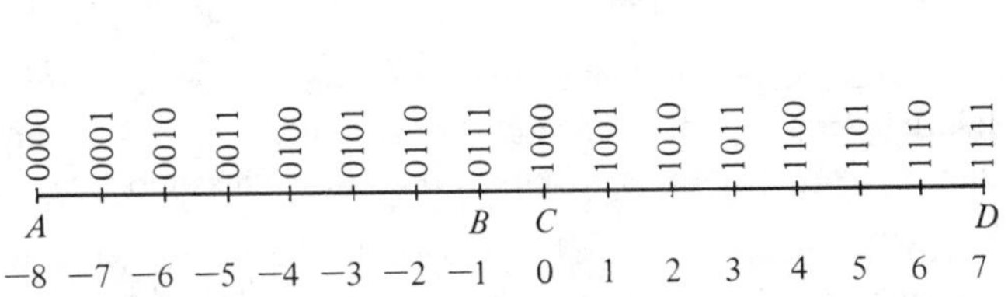

Figure 2.6
Offset retains both the order of the integers and the order of the binary values, but the representation of the positive values has the high-order bit set to one.

Exercises

1. When two k-digit positive numbers are added, they are said to *overflow* if the sum requires $k + 1$ bits. For example, the sum of 14 and 2 overflows in four-bit arithmetic because the sum, 16, requires five binary digits. For each of the four notations discussed in the text derive rules for adding two $(k-1)$-bit values. Your rules must properly set the sign of the result and must determine if an overflow has occurred. Consider adding positive values, negative values, and values of opposite sign. For what representation are the rules simplest?

2. Multiplication and division are frequently done by making both operands positive and adjusting the sign of the result. Determine whether multiplication can be done more directly for any of the four representations.

3. Explore the "signed-minitude" representation in which $-n$ is represented by complementing the high order bit of n and subtracting one from the result. Thus, with four bits, the representation of -1 is 1000. Moreover, there is only one representation of zero, and there are more negative than positive values. What is the addition algorithm? Is there a simple rule for deriving the representation of $-n$ from the representation of n? Express the signed-minitude of $-n$ as a function of n.

4. Show the representation of the following numbers in six-bit binary, using each of the four representation schemes: $0, 1, -1, -6, -12, -31, -32$.

5. Imagine two 32-bit words with four 8-bit characters packed in each. Under what conditions would integer comparison be unsatisfactory to determine which value was alphabetically larger?

6. In one's complement and signed magnitude there are two representations for zero. Computers that use these representations usually convert negative zero to positive zero in one or more of the following situations: after performing an arithmetic operation, before comparing two values, or before storing a value. Suppose we have three otherwise identical computers, each of which converts negative zero in a different one of the three cases. For each computer describe a program fragment that will perform as expected on that computer but fail on one of the others.

7. Note that there are more negative integers than positive integers with two's complement. Explain why a program containing the statement $x := -x$ may be incorrect. Describe precisely what this statement does on your computer.

8. Show that two's complement is "natural" in the following sense: when two integers of whatever sign are added, the result has the proper sign and representation if no overflow has occurred. Argue first with the number line and then with expressions involving 2^k and computations modulo 2^k.

2.3.2 Floating-Point

Conceptually, *real* values are those that can be expressed in *scientific notation*—that is, with a mantissa multiplied by ten raised to some *exponent*. Thus the following values in scientific notation are also *real* values:

6.02×10^{23} (Avogadro's number, the number of molecules in a mole).

3.34×10^{-9} seconds (the time for light to travel one meter).

6.96 years (the time for capital to double at 10 percent interest).

Hardware representations of real values are called *floating point* because each value includes the exponent that shows where the decimal point belongs in the final value. Also packed in a floating-point value are the mantissa and sign fields; the format used for Figure 2.1 was:

$$\boxed{\text{sign} \mid \text{exponent} \mid \text{mantissa}} \qquad (2.4)$$

where the exponent is a five-bit integer in two's-complement form and the sign is a one-bit field that gives the sign of the mantissa in signed-magnitude form. Since the values are represented in binary, it is more convenient to use the exponent as the position of the *binary point* of the value rather than the decimal point. The binary point of the mantissa is assumed to be at its left, so the value

$$0 \underbrace{0\,0\,0\,1\,0}_{\text{exponent}} 1\,0\,1\,0\,0\,0\,0\,0\,0\,0$$

is interpreted as $0.101_2 \times 2^{10_2}$ or, in decimal, 0.625×2^2, which is 2.5. An exponent shift rule applies to binary values, so the above value could be interpreted by shifting the binary point right two places and reducing the exponent to zero. This gives the binary value 10.1_2, which is indeed the binary for 2.5.

Almost every hardware design has utilized its own format for floating-point values. Many differ in their representation of negative exponents and negative mantissa. A few designs (notably those of IBM) treat the exponent as a power of sixteen rather than two. In the shift rule, then, the binary point moves four places for each change of one in the exponent. This scheme provides a wider range of exponent, but the accuracy of the mantissa is reduced because the mantissa must often begin with insignificant zeros. Greater accuracy is offered by the IEEE standard for floating point; it uses the exponent as a power of two and omits the first digit of the mantissa because it is always one (except for numbers of very small magnitude, which have special representations).

Not all values in scientific notation are values in floating point. In practice, the range of values is limited by the number of exponent bits, and the accuracy is limited by the number of mantissa bits. In addition, some hardware operations on floating values introduce additional problems. These will be illustrated in subsequent paragraphs, assuming a computer with decimal digits in the mantissa and exponent to avoid inconvenient conversions between decimal and binary.

To illustrate addition of floating values, consider adding 0.5×10^{-7} and 0.3×10^{-4}. First line up the decimal points by increasing the smaller exponent; this converts the first operand to 0.0005×10^{-4}. Next add the mantissas to get 0.3005×10^{-4}. In this case, we are done, but if the leftmost nonzero mantissa digit is not just after the decimal point we apply a third step. For instance in adding 0.3005×10^{-4} to -0.2991×10^{-4} the result of the first two steps is 0.0014×10^{-4}, which is adjusted by shifting the mantissa to get 0.14×10^{-6}.

This process of shifting the result is called *normalization* because it is considered "normal" to have a nonzero digit after the decimal point. It has the advantage of increasing the accuracy of multiplication (Exercise 3). Note that when a value is normalized by shifting left, zeros are inserted at the right, which may not be correct for the situation modeled with the floating value. In the last example above, both operands have four valid digits of information, but the result has only two.

The fact that only finite accuracy is available can lead to incorrect results and results that depend on the order of operations. To illustrate, consider adding 0.3003, 0.1×10^1, and 0.3007 with four-digit precision. Added in this order, the first partial sum is 0.1300×10^1 and the final result is 0.1600×10^1. However, if the two smaller values are added first, the result is 0.1601×10^1. The discrepancy is small here, but it can accumulate to a large value for a long chain of calculations, or lead to unexpected results when testing for equality.

It is a curious fact that floating-point values are "closer together" near zero. On our decimal computer, the closest value to 1.0 is at a distance of 0.1×10^{-3}, while the closest value to 0.1×10^{-50} is at a distance of only 0.1×10^{-53}. (What are the next larger and smaller values for each of 1.0 and 0.1×10^{-50}?) We can illustrate these facts by examining the number line in Figure 2.7 and labeling some of the points. Just as overflow can occur by adding values that produce an exponent

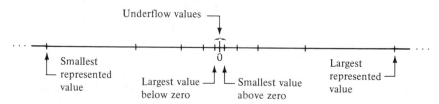

Figure 2.7
Number line.

larger than can be represented, a floating-point operation can also *underflow* by producing a value with an exponent too small to be represented, that is, in the gap between zero and the smallest nonzero value representable. Hardware often signals this error and automatically chooses the value zero if the program does not otherwise respond to the signal.

Exercises

1. Convert the following values to the binary floating-point representation (2.4), showing the result in hexadecimal: 1, -1, 0.5, 1024, 0.1, -0.2, 91.

2. Find the smallest and largest nonzero positive values that can be represented with (2.4). Express them in hexadecimal and decimal. Under what condition is it not possible to normalize a value?

3. Show in binary the result of multiplying 0.50390625 by 0.65625 with and without normalization. Which form of the answer is closer to the correct product of these values?

4. Suppose a floating-point value in format (2.4) is generated with zeros in the first two binary positions and random ones and zeros in the remaining fourteen positions. What is the expected value of the result?

5. Prove that a greater number of distinct values can be represented with a one-word **integer** variable than a one-word **real** variable. [*Hint*: Consider the representation of zero.]

6. The Newton-Raphson approximation to the square root of x is given by iteratively finding a new approximation r' from the old approximation r, using

$$r' = (r + x/r)/2$$

On one calculator this process never produces a result that is too large; on another the result is never too small. What is the difference between these calculators?

7. Write a procedure to perform a floating-point addition of two values represented as in (2.4). Assume the hardware has integer and logical operations but no floating-point operations.

2.3.3 Strings

One way to store a string of characters is to store one per word in an array. Access to characters is simple with this scheme, but it wastes space: with 32-bit words and eight-bit characters only one quarter of memory is utilized. The alternative is to pack multiple characters in each word. The string 'CURLY–MOE' would take nine words with the first scheme:

C	U	R	L	Y	–	M	O	E

but would take only three words when packed:

CURL	Y–MO	E

In the latter approach, the last word may be filled out with some special character that cannot be part of any string value, or left blank, with total length of the string indicated elsewhere.

Some representations of character strings include the length of the string as part of the first word of the packed value. Usually two character positions are enough for the length, since this offers a maximum length of 65,535 characters. Our string would now look like

9 CU	RLY–	MOE

where assuming, ASCII, the first word would appear as

$$0009435516_{16}$$

A character string can be used as an alternative to the binary form of Section 2.2 for storing integers. The value is represented as the sequence of characters that make up the printed version of the value. Thus the decimal value of the approximate population of the United States—250,000,000—could be stored in binary as the value $0EE6B280_{16}$, but it could equally well be stored as the string of characters '2 5 0 0 0 0 0 0'. In some situations this might be appropriate to avoid the expense of conversion to binary (see Exercise 3 of Section 2.3). A representation of integers intermediate between binary and character strings, called *packed decimal*, stores only four bits for each digit. With this scheme, the hexadecimal representations of the packed-decimal version of 250,000,000 is

$$25000000_{16}0xxxxxxx_{16}$$

where x indicates a value to be ignored. As with packed-character strings, the length of a packed-decimal value must be indicated somehow—either as a first digit or elsewhere.

With packed-decimal data two additional items may be encoded: the sign of the value and a decimal point. Convenient encodings for these are possible with four-bit values because the decimal digits require only ten of the sixteen possible values. We then assign four of the extra codes to $+$, $-$, ., and x. (In ASCII a natural choice would be B, D, E, and F. Why?) Unfortunately, most hardware does not make specific assignments to these codes, so any arithmetic with such values would have to be performed with a subroutine rather than a hardware instruction.

Two common character string data items are names and dates, both of which are problematic because humans are accustomed to a wide variety of forms. For example, Edward Bernard Grogan, Junior, may be referred to as E. B. Grogan, Jr., Ed Grogan, Mr. Grogan, Grogan, E. B., and many others. He may even receive a "personalized" letter from a fund raiser addressing him as Mr. Junior. If Grogan had a doctoral degree, he could also be referred to as Dr. Grogan or E. B. Grogan, Jr., Ph.D. Names with various heritages offer additional challenges: the surname is in the middle of Spanish names and at the beginning of many oriental names. Names sometimes have embedded blanks and capital letters, as in McDonald and da Vinci.

Any form of a name can be stored in a file, but the appropriate record can be recovered later only if the searcher has some idea of the form in which the name was originally entered. One suitable standard format might be:

- All titles and honorary suffixes are removed.
- The name is divided into three fields, a "last name," a "first name and initials," and an optional "suffix" (Jr., Sr., III, and so on). Suffixes are abbreviated.
- No field contains a comma. They may contain only letters, capitalization, spaces, hyphens, and periods.
- The name is written with last name, comma, and first name. If there is a suffix, it is placed at the end after a second comma.

For sorting names in this format, the names must first be transformed to remove spaces and convert lower case to upper case. (Why?) Then when the names are sorted according to the character sequence, they will be in alphabetic order. When the file is interrogated with an on-line query, the system converts the name to the above format and searches the file, using one of the search techniques of Chapter 7.

An appropriate encoding for dates must allow human reading, comparison of dates, and arithmetic to determine the elapsed time between two dates. Among the many date forms are

May 28, 1941	month-name dd, yyyy	Traditional. Month may be abbreviated.
5/28/41	mm/dd/yy	North American
28/5/41	dd/mm/yy	European
41/5/28	yy/mm/dd	Data processing standard
41.148	yy.ddd	"Julian;" ddd is the number of days past December 31.

The yy/mm/dd form provides for human readability and comparison, but it must be converted to perform arithmetic. The yy.ddd form is suitable for arithmetic but is not very readable by humans. For data bases it is best to adopt a standard form for date and time and convert all other forms to it for internal processing. One possibility is to count the number of milliseconds since the midnight beginning January 1 in the year that would be A.D. 0 by the Julian calendar. A six-byte field is sufficient to distinguish any millisecond between then and A.D. 8000. This form is excellent for comparison and arithmetic but makes no concession to human readability.

For many varieties of data items, standards exist and can be employed without the effort of developing a code. For example, the National Bureau of Standards has produced standard two-character codes for states of the United States. For more detailed geographic encoding, the Bureau of the Census has divided the country into county-sized units and has defined the extent of the large metropolitan areas. Additional codes have been developed under the auspices of the American National Standards Institute.

Exercises

1. Show the ASCII hexadecimal representation of the string 'Carrie H.' with the length in the first two bytes.

2. Write a procedure to select the kth character from a string packed with four characters per integer. Arguments to the procedure should be k and the array of integers. Assume that the length is stored in the first word of the string. The character selected should be returned in the rightmost bits of the result.

3. Write a procedure to add two packed-decimal values and replace the second with the sum. The four arguments to the procedure should be the length and an array of integers for each operand. Each integer is packed with eight digits. The procedure should return a result code indicating whether any error occurred during execution. Consider carefully what errors can occur. Do not expect decimal points and signs in the values.

4. It is not necessary to assign the values 8, 4, 2, 1 to the bits representing a digit; another possibility is -1, 2, 3, 6. Show the code for each digit using the latter values. Find another set of values that includes neither 1 nor -1.

5. Early RCA computers used a code where zero was 0011 and succeeding decimal digits had successively higher binary values, with 1100 representing nine. Why was this code called XS3? (Please do not groan too loudly.) Show the more-or-less simple rule for adding two decimal digits encoded in XS3 and determining whether to carry a one into the next higher digit position. In your judgment, is the simplicity of this rule a sufficient justification for choosing XS3 representation?

6. Write a procedure to check the form of names stored with the standard form sketched in the text. The input should be a name in an array of characters. The output should be a value indicating the nature of the first error detected, if any. The hardest part of this exercise is to develop the list of errors.

7. In some situations, such as airline reservations systems, it is valuable to encode names so they can be located even if the exact spelling is not known. One such code is used by many states for driver's license numbers. The code for a name starts with the first letter of the name. The remainder of the code is the first three digits derived from letters in this table:

BFPV	1
CGJKQSXZ	2
DT	3
L	4
MN	5
R	6
other	ignore

Double letters such as LL are reduced to a single letter, and the combination SC at the beginning of a name is absorbed by the initial S. Thus SHELL and SCHULL are both encoded as S400. Hansen is H525 and Reingold is R524.

(a) Encode your name in this code.

(b) Find three names that have at least four variant spellings each and show the encoding for all twelve names.

(c) Try to find a name with a variant spelling such that the encoding maps the variants into different codes.

8. Design a procedure to convert dates to the yy/mm/dd format. The input should be a date in an array, one character per array element; the output should be the date in another array in the prescribed format. Your routine should accept at least three different input formats, but it should assume that xx/xx/xx dates are in the order MMDDYY if the first two digits are not a year value (if they are, no conversion is needed). Complications to consider include dashes, spaces, commas, or slashes between date elements; alphabetic month specifications; year value absent (use current year) or specified with two or four digits; Julian dates.

9. The most common abbreviations for the names of the months are three and four characters long, but a shorter representation could save space. A one-character code would be too terse and artificial because more than one month starts with J and M. Devise a two-character alphabetic code for the month names. An overriding criterion should be recognizability by humans; a secondary concern is that humans ought to be able to encode month values quickly and reliably with little training.

10. In many situations a word typed to a computer is supposed to match one of a set of words. If the typed word is misspelled, a procedure can check to see if it is a misspelling of a correct word according to one of these possibilities:

- A letter has been omitted.
- A letter has been added.
- A letter has been changed to another.
- Two letters have been interchanged.

Write a procedure to check whether one word is a misspelling of another. The input for each word should be a length and an array with one character in each element. The output should be signals indicating whether there is a potential match, and if so, what and where the error is. [*Hint*: Use the lengths to determine which errors are possible.]

2.4 RELIABILITY AND EFFICIENCY

Previous sections have covered representations of values of various kinds. Two areas of mathematics deal with properties that such representations can have. One of these areas, *coding theory*, deals with the question of how message transmission can be made reliable; that is, how the sender of a message can ensure that the recipient gets the intended message instead of some garbled version. The other area, *information theory*, deals with the question of how efficiently information can be transmitted— how quickly and at what minimum cost. Reliability can be illustrated by computer memories, which often use *nine* bits to encode each 8-bit byte of memory. The ninth bit is called the *parity* bit and is set so that the total number of one bits is odd. As a result, if any bit of memory is accidentally changed, the change will be detected as a byte with an even number of one bits. A memory with parity is more reliable to the extent that, while it cannot reconstruct correct values, it will at least indicate that it does not have the correct value.

Efficiency is illustrated by the Morse code shown in Table 2.13, where different numbers of dots and dashes are sent for each character. For example, E and T are high-frequency letters and are represented by only one dot or dash. At the low-frequency end of the alphabet are letters such as J and Q with four dots or dashes each. If all codes were of the same length, each would have to be five dots or dashes just to distinguish among the letters and six of the ten digits. There would then be no provision for the other four digits or the punctuation marks.

In data base applications many non-numerical data items must be encoded as character strings: sex, language skills, warehouse location, product color, and so on. Design of such encodings must consider issues of reliability and efficiency. A one-bit code for sex occupies minimal space, but may be misinterpreted by a human. It

A ● ▬	N ▬ ●
B ▬ ● ● ●	O ▬ ▬ ▬
C ▬ ● ▬ ●	P ● ▬ ▬ ●
D ▬ ● ●	Q ▬ ▬ ● ▬
E ●	R ● ▬ ●
F ● ● ▬ ●	S ● ● ●
G ▬ ▬ ●	T ▬
H ● ● ● ●	U ● ● ▬
I ● ●	V ● ● ● ▬
J ● ▬ ▬ ▬	W ● ▬ ▬
K ▬ ● ▬	X ▬ ● ● ▬
L ● ▬ ● ●	Y ▬ ● ▬ ▬
M ▬ ▬	Z ▬ ▬ ● ●

Table 2.13
International Morse code. The ▬ (pronounced "dah") symbols are three times the
length of the ● (dit) symbols when the code is transmitted as sound signals. Codewords for letters are separated by letter space gaps as long as a dit; words are
separated by word spaces as long as a dah.

is more reliable to use the characters M and F; however, they make less efficient use
of space. Color codes will occupy minimum space if all colors are numbered sequentially, but users may prefer a numbering that indicates the mixture of the three primary colors. To suit both man and machine, codes can be stored compactly and
translated to and from a human readable form.

An encoding may be designed so all code values are the same length. This
tends to make programs more reliable because access to data is simpler; but it can
make inefficient use of space and lead to expansion problems: For many years US
Army personnel records have utilized fixed size fields exclusively. This has simplified programming, but massive conversions were necessary to change from three
digit APO codes to five digit ZIP codes and to expand the size of officer serial
numbers by one digit.

Account numbers, personnel numbers, part numbers, and other artificial identification schemes unambiguously identify a person or item with minimum storage
space, but are unreliable because they lack redundant cues like vowel-consonant order that people subconsciously check when writing down names and addresses. In-
teractive systems can aid data entry operators by displaying the complete identification of the individual or item after the number is entered.

To detect errors in account numbers, they must somehow include redundancy.
The common errors of omission and insertion of single digits are readily detected if
all account numbers are the same length. The other common errors—single digit
substitution and adjacent digit transposition—can both be detected by appending a
check digit to each account number. Here are three possible schemes; others are
discussed in the exercises.

Scheme 1—Modulo Nine. In this method the account number is divided by nine and the remainder is the check digit. This method is about 98 percent effective against substitution of one digit for another (Exercise 1) but is worthless against transpositions. (See Exercise 2.)

Scheme 2—Double Even. The check digit is chosen so the following process yields zero when the check digit is included in calculation:

1. Double the digits in the even positions (that is, the ones position, the hundreds position, and so on).

2. Add all digits in the results of (1) to all digits in odd positions.

3. Take the sum in (2) modulo 10.

Doubling the even position digits in 36415209 yields 12, 2, 4, 18, and the sum is $3+4+5+0+1+2+2+4+1+8$, which is 30, so it is a valid account number. The doubling protects against adjacent transpositions; the inclusion of the check digit in the calculation protects against transpositions with it; and the addition of the tens digit from the doubling avoids the difficulty that the low-order digit from doubling can be only 0, 2, 4, 6, or 8. Note, for example, that 4 and 9 are often confused in handwriting and yet when doubled both produce a low-order digit of 8.

Scheme 3—Divisible by Thirteen. In some cases it is possible to assign entirely new account numbers. If so, they can be chosen so they are all divisible by thirteen. Such numbers are protection against all single-digit replacements and transpositions across zero, one, two, and three positions (Exercise 4). Though there is no extra check digit with this protection scheme, account numbers will be somewhat longer than without it. The efficiency of the scheme can be measured by considering that it uses only one-thirteenth of all possible values with a given number of digits. This is about 0.0769, where the double-even scheme uses 0.1000 of all possible values (why?).

Exercises

1. Show that a modulo nine check digit will detect almost 98 percent of all instances where one digit is replaced by another.

2. The process of "casting out nines" is as follows: add together all of the digits of a decimal integer getting another integer. Repeat the process until the result is a single integer. Prove that the result is equal to the remainder when the original number is divided by 9. [*Hint*: $(10a+b)/9$ is equal to $(9a+a+b)/9$.]

3. (a) Suppose these are account numbers with the check digit represented by x: 472215x, 982327x, 111x. Compute the double-even check digit for each.

   (b) Using the same method, verify that the last digit is a correct check digit for these numbers: 123459, 00000, 99994.

4. (a) Show that divisible-by-thirteen account numbers protect against all possible single-digit replacements.

   (b) Show that divisible-by-thirteen account numbers provide protection against all transpositions between adjacent digits and digits separated by one, two, or three others.

5. Four familiar numbers in the United States are zip codes, social security numbers, driver's license numbers, and ten-digit phone numbers. All these codes have interesting features: zip codes have low error protection but gain some when combined with the two-letter state code; social security numbers are not unique (in fact, one particular number at one time served for twenty-nine different people); driver's license numbers often use the code of Exercise 7 of Section 2.3.3; and the second digit of area codes is either zero or one. For one or more of the above codes, do the following:

   (a) In many cases a number has components; a geographic code may use two digits for state, three for county, and two for town. For the code you are studying, describe the breakdown into components.

   (b) Find out what restrictions there are on the values in each component.

   (c) (Efficiency) Compute the number of possible codes when the restrictions are followed and how large a fraction that is of all codes if there were no restrictions.

   (d) (Reliability) Compute the probability of detecting an error caused by changing a single digit.

   (e) What is the cost of an error in interpretation of a codeword? Would this cost justify expansion of codewords to include a check digit?

6. The new machine readable passports now include check digits computed as follows: Each digit of the number (such as date of birth) is multiplied by the corresponding digit in the sequence 731731731...; these products are then added and the result modulo 10 is the check digit. Thus the date November 12, 1945 might be written 451112 and would yield the check digit

$$4\times7 + 5\times3 + 1\times1 + 1\times7 + 1\times3 + 2\times1 = 56 \equiv 6 \ (\text{mod } 10).$$

Comment on this method of computing a check digit. Why, for example, was the sequence 731731731... used? Are single digit errors detected? Are transpositions of adjacent digits detected?

7. On the back cover of this book is the ten-digit International Standard Book Number (ISBN) 0-316-73931-6. These numbers have been used on most books published throughout the world since about 1970. The first digit, 0, means the book was published in the English-speaking world (Germany would be 3, Israel 965, Denmark 87, and so on). The next group of digits, 316, identifies the publisher (in this case, Little, Brown and Company) which has chosen an identifying number 73931 for this particular book. The tenth digit, 6, is a check digit computed from the first nine digits so that the ISBN $d_1 d_2 \cdots d_{10}$ satisfies

$$10d_1 + 9d_2 + 8d_3 + 7d_4 + 6d_5 + 5d_6 + 4d_7 + 3d_8 + 2d_9 + d_{10} \equiv 0 \;(\mathrm{mod}\; 11)$$

If this requires that $d_{10} = 10$, then the character X is used. Discuss the extent to which this check digit protects against garbled numbers.

2.4.1 Reliable Codes

Reliability and efficiency problems have led to many interesting and deep mathematical analyses. Here we can only present the flavor of the subjects by considering a basic result in each area. For our formal model we hypothesize a *sender* transmitting *messages* to a *receiver* through a *channel*. Each message is chosen from a set (usually finite) of possible messages and transmitted over the channel by the sending of a *codeword*. A *code* is a table that specifies the relationship between the messages and the codewords; for example, Table 2.11 and 2.13 are codes for ASCII and Morse code, respectively. For our purposes, a codeword can be thought of as a sequence of binary digits, but the theory is general enough to encompass codewords composed of arbitrary symbols. Binary digits are sufficient here because they are the means of storing and transmitting information in computers.

Coding theory deals with reliability as one aspect of *block codes*. These are codes like ASCII, in which all codewords have the same length. The basis for analyzing such a code is the Hamming distance: The *Hamming distance* $d(c_1, c_2)$ between two codewords c_1 and c_2 in a block code is the number of bit positions in which the two codewords differ. For example, in ASCII, $d('H', 'R') = d(01001000, 01010010) = 3$ because the codewords differ in the fourth, fifth, and seventh positions. Exercise 1 shows that the Hamming distance behaves as we expect of a measure of distance. One way to think of it as a distance is to imagine the map of a country where the city names are binary numbers and a road exists between two cities only if they differ in one digit of their name. The Hamming distance between two cities is then the minimum number of roads that have to be traversed to get from one to the other.

The simplest reliability property of a code is its detection of errors; this can be done by a parity bit as described above. In terms of the imaginary map, parity partitions all cities into two classes such that it is impossible to get from a city in one class to another in the same class without going through a city of the other class.

Thus to change one code to another requires a transition to an error code and then another into valid code. Because a change in one bit position has a rather low probability, the change of two separate bits is far more improbable, so this code is sufficiently reliable for ordinary computer applications.

It is possible for codes to *detect* errors in more than one position.

Error Detection Theorem
Errors in k or fewer positions can be detected if all codewords of a code differ by Hamming distances at least $k + 1$.

Thus, in the parity example, all codewords differ by at least two, so any error in no more than one bit position can be detected. In general, the Error Detection Theorem divides the cities of a map into three classes: the original codewords, those within k steps of each original codeword, and those that may be further than k steps from any codeword. The codewords in the first class are accepted as being correct, while those in the latter two classes are taken as errors.

This same division into classes is the basis for construction of codes that *correct* errors in transmission:

Error Correction Theorem
Errors in k or fewer positions can be corrected by the receiver if all codewords of a code differ by Hamming distances at least $2k + 1$.

In an error-correcting code, the erroneous codewords are partitioned in groups so that each is interpreted as an error variation of some particular codeword. The situation is sketched in Figure 2.8, where each valid codeword is shown surrounded by a *neighborhood* of invalid codewords that are closer to it than to any other codeword. Each neighborhood is a "circle" of "radius" k. Since the distance between circle centers is at least $2k + 1$, the circles do not intersect, and any invalid code within a circle can be corrected to the valid code at the center.

One important question in coding theory is to determine how big the codewords have to be to encode information with a given degree of reliability. This problem can be approached by starting with Figure 2.8 and computing the number of codewords that can be encoded with a given length and a given minimum Hamming distance between codewords. With codewords n bits in length, the available number of codewords is 2^n. For k–bit error correction, the neighborhood of each codeword must include the codeword itself and all codewords reachable in k or fewer errors. In exactly j errors the number reachable is

$$\binom{n}{j} = \frac{n!}{j!(n - j)!},$$

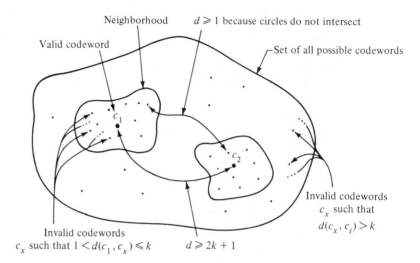

Figure 2.8
Neighborhoods within Hamming distance k of codewords

the number of ways to choose j items out of n. Thus, the number of codewords N is bounded by

$$N \leq \frac{\text{number of potential codewords}}{\text{number reachable in } k \text{ or fewer steps}}$$

$$= \frac{2^n}{\sum_{j=0}^{k} \binom{n}{j}} \tag{2.5}$$

Thus with messages of length sixteen, a code for at most 478 messages could be created that would detect and correct all errors in no more than two bit positions. Note that as shown by Exercise 3 it may not be possible to construct a code for the maximum number of codewords given by the equation.

Exercises

1. Verify that the Hamming distance behaves as one might expect a measure of distance to behave. That is, show that if c_1, c_2, and c_3 are codewords, then

   (a) $d(c_1, c_2) \geq 0$.

   (b) $d(c_1, c_2) = d(c_2, c_1)$.

(c) $d(c_1, c_2) = 0$ if and only if $c_1 = c_2$.

(d) $d(c_1, c_2) + d(c_2, c_3) \geq d(c_1, c_3)$.

2. Find two block codes for five messages each. The first must have Hamming distance two or greater between all pairs of codewords; the other must have distances of three or greater. (Codewords should be as short as possible.) What degree of error detection is afforded by each of these codes? Error correction?

3. Using Equation (2.5), determine the minimum number of bits required for codewords in a code that can send four messages in such a way that all errors of two or fewer bits can be detected and corrected. Show that no such code is possible with the minimum bit length. Find a suitable code using more bits.

4. The IBM 650 computer encoded information in a "two-out-of-five" code: five bits were used for each decimal digit; they had the values 0, 1, 2, 3, 6; and exactly two bits had to be set to represent a digit correctly. Since there are two possible representations for three with the above bit values, one of them was used to represent zero.

   (a) What is the reliability of this code? Prove your assertion from the viewpoints of the Hamming distance and of the design of the code itself.

   (b) What is the efficiency of this code? That is, of the possible values with the given number of bits, what fraction are actually available as codewords?

2.4.2 Efficient Codes

A codeword from a message source consumes resources, both space in storage and time on a transmission channel. One goal of information theory is to reduce this consumption by construction of more efficient codes. With block codes, every codeword has the same length, so the only way to reduce the resource requirement is to encode more than one message with some of the codewords. For example, English text could be represented more efficiently with eight-bit bytes if some of the unassigned codes were assigned to common letter pairs such as TH, AS, and ED. More often, efficient codes are constructed by using fewer bits for the more frequent messages, just as the Morse code of Table 2.13 uses fewer positions for the more frequent letters.

For the present discussion we require that codes be *instantaneously decodable*: no codeword is allowed to be an initial substring of another codeword. Note that Morse code fails this test because (for example) many codewords begin with dot, the codeword for E. With an instantaneously decodable code, a receiver can extract each codeword as soon as it is completely received, without waiting to see if subsequent bits transform it into a longer codeword. (Morse code delimits letters with a third "symbol" in messages, a pause between letters.)

The resource consumption of an encoding is measured by the expected number of bits to encode a message. (See the discussion of expected values in Section 1.3.2.) Thus if m messages have codewords with lengths t_1, t_2, ..., t_m and probabilities p_1, p_2, ..., p_m, then the expected length of the representation of a message is

$$\text{expected length} = \sum_{i=1}^{m} p_i t_i. \tag{2.6}$$

As an example, consider a source of messages for the outcome of hockey games. The possible messages might be: H—home team wins, A—away team wins, T—tie, or S—stoppage (riot, tornado, avalanche, or whatever). A block code for these messages might be

$$H = 10, \quad A = 01, \quad T = 11, \quad S = 00,$$

and the expected length for a message would be

$$2\,p_H + 2\,p_A + 2\,p_T + 2\,p_S = 2\,(p_H + p_A + p_T + p_S) = 2.$$

Since the message must be one of the four, the probabilities must sum to one, so the expected message length is two, as would be expected.

An instantaneously decodable variable-length code for the hockey outcomes is

$$H = 0, \quad A = 10, \quad T = 110, \quad S = 111$$

with expected length

$$1\,p_H + 2\,p_A + 3\,p_T + 3\,p_S.$$

If the messages are equally likely, the expected length is $(1+2+3+3)\,/\,4 = 2.25$, worse than the block code. In practice, however, wins are more common than ties, while stoppages are rare, so the probabilities might be something like

$$p_H = 0.47, \quad p_A = 0.44, \quad p_T = 0.07, \quad p_S = 0.02.$$

Now the average length with the variable-length code is 1.62, an improvement over the block code.

Since a change in the code has reduced the expected length, it is reasonable to ask whether some other encoding might do still better. There must be some lower limit, however, because clearly some number of bits must be used. Information theory shows that this lower limit is given by

$$\text{minimum expected length} = \sum_{i=1}^{m} -p_i \lg p_i \qquad (2.7)$$

which is called the *entropy* of the message source. The entropy of the hockey-outcomes code is

$$-0.47 \lg 0.47 - 0.44 \lg 0.44 - 0.07 \lg 0.07 - 0.02 \lg 0.02 = 1.41.$$

Thus the variable-length code above is 19 percent longer than the minimum, a level that is quite reasonable. To get closer to the entropy of a message source generally requires a more complex encoding.

Entropy is measured in units called *bits*, but we will use the longer term *information bits* here while we explore their relation to the *physical bits* that constitute computer memory. The rationale for the term "bit" in "information bit" is that entropy measures asymptotically, the minimum expected number of bits needed to represent a message. It is beyond our scope here to justify (2.7), but see Exercise 1.

In general, the information content of a physical bit may not be a full information bit, as we can show by computing the information capacity of a physical bit. Suppose we have a message source that produces exactly two possible messages. Since these can be encoded in a single bit, the entropy of this source describes the capacity of a physical bit. If the probability of one of the messages is p, then the probability of the other is $(1 - p)$, so the entropy is

$$-p \lg p - (1 - p) \lg (1 - p). \qquad (2.8)$$

This expression approaches a value of zero when p approaches zero or one. This corresponds to the idea that a message source does not give as much information if the probability of one message is large. The maximum value for the expression is one, its value when $p = \frac{1}{2}$. Thus, *the capacity of a physical bit is at most one information bit*; a physical bit may contain less than one bit of information, but never more.

A process called *Huffman's algorithm* computes the minimum entropy variable-length code for a set of messages with given probabilities. This process has two phases as illustrated in Figure 2.9. The first phase builds a diagram linking the messages; the second assigns a codeword to each message. Initially the diagram has an isolated element for each message with the probability p_i in the element. At each step of the first phase the two elements of smallest probability are paired together to form a new element whose probability is the sum of their probabilities. This construction ends when there is only a single element, which by definition has probability one. Figure 2.9(a) shows the outcome of this first phase. In the second phase we label one element of each pair with 1 and the other with 0. The codeword for a

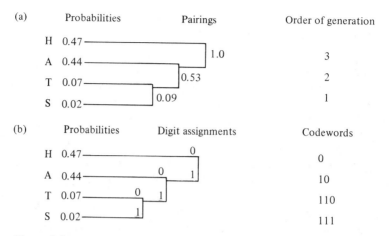

Figure 2.9
Illustration of Huffman algorithm. (a) The diagram is constructed in the order
shown. (b) After 0's and 1's have been assigned, the code for each message is
found by tracing the line from right to left and recording the bit values encountered. For this example, the expected number of bits per message is 1.62.

message is the sequence of labels encountered on the path to the message from the
final element, as shown in Figure 2.9(b). Huffman's algorithm minimizes entropy by
arranging that on average each bit will choose between message sets whose probabilities are as nearly equal as possible.

The algorithm can be proved correct by a recursive argument starting with
consideration of the two elements with the smallest probabilities. These elements
must differ by a single bit in at least one code that produces the minimum expected
length. This is so because the two smallest-probability codewords can be given messages of the same length, and these should be the longest codewords. After combining the two smallest elements, the same argument applies recursively to a set with
one element less.

The foregoing discussions suggest that a code can be either reliable or efficient
but not both. Actually, messages can be encoded first in a variable-length code, and
then the stream of variable-length segments can be split into fixed-length blocks.
Finally, each block can be encoded with enough extra bits to achieve the desired
degree of error protection. As an illustration, the hockey outcomes H, A, A, H, H,
T, A, H, S, T, A, H, A would be first encoded as 0, 10, 10, 0, 0, 110, 10, 0, 111,
110, 10, 0, 10 and then grouped together to form 01010001, 10100111, 11010010.
For single error detection, a parity bit could then be appended to each block:
010100011, 101001111, 110100100. Note that in this case the encoding takes only
one more bit than the two-bit block code for the messages, even though the latter
offered no error protection at all. (See Exercise 10.)

Exercises

1. Note that Equation (2.7) for entropy computes the expected value for the expression $-\lg p_i$. This quantity, $-\lg p_i$, is called the *information content* of message i; it depends only on the probability of that message.

   (a) Show that the information content in two independent messages is equal to the sum of the information contents for the two messages.

   (b) Suppose a source is capable of generating 2^m possible messages and all are equally likely. Show that messages can be encoded in m bits. Show that the information content of a message is m bits.

2. Show that the entropy in (2.8) cannot exceed one. This means that a bit cannot encode more than one "bit's worth" of information.

3. The nonnumeric component of a bridge bid has eight possibilities: Pass, Club, Diamond, Heart, Spade, No Trump, Double, Redouble.

   (a) Suppose these are equally probable; what is the expected length of a codeword to send one of these messages?

   (b) Suppose the probabilities have the following (more reasonable) values: 0.43, 0.10, 0.08, 0.10, 0.12, 0.12, 0.04, 0.01, respectively. What is the entropy of this message source? Use the Huffman algorithm to derive a code with one codeword for each message. What is the expected length of a message in your code?

4. If a code encodes four messages, only two essentially different sets of codewords can be derived by Huffman's algorithm. What are they? Under which conditions is each the result of the algorithm?

5. Show that the process of Huffman's algorithm gives the most accurate method to sum floating-point numbers. (See the example of summing three such numbers in Section 2.3.2.)

6. One way to reduce the bit requirement for messages is to send more than one message with each codeword. The kth extension of a message source is the set of all messages consisting of k messages chosen from the original set. The second extension for the hockey-outcome code is shown in Table 2.14 along with one possible code for the extended messages.

   (a) What is the expected number of bits per original message (H, A, T, or S) with the code shown in Table 2.14?

   (b) Use the Huffman algorithm to derive a more efficient code for the messages.

   (c) With your new code, what is the expected number of bits for an original message?

Information	Probability	Code
HH	0.2209	00
HA	0.2068	01
AH	0.2068	10
AA	0.1936	110
TH	0.0329	11100
HT	0.0329	11101
TA	0.0308	111100
AT	0.0308	111101
SH	0.0094	1111100
HS	0.0094	1111101
SA	0.0088	1111110
AS	0.0088	111111100
TT	0.0049	111111101
TS	0.0014	111111110
ST	0.0014	1111111110
SS	0.0004	1111111111

Table 2.14
Second extension of the hockey-outcome code. The code shown here is instantaneously decodable but is not optimum for the probabilities given.

7. The second extension in Table 2.14 uses sixteen codewords. One way to use fewer codewords is to represent only the high-probability pairs with special codewords. For example, we could have codewords for the messages HH, HA, AH, AA, H, A, T, and S, where H and A would be used only as the last codewords encoding a string of an odd number of H's and A's. When the probabilities of H, A, T, and S are 0.47, 0.44, 0.07, and 0.02, respectively, the probabilities of the eight codewords are

HH	0.2041778	HA	0.1911452	AH	0.1911452	AA	0.1789444
H	0.0390979	A	0.0366023	T	0.1235789	S	0.0353083

(T and S have increased probabilities because relatively fewer total codewords will be used for strings of H and A messages.)

(a) Use the Huffman algorithm to generate a code for the eight codewords above.

(b) Compute the expected number of bits required by the eight-codeword code to represent one of the original four messages (in a sequence).

★ (c) Derive the probabilities given above for the eight codewords. [*Hint*: Use Markov chains.]

8. Zipf's law states that the probability of using a word in a natural language is inversely proportional to its position in a list ordered according to frequency of use. Thus if there are n words, the probability of the ith most frequently used word is proportional to $1/i$ and is given by

$$p_i = \frac{1}{iH_n} \quad \text{where} \quad H_n = \sum_{i=1}^{n} \frac{1}{i} \approx \ln n.$$

H_n is the sum of the first n terms of the harmonic sequence 1, ½, ⅓, ...; it appears in the divisor of p_i to normalize the probabilities so they sum to one.

  (a) With a vocabulary of n words, how many bits would be required to express each if they were equally probable?

★ (b) Show that the entropy of the probabilities in Zipf's law is about $(\lg n)/2$.

  (c) How many bits per human word are implied by the relation in (b)? How does this compare with the number derived in (a)?

9. Computer memories typically contain many bytes with the value zero; one study showed that as many as forty percent were zero. Given this fact, the contents of a memory can be encoded by using a single zero bit for zero bytes and a one followed by the contents for the other bytes. Determine the saving in bits if memory is in fact forty percent zeros. What is the major disadvantage of this scheme?

10. In the example in the final paragraph of this section the thirteen messages averaged 2.077 bits each.

  (a) Compute the expected number of bits per message with this encoding. (It is less than 2.077.)

  (b) Write an expression that gives the expected number of bits when messages with expected length m are encoded in blocks of size b having p additional bits for protection.

11. One interesting property of a code is its *resynchronization distance:* if a stream of bits encoding messages is interpreted starting at an arbitrary point, how many bits will be examined before the bits are being correctly interpreted? For example, if the stream in the final paragraph of this section is interpreted starting with the third bit, only one bit will be incorrectly interpreted. However, if the start is at the fifteenth bit (ignoring parity bits), five bits will be misinterpreted. What is the expected number of bits that will be misinterpreted for the entire sequence, assuming the interpretation is equally likely to start at any of the 24 bits (ignoring parity bits)?

12. Discuss the advantages and disadvantages of storing a sequence of zeroes and ones as an array of integers that records the number of zeroes between successive ones. Under what conditions is memory saved? Consider the specific case in which the sequence of zeroes and ones indicates the locations of prime numbers, so that the array of integers records the differences between successive prime numbers.

2.5   REMARKS AND REFERENCES

The focus of this chapter has been on the programming side of bits and their interpretations as boolean, integer, real, and character values. A discussion of the machine architect's view of the same material can be found in

Mano, M. M., *Computer System Architecture,* 2nd ed. Englewood Cliffs, N.J.: Prentice-Hall, Inc., 1979.

The representation of numbers, and especially real numbers (as opposed to integers), is fraught with computational difficulty. See the October 1979 issue of the *ACM SIGNUM Newsletter*, which is a special issue devoted to the various difficulties in the choice of a representation.

The representation of characters or messages by bit sequences is an area of considerable depth in mathematics. See

MacWilliams, F. J., and N. J. A. Sloane, *The Theory of Error-Correcting Codes*, Vol. I (1977) and Vol. II (1980). Amsterdam: North-Holland Publishing Co.

This work has come to be known as the bible of coding theory.

Chapter 3

Elementary
Data Structures

A teacher who can arouse a feeling for one single good action, for one single good poem, accomplishes more than he who fills our memories with rows and rows of natural objects, classified with name and form.

Elective Affinities,   Goethe

Words as a data structure are built on a storage structure consisting of a sequence of bits, as we saw in Chapter 2. In this chapter we show that sequences of words serve as the storage structure for the elementary data structures of *arrays*, *records*, and *pointers*. In later chapters these will serve in turn as the storage structures for higher data structures.

We first describe arrays and records and their applications. Then we will show how each can be implemented in terms of memory words and addresses.

3.1   ARRAYS

An array is a sequence of elements each having the same data type. The storage structure is a sequence of instances of whatever data structure is chosen for the elements. The principal function on arrays is *subscription*: given an array A and an integer i the operation $A[i]$ returns the ith component of the sequence of elements in A. Values called the *lower* and *upper bounds* are associated with each array to indicate the subscript values of the first and last element in the array. Subscription is defined only if i has a value between the lower and upper bounds.

In Pascal an array is declared like this

signs: **array** [37..239] **of** *integer*;

	[37]	[38]	[39]	[40]			[238]	[239]
signs:	12	13	10	6		· · ·	22	35

Figure 3.1
An example of an array. As declared in the text, the array *signs* has 203 integer
elements with subscript values 37, 38, ..., 239. In this diagram, 12 is the value
in the array element with subscript value 37.

which specifies that *signs* is an array of 203 **integer** elements with subscripts ranging
from a lower bound of 37 to an upper bound of 239. We can picture this array as in
Figure 3.1.

It is not necessary that each element of an array occupy exactly one word. An
array of single bits is an important case and is called a *boolean array* or a *bit table*;
we will have occasion to use these in later chapters. An array of characters is called
a *string*. As we discussed in Section 2.3.3, considerable memory space can be saved
if we *pack* consecutive elements of the array so more than one is in each word (see
Exercise 10). Array elements can also be multiword values and even arrays and
records themselves. For efficient access it is preferable that each array element occupy the same amount of storage, a case we will cover in Section 3.3.1.

The strength of arrays is that elements can be accessed *sequentially* or at *random*. Sequential access considers each element in turn. For example, the total of all
elements in *signs* could be computed as

$$total := 0;$$
$$\textbf{for } i := 37 \textbf{ to } 239 \textbf{ do}$$
$$total := total + signs[i]$$

Similar sequential access would be used to print each element or to compute a function of the values in one array and store the results in another.

In access at random a reference to the ith location is not necessarily followed
by a reference to the $(i + 1)$th or $(i - 1)$th. Binary search, Algorithm 1.3, employs
access at random as do our next two examples. In both of these examples values in
one array, an *index*, are subscripts into another. We will access the index array
sequentially, but the other at random. First consider Algorithm 3.1 where we sort
the array *table* with a selection sort. Suppose elements of *table* are multiple words
so the assignment

$$t := table[i]$$

must be implemented with a loop. To avoid the execution time for this loop we use
an index array x, defined so that the ith element of the sequence is in $table[x[i]]$, as
illustrated in Figure 3.2. To sort *table*, we begin by setting $x[i]$ to i for $1 \leq i \leq$

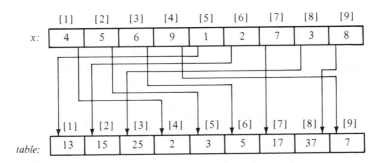

Figure 3.2
Example of an array used to index another array. The elements of *table* are data
values and the elements of *x* are subscript values indicating elements in *table*.
The values in *x* are such that they give the elements of table in ascending order.
Thus *x*[1] contains the value 4 and *table*[4] is the smallest data value.

nKeys. Comparisons are made between *table*[*x*[*i*]] and *table*[*x*[*j*]], but interchanges
are made only between *x*[*i*] and *x*[*j*]. Thus the first time through the outer loop will
set *x*[*nKeys*] to contain the one value *j* such that *table*[*j*] is the largest element in
table. Although selection sorting is generally inferior as a sorting algorithm, as we
will see in Chapter 8, the technique of making changes in an index array rather than
the one to be sorted can be used in conjunction with just about any sorting technique.

```
for i := nKeys downto 2 do begin
    j := 1;
    for k := 2 to i do
        if table[x[ j]] < table[x[k]] then
                j := k;
    t := x[i];
    x[i] := x[ j];
    x[ j] := t
end
```

Algorithm 3.1
Simple indirect selection sort. (Compare this with Algorithm 8.5)

An index array can form the basis of one way to implement sequences where
the elements are not all the same length—such an implementation can save space
when some elements are much longer than others. Names are usually short, but
occasionally long; so if the maximum space were allocated to each name, considerable space would be wasted. Instead, consider each name as a sequence of characters. We store all the characters of all names in a single sequence *chars* and store the

Figure 3.3
Names of varying lengths packed into a single long array with a second array
used as an index array to indicate element boundaries in the first array

subscript of the end of the ith name in $name[i]$. Then the ith name consists of the
characters

$$chars[name[i-1]+1], \ chars[name[i-1]+2], \ \ldots, \ chars[name[i]].$$

Figure 3.3 shows an example. Notice that $name[0]$ is 0 so the above expression is
correct even for $i = 1$.

To simplify expressions for subsequences of arrays we adapt the '..' of Pascal
array declarations for use in exposition and program comments. The expression
$A[t..v]$ means all elements of A from $A[t]$ to $A[v]$, inclusive. Thus the ith name in
$chars$ is given by

$$chars \ [name[i-1]+1 \ .. \ name[i]]$$

We will even use this notation in comparisons so $x < A[t..v]$ will be a shorthand for
$x < A[t], \ x < A[t+1], \ \ldots, \ x < A[v]$.

In addition to one-dimensional arrays, most programming languages allow multidimensional arrays. These are specified by giving more than one pair of dimension
limits in the description of the array. For example, the three-dimensional array shown
in Figure 3.4 could be declared by

$$A: \textbf{array} \ [1..2, \ 1..3, \ 1..3] \ \textbf{of} \ integer;$$

In general, the ranges of the subscripts can be arbitrary integers.

We will discuss representations of multidimensional arrays in Section 3.3.1.

Exercises

1. Suppose the array *signs* gives the number of billboards in each mile of Interstate
   I-94 from Ann Arbor to Chicago. Write a loop to find the cities along the interstate, assuming that a city will have a cluster of at least five consecutive miles

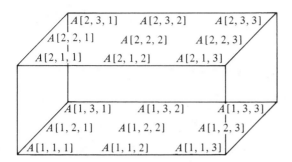

Figure 3.4
The elements of a three-dimensional array

where the number of signs is above average. Store the location of each city in an array *cities* by storing the number of the middle mile in the cluster.

2. Design a procedure to generate and print all *n*! permutations of the *n* elements $A[1..n]$. [*Hint*: Make your procedure recursive, choosing each element to be the first in turn and calling itself to generate all permutations of the remaining elements.]

3. Design a program to build and print histograms. The input is a sequence of integers with values between zero and 100 (say, grades on an exam). The output should be 101 lines, each containing an integer at the left and a row of asterisks proportional to the number of times that integer occurred in the input. The lines should be in order by the numerical values of the integers. [This exercise uses an array for both random access (counting the occurrences) and sequential access (printing the lines).]

4. Array subscript values can sometimes be calculated directly from data values. For example, a compiler must scan the input looking for identifiers, integers, and special characters; this is called *token scanning*. As part of this process it is useful to have a "type" value associated with each character to indicate whether it is a letter, a digit, or some other character. This is accomplished efficiently with an array *chtype* having one entry for each of the 256 possible character values:

chtype: **array** [0..255] **of** *integer*;

To determine the type of character *c*, the token scanner retrieves *chtype*[*ord*(*c*)]. *chtype* could be initialized with constants, but the program can be made machine independent if character constants in the program are used to generate the locations to store values. For example, to set the type for all letters we could use this program fragment:

$$alphabet := \text{'ABCDEFGHIJKLMNOPQRSTUVWXYZ'};$$
$$\textbf{for } i := 1 \textbf{ to } 26 \textbf{ do}$$
$$chtype[ord(alphabet[i])] := 1$$

(a) Write a program to initialize *chtype* so that the type of all digits is 3.

(b) Write a program to initialize *chtype* so the following special characters have the indicated value:

$$value: \quad 2 \quad 3 \quad 4 \quad 5 \quad 6 \quad 7 \: 8 \: 9 \: 10 \: 11 \: 12 \: 13$$
$$character: \quad E \: \uparrow \: . \: + \: - \: * \: / \: (\:) \: = \: , \: \text{space}$$

(c) Assume that *buffer* is a string and that *buffer*[*cursor*] contains the first digit of a sequence defining a non-negative integer, terminated by the first succeeding nondigit character. Write a procedure to find the value of the integer.

5. Rewrite Algorithm 8.1, the simple insertion sort, in a manner parallel to Algorithm 3.1.

6. Write a procedure to make an entry in a table represented as in Figure 3.3. Assume that the characters of the name to be added are in *new*[1..*n*], and that the first unused location in *name* is given by *free*.

7. (a) Write a procedure to compare two names represented as in Figure 3.3, indicating which of the names would be first in a telephone directory. (The names are in the standard form converted for comparison as discussed in Section 2.3.3.)

(b) Use the result of (a) along with Algorithm 3.1 to get a procedure to produce a sorted index array for a table of names represented as in Figure 3.3.

(c) Write a version of binary search for index arrays as in (b).

(d) Suppose that a search as in (c) discovered that a name was not in the table. Give an algorithm to insert it, keeping the index array up-to-date.

8. A simple alternative to the representation of names in Figure 3.3 is to have an array of fixed-length strings, each as long as the longest possible string. If the longest string has l characters and the average length of the n strings is $\bar{l}$, which approach is more economical?

9. Another alternative to the representation of Figure 3.3 is to use an array of characters, an array of subscripts *start*, and an array of lengths. If we have

chars: SELLSHELLSEASHOREBYTHE

$\uparrow$ $\uparrow$ $\uparrow$ $\uparrow$ $\uparrow$

1   5   10   18 20

then we can represent the popular tongue twister by

start: 5 1 10 5 18 20 10
length: 3 5   3 6   2   3   8

Note that values can overlap, as do SELLS and SHELL.

(a) The array *chars* contains 22 characters but represents a phrase with 30 non-blank characters, giving a compression of $22/30 \approx 73$ percent, neglecting the extra space for the arrays *start* and *length*. Encode some other phrases in the same manner and compute the compression ratios.

(b) It would be more realistic to compute the compression ratio including the space required for the arrays *start* and *length*. Do it for the example above and your examples in part (a).

(c) How would you sort a set of strings represented as above?

10. Packed arrays of bits and characters are examples of the general case of an array of k-bit values stored in sequences of w-bit words. In this data structure, subscription is implemented as two functions *Store* and *Retrieve*. *Store*(A, i, v) puts value v in array A as the ith element. *Retrieve*(A, i) returns the ith element in A. There are at least three possible storage structures for this data structure: one value per word, continuous without straddled words, and a continuous stream of bits, as shown below:

one value per word:

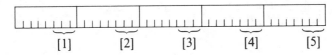

[1]   [2]   [3]   [4]   [5]

no straddled words:

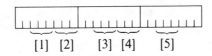

[1] [2]   [3] [4]   [5]

continuous bit stream:

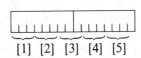

[1] [2] [3] [4] [5]

In this example, $k = 3$ and $w = 8$ with five values being stored. (In most Pascal implementations the **packed** attribute is treated as the no-straddled-words case.)

(a) Write *Store* and *Retrieve* procedures for each of the three storage structures, using logical operations to extract the proper bits (see Section 2.1).

(b) For each of the three cases, how many words are needed to store n elements for given values of k and w?

(c) Describe circumstances under which each of the approaches would be the best choice.

11. Continuous functions like temperature over a surface can often be computed approximately with an array. Suppose we wish to model an experiment in heating a copper sheet where three edges of the sheet are kept at 0°C and the fourth at 100°C. To determine the steady state interior temperatures, we represent the sheet as a collection of small squares, each with a uniform temperature, which we store as an element in a two-dimensional array. The computation begins with the edge squares at the given temperatures and two corners and all interiors at 50°C:

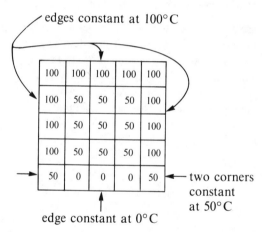

Then, each square not on the boundary has its temperature set to the average of the temperatures of the eight surrounding squares; this is done repeatedly until it yields only insignificant changes in the interior temperatures. Perform such a calculation using a 10×10 array. How much longer would it take to use a 100×100 array?

12. Write a program to print an organization chart. The input is a file of no more than 100 lines, each containing the name of an executive and the names of his subordinates; the lines are in alphabetical order by executive. Each name is limited to ten characters, and each executive is limited to a maximum of seven subordinates. The final line specifies which of the executives is the president—

it contains blanks in the first field and the name of the president in the second field. The output is to list one name per line, indented to indicate the number of executives above this person. The president's name is to be unindented on the first line. Subordinates' names are to appear in the listing below the name of their boss and before any other executive at the same level as their boss.

3.2   RECORDS AND POINTERS

A *record*, like an array, is a sequence of elements; unlike an array, the elements of a record, called *fields*, may be of diverse types and sizes. We imagine records as rectangles with subrectangles for the fields, as shown in Figure 3.5. Here the type of the record is *simpleDirectoryEntry*, and each such record has fields for name, address, and phone number.*

simpleDirectoryEntry

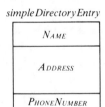

Figure 3.5
An example of a record containing three fields—*NAME*, *ADDRESS*, and *PHONENUMBER*. The subrectangles are shown in different sizes to reflect the different space requirements of each.

The storage structure for the record data structure is a sequence of the storage structures for the individual fields. The principle function on records is *field selection*, which returns a specified field from a record. In Pascal, field selection is written by placing a dot and field name after an expression for a record, so that if *current* is a *simpleDirectoryEntry* the value of the *PHONENUMBER* field is given by

   current.PHONENUMBER

and can be assigned a value with

   current.PHONENUMBER := 5551234

A Pascal program creates a record type in the **type** declaration section by writing the field declarations between **record** and **end**. The declaration for Figure 3.5 is

---

*In some programming languages, for instance PL/I and C, what we call a record is called a *structure*.

type
    simpleDirectoryEntry = **record**
        NAME: **array** [1..20] **of** *char*;
        ADDRESS: **array** [1..60] **of** *char*;
        PHONENUMBER: *integer*
    end;

Once a record type has been declared, the type name may be used in variable declarations as in

    current: *simpleDirectoryEntry*;

Note that the declaration of type *simpleDirectoryEntry* describes a layout of values in memory, but does not set aside any variable in memory having that layout. The latter is done only with a variable declaration or a call to procedure *new*, described later.

    A record variable is a variable and can appear wherever a variable can. We can assign or compare entire record values in a single expression. This makes programs more comprehensible, but not particularly faster since the assignment of the individual fields is only hidden, not eliminated. Because of the convenience of record assignment, it can be useful for a field itself to be a record. For example, if the *ADDRESS* field were a record composed of fields giving street, city, and zip code, then it would be easy to deal with the address as a unit and also to process its fields separately.

    Pointers. Despite the considerable utility of record variables for many applications, we have almost no use for them beyond this chapter. Instead we use records as the target of *pointers*. To introduce pointers, let us return to the phone directory example.

    Phone entries sometimes have subordinate entries; a physician lists his residence after his office or a parent lists the children's phone after the main number. Subordinate entries may have name, address, phone number, and even sub-subordinate listings (when the physician's residence has a children's phone), so we might try to write

    nestedEntry = **record**
        NAME: **array** [1..20] **of** *char*;
        ADDRESS: **array** [1..60] **of** *char*;
        PHONENUMBER: *integer*;
        SUBLISTING: *nestedEntry*   {This is wrong}
    end;

This fails! *SUBLISTING* cannot be of type *nestedEntry* because then variables of this type would occupy infinite storage, as we can see from Figure 3.6.

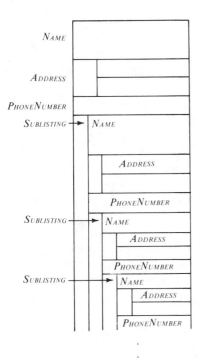

Figure 3.6
The storage layout for a *nestedEntry* requiring infinite storage

To declare subsidiary entries we need a field that might contain a subordinate listing or might contain nothing. We use a *pointer*. A pointer variable does not contain a record, but instead indicates the location of a record somewhere else in memory. One way to think of this is to imagine that each pointer variable is a rope and each record has a handle to which ropes can be attached. Assignment of a record value to a pointer variable causes the pointer's rope to be tied to that record. A special value, **nil**, can be assigned to a pointer to tie it to no record at all. With pointer variables, we can show a directory entry with two subordinate listings as in Figure 3.7.

In Pascal a field that points to a record of type T is declared to have type $\uparrow T$. The declaration for Figure 3.7 thus becomes

> *directoryEntry* = **record**
>   *NAME*: **array** [1..20] **of** *char*;
>   *ADDRESS*: **array** [1..60] **of** *char*;
>   *PHONENUMBER*: *integer*;
>   *SUBLISTING*: $\uparrow$ *directoryEntry*
> **end**;

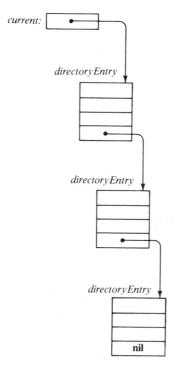

Figure 3.7
Feasible implementation of Figure 3.6 using pointers. In the rope metaphor the
arrows are ropes and the handles would be drawn in for the arrowheads to attach
to.

where the *SUBLISTING* field is a pointer. Pointer types also appear when declaring
pointer variables; the declaration

$$current: \uparrow directoryEntry;$$

makes *current* a pointer variable that can point to *directoryEntry* record values.

Until a value is assigned to it, a pointer variable is not connected to any record
value. Record values are created with the procedure *new*, which takes as its argument
a pointer variable, creates a new record with the type required for the pointer, and
ties a "rope" from the pointer variable to the new record value. We can create a
directoryEntry record value with the procedure

$$new(current)$$

The fields of the new record are not initialized.

To access the fields of a record value pointed to by a pointer, Pascal again uses the up-arrow. A pointer expression followed by an up-arrow is an expression for the record pointed at by the pointer. Usually we then extract a field by adding a dot and field name. The *NAME* field of *current* is accessed as in

$$current\uparrow.NAME := \text{'Dumpty, Humpty, Esq.'}$$

After the call to *new*, the *SUBLISTING* field does not point to a record, nor is it **nil**; its value is uninitialized. We can create subordinate listings for *current* with

$$new(current\uparrow.SUBLISTING);$$
$$current\uparrow.SUBLISTING\uparrow.NAME := current\uparrow.NAME;$$
$$new(current\uparrow.SUBLISTING\uparrow.SUBLISTING);$$
$$current\uparrow.SUBLISTING\uparrow.SUBLISTING\uparrow.NAME := current\uparrow.NAME$$

Finally we indicate there are no further subordinates by setting the innermost *SUBLISTING* field to **nil**:

$$current\uparrow.SUBLISTING\uparrow.SUBLISTING\uparrow.SUBLISTING := \textbf{nil}$$

The situation is now that given in Figure 3.7. (In future diagrams, a **nil** value will be shown as a diagonal line through the pointer rectangle.)

The standard Pascal function *new* allocates record values from a pool of available storage. A program can access records created by *new* only by traversing pointers from program variables. If we followed the statements above with

$$current\uparrow.SUBLISTING := \textbf{nil}$$

there would be no pointer to the second record and a pointer to the third only from that inaccessible second record. In Pascal, when record *p* is to be made inaccessible it should be returned to the pool of available storage by a call of the standard function *dispose*. We have done so in algorithms throughout this book; this occurs first in Algorithm 4.4. In each case *dispose(p)* must be called only when it is certain there are no other pointers to the record $p\uparrow$. The error of failure to dispose has the penalty of wasted storage; the penalty of the error of premature disposal, however, is much worse: the program will eventually fail in unpredictable and unrepeatable ways when the incorrectly disposed storage is reallocated for some other use by *new*. Implementation of *new* and *dispose*—and other approaches to management of allocatable storage—are discussed in Chapter 6.

Pointers can be compared for equality, just as other values can. Note, however, that comparison of two pointers does *not* compare the records to which they point!

Thus if A, B, C, and D are all pointers to directory listing records and they point as follows:

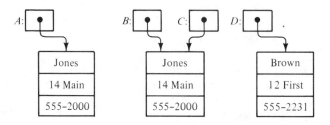

then A does not equal B (even though the records contain the same values); however, B does equal C (they both point to the same record). To compare the contents of two records, the up arrow selects the entire record attached to the pointer. The comparison

$$A\uparrow \; = \; B\uparrow$$

has the value **true**. Similarly, pointer assignment affects the pointers and not the records attached. $C := D$ makes C point to the same record that D points at, but does not affect B. However, the record value assignment $C\uparrow \; := \; D\uparrow$ changes the contents of the record attached to C. It does not cause C to point to a different record but alters memory so that the record pointed to by C *and* B contains new values. "Back-door" assignments like that to B can introduce subtle bugs into programs.

To summarize our discussion of pointers, note that they constitute a data structure: The storage structure is a single word (containing the address of the record value). The functions are $\uparrow$ to access the record attached to the pointer, *new* to create a new record value, and **nil**, the value for a pointer that points nowhere.

Exercises

1. Define a record type for playing cards; it should include fields for suit, rank, and whether the card is face up. Declare two variables for card records, one to represent the top card of a draw pile and the other to represent the top card of a discard pile. Imagine that cards are face down in the draw pile and face up in the discards, and assume that there is initially no card in the discard pile. Write a fragment of code to move the card from the draw pile to the discard pile; be sure to "turn it over" so it is face up.

2. A data base management system must keep a dictionary of the identifiers for each type of data the system stores. For example, a payroll record may have identifiers

such as *Name*, *DateOfBirth*, *Sex*, *PayGrade*, *DateHired*, *Address*, ... This dictionary is usually implemented as a set of records, with one for each identifier.

(a) Define a record type for dictionary entries. Each record should include at least the identifier and the field type.

(b) The *Address* field has subordinate fields *StreetNumber*, *StreetName*, *City*, and *Zip*. One way to represent this relationship is to store the name of the superordinate variable in the record for the subordinate name. Why is this simpler than storing the names of the subordinates?

(c) Instead of storing the name, we can store a pointer to the superordinate record. In what way would this be more efficient?

(d) Suppose we have an array of pointers to dictionary records. Write a procedure to find and print the names of all the subordinates of a given dictionary entry.

3. Write a procedure to create and initialize a *directoryEntry* and its subsidiaries, reading values for fields from the input. You may assume the existence of procedures to read values from the input: *ReadName*, *ReadAddress*, and *ReadNumber*. After the last record *ReadName* returns a value that begins with a period.

4. Consider the declarations

> **type**
>> *pTestcell* = ↑ *testcell*;
>> *testcell* = **record**
>>> *VALUE*: *integer*;
>>> *CHILD*, *SIB*: *pTestcell*
>>
>> **end**;
>
> **var**
>> *A, B, C, D*: *pTestcell*;

At the two places indicated in the following program fragment, show the configuration of the records. In particular, where do pointers point, which pointers are **nil**, and which records are no longer accessible?

> *new(A)*;
> *A*↑.*SIB* := **nil**;
> *new(B)*;
> *B*↑.*CHILD* := *A*;
> *new(C)*;
> *C*↑.*SIB* := *A*;
> *C*↑.*CHILD* := *B*;
> *D* := *C*↑.*CHILD*↑.*CHILD*;
> *D*↑.*CHILD* := **nil**;
> {What is the situation here?}

```
new(A);
A↑.CHILD := A;
new(B);
A↑.SIB := B;
B↑.SIB := B;
B↑.CHILD := C↑.CHILD;
new(C);
C↑.SIB := C;
C↑.CHILD := nil;
D := B↑.SIB↑.CHILD
{And here?}
```

5. Suppose we have an array of pointers to *testcell* records, as declared in the previous exercise. Write a procedure to sort the array of pointers so that the first points to the *testcell* record with the smallest value, and succeeding pointers point to *testcell* records with successively higher values. Do not examine or modify the *CHILD* or *SIB* fields.

6. Write a function to compute the depth of a *directoryEntry* value. The argument should be a pointer to a *directoryEntry*; if this value is **nil**, the depth is zero, otherwise it is one more than the depth of the *SUBLISTING* field.

7. At one point in a program for phone-directory maintenance it has been determined that the *directoryEntry L* must have a new subsidiary listing even though one may be there already. The new record is to have the existing subsidiary listing, if any, as its own subsidiary. Suppose that *N*, *A*, and *P* are, respectively, the name, address, and phone number for the new subsidiary listing. Write a sequence of assignment statements to make the insertion.

8. (a) Define a record type for representing a person. The information should be such that a program can determine for each person the name, date of birth, sex, and the location of records for parents and children.

   (b) Write a procedure to find a person's oldest sister. [*Hint:* You may want to redefine your structure for part (a) so that age ordering determines the order of children on lists.]

   (c) Write a procedure to find and print the names of a person's mother's brothers.

9. Most programming language implementations store real values directly in *real* variables. However, it is possible to implement them so a *real* variable is just a pointer to the real value. This would make sense if real values were multiword values, as is often the case in high precision calculations or in machines with small word lengths.

   (a) Unfortunately, a pointer implementation of *real* values must invoke *new* frequently. Show this by outlining a procedure to add two real values, assuming there is a subroutine to perform the actual addition. Explain why the result cannot be stored in one of the argument records.

(b) Suppose assignment is implemented by just copying one pointer into another. Can the system then have a "normalize" operation that does not call *new*? How about a procedure to increment a real value?

(c) Can we implement a system so that comparison of real values for equality is simply a process of comparing the pointers to the values? What are the disadvantages of this approach?

3.2.1 Examples of Records and Pointers

Records and pointers occur in many guises; this section considers four.

Random Access in Arrays. When a variable holds a subscript value, that variable is serving as a pointer to an element of an array. In binary search (Algorithm 1.3), the variables l and h point to the low and high ends of an array segment; m points to its middle. Similarly in Figure 3.2 each element of x is a pointer to an element of *table*. Algorithm 3.1 would change very little if x were an array of pointers to records, each containing a *KEY* field. The comparison would change to

$$\textbf{if } x[\,j\,]\!\uparrow\!.KEY < x[\,k\,]\!\uparrow\!.KEY \textbf{ then}$$

and t would be a pointer instead of an integer. (See Exercise 1.)

Variable-Parameters. When a procedure parameter F is declared without **var**, the formal parameter is a local variable of the procedure. When the procedure is called, F is initialized with the value of the actual parameter A. Thereafter, no operation on F has any effect on A. The addition of **var** to the declaration of F makes it a "variable-parameter," for which no space is allocated. Instead the local variable for F is a pointer to the actual parameter variable A, supplied by the call to the procedure. Any reference to F on the right or left of an assignment is treated as though it were $F\!\uparrow$, and the variable A becomes the source of the value or the target of the assignment, respectively.

Variable-Length Strings. In many applications strings need to vary dynamically in length, rather than have their exact length specified at the time of declaration. We can do this with records and pointers by implementing the string variable as a pointer to a record for the string value. This record can contain a length field followed by a string field containing the characters of the string. If the length of the string value is changed, *new* must be called to allocate a new string value.

For example, if *A* and *B* were strings with values 'CMU' and 'MICHIGAN', respectively, the situation would be this:

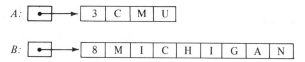

When *A* is assigned the value 'ILLINOIS', the situation becomes:

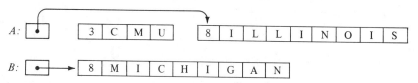

An assignment $A := B$ does not modify either record, but it makes *A* point to 'MICHIGAN' just as *B* does. In either of the above assignments, if there were no other pointer to the record for ┌─3─┬─C─┬─M─┬─U─┐ its space may be returned to the pool of available storage with *dispose*.

File Records. In traditional data processing, a *record* is the basic component of a file, which is just a sequence of records. In the file of Figure 3.8(a), the records are the phone company's list of customers. An input operation from this file makes a copy of one record value into a record variable like *current* as in Figure 3.8(b). It is then processed and possibly written to another file.

When files are on secondary storage, the term "record" has two meanings. It refers not only to actual data records but also to the block of data transferred to or from the storage device as a unit. These are not the same, because the high overhead in initiating and completing a transfer makes it more economical to move large numbers of data records together. This is called *blocking* the records. To distinguish the two kinds of records, the actual data records are called *logical records* while the groups transferred are called *physical records*.

When a physical record is read, it is transferred in its entirety from the storage device. To focus on one logical record at a time, we can choose *copy mode* or *locate mode*. In both, the physical record is copied from the file to a *buffer* area in memory. In copy mode the desired logical record is later transferred to a separate data record area for processing; *current* would indeed be a record variable. In locate mode *current* would be a pointer and the desired logical record would be chosen by attaching it to *current*. This avoids the time-consuming operation of copying the data.

Exercises

1. Write out in full the indirect selection sort of Algorithm 3.1 with *x* as an array of pointers to records. Show the state of *x* each time it changes in sorting five records with *KEY* values 10, 3, 12, 5, and 11.

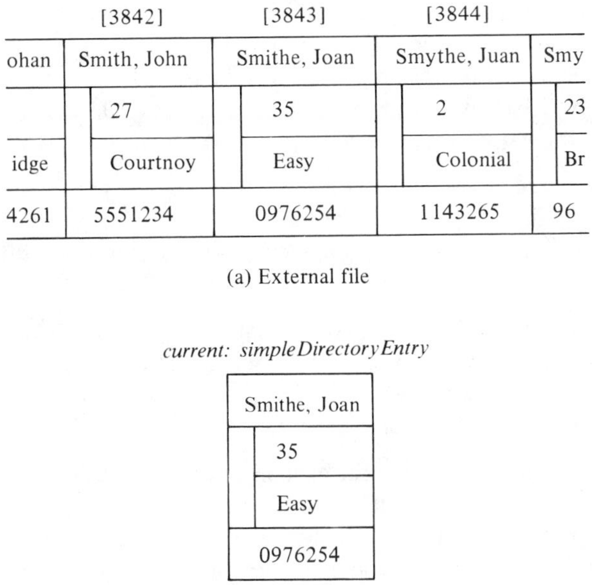

	[3842]	[3843]	[3844]	
ohan	Smith, John	Smithe, Joan	Smythe, Juan	Smy
	27	35	2	23
idge	Courtnoy	Easy	Colonial	Br
4261	5551234	0976254	1143265	96

(a) External file

current: simpleDirectoryEntry

Smithe, Joan
35
Easy
0976254

(b) In memory

Figure 3.8
In data processing an external file contains many different records of the same type (*simpleDirectoryEntry*, in this case). The record variable *current*—in memory—contains a copy of one record from the file.

2. Parameter-passing mechanisms are a considerable source of difficulty, both to programmers who must use them and compiler writers who must implement them. Consider this terror:

```
var
    temp: integer;
procedure Swap(var u, v: integer);
begin
    temp := u;
    u := v;
    v := temp
end
```

The terror springs from the unnecessary and inappropriate use of the global variable *temp* variable inside *Swap*. Explain what happens in executing the procedure body for the call *Swap(temp, x)*. Show the values of all variables before and after each statement is executed.

3. One alternative to variable-parameters is call-by-value-result. In this method a location is set aside for the parameter in the procedure itself. The actual parameter value is copied into the formal parameter space when the procedure is entered and the final value is copied back when the procedure terminates. Do the previous exercise assuming that u and v are passed with call-by-value-result.

4. Write a procedure to determine whether parameters are passed as variable-parameters or call-by-value-result. Do not use global variables (as was done in the previous two exercises). [*Hint*: Pass the same actual parameter to two different formal parameters.]

5. Suppose we call $Swap(i, A[i])$. Show the possible outcomes for various values of i and $A[i]$. Among the alternatives is whether to evaluate the subscript expression once on entry, or to reevaluate it every time an array reference is made. Consider both variable-parameters and call-by-value-result.

6. The principal operations on strings are concatenation and extraction of substrings. Assume that strings of undeclared length are implemented as in the text with a pointer to a record containing first the length and then the characters of the string. Show how to implement concatenation and extraction of substrings, given a version of *new* that takes an integer parameter specifying how long a string to create.

7. An alternate implementation of strings is to keep the actual characters in a separate area and implement each string value as a record containing the length of the string and a pointer to the first of the string characters. In this representation extraction of the substrings is especially simple; a new record is created describing the length and location of the substring. In some cases, however, a substring can also be used as the target for an assignment. Show how to implement the operation of replacing the third, fourth, and fifth characters of string C with another three characters. What happens if string C points to characters that are also part of some other string D? Suppose the replacement is four characters; can the operation be done?

8. (a) Implement a copy mode system. File F contains records of type R blocked ten to each physical record. Outline a procedure *Read* that will copy the next logical record into an area specified as a parameter to *Read*. *Read* should return **false** if an end of file is reached—that is, if the previous record returned was the last—and **true** otherwise. Assume that you have a procedure *ReadFile(buffer)* to transfer a physical record to *buffer* and that *ReadFile* will return the number of logical records transferred. It returns zero when end of file is reached. Specify initial values for all global variables referenced by your procedure.

   (b) Outline a *Write* procedure for the same file as in (a), assuming a procedure *WriteFile(buffer)* is given.

   (c) Do (a) and (b) using locate mode instead of copy mode.

3.2.2 Typical Programming Language Notations

Most modern programming languages provide facilities for records and pointers. In this section we compare these facilities in Pascal, PL/I, Algol 68, C, and Ada for a portion of the code implementing a symbol table for a compiler. Each record has fields giving the identifier for the variable, the number of occurrences of that identifier in the program, and a pointer to the next record of the same type in alphabetical order by identifier. After declaring a record type and a variable R to point to records of that type, the fragment gives a procedure to print all identifiers. The fragment goes on to show how to create a record, set R to point to it, initialize the number of occurrences to zero, increment the number of occurrences by one, and finally print the list of identifier records starting with the record pointed at by R. This fragment is presented in Pascal in Algorithm 3.2(a). Algorithms 3.2(b), (c), (d), and (e) give comparable fragments in PL/I, C, Algol 68, and Ada, respectively.

```
program example (input, output);
type pVariable =  ↑Variable;
      Variable = record
            IDENTIFIER: array [1..31] of char;
            FREQ: integer;
            NEXT: pVariable
      end;
var
      R: pVariable;
      . . .
procedure listing(P: pVariable);
begin
      while P ≠ nil do begin
            writeln(P↑.IDENTIFIER);
            P := P↑.NEXT
      end
end;
begin
      new(R);
      R↑.FREQ := 0;
      . . .
      R↑.FREQ := R↑.FREQ + 1;
      . . .
      listing(R);
      . . .
end.
```

Algorithm 3.2(a)
The fragment in Pascal

```
example: PROCEDURE;
        DECLARE 1 variable based,
                 2 identifier char(31),
                 2 freq fixed bin(31),
                 2 next pointer;

        DECLARE R pointer;
        ...

listing: PROCEDURE(P);
        DECLARE P pointer;
        DO WHILE(P ¬= NULL);
           PUT LIST(P –> identifier);
           P = P –> next,

        END;
        END listing;
        ...

ALLOCATE variable SET(R);
R –> freq = 0;
...
R –> freq = R –> freq + 1;
...
CALL listing(R);
...

END example;
```

Algorithm 3.2(b)
The fragment in PL/I

```
#include <stdio.h>
struct variable {
        char identifier[32];
        int freq;
        struct variable *next;}
struct variable *R;

        ...

listing(P) struct variable *P; {
        while (P!= NULL) {
           printf(''%s\n'', P–> identifier);
           P = P–> next;

        }

}
        ...

main () {
        R = (struct variable *)malloc(sizeof(struct variable));
        R–>freq = 0;
        ...
        R–>freq++;
        ...
        listing(R);
        ...

}
```

Algorithm 3.2(c)
The fragment in C

```
begin
  mode variable = struct (
    string identifier;
    integer freq;
    ref variable next);
  ref variable R;
  ...
  proc listing (ref variable P); begin
    ref variable T := P;
    while T/: /=: ref variable(nil) do begin
      print(identifier of T);
      T := next of T
    end
  end;
  R := heap variable := (skip, 0, nil);
  ...
  freq of R +:= 1;
  ...
  listing(R)
  ...
end
```

Algorithm 3.2(d)
The fragment in Algol 68

```
procedure example is
  type var_record;
  type variable is access var_record;
  type var_record is record
    identifier: string(1..31);
    freq: integer;
    next: variable;
  end record;
  R: variable;
  ...
  procedure listing(P: variable) is
    T: variable := P;
  begin
    while T /= null loop
      print(T.identifier);
      T := T.next;
    end loop
  end;
begin
  R := new variable(identifier = > '''',
                    freq = > 0,
                    next = > null);
  ...
  R.freq := R.freq + 1;
  ...
  listing(R);
  ...
end example;
```

Algorithm 3.2(e)
The fragment in Ada

Exercises

1. Work various exercises from Section 3.2 with the four additional languages used in this section.

2. Explore how the four additional languages treat record variables (as opposed to record values accessible only through pointers). Show how the languages distinguish declaration of pointer variables from declaration of record variables. In addition, determine how each language expresses copying and comparison of records.

3.3 IMPLEMENTATIONS IN MEMORY

In this section, we present the details of storage structures for implementing arrays, records and pointers. We begin with a brief discussion of the overall arrangement of memory. The memory of a computer is composed of a sequence of words, as illustrated in Figure 3.9. Each word is referred to by its unique *address*—that is, by its position in the sequence of words. The address of the first word is normally zero, since this allows a memory of 2^k words to have addresses that are k bits long. (See Exercise 1.)

A computer program is a sequence of instructions, each of which refers to words of memory by specifying the address of the desired word. Figure 3.10 shows a snapshot of the contents of memory as it might appear during execution of a program, although it is typical for more than one program to share the memory at a time. The first portion of memory contains the instructions and data that constitute the operating system—the monitor program responsible for starting and stopping programs and giving them access to system resources. Next come the instructions of the program and the data areas for variables, arrays, records, and input/output buffers.

We use the notation loc(*variable*) to represent the address to be used in an instruction referring to the variable. A compiler keeps track of how memory will be used at run-time. When it encounters a declaration for a variable, say x, the compiler implements x by setting aside one of the words of run-time memory as the location to store the value of x. The address of the word set aside is loc(x). If loc(x) is 21037, the assignment $x:=0$ would be compiled into a store-zero instruction:

stz 21037

In most computers each address value refers to a single byte: a thirty-two bit

word at 21036 would consist of the bytes 21036, 21037, 21038, and 21039. When
we speak of the width of an item in "words" in the next two subsections we are
really referring to its width in whatever the smallest unit that can be addressed on
the machine. In all byte-addressable computers, strings are stored with characters one
after another in bytes of increasing address. Integers are not treated as uniformly;
some computers place the high order byte of an integer in the lowest of the four
addresses; others place it in the highest. In the former the bytes of an integer read
from left to right in the same order as strings; in the latter strings and integers are
read in opposite order (see Exercise 5). This book is independent of the byte order;
the issue usually becomes a concern only when transferring data from a computer to
an external medium, especially for transfer to another computer.

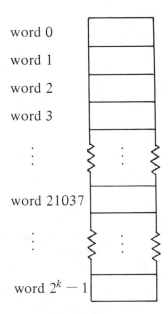

Figure 3.9
The sequence of locations in a computer memory

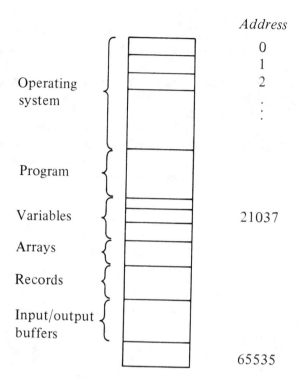

Figure 3.10
Snapshot of the contents of a computer memory with 2^{16} words

Exercises

1. Suppose a memory has 2^k words and addresses start with 1. How many bits are needed to express the address of the penultimate word of memory? How many bits are needed to express the address of the last word of memory?

2. Suppose a data area has d words of k bits and p pointers which point to other values in the data area. Show that the total space required (in bits) is not proportional to $d+p$ because pointers are implemented as addresses. Find an accurate expression for the space requirements.

3. Suppose you have a computer with 2^{16} words of sixteen bits each. Under what conditions will storing two variables A and B in successive words with A in the first and B in the second result in having the address of B numerically less than the address of A? This might be important if a program were doing address arithmetic to sequence through an array. For example, a loop might test for an address greater than the last in the array, but that address might be less than the beginning of the array. What approaches can be taken to avoid the problem?

4. If a program is moved from one area of memory to another (nonoverlapping) area, all the pointers in the program must be adjusted. Write a procecure to relocate a program. It has four arguments: the old location, the new location, the number of words in the program, and a bit map. The bit map has one bit for every word in the program; it is zero if the word does not contain a pointer, and one if it does. By what amount will pointers have to be adjusted? How many words does the bit table occupy?

5. Draw a diagram of part of memory holding two thirty-two-bit words: the integer $6789ABCD_{16}$ and the string 'abcd'. Give the address of each byte. Draw one diagram assuming that the computer puts the high-order byte of each integer into the lowest address; draw another diagram with the high-order byte in the highest address. How would two sixteen-bit integers appear in each of these computers?

3.3.1 Arrays

Given that memory is a contiguous sequence of words, we can conveniently store arrays by storing the elements in consecutive words. We then have the problem of interpreting array expressions, especially with multiple subscripts: for $A[i_1, i_2, \ldots]$ we must derive the address of the element from the address of the array and the subscript values.

Consider the one dimensional array

$$A: \textbf{array } [l..u] \textbf{ of } item$$

where *item* is w words long. A total of $(u - l + 1)w$ words are allocated to A beginning at loc($A[l]$) = L. Then, L, loc($A[l + 1]$) is $L + w$; loc($A[l + 2]$) is $L + 2w$; and so on up to loc($A[u]$) = loc($A[l + (u - l)]$) = $L + (u - l)w$. Thus we have the general expression for the location of $A[i]$ as

$$\begin{aligned} loc(A[i]) &= loc(A[l + (i - l)]) \\ &= loc(A[l]) + (i - l)w \\ &= L + (i - l)w, \end{aligned} \qquad (3.1)$$

as shown schematically in Figure 3.11.

In (3.1), the computation of the location of $A[i]$ requires a subtraction, a multiplication, and an addition. But suppose that instead of writing (3.1) in terms of L, the address of the first array element, we write it in terms of $L_0 = loc(A[0])$. If $l \le 0 \le u$, $A[0]$ will be somewhere among the stored elements; otherwise, it will be a conceptual location beyond one end of the array. In either case we can compute its location from (3.1):

$$L_0 = loc(A[0]) = L + (0 - l)w.$$

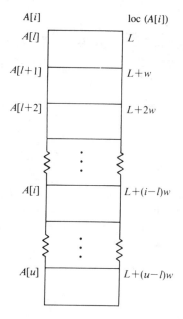

Figure 3.11

Diagram of an array $A[l..u]$ as arranged in memory, each element of the array requiring w words of storage. Observe that in all cases loc ($A[subscript]$) can be derived from $L + (subscript - 1)\, w$ as required by equation (3.1).

Solving for L and substituting in (3.1) we get

$$\text{loc}(A[i]) = L_0 - (0 - l)w + (i - l)w,$$

$$= L_0 + iw, \tag{3.2}$$

which requires only a multiplication and an addition.

Arrays of two or more dimensions must be "flattened" to fit them in the inherently one-dimensional space of computer memory. To do so the elements are placed in consecutive locations within subarrays, and the subarrays are themselves stored consecutively. Thus a 3×4 array B

$$B = \begin{bmatrix} b_{11} & b_{12} & b_{13} & b_{14} \\ b_{21} & b_{22} & b_{23} & b_{24} \\ b_{31} & b_{32} & b_{33} & b_{34} \end{bmatrix}$$

could be stored in the order

$$b_{11}\ b_{12}\ b_{13}\ b_{14}\ b_{21}\ b_{22}\ b_{23}\ b_{24}\ b_{31}\ b_{32}\ b_{33}\ b_{34}\ .$$

This is *row-wise* storage, the order we adopt below; the opposite approach is *column-wise*, wherein the leftmost subscript varies most rapidly. Expressions for the location of elements in a column-wise stored array can be derived by a simple transformation of the discussion below.

The general case is an n-dimensional array

$$C: \textbf{array } [l_1..u_1, \ldots, l_n..u_n] \textbf{ of } item$$

where we are to find a formula for $\text{loc}(C[i_1, \ldots, i_n])$ given that the array begins at L; that is, that $\text{loc}(C) = \text{loc}(C[l_1, \ldots, l_n]) = L$. Since we already have (3.1) as a solution to the one-dimensional case, we transform the problem for C to a series of one-dimensional problems.

The trick is to notice that C can be thought of as an array of subarrays. At the first level we have

$$C^1: \textbf{array } [l_1..u_1] \textbf{ of } [*, \ldots, *] \quad \{n - 1 \text{ stars}\}$$

where each element, say $C^1[i_1]$, has all elements of C whose first subscript has value i_1. In general, for any sequence of subscript values $i_1, \ldots, i_{k-1}$ there is a subarray

$$C^k: \textbf{array } [i_1, \ldots, i_{k-1}, l_k..u_k] \textbf{ of } [*, \ldots, *] \quad \{n - k \text{ stars}\}$$

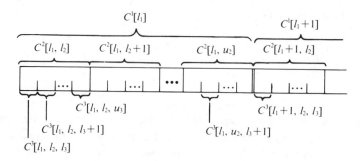

Figure 3.12
Nesting of subarrays of a multi-dimensional array

The nesting of subarrays is sketched in Figure 3.12.

To derive a formula for $\text{loc}(C[i_1, \ldots, i_n])$ note that it is within each of the arrays

$$C^1[i_1]$$

$$C^2[i_1, i_2]$$

$$\ldots$$

$$C^k[i_1, i_2, \ldots, i_k]$$

$$\ldots$$

$$C^n[i_1, i_2, \ldots, i_k, \ldots, i_n]$$

The general case of finding an element of C^k within an element of C^{k-1} can be depicted with this general nesting diagram:

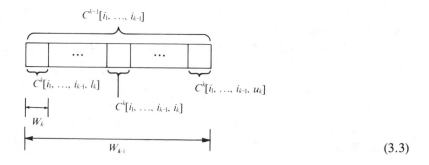

$$(3.3)$$

where W_k gives the number of words in each element of C^k. (W_k is a constant whose value we will compute below.) From this diagram and equation (3.1) we can see that

$$
\begin{aligned}
\text{loc}(C^k[i_1, &\ldots, i_k]) \\
&= \text{loc}(C^k[i_1, \ldots, i_{k-1}, l_k]) + (i_k - l_k)W_k \\
&= \text{loc}(C^{k-1}[i_1, \ldots, i_{k-1}]) + (i_k - l_k)W_k \qquad (3.4)
\end{aligned}
$$

The first term of the last line of (3.4) is in the same form as the first line, so we can apply the equation recursively, each time adding a term $(i_k - l_k)W_k$. The recursion halts when we reach $\text{loc}(C^1[l_1])$ which has value $\text{loc}(C)$. Thus we have,

$$
\begin{aligned}
\text{loc}(C[i_1, &\ldots, i_n]) \\
&= \text{loc}(C^n[i_1, i_2, \ldots, i_n]) \\
&= \text{loc}(C) + \sum_{k=1}^{n} (i_k - l_k)W_k \qquad (3.5)
\end{aligned}
$$

This can be simplified with the technique of equation (3.2) to eliminate the subtractions (see Exercise 2).

To compute W_k, the size of an element of C^k, we note first that the elements of C^n are elements of C itself so $W_n = w$. For other values of k consider again the general nesting diagram (3.3). In W_{k-1} there are $u_k - l_k + 1$ elements each have size W_k. Adding one to the subscripts we get

$$
W_k = \begin{cases} w, & \text{if } k = n \\ (u_{k+1} - l_{k+1} + 1)W_{k+1}, & \text{otherwise} \end{cases}
$$

At each step of the recursion we multiply by $(u_{k+1} - l_{k+1} + 1)$ so we can unravel the recursion to find that W_k is the product

$$
W_k = w \prod_{i=k+1}^{n} (u_i - l_i + 1) \qquad (3.6)
$$

For any given array the values of W_k are constants that depend only on w and the array bounds; thus they can be evaluated once and for all when the array is created.

Exercises

1. Simplify (3.5) and (3.6) for the following relatively common cases:
   (a) $n = 1$.
   (b) $n = 2$.

(c) $l_j = 0$ for all j.

(d) $l_j = 1$ for all j.

(e) $l_j = -u_j$ for all j.

2. Transform equations (3.5) and (3.6) by use of $C[0, 0, \ldots, 0]$ as was done for equation (3.2). Show that $\mathrm{loc}(C[i_1, i_2, \ldots, i_n])$ can be computed from n constant multipliers and a constant L_0 containing the location of $C[0, 0, \ldots, 0]$. Write a routine to initialize L_0 and the n constants; its arguments should be w, n, $\mathrm{loc}(C)$, and two one-dimensional arrays l and u containing $l_1 \ldots l_n$ and $u_1 \ldots u_n$, respectively. Write another routine to determine the location of $C[i_1, i_2, \ldots, i_n]$ given L_0, the n constants, and an array containing the subscript values.

3. Develop the columnwise analog of (3.5) and (3.6).

In Exercises 4 through 7 you are to design storage structures that allocate space only to nonzero elements.

4. A *lower triangular matrix* is a matrix $A = [a_{ij}]$ in which $a_{ij} = 0$ for $i < j$, and thus it is written

$$
A = \begin{pmatrix}
a_{11} & & & & \\
a_{21} & a_{22} & & & \\
a_{31} & a_{32} & a_{33} & & \\
\vdots & \vdots & \vdots & \ddots & \\
a_{n1} & a_{n2} & a_{n3} & \cdots & a_{nn}
\end{pmatrix}
$$

Design a sequential allocation for such matrices. The location of a_{ij} should be a simple function of i, j, and the location of a_{11}. Generalize your result for *tetrahedral arrays*: a k-dimensional tetrahedral array has the property that $a_{i_1 i_2 \cdots i_k}$ is nonzero only for $0 < i_k \leq i_{k-1} \leq \cdots \leq i_1 \leq n$.

5. A *tridiagonal matrix* is a matrix $A = [a_{ij}]$ in which $a_{ij} = 0$ if $|i - j| > 1$, and thus it is written

$$
A = \begin{bmatrix}
a_{11} & a_{12} & & & & \\
a_{21} & a_{22} & a_{23} & & & \\
 & a_{32} & a_{33} & a_{34} & & \\
 & & \ddots & \ddots & \ddots & \\
 & & & & & a_{m-1\,n} \\
 & & & a_{n,n-1} & & a_{n,n}
\end{bmatrix}
$$

Design a sequential allocation for such matrices. The location of a_{ij} should be a simple function of i, j, and the location of a_{11}.

6. Use your result from Exercise 5 to obtain a sequential allocation for

$$\begin{bmatrix} & & & a_{1,n-1} & a_{1,n} \\ & & & & a_{2,n} \\ & & \cdot & \cdot & \\ & \cdot & & \cdot & \\ a_{n-1,1} & & \cdot & & \\ a_{n,1} & a_{n,2} & & & \end{bmatrix}$$

7. We want to store values $A[1]$, $A[2]$, $\ldots$, $A[7]$ corresponding to the vertices of a triangular grid, as shown in Figure 3.13. There are three axes x, y, and z; however, a vertex is determined by specifying any two of its three coordinates. For example, $A[5]$ could be specified by $x = -1$, $z = 0$ or by $x = -1$, $y = 1$ or by $y = 1$, $z = 0$. Find three addressing functions $f(x, y)$, $g(x, z)$, and $h(y, z)$ that determine the array entry specified by given coordinates. In the example we would have $f(-1, 1) = g(-1, 0) = h(1, 0) = 5$.

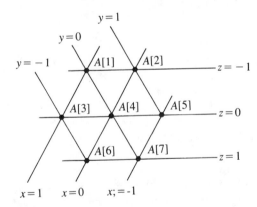

Figure 3.13
Exercise 7

8. In some FORTRAN implementations, arrays are stored in consecutive segments of memory. That is, if A and B are declared with

INTEGER A(100), B(50)

then 150 words are allocated with the first 100 devoted to A and the rest to B.

Since many of these implementations do not check the size of subscript values, it is possible to refer to elements of B with subscripts on A. Thus, for example, the following fragment initializes both A and B to zero:

$$\text{DO } 10 \text{ I} = 1,150$$
$$101 \text{ A(I)} = 0$$

What are the benefits and disadvantages of this trick? Consider space to store code, execution time, the probability of bugs, and the ability to move the code to another implementation of FORTRAN.

3.3.2 Records and Pointers

The implementation of records and pointers is simpler than that for arrays. A record is a consecutive block of words; a pointer value is the address of the first word in the block. Field selection is implemented as an offset from the pointer to the record, as we now show. Suppose a record is declared:

$$TypeName = \textbf{record}$$
$$FIELD_1: item_1;$$
$$FIELD_2: item_2;$$
$$\dots$$
$$FIELD_n: item_n;$$
$$\textbf{end};$$

where $item_i$ has length len_i words. If P is a pointer of type $\uparrow TypeName$, the address of $P\uparrow.FIELD_j$ is calculated from the length of the preceding $j-1$ fields. Thus the address of the jth field is given by

$$\text{loc}(P\uparrow.FIELD_j) = P + \sum_{i=1}^{j-1} len_i \tag{3.7}$$

This is illustrated in Figure 3.14. Note that equation (3.7) uses the value of P rather than $\text{loc}(P)$, since the value of P is the address of the record; compare this with equation (3.5).

We have been assuming that each field is an integral number of words. This is not so when we have packed records, and in this case field selection is more complex. As noted in Chapter 2, masking and shifting must be done to get the value from the field. More generally, fields may extend from the middle of one word through another word and on into a third or beyond. To permit this we consider the rightmost bit of one word to immediately precede the leftmost bit of the next word. In order to write a general procedure for field selection in packed records, we need a way to specify the location of the field. For unpacked records this is done by an offset to the word; for packed records we need a *descriptor* consisting of an offset giving the number of bits from the start of the record and the number of bits in the field (see Figure 3.15). Since these values will be fairly small compared to the maximum value for a word, they can themselves be packed into a single word. The descriptor might also contain an indication of the type of the field: *integer*, *real*, *character*, or whatever.

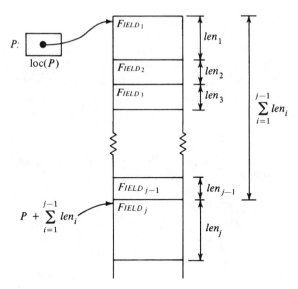

Figure 3.14
Layout of a record. Note that loc(P) is irrelevant to the location of the fields.

Field	Descriptors		Record

Field	Descriptors	
Ⓐ	0	21
Ⓑ	21	16
Ⓒ	37	62
Ⓓ	99	29
Ⓔ	128	32

Figure 3.15
Descriptors for fields in a packed record, assuming 32-bit words. The record has five fields, and each has a descriptor containing the start bit and length of the field. For example, the field C starts in the thirty-eighth bit of the record and is 62 bits long.

Exercise

Write out the details of the procedure for field selection in packed records. The arguments of the procedure are a pointer to the record, a pointer to the descriptor, and a pointer to an area in which to store the extracted field. Assume that there are w bits per word.

3.4 REMARKS AND REFERENCES

The problems involved in implementing arrays, records, and pointers are relatively simple in the static case—that is, when all size information is available at compile time. For declarations and allocations at run time the difficulties and possible trade-offs are many; some will be discussed in Chapter 6. Arrays with bounds known only at run time can be handled with *dope vectors*, a simple instance of records and pointers. See, for example,

Aho, A. V., and J. D. Ullman, *Compilers: Principles, Techniques, and Tools*. Reading, Mass.: Addison-Wesley Publishing Co., Inc., 1977.

This book also contains a discussion of the various parameter-passing mechanisms.

Chapter 4

Lists

I've got a little list, I've got a little list.

The Mikado, Gilbert and Sullivan

$\textbf{A}$ *list* data structure is a finite sequence of *elements*

$$s_1, s_2, \ldots, s_n. \tag{4.1}$$

For example, a shopping list is a list of items to purchase, a library catalog is a list of books, and a telephone book is a list of names, addresses, and telephone numbers. The *length* of the list is the number of elements on it—n in (4.1). Among the functions that can be defined for a list data structure are *insertion* and *deletion* of elements and an operation to find the *next* element after a given element. We will use the constant **nil** to represent the empty list—that is, the list with no elements. When *next* is applied to the last element of a list, **nil** is the value returned.

To illustrate these functions, consider writing a program to add an element *newphone* to a phone list L stored in order by phone number, where the *number* function applied to a list element returns its associated telephone number. The first portion of the program must find the proper position in the list for *newphone*:

$$x := L;$$
$$\textbf{while } number(x) < number(newphone) \textbf{ do}$$
$$x := next(x) \tag{4.2}$$

If we neglect the ends of the list, this loop will exit with the condition

$$number(\text{element before } x) < number(newphone) \leq number(x) \tag{4.3}$$

125

At this point the *insert* function is invoked to put *newphone* into place before x in L.

The simplest storage structure for a list such as (4.1) is *sequential allocation* in a one-dimensional array of records (see Chapter 3). If the elements of the list are in an array A, and s_1 is in $A[1]$, then s_i is in $A[i]$. Or, in general, if the first element is in $A[k]$, then s_i is in $A[k + i - 1]$. With sequential allocation, the algorithm for *next* is trivial: the subscript value is increased by one. In (4.2), x can be a subscript value, so the *next* operation is

$$x := x + 1 \qquad\qquad (4.4)$$

For this simple storage structure, the value of **nil** is one plus the number of elements in the list. With sequential allocation, however, the search of (4.2) could be replaced by the more efficient binary search of Section 1.3.

Unlike *next*, *insert* is cumbersome with sequentially allocated lists. For example, if the phone list of n elements is in an array A, the following loop is required to insert a record just before x:

> **for** $j := n$ **downto** x **do**
> $A[j+1] := A[j]$;
> $A[x] := newphone$

The time for this operation is generally proportional to n, the length of the list. There are also two additional costs of this *insert*. First, enough space must be allocated so that the array is large enough for the maximum number of elements that will ever be needed; in many cases programs are run with only a fraction of the maximum possible data, so this overhead may be large. Second, a graceful recovery is rarely possible if the number of elements allocated for the array turns out to be insufficient—the run must be restarted with a larger array. Since runs with more data generally take more time, the cost of restarting can be large. Fortunately, the problems of space and time can often be solved by the technique of linked lists introduced in this chapter. Linked lists are so important that the term "list" almost always refers to a linked-list implementation.

Exercises

1. Show that a dummy list element with phone number 999-9999 would enable program fragment (4.2) to deal with the end of the list. [*Hint*: Where in the list would this dummy element be?]

2. Using a sequential allocation, write a program to delete from the phone list the element for a phone that has been disconnected. Be sure to account for all special cases.

3. Expand condition (4.3) to include the situations at the ends of the list.

4. Explain how program fragment (4.2) can be used to sort a list as augmented in Exercise 1 into order.

5. Let us define *prepend* as a function of a value v and a list $x_2, x_3, \ldots, x_n$ which returns the list $v, x_2, x_3, \ldots, x_n$. Write a routine *reverse* of one argument l, a list, which uses *next* and *prepend* to produce a new list consisting of the elements of l in reverse order.

6. One way to represent an integer is as a "digit-list," a list of the decimal digits in the integer. Write a procedure *Add* to compute the sum of two digit-lists and return the result as a digit-list. (Use *next* and *prepend* as in Exercise 5.) Write a program using *Add* to calculate F_{85}, where F is the Fibonacci sequence, $F_0 = 0$, $F_1 = 1$, and for $i \geq 2$, $F_i = F_{i-1} + F_{i-2}$.

7. Show that if all the $n + 1$ possible locations for an insertion are equally likely, then the expected number of elements that must be moved for an insertion into a sequentially allocated list is $n/2$.

8. Show in detail how to implement the insertion into a phone list when the list is sequentially allocated and maintained in order by phone number. Include declarations and considerations of insertion at the ends of the list.

9. Explain why an assembly language version of (4.4) would be

$$x := x + a$$

where a is the number of words in each record.

★10. Suppose the number of elements actually occupied in an array R is a normally distributed random variable with mean μ and standard deviation σ.

    (a) Show that 97.7 percent of all runs will succeed if the space allocated for R is $\mu + 2\sigma$.

    (b) With the space allocated in (a), what is the expected percentage of the allocated space that is occupied?

4.1   LINKED LISTS

The inefficiency of inserting and deleting elements from a list that is sequentially allocated in an array occurs because the order of the list of elements is recorded *implicitly*. Adjacent records of the list must be in adjacent memory locations, so a number of records may have to be moved for an insertion or deletion. This movement can be avoided if the order of the elements is recorded explicitly instead of implicitly. In particular, a *linked-list* implementation associates with each list element s_i a pointer $NEXT_i$ to indicate the address at which s_{i+1} is stored. There is also a pointer

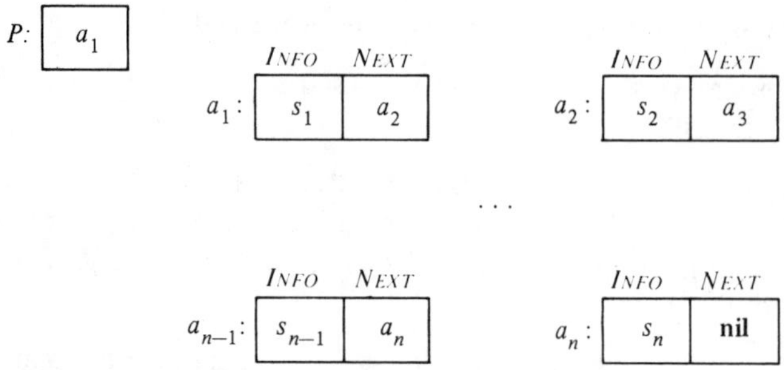

Figure 4.1
Representation of the list (4.1) as a linked list. Each record has an *INFO* field containing an element of the list and a *NEXT* field containing the address of the successor record. The end of the list is indicated by the value **nil** in the *NEXT* field.

P to the first element—the *head*—of the list; that is, P contains the address of s_1. These relationships are illustrated in Figure 4.1.

Each node (record) in Figure 4.1 consists of two fields, the list element itself in the *INFO* field and the pointer to its successor in the *NEXT* field as specified in Declarations 4.1. Since there is no successor to $s_n = a_n\uparrow.INFO$ we use **nil** as the value for $a_n\uparrow.NEXT$, where **nil** is the *empty* or *null* pointer. In diagrams we show **nil** as a diagonal line. The exact locations of $a_1, a_2, \ldots, a_n$ are unimportant in this context, so it is more common to depict the list of Figure 4.1 as shown in Figure 4.2.

This linked representation facilitates the operations of insertion and deletion of an element after s_i. All that is necessary is to change the values of some pointers. For example, to delete element s_2 from the list in Figure 4.2, it is only necessary to set $a_1\uparrow.NEXT := a_2\uparrow.NEXT$, and the element s_2 is no longer in the sequence (see Figure 4.3). To insert a new element $s_{1.5}$ into the sequence in Figure 4.2, it is only necessary to create a new node at some location $a_{1.5}$ with $a_{1.5}\uparrow.INFO = s_{1.5}$ and

```
type
    pList = ↑List;
    ValueType = "whatever this is a list of";
    List = record
        INFO: ValueType;
        NEXT: pList;
    end;
var
    P, t: pList;
```

Declarations 4.1

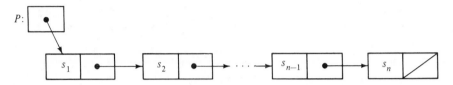

Figure 4.2
An alternate, more common way of depicting the list in Figure 4.1

$a_{1.5}\!\uparrow.NEXT = a_2$ and to set $a_1\!\uparrow.NEXT := a_{1.5}$ (see Figure 4.4). (What is required to add an element $s_{0.5}$ to the list?) Concatenation of lists and splitting a list into lists are also easy.

Use of linked lists implies the existence of some mechanism to allocate new records as needed and take care of records that are no longer needed. In Pascal, records are allocated by the function *new*; as discussed in Section 3.2, the statement *new(t)* assigns to *t* the address of a newly allocated record of whatever size is required for the type of *t*. The record allocated has no particular contents, so it must be initialized before it is attached to a list. Thus to add element $s_{1.5}$ as in Figure 4.4 we assume a prior step has set *prev* to the address a_1 and write

$$
\begin{aligned}
&new(t); &&\{\text{allocate a new record}\}\\
&t\!\uparrow.INFO := s_{1.5}; &&\{\text{initialize} \ldots \}\\
&t\!\uparrow.NEXT := prev\!\uparrow.NEXT; &&\{ \ldots \text{all fields}\}\\
&prev\!\uparrow.NEXT := t &&\{\text{attach to list}\}
\end{aligned}
$$

where $a_{1.5}$ is the value stored in *t* by *new*. Note that we must initialize $t\!\uparrow.NEXT$ before attaching *t* to the list. (Why?)

The possibility that a record may no longer be needed arises, for instance, when a list element is deleted, as was s_2 in Figure 4.3. In Pascal, an unneeded record *R* should be "released" to the storage management mechanism by calling *dispose(R)*. Thus if there are no other pointers to s_2 accessible directly or indirectly from program variables, then we should call dispose(a_2) after the deletion in Figure 4.3.

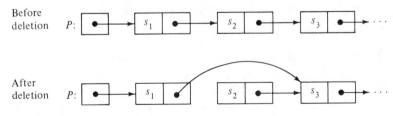

Figure 4.3
Deletion of an element from a linked list

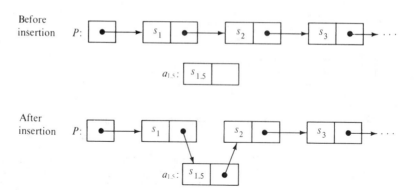

Figure 4.4
Insertion of an element in a linked list

It is instructive to consider the general case of moving an element from the middle of one list to the middle of another. Suppose x and y point to elements of lists and we want the element after x to be removed and inserted after y. A program fragment to do this is as follows:

$$
\begin{aligned}
t &:= x\uparrow.NEXT; &&\{\text{make } t \text{ point to element after } x\} \\
x\uparrow.NEXT &:= t\uparrow.NEXT; &&\{\text{link around } t \text{ to delete it}\} \\
t\uparrow.NEXT &:= y\uparrow.NEXT; &&\{\text{initialize } t \text{ for its new location}\} \\
y\uparrow.NEXT &:= t &&\{\text{attach } t \text{ after } y\}
\end{aligned}
\tag{4.5}
$$

The best way to devise such a fragment is shown in Figure 4.5, where before and after conditions are sketched, and then a sequence of assignments is devised to produce the desired result. Several principles are helpful in this regard:

1. Copy a pointer value and then replace it ($\cdots := \sim\uparrow.NEXT;\ \sim\uparrow.NEXT := \cdots$). Note that each $\sim\uparrow.NEXT$ in (4.5) appears first on the right side of an assignment to make a copy, and then on the left side of an assignment where its value is changed. The entire sequence of statements can be thought of as a circular "daisy chain," since the t at the beginning appears also at the end.

2. Disconnect a record before modifying it ($x\uparrow.NEXT := t\uparrow.NEXT$).

3. Initialize a record before attaching it ($t\uparrow.NEXT := y\uparrow.NEXT$).

Although correct programs can be written that violate them, these principles do give an order for assignments and help ensure that all necessary actions are taken: disconnection, modification, and attachment. The suggested order follows from considering a list as an entity in itself. If the rules are followed, the lists are always intact; the

(a) Before

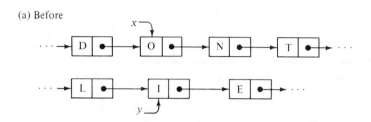

(b) Sequence of assignments

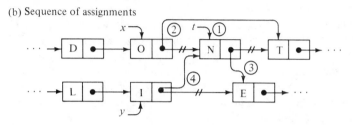

(c) After

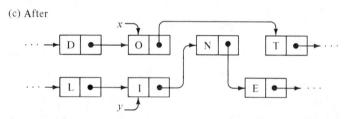

Figure 4.5
Moving an element from one list to another. The element N is moved from after *x* to be after *y*. Circled digits in (b) show the order of the assignments, and the slashes show the pointers that are destroyed by those assignments.

record moved is modified only while it is not part of any list. Such considerations are an aid in writing correct programs and are essential in cases where more than one process is accessing the list simultaneously.

The ease of insertion and deletion in linked lists is not without its cost. The fixed relationship between i and the location of s_i in a sequential allocation allows us, for example, to have immediate and direct access to any element of the list. In a linked allocation there is no such relationship, and access to list elements other than the first is indirect and inefficient. For instance, given the length of a list, it is easy to find the middle element for a binary search if the list is sequentially allocated, but relatively difficult if the list is linked. Furthermore, a price is paid in terms of storage overhead for the *NEXT* fields.

In choosing between sequential and linked allocation for a particular application, we must examine the types of operations that will be performed on the list and their relative frequencies in order to make an intelligent decision. If the operations are largely accessing random elements, searching for specific elements (see Chapter 7), or sorting the elements into order (see Chapter 8), then sequential allocation is usually better. On the other hand, linked allocation is preferable if the operations are largely inserting and deleting elements or concatenating and splitting lists.

As an example of the manipulation of linked lists, let us return to the telephone example and assume that *PhoneList* records have fields *NUMBER* and *NEXT*; *NEXT* and other pointers to such records are of type *pPhoneList*. Consider the problem of insertion of a record, *newphone*, in a list L whose elements are in order by *NUMBER*.* Our first problem is to find the proper position in the list, which means finding the first element p with a phone number larger than the new number. The new record is to be inserted just after the predecessor of p—that is, just after the record pointing to p. Accessing the predecessor of a selected element is a task that is often needed; the standard technique is to scan the list, keeping track of both the element currently being scanned *and* its predecessor in the list. Thus if p is the element currently being scanned and *pred* is its predecessor on the list, the loop would be

> **while** $p\uparrow.NUMBER$ < $newphone\uparrow.NUMBER$ **do begin**
> $pred := p$;
> $p := p\uparrow.NEXT$
> **end**

Notice that the relationship between p and *pred* is preserved with each iteration of the loop. When the loop ends, we insert the new record after *pred* by the assignments

> $newphone\uparrow.NEXT := pred\uparrow.NEXT$;
> $pred\uparrow.NEXT := newphone$

This, of course, is just the bare bones; we have left three important points unresolved: What if the new record belongs at the end of the list? What if it belongs before the first element? What if the list is empty?

For the first point—*newphone* goes at the end of the list—we change the test in the **while** loop to continue only if $p \neq$ **nil**. In order to stop when we reach the desired position, we set $p := $ **nil** when we get there. Although a conditional test is needed in many algorithms to determine why the loop ended, it is sufficient in this case to always insert the new element after *pred*, no matter how the loop ended. The algorithm is thus as given in Algorithm 4.1.

The crux of the second point—insertion before the first element—is that *pred* is necessarily undefined for the first element of the list: This possibility is handled by

---

*For economy of style we refer to an entire list by the pointer, L, to the first element of the list. To refer explicitly to the first record on the list we will use $L\uparrow$.

```
procedure insert (L, newphone: pPhoneList);
var p, pred: pPhoneList;
begin
        {Start-up tests here}
        begin
                pred := L;
                p := pred↑.NEXT;
                while p ≠ nil do
                        {Assert: The NUMBER field of each element of L prior to p
                        is less than newphone↑.NUMBER. p ≠ nil and p = pred↑.NEXT.}
                        if p↑.NUMBER ≥ newphone↑.NUMBER then
                                p := nil
                        else begin
                                pred := p;
                                p := p↑.NEXT
                        end;
                newphone↑.NEXT := pred↑.NEXT;
                pred↑.NEXT := newphone
        end
end
```

Algorithm 4.1
Insertion of a new record in a sorted list

not executing the **while** loop of Algorithm 4.1 if the number in *newphone* should precede that in the first element of the list. None of this will work, however, if the list is empty, so the third point is handled by a special test for $L = $ **nil**. The complete algorithm is derived from Algorithm 4.1 by replacing the comment "{Start-up tests here}" with

```
if L = nil then begin
        newphone↑.NEXT := L;
        L := newphone
end
else if newphone↑.NUMBER < L↑.NUMBER then begin
        newphone↑.NEXT := L;
        L := newphone
end
else
```

Notice that the two pairs of assignments are the same. We might consider combining the two conditions into

$$(L = \textbf{nil}) \text{ or } (newphone\!\uparrow\!.NUMBER < L\!\uparrow\!.NUMBER)$$

but Pascal defines **or** to always evaluate both operands. Thus even if L were **nil**, the second operand would be evaluated, causing an error.

This algorithm can be written more cleanly, however, if we introduce a *dummy element* as a perpetual first element in the list. The $INFO$ field of the dummy will have no particular value, but the $NEXT$ field will point to the first actual element of the list. Figure 4.6 shows both empty and nonempty lists with this dummy element. With the addition of the dummy element, the special tests for the second and third points can be omitted, and the entire algorithm is just as given in Algorithm 4.1, with no start-up tests to be added. Observe for yourself what happens if the list is empty or the new record belongs before the first element. Note that the extra space required for the dummy element can be considered repaid by the reduction in the space required for the algorithm.

The technique of designing (or modifying the design of) a data structure to simplify an accompanying algorithm is one that occurs frequently, and the reader should review this example carefully (and see Exercise 3).

Exercises

1. Follow the three principles given in the text to devise a program fragment that moves the first element of a list P to become the first element of a list Q.

2. Draw three versions of Figure 4.5(a) showing the pointers after each assignment to a $NEXT$ field in the program fragment (4.5).

3. Show how the **while** loop of Algorithm 4.1 can be simplified by the use of the dummy element 999-9999 of Exercise 1, page 126.

4. Write two versions of a program to delete an element from a phone list. One version should assume no dummy elements and the other should use dummy

(a) Empty list

(b) Nonempty list

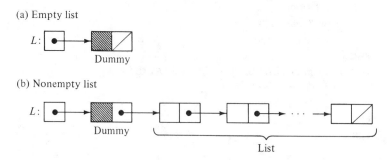

Figure 4.6
A linked list L with a dummy element. The shaded $INFO$ fields contain no meaningful information.

elements. If the element to be deleted is not found in the list, no action should be taken.

5. If P points to a linked list of elements having *INFO* and *NEXT* fields, what is the effect of the statement

$$P := Mystery5(P, \textbf{nil})$$

where the procedure *Mystery5* is

```
function Mystery5(x, y: pList): pList;
var t: pList;
begin
    if x = nil then
        Mystery5 := y
    else begin
        t := Mystery5(x↑.NEXT, x);
        x↑.NEXT := y;
        Mystery5 := t
    end
end
```

6. Let x and y each point to linked lists of the form described in the previous exercise. What list is returned by the following procedure?

```
function Mystery6 (x, y: pList): pList;
var t: pList;
begin
    if x = nil then
        Mystery6 := y
    else begin
        new(t);
        t↑.INFO := x↑.INFO;
        t↑.NEXT := Mystery6(x↑.NEXT, y);
        Mystery6 := t
    end
end
```

7. Rewrite the mysterious procedures in the previous two exercises as more straightforward, nonrecursive procedures.

8. Design a procedure that returns as its value a copy of the list given to it as an argument. Write your procedure in two different ways, one with recursion and one without.

9. State reasonable conditions under which the efficiency of storage utilization is
   (a) Better with sequential allocation than with linked allocation.
   (b) Better with linked allocation than with sequential allocation.

10. Suppose we want to insert an element *NewElement* into a list, but we have only
    a pointer *Current* to the element that is to follow the new one. Here is a code
    fragment for the task:

$$new(temp);$$
$$NewElement\uparrow.NEXT := temp;$$
$$temp\uparrow := Current\uparrow;$$
$$Current\uparrow := NewElement\uparrow;$$
$$dispose(NewElement);$$
$$NewElement := Current;$$
$$Current := temp$$

Under what conditions is this trick reliable? Show that it can lead to problems.
[*Hint*: Read Section 4.1.4.]

11. Discuss the pathological cases that can arise for program fragment (4.5). What
    happens if x or y is at the beginning or end of its list? What situations can arise
    if both point to elements of the same list?

4.1.1 Implementations of List Elements

Although we have so far always implemented a list element as a Pascal record,
an element is in fact a data structure with its own functions and several possible
storage structures. The principal functions are extraction of the contents of the element and creation of new elements. When records are the storage structure for elements, the algorithms for these functions are field selection and *new*, respectively. A
diagram of a typical record is in Figure 4.7.

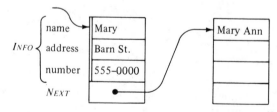

Figure 4.7
Example of a typical list element implemented as a record. A pointer to a second
record is also shown.

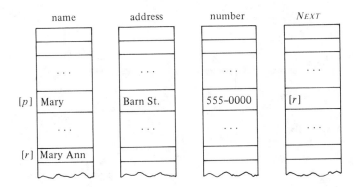

Figure 4.8
Implementation of elements in parallel arrays. The value *p* is a pointer to the
record in the row with subscript value *p*.

Another possible implementation is with *parallel arrays*, as were used in Chapter 1 to implement *Table*. There is a separate array for each component of the list element, as shown in Figure 4.8. A pointer to an element is a subscript value that selects a "row," one entry from each of the arrays. Selection of a component of an element is done by using the pointer as a subscript in the array containing the desired component. Creation of a new element can only occur if there is an unused row across the arrays. Often the initialization phase links together all rows of the array as a *free list* and each request for a new element is met by taking the first element off this list.

A third possibility is to implement each element as a list itself! To avoid confusion, we can temporarily call this a "minilist" composed of "mini-elements" with fields *DATUM* and *LINK*. The most extreme approach is to put each component in a separate mini-element. Done this way, elements in our phone-listing example would each require four mini-elements, as depicted in Figure 4.9. Field selection is implemented by the *next* operation on the minilist. Thus the name field of record *P↑* is accessed as *P↑.LINK↑.DATUM*. Creation of a record is done by a succession of *new* operations to construct the minilist.

It is usually unreasonable to implement an element of a list as its own tiny list. Not only is access more expensive, but the *LINK* fields can double the space required. Minilists, however, do have the advantage of simplicity, and the further advantage that *new* need be implemented to return only mini-elements of one specific size. This latter advantage eliminates some waste due to fragmentation, as we will see in Chapter 6.

Another advantage of minilists is that they provide a simple implementation with the property that the size of a particular element is determined only at the moment of its creation, rather than at the time the class of elements is defined. This

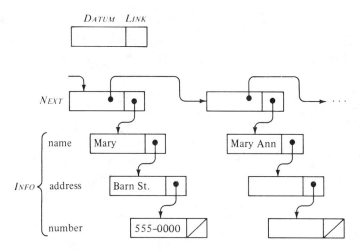

Figure 4.9
Implementation of list elements with a list of mini-elements, each having *DATUM*
and *LINK* fields

flexibility allows us, for example, to represent variable-length strings of characters,
without having to specify a length large enough for the longest possible string. In the
case of phone records, for example, we can allow names to be 40 characters long
without wasting space, even when the average length of a name is only eight characters. For similar reasons, the minilist implementation allows for optional fields: a
phone listing may have subsidiary numbers or it may have references to advertise-
ments, but it is wasteful to allow space for these in every record; they can be linked
into the minilist as required.

Exercises

1. Show how to do the insertion of Figure 4.4 using minilists.

2. Design a representation for variable-length strings using the minilist idea. Assume
   that the mini-elements consist of enough space to store the pointer and ten alphanumeric characters.

3. In one application, the observed record sizes were 5, 17, 20, 9, and 12, with the
   probabilities of occurrence being 0.3, 0.1, 0.1, 0.3, and 0.2, respectively. Suppose these records are implemented with a minilist scheme with fixed-size mini-
   elements. Show that the optimum mini-element size is five and that nine is nearly
   optimum.

4.1.2   Sublists and Recursive Lists

To derive the rowwise storage of a matrix in Section 3.3.1, we considered the elements in an array to be arrays themselves. We now return to that notion, examining some of the ramifications when we consider linked lists of linked lists.

With this in mind, we extend the definition of a list given at the beginning of this chapter: a *list* is a finite sequence of zero or more elements $(s_1, s_2, \ldots, s_n)$, each of which either is *atomic* or is a list itself, called a *sublist* of the list. "Atomic" means only that the element is not itself a list, not that it is otherwise indivisible; in practice it could be a record, a string, an array, and so on. In order to display the structure of lists and sublists properly, we will enclose the elements of a list in parentheses. Thus the list of zero elements, called the *empty* or *null* list, is written ( ). The list

$$((0, 1, 2), (\ ), (blue, red)) \tag{4.6}$$

is a list of three elements; the first is the list (0, 1, 2), the second is the empty list, and the third is the list (blue,red). Notice that ( ) and (( )) are not the same! The first is the empty list, while the second is a list of one element and that element is the empty list.

Linked representation of a list is just as before, only now the *INFO* field can be either an atomic element (as it has been previously) or a pointer to a sublist. Thus the list (4.6) would be represented as

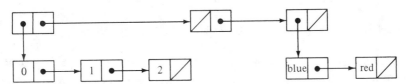

Notice that the second element of the list, the empty list, is represented by a **nil** pointer. This is consistent with our use of the **nil** pointer in the *NEXT* field of the last element of a list or sublist, because we consider the *NEXT* field of an element to point to the remainder of the list, which, for the last element, is the empty list.

To declare in Pascal that a field may be either a pointer or some other type, say a character, we use a variant record type declared like this

```
NodeType  =  (pointer, character, emptystring);
pPattern  =  ↑ Pattern;
Pattern  =  record
        NEXT: pPattern;
        case INFOKIND: NodeType of
            character: (INFOC: char);
            pointer:    (INFOP: pPattern)
end;
```

The *INFOKIND* field appears in every node to indicate whether the *INFO* field is really *INFOP* or *INFOC*, but for simplicity we will usually omit it from diagrams. The value *emptystring* in the *INFOKIND* field will be used in Pascal to represent ε, the empty string.

Because of the increased flexibility of such general lists (as compared to the linked structures so far discussed), they have very wide applicability and, in fact, have even been the basis for some programming languages. They are especially useful in representing structural information, as we will see in Section 4.3. In the present section, however, we will focus on one small yet important example in which they are used.

We want to describe classes of alphanumeric strings by writing patterns represented as lists. For example, the following simple pattern describes the class of strings that are one-letter codes for the compass directions:

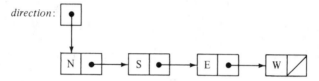

where *direction* is a pointer to the list. The list itself is viewed as a sequence of alternatives, an 'N', an 'S', an 'E', or a 'W'. In general, each of the alternatives in the list is a concatenation of strings. Thus Figure 4.10, written also as

$$((N, O, R, T, H), (S, O, U, T, H), (E, A, S, T), (W, E, S, T)),$$

is a pattern describing the four alternatives 'NORTH', 'SOUTH', 'EAST', 'WEST'. More generally still, each of the elements being concatenated is an alternation, **and** we have the following recursive definition of a pattern: a *pattern* is either

1. A single alphanumeric character or ε.

2. A linked list of alternatives. An alternative is a single alphanumeric character, or ε, or a linked list of patterns that are to be concatenated together.

To see the meaning of this definition, consider the following pattern:

$$(((c, b), a, t), ((d, h), o, g), (l, i, o, n)),$$

which would be drawn as in Figure 4.11. This pattern describes the set of strings 'CAT', 'BAT', 'DOG', 'HOG', and 'LION'. Notice that the lists alternate between alternation and concatenation, so that

alternate

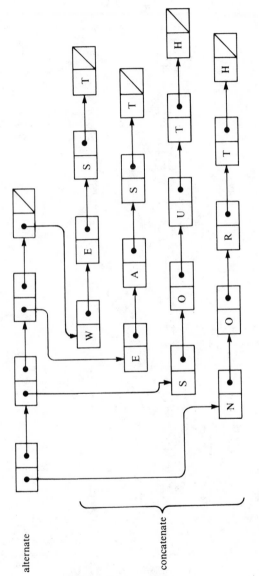

alternate

concatenate

Figure 4.10
A two level pattern

141

142

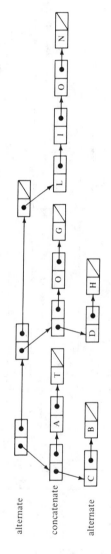

Figure 4.11
Pattern for a set of strings 'CAT', 'BAT', 'DOG', 'HOG', and 'LION'

or (A, T) describes the set of strings 'A' and 'T', while

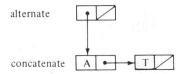

or ((A, T)) describes the string 'AT'. As a final example of this type, consider Figure 4.12 which uses the empty string ε in its description of the set of strings 'BED', 'BEST', 'BEAD', 'BEAST', 'LED', 'LEST', 'LEAD', 'LEAST', 'CHAR', 'CHAN', 'CHAIN', 'STAR', 'STAN', 'STAIR', 'STAIN', 'PAR', 'PAN', 'PAIR', and 'PAIN'.

Suppose we want to describe pairs of vowels. We could, of course, just create a list of 25 possibilities ((A, A), (A, E), ..., (U, U)), but instead we can define the lists

$$vowel = (A, E, I, O, U)$$
$$pair = ((vowel, vowel))$$

which would be drawn as in Figure 4.13. This list structure differs markedly from the previous ones because it contains a *shared sublist*—a list that is simultaneously a sublist of two different lists. This slight complication of the list structure offers self-evident economy.

The machinery introduced so far in this section allows us to construct only patterns that describe finite sets of strings. How can we describe infinite sets of strings such as all strings consisting of an even number of A's? We build such a pattern with a recursive definition: a string of A's has even length if it is empty, or consists of two A's followed by an even-length string of A's. Thus the pattern would be

$$even = ((A, A, even), ε),$$

drawn as shown in Figure 4.14(a). This illustrates a *recursive* list—one that is a sublist of itself. It is effectively the same as a list of infinite depth; in the case of *even* the equivalent list is shown in Figure 4.14(b). Unlike shared sublists, which are only a simple economy, recursive lists allow a new, more powerful use of linked lists.

It is instructive to examine an algorithm for the manipulation of recursive linked lists with shared sublists. The recursive nature of the lists usually imposes a recursive structure on algorithms for their manipulation, and you must learn to *think* about the algorithms with recursion, not iteration, in mind. An algorithm for match-

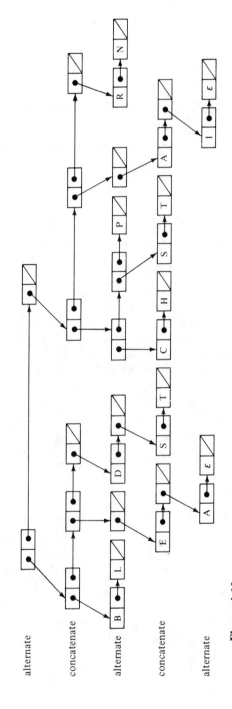

Figure 4.12
Use of the empty-string ε in a pattern

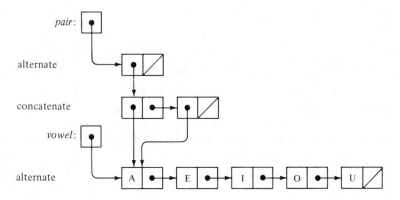

Figure 4.13
A pattern with a shared sublist

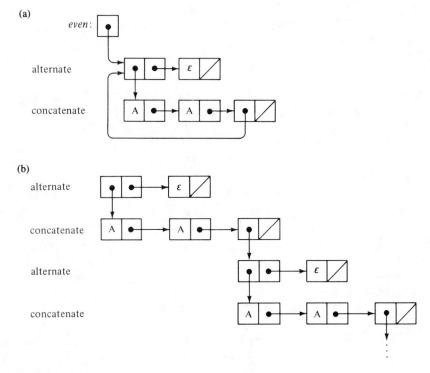

Figure 4.14
A recursive pattern (a) and its infinite equivalent (b)

ing strings to the patterns as represented on page 143 will exemplify this recursive algorithmic structure.

The idea of the pattern-matching algorithm is to match the pattern against the string by tracing through the pattern, simultaneously keeping track of the first unmatched character of the string. Mirroring the fact that a pattern either is atomic or is an alternation of concatenations of patterns, we have two recursive procedures. *Alternation*(P) takes pattern *P* represented as a list and matches it starting at the character of the string indicated by *cursor*. If *P↑.INFO* is a single character, the match involves only a comparison between the pattern character and the string character; if *P↑.INFO* is ε, the match succeeds trivially, since ε, the empty string, matches anyplace in any string. If *P↑.INFO* is not atomic, it is an alternation of concatenations, and we apply the parallel procedure *Concat* to each of the alternatives until one succeeds; if none succeeds, then the match fails. *Concat*(P) works identically, except that it applies *Alternation* to each of the patterns being concatenated, and all must succeed for the match to succeed. The procedure *Match* initiates the entire process. The details are given in Algorithms 4.2(a), (b), and (c). *StringType* is an array of *char*.

Our interest in Algorithm 4.2 is solely as an example of list manipulation, but we would be remiss if we did not point out that it has two serious shortcomings as a pattern-matching technique. First, many proper patterns and strings will cause the algorithm to go into an infinite loop. Consider, for example, the pattern in Figure

```
function Match (pat: pPattern; string: StringType; len: integer): boolean;
        {returns true if string (of length len) matches pattern pat}
var
    cursor: integer;  {index of position in string currently being matched}
        {cursor is used and modified within procedures Concat and Alternation.}
    function Concat (P: pPattern): boolean;  forward;


    {Algorithms 4.2(b) and 4.2(c) are nested in here}


begin
    cursor := 1;
    Match := false;
    if Alternation (pat) then
            {Found an alternative that matched. Whole string matches if cursor
            is at end of string.}
        Match := (cursor = len + 1)
end
```

Algorithm 4.2(a)
Driver for the procedures *Alternation* and *Concat* of Algorithms 4.2(b) and 4.2(c).

4.15(a). This pattern should match any string of balanced parentheses, but the use of recursion in the pattern is such that an infinite loop results on any attempted match. (This type of pattern is sometimes called *left recursive* because the first alternative begins with the pattern itself.) The pattern in Figure 4.15(b) avoids the difficulty, and Algorithm 4.2 will correctly match it with balanced strings of parentheses.

function *Alternation* (*P*: *pPattern*): *boolean*;

> {Match *string[cursor]*, *string[cursor + 1]*, ... with pattern *P* that is an alternation of patterns. Succeed if any one sub-pattern matches in the *string*. Upon success, set *cursor* to next character in *string* beyond the end of the match.}

var

> *savecursor*: *integer*;
> *finished*: *boolean*;

begin

> *savecursor* := *cursor*;
> *Alternation* := **true**;   {default: succeed}
> **repeat**
>> *finished* := **true**;   {default: quit}
>> *cursor* := *savecursor*;
>> {Assert: *P* points to one of the alternatives in the list given by the initial value of *P*. No prior pattern on the list matched *string[savecursor]*, *string[savecursor + 1]*, ...}
>> {Unless the value of *Alternation* or *finished* is changed, the loop will exit signaling that the present *P* matches.}
>> **if** *P* = **nil then**   {no more options}
>>> *Alternation* := **false**   {fail}
>> **else if** *P↑.INFOKIND* = *pointer* **then**
>>> **if** *Concat*(*P↑.INFOP*) **then**   {this option matched}
>>> **else** *finished* := **false**   {no match, try next}
>> **else if** *P↑.INFOKIND* = *emptystring* **then**
>>> {always matches}   {succeed}
>> **else** {is atom}
>>> **if** *cursor* > *len* **then**
>>>> *Alternation* := **false**   {off end of string}
>>> **else if** *string[cursor]* = *P↑.INFOC* **then**   {*P* matches}
>>>> *cursor* := *cursor* + 1   {go on to next char}
>>> **else** *finished* := **false**;
>> **if not** *finished* **then** *P* := *P↑.NEXT*   {try next alternative}
> **until** *finished*

end

> **Algorithm 4.2(b)**
> Procedure for the alternation levels of a pattern match

function *Concat* {(*P*: *pPattern*): *boolean*};

{Match *string*[*cursor*], *string*[*cursor* + 1], ... with pattern *P* that is a concatenation of patterns. Succeed only if all sub-patterns match successively in the *string*. Upon success, *cursor* is advanced to just beyond the end of the matches in *string*.}

var

    finished: *boolean*;

begin

    Concat := **false**;   {default: fail}

    repeat

        finished := **true**;   {default: quit}

        {Assert: *P* points to one element of the concatenation list that was pointed to by the original value of *P*. All prior elements on the list have matched consecutive pieces of *string*, and *cursor* now points to the next character after the last piece that matched.}

        {Unless the values of *Concat* and *finished* are changed the loop will exit with an indication that the match fails.}

        if *P* = **nil then** *Concat* := **true**   {all have matched}

        else if *P*↑.*INFOKIND* = *pointer* **then**

            if not *Alternation*(*P*↑.*INFOP*) **then**   {no match}

            else *finished* := **false**

        else if *P*↑.*INFOKIND* = *emptystring* **then**

            finished := **false**   {always matches}

        else {is atom}

            if *cursor* > *len* **then**   {string end}

            else if *string*[*cursor*] = *P*↑.*INFOC* **then begin**

                cursor := *cursor* + 1;   {advance in string}

                finished := **false**   {and in pattern}

            end

            else;   {no match, fail}

        if not *finished* **then** *P*   := *P*↑.*NEXT*

    until *finished*

end

    Algorithm 4.2(c)
    Procedure for the concatenation levels of a pattern match

A second difficulty with Algorithm 4.2 is that the strings matched will depend on the order of the alternatives in a list. This is quite a flaw, since we normally think of the operation "or" as commutative. In *balanced*$_2$ of Figure 4.15(b) for instance, interchanging the order of the alternatives makes the pattern useless as far as Algorithm 4.2 is concerned. It is always possible to redesign a pattern so that it will work correctly with Algorithm 4.2, and we give an important example of this in Exercise 4.

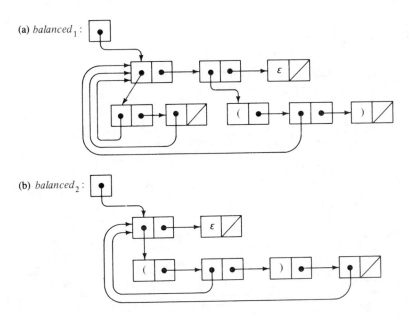

Figure 4.15
Patterns for balanced strings of parentheses. The pattern in (a) causes Algorithm
4.2 to go into an infinite loop; the pattern in (b) works correctly.

Algorithms that manipulate lists with shared or recursive sublists generally in-
volve the obvious sort of operations such as insertion, deletion, concatenation, splitting, and traversal. Since Algorithm 4.2 is not concerned with where the list representing the pattern came from, it illustrates only the traversal operation. In algorithms
that construct such lists (see, for example, Exercise 6), however, the other operations
are important and present a new difficulty with which we must cope. That difficulty
is that a shared or recursive sublist will be referred to from several places in the
overall structure; if we modify such a sublist, we must take care that all references
to it are properly updated.

Consider the example in Figure 4.16(a). We have a sublist L that is shared,
and we need to modify L by, say, adding A to the beginning. Since there are three
references to L, all three must be corrected to obtain the list shown in Figure 4.16(b),
4.16(b), where A is a new node that has been added to the structure.

In general it is difficult or impossible to locate all references to a sublist, so
we must find a different approach. We need to centralize the references to a sublist,
and we can do this by having a *header node* for each nonempty sublist. In the
example above, we would have instead the structure shown in Figure 4.16(c). To
add A to L now, we need only insert it after the header node of L. There is a

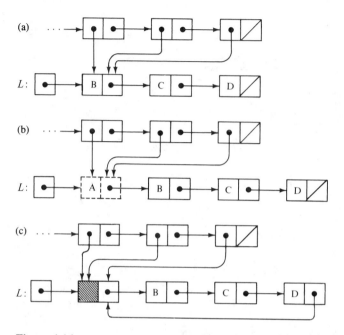

Figure 4.16
The difficulty of modifying lists with shared or recursive sublists. Inserting a new element into (a) to obtain (b) is difficult; the same insertion in (c) is relatively simple

slight overhead in memory locations for the header nodes, but this is often mitigated by various uses that can be made of their unused fields. For example, we will find in Chapter 6 that header nodes can be useful in keeping track of how many references there are to a sublist (see also Exercise 9).

Exercises

1. Design a list for a pattern to match the set of strings 'BED', 'BEDS', 'BEAD', 'BEADS', 'BEARD', 'BEARDS', 'ROT', 'ROTS', 'ROOT', 'ROOTS', 'ROOST', 'ROOSTS'.

2. Design a list for a pattern to match any string of an odd number of A's.

3. Design a list for a pattern matching any string of A's and B's in which the number of A's is equal to the number of B's.

4. The pattern in Figure 4.17 correctly describes syntactically correct arithmetic

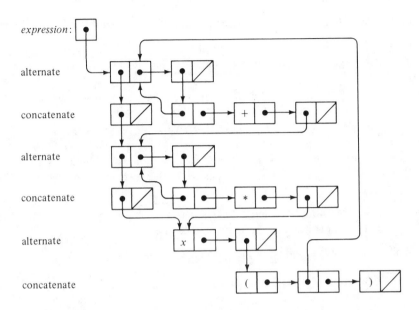

Figure 4.17
A pattern for arithmetic expressions

expressions constructed from x, $+$, $*$, (, and).

(a) Explain why Algorithm 4.2 will not work correctly with it.

(b) Redesign it so that Algorithm 4.2 *does* work correctly with it.

5. A pattern could have been defined somewhat differently, by the following sequence of definitions: A *pattern* is either

(i) a single alphanumeric character, or ε, the empty string, or
(ii) an alternative list.

An *alternative list* is either

(i) empty, or
(ii) a node N, where $N{\uparrow}.INFO$ is a concatenative list and $N{\uparrow}.NEXT$ is an alternative list.

A *concatenative list* is either

(i) empty, or
(ii) a node N, where $N{\uparrow}.INFO$ is a pattern and $N{\uparrow}.NEXT$ is a concatenative list.

(a) Redraw some of the patterns of this section according to this new definition (including some of the recursive patterns).

(b) Rewrite the matching procedures of Algorithm 4.2 for this new definition.

6. Design an algorithm to read list definitions in "parenthesis form" and convert them into linked lists. For example, upon reading the definitions

$$E = ((T), (E, +, T))$$
$$T = ((F), (T, *, F))$$
$$F = (x, ('(', E, ')'))$$

your algorithm should produce the list structure shown in Figure 4.17 above. [*Hint*: Include header nodes as suggested in the text and write the algorithm recursively.]

7. Design an algorithm to convert linked lists into parenthesis form, that is, to invert the transformation of the previous exercise.

8. What is the result of applying the procedure

```
function Mystery8 (x: pList): pList;
var t: pList;
begin
    if x = nil then
        Mystery8 := nil
    else begin
        new(t);
        t↑.INFO := x↑.NEXT;
        t↑.NEXT := Mystery8(x↑.INFO);
        Mystery8 := t
    end
end
```

to the following list *p*?

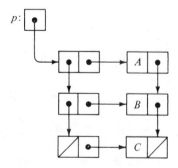

(*A*, *B*, and *C* are unspecified pointers.)

9. Design a recursive algorithm to copy a list structure that may have shared sublists and/or recursive sublists. Assume that sublists are always referenced through a header node that is distinguishable from ordinary nodes and that has sufficient room to store a pointer field and a few extra bits, if needed. [*Hint*: Use the pointer field of the header node to point to the copy of the sublist, after the copy has been made.]

10. Assuming the structure of lists described in the previous exercise, design an algorithm to test two lists for equality. First you must decide exactly what equality of lists should mean.

11. Modify Algorithm 4.2 so that it does the pattern match on strings represented by "minilists" as discussed in Section 4.1.1.

4.1.3 Common Variants of Linked Lists

A trivial modification of the linked list in Figure 4.2 gives a slightly more flexible linked list: if we set *NEXT* in the last node of the list to point to s_1, as shown in Figure 4.18 for list L, we obtain a *circular list*. This results in a simple type of recursive list in which it is possible to reach (albeit indirectly) any element of the list from any other element.

To familiarize ourselves with some of the ramifications of this modification, let us try to modify Algorithm 4.1 so it works correctly on a circular list. Notice that the test $p \neq$ **nil** in the **while** loop of Algorithm 4.1 needs to be changed, since in a nonempty circular list it will always be **true**. The corresponding test for circular lists is $p \neq L$, for we want the loop to stop when we have gone full circle around the list. As in the case of a noncircular list, everything works smoothly if we add a dummy element at the beginning of the circular list, as we did in Figure 4.6. Figure 4.19 shows the circular analogs of the lists in Figure 4.6. We leave it to the reader to satisfy himself that, after changing the three instances of **nil** to L, Algorithm 4.1 works properly for the circular lists of Figure 4.19.

As a second example of an algorithm that operates on circular lists, let us consider the problem of creating a copy of such a list. That is, we want to take

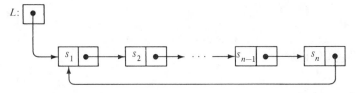

Figure 4.18
A circular list

(a) Empty circular list

(b) Nonempty circular list

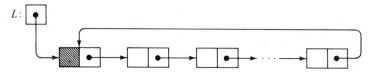

Figure 4.19
The circular analogs of the lists in Figure 4.6

records provided by *new* and form a list identical to the original list. The copy routine, Algorithm 4.3, keeps one pointer *y* pointing to an element of the original list and another pointer *x* pointing to the copy of *y↑*. Both pointers are advanced to their

function *CopyCircular* (*P*: *pList*): *pList*;
var
        y, t, x: pList   {*y* and *x* traverse *P* and the copy, respectively.
                            t↑ is the copy of *P↑.NEXT↑*}
begin
    new(*t*);
    x := *t*;
    y := *P↑.NEXT*;
    while *y* ≠ *P* **do begin**
        x↑.INFO := *y↑.INFO*;   {*x↑* is the copy of the current *y↑*}

        {Assert: All elements of *P* from *P↑.NEXT↑* through *y↑* have been copied to form list *t*.}

        new(*x↑.NEXT*);   {Think about this!}
        x := *x↑.NEXT*;
        y := *y↑.NEXT*
    end;
    x↑.NEXT := *t*;   {connect first element to second}
    CopyCircular := *x*
end

Algorithm 4.3
Copy a circular list of the type shown in Figure 4.19. Notice that the copying begins with the second element of the list.

successors at the same time. Pointer x can advance to its successor because, as part
of the initialization of the fields of $x\uparrow$, we initialize $x\uparrow.NEXT$ by calling *new* on it,
thus simultaneously allocating a new record and initializing the pointer to it. Notice
that this algorithm correctly copies an empty list as well as a nonempty one. (Why
is $P\uparrow.INFO$ not copied?)

It will often be necessary to be able to delete elements of a linked list, given
only a pointer to the element to be deleted. This, of course, is impossible in a simple
linked list containing only forward links (why; see also Exercise 4). Even in a circular list it is inconvenient, since it requires following links all the way around the
list in order to find the predecessor of the element to be deleted. The inherent difficulty can be eliminated by making it possible to go directly from an element to its
predecessor; this suggests lists with links going in both directions, or a *doubly linked
list*, as illustrated in Figure 4.20. Each node contains two pointers, $NEXT$ and $PREV$,
used as forward and backward links, respectively.

In the simplest case, given a doubly linked list and a pointer p to an element
in it, we can delete the element as follows:

$$p\uparrow.NEXT\uparrow.PREV := p\uparrow.PREV;$$
$$p\uparrow.PREV\uparrow.NEXT := p\uparrow.NEXT \qquad\qquad (4.7)$$

These statements are insufficient if the element is at one of the two ends of the list
(the list elements containing A or Z in Figure 4.20, for example), since one of the
links referred to does not exist. In general, we need

> **if** $p\uparrow.NEXT \neq$ **nil then**
> $p\uparrow.NEXT\uparrow.PREV := p\uparrow.PREV;$
> **if** $p\uparrow.PREV \neq$ **nil then**
> $p\uparrow.PREV\uparrow.NEXT := p\uparrow.NEXT$

Just as it is sometimes convenient to make a singly linked list circular, it also
is useful to have circular doubly linked lists. The doubly linked version of the circular list of Figure 4.18 is shown in Figure 4.21. Notice that statements in (4.7)
above also suffice for deletion of an element in a circular doubly linked list, *provided
that we are not deleting the element pointed to by the pointer to the list* (L in Figure
4.21). In fact, this could be a serious difficulty, and we are led to the doubly linked
analog of the circular list shown in Figure 4.22. The dummy element $D\uparrow$ again has

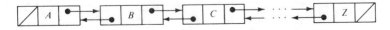

Figure 4.20
A doubly linked list

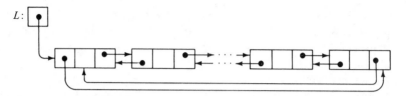

Figure 4.21
A doubly linked circular list

a form that is consistent with that of other list elements, but in this case that means it contains the *two* pointers *NEXT* and *PREV*.

Deleting an element x from the doubly linked circular list of Figure 4.22 is done exactly by the statements (4.7) above, even when the last element is being deleted to result in the empty list. Insertion of a new element *newelt* ↑ after an element y in the list is done by

$$newelt\uparrow.NEXT := y\uparrow.NEXT;$$
$$newelt\uparrow.PREV := y;$$
$$newelt\uparrow.NEXT\uparrow.PREV := newelt;$$
$$y\uparrow.NEXT := newelt$$

We leave it to the reader to verify that this works properly when the element is to be added to an empty doubly linked circular list.

Our example programs and diagrams have always shown as a simple variable the pointer to a list with a dummy element; in Figure 4.19 it is L, in 4.22, D. Once

(a) Empty doubly linked circular list

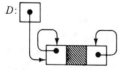

(b) Nonempty doubly linked circular list

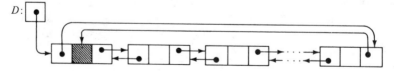

Figure 4.22
The doubly linked analog of the lists in Figure 4.19

in a while there is an advantage instead to declare this variable itself to be the dummy list element. This *might* be done in Pascal with the *List* type from Declarations 4.1:

$$L: List;$$

so *L* is itself a list element, rather than a *pList*, a pointer to a list element. The situation would then change from this

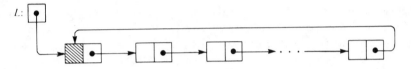

to this:

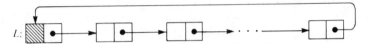

The advantages of having a dummy node still exist, of course. For instance, Algorithm 4.1 would still be used instead of the longer alternative with "Start-up tests." Unfortunately there is no way in standard Pascal to get loc(*L*), the address of variable *L*, so we can neither initialize *L.NEXT* to point to *L*, nor pass the address of *L* to a procedure like *insert*, Algorithm 4.1. Thus this technique is applicable only in other languages. (Why is there no ↑ in *L.NEXT*?)

Exercises

1. Design an algorithm to insert a new element s_0 as the first element of a circular list like that in Figure 4.18.

2. Write a nonrecursive algorithm to *reverse* a circular list of the type in Figure 4.19.

3. Suppose we want to maintain a circular list to be searched occasionally and in which the outside reference to the list (for example, *L* in Figure 4.18) is to be a "roving" pointer—after the list is searched, the pointer is left wherever the search ended. Furthermore, we want to be able to insert and delete elements of the list. Discuss the applicability of the various forms of circular lists we have presented. Choose the most suitable and design the needed algorithms for insertion and deletion.

4. Design an algorithm to delete an element from a list, given only a pointer to that element, by using the trick of Exercise 10, p. 136. Can this trick be applied to delete the last element of the list?

5. It is possible to achieve the effect of a doubly linked list with only one pointer field per record. Develop the following idea: The *NEXT* field of a node will contain a value *L* **xor** *R*, where *L* is the address in binary of the preceding node and *R* is the address in binary of the succeeding node. [*Hint*: ((*L* **xor** *R*) **xor** *L*) = *R* and ((*L* **xor** *R*) **xor** *R*) = *L*.]

4.1.4 Orthogonal Lists

Suppose that we need to organize the employee records of a company in which each employee falls into a job category 1, 2, ..., *j* and into a salary category 1, 2, ..., *s*. The records need to be examined with regard to both the job categories and the salary categories: it must be convenient, for example, to scan the records of all employees in job category *i*, for any *i*, or similarly to scan all records of employees in salary category *k*, for any *k*. Data of this type can be organized into *orthogonal lists* in which there are linked lists for each job category 1, 2, ..., *j* and for each salary category 1, 2, ..., *s*; each employee record is simultaneously an element of one of the job-category lists and one of the salary-category lists. Each record thus contains, in addition to whatever data fields there are, two pointer fields *JOBNEXT* and *SALNEXT* by which the linked lists are formed. Figure 4.23 shows such a config-

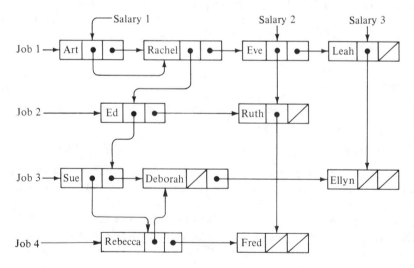

Figure 4.23
Employee records formed into lists by job and salary category. Each record has the form:

NAME	SALNEXT	JOBNEXT

uration, its structure illustrating why the lists are called orthogonal. Structures like these in which the elements are members of lists in accordance with some property or category are sometimes called *inverted lists*.

The example of an orthogonal list in Figure 4.23 is greatly oversimplified for purposes of illustration. A more typical such list would be a jumble of links impossible to portray legibly. So, in order to illustrate a fairly typical algorithm for orthogonal lists, we will restrict our attention to a more specialized type of orthogonal list having all the salient features, but easier to visualize. Suppose we want to represent *sparse matrices*—that is, matrices in which many or most of the entries are zero. In such a matrix it would be wasteful to allocate a position for each entry, and instead we will allocate positions only for the nonzero entries, the others being considered zero by omission. Of course we must also explicitly record the subscripts of the entries (they were implicit in the matrix representation discussed in Section 3.3.1; the subscripts could be deduced from the location and vice versa). Our representation here will use a record containing five fields for each nonzero entry:

> **type**
>> *pSparseNode* = ↑ *SparseNode*;
>> *SparseNode* = **record**
>>> *ROW, COL*: *integer*;   {subscripts for this element}
>>> *VALUE*: *real*;   {value of this element}
>>> *DOWN, RIGHT*: *pSparseNode*   {connections on two lists}
>> **end**;

We will draw such nodes like this:

ROW	COL	VALUE
DOWN		RIGHT

RIGHT and *DOWN* are pointers, used to form circular linked lists for each row and column, respectively, in which the nonzero entry appears. *ROW* and *COL* are integers, the row and column subscripts of the entry, and *VALUE* is the value of the matrix entry.

The *RIGHT* and *DOWN* pointers are used in the natural way. *RIGHT* points to the next nonzero entry to the right of the given entry; similarly, *DOWN* points to the next nonzero entry below the given entry. There are dummy elements for every row and column in which a nonzero entry appears. The dummy elements in the row lists have the value ∞ for *COL*; those in the column lists have the value ∞ for *ROW*. The *RIGHT* pointer in a row dummy element points to the first (leftmost) element in the row;

similarly, the DOWN pointer in a column dummy element points to the first (upper most) element in the column.

The row dummy elements themselves are formed into a circular list by their DOWN pointers: for a given row dummy element, the DOWN pointer points to the row dummy element of the next row down that has a nonzero entry. Similarly, the column dummy elements are formed into a circular list by their RIGHT pointers. The dummy element of both these lists is a "super dummy element" that has $ROW = COL = \infty$, RIGHT pointing to the leftmost column dummy element, and DOWN pointing to the highest row dummy element. The variable M points to this super dummy element. For example, the matrix

$$\begin{bmatrix} 59 & 0 & 0 & 0 \\ 71 & 0 & 9 & 0 \\ 0 & 0 & 0 & 0 \\ 2 & 0 & 1 & 6 \end{bmatrix} \tag{4.8}$$

is represented as shown in Figure 4.24.

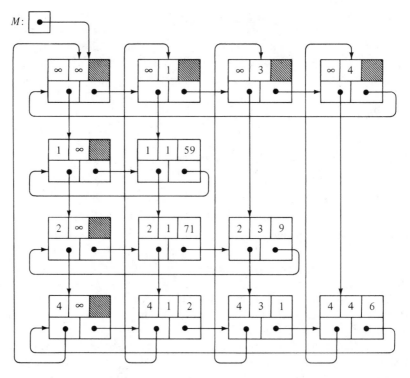

Figure 4.24
Representation of the matrix given in (4.8)

We have used the value ∞ for the *ROW* and *COL* fields of the dummy elements and chosen to have the circular lists go in ascending order (by row and column numbers). In some cases, however, it might be more convenient or natural to use 0 instead of ∞; this would probably make it more reasonable to have the circular lists go in descending order (why?).

As a simple example of an algorithm for manipulating orthogonal lists, we will present a procedure to delete the $[i, j]$ entry from the orthogonal-list representation

```
procedure Delete (M: pSparseNode; i, j: integer);
var
      prevRow, iRow, prevElt, ijElt, x, y: pSparseNode;
begin
      prevRow := predDOWN (M, i);
      iRow := prevRow↑.DOWN;
      if iROW↑.ROW = i then begin
            prevElt := predRIGHT(iRow, j);
            ijElt := prevElt↑.RIGHT;
            if ijElt↑.COL = j then begin
                  {Assert: iRow points to the correct row and ijElt points to the
                  correct element. prevRow and prevElt are their predecessors.}
                  prevElt↑.RIGHT := ijElt↑.RIGHT;   {delete [i, j] from row}
                  if prevElt↑.RIGHT = prevElt then begin
                        {Row i is empty, delete dummy element}
                        dispose (iRow)
                        prevRow↑.DOWN := iRow↑.DOWN;
                  end;
                  x := predDOWN(ijElt, i);
                  x↑.DOWN := ijElt↑.DOWN;   {delete [i, j] from column}
                  if x↑.DOWN = x then begin
                        {j column empty, delete its dummy element}
                        y := predRIGHT(x, j);
                        y↑.RIGHT := x↑.RIGHT;
                        dispose (x)
                  end;
                  dispose (ijElt)
            end
      end
end
```

Algorithm 4.4(a)
Deletion of the $[i, j]$ entry in a sparse matrix M represented by an orthogonal list as shown in Figure 4.24. The procedure *predDOWN* is given in Algorithm 4.4(b), and the analogous procedure *predRIGHT* is left to Exercise 1.

function *predDOWN*(*T*: *pSparseNode*; *k*: *integer*): *pSparseNode*;
var
    P, *pred*: *pSparseNode*;
begin
    P := *T*;
    repeat
        pred := *P*;
        P := *P*↑.*DOWN*
    until (*P*↑.*ROW* = *k*) **or** (*P* = *T*);
    predDOWN := *pred*
end

Algorithm 4.4(b)
Function to find the predecessor of row *k*, starting at *T*. What does it return if
there is no *k*th row?

of a sparse matrix as outlined above. Although simplified by the straightforward
nature of the underlying orthogonal list, this procedure [given as Algorithm 4.4(a)]
displays some of the typical intricacies of one that modifies a structure in which the
elements are simultaneously members of more than one list. The algorithm begins by
using the function *predDOWN* [Algorithm 4.4(b)] to scan down the column of *Row*
dummy elements to find the dummy element for the row preceding the *i*th row. The
algorithm then scans across the *i*th row to find the [*i*, *j*] entry (using a function
predRIGHT, which we leave for Exercise 1). This entry is then deleted from its row
and column lists. In both deletions we must be careful to delete the dummy elements
if the row and/or column becomes empty.

Exercises

1. Write out the details of the function *predRIGHT* omitted in the text.

2. Design an algorithm based on Algorithm 4.3, for copying a sparse matrix represented as an orthogonal list as illustrated in Figure 4.24.

3. Design an algorithm to insert an [*i*, *j*] entry in an orthogonal-list representation of a matrix in which that entry is missing.

4. Design an algorithm to multiply two sparse matrices represented as orthogonal lists; the product should also be represented as an orthogonal list. Can you do better than to use the result of Exercise 3?

5. Suppose we represent matrices as orthogonal lists in which the lists are circular and doubly linked. Rewrite Algorithm 4.4 for this case.

4.2 STACKS AND QUEUES

In this section we discuss two extremely important data structures that can be implemented with lists as the storage structure. The principal functions for each of them are the insertion of items and their later retrieval, with the order of the retrieval being dictated by the order of their insertion. A *push-down stack*, or *stack* for short, is a list in which all insertions and deletions occur at only one end, in this case called the *top* of the stack—the other end is the *bottom*. The list elements enter and leave the stack in a last-in, first-out order. A *queue* is a list in which all insertions are made at one end of the list (the *rear* or *back*), and all deletions are made at the other end (the *front*). In contrast to a stack, a queue operates in a first-in, first-out order. Figure 4.25 shows schematic diagrams of the operation of a stack and a queue.

The importance of stacks and queues lies in their use as bookkeeping devices. In order to perform some task, we may first have to perform a number of subtasks. Each subtask may, in turn, lead to other subtasks that must be performed. Both stacks and queues provide a mechanism for keeping track of the subtasks that are yet to be performed, and most importantly, the order in which they must be performed. In some cases that order is last-in, first-out, and so a stack is appropriate; in other cases the order is first-in, first-out and a queue is appropriate.

In the next two subsections we present two different storage structures for implementing stacks and queues, one based on sequentially allocated lists and the other on linked lists. In the final subsection we show some typical examples of the use of stacks and queues; many other important uses occur later in the book.

Regardless of which storage structure is chosen, stacks and queues have the following functions:

Push (*x, D*): Insert *x* in *D*. If *D* is a stack, *x* is added at the top. If *D* is a queue, *x* is added at the rear.

Pop (*D*): Return the value of the element at the top if *D* is a stack or at the front if *D* is a queue. *The element is deleted from D*. An error occurs if the stack or queue is empty.

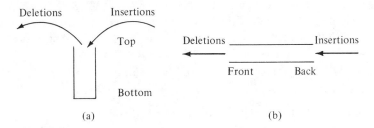

Figure 4.25
Schematic diagrams of (a) a stack and (b) a queue

Top (*D*): Like *Pop* except the element is *not* deleted from the stack or queue.

Empty (*D*): Initialize *D* to be the empty stack or queue.

IsEmpty (*D*): Return **true** if *D* is empty and **false** if not.

When we utilize stacks or queues, the names for the functions will be specialized; for instance, the operations on a stack of expressions will be *PushExpression* and *PopExpression*.

In coding these functions for particular situations, they may not appear as neatly as we give them here. In some cases it will be better to implement them by embedding appropriate sequences of code in programs where the function is required. At times the parameter *x* may be a tuple "(*a*, *b*, ...)", pushed and popped as a unit. The notation for popping, "(*a*, *b*, ...)" : = Pop(*S*), means that *a*, *b*, ... are each assigned the value of one component of the tuple popped off *S*. A tuple can be pushed by pushing each component and later popped by popping the components (in reverse order; why?) or the unit can be considered a record and implemented with any of the techniques discussed in Section 4.1.1.

Both stacks and queues are special cases of a data structure called a *priority queue*. In a priority queue each element has an associated number, its priority, and the structure operates on a highest-priority-out-first basis. Thus the order in which the elements are removed is determined solely by the associated priorities, not by the order of insertion. If the priority of each element inserted is higher than that of the preceding element we have a stack; if it is lower we have a queue. In general, priority queues cannot be efficiently implemented by the techniques discussed in this chapter; efficient implementation will be discussed in Chapter 7.

Exercises

1. Suppose letters arrive, one at a time in alphabetical order, from an input string. We can take an arriving letter and add it to the end of the output string, or we can put the arriving letter onto a stack. At any time we can remove the top stack entry and add it to the output string. Thus, for example, if the input string were AEPR, it could be permuted into the output string PEAR by stacking the A, stacking the E, adding the P to the output string, taking E off the stack and adding it onto the output string, taking A off the stack and adding it onto the output string, and finally adding R onto the output string.

   (a) Could AEPR be permuted into PARE? Into REAP? Into APER?

   (b) Into what English words can AELST be permuted?

2. Work Exercise 1 with "queue" substituted for "stack".

3. Write a program to sort a queue of elements *Q* using a stack *S* for temporary storage. At each step your procedure should pop an element off *S* or *Q* and

push it back onto one or the other. You may assume the elements initially on Q are terminated by a unique element with value *EndOfData*. Try to minimize the number of variables other than S and Q; none are needed. Prove that your program does not get in an infinite loop. [*Hint*: Put an element on the stack only if it is smaller than the top element.]

4. Suppose that as in Exercise 1 input values are pushed on a stack and the output is constructed by popping values off the stack.

   (a) Show that this scheme cannot be used to transform the integers 1, 2, ..., n into permutation $\pi_1, \pi_2, \ldots, \pi_n$ if and only if there are values for i, j, k such that $i < j < k \le n$ and $\pi_j < \pi_k < \pi_i$.

   ★(b) Determine how many of the $n!$ permutations of 1, 2, ..., n can be obtained.

5. In a "series" of stacks the top element of each serves as the input to the next. Show that if there are $\lceil \lg n \rceil$ *stacks in a series, then all n!* permutations of the input can be obtained (see Exercise 3).

4.2.1 Sequential Implementation

The natural storage structure for a stack is a list, and especially simple algorithms are possible for the stack operations when the list is implemented as an array. We need only the array S of m elements and an integer $t \le m$ to keep track of the top of the stack. At any time, the current stack contents are $S[1..t]$, and $t = 0$ means that the stack is empty (see Figure 4.26). The algorithms for the stack operations are simply

Push $(x, Stack)$:
    if $t \ge m$ **then** *overflow*
    else begin
        $t := t + 1$;
        $S[t] := x$
    end

Pop $(Stack)$:
    if $t = 0$ **then** *underflow*
    else begin
        "value of *Pop*" $:= S[t]$;
        $t := t - 1$
    end

Top $(Stack)$: "value of *Top*" $:= S[t]$ {if $t > 0$}

Empty $(Stack)$: $t := 0$

IsEmpty $(Stack)$: "value of *IsEmpty*" $:= (t = 0)$

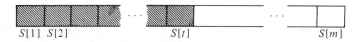

$S[1]$ $S[2]$ $S[t]$ $S[m]$

Figure 4.26
Sequential implementation of a stack. The shaded elements are the stack contents,
with $S[1]$ at the bottom and $S[t]$ at the top. For the empty stack, $t = 0$.

An *underflow* means that an attempt has been made to delete an element from an
empty stack; it is generally a meaningful end condition in an algorithm. Conversely,
an *overflow* means that there is no more room to add x to the stack, which usually
means trouble.

The sequential allocation of a queue is more complicated because it grows at
one end and shrinks at the other; if we are not careful, it can inch its way along and
try to overrun the locations set aside for it. Thus we use the m locations $Q[0 . . m - 1]$
allocated for a queue in a circular fashion, and we consider $Q[0]$ to follow
$Q[m - 1]$. Using f as a pointer to the location *just before* the front of the queue and
r as the pointer to the rear of the queue, the queue consists of the elements
$Q[f + 1 . . r]$. (See Figure 4.27.) With this definition, the empty queue corresponds
to $r = f$. We have

> *Push* (x, *Queue*):
> > $s := (r + 1)$ **mod** m;
> > **if** $s = f$ **then** *overflow*
> > **else begin**
> > > $r := s$;
> > > $Q[r] := x$
> >
> > **end**
>
> *Pop* (*Queue*):
> > **if** $r = f$ **then** *underflow*
> > **else begin**
> > > $f := (f + 1)$ **mod** m;
> > > "value of *Pop*" $:= Q[f]$
> >
> > **end**
>
> *Top* (*Queue*): "value of *Top*" $:= Q[(f + 1)\textbf{mod } m]$ {if $f \neq r$}
>
> *Empty* (*Queue*): $r := f$
>
> *IsEmpty* (*Queue*): "value of *IsEmpty*" $:= (f = r)$

As in the case of a stack, *underflow* is generally a meaningful end condition and
overflow is generally trouble.

Notice that *overflow* occurs while attempting to add an mth element to a queue
containing $m - 1$ elements; this means that one of the allotted m locations is wasted

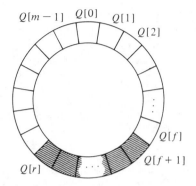

Figure 4.27
Sequential implementation of a queue. The shaded elements are the queue contents, with $Q[f + 1]$ at the front and $Q[r]$ at the rear. For the empty queue, $f = r$.

(see Exercise 1). The insertion algorithm is carefully designed to modify r only after it is certain there will be no *overflow*.

When *Push*, *Pop*, and other stack and queue operations are implemented as procedures with the stack or queue as a parameter, the parameter type must be a record having both the array and pointers. For example, a queue would be declared

type
     IntegerQueue = **record**
          front, rear: *integer*;
          Queue: **array** [0 . . *mminusone*] **of** *integer*
    end;

A procedure for a queue operation would declare its parameter a *var Q: Integer-Queue*, making it a variable parameter so the procedure can modify its fields. The calling procedure would pass an *IntegerQueue* record, rather than a pointer to a record as is done elsewhere in this text. (But see the description of variable parameters on p. 105.)

Generally speaking, sequentially allocated stacks and queues are simpler than the linked versions, less flexible, and more economical in memory usage. This situation exactly mirrors that of lists in general: when more than one stack or queue is required, it is usually more economical to use the linked implementations discussed in the next section. Two stacks can, however, coexist nicely in a single array. One stack grows from left to right, as did the example in Figure 4.26, while the other grows from right to left from the other end of the array. An *overflow* occurs when the tops of the two stacks collide—in other words, only when all the locations are full (Exercise 4). Other combinations of sequentially implemented stacks and/or queues are not as fortuitous, and *overflow* can occur even when there are still unused locations; this means that the stacks and queues need to be shifted around to make the free locations available where they are needed—a time-consuming operation. Techniques for simultaneous sequential implementation of stacks and queues that do not overflow until all locations are used are described in Exercise 6.

Exercises

1. Modify the algorithms for the sequential implementation of queues so *overflow* does not occur until the attempted insertion of the $(m + 1)$st element. [*Hint:* Use an extra flag bit.]

2. Rewrite the queue push/pop algorithms using **if-then-else** instead of the **mod** function. Under what conditions is the modified version faster than the original?

3. A *deque* (*d*ouble *e*nded *que*ue, pronounced "deck") is a list in which all insertions and deletions are made at the ends of the list. The queue operations given in this section suffice for "insert at rear" and "delete at front," so all that is needed to implement a deque are the operations "insert at front" and "delete at rear." Design algorithms for these operations.

4. Design push and pop algorithms for two stacks coexisting in a single array as described in the text.

5. Suppose that in addition to the insertion and deletion operations we want to be able to reverse the order of the elements in a queue. Suggest modifications to the sequentially allocated queue and the algorithms given in the text to facilitate the reversal operation.

6. We want to have *n* sequentially allocated stacks coexisting in a single array. "Local" *overflow* occurs if one stack runs out of space while the others still have space remaining; at that time the stacks are shifted around to give more space to the one that ran out. "Global" *overflow* occurs when all the space is used and hence reorganization is not possible.

   (a) Suppose the stacks are in the array as follows:

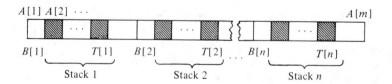

   with $B[i]$ pointing one position to the left of the base of the ith stack and $T[i]$ pointing to its top element, each stack growing from left to right. Design algorithms for push and pop of the ith stack, and design an algorithm to relocate the stacks when a local *overflow* occurs. The relocation process consists of assigning new locations for each stack and then actually moving them. Suggest various heuristics for the assignment phase and give algorithms for them. Are your algorithms sufficient if there is a mixture of stacks and queues instead of just stacks?

(b) Do part (a) so that the stacks grow toward each other in pairs.

7. Describe algorithms for the sequential implementation of a priority queue. How efficient are your algorithms?

8. Suppose it is known that the elements that will be put on the stack are all the same. Suggest a good way to implement the stack. What if it is a queue instead of a stack?

4.2.2 Linked Implementation

The linked implementation of a stack is as easy as the sequential implementation. We maintain a pointer t to the top stack element and use the *NEXT* field of a stack element to point to the element below it on the stack. The bottom stack element has the pointer **nil** in its *NEXT* field, and $t = $ **nil** corresponds to the empty stack. (See Figure 4.28.) We have

$Push$ $(x, Stack)$:
    $new(newnode)$;
    $newnode\uparrow.INFO := x$;
    $newnode\uparrow.NEXT := t$;
    $t := newnode$

Pop $(Stack)$:
    if $t = $ **nil then** *underflow*
    else begin
        "value of Pop" := $t\uparrow.INFO$;
        $temp := t$;
        $t := t\uparrow.NEXT$;
        $dispose$ $(temp)$ {Exercise 4}
    end

Top $(Stack)$: "value of Top" := $t\uparrow.INFO$ {if $t \neq$ **nil**}

$Empty$ $(Stack)$: **while** $t \neq$ **nil do** $u := Pop(Stack)$

$IsEmpty$ $(Stack)$: "value of $IsEmpty$" := $(t = $**nil**$)$

In this case, the *overflow* condition occurs in the operation *new* when no more records are available.

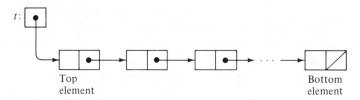

Figure 4.28
Linked implementation of a stack

For queues, the linked implementation is essentially the same as for stacks (that is, $x\uparrow.NEXT$ points to the element behind x in the queue), except that we use f instead of t as a pointer to the front, and we use r to point to the rear, as shown in Figure 4.29(a). To add an element to the queue we use

> *Push* (*x*, *Queue*):
>   *new(newnode)*;
>   *newnode*$\uparrow.INFO$:= *x*;
>   *newnode*$\uparrow.NEXT$:= **nil**;
>   *r*$\uparrow.NEXT$:= *newnode*;
>   *r* := *newnode*

As with the stack, the *overflow* condition is hidden in the call to *new*.

It would be convenient to have the empty queue represented by $f = $ **nil**, but we must insure that the value of r is such that the insertion algorithm above works properly even when the first element is inserted. The first three operations of the

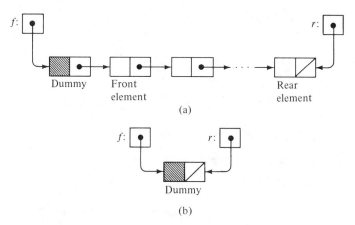

Figure 4.29
Linked implementation of a queue: (a) nonempty queue, (b) empty queue

insertion algorithm correctly construct the element to be inserted, and the last operation $r := newnode$ correctly sets r to point to that new last element. The operation $r\uparrow.NEXT := newnode$, however, will fail unless r points to an element of the list. To solve this problem we introduce a dummy element as the permanent front of the list. The empty queue is thus represented as shown in Figure 4.29(b), and deletion is accomplished by

> $Pop\ (Queue)$:
> $t := f\uparrow.NEXT$;
>   **if** $t = $ **nil then** *underflow*
>   **else begin**
>   "value of Pop" $:= t\uparrow.INFO$;
> $f\uparrow.NEXT := t\uparrow.NEXT$;
>   **if** $r = t$ **then**
> $r := f$;
> $dispose\ (t)$
>   **end**

We have also

> $Top\ (Queue)$: "value of Top" $:= f\uparrow.NEXT\uparrow.INFO$ $\{$if $f \neq r\}$
>
> $Empty\ (Queue)$: **while** $f \neq r$ **do** $t := Pop(Queue)$
>
> $IsEmpty\ (Queue)$: "value of $IsEmpty$" $:= (f = r)$

Exercises

1. Design a linked implementation and algorithms for a deque (see Exercise 3 of Section 4.2.1).

2. Design a linked implementation and algorithms for a priority queue and compare its efficiency to that of the sequential implementation of Exercise 7 of Section 4.2.1.

3. Suppose we need to keep track of the middle of a linked queue with a pointer M. M should point to the middle element if there are an odd number of elements on the queue, or just in front of the middle if there are an even number. Modify the insertion and deletion algorithms to keep track of M in such a way that the time required to do so is independent of the length of the queue. Be sure that your algorithms work for the empty queue.

4. For the linked list implementation of stacks, *Push* and *Pop* use one *new* and one *dispose* for every element pushed. We can reduce this storage management overhead by keeping a list of idle stack elements: *Push* does a *new* only if the list is empty; *Pop* puts the released element on the list. Write program fragments for

this version of the stack operations. Do similar fragments for the queue operations.

4.2.3 Applications of Stacks and Queues

The applications of stacks and queues are legion, and we will see many throughout this book. In this section we present three examples of the use of stacks that are more or less unrelated to the material of the other chapters. Some applications of queues are described briefly, but since queues are generally needed in situations that do not lend themselves to the extraction of simple examples, we do not give any specific algorithms. Specific examples using queues are found in Algorithms 4.9, 5.8, 5.9, and 8.8.

Stacks and Recursion. Throughout this book we develop and present recursive algorithms, and it is necessary to know how recursion can be implemented and how it can be transformed into iteration. Compilers implement recursive routines with a stack, and we can convert recursion to iteration by use of an explicit stack. Conversion to iteration is crucial if our programming language does not support recursion, but even if it does we might want to use iteration instead to take advantage of the idiosyncrasies of a particular situation. (See, for example, the discussion of quicksort, Section 8.1.2.) For the above reasons, our first application of stacks is to give iterative implementations of a very simple recursive procedure.

A recursive procedure is one that, in the process of doing its computations, invokes itself as a subprocess. By the nature of the computation, this subprocess must be completed before the computation can continue; in other words, the last invoked procedure must finish before any other procedure. This corresponds precisely to the last-in, first-out nature of a stack, and so a stack is the appropriate mechanism to save (and later restore) the values of parameters and local variables on a recursive call.

Consider the *Towers of Hanoi* problem. There are three poles named *left*, *middle*, and *right*. On pole *left* are n disks with diameters $1, 2, \ldots, n$ arranged in a pile in order by size; the other two poles are empty (see Figure 4.30). The problem is to move all n disks from *left* to *right*, moving only one disk at a time. At all times we must observe the rule that *no disk is ever placed on top of one of smaller diameter*; thus the final stack on *right* will be in the same order as the original stack.

In what order should the disks be moved? Actually, we should first ask *if* it is possible to solve the problem, but the fact that it is possible and the method of solution are entwined, and we will prove that it can be done by giving a way of doing it. If we had only one disk, the problem would be trivial, since we could simply move the disk from the source to the destination. With $m \geq 2$ disks we proceed as follows: recursively move $m - 1$ disks to the intermediate pole, move the mth disk to the final pole, and then recursively move the $m - 1$ disks from the intermediate pole to the final pole using the original pole as an intermediate. (Prove to

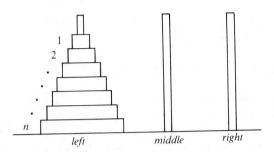

Figure 4.30
The Towers of Hanoi problem

yourself that, at all levels of the recursion, any disks on a pole are larger than those to be moved there while using it as an intermediate.) This technique tells us how to move the m disks, assuming we already know how to move $m-1$ disks, and we have the trivial case of moving one disk as the basis for the process. The recursive procedure that uses this method is given in Algorithm 4.5. That procedure has four parameters, one giving the number of disks to be moved, and the other three specifying the initial, intermediate, and final poles as values from the type $Pole = (left, middle, right)$.

> **procedure** *Hanoi* (*n: integer; start, temp, dest: Pole*);
>   {Move *n* disks from pole *start* to pole *dest* using pole *temp*.}
> **label** 1,2,3,4,5;   {used in the text}
> **begin**
>   **if** $n = 1$ **then**
> 1:   *writeln*(*start*, $'\rightarrow'$, *dest*)
>   **else begin**
> 2:   *Hanoi*(*n* − 1, *start*, *dest*, *temp*);   {move *n* − 1 disks to *temp*}
> 3:   *writeln*(*start*, $'\rightarrow'$, *dest*);
> 4:   *Hanoi*(*n* − 1, *temp*, *start*, *dest*);   {move *n* − 1 disks to *dest*}
> 5: **end**
> **end**

Algorithm 4.5
Recursive algorithm for the Towers of Hanoi problem

As an example, you are urged to verify that a call *Hanoi*(3, *left*, *middle*, *right*) produces the following sequence of moves:

$$
\begin{array}{lcl}
left & \rightarrow & right \\
left & \rightarrow & middle \\
right & \rightarrow & middle
\end{array}
$$

$$left \quad \rightarrow \quad right \quad \text{(move the bottom disk)}$$
$$middle \rightarrow left$$
$$middle \rightarrow right$$
$$left \quad \rightarrow \quad right$$

where "$x \rightarrow y$" means "move the top disk from pole x to pole y." You should also verify that this sequence of moves correctly solves the Towers of Hanoi problem with three disks.

When Algorithm 4.5 is executed, the code generated by the compiler utilizes an execution stack to distinguish the various nested invocations of *Hanoi*. Each time *Hanoi* (or any other procedure) is entered a *stack frame* is created on the execution stack. It contains values for the parameters and local variables of the procedure, and also a location to store the *return address*, a pointer to the code where execution is to continue after this invocation is completed.

For *Hanoi* each stack frame is a record with fields

RETURNADDRESS	N	START	TEMP	DEST

The call *Hanoi*(3, *left*, *middle*, *right*) first creates the stack frame:

external-call	3	left	middle	right

where the return address "external-call" indicates the location after the call. Execution begins in *Hanoi* and reaches the call at label 2; another stack frame is created and the stack becomes:

label 3	2	left	right	middle
external-call	3	left	middle	right

where "label 3" indicates the point to resume execution after this inner call.

Execution of this inner call on *Hanoi* soon reaches label 2 again and the stack becomes:

label 3	1	left	middle	right
label 3	2	left	right	middle
external-call	3	left	middle	right

The topmost execution on this stack now proceeds to label 1 (note the value of *n*) and generates the output

$$left \quad \rightarrow right$$

Execution of *Hanoi* for the topmost stack frame now terminates. Because the stack frame lists label 3 as the return address, we resume execution of the second *Hanoi* at that label. This immediately produces the output

$$left \quad \rightarrow middle$$

and continues to label 4 where a new invocation is made and a new stack frame is allocated:

label 5	1	*right*	*left*	*middle*
label 3	2	*left*	*right*	*middle*
external-call	3	*left*	*middle*	*right*

(Convince yourself that the values for *start*, *temp*, and *dest* are correctly generated from the values for those variables in the second stack frame.) This new stack frame executes to label 1, produces

$$right \quad \rightarrow middle$$

and exits. The second stack frame continues execution from label 5 and itself exits, this time to label 3 of the bottom stack frame. Here the output is

$$left \quad \rightarrow right$$

and execution continues to label 4 where the stack becomes

label 5	2	*middle*	*left*	*right*
external-call	3	*left*	*middle*	*right*

You should continue the simulation to observe how recursive execution finally returns to the external-call after having generated the rest of the output.

When recursion is not available, and sometimes when it is, it is valuable to have a general method of converting a recursive algorithm to iteration. We use a stack *S* to store values of the parameters on a recursive call and restore them afterward. For *Hanoi*, each stack element will be a quadruple (*n, start, temp, dest*); such an element means that the top *n* disks on *start* are to be moved to *dest* using *temp*.

The key idea is that *a call to Hanoi will be replaced by the insertion of the corresponding quadruple into the stack*. This idea is realized in Algorithm 4.6. Notice that the **else** clause in this algorithm differs in two essential ways from that in Algorithm 4.5. First, instead of saying *writeln* (*start, '→', dest*) it says *PushHanoi*("(1, *start, temp, dest*)", *S*). As stated above, this stack element means exactly that the top disk from pole *start* is to be moved to pole *dest*; it is put on the stack because this operation must be done *between* the two operations of moving the remaining *n* − 1 disks. The second difference is that the order in which the elements are added to the stack is the opposite of the order in which the recursive calls are made in Algorithm 4.5. This is necessary since the stack is last-in, first-out and we want (*n* − 1, *start, dest, temp*) to finish before beginning (*n* − 1, *temp, start, dest*).

You should convince yourself that when *n* is 3 the stack gets to five quadruples before generating any output and then pops four times generating a move with each pop.

```
procedure IterativeHanoi (n: integer; start, temp, dest: Pole);
var
      S: HanoiStack;
begin
      EmptyHanoi(S);
      PushHanoi("(n, start, temp, dest)", S);   {Initial quadruple}
      while not IsEmptyHanoi(S) do begin
            "(n, start, temp, dest)" : = PopHanoi(S);      {Assert: We are pro-
            cessing a move description tuple that moves the n smallest disks.
            All necessary prior moves have been done. The stack contains tu-
            ples that will generate subsequent moves.}
            if n = 1 then
                  writeln(start, '→', dest)
            else begin
                  PushHanoi("(n − 1, temp, start, dest)", S);
                  PushHanoi("(1, start, temp, dest)", S);
                  PushHanoi("(n − 1, start, dest, temp)", S)
            end
      end
end
```

Algorithm 4.6
Stack algorithm for the Towers of Hanoi problem

Stacks and Arithmetic Expressions. The problem of evaluating an arithmetic expression arises at all levels of computation, from hand calculations to using a pocket calculator to programming large computers. It is a nontrivial task to transform the expression into a sequence of simple arithmetic operations. In this section we examine two important algorithms for such manipulations of arithmetic expressions; both algorithms center around the use of stacks. In a sense, however, this material could fall under the previous heading of "stacks and recursion," since it is possible to view these algorithms as iterative implementations of their recursive counterparts (see Exercises 7 and 9).

Before constructing algorithms for any task, we must have a clear understanding of what the task is. For the evaluation of arithmetic expressions, what we want to do is fairly obvious, except for one thing: given the arithmetic expression $A + B*C$, we want to compute $A + (B*C)$ and *not* $(A + B)*C$. Without parentheses, how do we know which one we want? The answer lies in the notion of *precedence*. It is the convention that the multiplicative operations of multiplication and division take precedence over the additive operations of addition and subtraction; in other words, when there are no parentheses to make it otherwise, the multiplicative operations are done first, before the additive operations. All right, but how do we evaluate $A - B + C$? Should it be $A - (B + C)$ or $(A - B) + C$? Of course we want $(A - B) + C$, because it is also conventional that operations of equal precedence are performed from left to right. As a further example, $A/B*C$ would be evaluated as $(A/B)*C$ and *not* $A/(B*C)$.

Our problem is thus to evaluate arithmetic expressions that contain variables, $+$, $-$, $*$, $/$, and parentheses, with the conventions that $*$ and $/$ will be done before $+$ and $-$ (in the absence of parentheses, of course!) and that sequences of $+$'s and $-$'s or sequences of $*$'s and $/$'s will be done from left to right. This evaluation is tricky and can be done by a very clever recursive algorithm (see Exercise 7), but here we will do it by a simpler two-stage process that emphasizes the use of stacks. We will first show how to evaluate the expression, assuming it has been converted into an intermediate form, and then show how to do the conversion to that form.

The intermediate form is *Polish postfix* notation,[†] in which the operator follows its two operands, rather than separating them as in conventional notation. For example, instead of $A + B$ we would write $A\ B\ +$. (To eliminate the ambiguities possible when multicharacter variable names are adjacent to one another, we will insist that all variable names be single upper-case letters; this restriction is easy to overcome by using separator characters, but at the expense of some clarity of presentation.) For $A + B*C$ we would have $A\ B\ C\ *\ +$, which is interpreted as follows: The two operands for the $*$ are the B and C that precede it; the two operands of the $+$ are A and the expression $B\ C\ *$. If instead we want $(A + B)*C$, we write $A\ B\ +\ C\ *$, so that the two operands for the $+$ are the A and B that precede it,

---

[†]Named for the Polish logician Jan Łukasiewicz, who first suggested the notation.

while the two operands for the $*$ are the expression $A\ B\ +$ and C. The examples $A\ B\ C\ *\ +$ and $A\ B\ +\ C\ *$ illustrate the most important characteristic of Polish postfix notation: it does not need parentheses or precedence conventions to indicate the order of the computation; the order is defined completely by the relative order of the operands and the operators.

We can define the class of Polish postfix expressions recursively as follows: such an expression is either a simple variable, or consists of two Polish postfix expressions followed by an operator. The recursive definition gives us the key to the evaluation of postfix expressions. Consider, for example, the expression

$$A\ B\ +\ C\ D\ -\ E\ *\ F\ +\ *,$$

which corresponds to the expression

$$(A\ +\ B)\ *\ ((C\ -\ D)\ *E\ +\ F).$$

The order of evaluation is as follows:

The general rule used in this example is that whenever we find two operands followed by an operator, that operator is applied to those operands and the result replaces the substring consisting of the operands and operator. Thus, in the above example, we replaced the substring "$A\ B\ +$" by the value of $A\ +\ B$; then we replaced the substring "$C\ D\ -$" by the value of $C\ -\ D$; then we replaced the substring consisting of the value of $C\ -\ D$ followed by "$E\ *$" with the value of $(C\ -\ D)*E$, and so on, finally replacing the entire string with the value of $(A\ +\ B)\ *\ ((C\ -\ D)*E\ +\ F)$.

More precisely, the algorithm to evaluate postfix expressions operates by scanning the expression one character at a time from left to right. Operands are placed on a stack and operators are applied to the top two stack entries, which are deleted and replaced by the result of the operation. Algorithm 4.7 is a straightforward implementation of this process, assuming that a valid postfix expression is stored in an

```
function EvaluatePolish (P: PolishExpression; n: integer): Value;
var
      S: ValueStack;
      i: integer;
      x, y: Value;
begin
      EmptyValueStack(S);
      for i := 1 to n do
          if P[i] in ['A'..'Z'] then
              PushValue("value of variable in P[i]", S)
          else begin
              y := PopValue(S);        {note: y first}
              x := PopValue(S);
              PushValue("result of applying operator in P[i] to x and y", S)
          end;
      EvaluatePolish := PopValue(S)
end
```

Algorithm 4.7
Evaluation of Polish postfix expression $P[1..n]$

array P [$1..n$] of type *PolishExpression* = **array** [$1..max$] **of** *char*.

We are left with the problem of converting the usual infix expression into its equivalent Polish postfix form. To convert an expression into postfix form we must repeatedly replace an operand-operator-operand sequence by operand-operand-operator. For example, the following illustrates the transformation of

$$(A + B)*((C - D)*E + F)$$

into postfix form:

$$
\begin{array}{c}
(A + B) * ((C - D) * E + F) \\
\underline{\quad} \\
A\ B\ + \\
\underline{\quad} \\
C\ D\ - \\
\underline{\qquad} \\
C\ D\ -\ E\ * \\
\underline{\qquad} \\
C\ D\ -\ E\ *\ F\ + \\
\underline{\qquad\qquad} \\
A\ B\ +\ C\ D\ -\ E\ *\ F\ +\ *
\end{array}
$$

To do this as we scan the expression from left to right, we use a stack as follows. When we find an operator, then we know its left operand has already been converted to postfix and is in the output string. So, we store the operator on the stack and process its right operand. After finishing with its right operand, the operator will conveniently be at the top of the stack; we remove it and add it to the output string.

It is clear from this description of the process that operands must go directly into the output string and operators go into the stack. However, if we have just finished the second of the two operands of an operator, then that operator will be on top of the stack and we must recognize that it is time to put it into the output string. The end of the second of the operands for the operator at the top of the stack occurs one of three ways: at a closing parenthesis, at another operator for which the preceding was the first operand, or at the end of the input string. The case of another operator is handled by observing that, if this incoming operator has lower or equal precedence to the one on top of the stack, then we must have completed the second operand of the operator on top of the stack; that operator can now be popped off the stack and added to the output string. This process must be repeated for the new top stack element, and so on. We now have only finished the first operand for this incoming operator, and it is added to the stack. We handle the case of the end of the input string by adding a special end-of-string-marker, a $ that is treated as a very low precedence operator, causing the above outlined loop to dump out the stack when the $ is encountered.

Algorithm 4.8 embodies the procedure just outlined; it converts an expression in an array E to Polish form in array P (The type *InfixExpression* for E is the same as *PolishExpression*, an array of *char*.) In the algorithm the bottom of the stack is marked by the symbol # which is treated as an operator of even lower precedence than the $ that marks the end of the input string. This causes the $ to be put onto the stack, the end condition of the algorithm. The algorithm uses the precedence function

procedure *InfixToPolish* (*E*: *InfixExpression*; **var** *P*: *PolishExpression*);
    {Convert the infix expression in E to Polish postfix in P.}
var
S: *OperatorStack*;   {store operators during conversion}
i, j: *integer*;   {indices to E and P}
Ignore: *Operator*;
function *Prec* (*c*; *char*): *integer*:
begin
    "See Table 4.1"
end
                                                                           Cont'd

begin
    EmptyOperatorStack(S);
    PushOperator('#', S);   {bottom of stack marker}
    $j := 0$;   {pointer into the output P}
    $i := 0$;   {pointer into the input E}
    while *TopOperator(S)* ≠ '$' **do begin**
            {'$' is the end of input marker; its low precedence will cause the
            stack to be emptied before it is *Push*'ed on}
        {Assert: All single letter operands from $E[1..i]$ are in $P[1..j]$ in the same
        order. S contains, in the order encountered, operators whose left operand
        ends at or after $E[i]$; other operators from $E[1..i]$ are in P immediately
        after their right operand.}
        $i := i + 1$;   {move to next input character}
        if $E[i]$ **in** ['A'..'Z'] **then begin**   {operand: transfer to P}
            $j := j + 1$;
            $P[j] := E[i]$
        end
        else if $E[i]$ = '(' **then**
            PushOperator(E[i], S)
        else if $E[i]$ = ')' **then begin**   {empty stack to ')'}
            while *TopOperator(S)* ≠ '(' **do begin**
                $j := j + 1$;
                $P[j] := PopOperator(S)$
            end;
            Ignore := *PopOperator(S)*   {discard '('}
        end
        else if $E[i]$ **in** ['#', '$', '−', '+', '*', '/'] **then begin**
            {operator: empty stack down to first operator with lower pre-
            cedence, then put $E[i]$ on S}
            while $Prec(E[i])$ ≤ $Prec(TopOperator(S))$ **do begin**
                $j := j + 1$;
                $P[j] := PopOperator(S)$
            end;
            PushOperator(E[i], S)
        end
    end
end

Algorithm 4.8
Conversion of infix to Polish postfix

Prec as given in Table 4.1 to determine the relative precedences of two operators. Notice that the '(' has precedence lower than the arithmetic operations in order to keep it in the stack appropriately.

Algorithm 4.8 is really only the bare bones. To be useful, such an algorithm must check for syntactic errors (how does Algorithm 4.8 react to invalid expressions?) and allow for other operations such as exponentiation and unary minus. These issues are the subject of Exercises 10 and 11.

Character	Precedence
#	0
$	1
(	2
+, −	3
*, /	4

Table 4.1
The precedence function *Prec* used in Algorithm 4.8 for the conversion of infix expressions to their equivalent postfix form. The character # marks the bottom of the stack and $ marks the end of the input string.

Queues. Applications of queues tend to be too intricate to allow the extraction of a concise example. For example, queues are needed in the simulation of various business systems requiring processing customers, orders, jobs, or requests in the order that they arrive. The operation of some computer systems requires that jobs be executed in their order of submission; in this case, again, a queue is mandated. Within the computer itself, queues are needed to keep track of input/output requests—since they are so time consuming relative to internal operations, they can accumulate; if their order is not carefully adhered to, a program might end up, for instance, trying to read a record that has not yet been written. Our first application of a queue will occur in Section 4.3.1.

Exercises

1. In the Towers of Hanoi problem, how many moves are required to move the pile of n disks from the original pole to the final pole?

2. Modify Algorithms 4.5 and 4.6 to keep enough information so that after each move a picture can be printed of the current arrangement of the disks on the poles.

3. Modify Algorithm 4.5 so that the "basic" case is $n = 0$, not $n = 1$. Compare the efficiency of this modification to the original algorithm.

4. Suppose there are *n* disks and *four* poles. Design an algorithm to do the moving in this case. Your algorithm should generate fewer moves than Algorithm 4.5 (see Exercise 1).

5. Consider the following recursively defined sequences of integers: $T_1 = (1)$, $T_{n+1} = (T_n, n + 1, T_n)$. Thus, for example, $T_2 = (1, 2, 1)$ and $T_3 = (1, 2, 1, 3, 1, 2, 1)$. Design a nonrecursive algorithm based on a stack to generate T_n. Find a different algorithm based on divisibility by 2. What is the relation of this sequence T_n to the Towers of Hanoi problem?

6. Suppose you are given a partial solution to the Tower of Hanoi problem in the sense that various legal moves have been made, but the disks are not in their correct final positions. Specifically, you are given a legal configuration of disks in the form of a vector

$$tower: \textbf{array } [1..n] \textbf{ of } pole;$$

where *tower*[*i*] is the pole that disk *i* is on. Design a (recursive) procedure that generates the sequence of moves necessary to take the puzzle from its current state to the state of having all disks on pole *right*.

7. Suppose array *E* contains a (syntactically correct) arithmetic expression composed of + , *, parentheses, and variable names, terminated by a \$. If *i* initially points to the first symbol of this expression, a call to *Exp* returns the value of the expression:

```
function Term: integer; forward;
function Factor: integer; forward;
function Exp: integer;
var
      val: integer;
begin
      val := Term;
      while E[i] = ' + ' do begin
            i := i + 1;      {skip ' + '}
            val := val + Term
      end;
      Exp := val
end;
```

```
function Term {: integer};
var
        val: integer;
begin
        val := Factor;
        while E[i] = '*' do begin
            i := i + 1;        {skip '*'}
            val := val * Factor
        end;
        Term := val
end;
function Factor {: integer};
begin
        if "E[i] is a variable name" then begin
            Factor := "value of E[i]";
            i := i + 1
        end
        else begin {must be a parenthesized expression}
            i := i + 1;            {skip left parenthesis}
            Factor := Exp;         {evaluate enclosed expression}
            i := i + 1             {skip right parenthesis}
        end
end
```

(a) Explain the relationship between these procedures and the pattern given in Exercise 6 of Section 4.1.2.

(b) Modify the above procedures to include the operations $-$ and $/$.

(c) Modify them further to include the operation $\uparrow$ (exponentiation) so that $a \uparrow b \uparrow c$ is interpreted as $a \uparrow (b \uparrow c)$—that is, so that it associates from right to left, unlike the other operations.

8. Design an algorithm analogous to that of the previous exercise to evaluate Polish postfix expressions.

9. Design an algorithm analogous to those in the previous two exercises to convert an infix expression to postfix.

10. Algorithm 4.8 assumes that the input expression is syntactically correct. Modify it to recognize when the input expression is not syntactically correct.

11. Modify Algorithm 4.8 so that it will properly convert expressions with the $\uparrow$ operator [see Exercise 7(c) above for a description of how this operator associates]. The precedence of $\uparrow$ should be 5 in Table 4.1.

12. What would be the effect of changing $Prec(E[i]) \leq Prec(TopOperator(S))$ in Algorithm 4.8 to $Prec(E[i]) < Prec(TopOperator(S))$?

13. Show that by assigning the proper value as the precedence of $')'$, it is possible to combine the last two **else if**'s in Algorithm 4.8.

14. Peano's *dot notation* is used to define parenthesis-free expressions of a single operator "$*$" as follows. The largest number of consecutive dots in any expression divides the expression into its two principal subexpressions, and each subexpression is evaluated using the same rule recursively; ties are broken by going from left to right (that is, by doing the leftmost operator first). For example, the following are some expressions and dot notation equivalents:

Expression	Dot Form
$a * (b * c)$	a.bc
$a * b * c$	abc
$(a * b) * c * (d * (e * f))$	a.b.c...d..e.f

[Notice the notation is not unique: $a..b..c$ and abc both represent $(a * b) * c$.] Give an algorithm to convert a dot notation expression into its Polish postfix form. For example, $a.b.c...d..e.f$ should yield $ab*c*def***$.

15. Let $s_1 s_2 ... s_n$ be a sequence of operands and operators $+$, $-$, $*$, and $/$. Let f be a function defined by

$$f(0) = 0,$$
$$f(i) = \begin{cases} f(i-1) + 1 & \text{if } s_i \text{ is an operand,} \\ f(i-1) - 1 & \text{if } s_i \text{ is an operator.} \end{cases}$$

Prove that $s_1 s_2 ... s_n$ is a syntactically correct Polish postfix expression if and only if $f(i) \geq 1$ for $1 \leq i < n$ and $f(n) = 1$. To what does f correspond in Algorithm 4.7?

16. The *Polish prefix* form of an arithmetic expression is defined analogously to the postfix form, except that the operator precedes (rather than follows) the operands. Find a relationship between the prefix and postfix forms, and use this relationship to design an algorithm for the conversion of infix to prefix.

17. State and prove an analog of Exercise 15 for Polish prefix expressions.

4.3 GRAPHS

We end this chapter on lists with a discussion of an important application of linked lists. A *graph* $G = (V, E)$ consists of finite set of *vertices* $V = \{v_1, v_2, ...\}$ and a finite set of *edges* $E = \{e_1, e_2, \ldots\}$. To each edge there corresponds a pair of vertices; if the pair is *ordered* the graph is called *directed*; if the pair is *unordered* the graph is called *undirected*. The vertices corresponding to an edge are said to be *incident* on the edge. To draw a picture of a graph, we use dots for vertices and line segments for edges. If the graph is directed, the line segments have arrowheads showing the direction. Figure 4.31 shows examples of directed and undirected graphs.

Graphs are an extremely versatile mathematical structure. They can be used to represent diverse types of physical structures such as networks of roads between cities, connections among the components of an electrical circuit, or bonds in a chemical compound. They can also be used to represent abstract relationships such as social connections, priority of tasks, or flow of control. Their versatility makes the representation of graphs and the algorithms for their manipulation a most important application of the list structure technique presented in previous sections of this chapter. We begin by describing how graphs can be conveniently represented by linked lists, and we then present several basic algorithms on graphs so represented.

We will represent a graph as an *adjacency structure* in which all the "adjacencies" are explicitly recorded as pointers in a linked list. A vertex y in a directed graph is called a *successor* of another vertex x if there is an edge from x to y; in an undirected graph, two vertices are *neighbors* if there is an edge between them. The adjacency structure of a graph is a linked list for every vertex v of the successors (neighbors) of v; the relative order of the elements of the list is unimportant. The linked lists of successors are themselves formed into a linked list, as Figure 4.32 shows for the graphs of Figure 4.31.

Thus, each vertex is represented by a record

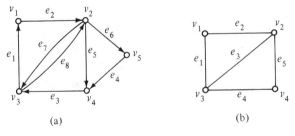

(a)   (b)

Figure 4.31
Examples of graphs: (a) a directed graph of five vertices and eight edges; (b) an undirected graph of four vertices and five edges

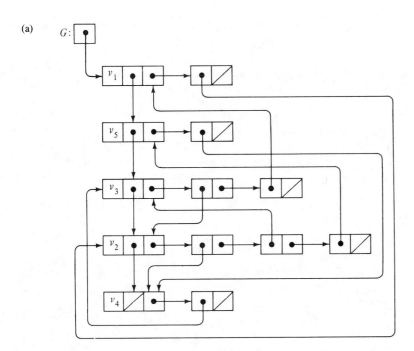

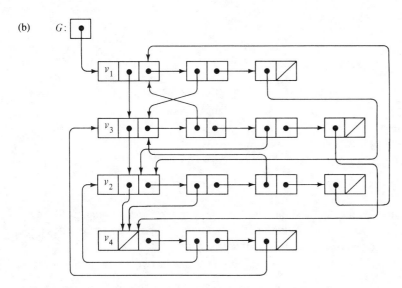

Figure 4.32
Adjacency structures: (a) the adjacency structure for the directed graph of Figure
4.31(a); (b) the adjacency structure for the undirected graph of Figure 4.31(b)

with possibly other information as needed for the vertex (coordinates, size, and so on), while in a list of edges each edge is a record of the form

SUCCESSOR	NEXTEDGE

with possibly other information as needed for the edge (a name, length, capacity, and the like). Declarations 4.2 show the Pascal versions of these records. Notice that the number of records required for an adjacency structure is $|V| + |E|$ for a directed graph and $|V| + 2|E|$ for an undirected graph (why?) where $|V|$ and $|E|$ are the number of vertices and edges, respectively.

type

    pVertex = ↑ *Vertex*;
    pEdge = ↑ *Edge*;
    Vertex = **record**
        NAME: **array**[1 .. 10] **of** *char*;
        NEXTVERTEX: *pVertex*; {next of the vertices in graph}
        EDGEList: *pEdge*;   {list of edges from this vertex}
             {The following fields are used in various applications below.}
        FINAL, *MARKED*: *boolean*;
        COMPNUM, *SEQNUM*: *integer*;
        DISTANCE: *real*
    end;
    Edge = **record**
        SUCCESSOR: *pVertex*; {vertex at other end of this edge}
        NEXTEDGE: *pEdge*;   {next edge on list of edges from a vertex}
             {The following fields are used in various applications below.}
        LENGTH: *integer*   {weight of edge}
    end;
    pGraph = *pVertex*;

Declarations 4.2

Exercises

1. (a) Explain how an electrical circuit could be represented as a graph. Is the graph directed or undirected? What kinds of additional information might be stored in the records for the vertices and edges?

   (b) Repeat part (a) but for a highway system instead of an electrical network.

2. (a) An edge of a graph is a *self-loop* if it begins and ends at the same vertex. Do adjacency structures allow the representation of graphs with self-loops?

   (b) Two edges are called *parallel* if they start and end at the same vertices (and have the same direction in a directed graph). Do adjacency structures allow the representation of graphs with parallel edges?

3. Show how a graph can be represented by a $|V| \times |V|$ bit matrix. Compare such representations to adjacency structures in terms of the storage required. Can parallel edges or self-loops be represented? When will the matrix be symmetric?

4. A graph is *weighted* if with every edge there is a number called the *weight* of the edge. Show how a weighted graph can be represented by a $|V| \times |V|$ matrix.

5. The *incidence matrix* of an undirected graph $G = (V, E)$ is the $|V| \times |E|$ bit matrix A defined by $A[i, j] = 1$ if and only if the ith vertex is incident on the jth edge; otherwise $A[i, j] = 0$. Can self-loops and parallel edges be represented? Can this idea be extended to directed graphs? What are the advantages and disadvantages of incidence matrices?

6. Design an algorithm to construct the adjacency structure described in the text from the incidence matrix described in the previous exercise. How many operations does your algorithm require?

7. Define a *sink* in a directed graph $G = (V, E)$ to be a vertex with $|V| - 1$ incoming edges and no outgoing edges. Find an algorithm that, given a directed graph represented as in Exercise 3, determines in proportional to $|V|$ bit inspections whether G contains a sink.

4.3.1 Breadth-First Search

All graph algorithms require systematic examination of the vertices and edges of a graph. In this section and the next we present two strategies for such an examination, along with some applications.

Perhaps the most natural method of exploring a graph is to start at an arbitrary vertex and fan outward, first examining the neighbors of the starting vertex, then the neighbors of those neighbors, then their neighbors, and so on. This technique, called *breadth-first search*, is extremely useful in designing algorithms for answering questions about distances between vertices in graphs. A sketch of this technique is given in Algorithm 4.9, which applies some unspecified process "*visit*" once to each vertex, starting with vertex *start*.

In this section we will consider only *weighted graphs* in which each edge has a positive number associated with it, its weight. Unweighted graphs can be considered a special case of weighted graphs in which every edge has weight 1. Weighted graphs can be represented with adjacency structures by including a field *WEIGHT* in the record corresponding to an edge. For our first example, however, we will consider the graph as representing a map and use *LENGTH*, the distance between the locations represented by the vertices, as the weight of each edge.

procedure *BreadthFirst* (*G*: *pGraph*; *start*: *pVertex*);
  {Visit each vertex of *G*, spreading outward from *start*.}
var
  Q: *VertexQueue*;
  t: *pVertex*; {current vertex}
  e: *pEdge*; {an edge from *t*}
  u: *pVertex*; {vertex at the other end of *e*}
begin
  "Set *MARKED* to **false** in all vertices of *G*";
  EmptyVertex(Q);
  start↑.*MARKED* := **true**;
  PushVertex(*start*, *Q*);
  while not *IsEmptyVertex*(*Q*) **do begin**
    {Assert: All vertices are either untouched, *MARKED* and visited, or
    MARKED and not yet visited. If a vertex has been visited, all its
    successors are *MARKED*. If a vertex has been *MARKED* and not yet
    visited, it is in *Q*. Vertices in *Q* are in order according to the min-
    imum number of edges that must be traversed from *start* to the
    vertex.}
    t := *Pop*(*Q*);
    "*visit* vertex *t*";
    e := *t*↑.*EDGELIST*;
    while *e* ≠ **nil do begin**
      u := *e*↑.*SUCCESSOR*;
      if not *u*↑.*MARKED* **then begin**
        u↑.*MARKED* := **true**;
        PushVertex(*u*, *Q*)
      end;
      e := *e*↑.*NEXTEDGE*
    end
  end
end

Algorithm 4.9
Breadth-first traversal of a graph. If a stack is used this becomes a "depth-first
traversal," which is more conveniently done with recursion—see Algorithms 4.11
and 4.12.

The questions we would like to be able to answer about a graph (given its
adjacency structure) are: What is the length of the shortest (least total weight) path
between two specified vertices? What is the path? What are the lengths of the shortest
paths from a specified vertex to *all* other vertices in the graph? What are the paths?
Various related questions are pursued in the exercises.

The first two questions, determining a shortest path and its length from a start-ing vertex s to a final vertex f, are answered by starting at s and fanning out until f is reached. As we fan out, the vertices encountered are labeled with their distance from s, so that when the distance of f has been determined we are done. Actually, each vertex will start out with a temporary label representing its distance from s using only some of the possible paths. As more and more paths are considered, the shortest ones are determined and the labels of vertices along them have their final values and are marked by setting *FINAL* to **true**. When the label of f becomes *FINAL*, the algo-rithm stops.

We begin by considering *none* of the paths, so that s is labeled by 0 and every vertex except s is labeled by ∞. We then iterate as follows, with each iteration mak-ing one of the temporary labels *FINAL*. Let *last* be the vertex whose label was just made final. Every vertex v with a temporary label is relabeled with the smaller of

1. The current label of v.

2. The sum of the label of *last* and the length from *last* to v.

Then the smallest of the temporary labels is found and made *FINAL*; in the case of a tie, any of the candidates is chosen. When the label of f becomes *FINAL*, the process ends—f having been labeled with its distance from s.

Why does this algorithm work? We can understand it by understanding the meaning of the labels. The label of a vertex v is the length of the shortest path from s to v that can be built from paths through vertices marked *FINAL*. Inductive reasoning verifies this assertion, for it is true initially when all labels except that of s are infinite and temporary and the label of s is 0 and *FINAL*. Furthermore, if this assertion is true on one iteration, it will be true on the next—the smallest of the temporary labels cannot get smaller by considering paths using other vertices, since all edges have positive length and all the as-yet-unconsidered vertices have labels at least as large (because they can only be reached from vertices with temporary labels). We leave it to Exercise 1 to demonstrate that the labels of the vertices are made *FINAL* in non-decreasing order of their distance from s.

A record of the path itself can be kept as the algorithm proceeds: whenever the *DISTANCE* to vertex v is reduced, $v\uparrow.PRE$ is set to the vertex from which v was reached at this new *DISTANCE*. When v is made final $v\uparrow.PRE$ is the vertex preceding v along the shortest path from s to f. The shortest path from s to f is thus

$$s, \ldots, \quad f\uparrow.PRE\uparrow.PRE\uparrow.PRE, \quad f\uparrow.PRE\uparrow.PRE, \quad f\uparrow.PRE, f.$$

We leave it to Exercise 3 to modify this idea to keep a record of *all* shortest paths from s to f.

Algorithm 4.10 gives the details of the above-outlined shortest-path algorithm. In addition to the fields described earlier and shown in Figure 4.32, each vertex record contains a numerical field *DISTANCE*, a pointer field *PRE*, and a boolean field *FINAL*. Each edge record additionally contains a numerical field *LENGTH*. Algorithm 4.10 executes the body of the outer **while** loop at most $|V| - 1$ times, and the number of operations required for each of those times is proportional to $|V|$ just to

procedure *ShortestPath* (*G*: *pGraph*; *s*, *f*: *pVertex*);
var
    v, *last*, *w*: *pVertex*;
    x: *pEdge*;
begin
        {initially, all distances are ∞ and temporary, except that of *s* which is 0 and *FINAL*}
    v := *G*;
    while *v* ≠ **nil do begin**
        v↑.*DISTANCE* := "∞";
        v↑.*FINAL* := **false**;
        v := *v*↑.*NEXTVERTEX*
    end;
    s↑.*DISTANCE* := 0;
    s↑.*FINAL* := **true**;
    last := *s*;
    while not *f*↑.*FINAL* **do begin**
        {breadth-first search until *f* gets its final distance}
        x := *last*↑.*EDGELIST*;
        while *x* ≠ **nil do begin**
            {update the *DISTANCE* of every temporary vertex to which there is a shorter path via *last*}
            v := *x*↑.*SUCCESSOR*;
            if not *v*↑.*FINAL*
                and (*v*↑.*DISTANCE* > *last*↑.*DISTANCE* + *x*↑.*LENGTH*) **then begin**
                v↑.*DISTANCE* := *last*↑.*DISTANCE* + *x*↑.*LENGTH*;
                v↑.*PRE* := *last*
            end;
            x := *x*↑.*NEXTEDGE*
        end;
    {Assert: In each vertex, *DISTANCE* is the length of the shortest path to the vertex from *s* through vertices that are *FINAL*.}

Cont'd

{Make *FINAL* the vertex with the smallest temporary distance because there can be no shorter path from s to it.}

    $w := f$;   {use $f\uparrow.DISTANCE$ as initial minimum}

    $v := G$;   {scan all of graph}

    while $v \neq$ **nil do begin**

        if not $v\uparrow.FINAL$ **and** $(v\uparrow.DISTANCE < w\uparrow.DISTANCE)$ **then**

            $w := v$;

        $v := v\uparrow.NEXTVERTEX$

    end;

    $w\uparrow.FINAL :=$ **true**;

    $last := w$

  end

end

Algorithm 4.10
Finds a shortest path from s to f in a graph $G = (V, E)$ represented as in Figure 4.32 with additional fields as described in the text

determine w, the vertex whose label will become *FINAL*. The total time required is thus proportional to $|V|^2$ operations.

Exercises

1. Show that Algorithm 4.10 labels the vertices final in nondecreasing order of their distance from s.

2. Would Algorithm 4.10 work properly if the lengths of the edges could be negative?

3. How should Algorithm 4.10 be modified to compute all shortest paths from s to f? [*Hint*: The difficult part of this exercise is to choose the proper data structure to represent the paths.]

4. Devise an algorithm comparable to Algorithm 4.10, but designed to work on a graph represented as a weight matrix W, where $W[i, j]$ is the length of the edge from vertex i to vertex j.

5. Design an algorithm to compute all shortest paths—that is, for all possible starting vertices and all possible final vertices. Assume the graph is represented as a weight matrix as in the previous exercise. As in Exercise 3, you must first decide how the paths are to be represented.

6. A *spanning tree* of a connected, undirected graph $G = (V, E)$ is a graph $T = (V, E')$, where $E' \subseteq E$ and T is *connected* and *acyclic*; that is, there is exactly one path in T between any pair of vertices.

(a) How many edges does T have?

(b) Give an algorithm to find a spanning tree of a graph G.

★(c) A *minimum spanning tree* of a weighted graph is a spanning tree with the additional property that the sum of the lengths of its edges is minimal. Give an algorithm to find a minimum spanning tree of a weighted graph G.

4.3.2 Depth-First Search

Instead of the breadth-first approach of the previous section, we could examine a graph by a *depth-first* strategy in which we attempt to go deeper and deeper into the graph before examining neighboring vertices. When we are examining a vertex v, we follow one of the edges (v, w) out of v. If all edges out of v have been

```
procedure ConnectedComponents (G: pGraph);
var
      v: pVertex;
      CurrentComponent: integer;
      procedure Comp (x: pVertex);
                  {Mark x as part of component Current Component and recursively
                  mark all successors of x.}
      var
            e: pEdge;     {an edge from x}
            u: pVertex;   {the vertex at the other end of e}
      begin
            x↑.COMPNUM := CurrentComponent;
            {explore vertices adjacent to x}
            e := x↑.EDGELIST;
            while e ≠ nil do begin
                  {Assert: All nodes reachable from x along edges prior to e in
                  x↑.EDGELIST have their COMPNUM = CurrentComponent.}
                  u := e↑.SUCCESSOR;
                  if u↑.COMPNUM = 0 then
                        Comp(u)
                  else ; {Assert: u.COMPNUM = CurrentComponent
                                          or graph is not undirected.}
                  e := e↑.NEXTEDGE
            end
      end; {Comp}
```

Algorithm 4.11
Numbering the vertices of G according to connected components—each connected component is assigned a unique number.

begin   {*ConnectedComponents*}
     {Give all vertices an initial component number of 0.}
     $v := G$;
     while $v \neq$ **nil do begin**
          $v\uparrow.COMPNUM := 0$;
          $v := v\uparrow.NEXTVERTEX$
     end;

     CurrentComponent $:= 0$;   {no components yet}
     {Apply depth-first search to each vertex of G.}
     $v := G$;
     while $v \neq$ **nil do begin**
          {Assert: All elements on list G prior to v have nonzero *COMPNUM*.}
          if $v\uparrow.COMPNUM = 0$ **then begin**
               {start a new component}
               CurrentComponent $:=$ *CurrentComponent* $+ 1$;
               Comp(v)
          end;
          $v := v\uparrow.NEXTVERTEX$
     end
end

   Algorithm 4.11, Cont'd

considered, we go back along the edge (u, v) that led to v and continue the exploration from u. The process ends when we attempt to back up from the vertex at which the whole exploration began. This can be done recursively or by Algorithm 4.9 with the queue replaced by a stack. In this section we will illustrate this important technique with two examples, one on undirected graphs and one on directed graphs.

Connected Components. An undirected graph is called *connected* if there is at least one path between every pair of vertices in the graph. A *connected component* of a graph is a maximal connected subgraph; that is, every vertex in a connected component is "reachable" from every other vertex in the component, and any vertex not in the component is not "reachable" from vertices in the component. In the undirected graph of Figure 4.31(b) there is only one connected component, the graph itself. Deleting edges e_4 and e_5 from that graph would leave a graph with two connected components: $(\{v_1, v_2, v_3\}, \{e_1, e_2, e_3\})$ is one and $(\{v_4\}, \emptyset)$ is the other.

   We want to use a depth-first search to label each vertex of the graph with a *component number* in such a way that all vertices in the same connected component have the same component number, and vertices in different connected components have different component numbers. This can be done by first assigning all vertices a component number of zero and then exploring the graph in a depth-first manner starting at every vertex in turn. If a vertex already has a nonzero component number, the search goes no deeper. If a vertex has a component number of zero, it is assigned the current component number, and the search continues deeper into the graph. Algorithm 4.11 gives the details. Each vertex record is assumed to have a numerical field *COMPNUM* in which the component number is stored.

The time required by Algorithm 4.11 is proportional to $|V| + |E|$. This can be understood by observing that, aside from the initialization which requires time proportional to $|V|$, each pointer in the adjacency structure is examined (that is, followed) exactly once. Moreover, the amount of work done before the next pointer is followed is bounded by a small constant.

Topological Numbering. We introduce this problem by an example. Suppose we need to schedule the individual tasks involved in a construction project. The various tasks are related by the fact that some tasks cannot be started until others have been completed; this precedence among tasks can be represented by a directed graph in which the vertices are the tasks and there is a edge from v to w if task v must be completed before task w is started. Figure 4.33 shows ten construction tasks and their relationships to one another. For simplicity, we assume that for some reason (such as inadequate manpower) it is possible to work on only one task at a time and that the tasks cannot be further subdivided. We would like to know the order in which the tasks should be performed by the work crew. In the case of the example in Figure 4.33, we can order the tasks as follows:

1. Fence site
2. Erect site workshops
3. Dig foundations
4. Install concrete plant
5. Bend reinforcement
6. Fabricate steelwork
7. Paint steelwork
8. Place reinforcement
9. Pour foundations
10. Erect steelwork

This arrangement has the property that no task requires a higher-numbered task to precede it. Such a numbering is called a *topological numbering* or a *topological sort* of the vertices of a graph. The general problem is to label the vertices of a directed graph $G = (V, E)$ with the sequence numbers $1, 2, \ldots, |V|$ so that if there is an edge from vertex v to vertex w, then $v\uparrow.SEQNUM < w\uparrow.SEQNUM$. If the directed graph contains a *cycle* of edges $v_0 \rightarrow v_1 \rightarrow \cdots \rightarrow v_0$, such a labeling is, of course, not possible, because it would require that $v_0\uparrow.SEQNUM < v_0\uparrow.SEQNUM$, a contradiction.

We can perform a topological numbering of the vertices of a directed, acyclic graph by a depth-first search strategy: recursively label all vertices "descended from" the current vertex in decreasing order, then label the current vertex with a number less than any number already used. Algorithm 4.12 embodies this idea by initially marking each vertex as yet unvisited and unlabeled; the depth-first labeling procedure *Visit* is then applied to each unvisited vertex in turn. This procedure first marks the vertex x and then recursively processes each vertex to which there is an edge from x. If one of those vertices has already been marked but is yet unlabeled with a *SEQNUM*, we have found a cycle in the graph—that is, we have determined that no topological numbering is possible. When we have finished all the descendants of x, we label x with the next lower *SEQNUM* and return. This algorithm is subtle, and you should trace through it carefully on the graph of Figure 4.33.

As in the case of Algorithm 4.11, Algorithm 4.12 requires only time proportional to $|V| + |E|$ because each edge and each vertex is "examined" only once.

Exercises

1. Simplify Algorithm 4.11 so that it only counts the number of connected components, without labeling the vertices with the component number.

2. Rewrite Algorithm 4.11 in an iterative fashion.

3. Why is j initialized to $|V| + 1$ instead of $|V|$ in Algorithm 4.12?

4. Rewrite Algorithm 4.12 in an iterative fashion.

5. Simplify Algorithm 4.12 so that all it does is to determine whether the graph has a cycle.

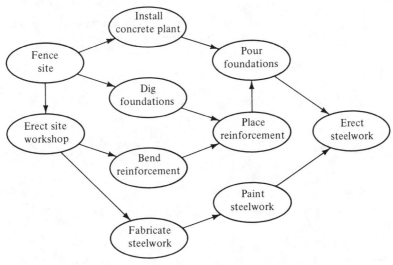

Figure 4.33
Tasks in a construction project, with their precedences shown by arrows

★6. A *bridge* in an undirected, connected graph is an edge whose removal disconnects the graph. Develop a depth-first search algorithm to determine all the bridges of a graph. [*Hint*: Assign the direction followed to an edge of the graph as it is "traversed" by the depth-first search method. Call an edge a *back edge* if it leads to an already visited vertex, and a *forward edge* otherwise. Number the vertices 1, 2,..., |V| in the order in which they are visited by the depth-first search, and define v↑.*LOWPT* to be the lowest-numbered vertex that can be reached from v by a sequence of zero or more (directed) forward edges followed by at most one (directed) back edge. Show that these *LOWPT* labels can be computed on a depth-first search and that they can be used to determine the bridges.]

procedure *TopologicalSort* (G: *pGraph*);
var
    v: *pVertex*;
    j: *integer*;   {value most recently given as a *SEQNUM*}

    procedure *Visit* (x: *pVertex*);
    var
        e: *pEdge*;   {an edge from x}
        u: *pVertex*;   {the vertex at the other end of e}
    begin
        x↑.*MARKED* := **true**;
        {process descendents of x}
        e := x↑.*EDGELIST*;
        while e ≠ **nil do begin**
            {Assert: If there are no cycles, all vertices that have edges entering them from to e↑.*SUCCESSOR* have either never been *Visit*'ed or have had *VISITED* set **true** and have *SEQNUM* ≠ 0.}
            u := e↑.*SUCCESSOR*;
            if u↑.*MARKED* **then**
                if u↑.*SEQNUM* = 0 **then**
                    "G has a cycle"
                else {okay}
            else
                Visit(e↑.*SUCCESSOR*);
            e := e↑.*NEXTEDGE*
        end;
        {Label x with a number less than that of any descendant.}
        j := j − 1;
        x↑.*SEQNUM* := j
    end; {*Visit*}

Algorithm 4.12
Topological numbering of the vertices in a directed graph

begin *{TopologicalSort}*
{Initialize all vertices as unmarked and labeled with 0.}
{Set *j* to 1 + (number of vertices in *G*).}
v := *G*;
j := 1;
while *v* ≠ **nil do begin**
    j := *j* + 1;
    v↑.*SEQNUM* := 0;
    v↑.*MARKED* := **false**;
    v := *v*↑.*NEXTVERTEX*
end;

{Process each unmarked vertex.}
v := *G*;
while *v* ≠ **nil do begin**
    {Assert: All elements of list *G* prior to *v* have *MARKED* = **true** and a non-zero *SEQNUM*.}
    if not *v*↑.*MARKED* **then**
        Visit(v);
    v := *v*↑.*NEXTVERTEX*
end
end

    Algorithm 4.12, Cont'd

★7. An *Eulerian path* in an undirected, connected graph is a path through the graph that traverses every edge of the graph exactly once.

  (a) Prove that a graph has such a path if and only if it has at most two vertices of odd degree. (The *degree* of a vertex is the number of edges going out of it.)

  (b) Design an algorithm to find an Eulerian path in a graph or determine that none exists.

4.4 REMARKS AND REFERENCES

Much of the material in this chapter was known for years only in the folklore of programming. It was in

Knuth, D. E., *The Art of Computer Programming*, Vol. 1, *Fundamental Algorithms*. Reading, Mass.: Addison-Wesley Publishing Co., 1st ed. 1968, 2nd ed. 1973.

that the various data structures and algorithms first coalesced; Knuth's book remains an encyclopedic source for material on lists, stacks, and queues, as well as trees and memory management, which we cover in the next two chapters.

The pattern-matching example of Section 4.1.2 was inspired by SNOBOL4, although it is enormously simpler than the pattern matching facility of SNOBOL4. See

Griswold, R. E., *The Macro Implementation of SNOBOL4*. San Francisco: W. H. Freeman and Co., 1972.

The difficulties of the pattern-matching strategy of Algorithm 4.2 are actually an instance of the problems that occur with parsing by recursive descent. For a general presentation of the method and a discussion of the possible solutions to its difficulties, see

Aho, A. V., and J. D. Ullman, *Compilers: Principles, Techniques, and Tools*. Reading, Mass.: Addison-Wesley Publishing Co., 1977.

This book is also recommended in regard to the evaluation of arithmetic expressions (given as an example in Section 4.2.3), which is a simple case of operator-precedence parsing. Other pattern matching algorithms are described in

Sedgewick, R., *Algorithms*. Reading, Mass.: Addison-Wesley Publishing Co., 1983.

In Section 4.3 we barely scratched the surface of the very broad and deep area of graph algorithms. For more comprehensive treatments, see

Reingold, E. M., J. Nievergelt, and N. Deo, *Combinatorial Algorithms: Theory and Practice*. Englewood Cliffs, N.J.: Prentice-Hall, Inc., 1977.

Tarjan, R. E., *Data Structures and Network Algorithms*. Philadelphia: Society for Industrial and Applied Mathematics, 1983.

Even, S., *Graph Algorithms*. Potomac, Md.: Computer Science Press, Inc., 1979.

Aho, A. V., J. E. Hopcroft, and J. D. Ullman, *The Design and Analysis of Computer Algorithms*. Reading, Mass.: Addison-Wesley Publishing Co., 1974.

Papadimitriou, C. H., and K. Steiglitz, *Combinatorial Optimization: Algorithms and Complexity*. Englewood Cliffs, N.J.: Prentice-Hall, Inc., 1982.

Chapter 5

Trees

I wonder about trees.

The Sound of Trees,   Robert Frost (1916)

In this chapter we will examine trees, a simple form of the general lists introduced in Section 4.1.2, discussing them in terms of the nonlinear, hierarchical organization they epitomize. Hierarchical organizations are so common and so useful that trees are one of the most important data structures covered in this book.

The best-known nontechnical example of a tree structure used to organize information is a *family tree*. In such a tree we show an individual and as many of his ancestors as known or needed. Consider the family tree in Figure 5.1. The principal of the tree, Gerhard Nothmann, is in the middle on the right. Just to his left are his parents, Rudolf Nothman and Margarete Caro; to their left are their parents, and so on; in each case a line is drawn to show the parent-child relationship.

A related nontechnical example is a *lineal chart*, in which we display a person's descendants, rather than his ancestors. Figure 5.2 gives a (partial) lineal chart for Johanna Caro; as in the family tree of Figure 5.1, the parent-child relationship is indicated by a line. In Figure 5.2, however, we have drawn the principal of the tree on the left, as is customary with lineal charts. This is consistent with Figure 5.1 in that the child appears to the right of the parent, and it is indicative of the generative character of the parent-child relationship since (in English) we read from left to right—that is, from parent to child.

Informally, a tree is a collection of elements, of which one is the *root* and the rest of which are partitioned into trees, called the *subtrees* of the root. For example, the root in the lineal chart of Figure 5.2 is Johanna Caro (nee Eger) and the subtrees of the root are lineal charts for her children (Berta Speyer, Friederike Fränkel, and so on). In terms of this recursive definition, a lineal chart for a person would be defined as the person's name (the root) and lineal charts for each of his or her children (the subtrees of the root).

Figure 5.3 shows two ways to depict another example of a tree structure, the

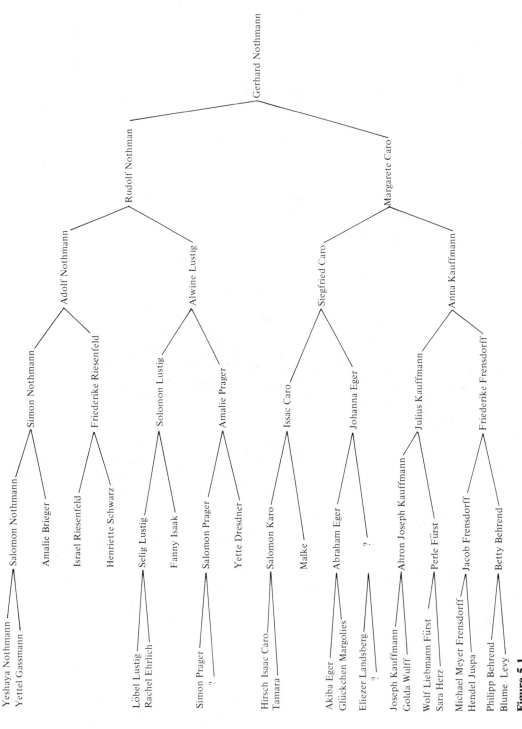

Figure 5.1
A family tree

various procedures that make up a modest compiler written in a block-structured programming language. Figure 5.3(a) shows the compiler's structure much as it would appear in actual code, in a representation by the indentation of the procedure names. Figure 5.3(b) shows the same tree, drawn in a more conventional manner.

There are so many common examples of tree structures used to present information that we could go on and on giving them: the Dewey decimal system, outlines, biological classification of organisms, organization charts, and so on. Whenever a hierarchy of elements is involved, there is a natural representation as a tree. In this and later chapters we shall see many ways in which trees can be used to organize information. Moreover, we will have other important uses of trees; in particular, we will see that trees are used in organizing hierarchical processes (such as knock-out tournaments, for example) and are an important device for the analysis or understanding of various algorithms.

Formally, a tree T is defined as a nonempty finite set of labeled nodes such that there is one distinguished node, called the *root* of the tree, and the remaining nodes are partitioned into $m \geq 0$ disjoint subtrees $T_1, T_2, \ldots, T_m$. Nodes that have no subtrees are called *leaves* or *external nodes*; the remaining nodes are called *internal nodes*. These concepts are illustrated in Figure 5.4, which shows a tree with eleven nodes labeled A through K. The nodes labeled D, E, F, H, J, and K are leaves; the other nodes are internal nodes. The node labeled A is the root.

In describing the relationships between nodes in a tree it has become customary to use the terminology of lineal charts. Thus all the nodes in a tree are said to be *descendants* of its root; conversely, the root is an ancestor of all of its descendants. Furthermore, we refer to the root as the *parent* of the roots in its subtrees; these nodes are, in turn, the *children* of the root. Children of the same node are called *siblings*. For example, in Figure 5.4; node A is the parent of nodes B, G, and I; J and K are the children of I; and C, E, and F are siblings.

Just as there are many species of natural trees, there are many possible variations on the tree structures we will be using. For instance, all the trees considered in this book will be *ordered*; that is, the relative order of the subtrees of each node is important. Thus we consider

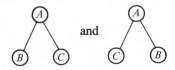

to be different trees, although this is not apparent from the definition. We can define a *forest* as an ordered set of trees and so rephrase the definition of a tree: a tree is a nonempty set of nodes such that there is one distinguished node, called the root of the tree; and the remaining nodes are partitioned into a forest of $m \geq 0$ subtrees of the root. A forest, a course, may also be considered a tree in which the root, although implicit, does not explicitly appear.

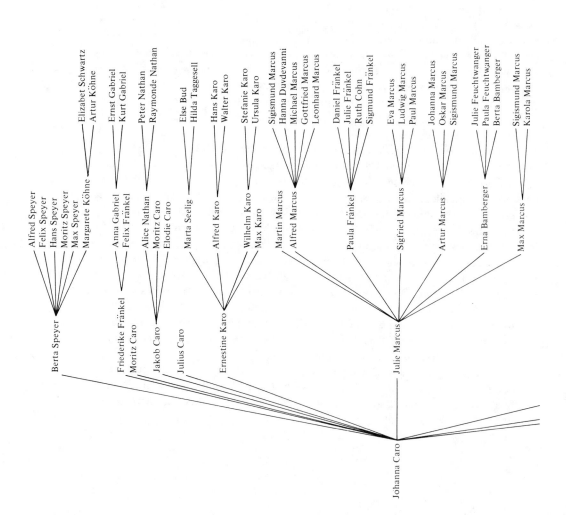

204

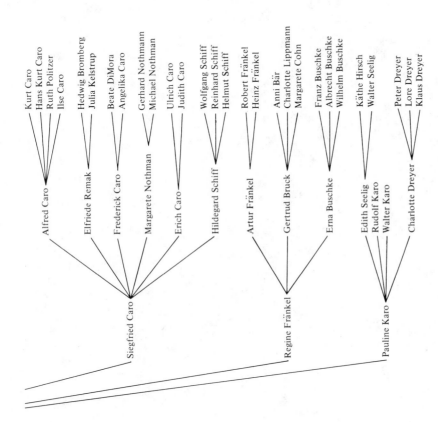

Figure 5.2
A lineal chart

205

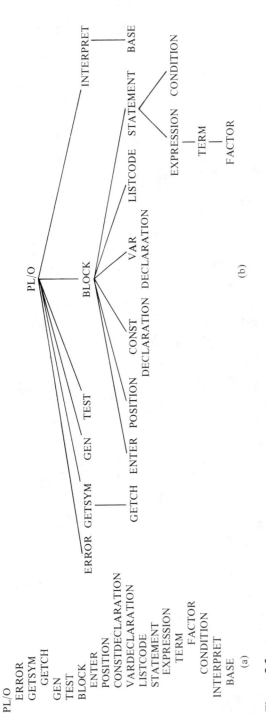

```
PL/O
  ERROR
  GETSYM
    GETCH
  GEN
  TEST
  BLOCK
    ENTER
    POSITION
    CONSTDECLARATION
    VARDECLARATION
    LISTCODE
    STATEMENT
    EXPRESSION
      TERM
        FACTOR
    CONDITION
  INTERPRET
    BASE
```

(a)

```
                          PL/O
        ┌──────┬────┬────┬────┼──────┐
      ERROR GETSYM GEN TEST BLOCK  INTERPRET
              │            ┌───┬──┬──┼──────┬──────┐       │
            GETCH      ENTER POSITION CONST VAR LISTCODE STATEMENT  BASE
                                  DECLARATION DECLARATION        ┌──────┴──────┐
                                                            EXPRESSION   CONDITION
                                                                 │
                                                                TERM
                                                                 │
                                                               FACTOR
```

(b)

Figure 5.3
Tree structures displaying the procedures that comprise a modest compiler

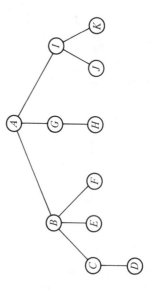

Figure 5.4
A tree with eleven nodes labeled *A* through *K*. The nodes *D*, *E*, *F*, *H*, *J*, and *K* are leaves; the other nodes are internal nodes. The node *A* is the root.

Perhaps the most important tree variant is the binary tree. A *binary tree T* either is *empty* or consists of a distinguished node called the root and two binary subtrees T_l and T_r, the left and right subtrees, respectively. Binary trees differ from the trees so far considered in two important ways: a binary tree may be empty while a tree cannot be, and, more importantly, the distinction of left and right causes

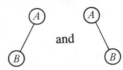

to be different binary trees; yet as trees they are both indistinguishable from

In this chapter we concentrate primarily on binary trees, since, as we shall see, trees and forests can be neatly encoded into binary trees. In later chapters, binary trees will prove more useful as a storage structure and as an analytical tool.

Exercises

1. Define the relationships "cousin," "uncle," and "second cousin once removed" in terms of trees.

2. The following is adapted from Knot II of Lewis Carroll's *A Tangled Tale*: The Governor of Kgovjni wants to give a very small dinner party, and invites his father's brother-in-law, his brother's father-in-law, his father-in-law's brother, and his brother-in-law's father. Find the minimum number of guests, assuming that no closer relations than first cousins may marry. [*Hint*: The governor and all of the guests should be descendants of one couple. Use a family tree/lineal chart to display filial and marital relationships.]

3. The *Strahler numbering* of nodes in a binary tree (useful in hydrology and botany) is defined as follows. The empty tree has Strahler number 0. If the binary tree T has subtrees T_l and T_r, the Strahler number $S(T)$ of T is defined as

$$S(T) = \begin{cases} \max[S(T_l), S(T_r)], & \text{if } S(T_l) \neq S(T_r), \\ S(T_l) + 1, & \text{otherwise.} \end{cases}$$

Compute the Strahler numbers of some binary trees. What is the smallest binary tree T with $S(T) = 3$?

4. Write down all the different trees that can be made from three nodes *A*, *B*, and *C*. Write down all the different binary trees that can be made from these nodes.

5. Show that if a binary tree has $n \geq 1$ nodes and each node has either 0 or 2 children (that is, no node has only 1 child), then *n* is an odd number. Show that such a tree has $(n - 1) / 2$ internal nodes (nodes with children) and $(n + 1) / 2$ external nodes (nodes without children).

5.1 LINKED REPRESENTATIONS

In Figures 5.1, 5.2, and 5.3 we have seen several ways of drawing trees. We have had the root at the right, the left, and the top, although not at the bottom as with trees in nature. The orientation of the trees in these figures has, in each case, arisen from the attempt to have the orientation depend on the nature of the information being represented. In the same way, different computer representations of trees are convenient, depending on the application.

In this section we will examine the fundamental ways of representing trees by nodes and pointers. Important variations will be introduced in later sections and chapters. Also, because sequential representations must, by their nature, impose a linear ordering on the nodes of the tree, we discuss such techniques in a later section.

5.1.1 *LEFT* and *RIGHT* Pointers

Almost all computer representations of trees are based on pointers that explicitly convey the hierarchical relationships. Thus each node of the tree consists of some information and some pointers; for simplicity assume that there is a single information field, *INFO*, and pointer fields as required by the particular linking techniques.

Most computer uses of trees require easy movement down a tree from ancestors to descendants. Such movement generally requires that the tree be represented with pointers that go from parents to children; this is complicated because, although a node has at most one parent, it can have arbitrarily many children. In other words, the nodes in the representation will need to vary in size—a definite inconvenience.

type
   pTree = ↑ *Tree*;
   Tree = **record**
         INFO: "contents of this node";
         LEFT, *RIGHT*: *pTree*   {pointers to left and right subtrees}
   end;

Declarations 5.1

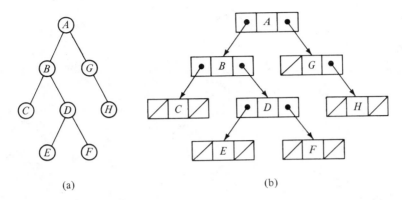

(a)   (b)

Figure 5.5
A binary tree (a) and its representation (b) by nodes with the three fields *LEFT*,
INFO, and *RIGHT*

For the moment we will ignore this problem by concentrating on binary trees, since
they are easily represented with nodes of fixed size. Each node has three fields, *LEFT*,
RIGHT, and *INFO*, as shown in Declarations 5.1 and illustrated in Figure 5.5.

An example of the use of such a structure is the decoding of characters represented in the International Morse Code (see Table 2.13, p. 75). The tree in Figure 5.6 represents this code in the following way. If we start at the root and follow
any valid sequence of dots (left branches) and dashes (right branches) down the tree,
the *INFO* field of the node at which we stop is the character represented by that
sequence of dots and dashes. Thus, for example, the sequence — • — • causes us to
go first right, then left, then right again, and finally left; the character thus found in
the *INFO* field is "C", and indeed, "C" is represented by — • — • in the International
Morse Code. If a sequence of dots and dashes does not correspond to a character,
then the path down the tree thus followed will end at a node with a blank *INFO* field
or will "fall off" the bottom of the tree. For instance, following • • — — • leads to
a blank node, while — • • — — leads off the tree; these two sequences do not, therefore, correspond to characters.

We can use the tree of Figure 5.6 to write a simple decoding algorithm. Suppose we are given the sequence of dots and dashes $d[1..n]$. To decode it, we use it
to follow links down the tree from the root, left and right accordingly, as indicated
by the $d[i]$. If we arrive at a blank node or fall off the tree, then $d[1..n]$ is not a
valid character; otherwise, it is the character found in the *INFO* field of the last node.
The algorithm is given formally by Algorithm 5.1(a).

Recursive routines are convenient for construction of binary trees. Suppose we
wish to construct the tree of Figure 5.6 by reading Table 2.13. We begin by estab-
lishing a root, *MorseTree*, and using *new (MorseTree)* to allocate a single node

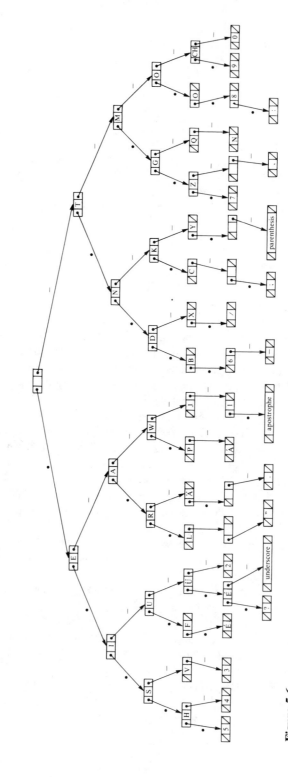

Figure 5.6
Tree used by Algorithm 5.1(a) for decoding Morse code (see Table 2.13)

function *DecodeMorse*(*d*: *MorseString*; *n*: *integer*): *char*;1
var
    i: *integer*;   {index into the string $d[1..n]$}
    p: *pTree*;   {pointer to a node in the Morse code tree}
begin
    $i := 0$;
    $p := MorseTree$;
    while $(i < n)$ **and** $(p \ne$ **nil**$)$ **do begin**
        $i := i + 1$;
        if $d[i] =$ '•' **then**
            $p := p{\uparrow}.LEFT$
        else $p := p{\uparrow}.RIGHT$
    end;1
    DecodeMorse := "invalid code";
    if $p \ne$ **nil then**
        if $p{\uparrow}.INFO \ne$ ' ' **then**
            DecodeMorse := $p{\uparrow}.INFO$

end

Algorithm 5.1(a)
Decoding a sequence $d[1..n]$ of dots and dashes into the corresponding character
in the international Morse code, using the tree in Figure 5.6

procedure *InsertMorse*(*c*: *char*; *d*:*Morse String*; *i*, *n*: *integer*; *p*: *pTree*)

    {Insert letter *c* in the Morse code subtree rooted at *p*, following the code
    given in $d[i..n]$.}
begin
  if $i > n$ **then**
    $p{\uparrow}. INFO := c$
  else if $d[i] =$ '•' **then begin**
    if $p{\uparrow}.LEFT =$ **nil then begin**
      new $(p{\uparrow}. LEFT)$;
      $p{\uparrow}.LEFT{\uparrow}.LEFT :=$ **nil**;
      $p{\uparrow}.LEFT{\uparrow}.RIGHT :=$ **nil**;
      $p{\uparrow}.LEFT{\uparrow}.INFO :=$ ' '
    end;
    InsertMorse $(c, d, i+1, n, p{\uparrow}.LEFT)$
  end
  else "similarly for $p{\uparrow}.RIGHT$".
end

Algorithm 5.1(b)
Creation of the Morse code decoding tree of Figure 5.6

whose *LEFT* and *RIGHT* fields we set to **nil**. Then for each line of the table we read the letter into *l* and the code string into *d*[1..*n*] and call

InsertMorse (l, d, 1, n, MorseTree)

where *InsertMorse* is Algorithm 5.1(b). At each step the Algorithm checks to see if the branch to be followed exists, and, if not, creates it. When there are no more symbols in the code string, *d*, the Algorithm inserts the letter in the current node. A simplification of the algorithm is given as Exercise 2.

Returning to the problem of representing trees in general, observe that we can represent trees as binary trees (using nodes of fixed size) by representing every node in a forest as a node consisting of *LEFT*, *INFO*, and *RIGHT* fields and by using the *LEFT* field of a node to point to the leftmost child of that node and the *RIGHT* field of a node to point to the next sibling of that node. For example, the forest shown in Figure 5.7(a) is transformed into the binary tree shown in Figure 5.7(b). Thus we use *LEFT* field of a node to point to a linked list of the children of that

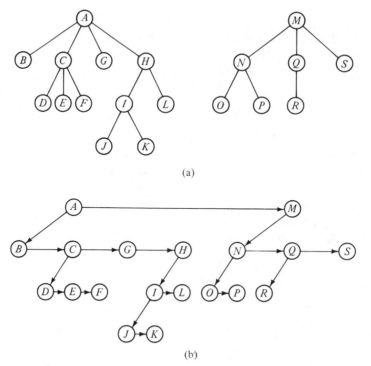

(a)

(b)

Figure 5.7
A forest (a) and its binary tree representation (b) under the natural correspondence

node; that list is linked together by *RIGHT* fields. We call this the *natural correspondence* between forests and binary trees; it will be useful and natural in several contexts.

Exercises

1. Draw a tree analogous to Figure 5.6 for the following code:

A	— — . —	J	— — — — . .	S	. — . —
B	. . — — . —	K	— — — — — . —	T	. . .
C	. — — . .	L	. — — — —	U	. — — — .
D	. . — .	M	. — — . —	V	. . — — . .
E	— . —	N	— — . .	W	. . — — — —
F	— — — — . .	O	— — — .	X	— — — — — — — . —
G	. . — — — .	P	— — — — . —	Y	— — — — — .
H	. — . .	Q	— — — — — — . .	Z	— — — — — — — —
I	— . . .	R	— . . —		

(This code was constructed using the Huffman algorithm of Section 2.4.2 with the frequency of occurrences of the letters in English text.) In what important way does the resulting tree differ from that in Figure 5.6? What does this difference mean in terms of the code?

2. As written, Algorithm 5.1(b) has two places where it calls *new* and initializes the resulting record. The same steps are needed a third time to initialize the root. Only one instance of these steps is needed if p is a variable-parameter to *InsertMorse*, because then the algorithm can begin by testing p and initializing it if it is **nil**. Write this version of the algorithm.

3. Write a non-recursive version of Algorithm 5.1(b).

4. Write a routine *DisposeMorse(p)* which calls *dispose* to free each node of the Morse decoding tree p.

5. What binary tree corresponds to Figure 5.8 under the natural correspondence?

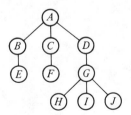

Figure 5.8
Exercise 5

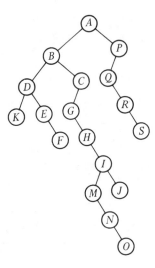

Figure 5.9
Exercise 6

6. To what forest does the binary tree in Figure 5.9 correspond, via the natural correspondence?

7. To what binary tree does the forest in Figure 5.10 correspond, via the natural correspondence? To what forest does it correspond (considering it as a binary tree)?

8. A book outline is a forest in which the children of a section are its subsections as indicated by an additional dot and digit in the section number. Write a procedure analogous to Algorithm 5.1(b) that will insert an element in a forest represented as a binary tree by the natural correspondence. The parameters to your procedure should include a value v for the *INFO* field of the node and an array *number* giving successive parts of the section number.

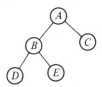

Figure 5.10
Exercise 7

5.1.2   Parent Pointers

There are occasions when trees will be used that will require easy movement *up* the tree from descendants to ancestors. In Section 5.2.2 we will see an indirect way of doing this within the context of *LEFT/RIGHT* pointers. In this section we will examine the direct way and an important application of it.

Figure 5.11 shows a linked representation of the tree in Figure 5.4 based on pointers from child to parent: each node consists of the *INFO* field and a single pointer, *PARENT*. This representation is useful if, as is occasionally the case, we need to move up a tree, from descendants to ancestors.

An important example of the usefulness of this representation is found in a set-manipulation problem that occurs frequently in combinatorial algorithms. Suppose that we want to manipulate disjoint subsets of a set $S = \{s_1, s_2, \ldots, s_n\}$. The operations to be performed are merging two of the disjoint subsets and, given an element s_i, finding which of the subsets contains s_i. At any given time, we thus have a partition of S into nonempty disjoint subsets.

For identification, each of the disjoint subsets of S will have a name. The name is simply one of the elements of the subset and can be thought of as a subset representative. When we refer to the name of a subset, we are referring to its subset representative. Consider, for example,

$$S = \{A, B, C, D, E, F, G, H, I, J, K\}$$

partitioned into four disjoint subsets

$$\{A, F, \textcircled{G}, H, K\}, \quad \{\textcircled{B}\}, \quad \{\textcircled{C}, D, E\}, \quad \{I, \textcircled{J}\}; \tag{5.1}$$

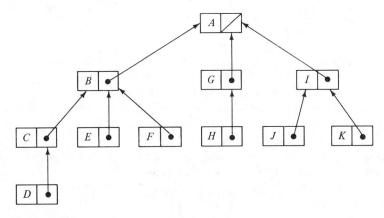

Figure 5.11
The tree in Figure 5.4 represented by nodes with an *INFO* field and a *PARENT* pointer

in each case the circled element is the name of the subset. If we ask to find the subset in which H is contained, the answer we expect is G, the name of the subset containing H. If we ask to take the union of the subsets named B and J, we want the resulting partition of S to be

$$\{A, F, \textcircled{G}, H, K\}, \quad \{\textcircled{C}, D, E\}, \quad \{\textcircled{B}\} \cup \{I, \textcircled{J}\},$$

in which the name of the set $\{B\} \cup \{I, J\}$ can be chosen as either B or J.

We assume that initially we have the partition of $S = \{s_1, s_2, \ldots, s_n\}$ into n singleton sets

$$\{\textcircled{s_1}\}, \quad \{\textcircled{s_2}\}, \quad \cdots, \quad \{\textcircled{s_n}\}, \tag{5.2}$$

in which each set is named after its only element. This partition is modified by a sequence of union operations in which find operations are intermixed. This seemingly contrived problem is quite useful in certain combinatorial algorithms; it was first motivated by the processing of EQUIVALENCE statements in FORTRAN.

We will give procedures $Union(x, y)$ and $Find(x)$ to implement the union and find operations. $Union(x, y)$ takes the names of two different subsets x and y and creates a new subset containing all the elements of x and y. $Find(x)$ returns as its value the name of the subset containing x. For example, if we want to cause the set containing a to be merged with the set containing b, we use the sequence of instructions

$$x := Find(a);$$
$$y := Find(b);$$
$$\textbf{if } x \neq y \textbf{ then}$$
$$\qquad Union(x, y)$$

Suppose that we have a sequence of u union operations intermixed with f find operations and we start with $S = \{s_1, s_2, \ldots, s_n\}$ partitioned into the singleton sets of (5.2). We want a data structure to represent the disjoint subsets of S so that such a sequence of operations can be efficiently performed. The data structure that we will use is a forest representation based on PARENT pointers, as illustrated in Figure 5.11. Each set element s_i will be a node in the forest, and the parent of set element s_i will be another element in the same subset as s_i. If an element has no parent (that is, is a root), then it is the name of its subset. Thus the partition (5.1) might be represented as shown in Figure 5.12.

With this representation, the operation $Find(x)$ consists of following parent pointers up from x to the root (i.e., name) of its subset. The operation $Union(x, y)$ consists of somehow hooking together the trees rooted at x and y; for example, this could be done by making y the parent of x.

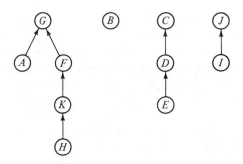

Figure 5.12
A forest representation of the partition (5.1)

After u union operations, the largest subset possible in the resulting partition of S contains $u + 1$ elements. Furthermore, since each union reduces the number of subsets by one, the sequence of operations can contain at most $n - 1$ unions; thus $u \leq n - 1$. Since each union operation changes the name of the subset containing some of the elements, we can assume that each union is preceded by at least one find, and hence we assume that $f \geq u$. The problem then is to perform efficiently a sequence of $u \leq n - 1$ union operations intermixed with $f \geq u$ find operations. The time required by the union operations is clearly proportional to u, because only the small constant amount of work needed to rearrange some pointers is necessary for each union operation. We can therefore concentrate on the time required by the f find operations.

If the operation $Union(x, y)$ is performed by making x the parent of y, then it is possible, after a sequence of u union operations, to produce the forest shown in Figure 5.13. In this case if the f find operations are done after all the union operations, and each find starts at the bottom of the chain of $u + 1$ set elements, it is clear that the time required by the find operations will be proportional to $f \times (u + 1)$. Obviously, it could not be worse than proportional to $f \times (u + 1)$.

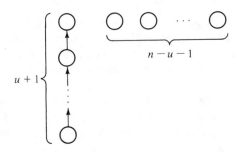

Figure 5.13
A possible forest resulting from u union operations

By being more clever we can reduce this worst case considerably. If the operation $Union(x, y)$ keeps the trees in the forest "balanced" by making the root of the larger subset the parent of the root of the smaller subset (ties can be broken arbitrarily), then we pay a slight premium in storage, since each node in the forest must contain information about the size of the subtree beneath it. However, we will see that the time required by the find operations will then be at most proportional to $f \lg(u + 1)$. First, we need some definitions.

The *level* of a node p in a tree T is defined recursively as 0 if p is the root of T, otherwise the level of p is 1 + (level of parent of p). The *height* $h(T)$ of a tree T is defined by

$$h(T) = \max_{\substack{\text{nodes} \\ p \text{ in } T}} level(p);$$

if T is nonempty. The height is not defined for the empty tree. The level of a node is thus its distance from the root, while the height of a tree is the distance from the root to the furthest leaf.

Going back to the *Union/Find* problem, for any s_i in S let $h(s_i)$ be the height of the subtree rooted at s_i and let $w(s_i)$ be the number of nodes in that subtree. Observe that we always have $w(s_i) \geq 2^{h(s_i)}$. This is clearly true for $u = 0$, since then each element s_i in S is the root of a tree consisting of a single node, and so we have $h(s_i) = 0$ and $w(s_i) = 1$. Suppose that $w(s_i) \geq 2^{h(s_i)}$ for $u = k$ and consider what happens on the $(k + 1)$st union operation, $Union(x, y)$. By induction, we have (before the union operation) $w(x) \geq 2^{h(x)}$ and $w(y) \geq 2^{h(y)}$. Without loss of generality, let $w(x) \geq w(y)$. Then $Union(x, y)$ causes x to become the parent of y, and the height of x after the union is $\max[h(x), h(y) + 1]$. After the union we will have $w(x) \geq 2w(y) \geq 2^{h(y)+1}$; and both before and after the union we have $w(x) \geq 2^{h(x)}$. We conclude that after u union operations each of the elements s_i satisfies

$$0 \leq h(s_i) \leq \lg(u + 1),$$

and thus f find operations will require time at most proportional to $f \lg(u + 1)$. Furthermore, since $f \geq u$, the *total* time for unions *and* finds is at most proportional to $f \lg(u + 1)$. It is easy to see that a tree of height $\lg(u + 1)$ can result from the u unions (how?), and therefore there is an example in which the finds can actually achieve the bound of $f \lg(u + 1)$.

We can improve the efficiency of the find operations by using *path compression*: after the operation $Find(x)$, x and all the vertices on the path between x and the root are made children of the root. For example, if we did $Find(H)$ on the forest in Figure 5.12, the value returned would be G as before, but in the meantime the forest would have changed to the one shown in Figure 5.14. Path compression causes only a minor increase in the cost of a find operation, and, as we will see, its use significantly affects the time required by a sufficiently large number of find operations.

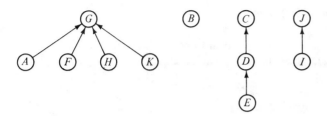

Figure 5.14
The result of *Find(H)* on the forest in Figure 5.12 when path compression is used

The union operation with balancing is given in Algorithm 5.2, and the find operation with path compression is given in Algorithm 5.3. In each algorithm we represent set element s_i with a *Subset* record consisting of three fields: *INFO* and *PARENT* as described with Figure 5.11, and *SIZE* giving $w(s_i)$, the number of elements in the subtree rooted at s_i. See Declarations 5.2.

type
    pSet = ↑ *Subset*;
    Subset = **record**
        INFO: "data for this element";
        PARENT: *pSet*;
        SIZE: *integer*   {number of elements in this subtree}
    end;

Declarations 5.2

The performance of Algorithms 5.2 and 5.3 is startlingly good. It can be shown, although the proof is beyond the level of this book, that the time required

procedure *Union(x, y: pSet)*;
            {x and y point to trees in the forest}
begin
    if x↑.*SIZE* < y↑.*SIZE* **then begin**
        x↑.*PARENT* := y;
        y↑.*SIZE* := y↑.*SIZE* + x↑.*SIZE*
    end
    else begin
        y↑.*PARENT* := x;
        x↑.*SIZE* := x↑.*SIZE* + y↑.*SIZE*
    end
end

Algorithm 5.2
The union operation with balancing

```
function Find(x: pSet): pSet;
var
        t, tt: pSet;    {traverse the path to be compressed}
        root: pSet;    {root of set containing x}
begin
        t := x;
        while t↑.PARENT ≠ nil do
                t := t↑.PARENT;
        Find := t;
        root := t;
        t := x;        {retraverse to compress}
        while t ≠ root do begin
                tt := t↑.PARENT;
                t↑.PARENT := root;
                t := tt
        end
end
```

Algorithm 5.3
The find operation with path compression. Note that the *SIZE* fields are not
maintained; see Exercises 3 and 4.

for $f \geq n$ finds and $n - 1$ unions is at most proportional to $n\alpha(f, n)$ where $\alpha(f, n)$ is
a function that grows so slowly that $\alpha(f, n) \leq 3$ for

$$n \leq 2^{2^{.^{.^{.^2}}}} \left.\right\} 65,537 \text{ twos}$$

Exercises

1. What structure results if we start with the sets $\{A\}, \{B\}, \{C\}, \{D\}, \{E\}, \{F\}, \{G\},$
   $\{H\}$ and perform the following sequence of operations with Algorithms 5.2 and
   5.3?

   Union(A, B)
   Union(Find(A), C)
   Union(D, E)
   Union(F, G)
   Union(H, Find(F))
   Union(Find(H), Find(D))
   Find(G)
   Find(B)
   Find(E)

2. Let $h(k)$ be the maximum height of a tree produced by a sequence of k union/find

operations with initially given sets $\{1\}$, $\{2\}$, ..., $\{2k\}$, when balancing (but not path compression) is used. Thus $h(0)=0$, $h(1)=h(2)=1$, $h(3)=2$, and so on. Prove that $h(2n + 1) \leq h(n) + 1$ for all $n \leq 0$.

3. Algorithm 5.3 does not maintain the *SIZE* fields in nodes subordinate to the root.

   (a) Will *Find* and *Union* continue to work correctly?

   (b) Modify the algorithm to place correct values in all *SIZE* fields.

4. Path compression has the disadvantage of requiring two passes over the path to the root—one pass to find the root and a second to do the compression (see Algorithm 5.3). An interesting alternative is *path halving*: when going up to the root make every other node on the path point to its grandparent. Rewrite Algorithm 5.3 to do path halving.

5.2   TRAVERSALS

In many applications of trees and forests it is necessary to traverse them—that is, to visit systematically each of the nodes and process each of them in some manner. The visit at each node might be as simple as printing its contents or as complicated as a major computation. The only assumption that we make about the visit is that it does not change the structure of the forest. Four useful basic traversal orders are *preorder*, *postorder*, *level order*, and, for binary trees, *inorder*.

   Preorder visits the nodes of a forest as described by the following recursive procedure.

   1. Visit the root of the first tree.

   2. Traverse the subtrees, if any, of the first tree in preorder.

   3. Traverse the remaining trees, if any, in preorder.

For instance, in the forest shown in Figure 5.7(a), the nodes would be visited in the order A, B, C, D, E, F, G, H, I, J, K, L, M, N, O, P, Q, R, S. The name "preorder" refers to the fact that we visit the root before traversing the remainder of a tree.

   For a binary tree, the recursive procedure simplifies to

   1. Visit the root of the binary tree.

   2. Traverse the left subtree in preorder.

   3. Traverse the right subtree in preorder.

In this case the empty tree is traversed by doing nothing. Notice that traversing a forest in preorder is exactly the same as the preorder traversal of the binary tree arising by the natural correspondence. This makes the correspondence "natural."

Postorder visits the nodes of the forest according to the following recursive procedure.

1. Traverse the subtrees of the first tree, if any, in postorder.

2. Visit the root of the first tree.

3. Traverse the remaining trees, if any, in postorder.

The name "postorder" refers to the fact that at the time a node is visited, all of its descendants have already been visited. In the forest in Figure 5.7(a) this order visits the nodes in the order *B, D, E, F, C, G, J, K, I, L, H, A, O, P, N, R, Q, S, M*. The recursive procedure for the postorder traversal applied to binary trees simplifies to

1. Traverse the left subtree in postorder.

2. Traverse the right subtree in postorder.

3. Visit the root.

Inorder or *symmetric order* is defined recursively for binary trees as

1. Traverse the left subtree in inorder.

2. Visit the root.

3. Traverse the right subtree in inorder.

This is also known as *lexicographic order* (for reasons that will become clear in Chapter 7). Notice that traversing a forest in postorder is equivalent to traversing the binary tree corresponding to the forest (by the natural correspondence) in inorder.

Comparing the recursive procedures for the preorder, inorder, and postorder binary tree traversals, we find considerable similarity. In all cases the left subtree is visited before the right subtree; only the time when the root is visited differentiates between the orders:

Preorder: before the subtrees
Inorder: between the subtrees
Postorder: after the subtrees

This similarity allows us to construct a general nonrecursive algorithm that can be adapted to each of these orders for binary tree traversal. We use a stack S to store pairs consisting of a node in the binary tree and a value telling which of the three operations of Table 5.1 (the first, second, or third) is to be performed when the pair reaches the top of the stack. This general algorithm is shown in Algorithm 5.4.

(Recall from Section 4.2 that we write tuple assignments with the tuple in quotation marks. For instance

$$\text{``}(p, state)\text{''} := PopStack(S)$$

pops a two-tuple off S and assigns its two components to p and $state$, respectively.)

It is straightforward to specialize Algorithm 5.4 to create specific traversal algorithms. For example, substitution from Table 5.1 of the column for preorder binary tree traversal yields Algorithm 5.5(a). We can simplify Algorithm 5.5(a) by noticing that when $(p, second)$ or $(p, third)$ comes to the top of the stack, the only thing that happens is that $(p{\uparrow}.LEFT, first)$, or $(p{\uparrow}.RIGHT, first)$ is put on the stack. This step can be done earlier, when we first visit node p, so we can simplify Algorithm 5.5(a) to Algorithm 5.5(b).

```
procedure GeneralTraverse(root: pTree);
var
        S: Stack; {a stack of 2-pairs to remember locations in tree}
        p: pTree; {pointer into the tree}
        state: (first, second, third); {choose an operation for p}
begin
        EmptyStack(S);
        PushStack("(root, first)", S);
        while not IsEmpty(S) do begin
                "(p, state)" := PopStack(S);
                {Assert: S contains, in order by depth, one pair for each node on
                the path from p to root. For nodes having p in their left subtree,
                the pair is (node, second); otherwise it is (node, third).}
                if p ≠ nil then
                        case state of
                        first: begin
                                        PushStack("(p, second)", S);
                                        "first operation"
                                end;
                        second: begin
                                        PushStack("(p, third)", S);
                                        "second operation"
                                end;
                        third:
                                        "third operation"
                        end
        end
end
```

Algorithm 5.4
General binary tree traversal, with operations as indicated in Table 5.1

	Traversal Order		
Operation	Preorder	Inorder	Postorder
First	visit node p	push LEFT	push LEFT
Second	push LEFT	visit node p	push RIGHT
Third	push RIGHT	push RIGHT	visit node p

Table 5.1
The operations for the general binary tree traversal of Algorithm 5.4. "Visit node p" means to perform some operation—such as printing—on the node pointed to by p; "push LEFT" means to push a 2-tuple with PushStack("$p\uparrow$.LEFT, first)" S); and similarly "push RIGHT" means PushStack("($p\uparrow$.RIGHT, first)", S).

Specializing Algorithm 5.4 for the inorder traversal of binary trees and simplifying the result as above, we get Algorithm 5.6. Specializing Algorithm 5.4 for the postorder results in Algorithm 5.7. (See Exercises 5 through 8 for further comments on these traversal algorithms.)

```
EmptyStack(S);
PushStack("(root, first)", S);
while not IsEmpty(S) do begin
     "(p, state)" := PopStack(S);
     if p ≠ nil then
             case state of
             first: begin
                             PushStack("(p, second)", S);
                             "visit node p"
                 end;
             second: begin
                             PushStack("(p, third)", S);
                             PushStack("(p↑.LEFT, first)", S)
                 end;
             third:
                             PushStack("(p↑.RIGHT, first)", S)
                 end
     end
```

Algorithm 5.5(a)
Straightforward specialization of Algorithm 5.4 to the preorder traversal of a binary tree

EmptyStack(S);
PushStack(root, S);
while not *IsEmpty(S)* **do begin**
    p := *PopStack(S)*;
    {Assert: For each ancestor of *p* that has *p* in its left subtree, the right child of the ancestor is in *S*. Nodes in *S* are in order of their depth in the tree. Visits have been made to the nodes that precede *p* in preorder and to no other nodes.}
    if *p* ≠ **nil then begin**
        "visit node *p*";
        PushStack(p↑.RIGHT, S);
        PushStack(p↑.LEFT, S)
    end
end

Algorithm 5.5(b)
Preorder binary tree traversal, a simplified version of Algorithm 5.5(a)

EmptyStack(S);
PushStack("(root, first)", S);
while not *IsEmpty(S)* **do begin**
    "*(p, state)*" := *PopStack(S)*;
    {Assert: For each ancestor of *p* having *p* in its left subtree, *S* contains one pair of the form. (ancestor, *second*). The pairs are in order by the depth of the ancestor they contain. Visits have been made to the nodes that precede *p* in inorder and to no other nodes.}
    if *p* ≠ **nil then**
        case *state* **of**
        first: **begin**
            PushStack("(p, second)", S);
            PushStack("(p↑.LEFT, first)", S)
        end;1
        second: **begin**
            "visit node *p*"
            PushStack("(p↑.RIGHT, first)", S)
        end;
    end
end

Algorithm 5.6
Inorder binary tree traversal, a simplified specialization of Algorithm 5.4

For forests represented by binary trees via the natural correspondence, the level-order traversal is a bit more complicated. At each node we must follow *RIGHT* links to visit the siblings and simultaneously keep track of the *LEFT* links ("eldest" children in the underlying forest). Thus we arrive at Algorithm 5.9.

The final traversal order is the *level order*. This traversal visits the nodes of the forest from the left to right, level by level from the roots down. Thus the nodes in the forest in Figure 5.7(a) would be visited in the order *A, M, B, C, G, H, N, Q, S, D, E, F, I, L, O, P, R, J, K*. In a binary tree this traversal is accomplished by having *S* be a queue instead of a stack in Algorithm 5.5(b) and by interchanging the last two *PushStack* statements (why?), yielding Algorithm 5.8.

```
EmptyStack(S);
PushStack("(root, first)", S);
while not IsEmpty(S) do begin
      "(p, state)" := PopStack(S);
      {Assert: S is as described in Algorithm 5.4. Visits have been made
      to all nodes that precede p in postorder and to no other nodes.}
      if p ≠ nil then
            case state of
            first: begin
                        PushStack("(p, second)", S);
                        PushStack("(p↑.LEFT, first)", S)
                  end;
            second: begin
                        PushStack("(p, third)", S);
                        PushStack("(p↑.RIGHT, first)", S)
                  end;
            third:
                        "visit node p"
            end
end
```

Algorithm 5.7   Postorder binary tree traversal, a specialization of Algorithm 5.4

procedure *LevelOrder* (*root*: *pTree*);
   var
        Q: *Queue*;
        p: *pTree*;
   begin
        EmptyQueue(*Q*);
        PushQueue(*root*, *Q*);
        while not *IsEmpty*(*Q*) **do begin**
            p := *PopQueue*(*Q*);
            {Assert: *Q* begins with the level-order sequence of those nodes that are on the same level as *p* and follow it in inorder; *Q* further contains—again in level order—all nodes that are one level deeper than *p* and precede it in inorder. Visits have been made to all nodes that precede *p* in level order and to no other nodes.}
            if *p* ≠ **nil then begin**
                "visit node *p*";
                PushQueue(*p*↑.*LEFT*, *Q*);
                PushQueue(*p*↑.*RIGHT*, *Q*)
            end
        end
   end

Algorithm 5.8   Level-order traversal of a binary tree

        EmptyQueue(*Q*);
        PushQueue(*root*, *Q*);
        while not *IsEmpty*(*Q*) **do begin**
            p := *PopQueue*(*Q*);
            while *p* ≠ **nil do begin**
                {Assert: *Q* contains—in forest-level order—the leftmost child of each node that both follows *p*'s parent in forest-level order and precedes *p* in that same order. Visits have been made to the nodes that precede *p* in forest-level order and to no other nodes.}
                "visit node *p*";
                if *p*↑.*LEFT* ≠ **nil then**
                    PushQueue(*p*↑.*LEFT*, *Q*);
                p := *p*↑.*RIGHT*
            end
        end

Algorithm 5.9   Level-order traversal of a forest represented as a binary tree via the natural correspondence

Exercises

1. Which of the traversal orders described is appropriate for computing the Strahler numbers of Exercise 2, page 207?

2. Find a simple relationship between the preorder traversal of a binary tree and the postorder traversal of its mirror image.

3. Is each of the following true or false? Prove your answers.

   (a) In a binary tree the node x is a descendant of the node y if and only if x follows y in preorder and precedes y in postorder.

   (b) In a binary tree the node x is a descendant of the node y if and only if x follows y in preorder and precedes y in inorder.

   (c) The leaves of a binary tree occur in the same relative order in preorder, inorder, and postorder. What about level order?

   (d) The leaves of a forest occur in the same relative order in preorder and postorder.

4. Research on Rhesus monkeys has shown that at birth females take their place in the dominance hierarchy directly below their mother, and above *all* of the females that their mother dominates, including any of their older sisters. Assuming that the daughters of a node are in decreasing order by age from left to right, to what forest traversal order does this dominance relation correspond?

5. In Algorithm 5.4, its specializations, and their simplifications much energy is expended moving the empty tree [that is, pairs (**nil,** *state*)] on and off the stack. Modify these algorithms so that only nonempty trees are put on the stack.

6. Why is the right child put on the stack before the left child in Algorithm 5.5(b)?

7. Design an inorder traversal algorithm that uses a stack to store tree nodes so that a node is put on and removed from the stack only once (as compared to Algorithm 5.6, in which each node is put on and removed from the stack twice). [*Hint*: Arrange it so that at the time a node is removed from the stack its left subtree has already been traversed; it is then sufficient to visit the node and then traverse its right subtree.]

8. Design a postorder traversal algorithm that uses a stack to store tree nodes so that a node is put on and removed from the stack only twice (as compared to Algorithm 5.7, in which each node is put on and removed from the stack three times).

9. Find all binary trees with the property that the preorder traversal and inorder traversal visit the nodes in the same order.

10. Describe the set of nonempty binary trees with the property that the preorder traversal and the level-order traversal visit the nodes in the same order.

11. Design an algorithm to reconstruct a binary tree from the preorder and inorder lists of nodes. Do corresponding algorithms exist for the preorder and postorder lists or the inorder and postorder lists?

12. Suppose the nodes of a tree are linked together in preorder with the *LEFT* pointers and in inorder in the *RIGHT* pointers. In other words, there is a linked structure of nodes like

preorder
successor of *N*   *N*   inorder
                                       successor of *N*

Devise an algorithm to traverse this list and transform it into the proper tree structure, using no additional nodes (see Exercise 11).

13. Design an algorithm for deleting a node in a tree in such a way that the inorder of the remaining nodes is unchanged. Design similar algorithms for preorder and postorder.

14. Consider binary trees represented with *LEFT* and *RIGHT* pointers in which each node also contains an additional one-bit field *BIT*. A *mixed-order traversal* of such a tree is defined recursively as

    (a) If *BIT* of the root is 0, then
        (1) Visit the root.
        (2) Traverse the left subtree in mixed order.
        (3) Traverse the right subtree in mixed order.
    (b) If *BIT* of the root is 1, then
        (1) Traverse the left subtree in mixed order.
        (2) Traverse the right subtree in mixed order.
        (3) Visit the root.

    For example, the mixed-order traversal of the tree in Figure 5.15 visits the nodes in the order *B, D, E, F, G, I, J, H, C, A*. Design a nonrecursive algorithm to traverse such a tree in mixed order.

15. Give a nonrecursive algorithm to traverse a binary tree in *dual order* defined recursively as

    (a) Visit the root for the first time.
    (b) Traverse the left subtree in dual order.
    (c) Visit the root for the second time.
    (d) Traverse the right subtree in dual order.

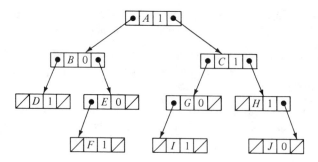

Figure 5.15
Exercise 14

16. Suppose we want to traverse a binary tree in preorder, inorder, and postorder *simultaneously* in the following recursively defined "triple-order, " traversal:

(a) Visit the root for the preorder traversal.

(b) Traverse the left subtree in triple order.

(c) Visit the root (again) for the inorder traversal.

(d) Traverse the right subtree in triple order.

(e) Visit the root (again!) for the postorder traversal.

Design an algorithm analogous to Algorithm 5.4 for the triple-order traversal of a binary tree.

17. The following seven operations can be rearranged in 7! = 5040 ways to yield recursive binary tree-traversal algorithms:

    (i) Visit the root.

    (ii) Visit the left child of the root, if it exists.

    (iii) Traverse the left subtree of the left child, if it exists.

    (iv) Traverse the right subtree of the left child, if it exists.

    (v) Visit the right child of the root, if it exists.

    (vi) Traverse the left subtree of the right child, if it exists.

    (vii) Traverse the right subtree of the right child, if it exists.

(a) Express preorder, inorder, and postorder in terms of the above steps.

(b) Can the following traversal be expressed in terms of the above steps? If so, do it; if not, explain why not.

(c) Design a general traversal analogous to Algorithm 5.4 but based on the above operations.

```
procedure Traverse17 (t: pTree);
begin
    if t ≠ nil then
        if t↑.RIGHT = nil then begin
                "visit node t";
                Traverse17(t↑.LEFT)
        end
        else begin
                Traverse17(t↑.RIGHT↑.LEFT);
                "visit node t";
                Traverse17(t↑.LEFT);
                "visit node t↑.RIGHT";
                Traverse17(t↑.RIGHT↑.RIGHT)
        end
end
```

18. In what order does the following algorithm traverse a binary tree?

```
        t := root;
    while t ≠ nil do
        if t↑.LEFT = nil then begin
            "visit node t";
            t := t↑.RIGHT
        end
        else begin
            p := t↑.LEFT;
            while (p↑.RIGHT ≠ nil) and (p↑.RIGHT ≠ t) do
                p := p↑.RIGHT;
            if p↑.RIGHT = nil then begin
                p↑.RIGHT := t;
                t := t↑.LEFT
            end
            else begin
                "visit node t";
                p↑.RIGHT := nil;
                t := t↑.RIGHT
            end
        end
```

Explain how the algorithm works. Design similar algorithms for other traversal
orders.

19. Let T be a binary tree in which associated with each edge $(v\uparrow.PARENT, v)$ there is a nonnegative *capacity*, $c(v\uparrow.PARENT, v)$, the amount of water that can flow from $v\uparrow.PARENT$ to v. Assume an infinite supply of water available at the root of T. A *flow* in T is a nonnegative function f on the set of edges such that

$$f(v\uparrow.PARENT, v) \leqslant c(v\uparrow.PARENT, v)$$

and

$$f(v\uparrow.PARENT, v) = f(v, v\uparrow.LEFT) + f(v, v\uparrow.RIGHT)$$

The *value* of a flow is defined as the total flow through the root—that is, the sum of $f(root, root\uparrow.LEFT) + f(root, root\uparrow.RIGHT)$. A flow is a *maximum flow* if its value is the largest possible.

(a) Explain why the value of a flow is equal to $\Sigma_{v\ \text{a leaf}} f(v\uparrow.PARENT, v)$.

(b) Devise an algorithm to compute the *value* of a maximum flow for a binary tree T with its associated capacity function. [*Hint*: Base your algorithm on a traversal.]

(c) Devise an algorithm to compute the values $f(v\uparrow.PARENT, v)$ for a maximum flow.

20. Define a *priority forest* as a forest of numerical values that either is empty or has the shape

where $m \geqslant 1$, $x_1, \ldots, x_m$ are values, and $F_1, \ldots, F_m$ are priority forests; furthermore, the preorder traversal of the forest yields the values in the nodes in *increasing order*. We will keep F_m empty, so this forest can be written as $(x_1\ F_1\ x_2 \ldots F_{m-1}\ x_m)$. The insertion of a new value into a priority forest is done by the following recursive strategy. Insertion of x into the empty forest yields (x). Insertion of x into $(x_1\ F_1 \ldots F_{m-1}\ x_m)$ yields $(x\ x_1\ F_1 \ldots F_{m-1}\ x_m)$ if $x \leqslant x_1$; or $(x_1 \ldots x_i\ \hat{F}_i\ x_{i+1} \ldots x_m)$ if $x_i < x \leqslant x_{i+1}$, where $\hat{F}_i$ is the result of recursively inserting x into F_i; or $(x_1\ F_1 \ldots F_{m-1}\ x_m\ x)$ if $x > x_m$. This recursive description of the algorithm insures that the values in the priority forest are always increasing in preorder; in particular, $x_1 < \cdots < x_m$, and the value of i is thus uniquely defined. It also insures that F_m is always empty.

(a) Show the priority forest that results from inserting 16, 11, 1, 3, 6, 2, 4, 5, 12, 15 into the originally empty forest.

(b) Suppose the priority forests are represented as binary trees according to the natural correspondence so that each node looks like

VALUE	
FIRSTCHILD	SIBLING

where *FIRSTCHILD* points to the leftmost child, if any, and *SIBLING* points to the next sibling to the right, if any. Assume further that the forest is pointed to by a header node *Head* of the same form where *Head↑.FIRSTCHILD* points to the root of the binary tree representing the forest. Give an algorithm to delete the element of a *nonempty* forest having the lowest *VALUE*. Your algorithm must leave the remaining values in a proper priority forest.

(c) Give both recursive and nonrecursive versions of the insertion algorithm described above.

21. A binary tree can be laid out compactly in the plane by the following technique:

Design traversal algorithms to assign the (x, y) coordinates to a node, as it will appear in the above examples.

5.2.1 Applications

The systematic traversal of the nodes of a tree is required in many applications. In this section we will examine some typical problems in which such traversals play a central role.

Copying a Binary Tree. Suppose we are given the root of a binary tree and we wish to create a copy of that tree. We can do so by traversing the tree in preorder, with the visit at a node copying its contents. It is easiest to understand the copying process when it is specified recursively: to copy a tree we create a new root, store in its *INFO* field the contents of the *INFO* field of the original tree, and then recursively copy the left and right subtrees of the original tree. Algorithm 5.10 embodies this process with a recursive procedure *Copy*. *Copy* has as its single argument the root of the tree to be copied and it returns as its value the root of the copy produced. The

```
function Copy(t: pTree): pTree;
var
        tcopy: pTree;
begin
        if t = nil then
                Copy := nil
        else begin
                new(tcopy);
                tcopy↑.INFO := t↑.INFO;
                tcopy↑.LEFT := COPY(t↑.LEFT);
                tcopy↑.RIGHT := Copy(t↑.RIGHT);
                Copy := tcopy
        end
end
```

Algorithm 5.10
A recursive procedure (based on a preorder traversal) to produce a copy of binary tree *T*

use of recursion in Algorithm 5.10 makes it clear that this procedure is just a preorder traversal, a fact obscured by the iterative version, which appears here as Algorithm 5.11.

In Algorithm 5.10, as in most algorithms in this book, the parameter is not modified by the procedure; but parameter modification can be useful. In Algorithm 5.11 the **var** parameter allows *CopyNode* to allocate a node with *new* and assign the pointer to it to the correct pointer field. In this algorithm the stack is used to store triples (*old, new, side*) where *old* points to a node *t* in the original tree, *new* is the copy of its parent, and *side* indicates whether *t* is to left or right of its parent.

Printing a Binary Tree. Suppose we want to print a binary tree so that its "shape" is properly displayed. For example, we might want to print the tree of Figure 5.5(a) as shown in Figure 5.16. The lines of the output must be printed from top to bottom; this requires that the tree be traversed in "reverse inorder." In other words, we need to traverse the tree according to the recursively defined order

1. Right subtree

2. Visit root

3. Left subtree

We will simplify the problem slightly by eliminating the connective lines between the nodes of the tree and also the characters that form the box around the

function *IterativeCopy(root: pTree): pTree*;
var

        S: Stack;
        newroot, oldnode, newparent: pTree;
        side: (CopyLeft, CopyRight);

    procedure *CopyNode(old: pTree*; **var** *newptr: pTree)*;
        {Copy node *old* and assign to *newptr* a pointer to the copy. Push
        onto *S* a tuple for each child of *old*.}
    begin
        if *old* = **nil then**
            newptr := **nil**
        else begin
            new(newptr);
            PushStack("(old↑.RIGHT, newptr, CopyRight)", S);
            PushStack("(old↑.LEFT, newptr, CopyLeft)", S)
        end
    end; {*CopyNode*}

begin {*IterativeCopy*}
    EmptyStack(S);
    CopyNode(root, newroot);
    while not *IsEmpty(S)* **do begin**
    "*(oldnode, newparent, side)*" := *PopStack(S)*;
        {Assert: Copies have been made of all nodes that precede *oldnode*
        in preorder. The pointer to each of these nodes from its corresponding
        parent has also been established. For each ancestor of *oldnode* having
        oldnode in its left subtree, there is a tuple in *S* with three fields:
        (ancestor↑.*RIGHT*, pointer to copy of ancestor, *CopyRight*).}
        if *side* = *CopyLeft* **then**
            CopyNode(oldnode, newparent↑.LEFT)
        else
            CopyNode(oldnode, newparent↑.RIGHT)
    end;
    IterativeCopy := *newroot*
end

Algorithm 5.11
An iterative procedure (based on a preorder traversal) to produce a copy of a
binary tree *T*

nodes. Since this "window dressing" is not too difficult to add, once the basic idea
is understood, we leave it to Exercise 3. Thus, consider the problem of printing the
tree of Figure 5.5(a) as shown in Figure 5.17.

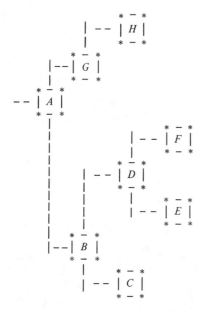

Figure 5.16
A "computer printed" version of Figure 5.5(a)

The basic idea is to write a recursive procedure, essentially a traversal in reverse inorder, that has an additional parameter, *indent*, whose value is the number of blanks to print prior to printing every line of this subtree. Initially *indent* is zero, but becomes larger as we go deeper in the tree. The recursive portion of this idea is shown in Algorithm 5.12; the entire tree would be printed by *PrintTree*(*root*, 0).

		H	
	G		
A			
			F
		D	
			E
	B		
		C	

Figure 5.17
A simplified version of Figure 5.16

procedure *PrintTree (s: pTree; indent: integer)*;
begin
    if *s* ≠ **nil then begin**
        PrintTree(s↑.RIGHT, indent + 1);
        write(' ':indent);   {write *indent* spaces}
        writeln(s↑.INFO);   {write *INFO* and end the line}
        PrintTree(s↑.LEFT, indent + 1)
    end
end

Algorithm 5.12
Printing a binary tree.

Arithmetic Expressions. In Section 4.2.3 we examined the conversion of an arithmetic expression from infix notation to postfix notation. If we now examine the process from the perspective of binary trees, we see that if we take an arithmetic expression and write it in an obvious way as a binary tree, then the postorder traversal of that tree produces the postfix form of the arithmetic expression. For example, consider the expression

$$(B - (B \uparrow 2 - 4 * A * C) \uparrow 0.5) / (2 * A).$$

As a binary tree we would write it as shown in Figure 5.18. A postorder traversal of this tree would visit the nodes in the order

$$B\,B\,2 \uparrow 4\,A * C * - 0.5 \uparrow - 2\,A * /,$$

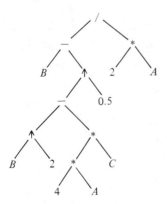

Figure 5.18
An arithmetic expression represented by a binary tree

exactly the postfix of the expression considered. Similarly, the preorder traversal of such a tree corresponds to prefix form of the expression, while the inorder traversal corresponds to the normal infix form with the parentheses deleted.

The connection between the postfix form of an arithmetic expression and the postorder traversal of the corresponding binary tree allows us to evaluate an arithmetic expression from its corresponding binary tree. We use a simple combination of postorder traversal and Algorithm 4.7, which computes the value of an arithmetic expression from its postfix form; the result is Algorithm 5.13. It is not difficult to apply Algorithm 5.7 to produce a nonrecursive version.

function *EvaluateTree* (*e*: *pTree*): *NumericValue*;
var
     x, *y*: *NumericValue*;
begin
     if "*e*↑.*INFO* is an operand" **then**
          EvaluateTree := *e*↑.*INFO*
     else begin
          x := *EvaluateTree*(*e*↑.*LEFT*);
          y := *EvaluateTree*(*e*↑.*RIGHT*);
          EvaluateTree := "value from applying
               operator *e*↑.*INFO* to *x* and *y*"
     end
end

Algorithm 5.13
Evaluation of an arithmetic expression represented as a nonempty binary tree

Exercises

1. Devise an algorithm that takes a binary tree represented with *LEFT* and *RIGHT* pointers and produces a binary tree with *PARENT* pointers. In other words, the tree

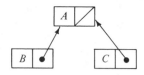

should be produced from

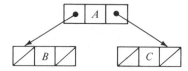

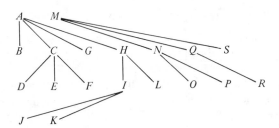

Figure 5.19
Exercise 4

2. Devise an algorithm to compute the height of a binary tree (see page 218).

3. Modify Algorithm 5.12 so it prints trees with all the window dressing of Figure 5.16.

4. Design an algorithm that prints forests by placing all nodes at a given level as far to the left as possible. For example, assuming that the tree was drawn on a plotter or that connecting lines were added by hand to printed output, the forest of Figure 5.7(a) would appear as in Figure 5.19.

5. How would Algorithm 5.12 print the tree in Figure 5.20? Design a tree-printing algorithm that produces a more aesthetic output! [*Hint*: Combine the idea of Algorithm 5.12 with that in the previous exercise.]

6. Rewrite Algorithm 5.12 using iteration and a stack in place of recursion.

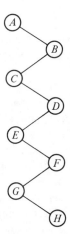

Figure 5.20
Exercise 5

7. Rewrite Algorithm 5.13 using iteration and a stack in place of recursion.

8. Write a program to implement Huffman's algorithm (see Section 2.4.2). The input, a sequence of probabilities, should be processed to form a list of trees where each tree has only a single node that contains an input probability. The first phase of the algorithm merges trees two at a time until the list has but one element, the final tree. The second phase traverses the tree assigning and printing codes. (Which traversal order is appropriate?)

9. Devise an algorithm that changes a tree into its mirror image (so that left and right are reversed).

5.2.2 Threaded Trees

In our conventional representation of trees with pointers from parents to children we find it generally inconvenient to move up from children to parents and to move laterally between siblings. Of course we might choose to use both *PARENT* pointers and *LEFT* / *RIGHT* pointers, giving us three pointers for each node in a tree. This would be overkill, however, because in most instances we need to move up or laterally in a tree in only restricted ways; in any case, the storage requirements for the pointers of the tree would then be increased by 50 percent. In this section we discuss a more economical means of facilitating upward and lateral movement in trees.

First of all, notice that any binary tree represented with *LEFT* / *RIGHT* pointers contains many unused pointers. In a binary tree with i nodes there are (obviously) $2i$ pointers. However, each of the nodes except the root has only one parent and hence only one pointer pointing at it. Thus only $i - 1$ of the pointers are nonnull, so that $2i - (i - 1) = i + 1$ of the *LEFT* / *RIGHT* pointers are unused in a binary tree of i nodes. We can utilize this wasted space.

For motivation, consider Figure 5.7(b), a forest being represented by a binary tree in the natural way. Observe that we could use the sibling pointer of the youngest child to point to its parent, as shown in Figure 5.21. This pointer is otherwise unused, and our use of it necessitates only that we be able to distinguish it from other sibling pointers. The distinction can be easily made by using an extra bit in each tree node to tell us whether the node is a youngest child—that is, whether the sibling pointer is being used to indicate the parent. Looking at Figure 5.21 more carefully and considering it as a binary tree, we notice that the newly added dashed right pointers indicate the successors of the respective nodes in inorder (ignore for the moment the dashed arrow from M, which leads nowhere). Furthermore, this suggests that any unused *LEFT* pointers might well be used to point to the inorder predecessors of the respective nodes. Figure 5.22 shows a binary tree in which the unused *LEFT* / *RIGHT* pointers are so utilized; such pointers are called *threads* and such trees are called *threaded binary trees*.

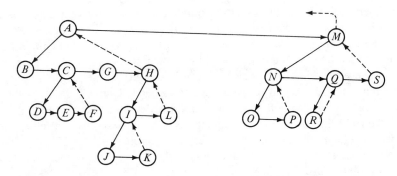

Figure 5.21
Figure 5.14 shown with extra pointers added from youngest child to parent

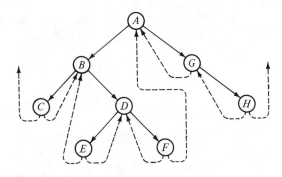

Figure 5.22
A threaded tree

type

    pThTree = ↑*ThTree*;
    ThTree = **record**
        INFO: "contents for node";
        LTH: *boolean*;   {**true** when *LEFT* is a thread}
        RTH: *boolean*;   {**true** when *RIGHT* is a thread}
        LEFT: *pThTree*;   {if **not** *LTH*, points to left subtree;
                                otherwise points to inorder predecessor}
        RIGHT: *pThTree*   {if **not** *RTH*, points to right subtree;
                                otherwise points to inorder successor}

    end;

Declarations 5.3

In order to distinguish the threads from the regular pointers we need to add two additional bits to each node: *LTH* and *RTH* are **true** or **false** according as *LEFT* and *RIGHT* are threads or pointers, respectively—see Declarations 5.3 and Figure 5.23(a). Thus the threaded tree of Figure 5.22 would be represented as in Figure 5.23(b). The addition of these two bits per node is an excellent investment, as we shall see.

We must decide what to do with the leftmost and rightmost threads—that is, the left thread from the node that has no inorder predecessor (the first node in inorder) and the right thread from the node that has no inorder successor (the last node in inorder). These are the threads that we left dangling in Figures 5.22 and 5.23(b). However, the decision will hinge on the various algorithms that use the threads, and so we will postpone the issue temporarily.

Given the nature of the threads, the most obvious algorithms to construct are those for determining the inorder successor and predecessor of a given node. These algorithms are, in a sense, mirror images of each other, so we arbitrarily choose to design the successor algorithm first. Given a node in a binary tree, where is its inorder successor to be found? Since inorder traverses the (unthreaded) tree in the order left subtree, root, and right subtree, the successor of a given node *n* with

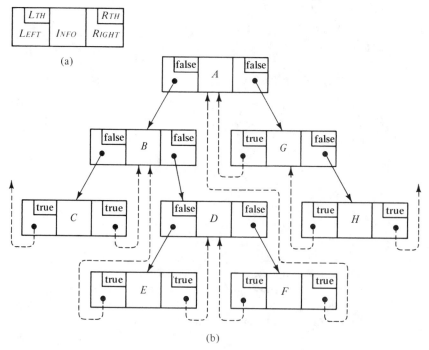

(b)

Figure 5.23
The form of a node (a) in a threaded tree and (b) a sample tree of such nodes

$n\!\uparrow\!.RIGHT \neq$ **nil** is the first node in the inorder traversal of its right subtree; thus if $n\!\uparrow\!.RIGHT \neq$ **nil** the inorder successor of n is found by repeatedly following *LEFT* pointers beginning at $n\!\uparrow\!.RIGHT$. If, on the other hand, the unthreaded tree had $n\!\uparrow\!.RIGHT =$ **nil,** the threaded-tree representation would have $n\!\uparrow\!.RIGHT$ pointing to the inorder successor. Recalling that in a threaded tree the test for an empty *LEFT* or *RIGHT* pointer becomes a test on the *LTH* or *RTH* fields, the procedure in Algorithm 5.14 for inorder successor becomes apparent.

For an algorithm to compute the inorder predecessor of a node n we observe that we are computing the inorder successor in the mirror-image tree (the tree obtained when *LEFT* and *RIGHT* are consistently interchanged. Thus the desired algorithm is obtained by reversing the roles of left and right in Algorithm 5.14, as shown in Algorithm 5.15.

With these two simple algorithms in mind, we can now resolve the question of what to do with the dangling threads of Figures 5.22 and 5.23(b). To do so, consider how we might use Algorithms 5.14 and 5.15 to find the first and last nodes (respectively) in inorder given a pointer t to a threaded tree. It would be convenient, for example, if *InorderSucc*(t) yielded the first node in inorder. This can work if t points to a header node that points in turn to the root element of the actual tree.

We first face a conflict. To find the first node using Algorithm 5.14 we could have the root as $t\!\uparrow\!.RIGHT$ and set $t\!\uparrow\!.RTH$ to **false.** But to find the last node with Algorithm 5.15 we would want the root as $t\!\uparrow\!.LEFT$ with $t\!\uparrow\!.LTH$ set **false.** We can store the root either on the *RIGHT* or *LEFT* but would prefer not to do both because this would introduce redundant pointers that would both have to be updated whenever there was a change to the root. The algorithms are symmetric, so we arbitrarily choose to store the root as $t\!\uparrow\!.LEFT$, which satisfies the *InorderPred,* Algorithm 5.15. We then trick Algorithm 5.14 into correct behavior by making $t\!\uparrow\!.RIGHT$ a pointer to

```
function InorderSucc(n: pThTree): pThTree;
var
        s: pThTree;
begin
        s := n↑.RIGHT;
        if not n↑.RTH then
                while not s↑.LTH do
                        {Assert: The inorder successor of n is the first node in inorder
                        in the left subtree of s.}
                        s := s↑.LEFT;
        InorderSucc := s
end
```

Algorithm 5.14
A procedure to compute the inorder successor of a node n in a threaded binary tree

function *InorderPred*(*n*: *pThTree*): *pThTree*;
var
      s: *pThTree*;
begin
      s := *n*↑.*LEFT*;
      if not *n*↑.*LTH* **then**
            while not *s*↑.*RTH* **do**
                  {Assert: The inorder predecessor of *n* is the last node in in-
                  order in the right subtree of *s*.}
                  s := *s*↑.*RIGHT*;
      InorderPred := *s*
end

Algorithm 5.15
A procedure to compute the inorder predecessor of a node *n* in a threaded binary
tree. The procedure is obtained from Algorithm 5.14 by interchanging the roles
of left and right.

the header itself. By setting both *t*↑.*LTH* and *t*↑.*RTH* to **false** we trick Algorithm 5.14
so *InorderSucc*(*t*) indeed yields the first node in inorder. This organization of the
header node will also turn out to be appropriate for other algorithms we will consider.

We have effectively established the header node *t* of a tree as the inorder predecessor of the first node in inorder and as the inorder successor to the last node in
inorder. Thus we set the dangling threads accordingly, and Figure 5.24 shows the
completed threaded tree of Figure 5.23(b).

How is the empty tree to be represented? The obvious choice is simply to set
the *LEFT* pointer of the header node, which points to the root of the tree, to be **nil**.
However, a threaded tree contains no **nil** pointers, since a pointer that would be **nil**
is used to point to the inorder successor or predecessor. For an empty tree both the
inorder successor and predecessor of the header node should be the header node
itself, and so to be consistent we choose to represent the empty tree by the header
node

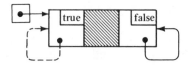

This choice insures that Algorithms 5.14 and 5.15 work correctly when applied to
the header node of an empty tree.

We can apply Algorithm 5.14 repeatedly to obtain an iterative algorithm for
inorder traversal that does not require a stack. This gives us Algorithm 5.16, whose
input is the header node of a threaded binary tree. Notice that this algorithm also
behaves properly on the empty tree.

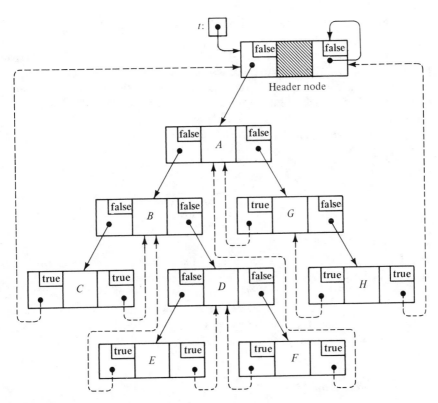

Figure 5.24
The completed threaded tree of Figure 5.23(b) in which the dangling threads have
been resolved

procedure *ThreadedInorderTraversal(head: pThTree)*;
var
    s: pThTree;
begin
    s := InorderSucc(head);
    while *s ≠ head* **do begin**
        "visit node *s*";
        s := InorderSucc(s)
    end
end

Algorithm 5.16
Inorder traversal of a threaded binary tree, given its header node *head*

It is hardly surprising that the inorder successor, predecessor, and traversal algorithms worked out so easily and neatly, since the threads are based on inorder. It *is* surprising that threaded trees also have similar algorithms for finding the parent, the preorder successor, and the postorder predecessor of a node, and slightly more complicated algorithms for the preorder predecessor and the postorder successor of a node. We will present algorithms for finding the parent of a node and the preorder successor of a node, leaving the remaining algorithms to the exercises.

To find the parent of a node n, consider the inorder sequence of nodes, and the subsequence consisting of n and all of its descendants:

$$\ldots, \; x, \; \ldots, \; \underbrace{n, \; \ldots, \; y,}_{\substack{\text{the inorder sequence of} \\ \text{the subtree rooted} \\ \text{at node } n}} \; \ldots$$

If n is the right child of its parent, then by the definition of inorder the parent of n must be x, the first node preceding the subtree rooted at n (why?). In this case we find x by first following *LEFT* pointers from n until we get to the "leftmost" descendant of n and then following the left thread from that node. Of course, we do not know if the node thus found is the parent of n, since n may have been the left child of its parent. So, we must check to see if n is the right child of the node thus found:

```
q := n;
while not q↑.LTH do
        {Assert: q is a descendant of n and precedes all previous
        values of q in inorder}
        q := q↑.LEFT;
q := q↑.LEFT;    {follow thread to inorder predecessor}
if q↑.RIGHT = n then
        "q is the parent"
```

If instead n is the left child of its parent, the final test above will fail and we know by the definition of inorder that the parent must be y, the first node following the subtree rooted at n. This node is then found in like manner, by following *RIGHT* pointers from n until we get to the "rightmost" descendant of n and then following the right thread from that node. The complete procedure is given in Algorithm 5.17.

Observe that in an unthreaded tree it would be necessary to traverse the entire tree to find the parent of a node (assuming, of course, that we knew the root of the tree; without that knowledge the problem would be impossible to solve). This would require time proportional to the number of nodes in the tree, while Algorithm 5.17 will require at most time proportional to the height of the tree. As will become clear in Section 5.3, this represents a considerable gain in efficiency. Moreover, unlike an

function *Parent*(*n*: *pThTree*): *pThTree*;
var
    q: *pThTree*;
begin
    q := *n*;
    while not *q*↑.*LTH* **do**
        q := *q*↑.*LEFT*;
    if *q*↑.*LEFT*↑.*RIGHT* = *n* **then**
        Parent := *q*↑.*LEFT*
    else begin {*n* is the left child of its parent}
        q := *n*;
        while not *q*↑.*RTH* **do**
            q := *q*↑.*RIGHT*;
        Parent := *q*↑.*RIGHT*
    end
end

Algorithm 5.17
Finding the parent of a node *n* in a threaded tree. For assertions see fragment on previous page.

algorithm based on one of the traversal algorithms for unthreaded trees, Algorithm 5.17 does not use a stack.

We leave it to the reader to verify that Algorithm 5.17 works correctly on the root of the tree, giving the header node as the result, and on the header node itself, giving the same result (see Exercise 1).

In order to derive an algorithm for the preorder successor of a node in a threaded tree, we need to characterize the node for which we are searching: The preorder successor of a node *n* is either

    1. its left child, if it exists,

    2. its right child, if it exists and the left child does not, or

    3. if *n* is a leaf, the right child of its lowest ancestor *q* such that *n* is in the left subtree of *q* and *q* has a right child.

The first two cases are obvious from the definition of preorder. To understand the third case, let *x* be the right child of the specified *q*. Now, observe that by the nature of preorder *x* must certainly appear somewhere after *n* in preorder; furthermore suppose there is a node *y* between them in preorder. The preorder is then

$$\ldots, q, \ldots, n, \ldots, y, \ldots, x, \ldots$$

and y must be a descendant of q (since both x and n are descendants and y comes between them in preorder), but since it precedes x, the right child of q, y must be in the left subtree of q. However, since it appears after n in preorder it cannot be an ancestor of n and it cannot be a descendant of n because we have assumed in case 3 that n is a leaf. Let a be the lowest common ancestor of n and y; we have just shown that such an a exists and is in the left subtree of q. Since a is the lowest such ancestor and since n precedes y in preorder, n must be in the left subtree of a and y in the right. This contradicts our assumption that q was the lowest ancestor of n such that n was in the left subtree of q and q had a right child. We conclude that no such y can exist and so, indeed, case 3 gives the correct preorder successor for a leaf.

Now we need to relate case 3 to the threads of a threaded tree: the inorder successor of a leaf n (that is, the node pointed to by the *RIGHT* thread) is the lowest ancestor r of n such that n is in the left subtree of r. This follows directly from the definition of inorder and an argument similar to one in the previous paragraph.

The desired algorithm is now apparent: the preorder successor of a node n that is not a leaf is the left child if it exists, and if not, the right child. If n is a leaf, the preorder successor is found by following *RIGHT* pointers as long as they are threads and then following one more *RIGHT* pointer. Algorithm 5.18 gives this procedure, simplified slightly by combining cases 2 and 3 in an obvious manner.

Like the other threaded tree algorithms presented in this section, Algorithm 5.18 works appropriately for the header node, the last node in preorder, and the empty tree. Like Algorithms 5.14, 5.15, and 5.17 it requires at worst time propor-

```
function PreorderSucc(n: pThTree): pThTree;
var
      q: pThTree;
begin
      if not n↑.LTH then
            PreorderSucc := n↑.LEFT
      else begin
            q := n;
            while q↑.RTH do
                  {Assert: n is the final node in preorder of all nodes
                  descended from q↑.RIGHT}
                  q := q↑.RIGHT;
            PreorderSucc := q↑.RIGHT
      end
end
```

Algorithm 5.18
Preorder successor of a node n in a threaded binary tree

tional to the height of the tree (instead of the number of nodes in the tree) and no stack.

We conclude this section with some assorted remarks about threaded trees. First, it is easy to insert new nodes at the leaves of a threaded tree or to delete leaves, keeping the tree properly threaded after the insertion or deletion. For example, to insert the node x as the left child of a node a (assuming that a has no left subtree) we need only do the following:

$$x\uparrow.LEFT := a\uparrow.LEFT;$$
$$x\uparrow.RIGHT := a;$$
$$x\uparrow.LTH := \textbf{true};$$
$$x\uparrow.RTH := \textbf{true};$$
$$a\uparrow.LEFT := x;$$
$$a\uparrow.LTH := \textbf{false}$$

The steps needed for deletion or insertion at other points in the tree are comparable (see Exercises 8 and 9).

Our second remark is that threaded trees do *not* make all traversals easy. For example, it does not appear to be much simpler to determine the preorder predecessor or the postorder successor of nodes in a threaded tree than it is in an unthreaded tree. The only advantages of threaded trees in these cases are that a stack is not needed and we do not need to know the root of the tree.

Our final remark is that it may be useful in certain circumstances to use trees that are only partially threaded. We might, for instance, have an application in which only *LEFT* threads were needed; in such a case we would not need the *RTH* field of a tree node, since we would let null *RIGHT* pointers remain null. We leave it as Exercise 10 to determine which of the various algorithms presented in this section would work (with minor modifications) for some form of partially threaded trees.

Exercises

1. Verify that Algorithm 5.17 works correctly for the root, header node, and empty tree.

2. Suppose that in writing Algorithm 5.17 we had chosen to test first if n was a left child of its parent (by reversing *LEFT* and *RIGHT* and *LTH* and *RTH*, respectively). How would the resulting algorithm behave when applied to the header node of a tree?

3. Prove that the right thread of a node points to its lowest ancestor a such that the node is in the left subtree of a. Prove a parallel result for left threads.

4. Devise an algorithm to thread an unthreaded tree whose nodes have the *LTH* and *RTH* fields available (but unused).

5. Prove that a node has a left thread pointing to it if and only if that node has a nonempty right subtree. Prove a parallel result for right threads.

6. Design an algorithm for determining the postorder predecessor of a node in a threaded tree. Your algorithm should not use a stack, and it should require at worst time proportional to the height of the tree.

7. Design an algorithm to copy a threaded binary tree. [*Hint*: Use Algorithm 5.18.]

8. Modify the program fragment given for inserting a node x as the left child of a so that if a already has a left child then x is added "between" a and its left child. That is,

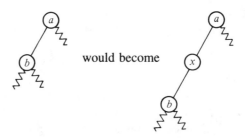

would become

9. (a) Give the code fragment necessary to delete a leaf in a threaded tree so that the tree remains properly threaded.
   (b) Use your answer to (a) to design an algorithm that deletes a given node x (not necessarily a leaf) from a threaded tree so that the inorder of the remaining nodes is unchanged and the tree remains properly threaded.

10. Determine which of the algorithms given in this section can be easily modified to work for partially threaded trees—that is, trees threaded only in either the *LEFT* or *RIGHT* pointers.

11. Examine the advantages and disadvantages of threads based on preorder, postorder, or some combination of the orders (for example, left threads pointing to the preorder successor and right threads pointing to the inorder successor).

12. Let $N_1, N_2, \ldots, N_n$ be the nodes of a threaded binary tree in preorder. Supposing $ord(\textbf{true}) = 1$ and $ord(\textbf{false}) = 0$, prove that

$$\sum_{i=1}^{k} [ord(N_i\uparrow.LTH) + ord(N_i\uparrow.RTH) - 1]$$

is 1 for $k = n$ and is at most 0 for $1 \leq k < n$.

13. (a) Let the nodes of two threaded binary trees T and U be $N_1, N_2, \ldots, N_n$ and $M_1, M_2, \ldots, M_m$, respectively, in preorder. Prove that T and U are identical

if and only if $n = m$ and for all i, $1 \leq i \leq n$, we have $N_i\uparrow.INFO$ = $M_i\uparrow.INFO$, $N_i\uparrow.LTH = M_i\uparrow.LTH$, and $N_i\uparrow.RTH = M_i\uparrow.RTH$. [*Hint*: Use the result of Exercise 12.]

(b) Use the result in (a) to design an algorithm for testing whether two threaded binary trees are identical.

5.2.3 Sequential Representations of Trees

The representations of trees considered in Section 5.1 are all based on explicitly storing pointers to the ancestors or descendants (or both) for each node of the tree. In this section, by contrast, we will examine three representations in which we have only a sequential list of the nodes (in one of the traversal orders) together with some limited additional information from which the structure of the tree can be deduced. These representations are not as useful as the linked representations already considered.

1.	Gerhard Nothmann	25.	Malke
2.	Rudolf Nothman	26.	Abraham Eger
3.	Margarete Caro	28.	Ahron Joseph Kauffmann
4.	Adolf Nothmann	29.	Perle Fürst
5.	Alwine Lustig	30.	Jacob Frensdorff
6.	Siegfried Caro	31.	Betty Behrend
7.	Anna Kauffmann	32.	Yeshaya Nothmann
8.	Simon Nothmann	33.	Yettel Gassmann
9.	Friederike Riesenfeld	40.	Löbel Lustig
10.	Salomon Lustig	41.	Rachel Ehrlich
11.	Amalie Prager	44.	Simon Prager
12.	Isaac Caro	48.	Hirsch Isaac Caro
13.	Johanna Eger	49.	Tamara
14.	Julius Kauffmann	52.	Akiba Eger
15.	Friederike Frensdorff	53.	Glückchen Margolies
16.	Salomon Nothmann	54.	Eliezer Landsberg
17.	Amalie Brieger	56.	Joseph Kauffmann
18.	Israel Riesenfeld	57.	Golda Wulff
19.	Henriette Schwarz	58.	Wolf Liebmann Fürst
20.	Selig Lustig	59.	Sara Herz
21.	Fanny Isaak	60.	Michael Meyer Frensdorff
22.	Salomon Prager	61.	Hendel Juspa
23.	Yette Dresdner	62.	Philipp Behrend
24.	Salomon Karo	63.	Blume Levy

Figure 5.25
A "genealogical numbering" for the family tree in Figure 5.1

Genealogists long ago discovered an interesting sequential representation of family trees. The principal of the tree (the one whose ancestors are being presented) is numbered 1; the others in the tree are numbered according to the rule that if a person is numbered i, his father is numbered $2i$ and his mother is numbered $2i + 1$. Thus we would encode the family tree of Figure 5.1 as the list of Figure 5.25. Notice that this numbering is according to the level-order traversal of the tree, with the missing numbers corresponding to missing nodes of the tree.

We can use this "genealogical numbering" to get a sequential representation of binary trees. We have a one-dimensional array, say A, and we store the root in $A[1]$; in general, the left child of $A[i]$ is stored in $A[2i]$ and the right child in $A[2i + 1]$. It is easy to move down, up, or laterally in a tree thus represented. For example, $A[floor(i + 2)]$ is the parent of $A[i]$, $A[i + 1]$ is the sibling of $A[i]$ if i is even, and so on. We will, in fact, have an important use for just this representation of a tree in Chapter 8, but for now let us only mention its major disadvantage: storing a tree of height h requires an array of about 2^{h+1} locations, regardless of the actual number of nodes in the tree. Thus to represent the tree

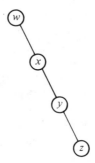

we would have to have an array $A[1..15]$ in which $A[1] = w$, $A[3] = x$, $A[7] = y$, $A[15] = z$, and the rest of the array is empty. It is clear that this representation is suitable only for short, full binary trees and not tall, scrawny ones.

A general sequential representation of (not necessarily binary) trees can be deduced from Polish notation for arithmetic expressions. In Section 4.2.3 we remarked that arithmetic expressions could be written uniquely in either prefix or postfix form, and in Section 5.2.1 we observed the connection between these forms and binary tree traversals. In effect, we can reconstruct the tree corresponding to an arithmetic expression from a list of its nodes in either preorder or postorder. Perhaps we can do that in general.

How do we know that, say, the prefix expression $*\,A + B\,C$ corresponds to the tree while we cannot tell whether the preorder traversal *uvwxy* corresponds to

or some other tree? The answer, of course, is that in *∗ A + B C* we know by inspection which nodes are operands and which are operators, while the preorder traversal *uvwxy* gives us no comparable information about which nodes are leaves and which are not. The key observation here is that in *∗ A + B C* we know the *degree* of each node—that is, how many children it has in the tree. If we add that information to the preorder list of nodes, we can reconstruct the tree.

Suppose we are given the lists

preorder:	A	B	C	D	E	F	G	H	I	J	K	L
degree:	4	0	3	0	0	0	0	2	2	0	0	0

We can retrieve the structure of the tree by reasoning as follows. Examining the lists from right to left and always remembering that the list is in preorder, we see that *I* must be the parent of *J* and *K*. With the same reasoning *H* must be the parent of *I* and *L*, *C* must be the parent of *D*, *E*, and *F*, and finally *A* must be the parent of *B*, *C*, *G*, and *H*. The tree is thus the one on the left of Figure 5.7(a).

The tree could also have been reconstructed from the lists

postorder:	B	D	E	F	C	G	J	K	I	L	H	A
degree:	0	0	0	0	3	0	0	0	2	0	2	4

by a similar process. Examining the lists from left to right this time, we see that *D*, *E*, and *F* must be children of *C*; *J* and *K* must be children of *I*; *I* and *L* must be children of *H*; and finally *B*, *C*, *G*, and *H* must be children of *A*.

These two sequential representations of trees are useful only rarely, the main example being the application to arithmetic expressions already discussed. Their usefulness is limited because it is impossible to identify the child or parent of a particular node except by reconstructing the entire tree.

Exercises

1. Write a routine to compute the index of the inorder successor of node *i* in a genealogically arranged array *A* with *n* elements. Assume that if an element is absent from the tree the corresponding cell in *A* has value 0.

2. How much additional information is needed per node to reconstruct a binary tree from a preorder list of nodes together with the *LTH* and *RTH* values for each node?

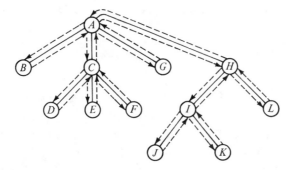

Figure 5.26
Exercise 5

3. Prove formally that the postorder list of nodes and their associated degrees uniquely determine the forest from which they were derived.

4. Design an algorithm to construct the binary tree corresponding (via the natural correspondence) to the forest represented by the arrays *Info*[i] and *Degree*[i] given in preorder.

5. Given a (not necessarily binary) tree, we will walk around it as shown in Figure 5.26 by dashed lines, writing the sequence of up and down moves as we walk:

DUDDUDUDUUDUDDDUDUUDUU.

We add an extra U at the end of this sequence and consider the sequence to be the preorder list of nodes of a binary tree in which each D is an internal node (with two children) and each U is a leaf. Using the method discussed in this section, we can reconstruct the binary tree of D's and U's. What is the relationship between the binary tree thus constructed and the original tree? Prove your answer.

5.3 QUANTITATIVE ASPECTS OF BINARY TREES

In addition to finding trees invaluable as a data structure when dealing with hierarchical information, we will also find them useful as a tool in the analysis of various searching and sorting algorithms. In this context we will need quantitative measures of certain aspects of binary trees.

Two important quantitative aspects of trees have already been introduced and used in Section 5.1.2. There we defined the *level* of a node N to be 0 if N is the root of the tree and 1 + (level of N's parent) otherwise. We also defined the *height* $h(T)$

of a tree T to be the maximum level of any node in T if T is nonempty. No height is defined for the empty tree.

To understand the usefulness of these and the other quantitative measures that will be introduced, we will make a brief digression to the binary search procedure (Algorithm 1.3) presented in Section 1.3. Binary trees and the results discussed in this section will provide the techniques needed for the analysis of this important procedure.

It is useful to describe as a binary tree the sequence of comparisons "$z : x_i$" made by binary search in looking for z in $x_1, x_2, \ldots, x_n$. The first comparison is the root of the tree

and the left and right subtrees are the tree structures for the succeeding comparisons when $z < x_{\lfloor (n+1)/2 \rfloor}$ and $z > x_{\lfloor (n+1)/2 \rfloor}$, respectively. The tree corresponding to a binary search of the range $x_l, x_{l+1}, \ldots, x_h$ is defined recursively by Equation (5.3):

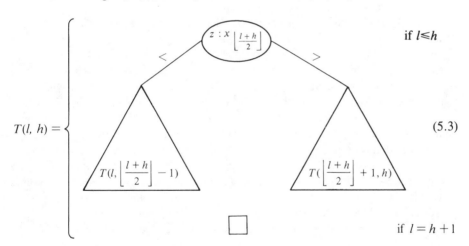

$$T(l, h) = \qquad (5.3)$$

Thus $T(1, 10)$, the tree corresponding to a binary search for z in a table containing ten names, is shown in Figure 5.27.

We can consider such a tree to be a flowchart of the binary search algorithm. The algorithm stops when it finds $z = x_i$ or when it reaches a leaf. The leaves correspond to the "gaps" between x_i and x_{i+1} in which z might lie, with the obvious interpretation for the leftmost and rightmost leaves. For example, in Figure 5.27 the

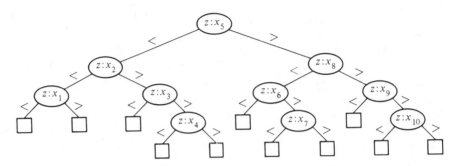

Figure 5.27
$T(1, 10)$, the tree corresponding to binary search in a table with ten names

left and right children of the node $(z : x_4)$ are nodes corresponding to the conditions $x_3 < z < x_4$ and $x_4 < z < x_5$, respectively.

The height of the tree just derived from binary search has an important significance: it is the number of comparisons that will be made by the algorithm in the worst case on a search that ends unsuccessfully (that is, without finding z among x_1, x_2, ..., x_n). This leads us to ask what the height of the tree $T(1, n)$ is, or, more generally, what the height of the tree $T(l, h)$ is. We leave it as Exercise 1 to prove by induction that $T(l, h)$ has height $\lceil \lg(h - l + 2) \rceil$. Thus $T(1, n)$ has height $\lceil \lg(n + 1) \rceil$, and this then is the number of comparisons made by binary search in the worst-case unsuccessful search. The worst-case successful search (in which z is found among $x_1, x_2, ..., x_n$) will require the same number of comparisons (why?).

To analyze the average behavior of binary search we need some more machinery—some additional quantitative measures of binary trees. For U_n, the average number of comparisons $z : x_i$ in an unsuccessful search of $x_1, x_2, ..., x_n$, we need to compute the average distance from the root to one of the square nodes at the bottom of the corresponding tree $T(1, n)$. In computing this average we will assume that each of the possible unsuccessful outcomes is equally probable, so that the probability of having the search end at any one of the $n + 1$ square nodes is $1/(n + 1)$. Thus the average number of comparisons for an unsuccessful search is

$$U_n = \frac{\text{sum of levels of the } n + 1 \text{ square nodes}}{n + 1}$$

For example, for $n = 10$, Figure 5.27 tells us that this value is

$$U_{10} = \frac{3 + 3 + 3 + 4 + 4 + 3 + 4 + 4 + 3 + 4 + 4}{11} \approx 3.55,$$

and so the average unsuccessful search will require about 3.55 comparisons $z : x_i$.

For S_n, the average number of comparisons $z : x_i$ in a successful search of x_1, $x_2, \ldots, x_n$, we need the average distance from the root to one of the circular nodes in the tree $T(1, n)$. In parallel to the case of U_n, we will assume that each of the possible successful outcomes is equally probable, so that the probability of having the search find that $z = x_i$ is $1/n$ for $i = 1, 2, \ldots, n$. Thus the average number of comparisons for a successful search is

$$S_n = \frac{\text{sum of } (1 + \text{level}) \text{ of each of the } n \text{ circular nodes}}{n}$$

In our example $n = 10$ we find that

$$\begin{aligned}
S_{10} &= [(1+0) + (1+1) + (1+1) + (1+2) + (1+2) \\
&\quad + (1+2) + (1+2) + (1+3) + (1+3) + (1+3)] / 10 \\
&= 2.9,
\end{aligned}$$

and so the average successful search will require 2.9 comparisons $z : x_i$.

Before continuing our analysis, it is important to understand exactly what the analysis describes. We have made an assumption that is not generally true: only rarely will each of the x_i be the search object with equal likelihood or will the "gaps" (square nodes) be equally likely. Why bother, then, with an analysis whose cornerstone is improbable? The answer is that in writing the binary search procedure we have assumed implicitly that we knew nothing about the probabilities involved. In fact, as we will see in Chapter 7, if something is known about the probabilities we will be able to construct much more efficient search techniques. In the absence of any such knowledge we have made the only reasonable assumption, and we expect it to provide us with the right order of magnitude in the general case.

With the above introduction as motivation, we now backtrack slightly to introduce some general concepts and results that will be applied to binary search at the end of this section. Suppose we are given a binary tree (of circular nodes) as in Figure 5.28(a). We extend the tree by adding a square node, usually called an *external node* or *leaf*, in place of every empty subtree to obtain an *extended binary tree* as in Figure 5.28(b). The circular nodes are then called *internal nodes*. An extended binary tree of n internal nodes always contains $n + 1$ external nodes (Exercise 2).

The *external path length* $E(T)$ of an extended binary tree T with n internal nodes is the sum of levels of all the external nodes; the *internal path length* $I(T)$ is

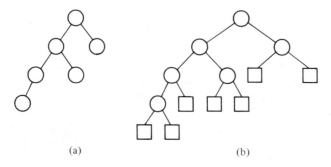

Figure 5.28
(a) A binary tree and (b) the same tree extended by the addition of external nodes

the sum of the levels of all the internal nodes. Therefore in Figure 5.28(b) the external path length is 21 and the internal path length is 9. These sums divided by the number of external nodes or the number of internal nodes, respectively, give the averages needed for the analysis of binary search:

$$\text{average distance to an external node } = \frac{E(T)}{n + 1},$$

$$\text{average distance to an internal node } = \frac{I(T)}{n}.$$

It is easy to define both $E(T)$ and $I(T)$ recursively for an extended binary tree T with n internal nodes:

$$I(\square) = 0,$$

$$I\left(T = \quad\quad \right) = I(T_l) + I(T_r) + n - 1, \tag{5.4}$$

$$E(\square) = 0,$$

$$E\left(T = \quad\quad \right) = E(T_l) + E(T_r) + n + 1. \tag{5.5}$$

To understand the recursive part of the definition (5.4) notice that T_l and T_r contain between them $n - 1$ internal nodes and that adding an internal node above them as the root increases the level of each by 1. Similar reasoning explains the recursive part of the definition (5.5). We can relate $E(T)$ and $I(T)$ by considering the difference $D(T) = E(T) - I(T)$. Using (5.4) and (5.5), we find the results,

$D(\square) = 0$

$$D\left(T = \overset{\circ}{\underset{T_l}{\triangle} \quad \underset{T_r}{\triangle}}\right) = D(T_l) + D(T_r) + 2, \tag{5.6}$$

which tell us (Exercise 3) that $D(T) = 2n$ for an extended binary tree T with n internal nodes. Thus

$$E(T) = I(T) + 2n, \tag{5.7}$$

and hence we need only study one of $E(T)$ or $I(T)$ to determine the properties of both.

We are particularly interested in the range of values of $E(T)$ and $I(T)$. For instance, over all extended binary trees with n internal nodes, one with the maximum value of $I(T)$ is the tree shown in Figure 5.29. In this case

$$I(T) = \sum_{i=0}^{n-1} i = n(n-1)/2$$

and

$$E(T) = n(n+3)/2.$$

(See Exercise 4.)

Deriving the minimum values of $I(T)$ and $E(T)$ is more complicated, but we will need these results for the analysis of binary search in the average case, as well as for a benchmark against which to compare the binary search trees of Chapter 7. The derivation is based on two observations and some elementary algebra:

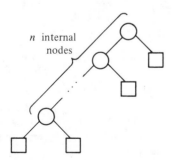

n internal nodes

Figure 5.29
An extended binary tree with the largest possible internal and external path lengths

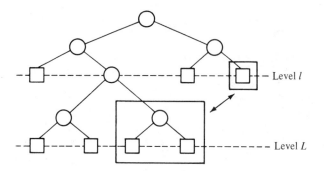

Figure 5.30
An example of how the external path length can be decreased if $L \geq l + 2$ in Observation 1

Observation 1

An extended binary tree of n internal nodes with minimum external path length has all of its external nodes on levels l and $l + 1$, for some l. Such a tree is called a *completely balanced binary tree* of n internal nodes.

Proof

Let T be an extended binary tree with minimum external path length and let L and l be the maximum and minimum, respectively, of all levels on which external nodes appear, $L \geq l$. Suppose $L \geq l + 2$. Remove two external nodes that are siblings from level L and make their parent an external node. Then put them below an external node on level l, which thus becomes an internal node. This process is shown in Figure 5.30. Such a modification of the tree preserves the number of internal and external nodes, but it decreases the external path length by $L - (l + 1)$, which is positive since $L \geq l + 2$. This contradicts the minimality of the external path length of T.

Observation 2

If $l_1, l_2, \ldots, l_{n-1}$ are the levels of the $n + 1$ external nodes in an extended binary tree with n internal nodes, then $\sum_{i=1}^{n+1} 2^{-l_i} = 1$.

Proof

The proof is by mathematical induction on the height of an extended binary tree T. If the height of T is 0, then $T = \square$, $n = 0$, $l_1 = 0$, and indeed $2^0 = 1$. If the height of T is at least 1, we can write

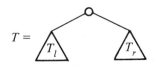

Since the level of each external node of T_l and T_r is one greater with respect to T than with respect to T_l and T_r, we see that if $l_1, l_2, \ldots, l_{k+1}$ are the levels in T of the $k_1 + 1$ external nodes in T_l and similarly $l_{k+2}, l_{k+3}, \ldots, l_{n+1}$ are the levels in T of the $(n + 1) - (k_1 + 1)$ external nodes in T_r, then

$$\sum_{i=1}^{n+1} 2^{-l_i} = \sum_{i=1}^{k+1} 2^{-l_i} + \sum_{j=k+2}^{n+1} 2^{-l_j}$$

$$= \frac{1}{2}\left(\sum_{i=1}^{k+1} 2^{-(l_i-1)} + \sum_{j=k+2}^{n+1} 2^{-(l_j-1)}\right)$$

$$= \frac{1}{2}(1 + 1) \qquad \text{(by induction because } l_j - 1 \text{ is the level of node } i \text{ in } T_l \text{ and } l_j - 1 \text{ is the level of node } j \text{ in } T_r)$$

$$= 1 \qquad \text{as desired.}$$

Now we are ready to compute the minimum external path length of an extended binary tree with n internal nodes and $n + 1$ external nodes. Using the first observation, let there be k external nodes on level l and $n + 1 - k$ on level $l + 1$, $1 \le k \le n + 1$ (that is, all the external nodes may be on level l). The second observation tells us that

$$k2^{-l} + (n + 1 - k)2^{-l-1} = 1$$

and hence

$$k = 2^{l+1} - n - 1. \tag{5.8}$$

Since $k \ge 1$, $2^{l+1} > n + 1$ and, since $k \le n + 1$, we have $2^l \le n + 1$; that is,

$$l = \lfloor \lg(n + 1) \rfloor. \tag{5.9}$$

Combining (5.8) and (5.9) gives

$$k = 2^{\lfloor \lg(n+1) \rfloor + 1} - n - 1,$$

and the minimum external path length is thus

$$lk + (l + 1)(n + 1 - k) = (n + 1)\lfloor \lg(n + 1) \rfloor + 2(n + 1) - 2^{\lfloor \lg(n+1) \rfloor + 1}.$$

Letting $\theta = \lg(n + 1) - \lfloor \lg(n + 1) \rfloor$, $0 \le \theta < 1$, the minimum external path length becomes

$$(n + 1)\lg(n + 1) + (n + 1)(2 - \theta - 2^{1-\theta}). \qquad (5.10)$$

The function $f(\theta) = 2 - \theta - 2^{1-\theta}$ is small on the interval $0 \leq \theta < 1$; more precisely, $0 \leq f(\theta) \leq 0.0861$ on this interval.

In light of the above discussion, we can conclude our analysis of binary search by observing that

$$S_n = 1 + \frac{1}{n} [\text{internal path length of } T(1, n)]$$

and similarly

$$U_n = \frac{1}{n + 1} [\text{external path length of } T(1, n)].$$

Combining these equations, Equations (5.6) and (5.10), and the fact that $T(1, n)$ is a completely balanced binary tree with n internal nodes (why?), we derive

$$U_n = \lg(n + 1) + 2 - \theta - 2^{1-\theta}$$

$$S_n = \left(1 + \frac{1}{n}\right)[\lg(n + 1) + 2 - \theta - 2^{1-\theta}] - 1,$$

where $\theta = \lg(n + 1) - \lfloor \lg(n + 1) \rfloor$, as before.

Exercises

1. Prove that the height of $T(l, h)$ is $\lceil \lg(h - l + 2) \rceil$. [*Hint*: Use mathematical induction on $h - l$.]

2. Explain why an extended binary tree with n internal nodes contains $n + 1$ external nodes.

3. Prove that $D(T) = 2n$, where T is an extended binary tree with n internal nodes and $D(T) = E(T) - I(T)$.

4. Prove that the extended binary tree of Figure 5.29 has the largest possible internal and external path lengths of all binary trees of n internal nodes.

★5. Consider the sequence of extended binary trees $T_0, T_1, T_2, \ldots$ defined by $T_0 = \square$, $T_1 = $, and $T_n = $ for $n > 1$. Com-

(a)   (b)

pute the height, the number of internal and external nodes, and the internal and external path lengths of T_n, in terms of n.

6. A t-ary tree is defined in the same way as a binary tree, except that every internal node has t subtrees, any or all of which may be empty.
   (a) Find a formula analogous to Equation (5.7) for *extended t-ary trees* with n internal nodes.
   (b) Find the formula for the minimum and maximum internal and external path lengths for extended t-ary trees.

7. Let $l_1, l_2, \ldots, l_{n+1}$ be the levels of the $n + 1$ external nodes in an extended binary tree, and let $s_1, s_2, \ldots, s_n$ be the numbers of external nodes descended from the n internal nodes. Prove that

$$\sum_{i=1}^{n} s_i = \sum_{i=1}^{n+1} l_i.$$

8. What does Observation 1 imply about binary search?

9. Define $F(T)$ as

$$F(\square) = 0,$$
$$F(T) = \qquad = F(T_l) + F(T_r) + \min[h(T_l), h(T_r)],$$

where $h(T)$ is the height of T. Find a simple closed formula for $F(T)$. Generalize your result for t-ary trees and for forests, replacing "min" by "sum-of-all-but-the-largest."

10. Let T be the completely balanced, extended binary tree of height h with $2^{(h+1)} - 1$ nodes (both external and internal) numbered in the order visited by the inorder traversal. Let u and v be the numbers of two nodes in T neither of which is a descendant of the other. Prove that the subtree rooted at the lowest common ancestor of u and v is $\lfloor \lg(ord(logical(u) \ \mathbf{xor} \ logical \ (v))) \rfloor$.

5.4 REMARKS AND REFERENCES

This chapter has only scratched the surface of the large volume of material on trees. We will go into the application of trees to the organization of data in Chapter 7. In these remarks, therefore, we concentrate on their structural and mathematical aspects.

In Chapter 2 of

Knuth, D. E., *The Art of Computer Programming*, Vol. 1, *Fundamental Algorithms*. Reading, Mass.: Addison-Wesley Publishing Co., 1st ed. 1968, 2nd ed. 1973.

the reader will find a great wealth of material on trees, their representations, mathematical properties, and some applications. By and large, the only topics lacking in this work are some recent innovations in algorithms for tree traversals (for example, see Exercise 18 of Section 5.2), which are not of fundamental importance.

For more detailed presentations of the union/find application of Section 5.2 the reader is referred to

Reingold, E. M., J. Nievergelt, and N. Deo, *Combinatorial Algorithms: Theory and Practice*. Englewood Cliffs, N.J.: Prentice-Hall, Inc., 1977.

Aho, A. V., J. E. Hopcroft, and J. D. Ullman, *The Design and Analysis of Computer Algorithms*. Reading, Mass.: Addison-Wesley Publishing Co., Inc., 1974.

Tarjan, R. E., *Data Structures and Network Algorithms*. Philadelphia, Pa.: Society for Industrial and Applied Mathematics, 1983.

Very deep mathematical analyses can be found in

Tarjan, R. E., "Efficiency of a Good but Not Linear Set Union Algorithm," *J. ACM,* **22** (1975), 215–225.

Tarjan, R. E., "Applications of Path Compression on Balanced Trees," *J. ACM,* **26** (1979), 690–715.

Knuth, D. E., and A. Schönhage, "The Expected Linearity of a Simple Equivalence Algorithm," *Theoretical Comp. Sci.,* **6** (1978), 281–315.

Chapter 6

Storage Management

Your borrowers of books—those mutilators of collections, spoilers of the symmetry of shelves, and creators of odd volumes.

"The Two Races of Men," Essays of Elia,
Charles Lamb

In previous chapters we have used the Pascal standard procedure *new* to allocate records. To respond to this request, Pascal's run-time support routines manage a pool of available storage and find a sufficiently large section of memory to satisfy the request. In turn, these routines acquire memory by requesting it from the operating system, which manages all memory. In this chapter we present the basic techniques applicable to both levels of storage management and to storage management within application programs, as well. Different mechanisms of implementation have different strengths and weaknesses, and we must understand them to select an appropriate method for a given situation.

After a record has been allocated and used, the program may eventually no longer need it. If nothing is done to release records for reuse, the program may eventually fail from lack of memory. In a virtual memory environment it might continue working, but records can become scattered and execution slowed by excessive disk operations (as we will see in Section 6.2.3). One way records are reused is by calling the standard Pascal procedure *dispose*: *dispose(p)* releases the space of $p\uparrow$. This chapter will consider, in addition, a number of other techniques for releasing unneeded records.

The combination of a storage allocation technique and a plan for reuse of allocated records that are no longer needed is called a *storage management regime*. A number of factors determine which regime is appropriate for an application: whether or not all records are the same size, whether the run-time system can find all pointers, whether it can safely move records from one location to another, and whether virtual memory is in use. As we discuss the various storage management regimes we will see many interactions among these factors.

All the techniques use the same basic idea and terminology: when a record is in use it is called *active*. A linked list is kept of all *inactive* records—that is, those available for use. This list, called the *free list* or the *list of available records*, is used to dispense records as requested and to keep track of records that have been released. Since "record" is a reserved word in Pascal, we have named the data type in our examples a *block*, and we use the terms interchangably. The space managed by a storage management regime may be contiguous or scattered. For our purposes we model the space as a contiguous array *pool* or *word*. In a few cases we use the notation "loc(x)" to mean the pointer to the space allocated for variable x. In particular, a pointer to element i of array A is given by loc($A[i]$).

6.1 UNIFORM SIZE RECORDS

A call *new(p)* allocates blocks of diverse size, depending on the size needed for a record of type $p\uparrow$. For simplicity, let us assume in this section that all records are of the same, uniform size. In this way we can concentrate on techniques for identifying records that are no longer active and need to be returned to the free list. Later sections will describe how to manage storage for records of diverse size.

Since the records are of uniform size, we can model an allocatable storage of

const
        m = "number of records in storage pool";
        nPtrs = "number of pointers in each record";
type
        ptr = ↑ *block*;
        blockType = (*freeBlock*, *activeBlock*);
        block = **record**
            "EveryBlock"; {here some regimes have additional fields
                that appear in every record, both active and inactive}
            case *blockType* **of**
                freeBlock: (*NEXT: ptr*);   {link together free records}
                activeBlock: ("fields needed by the application";
                    PTRS: **array** [1..*nPtrs*] **of** *ptr*)
        end;
var
        free: ptr;   {points to list of free records}
        pool: **array** [1..*m*] **of** *block*;   {the records to allocate}

Declarations 6.1
Declarations for management of records of uniform size

procedure *InitializePool*;
var *i*: *integer*;
begin
    for *i*:= *2* **to** *m* **do**
        {Assert: Records *pool*[1 .. *i* − 1] are linked into a list.}
        {connect from each record to the next}
        pool[*i* − 1].*NEXT* := "loc(*pool*[*i*])";
    pool[*m*].*NEXT* := **nil**;   {end of list}
    free := "loc(*pool*[1])"   {point to start of list}
end

Algorithm 6.1
Initialization of the list of available records

m records as an array *pool*. Any record will satisfy a request, so it suffices to maintain the free list as a simple list with a pointer *free* to its first element. Each inactive record has a field *NEXT* for linking the free list; in active records this space is used for other purposes. We will need to traverse all pointers from each active record, so we decree that these pointers be arranged consecutively within the record where they can be accessed as an array. For our model we simply declare these pointers as the array *PTRS*. All these considerations lead to the storage structure shown in Declarations 6.1; initial conditions are established by Algorithm 6.1.

A request for a record, *NewUniform*(*p*), is handled by Algorithm 6.2. Notice that when all the records have been allocated, the allocation procedure indicates an overflow condition. If records are never made inactive, or *released*, by the requesting program, *Overflow* will be called on the (*m* + 1)st call to *NewUniform*. Usually,

procedure *NewUniform*(**var** *newrecord*: *ptr*);
var
    i: 1..*nPtrs*;
begin
    newrecord := *free*;
    if *free* = **nil then**
        Overflow   {no free record available}
    else begin
        free := *free*↑.*NEXT*;
        for *i* := 1 **to** *nPtrs* **do**
            newrecord↑.*PTRS*[*i*] := **nil**
    end
end

Algorithm 6.2
Implementation of *new* for records of uniform size

however, programs release unneeded records either explicitly—as with Pascal's *dispose*—or implicitly. In implicit release regimes, the application program does nothing to an inactive record except change pointers so none refers to the record. It is up to the storage management routines to find inactive records and reuse their space. In Algorithm 6.2, unlike Pascal's *new*, pointers in the record are initialized to **nil**; this is essential for the implicit release regimes, which must traverse every pointer in active records. Explicit and implicit release are discussed in the two subsections that follow.

Exercises

1. If *p* and *t* are of type *ptr*, *i* is an integer, and *m* is 7 in Declarations 6.1, show the result of executing

    > *InitializePool*;
    > *NewUniform(t)*;
    > **for** *i* := 1 **to** 4 **do begin**
    >   *NewUniform(p)*;
    >   *p↑.NEXT* := *t*
    > **end**;
    > *t↑.NEXT* := **nil**

    In a diagram indicate which records are active, which are free, and which are on the free list. Show where *p* and *t* point and the values of all *NEXT* fields.

2. Modify Algorithm 6.2 so that Algorithm 6.1 is reduced to a single assignment. In other words, rewrite Algorithm 6.2 so that it initially allocates records *sequentially* from *pool*[1..*m*], switching to linked allocation only later.

6.1.1   Reference Counts

In the simplest storage management regimes, records are explicitly released when they are no longer needed. When an application no longer needs a record, say *p↑*, it releases it with simple list operations:

> *p↑.NEXT* := *free*;
> *free* := *p*

Although this method is trivial for the storage management routines, it can be inconvenient for the program using the records. For example, to release an entire list of records it is necessary that they be released one by one, unless they are (fortuitously) already linked together by the *NEXT* field (see Exercise 1). Furthermore, since each record can be part of several structures simultaneously, it is not always clear when a record should be released. Worse, if a record is mistakenly released too early, the program may continue to behave correctly for some time beyond the erroneous operation, making it exceedingly difficult to find the source of the inevitable failure.

One (seemingly) simple way to know when a record is no longer needed is to keep track of how many pointers currently point to it. This information can be stored in the record itself in a reference count field *REF*, declared at "EveryBlock" in Declarations 6.1. *REF* is initialized to zero when the record is allocated (this is added to Algorithm 6.2), incremented when a pointer is made to point to the record, and decremented when a pointer to the record is made to point elsewhere. In this regime we consider a record to be inactive when its *REF* field again becomes zero.

Reference counts seem less simple when we note that to maintain the *REF* fields, every pointer assignment which was formerly just $p:=q$ must now be done as

$$
\begin{aligned}
&q\uparrow.REF := q\uparrow.REF + 1;\\
&p\uparrow.REF := p\uparrow.REF - 1;1\\
&\textbf{if } p\uparrow.REF = 0 \textbf{ then}\\
&\qquad DisposeRefs(p);\\
&p := q
\end{aligned}
\tag{6.1}
$$

where *DisposeRefs* is given as Algorithm 6.3.

One requirement for *DisposeRefs* will occur for later algorithms as well: every pointer value must be valid. This is because the storage management routines will attempt to use the value as a pointer; if it is invalid the routines will at best attempt to access an invalid address and at worst decrement some field whose erroneous value will not be detected until much later. It is to avoid these problems that the procedure *NewUniform* initializes all pointers to **nil**.

Another aspect of reference counts is that the application program no longer calls *dispose* explicitly because it may not know when the target of a pointer is truly free. Instead it sets the pointer to **nil**, using (6.1). Note, however, that as (6.1) is written the assignment $p := $ **nil** will add one to **nil**$\uparrow.REF$. To avoid having a test for **nil** in sequence (6.1), we have assumed that the value representing **nil** is the address of a unique physical record, one with at least a *REF* field. Algorithm 6.3 checks specifically for **nil** and makes its reference count large so further attempts to dispose it will be stymied for some time to come. (See Exercise 4.)

The time and space overheads of reference count regimes are significant, but similar overheads are encountered in all regimes. With reference counts the execution cost rises from one for a simple assignment to these twelve for (6.1): $\uparrow$, $\uparrow$, $+$, $:=$, $\uparrow$, $\uparrow$, $-$, $:=$, **if**, $\uparrow$, $=$, $:=$. In later sections we will compare this execution time with that of other regimes, but we note a space-time tradeoff here: if the sequence (6.1) is coded for every pointer assignment, the space for the code will be larger by a considerable factor. We could trade this space for extra time by writing

```
procedure DisposeRefs(p: ptr);
        {Place record p↑ on free list and decrement reference counts of
        records it points at.}
var
      i: integer;
      t: ptr;
begin
      if p = nil then              {never dispose nil}
          p↑.REF := 1000           {don't even try for a long time}
      else begin
          for i := 1 to nPtrs do begin
                {reduce reference counts of children}
                t := p↑.PTRS[i];
                t↑.REF := t↑.REF − 1;
                if t↑.REF = 0 then
                      DisposeRefs(t)
          end;
          p↑.NEXT := free;   {finally, free the record}
          free := p
      end
end
```

Algorithm 6.3
Dispose operation for the reference count regime. The pointer assignments here
are *not* done with sequence (6.1).

each assignment as a procedure call. Considerable extra storage is occupied by the
REF fields. This can be reduced somewhat by using *REF* fields only in the header
nodes of lists or trees; but then our use of pointers into the list or tree would be
restricted—we would not be able to have shared sublists or subtrees.

Reference counts are usually unacceptable not for any of the reasons discussed
so far, but because they cannot handle circular lists and other structures that contain
cyclic chains of pointers. In each cycle no record will ever have a reference count
value of zero, so the entire structure will never be recognized as inactive, even if it
is unreachable by any pointer outside the structure. If an application creates and later
detaches many circular structures, memory will be filled with inactive structures
whose space cannot be reused. This inability to guarantee reclamation of inactive
records limits the utility of reference counts to special circumstances (see Exercise 6).

Exercises

1. Design an algorithm to return the records in a circular linked list to the list of
   available records. Assume that the list records are connected by the *NEXT* field.

Your algorithm should require only a constant number of operations, no matter the length of the list.

2. What error could occur if the increment of $q\uparrow.REF$ were moved from first to last in sequence (6.1)?

3. Repeat Exercise 1 on page 268 but using reference counts. Show the reference count for each record in a diagram of the final state of memory.

4. The text assumed that **nil** is implemented as a pointer to a unique physical record with a REF field. Suppose it is not a valid pointer. Give revised versions of (6.1) and Algorithm 6.3 for this case.

5. Consider the recursive call $DisposeRefs(t)$ in Algorithm 6.3. Explain why t cannot point to a record that is already being released by a call to $DisposeRefs$ at a higher level in the recursion.

6. Using circular structures with reference counts requires a way to indicate to the storage management system when a circular structure is no longer accessible. Describe how this might be done. Discuss the advantages and disadvantages.

6.1.2   Garbage Collection

Instead of having a program explicitly release records it no longer needs, it is more convenient for the program simply to request records as needed and to ignore those records no longer needed. Of course, sooner or later the list of available records will become empty and a request will lead to *Overflow* in Algorithm 6.2. When this happens, the *new* routine for this regime will begin a process called *garbage collection*, in which all the inactive records are located and gathered together to form a new list of available records. Garbage collection is accomplished by *marking* all the active records, that is, all those that can be reached (via a sequence of pointers) from pointer variables within the program. The records that remain unmarked after this process are considered to be inactive ("garbage") and are collected to build a new free list.

To mark all active records we must be able to find all program variables that are pointers. This stringent requirement causes many implementation problems, but unfortunately there is no other way to locate and mark all active records. We cannot write such a routine in Pascal, so we describe it by introducing the construction

"**foreach** pointer variable p; let $pvar = \text{loc}(p)$ **do**"
        statement

which means that *statement* is executed once for each pointer variable and that $pvar$ will point to that variable. The type of $pvar$ is $\uparrow ptr$ so the value of the program variable itself is given by $pvar\uparrow$ and the record actually referred to is $pvar\uparrow\uparrow$.

Algorithms 6.4 and 6.5(a) give procedures to mark all the active records and

procedure *GarbageCollect*;
        {Find all inactive records and build them into a free list.}
var
    p: *ptr*;
    pvar: ↑*ptr*;
    i: *integer*;
begin
    for *i* := 1 **to** *m* **do**   {start with all free}
        pool[*i*].*ACTIVE* := **false**;
    "**foreach** pointer variable *p*; let *pvar* = loc(*p*) **do**"
        Mark(*pvar*↑);   {mark all active records}
    free := **nil**;
    for *i* := 1 **to** *m* **do**
        {Assert: *Free* points to a list, in reverse order, of all non-*ACTIVE*
        records in *pool*[1 .. *i* − 1].}
        if not *pool*[*i*].*ACTIVE* **then begin**
        pool[*i*].*NEXT* := *free*;   {put free record on list}
        free := "loc(*pool*[*i*])"
        end;
    if *free* = **nil then**
        Overflow
end

Algorithm 6.4
Garbage collection

collect all inactive records. The marking is done by a recursive traversal algorithm reminiscent of a recursive preorder tree traversal (see Section 5.2). It performs a depth first search as would be done by Algorithm 4.9 with a stack. As each record *r* is visited it is marked by setting the bit *r*↑.*ACTIVE* to **true**; initially, of course, all these bits are set to **false**. The bits used for marking constitute a one-bit-per-record overhead necessary in all garbage collection schemes. These bits may be stored in the records themselves (by a field in "EveryBlock" in Declarations 6.1) or in a separate bit table. The collection phase links all records marked **false** into the new list of available records. Notice that if we still have *free* = **nil** after the collection procedure, there is an *Overflow*.

    The marking method of Algorithm 6.5(a) has a very serious shortcoming: because it is recursive it will need (implicitly) a push down stack at the very moment that memory is at a premium (otherwise, why would we be collecting the inactive records?). However, we can eliminate the stack by making the algorithm nonrecursive and reserving a few extra bits per record for a clever programming trick.

    The trick is to store the stack in the pointer fields of the very records being

procedure *Mark*(*p*: *ptr*);
        {Mark record $p\uparrow$ and all records reachable from it.}
var
    i: *integer*;
begin
    if *p* ≠ **nil then**
        if not $p\uparrow$.*ACTIVE* **then begin**
            $p\uparrow$.*ACTIVE* := **true**;
            for *i* := 1 **to** *nPtrs* **do**
                Mark($p\uparrow$.*PTRS*[*i*])
        end
end

Algorithm 6.5(a)
Marking for garbage collection

marked; the few extra bits per record allow us to do this without loss of information. We use them for a *COUNT* field in the *activeBlock* variant of every record. This field must be large enough to hold a value from 1 to *nPtrs*, the number of pointers per record; the purpose of this field will be clear in a moment. The heart of the trick is the use of the pointer fields of the records being traversed as the stack: each pointer is "inverted" as we follow it from one record to the next; the pointers are restored to their original values as we retrace our way back. At any moment a record will have at most one pointer whose value has been modified—the value of the *COUNT* field indicates which. Algorithm 6.5(b) shows the details of this marking technique.

It is best to think of the algorithm as a traversal of the records in which the pointer *v* indicates the current record and the pointer *u* indicates its parent, which is also the top record on a stack that keeps track of the path from *v* to *p*, the starting record. The path consists of v, u_0, u_1, u_2, ..., u_k, p, where $u_0 = u$, $u_{i+1} = u_i\uparrow.PTRS[u_i\uparrow.COUNT]$, and $p = u_k\uparrow.PTRS[u_k\uparrow.COUNT]$; notice that $p\uparrow.PTRS[p\uparrow.COUNT]$ = **nil**; thus when *u* = **nil** the stack is empty. Figure 6.1 shows a typical list structure with a stack stored in it by this trick. Since it temporarily modifies the structure in memory, Algorithm 6.5(b) must be used with great care in situations where multiple processes share the same data.

Can analysis show that either reference counts or garbage collection is preferable? The space overheads in each are comparable—*REF* versus *COUNT*, so we need only try to compare the times. The time overhead for reference counts is two extra operations during *new* (for *newrecord*$\uparrow$.*REF* := 0) and eleven extra operator executions for each assignment. For garbage collection the time overhead for marking is about $11m + 5a + 34p$ where *m* is the total number of records, *a* is the number of active records, and *p* is the number of pointers in active records. The time for actually releasing records is the same in both regimes.

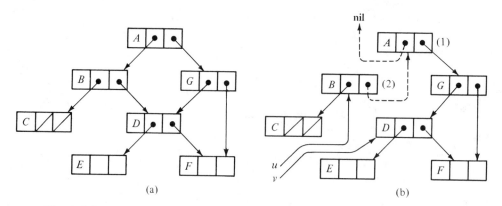

Figure 6.1
Storing the stack within the structure being traversed, as in Algorithm 6.5(b): (a) the
structure; (b) the structure while processing node D. The stack is shown by dashed
pointers; nonzero *COUNT* fields are in parentheses.

We need then to compare the number of garbage collections to the number of
pointer assignment operations in the class of programs for which the storage management regime is being designed. We introduce the parameter $\alpha = a/m$ to represent
the fraction of memory occupied with active records. Assuming α remains roughly
constant, the number of allocations with *new* between garbage collections is about
$m(1 - \alpha)$ [why?] and the cost of the garbage collection is $m(11 + 5\alpha + 34\alpha n)$,
where n is the average number of pointers per record. Apportioning the cost of the
garbage collection over the $m(1 - \alpha)$ calls to *new* gives the approximate garbage
collection cost per *new* as

$$\frac{11 + 5\alpha + 34\alpha n}{1 - \alpha} \tag{6.2}$$

Let s be the average number of pointer assignments with (6.1) between calls to *new*;
then the cost per *new* for the reference count regime is

$$11s + 2 \tag{6.3}$$

procedure *MarkInPlace*(p: *ptr*);
var

v: *ptr*;	{pointer to current record on traversal}
u: *ptr*;	{points to parent of $v\uparrow$}
down: *boolean*;	{current direction of traversal}
T: *ptr*;	
i: *integer*;	

begin
    u := **nil**;   {bottom of "stack"}
    v := p;   {start with record at p as current}
    down := **true**;   {and start descending}
    repeat {until u = **nil**}
        {Assert: The path from $v\uparrow$ to root is u_0, u_1, ..., u_k, p, as given in the text. For $0 \leq i \leq k$, all children of u_i have been marked *ACTIVE* if they are referred to by $u_i.PTRS[j]$ where $1 \leq j < u_i\uparrow.COUNT$. *Down is* **true** unless $v\uparrow$ was found to be *ACTIVE* or **nil**.}
        if *down* **then** {descend if possible}
            if v = **nil then** *down* := **false**
            else if $v\uparrow.ACTIVE$ **then** *down* := **false**
            else begin {mark and continue downward}
                $v\uparrow.ACTIVE$:= **true**;
                $v\uparrow.COUNT$:= 1;
                T := $v\uparrow.PTRS[1]$;
                $v\uparrow.PTRS[1]$:= u;   {save pointer to parent}
                u := v;   {move (u, v) down}
                v := T {$u\uparrow$ is still parent of $v\uparrow$}
            end
        else {not down, try sibling or parent}
            if $u\uparrow.COUNT$ < $nPtrs$ **then begin** {advance v to next sibling}
                i := $u\uparrow.COUNT$;
                $u\uparrow.COUNT$:= i + 1;
                T := $u\uparrow.PTRS[i]$;   {get pointer to parent of $u\uparrow$}
                $u\uparrow.PTRS[i]$:= v;   {restore original value}
                v := $u\uparrow.PTRS[i + 1]$;   {point v at next sibling}
                $u\uparrow.PTRS[i + 1]$:= T;   {save pointer to parent of $u\uparrow$}
                down := **true**   {go down through sibling}
            end
            else begin   {$v\uparrow$ is last child of $u\uparrow$, go up}
                T := $u\uparrow.PTRS[nPtrs]$;   {get pointer to parent of $u\uparrow$}
                $u\uparrow.PTRS[nPtrs]$:= v;   {restore original value}
                v := u;   {*move (u, v) up*}
                u := T {$u\uparrow$ is still parent of $v\uparrow$}
            end
    until u = **nil**
end

Algorithm 6.5(b)
Marking for garbage collection with pointer swapping to store the stack

When (6.2) is less than (6.3) garbage collection is preferable. Since (6.3) increases with s, we can set (6.2) equal to (6.3) and solve for s to find the break-even point between garbage collection and reference counts. We find that for

$$s > \frac{(11 + 5\alpha + 34\alpha n)/(1 - \alpha) - 2}{11}$$

garbage collection is preferable. When there are two pointers per record ($n = 2$) and memory is half full ($\alpha = 0.5$), the break-even value of s is 8. For larger n and α the break-even value can be much larger, so from this point of view reference counts will be more desirable than garbage collection.

The costs for assignments, *new*, and garbage collection are not the only factors, however. Reference counts will be more expensive if a subroutine call is used for each assignment, or the code will be considerably expanded if the assignment sequence is repeated for each assignment. (Larger code can lead to increased paging in virtual memory and consequent poor performance.) Still, the most significant barrier to the use of reference counts is their inability to handle circular structures.

Exercises

1. Rewrite Algorithm 6.5(a) so that it uses an explicit stack instead of recursion.

2. Write code for a marking algorithm based on "sweeping" memory. Begin by marking *ACTIVE* all records directly accessible from program pointer variables. Then scan $pool[1 .. m]$ with a pointer p that begins pointing at $pool[1]$. On each step check if $p\uparrow$ is *ACTIVE* and if so mark *ACTIVE* any children not already so marked. If $p\uparrow$ was not *ACTIVE*, advance p to the following record; otherwise set p to the smallest address among that of the following record and those of all children that were just made *ACTIVE*.

3. Combine the ideas in the algorithms of the previous two exercises to obtain an algorithm in which a stack of *fixed size* is used until it is full, at which point the strategy of Exercise 2 is employed.

4. In what order are the nodes in Figure 6.2 marked by Algorithm 6.5(b), assuming the algorithm starts at A?

5. Specialize Algorithm 6.5(b) for the case of one pointer per record (called *NEXT*).

6. Specialize Algorithm 6.5(b) for the case of two pointers per record (called *LEFT* and *RIGHT*).

7. Design an inorder binary tree-traversal algorithm based on the idea of Algorithm 6.5(b)—that is, one that temporarily modifies the tree during the traversal, instead of using recursion or a stack.

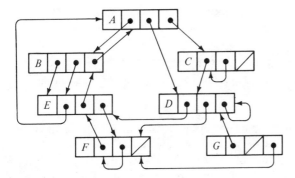

Figure 6.2
Exercise 4

8. Design a recursive algorithm to copy an arbitrary list structure. Assume that each record has an unused pointer field *NEWLOC* that can be used during the copying. Assume further that all the *NEWLOC* fields are initially **nil**. [*Hint*: Look at Algorithm 6.5(a).]

9. Why is there no need for the statement *free* := **nil** in *GarbageCollect*, Algorithm 6.4? What undesirable condition would it cause if *GarbageCollect* were called directly from an application program?

10. Count the operators executed in Algorithm 6.5(b) when the path "advance *v* to next sibling" is taken. Explain why this count is close to the sum of the counts for the other two main paths through the loop and why it is the per-pointer cost for the algorithm.

6.2   DIVERSE SIZE RECORDS

In most applications the records needed at different times have diverse sizes, hence the uniform size techniques discussed in the previous section are limited in usefulness. We can get around this problem by choosing a uniform size large enough to satisfy any possible demand that could occur, but this could waste a great deal of memory due to *internal fragmentation*: the unavailability of memory because it is scattered around, unused and unusable, in active records throughout memory. The amount of internal fragmentation could be reduced by maintaining several lists of available records, one for each of a few possible record sizes. This strategy is worthwhile only when there are a limited number of possible record sizes. In this section we discuss the problem of allocating diverse size records when there will be too many sizes for the multiple-list approach to be feasible. In Section 6.3 we discuss a limited form of the multiple-list technique.

0   15,000   35,000   55,000   75,000   90,000 100,000

Figure 6.3
A possible memory configuration. The dark regions are active; there are 50,000
inactive words, but no request larger than 20,000 words can be filled due to
external fragmentation.

The storage management strategies discussed in this section suffer very little
from internal fragmentation (but see the discussion of ε in Section 6.2.1). However,
they do suffer from some degree of *external fragmentation*: the inactive areas of
memory may become broken into pieces that are too small to satisfy most requests.
To understand this pervasive problem, consider the following situation. Suppose
100,000 words are available to our storage management regime and through requests
and releases the inactive words are spread throughout memory as shown in Figure 6.3. If a request for 25,000 words occurs, it cannot be filled because there is no
contiguous block of words large enough, even though in total 50,000 words of storage are inactive.

In Section 6.1 we did not face problems of external fragmentation because the
records were of uniform size and any request could be satisfied by any available
record. In this section the main emphasis is on how to avoid or minimize external

```
const
        m = "size of memory to be allocated from";
        epsilon = "size of smallest free record allowed";          {ε}
type
        ptr =  ↑ block;
        blockType = (activeBlock, freeBlock);
        block = record
                "EveryBlock"; {here some regimes have additional fields
                        that appear in every record, both active and inactive}
                SIZE: integer;   {size of this record}
                case blockType of
                        freeBlock: (NEXT: ptr);     {link free list}
                        activeBlock: ("contents, as required")
        end;
var
        free: ptr;     {pointer to list of inactive records}
        word: array[1..m{+ words for a dummy record}]
                        of "places where record can start";
```

Declarations 6.2
Global types and variables for management of records of diverse size

fragmentation. One technique is to keep a *list of free blocks* and search it for each request. The alternative is *memory compaction*: all active records are moved so that there is only one free block. While compacting memory it is also possible to *rearrange* all records to reduce paging. These three approaches are discussed in the next three subsections.

Rather than a pool of records available for allocation, as we had with uniform size allocation, we assume here that allocation takes place from a memory of m words *word*[1..m]. As shown in Declarations 6.2, each of these words is taken to be a place at which a record could start. A pointer to a record occupying *word*[$l..h$] is represented by the address "loc(*word*[l])". Although it is a violation of the strong typing rules of Pascal, we will define the addition "$p + n$" of a pointer p and an integer n to yield a pointer to the word n words beyond the one addressed by p. In particular, the phrase "$p + p\uparrow.SIZE$" gives the address of the record following the one pointed at by p. It is an important characteristic of these algorithms that every record is directly followed by another record—free or active—so we can scan the entire set of records by repeatedly setting $p := "p + p\uparrow.SIZE"$.

Exercises

1. Suppose *word*[0..7] are available for allocation and that k words have been allocated at random.

   (a) Show that L, the expected size of the largest free block, is 5.5 for $k = 1$ and 4.036 for $k = 2$.

   (b) What is L for $k = 7$ and $k = 8$?

   (c) Write a program to evaluate L for $k = 3, 4, 5,$ and 6. Try it with other memory sizes.

   (d) Extend your program to determine, for a given k, the probability of being able to allocate a record of size n for $1 \leq n \leq (8 - k)$. Is the probability linear as a function of n or does it rise more steeply for low or high n? (This probability distribution is a rough measure of the potential for external fragmentation.)

2. (a) Suppose *word*[1..23] are available for allocation and suppose that all requests are for records of one or two words. Develop an allocation scheme that will not overflow if there are never more than sixteen allocated words.

   (b) Suppose there are only 22 words available. Prove that *any* allocation scheme can be forced to reach a state in which only fourteen of the words are allocated, but a request for a record of two words cannot be honored.

3. As in Exercise 2(a) above, determine, as a function of n, the minimum number of words needed to guarantee that any request for one- or two-word records can be honored, as long as there are never more than n allocated words.

6.2.1 Allocation by Search

As in the case of uniform size records, it is convenient to maintain a list of available blocks of words. Initially the list consists of a single record containing all m words. In general, a request for a record is filled by choosing some available record from the list and, if necessary, breaking it into two pieces, one to be allocated and the other to be put back on the list of available records. Although this is the general outline, we need to resolve various questions of implementation such as how to choose a record from the list, in what order to maintain the list, and how to return a released record. It is not surprising that these issues are interrelated and must be considered together rather than individually.

To begin, consider the process of allocating a record of n words to fill a request. In searching through the list of available records, should we be looking for the record closest in size and no smaller than the request (*best fit*) or should we stop at the first record large enough that is encountered (*first fit*)? While the best-fit strategy is plausible, it performs poorly in practice: in order to find the best fit we must search the entire list of available records, or if it is ordered by size, about half of it on the average, to do the allocation (see Section 7.1.1). This can be expensive! Furthermore, by choosing the smallest record large enough to fill the request and making the excess into a new record, we may be causing a proliferation of small, unusable records. The first-fit technique works much better, and we will present a variation of it.

When first fit is used and the search for the record to be allocated is always started at the beginning of the list of available records (that is, from *free*), whatever small records occur through division of large records to satisfy small requests will tend to occur at the front of the list of available records, cluttering it up and increasing the average time required to find a suitable record. It is thus a good idea to keep the list of available records as a circular list and to have *free* point to a "random" record in the list. This can be achieved by just leaving *free* wherever it is after an allocation and beginning the search for the next allocation at that point. We call this method *next fit*.

We can further inhibit the occurrence of small, unusable records by not dividing a record when it is only a little larger than the record requested. In other words, we establish a minimum size for records on the list of available space, say ε. Whenever a record of n words is requested and a record of size $k > n$ is found for the allocation, we leave a free record of size $k - n$ only if $k - n \geq \varepsilon$; otherwise we fill the request with the entire record of k words.

These ideas are embodied in the allocation procedure given in Algorithm 6.6(a). In this algorithm we have made the list of available records into a circular list using the pointer *NEXT*; in addition to *NEXT*, each record on the list contains a field *SIZE* that gives its size and is unchanged while the record is active. (The number of words used for fields in free records determines a minimum value for ε. Why?

procedure *NewNextFit*(*n*: *integer*; **var** *newrecord*: *ptr*);
    {Allocate a record of size at least *n* and set *newrecord* to point at it.}
var
    p, *pred*: *ptr*;
begin
    {Search for a large enough free record. The list cannot be empty because
    the free list contains a dummy element with *SIZE* zero.}
    p := *free*↑.*NEXT*;
    pred := *free*;
    while (*p* ≠ *free*) **and** (*p*↑.*SIZE* < *n*) **do begin**
        {Assert: No free block on the list from *free*↑.*NEXT* to *p* has size *n*
        or larger. *pred*↑.NEXT = *p*}
        pred := *p*;
        p := *p*↑.*NEXT*
    end;
    if *p*↑.*SIZE* < *n* **then**
        {The search went all the way around and did not find a large
        enough record.}
        Overflow
    else begin
        {allocate from record at *p*}
        if *p*↑.*SIZE* − *n* < *epsilon* **then begin**
            {allocate entire record, removing it from free list}
            pred↑.*NEXT* := *p*↑.*NEXT*;
            free := *pred*
            {*SIZE* remains unchanged and will be needed when the record
            is freed; the record may be larger than *n*}
        end
        else begin
            {split *p*↑ and free the left end}
            free := *p*;
            p↑.*SIZE* := *p*↑.*SIZE* − *n*;
            p := "*p* + *p*↑.*SIZE*";
            p↑.*SIZE* := *n*
        end;
        {*p*↑.*SIZE* ≥ *n* and a record of length *p*↑.*SIZE* has been allocated be-
        ginning at *p*}
        newrecord := *p*
    end

end

Algorithm 6.6(a)
Next-fit allocation procedure for diverse size records

Also, see Exercise 6.) In order for the algorithm to work properly we include a dummy record of *SIZE* zero on the list of available records; this insures that the list is never empty. Without such a dummy we would have to complicate the algorithm slightly to compensate for the different things that would need to be done when the final free record was allocated. The initial conditions are established by

$$free := \text{``loc}(word[m + 1])\text{''};$$
$$free\uparrow.SIZE := 0;$$
$$free\uparrow.NEXT := \text{``loc}(word[1])\text{''};$$
$$\text{``loc}(word[1])\text{''}\uparrow.SIZE := m;$$
$$\text{``loc}(word[1])\text{''}\uparrow.NEXT := free$$

We must now devise the procedure to return a released record to the list of available records. The most simplistic technique is to insert the record at an arbitrary position on the list, say at *free*. Unfortunately this will work poorly, since the records of storage available will become smaller and smaller through splittings, until all are too small to satisfy requests of even moderate size. The procedure to return released records must therefore recombine adjacent available records. In order to do the recombination for a newly released record p we must find the records physically adjacent to p in memory; the record p may be combined with one or both, depending on which are currently unallocated.

One approach to the problem of finding the physical neighbors of p is to search the list of available records. We reject this approach immediately, since we want to avoid the time overhead involved in such searches; even if the list of available records were kept in order of physical location we would have to search about half the list, on the average (see Section 7.1.1).

Actually, we can easily determine the record physically following p: it begins in $word[\text{``}p + p\uparrow.SIZE\text{''}]$. The problem is how to know whether it is allocated. By using one extra bit per record we can keep this information in the record itself. We will assume that each record r has a field $r\uparrow.ACTIVE$ that is **true** if the record is currently allocated and **false** if the record is on the list of available records. We are not quite done, however, because just knowing that a record q is on the list does not allow us to delete it easily—we must know its predecessor on the list. For this reason we will maintain the list of available records as a *doubly linked* circular list, recalling that in such a list we can easily delete any element without a search. Thus we will consider each record to have fields *SIZE*, *ACTIVE*, *NEXT*, and *PREV*, where *PREV* points to the predecessor of the record on the list of available records. Fields *SIZE* and *ACTIVE* are needed in all records, active or not, but *NEXT* and *PREV* are used only in inactive records.

Getting to the record physically preceding record p is only slightly more complicated. We have direct access to the last word in that record, $word[p - 1]$, and so we can store in that location a pointer *FRONT* to the first word of the record. Then the first word of the record physically preceding *p* is *word*[("*p* − 1")↑.*FRONT*]. Of course since our goal is the recombination of available records, we will only need to reach this word if the preceding physical record is inactive; furthermore, it is definitely undesirable to have unusable space in the last word of an active record. It is thus better to have the field *FRONT* defined only for inactive records and to store a copy of the *ACTIVE* bit of a record in the physically following record. We will call this bit *PREACTIVE* and extend the declaration of *block* to be:

```
block = record
      SIZE: integer;                    {size of this record}
      ACTIVE: boolean;                  {true when this record is in use}
      PREACTIVE: boolean;               {true when preceding record is in
                                        use}
      case blockType of
           freeBlock: (NEXT, PREV: ptr;   {link free list}
                          ". . ."
                              FRONT: ptr);   {last word points to start of record}
           activeBlock: ("contents, as required")
end;
```

The structure of a record is thus as shown in Figure 6.4. We have used some additional space per record for these new fields, but only two extra bits in active

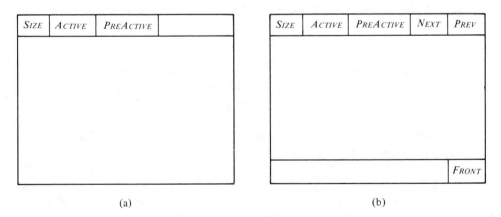

(a)   (b)

Figure 6.4
The structure of records for memory management by Algorithms 6.6(b) and 6.7:
(a) an active record—*ACTIVE* is **true**; (b) an inactive record—*ACTIVE* is **false**
and *FRONT* points to the first word of the record

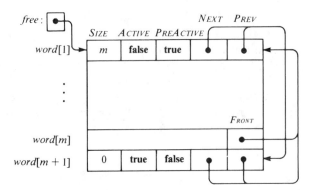

Figure 6.5
The initial configuration of memory for the boundary-tag method of dynamic
storage allocation

records, and we gain the important advantage of being able to release records and
recombine them without searching the list of available records.

The modified version of Algorithm 6.6(a) necessary for this new structure is
given as Algorithm 6.6(b). Algorithm 6.7 gives the procedure to release a record,
recombining it with its physical neighbors if necessary. After satisfying a request
from element p of the free list, the allocation algorithm implements *next fit* by setting
free so $p\uparrow.NEXT$ will be the first block checked for the next allocation. Similarly, if
the release algorithm changes *free* the new value is such that the next search will
begin at the successor to the block just freed. To simplify the release algorithm we
have established a dummy record in $word[m + 1]$; this record is considered allocated
and thus allows us to use the same algorithm for releasing records at the boundaries
and in the interior. We have also used the record in $word[m + 1]$ as the dummy
record on the list of available records. Figure 6.5 shows the initial situation. Because
of the additional information kept at the boundaries of each record, this technique
has become known as dynamic storage allocation with *boundary tags*.

We can combine the ideas presented in this section with those presented in our
discussion of garbage collection to eliminate the need for an explicit release procedure. When overflow occurs on an attempted allocation, we initiate a marking phase
and follow it by a sequential scan of all records to combine adjacent available records
and reform them into a list of available space. Since the marking phase requires the
ability to recognize all the pointers in a record, and since such an ability would also
allow us the flexibility needed to relocate active records, we will discuss this topic
together with compaction in Section 6.2.2.

Performance. Almost no analytical results are known about the performance
of Algorithms 6.6(b) and 6.7. Instead, we must rely on empirical evidence that

procedure *NewTags* (*n*: *integer*; **var** *newrecord*: *ptr*);
var
      p: *ptr*;
begin
      p := *free*;
      {scan free list looking for a large enough record}
      while (*p* ≠ *free*↑.*PREV*) **and** (*p*↑.*SIZE* < *n*) **do**
            {Assert: No record on list from *free* to *p* has size *n* or larger.}
            p := *p*↑.*NEXT*;
      if *p*↑.*SIZE* < *n* **then**
            Overflow   {no free record is large enough}
      else begin
            free := *p*↑.*NEXT*;   {set *free* for next allocation}
            if *p*↑.*SIZE* − *n* < *epsilon* **then begin**
                  {allocate entire record; remove it from free list}
                  p↑.*NEXT*↑.*PREV* := *p*↑.*PREV*;
                  p↑.*PREV*↑.*NEXT* := *p*↑.*NEXT*
            end
            else begin
                {split *p*; allocate the tail end, leaving the rest free}
                p↑.*SIZE* := *p*↑.*SIZE* − *n*;
                "*FRONT* pointer at end of *p*↑" := *p*;
                p := "*p* + *p*↑.*SIZE*";
                p↑.*SIZE* := *n*;
                p↑.*PREACTIVE* := **false**
            end;
            {*p*↑.*SIZE* ≥ *n* and a record of length *p*↑.*SIZE* has been allocated, beginning at *p*}
            p↑.*ACTIVE* := **true**;
            "(*p* + *p*↑.*SIZE*)"↑.*PREACTIVE* := **true**;
            newrecord := *p*   {return a pointer to the new record}
      end
end

Algorithm 6.6(b)
Next-fit allocation procedure with boundary tags

comes from extensive simulations. For example, it has been observed that, on the average, the **while** loop of Algorithm 6.6(b) goes through less than three iterations. Thus the next-fit technique of having *free* be a "roving" pointer pays off. The rest of the allocation procedure clearly requires only a small constant amount of time, as does the release procedure.

procedure *DisposeTags*(*p*: *ptr*);
var
t: *ptr*;
begin
$t := "p + p\uparrow.SIZE"$; {$t\uparrow$ is the next record after $p\uparrow$ in *word*}
if not $t\uparrow.ACTIVE$ **then begin**   {$t\uparrow$ is free}
 {merge $p\uparrow$ and $t\uparrow$, removing $t\uparrow$ from free list}
 $t\uparrow.NEXT\uparrow.PREV := t\uparrow.PREV$;
 $t\uparrow.PREV\uparrow.NEXT := t\uparrow.NEXT$;
 if $t = free$ **then**
  $free := t\uparrow.NEXT$;
 $p\uparrow.SIZE := p\uparrow.SIZE + t\uparrow.SIZE$
 end
 else $t\uparrow.PREACTIVE := $ **false**;
 if not $p\uparrow.PREACTIVE$ **then begin**
  {merge $p\uparrow$ with physically preceding record, which is already on the free list}
  $t := "FRONT$ pointer from word just before $p\uparrow"$;
  $t\uparrow.SIZE := t\uparrow.SIZE + p\uparrow.SIZE$;
  $"FRONT$ pointer at end of $t\uparrow" := t$
 end
 else begin
  {put p on free list}
  $p\uparrow.ACTIVE := $ **false**;
  $"FRONT$ pointer at end of $p\uparrow" := p$;
  $p\uparrow.PREV := free\uparrow.PREV$;
  $p\uparrow.NEXT := free$;
  $free\uparrow.PREV := p$;
  $p\uparrow.PREV\uparrow.NEXT := p$
 end
end

Algorithm 6.7
Release procedure for the boundary-tag method

The more important question, however, is the degree to which external fragmentation prevents the memory available from being fully utilized. To write a simulation to study this question we begin with an array to simulate the memory being allocated and an *event list* of pending deallocations. We characterize each allocation request by two parameters, the size of the record and its *lifetime*. Since nothing else is going on in the simulated environment, it is sufficient to measure the lifetime of a record by the number of subsequent allocations for which it remains allocated after that time it is released. The event list contains, for each allocated record, a pair

(p, T) consisting of p, the address of the record, and T, the time when it is to be released.

The basic simulation algorithm is then

```
for t := 1 to NumberOfAllocations do begin
      "for each event pair (p, T) having T = t do" begin
            {deallocate the record}
            DisposeTags(p);
            "delete pair (p, T) from the event list"
      end;
      {now allocate a record}
      l := "randomly chosen lifetime";
      s := "randomly chosen size";
      NewTags(s, p);
      "insert pair (p, t + l) on event list"
end
```

Let *MeanLifetime* be the mean of the distribution of lifetimes. Experience has shown that a choice of $10 \times MeanLifetime$ for *NumberOfAllocations* gives a reasonable picture of the behavior that can be expected in practice. It has been common to choose a uniform or exponential distribution for s and l. An exponential distribution for l is close enough to those observed in practice, but the observed distributions for s are far more "quirky" than can be described by formula. For example the distribution in Figure 6.6 was generated by observing the pattern of storage requests made by a compiler: the peak at 512 is for storage of records from secondary storage; the peak at 32 is for file control blocks, which are required for reading from storage; other requests are distributed sporadically all the way from the teens to 8,000.

The basic measure for performance for an algorithm is the *memory load* it can sustain. This is simply the expected amount of the memory occupied and is given by

$$MeanSize \times MeanLifetime$$

where *MeanSize* is the mean of the size distribution. This measure is highly dependent on the exact nature of the size distribution; if there are large sizes, external fragmentation is more likely to halt the simulation.

In preparation of this section a series of experiments was run utilizing the above driver and Algorithms 6.6(b) and 6.7. Lifetimes were exponentially distributed with means of 75, 100, 125, 150, and 200. Request sizes were exponentially distributed with a mean chosen to generate loads of 45, 50, 55, ..., 90 percent. However the request size distribution was also truncated by setting a maximum size varying between m/50 and m/10; this truncation resulted in observed mean requests lower than

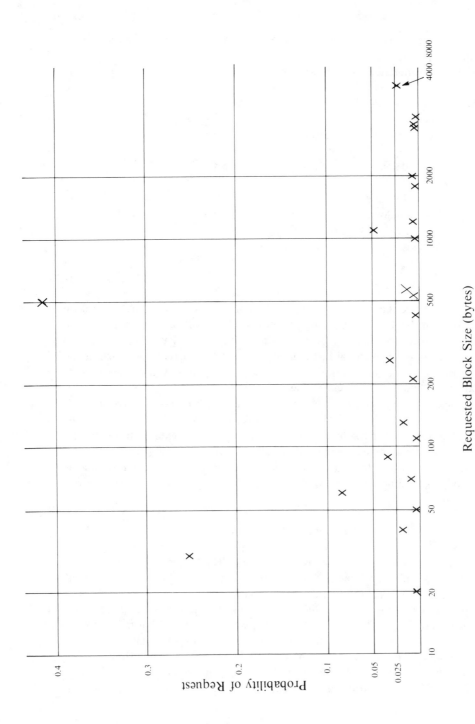

Figure 6.6
An observed probability distribution for the size of memory requests by a Pascal compiler. Each point represents a range of request sizes, although for most ranges only one or two sizes in the range were requested.

the mean of the distribution. Each experiment was run ten times and the observations were averaged.

A striking pattern emerged from the experiments. The simulation would run to completion if and only if the observed average memory load was less than $0.55m$. At higher memory loads a few runs would succeed, but by $0.65m$ most runs failed about half-way through ($5 \times$ *MeanLifetime* allocations).

Memory loads observed in practice are often higher than 0.55 due to three factors not modelled by the above simulation. First, many programs do few *dispose*'s; there is a tendency to build large structures, and then just traverse them to compute results. Second, programs that do *dispose* many small records keep lists of idle records and reuse them; for an example, see Exercise 4 of Section 4.2.2. Third, modern operating systems usually provide some mechanism so a program can request an increase in its allocatable storage; thus providing a solution for the occasional large request that cannot be satisfied from a fragmented memory.

Exercises

1. Find sequences of requests and releases with the property that:
   (a) Best fit succeeds where both first fit and worst fit fail.
   (b) First fit succeeds where both best fit and worst fit fail.
   (c) Worst fit succeeds where both best fit and first fit fail.
   (Worst fit always uses the largest available block to fill a request.)

2. Suppose that requests and releases are made in a last-in, first-out manner so that no allocated record is released until after all subsequently requested records have been released. Design a memory management strategy for this case. Does the first-fit/best-fit distinction make sense?

3. Rewrite Algorithm 6.6(a) so that it uses best fit instead of next fit.

4. Write a routine to initialize *word* for Algorithms 6.6(b) and 6.7.

5. Rewrite Algorithms 6.6(b) and 6.7 so the first test in the **while** predicate is $p \neq free$. Your revised versions should continue to have the property that when a block is allocated from or inserted on the free list then the succeeding block is the first one checked for the next allocation.

6. (a) Explain why *epsilon*, the minimum size of a record in Algorithm 6.6(b), must be large enough to hold a size header and three pointers.
   (b) Design and write the routines for a storage manager in which *epsilon* need only be enough for a size header and one pointer. [*Hint*: The *dispose* routine will keep the free list in order by address. To do so, a search of the free list is required for each *dispose*.]

(c) Design and write the routines for a storage manager in which *epsilon* need only be large enough for a size header. [*Hint*: The *new* routine must examine *all* blocks, both active and free.]

7. Simulate the behavior of Algorithms 6.6(b) and 6.7. Test the claim that the while loop in *NewTags* averages less than three iterations. Determine for two artificial distributions of size requests whether a memory load of $0.55m$ can be sustained.

6.2.2 Compaction

We can combine the flexibility of the allocation procedure for diverse size records given in the previous section with the convenience of a garbage-collection technique instead of explicit release. Recall that garbage collection requires the ability to recognize all the pointers both within records and from pointer variables in the program; it is not unreasonable to expect this ability in records of uniform size as in Section 6.1.2, but it is not so reasonable for records of varying sizes. If we do have that ability, however, then we can both perform garbage collection and relocate active records. Relocating active records means that we can compact all active records into a contiguous area of memory. This is of little consequence for records of uniform size, since in that case it makes no difference which particular record is used to fill a request, but for records of diverse sizes this is of great consequence, since it allows us to combine all available records into a single large record and completely eliminate external fragmentation. It is also beneficial in virtual memories, as we discuss in the next section.

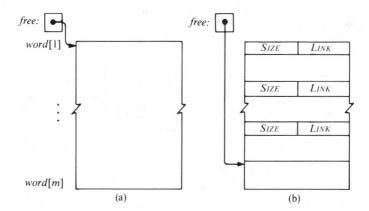

Figure 6.7
The structure of the: allocatable memory: (a) initially and (b) in general

In this section we will use a very simple allocation scheme: there is only one available block at any time, pointed to by *free*. Everything physically before *free* in memory is assumed to be active (although parts of it may be inactive), and a request for a record is handled by allocating the front part of the only available record, the remainder of which then becomes the available record. For convenience, each allocated record is assumed to have a *SIZE* field as before and a *LINK* field to be used during marking and compaction. Initially we would have the configuration of Figure 6.7(a) with the general case shown in Figure 6.7(b).

Since all pointers must be known to the storage management routines, we adapt the *PTRS* scheme used for Algorithm 6.5, extending it to include in every record a field *NUMPTRS* giving the number of pointers in that record. We no longer need the *NEXT* field so the full declaration of a record is

```
block = record
      SIZE: integer;          {size of this record}
      LINK: ptr;              {used during Compact}
      NUMPTRS: integer;       {number of pointers in this record}
      PTRS: array [1.."NUMPTRS"] of ptr;
      "other contents, as required"
end;
```

Note that a variable upper bound is given for *PTRS*. Since the application is allocating arbitrary size records—which it could not do in Pascal, we may as well allow it to choose the upper bound at the time of record allocation—which is also not valid Pascal.

With the storage structure we have just described, the allocation procedure is as given by Algorithm 6.8. The *LINK* field is set to **nil** for later use—it will always be **nil** except during garbage collection, when it is used to store the stack (see Section 6.1.2), and during relocation, when it is used to store the new location of the record. The last location of *word* is not allocated; this location is used during the *Mark* phase of compaction.

The procedure *Compact* given as algorithm 6.9 has four phases. The first, Algorithm 6.9(b), marks all records with a technique similar to Algorithm 6.5(b), but stores the stack in the *LINK* fields; the *LINK* field of each active record is thus left non-**nil**, marking it as active. The next three phases—*Assign*, *Change*, and *Move*— all have the same structure; they go through the memory one record at a time, processing each active record. *Assign* stores in the *LINK* field the address the record will have after the compaction; *Change* changes all pointers to point where they must after the compaction; and *Move* finally moves all records. Notice we implicitly assume that pointers point only to the beginning of records.

```
procedure NewCompact(n, nptrs: integer; var newrecord: ptr);
var
      i: integer;
begin
      if "free + n" > m then
            Compact;
      if "free + n" > m then
            Overflow        {Compact did not help}
      else begin
            {allocate a record of n words at free}
            newrecord := free;
            free := "free + n";
            newrecord↑.SIZE := n;
            newrecord↑.LINK := nil;
            newrecord↑.NUMPTRS := nptrs;
            for i := 1 to nptrs do
                  newrecord↑.PTRS[i] := nil
      end
end
```

Algorithm 6.8
Allocation of a record of size *n* with *nptrs* pointers

The last three phases of *Compact* all scan memory in the same manner, so we can simplify the algorithm considerably by introducing the special form

"**foreach** active record; let *p* point to the record **do**" *STATEMENT*

which is shorthand for

```
p := "loc(word[1])";
while p ≠ free do begin
      if p↑.LINK ≠ nil then
            STATEMENT;
      p := "p + p↑.SIZE"        {see Exercise 1}
      {Assert: All active records in word[1..p − 1] have had STATE-
      MENT done for them.}
end
```

Since records follow one another in *word* and *free* points to just past the last allocated record, this sequence performs the **if** test once for every record. The *LINK* fields are non-**nil** in the active records so the loop executes *STATEMENT* once for every active record.

procedure *MarkWithLinks*; *forward*;

procedure *Compact*;
{Restructure free space by moving all active records to the front
end of array *word*. Before and after *Compact*, all *LINK* fields have
value **nil**.}
var
newfree: *ptr*; {value for *free* after compaction}
p, *newloc*: *ptr*;
i: *integer*;
pvar: ↑*ptr*;   {points at a program pointer variable}
begin {*Compact*}
{Phase 1: *Mark*—Mark all active records}
MarkWithLinks;   {Algorithm 6.9(b)}
{Phase 2: *Assign*—Store in *p*↑.*LINK* the new address for *p*↑}
newloc := "loc(*word*[1]);"
"**foreach** active record; let *p* point to the record **do**" **begin**
p↑.*LINK* := *newloc*;   {assign new address}
newloc := "*newloc* + *p*↑.*SIZE*"
end;
newfree := *newloc*;
{Phase 3: *Change*—Change all pointers to their correct new values}
"**foreach** active record; let *p* point to the record **do**"
for *i* := 1 **to** *p*↑.*NUMPTRS* **do**
if *p*↑.*PTRS*[*i*] ≠ **nil then**
p↑.*PTRS*[*i*] := *p*↑.*PTRS*[*i*]↑.*LINK*;
"**foreach** pointer variable *p*; let *pvar* = loc(*p*) **do**"
if *pvar*↑ ≠ **nil then**
{change program pointer variable}
pvar↑ := *pvar*↑↑.*LINK*;
{Phase 4: *Move*—Move all records to their new locations}
{see Exercise 1}
"**foreach** active record; let *p* point to the record **do**" **begin**
newloc := *p*↑.*LINK*;
p↑.*LINK* := **nil**;
newloc↑ := *p*↑   {move *p*↑ to its new location}
end;
free := *newfree*
end {*Compact*}

Algorithm 6.9(a)
Compaction of active records

procedure *MarkWithLinks*;
　　　　　{Mark all active records by setting *LINK* fields to other than **nil**. The *LINK* fields are used to keep the stack of records known to be active, but whose children are not yet marked.}
var
　　p: *ptr*;　　{points to record being processed}
　　top: *ptr*;　　{points to top of "stack" during marking}
　　i: *integer*;
　　pvar: ↑*ptr*;
begin
　　top := *free*;
　　free↑.*LINK* := **nil**;　　{end of stack indicator}
　　"**foreach** pointer variable *p*; let *pvar* = loc(*p*) **do**"
　　　　{mark all records pointed at by pointer variables}
　　　　if *pvar*↑ ≠ **nil then**
　　　　　　if *pvar*↑↑.*LINK* = **nil then begin**　　{not marked}
　　　　　　　　pvar↑↑.*LINK* := *top*;　　　　{mark it ...}
　　　　　　　　top := *pvar*↑　　　　　　{... and link onto stack}
　　　　　　end;
　　p := *top*;　　　　{take first record from stack}
　　top := *top*↑.*LINK*;
　　while *top* ≠ **nil do begin**
　　　　{Assert: All active records are either marked with a nonzero value in the *LINK* field or are reachable from records in the list starting from *top* and connected by the *LINK* field. A marked record which has been removed from the list will not be put back on.}
　　　　{check children of top record from stack}
　　　　for *i* := 1 **to** *p*↑.*NUMPTRS* **do**
　　　　　　if *p*↑.*PTRS*[*i*] ≠ **nil then**　　　　{check *p*↑.*PTRS*[*i*]↑}
　　　　　　　　if *p*↑.*PTRS*[*i*]↑.*LINK* = **nil then begin**　　{not marked}
　　　　　　　　　　p↑.*PTRS*[*i*]↑.*LINK* := *top*;　　{*mark it ...*}
　　　　　　　　　　top := *p*↑.*PTRS*[*i*]　　　　{... and link onto stack}
　　　　　　　　end;
　　　　p := *top*;　　　　　　{get next stacked record}
　　　　top := *top*↑.*LINK*
　　end
end

Algorithm 6.9(b)
Marking active records for compaction

Exercises

1. Show that for the *Move* phase of Algorithm 6.9(a) the expansion of "**foreach** active record ..." must have $p := $ "$p + newloc\uparrow.SIZE$" instead of $p := $ "$p + p\uparrow.SIZE$".

2. Suppose we have records of fixed size containing two pointers each, *LEFT* and *RIGHT*. Design an algorithm for compaction. You may not use an explicit stack, and there is no *LINK* field as used in Algorithm 6.9, but your algorithm is to move and compact the structure into an entirely new area of memory, and you can distinguish between addresses in the new and old areas.

3. The *Assign*, *Change*, and *Move* phases of Algorithm 6.9 all scan memory and skip inactive records. The latter two phases can be made faster if the *Assign* phase combines adjacent free records so the later phases can skip over each group in one step. Augment the *Assign* phase so it combines adjacent free records.

4. If *MarkWithLinks*, Algorithm 6.9(b), does not need the *LINK* field, it can be eliminated from the other phases as well. To do so, a table is built relating pre-compaction addresses to new ones. Describe circumstances in which this table can be kept in the free records themselves. Show that each group of consecutive free records gives rise to one entry in the table. What two values are needed in each entry? How is the entry used to update pointers that refer to records between this free group and the next? (See also Exercise 14 in Section 7.1.2.)

5. The fields *SIZE* and *NUMPTRS* required in every active record constitute a considerable overhead if records are small. If an application requires only a limited number of varieties of record, these overhead fields can be replaced by a few-bit *TYPE* field that indexes into an array of descriptors, one for each variety of record. Show the implementation of

   "**foreach** active record; let p point to the record **do**"

   when *TYPE* fields are used. Be sure to show your declaration for the descriptor array.

6. In this and the next exercise you will design a curious algorithm for the *Assign*, *Change*, and *Move* phases that requires only two passes through the memory and utilizes pointers to pointer fields. The basic approach is to build a list of the pointers to any given record, say $p\uparrow$, by swapping the contents of $p\uparrow.LINK$ with each of the pointers in turn. As a result, *LINK* points to the first pointer and each remaining pointer points to the next.

   (a) Write a procedure *NoteReferenceFrom(pvar: ↑ptr)* that interchanges the contents of pointer $pvar\uparrow$ with $pvar\uparrow\uparrow.LINK$. (This procedure cannot be written in pure Pascal.)

(b) Write a procedure *UpdateReferencesTo*(*p*, *newloc*) that follows the chain from *p*↑.*LINK*, changing all pointers on the list to point to *newloc*, the location *p*↑ will occupy after the compaction. The *LINK* field should wind up **nil** again.

(c) Utilize the procedures from (a) and (b) to build a two pass procedure for *Assign*, *Change*, and *Move*. The first pass should call *NoteReferenceFrom* for each pointer and *UpdateReferencesTo* for all link fields. The second pass should call *UpdateReferencesTo* again and actually move the records.

(d) Show that the call to *UpdateReferencesTo* in the first pass of (c) updates only pointers that refer to records of higher address than their own and the call in the second pass updates all other pointers. Explain why we must do *UpdateReferencesTo* in both passes.

(e) Consider the memory whose initial state is shown in Figure 6.8(a). When the algorithm in (c) has first passed record *B*, the state becomes that given in Figure 6.8(b). Draw the state after completion of the first pass, after finishing record *A* in the second pass, and at completion of the algorithm.

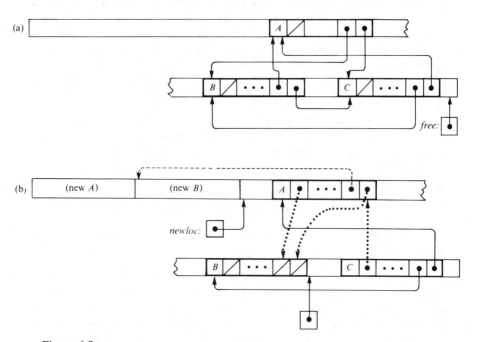

Figure 6.8
Exercises 6 and 7. (a) Initial conditions. Each cell has *VAL* and *LINK* fields, other data, and two pointer fields. (b) After first scan has processed nodes *A* and *B*. Dotted pointers form lists that start at a *Link* field and connect all pointer fields known to refer to the record at the start of the list. The dashed pointer is one that has already been corrected.

7. The technique of Exercise 6 makes possible the reduction of the *LINK* field to an *ACTIVE* bit and two other bits. The trick is that the initial value in the *LINK* field is only needed to determine when the end of list is reached in *Update-ReferencesTo*, so if we have another means to find the list end, the *LINK* field can be any nonpointer portion of the record. Its value is restored by *Update-ReferencesTo*. Thus we can get away with just two bits to indicate the length of the list. They clearly suffice to distinguish list lengths of 0, 1, and 2 from all others. Show that longer lists are in order of memory location and that the order of the last two elements can be reversed to signal the end of the list. Write versions of *NoteReferenceFrom* and *UpdateReferencesTo* that use this scheme.

6.2.3 Rearrangement

So far we have treated active records by leaving them where they are or by compacting them together in order. In this section we present an algorithm that compacts them and also reorders them. This algorithm is actually faster than Algorithm 6.9 and has a number of other advantages, but it uses twice as much memory! Because this algorithm has its greatest impact in virtual memory environments, let us describe them first.

A virtual memory operating system simulates a very large address space for program execution. The bits and bytes of information represented in that space are physically stored in external storage, say on a disk. The hardware and operating system interact to copy portions called *pages* of this disk space into physical locations in main memory when they are accessed by the program. (Note that the operating system manages the disk storage and physical storage by uniform size allocation with explicit release.)

The vast size of virtual memory raises the hope that a storage management regime could merely allocate memory and never release it. Unfortunately, list and tree processing programs perform poorly in virtual memory systems when the storage structures become scattered over many pages. Traversals over the structure access multiple pages and thus entail many disk operations to transfer information between memory and disk.

One simple measure of the degree to which a storage structure has become unsuitable to a virtual memory is to count the number of *off-page* pointers, that is, those that point from a record on one page to a record on another. This measure is not accurate, however, because it ignores the possibility of all the children of a node being together on a page remote from the node itself; in this case only two pages need reside in main memory to process the node and its children, but all pointers from the node would be counted as off-page pointers.

The best way to estimate paging cost is to begin by recording the sequence of pages referenced as a sample of programs is executed. This data can then be scanned by examining every subsequence of some given length and noting the number of distinct pages referenced in that subsequence. The maximum value is the number of pages of physical memory needed to ensure that subsequences of the chosen length can be run without loading a given page more than once. In choosing among storage management regimes, then, we would choose the one that required the smallest number of pages for a given subsequence length. If the choice were close we would choose a regime that worked for a wide range of lengths over one that worked for just a few.

How can a storage reorganization algorithm reduce paging? We have already seen Algorithm 6.9, which can reduce paging simply by compacting all records to fewer pages. Even fewer pages will need to reside simultaneously in main memory if we rearrange records so related records are together on one or two pages. Such rearrangement is exactly the result of the algorithm we now present. It not only rearranges records, but it also eliminates the need for the *LINK* or *PREACTIVE* fields in every active record. The central idea is that the algorithm copies the active records from the old memory area to a new one.

Although we have pointed out already that storage reorganization occurs precisely when memory is the scarcest resource, the assumption that we have two copies of memory is not unworkable; Exercise 3 offers one solution and virtual memory offers another. To get twice as much memory, we simply ask the operating system for another chunk of address space. After doing the storage reorganization we can return the original address space for reuse.

Of the fields we have used before in records we need here only *ACTIVE*—which is used to mark a record that has been copied; and *SIZE*, *NUMPTRS*, and *PTRS*—which may be implicit in the record type. In addition, we need in every record a *NEWLOC* field, but it can overlay onto any portion of the record other than the *ACTIVE* bit. *NEWLOC* is used during the storage rearrangement to point from a record in the old memory to the location of the copy of the record in the new memory. Thus it can overlay other fields because we can refer to the data in the copy instead.

The procedure is shown as Algorithm 6.10, requiring as its argument a pointer to the new area of memory to be used for the copies. The heart of the algorithm is the function *GetNewAddress(old)*, which makes sure that the record at *old* has been copied to the new memory and then returns its address. The main body of the algorithm first calls *GetNewAddress* for each program pointer variable to ensure that all records that can be directly reached are copied to the new memory. Then a scan is made *through the new memory*, updating all pointers by applying *GetNewAddress*. As this happens, records that had not been copied are copied over to the end of the new memory and are updated as the scan reaches them. The scan ends when there are no more records to copy and the addresses in the last copied record have been updated; at this time, the scan pointer p finally catches up to the pointer *whereto*, which has been indicating where to put the copies of records. Notice that the new memory is accessed very nicely for a virtual memory environment: it is accessed only sequentially as p and *whereto* advance.

procedure *RearrangeMemory(newmemory: ptr)*;
var
      whereto: *ptr*;   {where to put next record in new memory}
      p: *ptr*;   {pointer for scan of new memory}
      i: *integer*;
      pvar: ↑*ptr*;
      function *GetNewAddress(old: ptr): ptr*;
                    {Ensures that the record at *old* has been copied to the new
                    memory and returns its address there. If it had not been cop-
                    ied, it is copied and marked, and then its *NEWLOC* field is
                    replaced by its new address.}
      begin
          if *old* = **nil then**
              GetNewAddress := **nil**
          else if *old*↑.*ACTIVE* **then**   {old↑ has been copied}
              GetNewAddress := *old*↑.*NEWLOC*
          else begin
              whereto↑ := *old*↑ ;   {copy *old*↑}
              GetNewAddress := *whereto*;
              old↑.*NEWLOC* := *whereto*;   {save new address}
              old↑.*ACTIVE* := **true**;   {and mark it as copied}
              whereto := "*whereto* + *whereto*↑.*SIZE*"
          end
      end; {*Get New Address*}
begin {*RearrangeMemory*}
      whereto := *newmemory*;
      "**foreach** pointer variable *p*; let *pvar* = loc(*p*) **do**"
          pvar↑ := *GetNewAddress(pvar*↑);
      p := *newmemory*;
      while *p* ≠ *whereto* **do begin**
              {Assert: Records known to be active have been copied into the re-
              gion between *newmemory* and *whereto* − 1. The *ACTIVE* field in the
              original of the copied record is **true**. The *NEWLOC* field in the orig-
              inal points to the copy. All records in *newmemory* ... *p* − 1 have
              had their children copied and have correct pointers to the copies.}
                  for *i* := 1 **to** *p*↑.*NUMPTRS* **do**
             p↑.*PTRS*[*i*] := *GetNewAddress(p*↑.*PTRS*[*i*]);
             p := "*p* + *p*↑.*SIZE*"
      end
end

Algorithm 6.10
Memory rearrangement while collecting the active records

Operator count analysis shows that Algorithm 6.10 has low overhead. The combined cost of marking, moving, and updating is only 26 operations the first time a pointer to a given record is encountered and 17 operations for every subsequent pointer to that record. This is competitive with the cost of reference counts even with as few as five pointer assignments per *new*. (The cost can be even lower; see Exercise 2.)

Exercises

1. Consider execution of Algorithm 6.10 operating on the structure in Figure 6.1. Assume that program pointer variables refer to records A and B and that *NEWLOC* occupies the second word of each cell. Draw diagrams of the state of old and new memory just after the first loop of the main body, after four records have been copied, and at the end.

2. The operator counts cited in the text counted the function calls to *GetNewAddress*. These can easily be eliminated by copying the body of the procedure to the two places it is called. What would the operator counts be then?

3. Rewrite Algorithm 6.10 so it copies the records to secondary storage, reads and writes them for the scan, and finally reads them in after completing its work. Your routine should assemble the records for secondary storage into physical records of a thousand words. (See Section 3.2.1.) You may assume the read and write operations to secondary storage have parameters that specify the desired physical record as an index within the file. Be wary of the case in which *whereto* and p both point into the same physical record.

4. Perform a simulation of the behavior of Algorithm 6.10 operating on a simulated structure being built by random replacement of pointer fields with new records. Study the degree to which a preorder traversal of the structure [as in Algorithm 6.5(a)] has greater or lesser locality of reference. For instance, try a page size ten times the average record size and a four-page memory. Determine the number of paging operations for the traversal before and after the first rearrangement that occurs after the structure reaches 200 records. Compare this to the number of paging operations after compaction by Algorithm 6.9.

6.3 THE BUDDY SYSTEM

In the two previous sections we have presented storage management techniques for uniform record size (Section 6.1) and for diverse record sizes (Section 6.2); in this section we describe a system that compromises between these two extremes. In the *buddy system* there is a sequence $s_0, s_1, s_2, \ldots, s_t$ of possible record sizes. Of course, we could use the techniques of Section 6.1 by maintaining entirely separate areas for each record size, but it would then be difficult to use the words of memory for different size records at different times. The key idea of the buddy system is that records are allowed to be split or recombined in a carefully controlled manner: In general for some j we have $s_n = s_{n-1} + s_{n-j}$, so that a record of s_n words can be split only into two records of s_{n-1} and s_{n-j} words, respectively. The two records are called *buddies*. One of the buddies will be used to satisfy the request (with further splittings as needed) and the other will be free. If, as a result of a release, two buddies are both free, they are combined to restore the original record (which may be further recombined).

The buddy system, if properly implemented, allows easy access to the buddy of a newly released record. Of particular interest in this regard is the *binary buddy system*, in which $s_n = s_{n-1} + s_{n-1}$, $s_0 = 1$, and hence $s_k = 2^k$. This method is well suited to binary computers because there is a simple relationship between the size of a record, its location (that is, the location of its first word), and the location of its buddy. To derive this relationship, consider a memory of $2^4 = 16$ locations *word*[0..15]. These 2^4 locations split into buddies as shown in Figure 6.9. This small example suggests that the first word of a record of 2^k words is at a location divisible by 2^k. Indeed, this is true in general, for it is true initially and if a block of 2^{k+1} words begins at *word*[l], it splits to buddies of 2^k words each at locations l and $l + 2^k$; since 2^{k+1} divides l, it follows that 2^k divides both l and $l + 2^k$. We thus know that the buddy of a record of 2^k words beginning at location l begins at either $l + 2^k$ or $l - 2^k$. Which one? The answer depends on l: If 2^{k+1} does not divide l, then l cannot be the first location of a record of 2^{k+1} words; that is, it cannot be the first of two buddies. Hence

$$\begin{array}{l} \text{first word of the} \\ \text{buddy of a record of} \\ 2^k \text{ words beginning} \\ \text{at location } l \end{array} = \begin{cases} l + 2^k, & \text{if } 2^{k+1} \text{ divides } l, \\ l - 2^k, & \text{if not.} \end{cases}$$

The advantage of the binary buddy system on a binary computer now becomes apparent: the address of the buddy is easily computed from the binary representation of the address of the first word of the record: it is l **xor** 2^k. To take advantage of this relation we describe *ptr* values for the buddy system as indices into *word* (but see Exercise 4).

In the remainder of this section we outline the rather straightforward algorithms for allocation and release in the binary buddy system. Suppose we have $m = 2^{maxx}$ words. We will maintain $maxx + 1$ linked lists *free*[0...*maxx*] for the available records of sizes 2^0, 2^1, ..., 2^{maxx}, respectively. In addition, to speed up the reservation algorithm we will have a dummy list *free*[*maxx* + 1], which is always non-**nil**. Initially all of the $maxx + 2$ lists are empty except *free*[*maxx*] which contains the

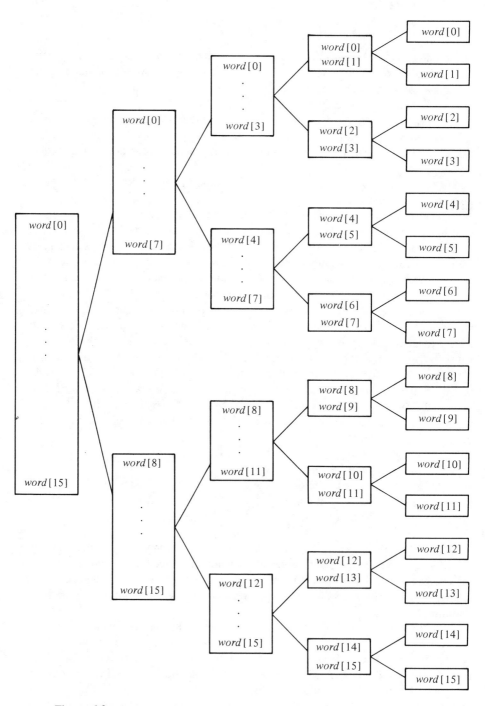

Figure 6.9
A tree showing how $2^4 = 16$ words are split into buddies of sizes 8, 4, 2, and 1

single record of 2^{maxx} words that comprises the available memory. To fill a request for an n-word record we first find the smallest $x \leqslant maxx$ such that $2^x \geqslant n$ (that is, $x \geqslant \lceil \lg n \rceil$) and $free[x]$ is not empty. If no such x exists, the request cannot be filled and an *Overflow* condition is indicated. If such an x does exist, the first record on $free[x]$ is removed and is used to fill the request. If $n > 2^{x-1}$, the entire record is allocated, otherwise it is split into buddies of 2^{x-1} words; one of these buddies is used to fill the request (with further splitting if $2^{x-2} \geqslant n$) and the other is put onto $free[x - 1]$.

When a record of 2^x words is released, we see if its buddy is on $free[x]$. If so, we combine the buddies and continue further combinations with buddies as possible. When all such combinations (if any) are done, the record is then added to the appropriate list.

As in other memory allocation schemes, it is convenient to maintain the lists of available records as doubly linked lists, since it is then easy to delete an element at any point in the list without knowing its predecessor. As in the other schemes also, the size of a record will be stored in all records, but here it is only necessary to store a *size index*, the exponent of 2 for the size. The structure of the records in the binary buddy system is shown in Figure 6.10 and described in Declarations 6.3.

Algorithms for allocation and release in the binary buddy system are given as Algorithms 6.11 and 6.12, respectively. They work in a straightforward manner, and the details left to Exercise 1 are not too difficult to work out.

In the more general buddy system (that is, when we have $s_n = s_{n-1} + s_{n-j}$), it is necessary to store in a block an indication of whether it is a left or right buddy. This could be done with a single bit, *LEFT*, but the problem arises of how to set the bit in a block resulting when two buddies are recombined into a larger block. To solve this problem, we introduce a *storage bit, S*. When a block is split, its *LEFT* bit is stored in the S bit of its left son and its S bit is stored in the S bit of its right son. When the buddies are recombined, their S bits are used to set the S and *LEFT* bits of the resulting block. (See Exercise 6.)

(a)
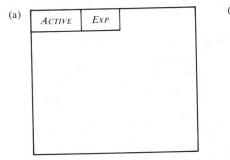

(b)
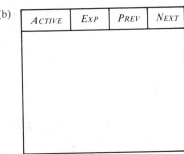

Figure 6.10
The structure of records in the binary buddy system: (a) active, (b) inactive. The *EXP* field is the size index giving the exponent of 2 of the size of the record.

const
    $maxx$ = "memory size index"; {memory is 2^{maxx} words}
    $maxxPlus1$ = "$maxx$ + 1";
    m = "2^{maxx}";   {upper bound on memory}

type
    $sizeindex$ = $0..maxxPlus1$;
    ptr = ↑ $block$;   {a value $0..m$; an index into $word$}
    $blockType$ = ($activeBlock$, $freeBlock$);
    $block$ = **record**
        $ACTIVE$: $boolean$;   {true when record is in use}
        EXP: $sizeindex$;   {record size is 2^{EXP}}
        case $blockType$ **of**
            $freeBlock$: ($NEXT$, $PREV$: ptr);   {link free lists}
            $activeBlock$: ("contents, as required")
    end;

var
    $free$: **array** [$0..maxxPlus1$] **of** ptr;
    $word$: **array** [$0..m$] **of** "places where a record can start";

Declarations 6.3
Types and global variables for binary buddy system. Note that $word[m]$ will not be allocated, but $DisposeBinaryBuddy$ may access its $ACTIVE$ and EXP fields.

procedure $NewBinaryBuddy$(n: $integer$; **var** $newrecord$: ptr);
        {Returns a pointer to a record large enough to hold n words.}
var
    $wantx$: $sizeindex$;   {size index of desired record}
    x: $sizeindex$;   {size index of current record}
    $result$, $buddy$: ptr;
begin
    $wantx$:= $ceiling(lg(n))$;
    x := $wantx$;
    while $free[x]$ = **nil do**   {find smallest sufficient free record}
        {at worst this stops because $free[maxx + 1]$ ≠ **nil**}
        x := x + 1;
    if x = $maxx$ + 1 **then**
        $Overflow$
    else begin {allocate a record, splitting as needed}
        $result$:= $free[x]$;
        "remove first element ($result$) from $free[x]$"; {see Exercise 1}
        while x > $wantx$ **do begin**
            {Assert: The record $result$ is not on any free list and is larger than needed to satisfy the request for size n. All free lists and

> record fields are correct except those of *result*.}
> {split *result*, freeing one half}
> $x := x - 1;$
> $buddy := \text{``}result \text{ } \textbf{xor} \text{ } 2^x \text{''};$
> $buddy\uparrow.ACTIVE := \textbf{false};$
> $buddy\uparrow.EXP := x;$
> "add *buddy* to empty list *free*[*x*]" {see Exercise 1}
> {How do we know that *free*[*x*] is empty?}

    end;
    $result\uparrow.ACTIVE := \textbf{true};$
    $result\uparrow.EXP := wantx;$
    $newrecord := result$
    end
end

Algorithm 6.11
Allocation in the binary buddy system

procedure *DisposeBinaryBuddy* (*unused*: *ptr*);
> {Return record at *unused* to free list, combining buddies as needed.}

var
    curx: *sizeindex*;   {size of record currently being released}
    buddy: *ptr*;
begin
    $curx := unused\uparrow.EXP;$ {get size of released record}
    $buddy := \text{``}unused \text{ } \textbf{xor} \text{ } 2^{curx}\text{''};$ {find its buddy}
    while $(curx \neq maxx)$ **and not** $buddy\uparrow.ACTIVE$
            and $(buddy\uparrow.EXP = curx)$ **do begin**
> {Assert: All free lists and record fields have correct values except possibly *unused*↑, which is not on a free list. *Buddy* and *unused* are buddies. *Buddy* is not active.}
> {combine *unused* with *buddy*}
> "delete *buddy* from list *free*[*curx*]"; {see Exercise 1}
> $curx := curx + 1;$
> $unused := \text{``}min(unused, buddy)\text{''};$
> $buddy := \text{``}unused \text{ } \textbf{xor} \text{ } 2^{curx}\text{''}$

    end;
    $unused\uparrow.ACTIVE := \textbf{false};$
    $unused\uparrow.EXP := curx;$
    "add *unused* to list *free*[*curx*]"   {Exercise 1}
end

Algorithm 6.12
Release in the binary buddy system

Exercises

1. Write a routine to initialize *free* and *word* appropriately. Fill in the list-manipulation details that have been omitted from Algorithms 6.11 and 6.12. See Section 4.2.1 for two possible implementations of doubly linked lists. What changes (if any) need to be made to the algorithms if dummy elements are used?

2. Can it happen that two records of 2^k words each can be adjacent and inactive simultaneously (that is, not buddies)?

3. How can the test in the **while** loop of Algorithm 6.12 be simplified by having a dummy record in $word[2^{maxx}]$?

4. Rewrite the expression "*result* **xor** 2^x" for the case where *result* is a memory address rather than an index into *word*.

5. Find a formula in terms of i and j for the size of the smallest buddy that contains both $word[i]$ and $word[j]$. [*Hint*: See Exercise 10 of Section 5.3.]

6. By experiments determine whether the binary buddy system is superior to the *Fibonacci buddy system*, where the block sizes are given by the recurrence $F_1 = 1, F_2 = 2, F_n = F_{n-1} + F_{n-2}$.

7. Use the *LEFT* and S bit approach to implement the Fibonacci buddy system of Exercise 5.

8. Perform simulation experiments to determine if the binary buddy method supports a greater or lesser memory load than Algorithms 6.6(b) and 6.7.

9. Buddy methods can permit a choice of sizes for the buddies in a split. For example, we could allow records whose size is a power of two to be split either $\frac{1}{2}:\frac{1}{2}$ or $\frac{1}{4}:\frac{3}{4}$ while records whose size is a multiple of three are always split $\frac{1}{3}:\frac{2}{3}$. The sequence of possible sizes is 1, 2, 3, 4, 6, 8, 12, 16, 24, ...

   (a) Show how to use three bits, *LEFT*, S, and T, in each record so the bits of a record can be reconstructed from the six bits of the two buddies it has been split to. In conjunction with the *EXP* field, use the three bits of a record to determine the size and address of its buddy.

   (b) Simulate this method and test the claim that it results in a greater memory load than the binary buddy method but less than that of Algorithms 6.6(b) and 6.7.

6.4 REMARKS AND REFERENCES

The particular needs of any system will necessarily make memory management idiosyncratic, so in this chapter we have introduced only the basic and most general techniques. For general purposes we recommend: (*i*) boundary tags, Algorithms 6.6(b) and 6.7, if the storage management regime cannot be sure of finding all pointers; (*ii*) compaction, Algorithms 6.8 and 6.9, if all pointers are known and memory is not virtual; and (*iii*) rearrangement, Algorithms 6.8 and 6.10, if all pointers are known and virtual memory is in use. For special applications reference counts, Algorithms 6.1, 6.2, and 6.3 are appropriate if there are no circular structures and relatively few assignments of pointer variables. In a special application with only a small variety of block sizes, storage management can be done with one free list per size or with one of the buddy methods like Algorithms 6.11 and 6.12. Even with a general purpose regime an application may choose to keep a list of unallocated blocks of some particular size; see, for example, Exercise 4 of Section 4.2.2.

A great many other storage management strategies have been proposed, and the reader is referred to the following for detailed discussions of implementations and simulation results:

Knuth, D. E., *The Art of Computer Programming*, Vol. 1, *Fundamental Algorithms*. Reading, Mass.: Addison-Wesley Publishing Co., 1st ed. 1968, 2nd ed. 1973.

Standish, T. A., *Data Structure Techniques*. Reading, Mass.: Addison-Wesley Publishing Co., Inc., 1980.

These books contain extensive bibliographies that the reader may find useful. Further references may be found in

Cohen, J., "Garbage Collection of linked data structures," *Comput. Surv. 13* (1981) 341–367.

Chapter 7

Searching

Thou preparest a table before me.

Psalms 23:5

This chapter examines various techniques for organizing data to be searched efficiently. Rather than introduce new storage structures, we will demonstrate the *use* of structures such as arrays, linked lists, and trees in the organization of tables to be searched. For a given problem, the particular choice of a storage structure depends on the nature of the storage medium (internal memory, magnetic tape, disk, or whatever), on the nature of the data being organized (does it change through insertions or deletions, is it alphabetic or numeric, are some elements more likely to occur as search objects than others, and so on), and on the requirements of the search (must it be as fast as possible on the average or in the worst case, how much information is available, and the like). We will present the most important table organizations and discuss their relative strengths and weaknesses.

Throughout this chapter we will assume that we are searching a *table of elements*, where each element has a collection of values associated with it, one value for each of a number of *attributes*. One of these attributes is special and will be called the *key* or *name* that is used to refer to the element. For example, the key might be a person's name and the other attributes might be the address, phone number, age, sex, salary, and so on. A *search* will consist of examining the table to find the element (or elements) containing some particular value for the key. For simplicity of presentation, our storage structures will consist *only* of the values of the key. If the structure is a record, other attributes can be imagined to be stored in additional fields; if the structure is an array, other attributes can be stored in parallel arrays (see Sections 1.3 and 4.1.1). The value of the key for which we are searching will be assumed to be in the variable z. We will code comparison and assignment as if keys and table entries were integers; in an application in which keys are actually strings, these operations would be implemented with loops. The result of each search routine will be either the location of z or the value 0 or **nil** to indicate z is not in the table. These assumptions are summarized in Declarations 7.1.

> **const**
> 　　　*TableSize* $=$ "size of table if it is an array";
> **type**
> 　　　*KeyType* $=$ "type of each key";
> 　　　*Table* $=$ **array** $[0..TableSize]$ **of** *KeyType*;
> 　　　*pList* $=$ $\uparrow$*List*;
> 　　　*List* $=$ **record**
> 　　　　　*Key*: *KeyType*;
> 　　　　　*Next*: *pList*
> 　　　**end**;
> **var**
> 　　　*z*: *KeyType*;　　　{the key we are seeking}
> 　　　*x*: *Table*;　　　　{search either in *Table*}
> 　　　*L*: *pList*;　　　　　　{or in *List*}
> 　　　*result*: *integer*;　{location of found key. 0 if not found}
> 　　　　　　　　　　　　{When searching in *L*, *result* is of type *pList* and has value **nil** if not found.}

Declarations 7.1

O **Notation.** In order to compare searching and sorting algorithms, we will need to analyze their behavior under various assumptions. Often, such an analysis is difficult or impossible to do precisely and we will need some notation (in this and the following chapter) that allows us to describe an analysis in terms of the *growth rate* of a function. We will write the equation $f(n) = O(g(n))$, read "$f(n)$ is big-oh of $g(n)$," to mean that $f(n)$ grows no faster than $g(n)$ as n gets large. Specifically, it means that as n gets bigger and bigger, the value of $|f(n)/g(n)|$ does not grow without bound. The similar notation $f(n) = o(g(n))$ ("little-oh") means that as n gets bigger and bigger, the value of $|f(n)/g(n)|$ gets closer and closer to zero; in other words, $f(n) = o(g(n))$ means that $f(n)$ grows strictly more slowly than $g(n)$.

The equation $f(n) = h(n) + O(g(n))$ is shorthand for $f(n) - h(n) = O(g(n))$ and, similarly, $f(n) = h(n) + o(g(n))$ is shorthand for $f(n) - h(n) = o(g(n))$. Thus, for example, when we state that the average number of "probes" into a table is $\lg(n + 1) + o(1)$, we are saying that the number of probes differs from $\lg(n + 1)$ by an amount that becomes vanishingly small as n gets big. When we state that the external path length of some trees is $E_n = (2 \ln 2)n \lg n + O(n)$, we are saying that E_n differs from $(2 \ln 2)n \lg n$ by an amount that grows no faster than n as n gets larger.

These notations, once they are mastered, give us a way to describe the dominant behavior of an algorithm without getting mired in minutiae.

7.1   SEARCHING LISTS

In many cases the simplest and most obvious storage structure for a table is a list data structure. The algorithms are short and there is little overhead in wasted space; there is *no* wasted space if an array of the proper size is used to implement the list. The simplicity is deceptive, however, since a number of subtleties need examination.

Given that we are going to organize a table as a linear list, we can vary only two things: the order of the elements in the list and the implementation as either sequential or linked. The elements may be in no particular order, in an order based on their frequencies as search objects, or in their natural order (alphabetic or numeric). The cases in which the elements are in no particular order or in an order based on their frequencies are similar, and we treat them together in Section 7.1.1. The case of a list in natural order is the subject of Section 7.1.2.

We will find the same trade-off as in Chapter 4 between sequential and linked lists: the ease with which we can directly access any element in a sequential list makes it an ideal structure under certain conditions, while under other conditions the ease of insertion and deletion makes a linked list more appropriate. Situations also occur in which both efficient access and ease of modification are needed simultaneously. Such situations cannot be properly handled by the techniques presented here, since they require a compromise between the two conflicting properties; techniques for these situations are discussed in Section 7.2.2.

7.1.1   Sequential-Search Techniques

The essence of sequential search is obvious: begin at the start of the list and examine each element in turn to see if it is the one sought. This process continues either until the element is found or until all the elements in the list have been checked. For a sequential list (array) $x_1, x_2, \ldots, x_n$ and a search object z this amounts to the loop given in Algorithm 7.1(a). When the list is linked rather than sequential and L points to its first element, we have the loop of Algorithm 7.1(b) instead. In either case the order of the elements in the list does not affect the correctness of these algorithms, only the amount of time they require.

In order to compare the performance of linear search under various orderings, we must establish some basis of comparison. The basis that we choose is the number of probes into the list: a *probe* is a comparison between the search object z and the key of some element of the table being searched. We will evaluate search strategies by the number of probes required to find an object, both in the worst case and on the average. The amount of work in searching for an element is not entirely in the

$i := 1;$
$result := 0;$
while $i \leqslant n$ **do**
      {Assert: z is not in $x[1..i-1]$}
      if $z = x[i]$ **then begin**
          $result := i;$
          $i := n + 1$ {stop the loop}
      end
      else $i := i + 1$

(a) Sequential-list search

$p := L;$
$result := $ **nil**;
while $p \neq $ **nil do**
      {Assert: If z is in L, it is in the list starting at p.}
      if $z = p\uparrow.KEY$ **then begin**
          $result := p;$
          $p := $ **nil**   {stop looping}
      end
      else $p := p\uparrow.NEXT$

(b) Linked-list search

Algorithm 7.1
Sequential search of a list for the element z

probes, of course, but the total work done is usually proportional to the number of probes, since only a constant number of operations are done per probe. Thus if one method requires n probes and another $\lg n$ probes, the constants of proportionality are not too important, since $\lg n$ grows so much more slowly than n. The constants of proportionality become important only when comparing methods with comparable numbers of probes, or when the constant is so large as to make a method impractical for table sizes occurring in practice. The number of probes will be our measure of efficiency, not only for the linear search algorithms of this section but throughout the chapter.

Let us examine Algorithm 7.1, the simple linear-search algorithm, from the perspective of the number of probes. In this case a probe is a comparison $z = x_i$ or $z = p\uparrow.KEY$. In the worst case each of the n elements in the table must be compared to the search object; thus n probes will be required for the worst-case search, no matter whether it ends successfully or unsuccessfully. In the best case a successful search will end after a single probe (this is true for all search strategies), but an unsuccessful search will still require n probes. To consider the behavior on an "average" search, we must have a precise notion of what an "average" instance of a search is. For example, on an unsuccessful search, n probes will always be required, so that the worst case, best case, and average behavior coincide—all are n probes. A successful search will end having found z in the table, and the average such search will depend on the probability that x_i is the search object. If $p_i = $ Pr $(z = x_i)$, that is, p_i is the probability that $z = x_i$, then the expected number of probes required is

$$1p_1 + 2p_2 + 3p_3 + \cdots + np_n \qquad (7.1)$$

since i probes are required to find z if it is x_i, an event which happens with probability p_i. We can summarize the behavior of linear search with the following table:

	Worst Case	Best Case	Average Case
Search Ends Successfully	n probes	1 probe	$\sum_{i=1}^{n} ip_i$ probes
Search Ends Unsuccessfully	n probes	n probes	n probes

Usually we are most concerned with the average behavior of a search strategy, and this means evaluating formula (7.1) for particular probabilities $p_1, p_2, \ldots, p_n$. In the absence of any other information we may as well assume that each x_i is equally likely to be the object of the search—that is, that $p_i = 1/n$ for all i, $1 \le i \le n$. Formula (7.1) becomes

$$1 \times \frac{1}{n} + 2 \times \frac{1}{n} + \cdots + n \times \frac{1}{n} = \frac{1}{n} \sum_{i=1}^{n} i = \frac{1}{n} \frac{n(n+1)}{2} = \frac{n+1}{2}$$

which tells us that an average successful search will use $(n + 1)/2$ probes—that is, it will examine about half the entries in the table.

From the table above it is clear that the only possibility for improving the linear-search strategy is to arrange the list so that the value of formula (7.1) is made small. The minimum value occurs when

$$p_1 \ge p_2 \ge \cdots \ge p_n$$

To understand why, suppose that $p_2 > p_1$. Then, $p_1 + 2p_2 > p_2 + 2p_1$ and the value of (7.1) is reduced if we interchange the elements x_1 and x_2 (and hence p_1 and p_2). Similarly, if any $p_i > p_j$, for $i > j$, then $ip_i + jp_j > ip_j + jp_i$ so the value of (7.1) is reduced by interchanging x_i and x_j. It follows that for (7.1) to be minimized there can be no $p_i > p_j$ for $i > j$. In other words, the best arrangement of the table elements is in nonincreasing order of their probabilities as search objects.

Changing the order of the elements can have an enormous effect on the number of probes in an average successful search. Consider, for example, $p_1 = \frac{1}{2}$, $p_2 = \frac{1}{4}$, $p_3 = \frac{1}{8}$, ..., $p_{n-1} = 1/2^{n-1}$, $p_n = 1/2^{n-1}$. If the elements are in decreasing order of probability, then the expected number of probes for a successful search is

$$\sum_{i=1}^{n} ip_i = \sum_{i=1}^{n-1} \frac{i}{2^i} + \frac{n}{2^{n-1}} = 2 - \frac{1}{2^{n-1}} < 2$$

If the elements are in increasing order of probability, this value becomes

$$\sum_{i=1}^{n} ip_{n+1-i} = \sum_{i=2}^{n} \frac{i}{2^{n+1-i}} + \frac{1}{2^{n-1}} = n - 1 + \frac{1}{2^{n-1}}$$

The difference is staggering; in the first case only a small constant number of probes are expected on a successful search, while in the second case the entire table generally needs to be examined. In practice, of course, such extreme probabilities are unlikely, but it is just as unlikely that the probabilities will be uniform (all equal to $1/n$). Thus it is worthwhile, when possible, to arrange in decreasing order of probability a table that will be searched sequentially. (Exercise 4 describes a generalization of this result that is applicable when searching tables stored on tape.)

Just as few tables are governed by uniform access probabilities, it is seldom possible to determine the access probabilities a priori. Even empirical observation may not give an accurate picture of the probabilities if they fluctuate in time. We can still take advantage of nonuniform access probabilities, however, by allowing the order of the elements in the table to change in such a way that those frequently accessed move to the front of the table while those infrequently accessed move toward the rear. Such a table is called *self-organizing*.

The basic idea is that when an element z is accessed, it is moved to a position closer to the beginning of the table. The amount of work to do this movement must be reasonable, and so the possibilities are limited. If the table is a sequential list, we can interchange z with its predecessor, the *move-ahead-one strategy*, or we can interchange z with the first element of the list, the *interchange-to-the-front strategy*. If the table is a linked list we can, in addition, simply move z to the front of the table, the *move-to-front strategy*. (This strategy is too time-consuming in sequential lists.)

The move-ahead-one strategy, applicable to either linked or sequential lists, works very well to keep the table well arranged if the table order is not too far from the desired order. However, it will take quite a while initially for the popular elements to move to the beginning of the list, since they move so slowly. On the other hand, the move-to-front strategy, applicable only to linked lists, works well to order the elements quickly when they are far out of order, but it causes erratic behavior in a table that is nearly in order. The interchange-to-the-front strategy is even worse in this regard. Thus it is most reasonable to apply the move-to-front strategy initially until the table order settles down a bit and continue thereafter with the move-ahead-one strategy.

Exercises

1. We can make Algorithm 7.1(a) a bit faster on unsuccessful searches by first adding z, the object of the search, at the end of the list and rewriting the loop:

   $x[n + 1] := z;$
   $i := 1;$
   while $z \neq x[i]$ **do**
   $\quad i := i + 1;$
   if $i \leq n$ **then** $result := i$ $\{z = x[i]\}$
   else $result := 0$ $\{z$ is not in table$\}$

   Compare the efficiency of this algorithm with that of Algorithm 7.1(a). Use the operator count analysis of Section 1.4.2.

2. Suppose the access probabilities for $x_1, x_2, \ldots, x_n$ are $p_i = c/i$, $1 \leq i \leq n$, where $c = 1/(\Sigma_{i=1}^{n} 1/i)$. Compare the behavior of sequential search when the table is in decreasing order by access probability to that when the table is in increasing order by access probability. [*Hint*: You may consider that $\Sigma_{i=1}^{n} 1/i \approx \ln n$.]

3. Design and analyze the behavior of a sequential-search algorithm on a circular linked list in which the search begins wherever it left off on the previous search [see Algorithm 6.6(b)].

4. Assume there is a cost c_i involved in examining an element x_i *after* the position of x_i has been found. Prove that for successful searches the minimum average total cost is achieved when the elements are arranged so that

$$\frac{p_1}{c_1} \geq \frac{p_2}{c_2} \geq \cdots \geq \frac{p_n}{c_n}$$

5. Perform simulations to determine the behavior of the various strategies for self-organizing lists.

7.1.2   Lists in Natural Order

In many instances it is possible to maintain the list in some natural order (such as numeric or alphabetic) and it is almost always advantageous to do so. Algorithm 7.1 can be speeded up somewhat for *unsuccessful* searches because it can now stop when it discovers the first element beyond z in the natural order, rather than go all the way to the end of the list. The algorithm becomes somewhat simpler, too, if we append an element with the key value ∞ at the end of the list (compare this with Exercise 1 of Section 7.1.1). Algorithm 7.2 gives this modified version of Algorithm 7.1. The behavior of Algorithm 7.2 is no different from that of Algorithm 7.1 with respect to *successful* searches.

> $i := 1$;
> **while** $z > x[i]$ **do**
>> {Assert: z is not in $x[1..i]$}
>> $i := i + 1$;
> **if** $z = x[i]$ **then** *result* $:= i$
> **else**
>> {z not found, but would have been just before $x[i]$}
>> *result* $:= 0$

(a) Sequential-list search in an ordered list

> $p := L$;
> **while** $z > p\uparrow.KEY$ **do**
>> {Assert: If z is in L, it must be in list starting at $p\uparrow.NEXT$.}
>> $p := p\uparrow.NEXT$;
> **if** $z = p\uparrow.KEY$ **then** *result* $:= p$
> **else**
>> {z not found,
>> but would have been just before the element pointed to by p}
>> *result* $:=$ **nil**

(b) Linked-list search in an ordered list

Algorithm 7.2
Sequential search of an ordered list for the element z. *The list is assumed to contain a dummy final element whose value is* ∞. If implemented as functions, these routines would return *result* as their value and set a **var** parameter to indicate the proper location for z in the table.

The improvement for unsuccessful search times in tables in the natural order is minor in contrast to the fact that a single probe into the table can now get a good deal more information than when the table is in some other order. If we find that $z > x_i$, then z cannot be one of $x_1, x_2, \ldots, x_i$, or if we find that $z < x_i$, then z cannot be one of $x_i, x_{i+1}, \ldots, x_n$. This observation is behind the binary search procedure, Algorithm 1.3, discussed in Sections 1.3.1 and 5.3. For convenience we repeat binary search here as Algorithm 7.3 and summarize the results of Section 5.3 with the following table:

	Worst Case	Best Case	Average Case
Search Ends Successfully	$\lceil \lg(n+1) \rceil$ probes	1 probe	$\left(1 + \dfrac{1}{n}\right)\lg(n+1) + o(1)$ probes
Search Ends Unsuccessfully	$\lceil \lg(n+1) \rceil$ probes	$\lfloor \lg(n+1) \rfloor$ probes	$\lg(n+1) + o(1)$ probes

Recall that binary search requires the direct access to all parts of the list that sequential representation allows, but linked representation does not. This means that Algorithm 7.3 cannot be adapted to linked lists and so it may not be applicable in certain circumstances. For example, when the order of the list is important, it is easy to allow insertions and deletions if the table is implemented as a linked list; in the case of a sequential list, as required by binary search, the insertion or deletion of an element is a time-consuming operation. This is only the first instance in this chapter of the conflict between fast search times and ease of modification—this conflict is ubiquitous in designing search algorithms.

```
function BinarySearch(x: Table; n: integer; z: KeyType): integer;
var
    l, h: integer;          {low and high bounds or region}
    m: integer;             {midpoint of the region}
    found: boolean;
begin
    l := 1;                 {initial region is x[1..n]}
    h := n;
    found := false;
    while (l ≤ h) and not found do begin
        {Assert: 1 ≤ l ≤ h ≤ n
                and z is not in either x[1..l−1] or x[h+1..n]}
        m := (l + h) div 2;
        if      z < x[m] then   h := m − 1
        else if z > x[m] then   l := m + 1
        else                    found := true

    end;
    if found then BinarySearch := m
    else
        {here l = h + 1 and x[h] < z < x[h + 1]}
        BinarySearch := 0
end
```

Algorithm 7.3
Binary search

Recall also that the values given for the number of probes in the average successful and unsuccessful searches were based on the assumption that for successful searches each of the n elements was equally probable as the place for the search to end. As we mentioned in discussing the average behavior of sequential search, this assumption is rarely justified in practice but is the only reasonable one in the absence of any information. When the access probabilities are known, it is possible to use the analogs of binary search discussed in Section 7.2.1.

So far we have considered only the frequency with which various elements will be the object of a search or the frequency with which the search will fail in a specified way. There are, however, other useful statistical properties that the table elements often have in practice. For example, in looking up the name "Smith" in a phone book we would be unlikely to probe first at the half point and then at the three-quarters point, and so on, as in binary search. Instead, we would assume that under normal conditions the name "Smith" would be found near the end of the listings, and we would begin our search nearer to the expected location of the search object. This idea leads to *interpolation search*.

For simplicity let us assume that we are dealing with numeric values $x_1 < x_2 < \cdots < x_n$ that are uniformly distributed in the range (x_0, x_{n+1}); extensions to nonnumeric keys and nonuniform distributions are not difficult (see Exercise 13, for example). If we are searching such a table for z, where $x_0 < z < x_{n+1}$, the uniform distribution suggests that we interpolate linearly to determine the expected location of z. That expected location is $n(z - x_0)/(x_{n+1} - x_0)$, and this is where we should probe first. In general, assume we know that $x_l < z < x_h$; then we should probe at location

$$l + \frac{z - x_l}{x_h - x_l} (h - l - 1)$$

Following a style similar to binary search, Algorithm 7.4 implements interpolation search. Notice, however, that it is more convenient to begin at $l = 0$ and $h = n + 1$ and have the condition for continuing the loop be $h - l > 1$; this happens because the range under consideration, x_l to x_h, is now exclusive of the endpoints, while in binary search it was inclusive of the endpoints.

The number of probes in the best and worst cases of interpolation search is obvious, and the analysis of the average number involves mathematics that is well beyond the level of this book, so we will simply summarize the results in the following table:

	Worst Case	Best Case	Average Case
Search Ends Successfully	n probes	1 probe	lg lg n probes
Search Ends Unsuccessfully	n probes	2 probes	lg lg n probes

```
function InterpolationSearch(x: Table; n: integer; z: KeyType): integer;
var
     l, h, m: integer;
     found: boolean;
begin
     l := 0
     h := n + 1;
     found := false;
     while (h − l > 1) and not found do begin
          {Assert: l < h − 1 and z is not in x[1..l] or x[h..n]}
          m := ceiling(l + (h − l + 1)*(z − x[l])/(x[h] − x[l]));
          if      z < x[m] then h := m
          else if z > x[m] then l := m
          else                  found := true

     end;
     if found then InterpolationSearch := m
     else   {here h = l + 1 and x[l] < z < x[l + 1]}
          InterpolationSearch := 0
end
```

Algorithm 7.4
Interpolation search for z, $x_0 < z < x_{n+1}$ in a table $x_1 < x_2 < \cdots < x_n$ of elements
uniformly distributed over (x_0, x_{n+1})

It is crucial to understand that the average behavior of interpolation search is a much
different "average" than was considered for either sequential search or binary search.
In those cases the table of elements was fixed and the average was over the occurrences of the various elements as search objects; in this case the average is over
search objects *and* tables whose elements follow a certain statistical pattern. This
means that if a particular table does not follow that pattern, the average search in
that table may be much poorer than expected.

Simulation results suggest that interpolation search is inferior to binary search
unless the tables are much larger than most tables that occur in practice in internal
memory. The difficulty stems from the greatly increased cost per probe in interpolation search as compared to binary search, where a probe can be made in only a few
machine instructions. Thus, for example, in a table of 4000 elements binary search
will need twelve probes and interpolation search an average of four probes, but since
each of the latter probes is at least four times as costly, there will be no savings (in
fact, interpolation search will be *slower* than binary search on such small tables).
However, for larger tables, the fact that lglg$n$ grows so much more slowly than
lg$n$ will outweigh the increased cost per probe, making interpolation search worthwhile, at least for the first few probes.

Exercises

1. Under whatever probabilistic assumptions you deem reasonable, analyze the average unsuccessful search time for Algorithm 7.2

2. Not all of the results in the table summarizing the performance of binary search were derived in Section 5.3. Derive the number of probes in the best case for both successful and unsuccessful searches and the worst case for successful searches.

3. What happens if we change the statement $m := (l + h)$ **div** 2 to $m := l$ in Algorithm 7.3? What about $m := h$?

4. In first attempts at writing a binary search routine, novice programmers often use $h := m$ and $l := m$ instead of $h := m-1$ and $l := m+1$, respectively. What kind of error does this cause in Algorithm 7.3? Modify the rest of the Algorithm so it works correctly with $h := m$ and $l := m$.

5. Give a proof that Algorithm 7.3 works correctly for both successful and unsuccessful searches.

6. Rewrite Algorithm 7.3 so that instead of three pointers, l, h, and m, only two values are kept—the current position m and its rate of change *delta*. After an unequal comparison the algorithm should increment or decrement m by *delta* and set *delta* := *delta* **div** 2. Analyze this search algorithm.

★7. Analyze the behavior of Algorithm 7.3 with the statement $m := (l + h)$ **div** 2 changed to $m := rand(l,h)$ where $rand(l,h)$ is a randomly chosen integer, $l \le rand(l,h) \le h$.

8. Algorithm 7.3 requires a division by 2 at each iteration to evaluate $(l + h)$ **div** 2. Use the relation $F_h = F_{h-1} + F_{h-2}$, $F_0 = 0$, $F_1 = 1$ to replace the division by 2 by a subtraction. Analyze the worst- and average-case behavior of the resulting search algorithm. [*Hint*: The search effectively bisects the interval at the $(\sqrt{5} - 1)/2$ point rather than in the middle.]

9. Under what conditions will binary search be less efficient than sequential search, considering the *total search time*, not just the number of probes? (See Exercise 13 of Section 1.4.3.)

10. Let $x[1..n]$ be an array of integers in increasing order. Give an algorithm that requires only time proportional to log n time to determine if any $x[i] = i$, finding such an i if one exists. Can it be done in less than a logarithmic number of probes?

11. Design a search technique requiring at most 2 lg n probes in the worst case and 2 lg lg n probes on the average. [*Hint*: Use a hybrid of binary search and interpolation search.] When might such a technique be useful?

12. Analyze the average-, worst-, and best-case behavior of the following variant of interpolation search. The first probe is at $x_{[pn]}$, $p = (z - x_0)/(x_{n+1} - x_0)$. If $z > x_{[pn]}$, then z is successively compared with $x_{[pn+i\sqrt{n}]}$, $i = 1, 2, \ldots$. Similarly, if $z < x_{[pn]}$, z is successively compared with $x_{[pn-i\sqrt{n}]}$, $i = 1, 2, \ldots$. In any case, the subtable of size $\sqrt{n}$ thus found is then searched by applying the same technique recursively.

★13. Modify Algorithm 7.4 so that it interpolates correctly for any probability distribution over the table elements, subject to the restriction that the cumulative distribution function $F(x) = \Pr(X \leq x)$ is continuous. [*Hint*: The distribution of $F(x)$ is uniform over $(0, 1)$ and F is order preserving.]

14. Suppose values in an ordered array A are known to lie in the range $[a,b]$. We can reduce the cost of searching for z in A with an auxiliary array $L[0..m+1]$ having entries chosen so that z is in $A[L[z \text{ div } m]..L[1 + (z \text{ div } m)]]$. (By making m a power of two the **div** operations can be done with *shift_left*.) Develop an algorithm based on this trick. Show how it can be applied to the address mapping problem in Exercise 4, Section 6.2.2.

7.2 BINARY SEARCH TREES

As we saw in Section 5.3, the order in which the elements are examined by binary search is governed by an implicit binary tree on the table elements (see Figure 5.27, for an example). Similarly, we could view linear search on a table in natural order and interpolation search in terms of a binary tree. For linear search the implicit tree is as shown in Figure 7.1, and for interpolation search the tree varies with the search argument—$x_{\lceil pn \rceil}$ is the root, $p = (z - x_0)/(x_{n-1} - x_0)$, and so on. In this section we will discuss the benefits of making such a binary tree structure explicit instead of

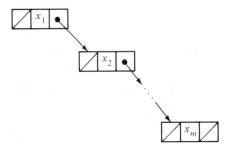

Figure 7.1
The implicit tree corresponding to linear search

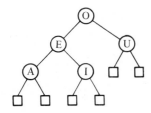

Figure 7.2
A binary search tree: the inorder traversal gives the elements in the natural order

implicit. Those benefits are twofold. For tables in which the elements do not change through insertions and deletions (*static tables*), an explicit tree structure can be used to take advantage of a known distribution of the frequency of access of the elements. For *dynamic tables* that change through insertions and deletions, an explicit tree structure gives us the flexibility to search the table in logarithmic time and to make insertions and deletions also in logarithmic time.

A *binary search tree* is a binary tree in which the inorder traversal of the nodes gives the elements stored therein in the natural order. In other words, every node p in the tree has the property that elements in its left subtree are before $p\uparrow.KEY$ in the natural order and those in its right subtree are after $p\uparrow.KEY$ in the natural order. For descriptive purposes we will consider a binary search tree to be an extended binary tree (see Figure 5.28), that is, a tree with explicit nodes for empty subtrees. In practice, these nodes are not implemented; the pointers to them are simply **nil**. Figure 7.2 shows a binary search tree for the set of keys {A, E, I, O, U}.

The structure of the binary search tree makes it easy to search for an element z. We compare z to the root; if it is equal, the search ends successfully, and if it is not, we search the left or right subtree according to whether z is less than or greater than the root, respectively. Algorithm 7.5 gives this procedure explicitly, using the types shown in Declarations 7.2. Observe that unsuccessful searches terminate at external nodes of the extended tree. Also, notice the similarity between this algorithm and binary search.

```
type
    pTree = ↑Tree;
    Tree = record
        KEY: KeyType;
        LEFT, RIGHT: pTree
    end;
```

Declarations 7.2

```
function BinarySearchTree (T: pTree; z: KeyType): pTree;
var
        p: pTree;
        found: boolean;
begin
        p := T;   {start with the root of the tree}
        found := false;
        while (p ≠ nil) and not found do
                {Assert: If z is in T, it is in the subtree rooted at p.}
                if      z < p↑.KEY then p := p↑.LEFT
                else if z > p↑.KEY then p := p↑.RIGHT
                else                        found := true;
        BinarySearchTree := p   {p will be nil if z is not in the tree}
end
```

Algorithm 7.5
Searching a binary search tree T for the element z

In sections 7.2.1 and 7.2.2 we will examine the two aspects of binary search trees—their application to static tables and to dynamic tables.

Exercises

1. How would we produce a list of the elements of a binary search tree in their natural order?

2. Does Algorithm 7.5 work if T is an empty tree?

★3. Given n elements, how many possible different binary search trees are there?

4. Suppose $x_1 < x_2 < \cdots < x_n$ are formed into a binary search tree and x_i, for some $i \geq 2$, has $x_i↑.LEFT = $ **nil**. Prove that a search for x_i by Algorithm 7.5 will make a probe at x_{i-1}.

5. Suppose $x_1 < x_2 < \cdots < x_n$ are formed into a binary search tree. Prove that a search for z, $x_i < z < x_{i+1}$, by Algorithm 7.5 will make probes at both x_i and x_{i+1}.

6. Given a binary search tree T and a new element x not in the tree, how many possible ways are there to insert x into the tree so that it remains a binary search tree? Consider two cases: (a) x must be inserted at a leaf, and (b) x can be inserted anywhere. In case (b), consider only those insertions that can be accomplished by changing a single pointer in the tree (along with the two pointers in the new node).

7.2.1 Static Trees

The application of binary search trees to static tables is concerned entirely with arranging the tree so as to minimize search time; we assume that the table is constructed once and that its contents will never change or will change so infrequently that it will be possible to reconstruct the entire table to make the change. If we want to minimize the worst-case search time, we simply use the tree corresponding to binary search (why?), and we do not need an explicit tree at all. The more difficult problem is to minimize the average search time, given some distribution of how the search will end. If the table consists of elements $x_1 < x_2 < \cdots < x_n$, then the search can end successfully at any of the x_i (internal nodes) and unsuccessfully in any of the $n + 1$ gaps between the x_i and at the endpoints (external nodes y_i). Throughout this section we assume that we have values $\beta_1, \beta_2, \ldots, \beta_n$ and $\alpha_0, \alpha_1, \ldots, \alpha_n$, where β_i is the relative frequency with which a search will end successfully at x_i and α_i is the relative frequency with which the search for z will end unsuccessfully at y_i, that is, with $x_i < z < x_{i+1}$ (defining $x_0 = -\infty$ and $x_{n+1} = \infty$). As a continuing example, we will use the vowels A, E, I, O, U as table elements with their frequencies of occurrence in English text as the β_i and the frequencies of occurrence of the intervening letters as the α_i. These frequencies are shown in Figure 7.3. Notice that the α_i and β_i are *not* probabilities; to compute the equivalent probabilities it is necessary to divide each α_i and β_i by the sum $\alpha_0 + \beta_1 + \alpha_1 + \cdots + \beta_n + \alpha_n$.

A	E	I	O	U
$\beta_1 = 32$	$\beta_2 = 42$	$\beta_3 = 26$	$\beta_4 = 32$	$\beta_5 = 12$
$\alpha_0 = 0$	$\alpha_1 = 34$	$\alpha_2 = 38$	$\alpha_3 = 58$	$\alpha_4 = 95$	$\alpha_5 = 21$

Figure 7.3
A sample set of frequencies. The β_i are the approximate frequencies of occurrence of vowels in English text and the α_i are the approximate frequencies of occurrence for the intervening letters.

The problem is to choose among the many possible binary trees with n internal nodes for a particular set of values α_i and β_i. We will measure the desirability of a tree by the cost of an average search; as before, the cost will be the number of probes. In Section 5.3 we introduced such a measure, the internal path length (or the related external path length). That measure is not sufficient for our purpose here because it does not take the varying frequencies into account. However, we can generalize the notion of path length as follows: the *weighted path length* of a binary tree T with internal nodes $x_1, x_2, \ldots, x_n$, external nodes $y_0, y_1, \ldots, y_n$, and α_i and β_i as defined above is

$$\sum_{i=1}^{n} \beta_i \, [1 + \text{level}(x_i)] + \sum_{i=0}^{n} \alpha_i \, \text{level}(y_i) \tag{7.2}$$

Notice that this is $\Sigma \alpha_i + \Sigma \beta_i$ times the average search time, since the search ends successfully at internal node x_i with frequency β_i and a cost of $[1 + \text{level}(x_i)]$ probes and unsuccessfully at external node y_i with frequency α_i and a cost of $\text{level}(y_i)$ probes. As in the cases of the external and internal path lengths, it is convenient to define the weighted path length recursively.

$$W(\square) = 0$$

$$W(T = \;\overset{}{\underset{T_l}{\triangle}}\;\overset{}{\underset{T_r}{\triangle}}\;) = W(T_l) + W(T_r) + \Sigma \alpha_i + \Sigma \beta_i \qquad (7.3)$$

where the summations $\Sigma \alpha_i$ and $\Sigma \beta_i$ are over all α_i and β_i in T. (Exercise 1 is to prove that these two definitions of weighted path length are equivalent.)

Let us consider the tree of Figure 7.2 as an example. Figure 7.4 shows the same tree, but with the corresponding frequencies from Figure 7.3 given below each node. The weighted path length of this tree is computed as follows:

$$\sum_{i=1}^{n} \beta_i [1 + \text{level}(x_i)] = 32 \times 3 + 42 \times 2 + 26 \times 3 + 32 \times 1 + 12 \times 2$$

$$= 314$$

and

$$\sum_{i=0}^{n} \alpha_i \, \text{level}(y_i) = 0 \times 3 + 34 \times 3 + 38 \times 3 + 58 \times 3 + 95 \times 2 + 21 \times 2$$

$$= 622$$

The weighted path length is thus $314 + 622 = 936$. If we divide this by $\Sigma \alpha_i +$

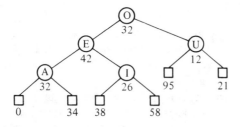

Figure 7.4
A weighted version of the binary search tree of Figure 7.2 using the weights from Figure 7.3. The weighted path length is 936 and the number of probes on an average search is $936/390 = 2.4$. It turns out that this tree is optimal for the given weights.

$\Sigma \beta_i = 390$, we find that the number of probes in the table on an average search will be $936/390 = 2.4$.

Our problem is to determine a binary search tree that has an optimal (minimal) weighted path length, given the frequencies α_i and β_i. Since the number of possible trees is *exponentially* large as a function of n (Exercise 3 of Section 7.2), we cannot do the obvious of examining all possibilities, computing the weighted path length of each, and choosing the smallest. In fact, the large number of possibilities makes it seem doubtful that there is any reasonable way to make the determination. However, a simple but crucial observation about the nature of the weighted path length of a tree will show us the way to proceed.

The observation is that subtrees of an optimal tree must themselves be optimal. More precisely, if T is an optimal binary search tree on weights α_0, β_1, α_1, ..., β_n, α_n and it has weight β_i at the root, then the left subtree must be optimal over weights α_0, β_1, α_1 ..., β_{i-1}, α_{i-1} and the right subtree must be optimal over weights α_i, β_{i+1}, α_{i+1}, ..., β_n, α_n. To see why this *optimality principle* must hold, suppose that some tree over α_0, β_1, α_1, ..., β_{i-1}, α_{i-1} had lower weighted path length than the one that is the left subtree of T. Then by (7.3) we could get a tree T' with lower weighted path length than T by replacing the left subtree of T by the one of lower weighted path length we have supposed to exist. This contradicts the assumed optimality of T. We can argue similarly about the right subtree of T, and in fact *any* subtree of T. This optimality principle is the basis of a technique called *dynamic programming*, which we will use to compute optimal binary search trees and which in general is an extremely powerful technique in combinatorial algorithms.

The optimality principle together with (7.3) allows us to write the following recursive description of optimal binary search trees: Let C_{ij}, $0 \leq i \leq j \leq n$, be the cost of an optimal tree (although the minimum cost is unique, it may be achieved by more than one tree) over the frequencies α_i, β_{i+1}, ..., β_j, α_j. Then

$$C_{ii} = 0$$

and

$$C_{ij} = \min_{i < k \leq j} (C_{i,k-1} + C_{kj}) + \sum_{t=i}^{j} \alpha_t + \sum_{t=i+1}^{j} \beta_t$$

by (7.3), since the optimality principle guarantees that if x_k is the root of the optimal tree, then $C_{i,k-1}$ and C_{kj} are the costs of the left and right subtrees, respectively. Defining

$$\begin{aligned} W_{ii} &= \alpha_i \\ W_{i,j} &= W_{i,j-1} + \beta_j + \alpha_j, \ i < j \end{aligned} \tag{7.4}$$

so that $W_{ij} = \alpha_i + \beta_{i+1} + \cdots + \beta_j + \alpha_j$, we get

$$C_{ii} = 0,$$
$$C_{ij} = W_{ij} + \min_{i < k \leqslant j} (C_{i,k-1} + C_{kj}) \qquad (7.5)$$

Equations (7.4) and (7.5) form the basis of our computation of the optimal search tree; in evaluating (7.5) to get C_{0n}, the cost of the optimal tree over $\alpha_0, \beta_1, \ldots, \beta_n,$ α_n, we need only keep track of the choices of k that achieve the minimum in (7.5). We thus define

$$R_{ij} = \text{a value of } k \text{ that minimizes } C_{i,k-1} + C_{kj} \text{ in (7.5)} \qquad (7.6)$$

R_{ij} is the root of an optimal tree over $\alpha_i, \beta_{i+1}, \ldots, \beta_j, \alpha_j$.

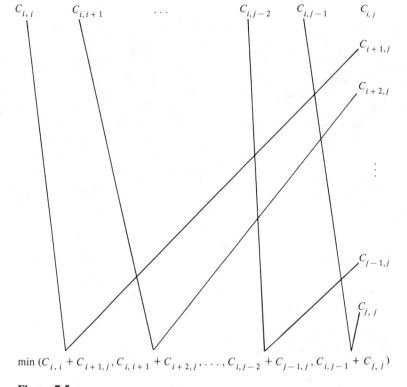

$$\min (C_{i,i} + C_{i+1,j}, C_{i,i+1} + C_{i+2,j}, \ldots, C_{i,j-2} + C_{j-1,j}, C_{i,j-1} + C_{j,j})$$

Figure 7.5
The "flow" of data in the computation of C_{ij} from Equation (7.5). The expression at the bottom is used in computing C_{ij} for the upper right corner. Note that all entries in the matrix are above the main diagonal and below the diagonal containing C_{ij}.

We are left with the problem of organizing the computation from (7.4), (7.5), and (7.6). Of course, we could simply make (7.4) and (7.5) into recursive procedures as they stand, but that would lead to an exponential time algorithm because many computations would be repeated over and over. For example, the computation of $C_{1,3}$, the optimal subtree over $\alpha_1, \beta_2, \alpha_2, \beta_3, \alpha_3$ of Figure 7.3, would be done in the computation of $C_{0,3}$ and $C_{1,4}$; in larger examples the number of repeated computations becomes staggering. The obvious way to avoid this difficulty is to insure that each C_{ij} is computed only once. We do this by observing that the value of C_{ij} in (7.5) depends only on values below and/or to the left of C_{ij} in an $(n + 1) \times (n + 1)$ matrix, as illustrated in Figure 7.5. We thus compute the matrix C (and, in parallel, W and R) starting from the main diagonal and moving up one diagonal at a time. First, $C_{ii} = 0, 0 \le i \le n$ by (7.5). Then we compute $C_{i,i+1}, 0 \le i \le n - 1$, then $C_{i,i+2}, 0 \le i \le n - 2$, and so on. Algorithm 7.6 embodies this idea.

An example of the computations of Algorithm 7.6 is shown in Figure 7.6. The frequencies used are those given for sample problem of Figure 7.3. To recover the

	0	1	2	3	4	5
0	$R_{00} = 0$ $W_{00} = 0$ $C_{00} = 0$	$R_{01} = 1$ $W_{01} = 66$ $C_{01} = 66$	$R_{02} = 2$ $W_{02} = 146$ $C_{02} = 212$	$R_{03} = 2$ $W_{03} = 230$ $C_{03} = 418$	$R_{04} = 3$ $W_{04} = 357$ $C_{04} = 754$	$R_{05} = 4$ $W_{05} = 390$ $C_{05} = 936$
1		$R_{11} = 1$ $W_{11} = 34$ $C_{11} = 0$	$R_{12} = 2$ $W_{12} = 114$ $C_{12} = 114$	$R_{13} = 3$ $W_{13} = 198$ $C_{13} = 312$	$R_{14} = 3$ $W_{14} = 325$ $C_{14} = 624$	$R_{15} = 4$ $W_{15} = 358$ $C_{15} = 798$
2			$R_{22} = 2$ $W_{22} = 38$ $C_{22} = 0$	$R_{23} = 3$ $W_{23} = 122$ $C_{23} = 122$	$R_{24} = 4$ $W_{24} = 249$ $C_{24} = 371$	$R_{25} = 4$ $W_{25} = 282$ $C_{25} = 532$
3				$R_{33} = 3$ $W_{33} = 58$ $C_{33} = 0$	$R_{34} = 4$ $W_{34} = 185$ $C_{34} = 185$	$R_{35} = 4$ $W_{35} = 218$ $C_{35} = 346$
4					$R_{44} = 4$ $W_{44} = 95$ $C_{44} = 0$	$R_{45} = 5$ $W_{45} = 128$ $C_{45} = 128$
5						$R_{55} = 5$ $W_{55} = 21$ $C_{55} = 0$

Figure 7.6
The computation of Algorithm 7.6 to obtain the optimal binary search tree for the sample problem of Figure 7.3. The tree obtained is that shown in Figure 7.4.

tree from the data in Figure 7.6, we look at the $(0, 5)$ matrix entry and see that $R_{0,5} = 4$; this tells us that x_4, corresponding to O, is the root of the tree. The left and right subtrees are found similarly, looking at the $(0, 3)$ and $(4, 5)$ matrix entries, respectively. The optimal tree thus computed turns out to be the one shown in Figure

```
procedure OptimalBST(alpha, beta: FrequencyArray; var R: SubscriptMatrix);
var
      i, j, k, d, opt: integer;
      C, W: CostMatrix;
begin
      {Initialize the main diagonal}
      for i := 0 to n do begin
            R[i, i] := i;
            W[i, i] := alpha[i];
            C[i, i] := 0.0
      end;
      {visit each of the n upper diagonals}
      for d := 1 to n do
            {visit each entry in the dth diagonal}
            for i := 0 to n − d do begin
                  {Assert: R[u,v], C[u,v], and W[u,v] are complete for cells
                  with v − u < d and for those having v − u = d where u < i.}
                  j := i + d;  {for dth diagonal, j − i = d}
                  opt := i + 1;
                  for k := i + 2 to j do
                        if C[i, k − 1] + C[k, j] < C[i, opt − 1] + C[opt, j]
                              then opt := k;
                  {Assert: opt is a value of k, i < k ≤ j minimizing
                              C[i, k − 1] + C[k, j]}
                  {compute [i, j] entries}
                  R[i, j] := opt;
                  W[i, j] := W[i, j − 1] + beta[j] + alpha[j];
                  C[i, j] := C[i, opt − 1] + C[opt, j] + W[i, j]
            end
end
```

Algorithm 7.6
Construction of an optimal binary search tree over the frequencies $\alpha_0, \beta_1, \alpha_1, \ldots, \beta_n, \alpha_n$
  $R[i, j]$: index of the root of the optimal tree over $\alpha_i, \beta_{i+1}, \ldots, \beta_j, \alpha_j$
  $W[i, j]$: $\alpha_i + \beta_{i+1} + \cdots + \beta_j + \alpha_j$
  $C[i, j]$: cost of an optimal tree over $\alpha_i, \beta_{i-1}, \ldots, \beta_j, \alpha_j$

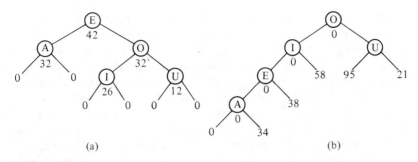

Figure 7.7
Optimal binary search trees for the frequencies in the example of Figure 7.3 with
(a) successful searches only and (b) unsuccessful searches only. For (a) the average number of probes is 284/144 ≈ 1.97 and for (b) 598/246 ≈ 2.43.

7.4. Figure 7.7 shows optimal trees constructed for the frequencies of the example
in Figure 7.3 with successful searches only [Figure 7.7(a)] and unsuccessful searches
only [Figure 7.7(b)]; notice that the shape of the optimal tree is different in each
case, and each is different from the optimal tree of Figure 7.4.

The running time of Algorithm 7.6 will be roughly proportional to the number
of comparisons $C[i, k - 1] + C[k, j] < C[i, opt - 1] + C[opt, j]$ made in the
innermost loop. That **if** statement is executed

$$\sum_{d=1}^{n} \sum_{i=0}^{n-d} \sum_{k=i+2}^{i+d} 1 = \sum_{d=1}^{n} \sum_{i=0}^{n-d} (d - 1)$$

$$= \sum_{d=1}^{n} (n - d + 1)(d - 1)$$

$$= n^3/6 + O(n^2) \tag{7.7}$$

times. Algorithm 7.6 thus runs in time proportional to n^3—not very acceptable in
constructing search trees of several thousand elements.

Algorithm 7.6 can be speeded up considerably by an important observation:
there is an optimal tree over $\alpha_i, \beta_{i+1}, \ldots, \beta_j, \alpha_j$ whose root R_{ij} satisfies $R_{i, j-1} \leq$
$R_{ij} \leq R_{i+1, j}$, where $R_{i,j-1}$ and $R_{i+1,j}$ are roots of optimal trees over $\alpha_i, \beta_{i+1}, \ldots,$
$\beta_{j-1}, \alpha_{j-1}$, and $\alpha_{j+1} \beta_{i+2}, \ldots, \beta_j, \alpha_j$, respectively (see Exercise 7). Based on
this observation we can replace the statement $opt := i+1$ by $opt := R[i, j - 1]$
and the innermost loop **for** $k := i+2$ **to** j by **for** $k := opt+1$ **to**
$R[i + 1, j]$. Equation (7.7) now becomes

$$\sum_{d=1}^{n} \sum_{i=0}^{n-d} \sum_{k=R_{i,j-1}}^{R_{i+1,j}} 1 \tag{7.8}$$

which, after some calculation (Exercise 8), is at most proportional to n^2. In other words, the modified Algorithm 7.6 runs in time proportional to n^2.

Even the improved version of Algorithm 7.6, however, may not be efficient enough in certain circumstances. If n is several thousand, it may be quite expensive to construct the optimal tree; furthermore, the frequencies α_i and β_i are rarely known with any accuracy and it would be foolish to invest much computation time to get an optimal tree from inaccurate frequencies. In such cases a tree that approximates the optimal tree may be satisfactory and will certainly be less expensive to construct. We now examine heuristics for the construction of "near-optimal" binary search trees.

Given frequencies α_i and β_i, two heuristics immediately suggest themselves; we discuss them in turn. The *monotonic* rule constructs a binary search tree by choosing the root to be x_i, where β_i is the largest β value, and then proceeding recursively on the left and right subtrees. Figure 7.8 shows the tree resulting when the monotonic rule is applied to the sample problem of Figure 7.3. This tree costs more than the optimal tree, but perhaps this is because the large α_i ends up too far from the top of the tree; in fact, the optimal tree when all $\alpha_i = 0$ [Figure 7.7(a)] is exactly the tree of Figure 7.8. This suggests that perhaps the monotonic rule may work very well in the special case of only successful searches occurring. Unfortunately, that is not the case: the monotonic rule produces poor trees in general, even when all the $\alpha_i = 0$: *on the average a tree constructed according to the monotonic rule is no better than a tree constructed at random!* (See Exercises 9 and 10.)

The second heuristic is the *balancing rule*: choose the root so as to equalize (as much as possible) the sum of the frequencies in the left and right subtrees, breaking ties arbitrarily. Figure 7.9 shows the tree constructed by the balancing rule for the example of Figure 7.3. The cost of the resulting tree is almost exactly that of the optimal tree; is this coincidental? No, the cost of the tree resulting from the balancing rule is always extremely close to the cost of the optimal tree. In particular, suppose the frequencies are normalized so that $\Sigma\alpha_i + \Sigma\beta_i = 1$ and let*

$$H = \sum_{i=0}^{n} \alpha_i \lg \frac{1}{\alpha_i} + \sum_{i=1}^{n} \beta_i \lg \frac{1}{\beta_i}$$

H is called the entropy of the frequency distribution. Then it can be shown that

$H - \lg H - \lg e + 1$
        $\leq$ weighted path length of the optimal tree
        $\leq$ weighted path length of the tree derived by the balancing rule
        $\leq H + 2$.

Since the maximum value of H is $\lg(2n+1)$, which occurs for $\alpha_j = \beta_i = 1/(2n+1)$, the balancing rule always comes within $\lg H + 2.443 \approx \lg \lg (2n+1) + 2.443$ of giving the optimal weighted path length. (See also Exercises 11 and 12.)

---

*$0 \lg \dfrac{1}{0}$ is taken as 0, since $\lim\limits_{x \to 0} -x \lg x = 0$.

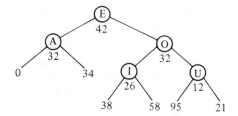

Figure 7.8
The tree constructed by the monotonic rule for the example in Figure 7.3. The weighted path length is 988, so the expected number of probes is 988/390 ≈ 2.53.

That the balancing rule does so well is even more remarkable since it can be implemented in time proportional to n, the number of elements in the table! We want to choose the root to equalize as much as possible the total frequencies of the left and right subtrees. In other words, we need to find an i such that $|(\alpha_0 + \beta_1 + \cdots + \beta_{i-1} + \alpha_{i-1}) - (\alpha_i + \beta_{i+1} + \cdots + \beta_n + \alpha_n)|$ is minimized, and we must repeat the computation recursively for $\alpha_0, \beta_1, \ldots, \beta_{i-1}, \alpha_{i-1}$ and $\alpha_i, \beta_{i+1}, \ldots, \beta_n, \alpha_n$ to find the left and right subtrees, respectively. The computation is organized as follows. We first compute the W_{0i} of Algorithm 7.6

$$W_{0i} = \alpha_0 + \beta_1 + \cdots + \beta_i + \alpha_i, \qquad 0 \leqslant i \leqslant n$$

by the recurrence relation

$$W_{00} = \alpha_0,$$
$$W_{0,i+1} = W_{0i} + \beta_{i+1} + \alpha_{i+1}$$

The computation of the W_{0i} thus requires only time proportional to n. Given the W_{0i}, we can immediately get any needed W_{ij} with two subtractions, since

$$W_{ij} = \alpha_i + \beta_{i+1} + \cdots + \beta_j + \alpha_j$$
$$= W_{0j} - W_{0,i-1} - \beta_i$$

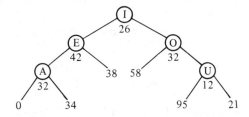

Figure 7.9
The tree constructed by the balancing rule for the example in Figure 7.3. The weighted path length is 948, so the expected number of probes is 948/390 ≈ 2.43, only slightly worse than for the optimal tree of Figure 7.4.

We will describe the computation for the root of the entire tree; the process is identical when applied to subtrees. To find where $|W_{0,i-1} - W_{in}|$ is minimized, we need to find where $W_{0,i-1} - W_{in}$ changes sign; the i we want will be on either side of the sign change. More exactly, if $W_{0,k-1} - W_{kn} \leq 0 < W_{0k} - W_{k+1,n}$, then we want either $i = k$ or $i = k + 1$, depending on whether or not $|W_{0,k-1} - W_{kn}|$ is less than $|W_{0k} - W_{k+1,n}|$. We can find k by a binary search type of process. Initially we know that $1 \leq k \leq n$; in general, if $l \leq k \leq h$, check the sign of $W_{0,m-1} - W_{mn}$, where $m = [(l + h)/2]$. If it is positive, set $h:=m$, or if negative set $l:=m$ and continue; if it is zero we are done. (By using $h:=m$ and $l:=m$ instead of $h:=m-1$ and $l:=m+1$, respectively, we ensure that the differences of W's have opposite signs at the end points.) Finding i in this way will require work proportional to $\lg n$ (why?), and the total amount of work will be given by the recurrence relation:

$$T(n) \leq \max_{1 \leq i \leq n} [T(i - 1) + T(n - i) + c \lg n]$$

where the $T(i - 1)$ and $T(n - i)$ are the work to find the left and right subtrees, respectively, once the root is found. The $c \lg n$ term is the time required to find the root i. $T(0)$ is some constant. The solution to this recurrence relation gives $T(n)$ proportional to $n \lg n$ and *not* to n as was promised.

We can reduce the computation time needed by searching for i in a slightly different way. We find the spot where $W_{0,k-1} - W_{kn}$ changes sign by checking $k = 1, k = n, k = 2, k = n - 1, k = 4, k = n - 3, k = 8, k = n - 7,\ldots$. In other words, we check from the left and right simultaneously, doubling the interval at each step. In this way we spend time proportional to $\min[\lg i, \lg(n - i)]$ to find an interval containing i. This interval has length proportional to $\min[i, n - i]$ and i can be located by binary search in time proportional to $1 + \min[\lceil \lg i \rceil, \lceil \lg(n - i + 1) \rceil]$. The recurrence relation for $T(n)$ becomes

$$T(n) \leq \max_{1 \leq i \leq n} \{T(i - 1) + T(n - i) + d(1 + \min[\lceil \lg i \rceil, \lceil \lg (n - i + 1) \rceil])\},$$

and the solution of this gives $T(n)$ proportional to n, as desired. We leave the details to Exercises 14 and 15.

Exercise 16 describes a variant of the balancing heuristic whose behavior is slightly better.

Exercises

1. Show the equivalence of the two definitions (7.2) and (7.3) for weighted path length.

2. Assuming successful searches only, to what does the weighted path length of the Morse code tree of Figure 5.6 correspond?

3. In what way is the Morse code tree of Figure 5.6 a binary search tree?

4. By hand calculation determine the optimal binary search tree for the frequencies $\alpha_0 = 17$, $\beta_1 = 6$, $\alpha_1 = 5$, $\beta_2 = 10$, $\alpha_2 = 14$, $\beta_3 = 1$, $\alpha_3 = 0$, $\beta_4 = 11$, $\alpha_4 = 3$, $\beta_5 = 7$, $\alpha_5 = 3$. Determine the trees that result from the monotonic and balancing rules.

5. Modify Algorithm 7.6 so that it computes *all* optimal binary search trees instead of just one of them.

6. Find a set of frequencies that have the tree shown in Figure 7.10 as their optimal search tree.

7. (a) Prove that the W_{ij} defined by Equation (7.4) satisfy

$$ W_{ij} + W_{i'j'} = W_{i'j} + W_{ij'} \qquad \text{for } i \le i' \le j \le j'. $$

★(b) Prove that the C_{ij} defined by Equation (7.5) satisfy

$$ C_{ij} + C_{i'j'} \le C_{i'j} + C_{ij'} \qquad \text{for } i \le i' \le j \le j'. $$

[*Hint*: Use induction on $j' - i$ and the result from part (a), considering the four cases $i = i'$, $j = j'$, $i < i' = j < j'$, and $i < i' < j < j'$.]

(c) Modify Equation (7.6) so that R_{ij} is the *largest* value of k that minimizes $C_{ik-1} + C_{kj}$ in Equation (7.5). Using part (b), show that $R_{i,j-1} \le R_{ij} \le R_{i+1,j}$ for $i < j$.

8. Evaluate the triple summation to verify that Formula (7.8) is $O(n^2)$.

9. Find a set of frequencies for which the monotonic rule produces a tree with weighted path length proportional to n, but the balancing rule produces a tree

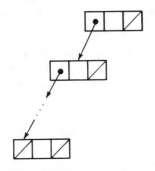

Figure 7.10
Exercise 6

with weighted path length proportional to log n. [*Hint*: Let the $\alpha_i = 0$ and the β_i be almost all equal, but differing from each other by enough so that the monotonic rule produces a tree that is essentially a linear list.]

10. Suppose the $\alpha_i = 0$ and the β_i are drawn at random from some distribution over the nonnegative real numbers with average $\bar{\beta}$. Let R_n be the expected weighted path length of a random binary search tree on n nodes, defined by the property that each of the n elements has equal probability $1/n$ of being the root, and if β_i is the root, then it has a random binary search tree of elements $\beta_1, \ldots, \beta_{i-1}$ as its left subtree and a random binary search tree of elements $\beta_{i+1}, \ldots, \beta_n$ as its right subtree.

(a) Verify the recurrence relation

$$R_n = \bar{\beta}n + \frac{1}{n} \sum_{i=1}^{n} (R_{i-1} + R_{n-i})$$

(b) What is R_0?

(c) Show how to transform the recurrence relation to

$$R_n = \bar{\beta}n + \frac{2}{n} \sum_{i=0}^{n-1} R_i$$

(d) Show that the solution to this recurrence relation is

$$2\bar{\beta}\,(n + 1)H_n - 3\bar{\beta}n, \qquad \text{where } H_n = \sum_{i=1}^{n} \frac{1}{i} \approx \ln n$$

This shows that $R_n \approx (2 \ln 2)\bar{\beta}n \lg n$. Defining M_n to be the weighted path of the tree resulting from applying the monotonic rule to n weights drawn at random from the same distribution as above, it can be shown that $M_n \approx (2 \lg 2)\bar{\beta}n \lg n$, so that the monotonic rule is (in a probabilistic sense) no better than constructing a random tree!

★11. Compute B_n, the expected cost of the tree that results from applying the balancing rule to n weights drawn from a distribution with average $\bar{\beta}$. [*Hint*: First show that on average $B_n = n\bar{\beta} + B_{\lfloor (n-1)/2 \rfloor} + B_{\lceil (n-1)/2 \rceil}$. Approximate this with $B_n = \bar{\beta}n + 2B_{n/2}$; your answer should be that $B_n \approx \bar{\beta}n \lg n$.]

★12. Compute O_n, the expected cost of the tree that results from applying Algorithm 7.6 to n weights drawn from a distribution with average $\bar{\beta}$.

13. Compute the entropy H for the frequencies of the example in Figure 7.3. [*Hint*: Remember to convert them to probabilities first.]

14. Write out the details of the algorithm to compute a binary search tree by the balancing rule.

15. Prove that the second recurrence relation given for $T(n)$, the time required to implement the balancing heuristic, is proportional to n.

16. Consider the following variation on the balancing heuristic. Suppose $\Sigma\alpha_i + \Sigma\beta_i = 1$. Define

$$s_i = \alpha_0 + \beta_1 + \cdots + \alpha_{i-1} + \beta_i + \frac{\alpha_i}{2}, \qquad 0 \leqslant i \leqslant n$$

The root of the search tree is chosen as x_k, where $s_{k-1} \leqslant \frac{1}{2}$ and $s_k \geqslant \frac{1}{2}$, and the heuristic continues on $s_0, \ldots, s_{k-1}$ and $s_k, \ldots, s_n$ using $\frac{1}{4}$ and $\frac{3}{4}$, respectively, in place of $\frac{1}{2}$, and so on for smaller intervals. Show that this heuristic can be implemented in time proportional to n. It can be shown that the weighted path length of the tree produced by this heuristic is at most $H + 1 + \Sigma\alpha_i$.

17. Study the properties of the *min-max* heuristic: choose as the root of $x_i, x_{i+1}, \ldots, x_j$ the element x_k for which $\max(W_{i,k-1}, W_{kj})$ is minimized.

7.2.2 Dynamic Trees

In the previous section we used binary search trees to improve the binary search technique in the case of a static table with nonuniform access frequencies. In this section we will show how binary search trees can be used to get a binary search technique in dynamic tables—that is, tables whose contents change because of insertions and deletions. There is a conflict between fast-search algorithms and fast-modification algorithms: Fast search requires a rigid structure, while fast modification obviously needs a flexible structure; binary search trees provide a compromise between the two requirements.

Inserting a new element z into an existing binary search tree T is not difficult if we do not care what the effect is on the shape of the tree. If the elements in the tree are $x_1 < x_2 < \cdots < x_n$ and $x_i < z < x_{i-1}$, $0 \leqslant i \leqslant n$ (with x_0 and x_{n-1} considered as $-\infty$ and ∞, respectively), then the ith external node can simply be replaced with

For example, adding the letter Y to the tree of Figure 7.2 yields the tree of Figure 7.11. Thus, given a binary search tree and a new element z to be inserted, there is a unique external node at which to insert the element because the element falls into a unique gap between some x_i and x_{i+1}. Furthermore, the external node corresponding

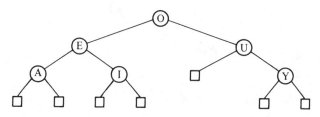

Figure 7.11
The tree of Figure 7.2 with the letter Y added at its proper place

to that gap is the one at which Algorithm 7.5 (searching a binary search tree) ends in its unsuccessful search for z in the tree. This fact allows us to use a minor modification of Algorithm 7.5 to do the insertion, since after the search we need only get a new record for z and link it on the proper side of the last node visited during the unsuccessful search. The corresponding statements cannot just be added to Algorithm 7.5, however, because on normal termination of the **while** loop p no longer points to the last node visited but instead has the value **nil**. So we must keep track of the parent of p and whether p is a left or right child or was the root itself. The modifications necessary for Algorithm 7.5 to insert the element z are now apparent and are shown in Algorithm 7.7.

What happens if we use this algorithm to construct search trees? In the worst case, of course, the tree can degenerate into a linear list; this happens, for example, if the order of insertion is A, E, I, O, U. (Even more innocent looking insertion orders can be problematic; consider A, U, E, O, I.) Are things really that bad on the average? If we have a random insertion order, what will the average search time be in the tree constructed? To answer, we recall that the external path length is the measure of the average search time (since it is the sum of the number of probes over all possible unsuccessful searches and differs only slightly from the internal path length, which is the sum of the number of probes over all possible successful searches). We want to compute the expected external path length in a tree constructed by Algorithm 7.7 for random insertion order. Without further information, we may as well assume that each of the $n!$ permutations of the n elements is equally likely as the insertion order. Let E_n be the expected external path length in a tree constructed from n elements taken in a random order. [The nonmathematical reader should skip to Equation (7.16).] To develop a recurrence relation for E_n we observe that if the n elements are in random order, then the probability that any particular one is first is $1/n$, and that the remaining $n - 1$ are again in random order. Furthermore, if the first one happens to be x_i, the ith element of the n elements (in the natural order), then those elements less than x_i (that is, $x_1, x_2, \ldots, x_{i-1}$) are in a random order, as are those larger than x_i (that is, $x_{i+1}, x_{i+2}, \ldots, x_n$). Thus if x_i happens to be the first element inserted into the tree (as the root), it will have, by the nature of the insertion process of Algorithm 7.7, a random tree made up of $x_1, x_2, \ldots, x_{i-1}$ as its left

function *InsertInBST*(**var** *T*: *pTree*; *z*: *KeyType*): *pTree*;
    {find or insert a node for *z*; return a pointer to the node}
var
    p, *parent*: *pTree*;
    direction: (*left*, *right*, *root*);
    found: *boolean*;
begin
    p := *T*;
    direction := *root*;
    found := **false**;
    while ($p \neq$ **nil**) **and not** *found* **do**
    {Assert: *z* belongs in subtree rooted at *p*. If $p \neq T$, *p* is the child of
    parent on the side given by *direction*.}
        if $z < p\uparrow.KEY$ **then begin**
            direction := *left*;
            parent := *p*;
            p := $p\uparrow.LEFT$
        end
        else if $z > p\uparrow.KEY$ **then begin**
            direction := *right*;
            parent := *p*;
            p := $p\uparrow.RIGHT$
        end
        else *found* := **true**;
    if not *found* **then begin**
        {insert a new node for *z*}
        new(*p*);
        $p\uparrow.LEFT$:= **nil**;
        $p\uparrow.RIGHT$:= **nil**;
        $p\uparrow.KEY$:= *z*;
        case *direction* **of**
            root: *T* := *p*;
            left: $parent\uparrow.LEFT$:= *p*;
            right: $parent\uparrow.RIGHT$:= *p*
        end
    end;
    InsertInBST := *p*
end

Algorithm 7.7
Insertion of a new element *z* into a binary search tree

subtree and a random tree made up of $x_{i+1}, x_{i+2}, \ldots, x_n$ as its right subtree. Together with Equation (5.5) this gives us

$$E_0 = 0,$$

$$E_n = \sum_{i=1}^{n} (n + 1 + E_{i+1} + E_{n-i})\Pr(i \text{ will be the root})$$

Since the probability that i will be the root is equal for all i, it is $1/n$, and the above equation becomes

$$E_n = \sum_{i=1}^{n} \frac{1}{n} (n + 1 + E_{i-1} + E_{n-i})$$

which by some elementary algebra can be rewritten as

$$E_n = n + 1 + \frac{2}{n} \sum_{i=0}^{n-1} E_i$$

Recurrence relations of this type are not difficult to solve if one knows the trick, and since they occur not only here but also in Chapter 8, we now make a short detour to solve

$$t_n = an + b + \frac{2}{n} \sum_{i=0}^{n-1} t_i, \qquad n \geq n_0 \tag{7.9}$$

for t_n in terms of $n, a, b, n_0, t_0, t_1, \ldots, t_{n_0-1}$.

To eliminate the summation from (7.9) we first multiply each side by n to obtain

$$nt_n = an^2 + bn + 2 \sum_{i=0}^{n-1} t_i, \qquad n \geq n_0 \tag{7.10}$$

Replacing n by $n - 1$, we get

$$(n - 1)t_{n-1} = a(n - 1)^2 + b(n - 1) + 2 \sum_{i=0}^{n-2} t_i, \qquad n \geq n_0 + 1 \tag{7.11}$$

Subtracting (7.11) from (7.10) gives

$$nt_n - (n - 1)t_{n-1} = 2t_{n-1} + 2an + b - a, \qquad n \geq n_0 + 1$$

or

$$nt_n - (n + 1)t_{n-1} = 2an + b - a, \qquad n \geq n_0 + 1$$

Divide this by $n(n + 1)$ and we have

$$\frac{t_n}{n + 1} - \frac{t_{n-1}}{n} = \frac{3a - b}{n + 1} + \frac{b - a}{n}, \qquad n \geq n_0 + 1$$

Replacing n by i and summing gives

$$\sum_{i=n_0+1}^{n} \left(\frac{t_i}{i + 1} - \frac{t_{i-1}}{i} \right) = \sum_{i=n_0+1}^{n} \left(\frac{3a - b}{i + 1} + \frac{b - a}{i} \right) \qquad (7.12)$$

The left-hand side is the telescoping sum

$$\frac{t_n}{n + 1} - \frac{t_{n-1}}{n} + \frac{t_{n-1}}{n} - \frac{t_{n-2}}{n - 1} + \cdots - \frac{t_{n_0+1}}{n_0 + 2} + \frac{t_{n_0+1}}{n_0 + 2} - \frac{t_{n_0}}{n_0 + 1}$$

$$= \frac{t_n}{n + 1} - \frac{t_{n_0}}{n_0 + 1}$$

and the right-hand side can be rewritten as

$$2aH_n - 2aH_{n_0} - (3a - b)\left(\frac{1}{n_0 + 1} - \frac{1}{n} \right),$$

where

$$H_n = \sum_{i=1}^{n} \frac{1}{i} \qquad (7.13)$$

are called the *harmonic numbers*. Thus (7.12) yields

$$t_n = 2anH_n + n \left(\frac{t_{n_0} - 3a + b}{n_0 + 1} - 2aH_{n_0} \right) + 2aH_n$$

$$+ \frac{t_{n_0} - 3a + b}{n_0 + 1} + 3a - b - 2aH_{n_0}, \qquad (7.14)$$

where

$$t_{n_0} = an_0 + b + \frac{2}{n_0} \sum_{i=0}^{n_0-1} t_i$$

from (7.9). Since $H_n = \ln n + O(1)$ (see Exercise 1), (7.14) tells us that

$$\begin{aligned} t_n &= 2an \ln n + O(n) \\ &= (2a \ln 2)n \lg n + O(n) \end{aligned} \tag{7.15}$$

For E_n, this yields

$$\begin{aligned} E_n &= (2 \ln 2)n \lg n + O(n) \\ &\approx 1.38n \lg n \end{aligned} \tag{7.16}$$

Equation (7.16) tells us that in binary search trees built at random, the average search time will be about 1.38 lg n, or about 38 percent longer than in an optimal tree with equiprobable keys. The simplicity of Algorithm 7.7 would make it acceptable in spite of the increase over the minimum search time, except for an important fact: our analysis assumed that the insertion order was random, and this is almost never true in practice, since there are often sequences of elements arriving in their natural order. Thus, despite Equation (7.16), Algorithm 7.7 must be considered unreliable except in truly random circumstances.

So far we have considered only insertions. What about deletions? Deletions are somewhat more complex than insertions, because insertions cause changes only in the external nodes, but a deletion affects the internal nodes as well. Suppose the element y is to be deleted. There is no problem if y has two **nil** children; we just replace the pointer to y by **nil**. Also, if y has only one **nil** child, we replace the pointer to y with a pointer to its single child. These two easy cases are illustrated in Figure 7.12. What if y has two non-**nil** children? Then y has both an inorder predecessor which has a **nil** right child and an inorder successor which has a **nil** left child (Exercise 3). Thus we can replace y by either its predecessor or its successor, deleting that element's node as shown in Figure 7.12. The details of the entire process are left to Exercise 4.

There is little known analysis of the expected search time in binary search trees constructed through random insertions and deletions, as we gave above for the case of random insertions only. But it is unlikely that results more favorable than (7.16) are true, especially since there is an inherent asymmetry in the deletion algorithm (do we replace an element with two children by its predecessor or successor?). Furthermore, the possibility of biased sequences of insertions and deletions is very real in practice and makes these algorithms unreliable. Suitably adapted by the techniques described below, however, these algorithms form the basis of very flexible table organizations that have logarithmic search and insertion/deletion times even in the worst case.

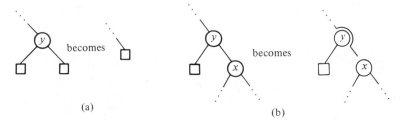

Figure 7.12
Deletion of an element y with (a) two **nil** children and (b) one **nil** child. Deletion of an element with two non-**nil** children reduces to one of these cases. (In either case, y should be *dispose*'d if there is no other pointer to it.)

Logarithmic search times can be achieved by keeping the tree perfectly balanced at all times (as is implicit in binary search). Unfortunately, when the tree is thus constrained, it is more costly to insert or delete an element than to rearrange elements in the sequentially allocated arrays required by binary search. Instead, our goal is to allow more flexibility in the shape of the tree so that insertions and deletions will not be so expensive, yet search times will remain logarithmic. In the remainder of this section we present two techniques that achieve this goal. Both techniques keep the trees "balanced" so that they cannot become too skewed (and hence degenerate to linear search times). The height of such trees of n elements will be $O(\log n)$, so that search times are logarithmic and insertions and deletions will require only local changes along a single path from the root to a leaf, requiring only time proportional to the height of the tree—that is, $O(\log n)$.

Height-Balanced Trees. An extended binary tree is *height-balanced* if and only if it consists of a single external node, or the two subtrees T_l and T_r of the root satisfy

1. $\mid h(T_l) - h(T_r) \mid \leq 1$, and

2. T_l and T_r are height-balanced.

In other words, at any node in a height-balanced tree the two subtrees of that node differ in height by at most one. Figure 7.13 shows two trees, one height-balanced and the other not.

We want to use height-balanced trees as a storage structure for dynamic tables, but in order for height-balanced trees to be useful we must demonstrate that search times are at worst $O(\log n)$ and that insertions and deletions are easily and efficiently accommodated. Once we have shown that a height-balanced tree of n nodes has height $O(\log n)$, then the worst-case search time is $O(\log n)$ and, since the insertion/deletion time will also be proportional to the height, we will be done.

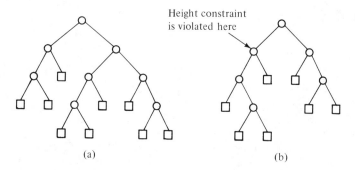

Figure 7.13
Two extended binary trees: (a) height-balanced and (b) not height-balanced

What is the height of the tallest height-balanced tree containing n internal nodes and $n + 1$ external nodes? To answer this question we will turn it around and ask what is the least number of internal nodes necessary to achieve height h in a height-balanced tree.

Let T_h be a height-balanced tree of height h with n_h internal nodes, the fewest possible. Obviously,

$$T_0 = \square, \qquad n_0 = 0$$

and

$$T_1 = \overset{\bigcirc}{\underset{\square \quad \square}{\diagup \diagdown}}\quad , \qquad n_1 = 1 \tag{7.17}$$

since these are the only extended binary trees with heights 0 and 1, respectively. Now consider T_h, $h \geq 2$. Since T_h is height-balanced and has height h, it must have a tree of height $h - 1$ as its left or right subtree and a tree of height $h - 1$ or $h - 2$ as its other subtree. For any k, a tree of height k has a subtree of height $k - 1$ and thus $n_k > n_{k-1}$; this tells us that T_h has one subtree of height $h - 1$ and the other of height $h - 2$, for if T_h had two subtrees of height $h - 1$, we would replace one of them by T_{h-2} and, since $n_{h-1} > n_{h-2}$, this would contradict the assumption that T_h had as few nodes as possible for a height-balanced tree of height h. Similarly, the two subtrees of T_h must be height-balanced and have the fewest nodes possible, for otherwise we could replace one or both subtrees with same height subtrees of fewer nodes, again contradicting the assumption that T_h has as few nodes as possible. Thus T_h has T_{h-1} as one subtree and T_{h-2} as the other,

$$T_h = \overset{\bigcirc}{\underset{T_{h-1} \quad T_{h-2}}{\diagup \diagdown}}\quad , \qquad n_h = n_{h-1} + n_{h-2} + 1 \tag{7.18}$$

Readers familiar with Fibonacci numbers will notice the resemblance of the construction of T_h and the recurrence relation for n_h to those for the Fibonacci numbers.

The solution of n_h in terms of h can be shown to be

$$n_h = \frac{1}{\sqrt{5}} \left(\frac{1 + \sqrt{5}}{2} \right)^{h+2} - \frac{1}{\sqrt{5}} \left(\frac{1 - \sqrt{5}}{2} \right)^{h+2} - 1$$

or, one less than the $(h + 2)$nd Fibonacci number. Since $|(1 - \sqrt{5})/2| < 1$, the term $[(1 - \sqrt{5})/2]^{h+2}/\sqrt{5}$ is always quite small, so that

$$n_h + 1 = \frac{1}{\sqrt{5}} \left(\frac{1 + \sqrt{5}}{2} \right)^{h+2} + O(1)$$

Since the tree of height h with the fewest nodes has n_h nodes, it follows that any tree with fewer than n_h nodes has height less than h. Therefore, if a height-balanced tree of n nodes has height h, then

$$n + 1 \geqslant n_h + 1 = \frac{1}{\sqrt{5}} \left(\frac{1 + \sqrt{5}}{2} \right)^{h+2} + O(1)$$

implying that

$$h \leqslant \frac{1}{\lg \dfrac{1 + \sqrt{5}}{2}} \lg(n + 1) + O(1)$$
$$\approx 1.44 \lg(n + 1)$$

(we have written $n + 1$ and not n so the function will be properly defined for $n = 0$, that is, a tree with only a single external node).

Thus in the worst case the number of probes by Algorithm 7.5 into a height-balanced tree of n internal nodes will be about $1.44 \lg(n + 1)$ and the total search time will be logarithmic, as desired. It remains to be seen, however, whether insertions and deletions can be done efficiently so that a height-balanced tree remains height-balanced afterward.

To make an insertion or deletion we will use the method outlined above for the case when the tree can change in an unconstrained manner, but we will follow it with a rebalancing pass that verifies or restores the height-balanced state of the tree. In order to verify/restore the tree we need to be able to test whether the element inserted or deleted has changed the relationship between the heights of the subtrees of a node so as to violate the height constraints. For this purpose, we will store a *condition code* in each node of a height-balanced tree. The condition code is one of the following:

/ Means the left subtree of this node is taller (by one) than its right subtree.
= Means the two subtrees of this node have equal height.
\ Means the right subtree of this node is taller (by one) than its left subtree.

Storing condition codes requires an extra two-bit field per node in the tree. This very modest additional storage requirement can be made even more modest by the techniques of either Exercise 15 or Exercise 16, which reduce the condition code to a single bit, but at the expense of the efficiency and (relative) simplicity of the algorithms for rebalancing a tree that has become unbalanced through an insertion or deletion.

Roughly speaking, the rebalancing pass consists of retracing the path upward from the newly inserted node (or from the site of the deletion) to the root. If *PARENT* pointers are available, they are the most efficient way to accomplish this. If they are not available—and they usually are not—then we have two choices: either store the path, node by node, on a stack as we go down the tree from the root to the site of the modification, or use the trick of Algorithm 6.5(b) (see Exercise 6 of Section 6.1.2) to change the pointers as we go down the tree; this latter choice will require an additional two bits per node. In the case of an insertion there is a third possibility, that of simply retracing a portion of the path downward—see Exercise 11.

As the path is followed upward, we check for instances of the taller subtree growing taller (on an insertion) or the shorter subtree becoming shorter (on a deletion). When we find such an occurrence, we apply a local transformation to the tree at that point. In the case of an insertion it will turn out that applying the transformation at the first such occurrence will completely rebalance the tree. In the case of a deletion the transformations may need to be applied at many points along the way up to the root. We must be careful that any transformation made does not affect the inorder of the nodes in the tree (why?).

Since the rebalancing after an insertion is a bit simpler than after a deletion, we consider it first. What could have happened using Algorithm 7.7 to add an element to a height-balanced tree? The only difficulty is that the new element may have been added to the bottom of the taller of two subtrees of some node. Without loss of generality, suppose the right subtree was the taller before the insertion, as in Figure 7.14.

The way to repair the newly created imbalance depends on where within the taller subtree T the insertion was made. Suppose it was in the right subtree of T; we then have a situation that can be repaired as shown in Figure 7.15(a). The transformation shown there is called a *rotation*, and it is considered to be applied to the element A. Obviously, if the left subtree in Figure 7.14 had been taller and the

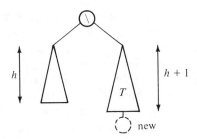

Figure 7.14
Insertion making a node unbalanced

insertion made it even taller, we would have to rotate in the other direction, using the mirror image of the transformation shown in Figure 7.15(a).

The transformation of Figure 7.15(a) would not have helped if the insertion had been to the left subtree of T in Figure 7.14—that is, to T_2 in Figure 7.15(a). In this case the repair is made as shown in Figure 7.15(b). This transformation, called

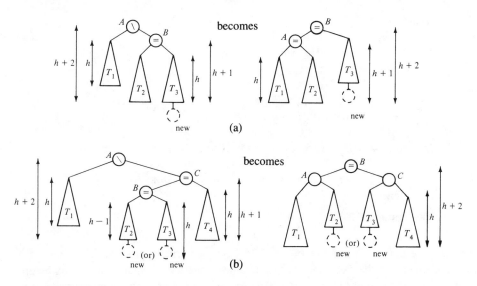

Figure 7.15
The transformations used to rebalance a height-balanced tree after the insertion of a new element: (a) rotation around A, (b) double rotation around A. The height condition codes in A and C in the right-hand drawing of (b) depend on whether the new element is at the bottom of T_2 or T_3. Both T_2 and T_3 are empty when B is the new element (see also Exercise 9). Notice that in each transformation the inorder of the tree is unchanged and the height of the tree *after* the transformation is the same as the height of the tree *before* the insertion. In each case, there are corresponding mirror-image transformations.

a *double rotation*, is considered to be applied at A. The new element can be at the bottom of either T_2 or T_3. Both T_2 and T_3 can be empty, in which case B is the new element (see Exercise 9). Again, a mirror-image transformation would be needed in the comparable case where the left subtree in Figure 7.14 was the taller.

Before continuing, the reader should try enough examples to be convinced that Figures 7.15(a) and (b), along with their mirror images, are the only possible cases.

We will generally show rotations in diagrams rather than program fragments, but the corresponding fragments are not intricate; they have no loops and few conditional tests. Here, for instance, is the code for Figure 7.15(a):

```
A↑.RIGHT  :=  B↑.LEFT;
B↑.LEFT  :=  A;
A↑.CONDITION  :=  " = ";
"pointer to A"  :=  B
```

We utilize here and below the identifiers shown in Declarations 7.3.

```
type
        BalanceType  =  (" ∕ ", " = ", " ∖ ");
        pHbTree  =  ↑HbTree;
        HbTree  =  record
                KEY: KeyType;
                LEFT, RIGHT: pHbTree;
                CONDITION: BalanceType
        end;
        PathStack  =  record    {used to record the nodes on path from root}
                TOP: integer;    {if TOP is − 1, the stack is empty}
                STACK: array [0.."maximum depth"] of pHbTree
        end;
```

Declarations 7.3

The transformations of Figure 7.15 have two critical properties: the inorder of the elements of the tree remains the same after the transformation as it was before, and the overall height of the tree is the same after the transformation as it was before the insertion. The first property is necessary if we are to be able to search the tree properly by Algorithm 7.5. The second property means that after the insertion the appropriate transformation needs to be applied *only* at the lowest unbalanced spot in the tree.

The insertion algorithm is thus as follows. Use Algorithm 7.7 to insert the new element into its proper place, setting its condition code to = and storing the path followed down the tree, node by node, in a stack (the new element ends up as the top stack entry and the root is the bottom stack entry). Then, retrace that path backward, up the tree, popping nodes off the stack and correcting the height-condition codes until either the root is reached and its height-condition code corrected, or we reach a point when no more height-condition codes need to be corrected, or we reach a point at which a rotation or double rotation is necessary to rebalance the tree. More specifically, we follow this path backward, node by node, taking actions as defined by the following rules, where *current* is the current node on the path, *child* is the node before *current* on the path (that is, its child), and *grandchild* is the node before *child* on the path (the grandchild of *current*). Initially *child* is the new element just inserted, *current* is its parent, and *grandchild* is **nil**. These rules are expanded to Pascal in Algorithm 7.8.

1. If *current* has height condition $=$, change it to $\searrow$ if *child* $=$ *current*↑.*RIGHT* and to $\diagup$ if *child* $=$ *current*↑.*LEFT*. In this case the subtree rooted at *child* grew taller by one unit, causing the subtree rooted at *current* to grow taller by one unit, so we continue up the path, unless *current* is the root, in which case we are done. To continue up the path we set *grandchild* $:=$ *child*; *child* $:=$ *current*, and *current* to the top stack entry, which is removed from the stack.

2. If *current* has height condition $\diagup$ and *child* $=$ *current*↑.*RIGHT* or *current* has height condition $\searrow$ and *child* $=$ *current*↑.*LEFT*, change the height condition of *current* to $=$, and the procedure terminates. In this case the shorter of the two subtrees of *current* has grown one unit taller, making the tree better balanced.

3. If *current* has height condition $\diagup$ and *child* $=$ *current* ↑.*LEFT* or *current* has height condition $\searrow$ and *child* $=$ *current*↑.*RIGHT*, then the taller of the two subtrees of *current* has become one unit taller, unbalancing the tree at *current*. A transformation is performed according to the following four cases:

	grandchild $=$ *child*↑.*RIGHT*	*grandchild* $=$ *child*↑.*LEFT*
child $=$ *current*↑.*RIGHT*	Rotate around *current* using Figure 7.15(a)	Double-rotate around *current* using Figure 7.15(b)
child $=$ *current*↑.*LEFT*	Double-rotate around *current* using the mirror image of Figure 7.15(b)	Rotate around *current* using the mirror image of Figure 7.15(a)

In each case, the height conditions are set as shown in Figure 7.15. The procedure terminates, having rebalanced the tree at its lowest point of imbalance.

procedure *RebalanceAfterInsert*(**var** *S*: *PathStack*);
{rebalance a height-balanced tree whose most recent insertion path
is recorded in *S*}
var
current, child, grandchild: *pHbTree*;
balancing: *boolean*;
begin
child := *Pop*(*S*);
current := *Pop*(*S*);
grandchild := **nil**;
balancing := **true**;
while *balancing* **do begin**
{Assert: *S* has the path from *current* to root. *current* is the parent
of *child*. *child* is the parent of *grandchild*. The insertion was made
in subtree at *child* which is height-balanced.}
if *current*↑.*CONDITION* = " = " **then begin**
{Rule 1: *current* was balanced:
propagate imbalance up tree}
if *child* = *current*↑.*RIGHT* **then**
current↑.*CONDITION* := " \ "
else *current*↑.*CONDITION* := " / ";
if *IsEmpty*(*S*) **then**
balancing := **false**
else begin
grandchild := *child*;
child := *current*;
current := *Pop*(*S*)
end
end
else if ((*current*↑.*CONDITION* = " / ")
and (*child* = *current*↑.*RIGHT*))
or ((*current*↑.*CONDITION* = " \ ")
and (*child* = *current*↑.*LEFT*)) **then begin**
{Rule 2: short side of *current* grew taller:
now better balanced}
current↑.*CONDITION* := " = ";
balancing := **false**
end

```
                else begin
                    {Rule 3: tall side of current grew taller: do a rotation}
                    if child = current↑.RIGHT then
                        if grandchild = child↑.RIGHT then
                            {rotate around current}
                            "apply Figure 7.15(a)"
                    else
                            {double-rotate around current}
                            "apply Figure 7.15(b)"
                else
                    if grandchild = child↑.RIGHT then
                        {double-rotate around current}
                        "apply the mirror image of Figure 7.15(b)"
                    else
                        {rotate around current}
                        "apply the mirror image of Figure 7.15(a)";
                balancing := false
            end
        end
end
```

Algorithm 7.8
Rebalance a tree after the insertion whose path has been recorded in a stack

As an example of the insertion process, consider inserting the letter T into the tree of Figure 7.16. Algorithm 7.7 inserts T as the right child of S, and the path back up the tree is T, S, R, P, K, U, H. We thus begin rebalancing with $current = S$, $child = T$, and $grandchild = $ **nil**, while the stack contents are R, P, K, U, H. Case 1 applies to $current$, so we change the condition code of S to $\searrow$ and set $grandchild := T$, $child := S$, and $current := R$ from the top of the stack. Again case 1 applies to $current$, so we set the condition code of R to $\searrow$, $grandchild := S$, $child := R$, and $current := P$ from the top of the stack. Again case 1 applies, so we set the condition code of P to $\searrow$, $grandchild := R$, $child := P$, and $current := K$ from the top of the stack. Now case 3 applies and, since $child = current↑.RIGHT$ and $grandchild = child↑.RIGHT$, we apply the rotation of Figure 7.15(a) to the node $current = K$, setting the height-condition codes of K and P to $=$, as indicated in Figure 7.15(a). The procedure then terminates (ignoring the remainder of the stack contents). If we had been inserting O instead, then upon reaching the node K we would apply the double rotation of Figure 7.15(b).

The deletion process is more complex than insertion because it will not always be sufficient to apply a transformation only at the lowest point of imbalance; transformations may need to be applied at many levels between the site of the deletion and the root. To delete a node we may need to begin, as with unconstrained trees, by replacing it with the contents of another node, which is then deleted. If the node has two non-**nil** children, it is replaced by its inorder successor or predecessor, which is guaranteed to have at most one non-**nil** child (see Figure 7.12). In the case of a height-balanced tree, however, if a node has only one non-**nil** child, it must look like

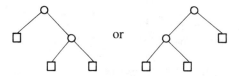

because the height constraint. In either case, replacing the node by its only child has the identical effect on the heights as deleting the node with no children. We thus need consider *only* the case of deleting a node with two null children.

As in the insertion algorithm, we store on a stack the path followed down the tree to the site of the node to be deleted, then we retrace the path backward up the tree, popping nodes off the stack, correcting height-condition codes, and making transformations as needed. As we go back up the path, actions are taken as defined by the following rules, where (as before) *current* is the current node on the path and *child* is the node before *current*. Initially, *child* is the node to be deleted and *current* is its parent, if any. The actual deletion occurs after the rebalancing because the algorithm may need to test the pointer from parent to deleted child. A Pascal version of these rules is given as Algorithm 7.9.

1. If *current* has height condition =, then shortening either subtree does not affect the height of the tree rooted at *current*. The condition code of *current* is changed to \ if *child* = *current*↑.LEFT and to / if *child* = *current*↑.RIGHT. The procedure then exits from the balancing process.

2. If *current* has height condition \ and *child* = *current*↑.RIGHT or *current* has height condition / and *child* = *current*↑.LEFT, the condition code of *current* is changed to =.

3. If *current* has height condition \ and *child* = *current*↑.LEFT, then the height constraint is violated at *current*. There are three subcases, depending on the height-condition code at *current*↑.RIGHT, the sibling of *child*. The subcases are as given in Figure 7.17.

4. If *current* has height condition / and *child* = *current*↑.RIGHT, then the height constraint is violated at *current*. There are three subcases, depending on the height-condition code at *current*↑.LEFT, the sibling of *child*. The subcases are the mirror images of those given in Figure 7.17, and we leave them as Exercise 12.

5. The balancing process may have terminated in step 1, 3(a), or 4(a); otherwise the height of the subtree rooted at *current* is now one less than it was before the deletion, so we continue up the path, unless *current* is the root, in which case we are done. To continue up the path we set *child* := *current* and set *current* by popping the top element off the stack. We then repeat this set of rules.

As an example of the deletion procedure, consider deleting the node *B* from the tree of Figure 7.16. Case 2 applies to the node *A* and then case 3(c) applies to the node *C*, so a double rotation is applied there. Then case 3(a) applies to the node *H* and a rotation is applied there. The tree is then completely rebalanced. The reader can become familiar with the algorithm by going through the steps necessary to delete *D* or *X* from the tree of Figure 7.16.

The deletion algorithm will clearly require only time proportional to the height of the tree; thus deletion can be accomplished in $O(\log n)$ time, as can insertion. An insertion, however, will need at most one rotation/double rotation to rebalance the tree, while a deletion from a height-balanced tree of height h can require as many as $\lfloor h/2 \rfloor$ rotations/double rotations, but no more (Exercise 14).

What do height-balanced trees look like "on the average"—that is, when they are generated by a random sequence of insertions and deletions? There is no known mathematical analysis to answer this question, but empirical evidence strongly suggests that the average search time in such a tree is $\lg n + O(1)$ probes. This suggests that on the average height-balanced trees are almost as good as the completely balanced trees that correspond to binary search. Of course, unlike the case of binary search, height-balanced trees can be modified by insertions and deletions in logarithmic time.

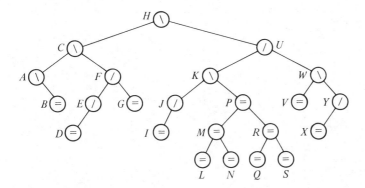

Figure 7.16
A height-balanced tree to illustrate the rebalancing algorithms after an insertion or a deletion

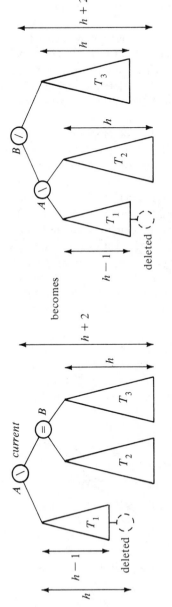

becomes

(a) Apply the rotation of Figure 7.15(a) to *current* and exit from the balancing operation since the height-balance has been restored and the height of the tree after the transformation is the same as it was before the deletion. (See also Exercise 13.)

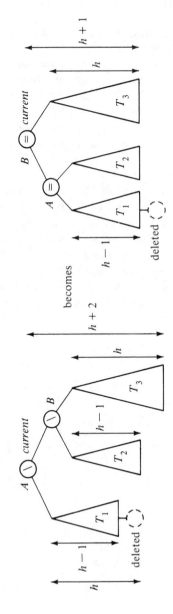

becomes

(b) Apply the rotation of Figure 7.15(a) to *current* and change *current* to point to *B*.

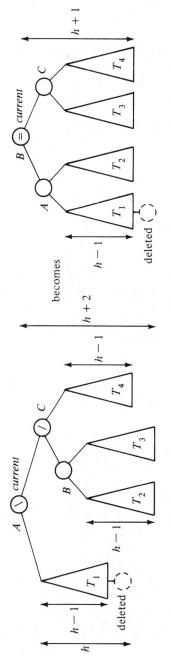

(c) Apply the double rotation of Figure 7.15(b) to *current* and change *current* to point to B. The height-condition codes of A and C are both = if that of B was =. If B was \, then A is / and C is =. If B was /, then A is = and C is \.

Figure 7.17
The three rotations utilized in Algorithm 7.9 when *current* has height condition \ and *child* = *current*↑.*LEFT*. Three more required rotations are derived as mirror images of those here (Exercise 12).

procedure *RebalanceAndDelete*(**var** *T*: *pHbTree*; **var** *S*: *PathStack*);
var
      current: *pHbTree*;   {node currently considered}
      child: *pHbTree*;   {*current*↑.*LEFT* or ↑.*RIGHT*}
      balancing: *boolean*; {loop control flag}
      bereft: *pHbTree*;   {node whose leaf is to be deleted}
      wasLeft: *boolean*; {which side of *bereft* to delete}
begin
      child := *Pop*(*S*);
      if *IsEmpty*(*S*) **then**
          T := **nil**
      else begin
          current := *Pop*(*S*);
          bereft := *current*;
          wasLeft := (*child* = *bereft*↑.*LEFT*);
          balancing := **true**;
          while *balancing* **do begin**
              {Assert: *S* has path from *current* to root. *bereft* is parent of
              the node to be deleted. *current* is the parent of *child*. *bereft*
              is in the subtree rooted at *child*.}
              if *current*↑.*CONDITION* = '' = '' **then begin**
                  {Rule 1: deletion from either subtree can be absorbed
                  here}
                  if *child* = *current*↑.*LEFT* **then**
                     current↑.*CONDITION* := ''\''
                  else *current*↑.*CONDITION* := '' / '';
                  balancing := **false**
             end
             else if ((*current*↑.*CONDITION* = ''\'')
                    and (*child* = *current*↑.*RIGHT*))
                 or ((*current*↑.*CONDITION* = '' / '')
                    and (*child* = *current*↑.*LEFT*))   **then**
                {Rule 2: *current* becomes balanced, but its subtree is
                shorter so imbalance must be propagated up}
                current↑.*CONDITION* := '' = ''
             else {Rules 3 and 4: Rotate}
                if (*current*↑.*CONDITION* = ''\'')
                    and (*child* = *current*↑.*LEFT*) **then**
                  ''apply the rotations of Figure 7.17''
                else ''apply the mirror images of the rotations in
                      Figure 7.17'';

{the rotations may have set *balancing* to *false*, otherwise we continue up the tree}
if *balancing* **then**   {**Rule 5**}
    if *IsEmpty(S)* **then**
        {we are at *root*; it remains unbalanced}
        balancing := **false**
    else begin
        child := *current*;
        current := *Pop(S)*
    end
end;
{Delete designated node}
if *wasLeft* **then**
    bereft↑.LEFT := **nil**
else *bereft↑.RIGHT* := **nil**
end
end

Algorithm 7.9
Rebalance a height-balanced tree and complete a deletion. The path to the node to be deleted has been recorded in stack S. Note that the deletion is not actually performed until after the rebalancing.

Weight-Balanced Trees. We now consider another class of balanced trees having the properties that the height of a tree is logarithmic in the number of nodes and that insertions and deletions can be accomplished in logarithmic time. The difference between the trees considered here and height-balanced trees is the constraint used to balance the trees. In addition, the algorithms for rebalancing the trees after an insertion or deletion are simpler and, most important, allow an explicit trade-off to be made between search times and rebalancing times.

Let T be an extended binary tree, so that T either is a single external node $\square$ or consists of a root and left and right subtrees T_l and T_r, respectively. Let $|T|$ be the number of external nodes in T. The *balance* of the root of a tree is defined as

$$\beta(T) = \begin{cases} \dfrac{1}{2}, & \text{if } T = \square, \\[2ex] \dfrac{|T_l|}{|T|}, & \text{otherwise} \end{cases}$$

Notice that $\beta(T)$ roughly indicates the relative number of nodes (internal or external) in the left subtree of T. If the balance is ½, then half the nodes are in each of the two subtrees, and this is the ideal balance; this explains our setting $\beta(\square) = \frac{1}{2}$, since the tree $\square$ is (trivially) well balanced. Obviously, $0 < \beta(T) < 1$ for any extended binary tree T.

A tree T is said to be of *weight-balance* α, or in the set WB[α], for $0 \leq \alpha \leq \frac{1}{2}$, if

1. $\alpha \leq \beta(T) \leq 1 - \alpha$.

2. If $T \neq \square$ then both T_l and T_r are in WB[α].

In other words, at any node in a WB[α] tree the balance factor lies between α and $1 - \alpha$. Figure 7.18 shows four examples of weight-balanced trees for various values of α; in each case the balance of every subtree is given in the root of the subtree (except leaves).

Clearly WB[α_1] is a subset of WB[α_2] for $\alpha_1 \geq \alpha_2$, hence the set WB[α] becomes more and more restricted as α goes from 0 to $\frac{1}{2}$. Since $\alpha = 0$ imposes no restriction at all on the trees, WB[0] is the set of *all* extended binary trees. On the other hand, $\alpha = \frac{1}{2}$ forces the subtrees of every node to contain equal numbers of leaves, implying that the trees contain 2^h leaves and are completely balanced. For any α, $\frac{1}{3} < \alpha < \frac{1}{2}$, WB[$\alpha$] = WB[$\frac{1}{2}$]. To prove this, suppose that a tree T is not in WB[$\frac{1}{2}$]—that is, is not completely balanced. Since T is not in WB[$\frac{1}{2}$], it contains some subtree not in WB[$\frac{1}{2}$]; consider the smallest subtree T' of T not in WB[$\frac{1}{2}$]; both its left and right subtrees must be in WB[$\frac{1}{2}$]. Thus the number of leaves each contains must be a power of 2, say 2^l in the left subtree of T' and 2^r in the right subtree of T'. Without loss of generality, suppose $l < r$. Then

$$\beta(T') = \frac{2^l}{2^l + 2^r} = \frac{1}{1 + 2^{r-l}} \leq \frac{1}{3}$$

and T cannot be in WB[α] for $\alpha > \frac{1}{3}$.

Two observations are in order here, to demonstrate that weight-balanced trees bear no relation to height-balanced trees. First, consider the tree of Figure 7.18(b), which is in WB[$\frac{1}{3}$]. Since WB[α] = WB[$\frac{1}{2}$] for $\alpha > \frac{1}{3}$, the tree is as weight-balanced as it can be without being in WB[$\frac{1}{2}$] and it is *not* height-balanced. Thus we cannot in general conclude anything about the height-balance of a weight-balanced tree. Second, there are height-balanced trees that are not weight-balanced, as can be seen by considering the tree with a completely balanced tree of 2^h leaves as its right subtree and the tree T_h of (7.18) as its left subtree. Such a tree is height-balanced, but the weight-balance at the root goes to zero as $h \to \infty$ (why?). Thus we cannot conclude anything about the weight-balance of a height-balanced tree. The two concepts are therefore independent.

We need to prove that weight-balanced trees have only logarithmic height, and further that their weight-balanced state can be maintained efficiently under insertions

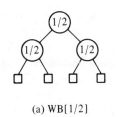

(a) WB[1/2]

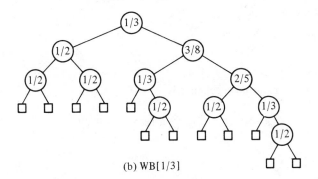

(b) WB[1/3]

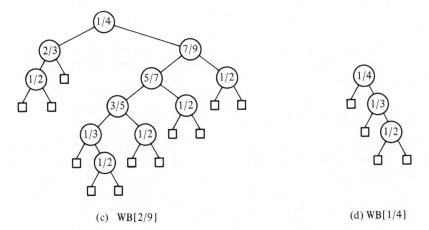

(c) WB[2/9]   (d) WB[1/4]

Figure 7.18
Examples of weight-balanced trees in WB[α], for various values of α

and deletions. We will outline such a demonstration for $0 < \alpha < 1 - \sqrt{2}/2 \approx 0.29289$ with insertions but no deletions. For deletions we will require $\frac{2}{11} < \alpha < 1 - \sqrt{2}/2$, approximately $0.18182 < \alpha < 0.29289$.

What is the height of the tallest possible WB[α] tree with $n + 1$ external nodes (and hence n internal nodes)? Let it be $h_\alpha(n + 1)$. By Exercise 20, $h_\alpha(n + 1) \geq h_\alpha(n)$, so the tallest WB[$\alpha$] tree is the one formed by putting as many of the nodes as possible on one side, say the right side. Since the tree must be in WB[α], if it has $n + 1$ external nodes at most $\lfloor(1 - \alpha)(n + 1)\rfloor$ of them can be in either subtree and thus

$$h_\alpha(n + 1) = 1 + h_\alpha(\lfloor(1 - \alpha)(n + 1)\rfloor)$$

and trivially

$$h_\alpha(1) = 0$$

The solution to this recurrence relation is

$$h_\alpha(n + 1) = \log_{1/(1-\alpha)}(n + 1) + O(1)$$

$$= \frac{1}{\lg \dfrac{1}{1 - \alpha}} \lg(n + 1) + O(1).$$

For $\alpha = \frac{1}{2}$, we have

$$h_{1/2}(n + 1) = \lg(n + 1) + O(1)$$

as we should, since WB[$\frac{1}{2}$] trees are the completely balanced trees in which $n + 1 = 2^t$, for some t. For $\alpha = 1 - \sqrt{2}/2$, the largest value for which the rebalancing algorithms will work, we have

$$h_{1-\sqrt{2}/2}(n + 1) = 2 \lg(n + 1) + O(1)$$

so the worst-case number of probes is just twice as many as the minimum possible. For $\alpha = \frac{2}{11}$, the smallest value for which the rebalancing algorithms will work in the case of a deletion, we have

$$h_{2/11}(n + 1) \approx 3.45 \lg(n + 1) + O(1)$$

or about $3\frac{1}{2}$ times the optimal. In any case, the height of a WB[α] tree is clearly logarithmic in its number of nodes, as desired.

In weight-balanced trees we can also say something about the average number of probes to search a WB[α] tree, whereas in height-balanced trees no such analytical results are known. We leave it to Exercise 22 to verify that the internal path length of a tree in WB[α] is at most

$$\frac{1}{H(\alpha)} (n + 1)\lg(n + 1) - 2n$$

where $H(\alpha) = -\alpha \lg \alpha - (1-\alpha) \lg (1-\alpha)$ is a simple instance of the entropy function introduced in Section 7.2.1. This bound tells us that the average number of probes for any WB[α] will be at most

$$\frac{1}{H(\alpha)} \lg(n + 1) + O(1)$$

assuming each of the keys is equally likely to be the object of the search. For $\alpha = 1 - \sqrt{2}/2$, $1/H(\alpha) \approx 1.15$ so that the average search time will be no more than 15 percent larger than the optimal. For $\alpha = 2/11$, $1/H(\alpha) \approx 1.46$ so that the average search time will be no more than 46 percent larger than the optimal. These bounds hold for *any* WB[α] tree, so the average search time in the *average* WB[α] tree is surely much better, but there is no mathematical analysis known for this case.

When the insertion or deletion of an element in a WB[α] tree causes the balances at various nodes to be outside the range [α, $1 - \alpha$], the tree can be rebalanced in logarithmic time using rotations and double rotations. Figure 7.19 shows the effects of these transformations on the balances of the subtrees involved. The formulas for the balances given in Figure 7.19(a) can be verified by starting from β_A and β_B, the weight balances of the trees rooted at A and B, respectively:

$$\beta_A = \frac{|T_1|}{|T_1| + |T_2| + |T_3|} \quad \text{and} \quad \beta_B = \frac{|T_2|}{|T_2| + |T_3|}.$$

Since

$$|T_1| + |T_2| = (|T_1| + |T_2| + |T_3|) \times$$

$$\left[\frac{|T_1|}{|T_1| + |T_2| + |T_3|} + \left(1 - \frac{|T_1|}{|T_1| + |T_2| + |T_3|} \right) \frac{|T_2|}{|T_2| + |T_3|} \right]$$

$$= (|T_1| + |T_2| + |T_3|)[\beta_A + (1 - \beta_A)\beta_B],$$

we have

$$\beta'_A = \frac{|T_1|}{|T_1| + |T_2|} = \frac{|T_1|}{|T_1| + |T_2| + |T_3|} \frac{1}{\beta_A + (1 - \beta_A)\beta_B}$$

$$= \frac{\beta_A}{\beta_A + (1 - \beta_A)\beta_B}$$

and

$$\beta'_B = \frac{|T_1| + |T_2|}{|T_1| + |T_2| + |T_3|} = \beta_A + (1 - \beta_A)\beta_B.$$

We leave the similar verification of the balances in Figure 7.19(b) as Exercise 23. An alternate derivation of these formulas is the object of Exercise 24.

type
  $pWbTree = \uparrow WbTree$;
  $WbTree =$ **record**
      KEY: *KeyType*;
      LEFT, *RIGHT*: *pWbTree*;
      CONDITION: *BalanceType*;
      SIZE: *integer*   {one less than the number of leaves in this subtree}
  end;
Declarations 7.4

We use rotations and double rotations as follows to rebalance a tree during an insertion or deletion. As in the case of height-balanced trees, we search the tree starting at the root for the site of the insertion or deletion. As each node on this downward path is visited, we can tell immediately whether the insertion or deletion will disturb the balance at the node enough to throw the tree out of WB[α]. We make this determination by a simple calculation on the *SIZE* fields that we maintain in every node as shown in Declarations 7.4: $p\uparrow.SIZE$ is one less than the number of leaves in the subtree rooted at p. (See also Exercise 27.) As each node is visited, its size information is updated, and if this results in an imbalance, a transformation is made to rebalance the tree according to the following rules. Let T be a binary tree with left and right subtrees T_l and T_r, respectively:

1. A rotation as shown in Figure 7.19(a) rebalances T if $|T_l|/|T| < \alpha$, $\beta(T_r) \leq 1/(2 - \alpha)$, and either $|T_l|/(|T| - 1) \geq \alpha$ (T was in WB[α] and an insertion into T_r threw it out of balance) or $(|T_l| + 1)/(|T| + 1) \geq \alpha$ (T was in WB[α] and a deletion from T_l threw it out of balance).

2. A double rotation as shown in Figure 7.19(b) rebalances T if in case 1 we have instead that $\beta(T_r) > 1/(2 - \alpha)$.

3. The mirror image of the rotation in Figure 7.19(a) rebalances T if $|T_l|/|T| > 1 - \alpha$, $\beta(1T_l) \geq (1 - \alpha)/(2 - \alpha)$, and either $(|T_l| - 1)/(1T| - 1) \leq 1 - \alpha$

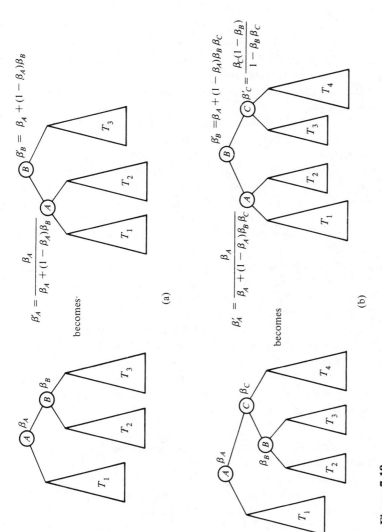

Figure 7.19
The effects in weight-balanced trees of (a) a rotation and (b) a double rotation on the subtrees involved

(T was in WB[α] and an insertion into T_l threw it out of balance) or $|T_l|/(|T| + 1) \leq$ $1 - \alpha$ (T was in WB[α] and a deletion from T_r threw it out of balance).

4. The mirror image of the double rotation in Figure 7.19(b) rebalances T if in case 3 we have instead that $\beta(T_l) < (1 - \alpha)/(2 - \alpha)$.

The verification that these rules do indeed always rebalance the tree for $0 < \alpha \leq 1 - \sqrt{2}/2$ in the case of an insertion and $2/11 < \alpha \leq 1 - \sqrt{2}/2$ in the case of a deletion is elementary but very tedious, and we leave it for Exercises 25 and 26. Notice the crucial fact that the *SIZE* fields are easy to maintain as the tree undergoes rotations and double rotations.

Of course, storing the *SIZE* fields will require more than the two bits required for the height-condition codes in height-balanced trees. But, as we will see in the applications discussed below, that information is useful, and in certain cases we would have the *SIZE* fields (or something equivalent) even in height-balanced trees. The extra storage per node, therefore, need not be an impediment to using weight-balanced trees. However, the extra arithmetic required in the rebalancing operations may not be worth its expense. The primary advantage of weight-balanced trees is that the parameter α can be chosen to give some desired trade-off between search time and rebalancing effort.

There is one result known about weight-balanced trees for which no comparable result is known for height-balanced trees: given any sequence of n insertions and deletions on an initially empty weight-balanced tree, the total number of rotations and double rotations required by the n insertions and deletions is $O(n)$. In other words, on *any* single such sequence, the average number of transformations per insertion or deletion is constant. All that is known for height-balanced trees is that on the average over *many* different sequences of insertions and deletions, the number of transformations per insertion or deletion *seems* (on the basis of empirical evidence) to be constant. The statement made for weight-balanced trees is clearly much stronger than that made for height-balanced trees.

Applications of Balanced Trees to Lists. The size fields that we used for weight-balanced trees allow us to perform efficiently a search by *index position* of the elements, in addition to the search of Algorithm 7.5 which is by their alphabetic or numeric value. That is, we can find the kth element in inorder with the *SIZE* fields as follows. Compute the index position of the element at the root—it is $rank = 1 + root\uparrow.LEFT\uparrow.SIZE$. If this is equal to k, we are done. If it is greater than k, search the left subtree for the kth element; otherwise, search the right subtree for the $(k - rank)$th element. Algorithm 7.10 specifies this process more precisely.

Of course, we do not need weight-balanced trees to use Algorithm 7.10. It will work correctly in any binary tree that has correct *SIZE* fields. We have these fields already in weight-balanced trees because we need them to do the rebalancing after an insertion or deletion, but we could easily add them to nodes in height-balanced

function *IndexSearch(T*: *pWbTree*; *k*: *integer*): *pWbTree*;
{Return a pointer to the *k*th node in *T* in inorder. Return **nil** if
k < 1 or *k* > number of elements in the tree.}
var
    m, rank: *integer*;
    p: *pWbTree*;
    found: *boolean*;
begin
    m := *k*;
    p := *T*;
    found := **false**;
    while (*p* ≠ **nil**) **and not** *found* **do begin**
        {Assert: The *k*th node in *T* is the *m*th node in *p*.}
        {compute the relative index of *p*↑ in its subtree}
        if *p*↑.*LEFT* = **nil then**
            rank := 1
        else *rank* := 1 + *p*↑.*LEFT*↑.*SIZE*;
        {check for location of *k*th node}
        if *m* < *rank* **then**
            p := *p*↑.*LEFT*
        else if *m* > *rank* **then begin**
            m := *m* − *rank*;
            p := *p*↑.*RIGHT*
        end
        else *found* := **true**
    end;
    IndexSearch := *p*
end

Algorithm 7.10
Tree search by inorder index position

trees and maintain them just as in weight-balanced trees (in that case, however, it might be more natural to store the rank information directly, not the size—see Exercise 28). Algorithm 7.10 requires time proportional to the height of the tree, and for height- or weight-balanced trees this will be logarithmic in the number of elements in the tree. Furthermore, it is clear that Algorithm 7.10 can be combined with the insertion, deletion, and rebalancing algorithms, allowing us to make insertions and deletions by index position [for example, to insert a new element between the *k*th and (*k* + 1)st elements or to delete the *k*th element] in $O(\log n)$ time.

We can therefore use weight-balanced trees or height-balanced trees augmented with *SIZE* fields as a compromise between the linked and sequential storage structures for representing linear lists. The normal sequential storage structure (Section 4.1) could be easily searched by index position but was expensive to modify, while the normal linked structure (Section 4.2) was easy to modify once the location was known but expensive to search. Both searching by index position and insertions/deletions can be done with height- or weight-balanced trees in logarithmic time. This compromise is especially useful in implementing a priority queue (see the introduction to Section 4.2) which operates in a first-in, highest-priority-out-first order. As the elements arrive they are inserted into the tree according to their value by Algorithm 7.7 and the appropriate rebalancing scheme. The element deleted is always the one with the highest priority. In this case we do not even need the full power of Algorithm 7.10 to find the element to be deleted (why?).

Using balanced trees as a storage structure for linear lists suggests the need to be able to concatenate them together and split them apart, just as we can do with linked lists. Can these operations also be done in logarithmic time? Yes they can for both height- and weight-balanced trees, although the operations are slightly more complex for weight-balanced trees (see Exercise 31).

Suppose, first, we want to concatenate height-balanced tree U to the right of height-balanced tree T and have the result be a height-balanced tree. We proceed as follows. Compute the heights of T and U in logarithmic time (see Exercise 17). Assume that $heightHB(T) \geqslant heightHB(U)$; the other case is essentially the mirror image. Delete the leftmost inorder element of U, call it q, and rename the remaining tree V. Then use a *paste* operation to paste everything together:

$$PasteHB(T, q, V)$$

This routine constructs a height-balanced tree from node q and trees T and V given that all nodes of T precede q in inorder and q precedes all nodes of V.

In *PasteHB*, Algorithm 7.11, we first compute the heights of the two trees and determine the taller so we can insert q and the smaller tree at a place of proper height in the taller. By assumption above, T is the taller. We descend within T following *RIGHT* links to a node p at about the same height as the height of V. The computation begins with the initial height of T and at each node subtracts either 1 or 2 depending on the height-condition code, 1 if the code was $=$ or $\setminus$ and 2 if it was $\diagup$ (why?). This continues until we find a node p in T such that

$$0 \leqslant heightHB(p) - heightHB(V) \leqslant 1$$

(see Exercise 32). The node

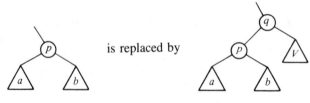

function *PasteHB*(*T*, *q*, *V*: *pHbTree*): *pHbTree*;

    {Construct a height-balanced tree from trees *T* and *V* and node *q*. If the result is to be in inorder, we must have the initial inorder condition: $last(T) \leq q \leq first(V)$}

var

    p, *parent*: *pHbTree*;

    hT, *hV*, *hp*: *integer*;   {heights of the subtrees}

    S: *PathStack*;

begin

    hT := *heightHB*(*T*);

    hV := *heightHB*(*V*);

    if $hT \geq hV$ **then begin**

        Empty(*S*);

        p := *T*;

        hp := *hT*;

        parent := **nil**;

        while $(hp - hV) > 1$ **do begin**

            {Assert: *S* contains the nodes on the path from *p* to root. *p* is right child of *parent*. *hp* is height of tree rooted at *p*.}

            Push(*p*, *S*);

            if *p*↑.*CONDITION* = " $\diagup$ " **then**

                hp := *hp* − 2

            else *hp* := *hp* − 1;

            parent := *p*;

            p := *p*↑.*RIGHT*

        end;

        q↑.*LEFT* := *p*;

        q↑.*RIGHT* := *V*;

        if *hp* = *hV* **then** *q*↑.*CONDITION* := " = "

        else *q*↑.*CONDITION* := " $\diagup$ "

        if *parent* ≠ **nil then** *parent*↑.*RIGHT* := *q*;

        Push(*q*, *S*);

        PasteHB := *RebalanceAfterInsert*(*S*)   {Exercise 33}

    end

    else begin

        "this case is a mirror-image of the above"

    end

end

Algorithm 7.11

Concatenate two height-balanced trees by pasting a node between them with the height-condition code of q being either $=$ or $\diagup$ depending on $heightHB(p) - heightHB(V)$. Having stored the nodes encountered along the right boundary of T on a stack we conclude by going up that boundary beginning at the original parent of p, correcting height-condition codes and performing a rotation or double rotation as though we had done an insertion into the subtree rooted q and had thereby increased its height by one unit.

The problem of splitting a tree in two, corresponding to splitting a linked list into two pieces, is solved by disconnecting portions of the tree and reassembling them with *PasteHB*. To understand the idea, consider the tree of Figure 7.20. The list represented is the inorder of the tree, $S_1aS_2bS_3cS_4dT_1eT_2fT_3$, and suppose this is to be split into two lists $S_1aS_2bS_3cS_4d$ and $T_1eT_2fT_3$; in other words, the list is to be split after node d, as shown in Figure 7.20 by the dashed line. Assume that in tracing the path from the root to d the nodes have been stored on a stack, as in the other height-balanced tree algorithms. We now go back up that path toward the root, breaking the tree apart and concatenating the pieces together to form the desired lists. First d is inserted at the extreme right of S_4, to give S_4d. S_3 and S_4d are then concatenated using c as the paste node in the concatenation algorithm to form S_3cS_4d. *The node e is then used as the paste node in concatenating T_1 and T_2 to form T_1eT_2.* The node b is then used as the paste node in concatenating S_2 to S_3cS_4d, giving $S_2bS_3cS_4d$, which is in turn concatenated to S_1 using a as the paste node, giving $S_1aS_2bS_3cS_4d$.

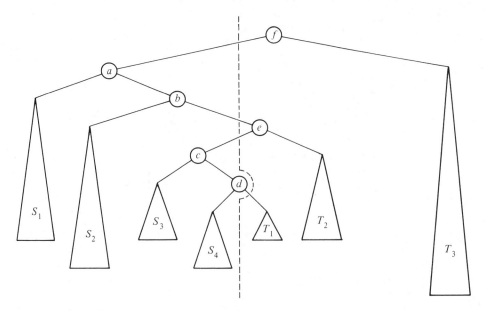

Figure 7.20
An example of splitting a binary tree into two pieces based on the inorder of the nodes

On the last step, f is used as the paste node in concatenating T_3 to $T_1 e T_2$, giving $T_1 e T_2 f T_3$.

Algorithm 7.12 gives an outline of the procedure in general. Notice that the algorithm as outlined will work to split any binary tree, not just a height-balanced tree. For example, using the insertion and concatenation procedures for weight-balanced trees, Algorithm 7.12 serves to split a weight-balanced tree, resulting in two weight-balanced trees. The time required by Algorithm 7.12 will be proportional to the total required by the insertion and the sequence of concatenations. In height- or weight-balanced trees these are potentially $O(\log n)$, and the concatenation process requires $O(\log n)$ time, suggesting that the splitting algorithm might require time proportional to $(\log n)^2$ in the worst case for such balanced trees. Fortunately, however, the concatenation algorithm requires logarithmic time only to delete the node that will be used to paste the trees together. If given that node, as is the case in the concatenations done in the splitting process, the concatenation will require only time proportional to the difference in height of the two trees being concatenated. This leads to a logarithmic worst-case time for splitting balanced trees (Exercise 34).

```
procedure SplitTree(var P: PathStack; var S, T: pHbTree);
            {P contains the nodes on the path to a split node. Construct two
            trees in S and T from those nodes. The split node will be at the end
            of S.}
var
        current, child: pHbTree;
begin
        current := Pop(P);
        S := current↑.LEFT;
        T := current↑.RIGHT;
        S := PasteHB(S, current, nil);    {insert current in left result tree}
        while not IsEmpty(P) do begin
            {Assert: P has path from current to root. S and T contain, respec-
            tively, the left and right results of splitting the subtree at current in
            such a way as to keep the original split node at the end of S.}
            child := current;
            current := Pop(P);
            if child = current↑.RIGHT then
                    S := PasteHB(current↑.LEFT, current, S)
            else
                    T := PasteHB(T, current, current↑.RIGHT)
        end
end
```

Algorithm 7.12
Splitting a binary tree in two pieces based on the inorder of the nodes

Two final remarks about representing lists by trees are in order. First, the algorithms described can be used *without* the rebalancing parts, essentially allowing the trees to grow randomly. If the insertions, deletions, concatenations, splittings, and searches were all random, the resulting trees would probably maintain logarithmic height on the average. But in most applications it is extremely unlikely that the sequences of operations would be truly random; rather, biases would occur that would cause the trees to deteriorate badly. Second, if possible when using binary trees to represent lists, *PARENT* pointers should be maintained in the nodes. This will greatly facilitate the algorithms that require retracing the path from a node to the root: insertion, deletion, concatenation, and splitting. Furthermore, it will allow the deletion of a node given only a pointer to the node; in this sense *PARENT* pointers give something of an analog to doubly linked lists.

Exercises

1. Use elementary integral calculus to show that $H_n = \sum_{i=1}^{n} 1/i \approx \ln n$. [*Hint*: Compare H_n to $\int_1^n dx/x$ and use the rectangle rule.]

2. This exercise is an alternative way of deriving the result of Equation (7.16), which gives the external path length of a randomly constructed binary search tree of n elements. Let U_n be the average number of probes in an unsuccessful search in a given binary search tree T of n nodes. Let U_{n+1} be the average number of probes in an unsuccessful search after a random insertion has been made in T.

   (a) What is U_1?

   (b) What is the relationship between U_n and the E_n of Equation (7.16)?

   (c) Prove that $U_{n+1} = U_n + 2/(n + 2)$. [*Hint*: If the insertion is at level i, by how much does the external path length increase? What is the average level of a leaf in the tree?]

   (d) Use the above results, along with Exercise 1, to obtain (7.16).

   (e) Let S_n be the average number of probes in a successful search of a randomly constructed binary search tree of n elements. Prove that $S_n = 1 + (U_0 + U_1 + \cdots + U_{n-1})/n$.

3. Prove that if a node X in a binary tree has a non-**nil** left (right) child, then its inorder predecessor (successor) has a **nil** right (left) child.

4. Write out the details of the algorithm to delete an element from a binary search tree. (See page 340.)

5. Derive a recurrence relation for N_h, the number of distinct height-balanced trees of height h. How fast does N_h grow?

6. Compute the external path length of the tree T_h as defined by (7.17) and (7.18).

7. Find height-balanced trees whose internal path length is close to $(1 - \sqrt{5}/20)/\lg[(1 + \sqrt{5})/2] \approx 1.28$ times that of the completely balanced tree of Section 5.3.

8. In a height-balanced tree of n internal nodes, at least how many *must* have = as their height-condition code? (*Answer*: $[(3 - \sqrt{5})/2]n \approx 0.38n$.)

9. Can either or both of T_1 and T_4 in Figure 7.15(b) be empty?

10. Explain how the transformations of Figure 7.15 might be used to implement *self-organizing binary search trees*, in which the more an element is accessed the closer it moves to the root.

11. The backward scan up the tree from the site of the insertion in a height-balanced tree can be eliminated at the expense of retracing part of the path down the tree. This can be done roughly as follows. As we go down in the tree to the site of the insertion, keep track of the node S that is the latest one along the path to have height condition code $\searmon$ or $\nearrow$. When the insertion is made, each of the elements between S and the newly inserted element has height-condition code = and each must be changed to $\searmon$ or $\nearrow$. It is at S that a rotation or double rotation may be needed. Work out the details of this insertion algorithm.

12. Draw the trees for the mirror images of Figure 7.17 in the algorithm for deletion from a height-balanced tree.

13. Under what conditions does a double rotation also rebalance the tree in Figure 7.17(a) in the algorithm for deletion from a height-balanced tree?

14. Prove that the deletion algorithm for height-balanced trees may require as many as $\lfloor h/2 \rfloor$ rotations and double rotations for a tree of height h, but no more.

15. Devise a technique for height-balanced trees that requires only one bit per element for the height-condition code. [*Hint*: If a node in the tree has two children then its two-bit height-condition code can be stored with one bit in each child. What if a node has zero or one child?]

16. As an alternative to the two-bit height-condition code or the complication of Exercise 15, we can insist that if one subtree is taller than its sibling, it must be the right subtree. Thus a *one-sided, height-balanced tree* always has $0 \le h(T_l) - h(T_r) \le 1$. Obviously, a single bit suffices in this case for the height-condition code. Develop insertion and deletion algorithms for these trees.

17. Give an $O(\log n)$ function *heightHB* to determine the height of a height-balanced tree.

18. Determine the exact shape of the height-balanced tree that results from insertion of n elements in increasing order.

19. Develop, in parallel with the presentation given in the text for height-balanced trees, the notion of height-balanced trees in which the heights of the left and right subtrees can differ by at most 2.

20. Show that for all α, $0 < \alpha \leq \frac{1}{3}$, the tallest possible WB[α] tree containing $n + 1$ internal nodes is at least as tall as the tallest possible WB[α] tree containing n internal nodes. (*Hint*: Show that, given a WB[α] tree, a node can be added without throwing the tree out of WB[α].)

21. What is the least number of nodes in a tree of height 10 in (a) WB[$\frac{1}{2}$], (b) WB[$\frac{1}{3}$], (c) WB[$1 - \sqrt{2}/2$], (d) WB[$\frac{1}{4}$], (e) WB[$\frac{2}{11}$]?

22. Use induction on the number of nodes to prove that the internal path length of a tree in WB[α] is at most

$$\frac{1}{H(\alpha)} (n + 1)\lg(n + 1) - 2n$$

where $H(\alpha) = -\alpha \lg \alpha - (1 - \alpha)\lg(1 - \alpha)$.

23. Verify the formulas for the balances β'_A, β'_B, and β'_C in Figure 7.19(b).

★24. Interpreting β_A, β_B, and β_C as probabilities, derive the formulas for β'_A, β'_B, and β'_C in Figures 7.19 by using the law of *conditional probability*. [*Hint*: In Figure 7.19(a) β_A is the probability that an external node is in T_1. What is the conditional probability that an external node is in T_2, given that it is in either T_2 or T_3?]

25. Does the rebalancing algorithm for weight-balanced trees work in the case of a deletion for $\alpha = \frac{2}{11}$?

26. Verify that the rebalancing algorithms for weight-balanced trees really do restore the balances properly for $0 < \alpha \leq 1 - \sqrt{2}/2$ in the case of an insertion and $\frac{2}{11} < \alpha \leq 1 - \sqrt{2}/2$ in the case of a deletion.

27. Suppose that, instead of using a field *SIZE* in a node giving the number of nodes in the subtree rooted at that node, we use a field *RANK* that gives the number of nodes in the left subtree of that node plus one. Suppose further that the tree is stored as the left child of the header node and that a header node contains a *RANK* field, the value of which would be, naturally, the number of nodes in the tree T plus one. Show that these *RANK* fields are sufficient to maintain weight-balanced trees.

28. Show that both the *SIZE* and *RANK* fields can be properly maintained in logarithmic time in height- or weight-balanced trees under the various operations presented.

29. Give the details of the algorithms for insertion and deletion from a weight-balanced tree.

★30. Assuming that the balance of each node in a WB[α] tree is uniformly distributed over the interval [α, $1 - \alpha$], independently of the balances of other nodes, show that the expected number of rotations and double rotations required to insert or delete a node is less than $2/(1 - 2\alpha)$.

31. Show that weight-balanced trees can be concatenated in logarithmic time.

32. In the algorithm to concatenate height-balanced trees we require that $0 \le heightHB(p) - heightHB(U) \le 1$. Why don't we allow $heightHB(p) - heightHB(U) = -1$?

33. Revise *RebalanceAfterInsert*, Algorithm 7.8, to return the root of the resulting tree for use in Algorithm 7.11. Write out the procedure in full, including the details of the rotations.

34. Verify that Algorithm 7.12 for splitting a tree requires only $O(\log n)$ time for height-balanced trees. Is this also true for weight-balanced trees?

35. What changes would be necessary to Algorithm 7.12 if we wanted to split the tree *before* (rather than after) the splitting node?

36. In the application of representing a list as a binary tree, it might be more natural to keep a field *INDEX* rather than *SIZE* or *RANK*, where the *INDEX* field of the *i*th element in the list being represented is *i*. Comment on the advisability of this suggestion.

37. Consider the following memory management problem. Memory consists of an infinite number of locations that are to be allocated according to the first-fit rule: when *k* locations are requested, they are to be allocated from the *leftmost* (lowest-address) block of locations currently available. Describe a data structure and algorithm for implementing reservations and releases so that each of these operations requires only time proportional to log *n*, where *n* is the number of blocks currently available.

38. Consider *n* elements $x_1 < x_2 < \cdots < x_n$ organized into the following data structure. A subset of $l - 1$ elements $x_{i_1} < x_{i_2} < \cdots < x_{i_{l-1}}$ divides the rest of the keys into *l* subfiles; the *j*th subfile consists of elements between $x_{i_{j-1}}$ and x_{i_j}. A *file tree* is the structure obtained linking these $l - 1$ elements and *l* subfiles together, where each subfile is organized as an ordered sequential list. The elements x_{i_1}, x_{i_2}, ..., $x_{i_{l-1}}$ are organized as a height-balanced binary tree. The

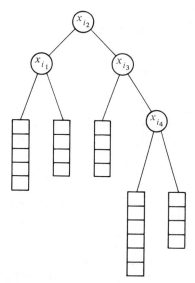

Figure 7.21
Exercise 37

resulting structure looks like the structure in Figure 7.21. There is an additional restriction that none of the subfiles can have more than $3m$ elements or less than $2m$ elements. (In the above example $m = 2$.) To search a file tree for z we search as in binary search trees to find the proper subfile and then search that subfile sequentially.

(a) Describe a procedure to insert a new element into a file tree so that it remains a file tree.

(b) How many key comparisons are required in the worst case for your procedure?

39. Suppose we want to represent a priority queue that will never contain more than ten elements. Should we use the balanced-tree representation presented here?

40. Develop algorithms that keep trees balanced by bounding the amount by which the external path lengths of the two subtrees of a node can differ.

41. Develop algorithms that keep trees balanced by performing a rotation or double rotation where it will decrease the internal path length of the tree. Analyze the worst and average search times in such trees.

42. Develop logarithmic time algorithms for the operations of insertion, deletion, concatenation, and splitting of linear lists represented by balanced binary trees in which the external nodes are the list elements and internal nodes correspond to the links in the list.

7.3 DIGITAL SEARCH TREES

We can use trees to organize tables based on the representation of the elements, rather than on the ordering of the elements as in the previous section. Actually, we have already seen a simple example of such an organization: Figure 5.6 shows how a binary tree could be used to store a table for decoding characters in Morse code. The principal idea there is to go down the tree starting at the root, going left or right based on whether the next symbol is a dot or a dash, respectively. This idea is easily extended to larger alphabets, say decimal digits or alphabetic characters, in place of dots and dashes. If the alphabet contained c characters, each node in the tree would be a c-way branch—one branch for each possible character. The structure thus obtained, called a *digital search tree* or *trie* (taken from the middle letters of the word "re*trie*val," but pronounced "try"), is illustrated in Figure 7.22 which shows 30 common English words.

To explain Figure 7.22 we will describe how to search it. Suppose we are given the word HAVE as the object of the search. We consider each of the letters H, A, V, E in turn, starting at the root of the tree and proceeding as follows. Follow the branch labeled H out of the root; at the next node follow the branch labeled A, then the branch labeled V, and finally the branch labeled E. At that point we are at the bottom of the tree and the letters of the search object are exhausted, so we have successfully found HAVE in the tree. If the search object had been HAVING, we would have followed down branches in the tree corresponding to H, A, and V, but then there would be no branch labeled I, indicating that HAVING is not in the tree. If needed, we could store information about the word in a record pointed to by the last letter. A digital search tree is only a thumb-index arrangement in the extreme: at the top level there is a section for each initial character, within each initial letter there is a section for each possible second character, and so on.

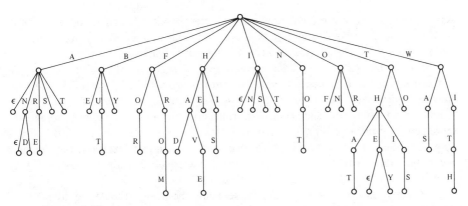

Figure 7.22
A digital search tree consisting of 30 common English words

Notice at the extreme lower left of Figure 7.22 there are branches of the tree labeled ε. This special symbol is used to distinguish between words in the tree that are prefixes of one another. In Figure 7.22 for example, we have the words A, AN, and AND. The ε as a possible character after taking the branch labeled A from the root means that A itself is an element of the tree. We thus need to modify the search algorithm outlined above as follows. To search for an object $C_1C_2\cdots C_k$ in the tree, we follow the branch out of the root labeled C_1, then follow the branch labeled C_2, and so on. After following the branch for C_k, if the node reached has no outgoing branches or has a branch labeled ε then we have successfully found the object. Otherwise, the search fails. The search also fails if at any point along the way there was no branch labeled C_i as required. When a search object is not in the tree, the search procedure finds the element in the tree that has the longest match of initial characters with the search object.

The advantage of a digital search tree is that in many circumstances the multiway branch required at every node of the tree will require little or no more time than a binary decision. In c-way branching, on the average only $\log_c n = \lg n/\lg c$ tests would be needed instead of, say, $\lg n$ for binary search. For example, in the case of alphabetic information $c = 27$ (why not 26?) and $1/(\lg 27) \approx 0.21$, indicating that only about a fifth as many tests would be made in a digital search tree based on letters as would be made by binary search. Of course, if the 27-way branch were five times as expensive as a two-way branch, there would be no savings. Typically, though, by using subscripts into an array it is possible to implement a c-way branch in only slightly more time than is required by a two-way branch. In the case of alphabetic characters each tree node could be of the form

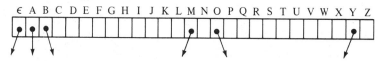

Assuming the binary representations of the letters A, B, C, and so on are 00001, 00010, 00011, ..., we can choose 00000 as the binary representation for ε and use these "values" of the letters as indices into the particular record.

For the tree of Figure 7.22 we would need 27 such records, one for each node in the tree that has a descendant. Each record has room for 27 pointers, so the total storage requirements are about $27 \times 27 = 729$ pointers to represent a table of 30 words totaling only 79 characters. Unfortunately, this rather excessive storage requirement is typical of digital search trees! It arises from the fact that with records as shown above for tree nodes, there is an enormous amount of room for elements *not* in the table (why?). It is precisely this characteristic that allowed us the c-way branches that lead to $\log_c n$ average search times.

There is an obvious possibility for reducing the heavy storage requirements of digital search trees. We could use the natural correspondence (see Section 5.1.1) to represent the tree of Figure 7.22 as the binary tree shown in Figure 7.23. Searching

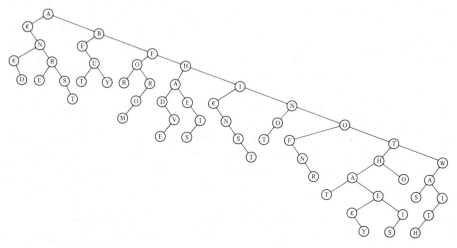

Figure 7.23
The binary tree resulting from the digital search tree of Figure 7.22 by the natural
correspondence

the tree in this form means going to the *RIGHT* zero or more times until the desired
character is found, going *LEFT* one step, and then repeating the process for the subsequent characters of the search object (Exercise 3). This process has replaced c-way
branches by two-way branches, and we know from Section 5.3 that the average and
worst-case number of such branches examined in searching such a tree cannot be less
than $\lg n$, quite poor in comparison to $\log_c n$. This method for reducing the storage
requirement of digital search trees is thus *not* to be recommended.

A second method of reducing storage requirements in digital search trees is to
collapse sequences of nodes in which no branching occurs into a single node. In
Figure 7.22, for example, we could replace ⌇ T by ⌇ TH , eliminating one node from
the tree, at the expense of a slight complication of the algorithm. Even in this small
example the payoff for the additional complication is significant (we could make 14
such changes to the tree, saving 14 nodes, or more than half of the space); in many
cases the savings would be even more dramatic (see Exercise 2). This collapsing
need not be done just at the bottom of the tree. If we had a digital search tree of
names of fish containing both REDFIN and REDFISH, we could use

A third, even more useful strategy to reduce the storage requirements is to take a cue from the thumb-index analogy and use a digital search tree only for the few top levels, changing to some other technique when the number of elements is small enough.

Another weakness of digital search trees is that it would take a relatively long time to distinguish between almost identical words such as IRRESPONSIBLE and IRRESPONSIBILITY, while binary search would do so in only one comparison. In the nonrandom elements found in many practical applications such identical sequences of initial characters are common. Given a set of elements to be organized into a digital search tree, it may therefore be advantageous to base the tree on a different order of the characters in an element—for example, taking the characters of an element from right to left rather than left to right. In general the problem of determining the *optimal* order in which the characters should be considered (given some probability distribution for the search objects) is computationally intractible.

Finally, digital search trees can be used for dynamic tables, since insertions and deletions are not hard to accommodate. The time for such operations cannot be guaranteed to be logarithmic in the table size, however.

Exercises

1. Give a digital search tree for the following approximations to well-known mathematical constants: $\sqrt{2} \approx 1.414$, $1/\ln 2 \approx 1.44$, $(1 + \sqrt{5})/2 \approx 1.6$, $\ln 10 \approx 2.3$, $e \approx 2.718$, $\pi \approx 3.14159$, $\gamma \approx 0.57722$, and $\cos 1 \approx 0.5403$. Do the same for these approximations in octal.

2. Give a digital search tree for the names of the books of the Old Testament of the Bible. Modify the tree by collapsing sequences of two or more nodes that have no branches and compute the amount of storage thus saved.

3. Give the complete algorithm to search a digital search tree that is represented by the binary tree arising from the natural correspondence.

4. Give the digital search tree for the same elements as in Figure 7.22, except with the letters of the elements in reverse order. Which of these two trees is more efficient? Consider space and average search time with some reasonable distribution of search objects.

★5. Prove or disprove: In an alphabet of c characters the average length of n distinct equally probable strings of characters cannot be much less than $\log_c n$ as n gets large.

7.4 HASHING

We now examine a class of table organizations in which we attempt to store elements in locations that are easily computed from the value or representation of the elements.

This contrasts markedly with the techniques presented in previous sections of this chapter; in those sections we based a search on comparisons (usually binary), and the location in which an element was stored depended on its position in an *ordered* arrangement of the elements. In this section we discuss techniques based on *directly* transforming the element into an address at which it will be stored.

A very simple version of this technique has already been presented in the discussion of multidimensional arrays in Section 3.1.1. There we considered the layout in memory of an array $A[l_1..u_1, l_2..u_2, \ldots, l_n..u_n]$ and gave a formula for the location of $A[i_1, i_2, \ldots, i_n]$ as a function of $i_1, i_2, \ldots,$ and i_n. Considering the n-tuple $(i_1, i_2, \ldots, i_n)$ as the key z and the associated array value $A[i_1, i_2, \ldots, i_n]$ as some additional information to be carried in a field in the corresponding record, the problem of finding z reduces to the problem of computing the location from the n-tuple comprising z; that is where $A[z]$ will be found. Because there is a one-to-one correspondence between n-tuples $(i_1, i_2, \ldots, i_n)$ and locations, we do not need to store the n-tuple itself, only the array value. For the same reason, we need not worry about two different n-tuples yielding the same location.

More generally, we will suppose that we have an array of m table locations $T[0..m-1]$, say, and given an element z to be inserted we transform it to a location $h(z)$, $0 \leqslant h(z) < m$; h is called a *hash function*. We then examine $T[h(z)]$ to see if it is empty. Most of the time it will be, so we set $T[h(z)] := z$ and we are done. If $T[h(z)]$ is not empty, a *collision* has occurred and we must resolve it somehow. Taken together, the hash function and the collision resolution method are referred to as *hashing* or *scatter storage* schemes. In Section 7.4.1 we discuss various possible hash functions, and in Section 7.4.2 we discuss alternative strategies for resolving collisions.

For ease of presentation we will assume that the elements to be stored in the hash table are small enough to be stored in their entirety in the table locations. In practice, if the elements are large records, we would instead store only pointers to the actual records, supplied by *new*, in the table locations. This procedure slows down access into the table slightly because we must follow an extra pointer to reach the record contents. It also increases the storage overhead. It is advantageous, however, because it allows us to use a larger table size m which in turn will lead to better performance, as we will see.

Under the proper conditions, hashing is unsurpassed in its efficiency as a table organization, since the average times for a search or an insertion are generally *constant, independent of the size of the table*. However, some important caveats are in order. First, hashing requires a strong belief in the law of averages, since in the worst case collisions occur every time and hashing degenerates into linear search! Second, while it is easy to make insertions into a hash table, the full size of the table must be specified *a priori*, because it is usually closely connected to the hash function used; this makes it extremely expensive to change dynamically: choose too small a size and the performance will be poor or the table may overflow, but choose too large a size and much memory will be wasted. Third, deletions from the table are not easily accommodated in most schemes. Finally, the order of the elements in the table is unrelated to any natural order that may exist among the elements, and so an unsuccessful search results only in the knowledge that the element sought is not in the table, with no information about how it relates to the elements that are in the table.

7.4.1 Hash Functions

The hash function takes an element to be stored in a table and transforms it into a location in the table. If this transformation makes certain table locations more likely to occur than others, the chance of collision is increased and the efficiency of searches and insertions is decreased. The phenomenon of some table locations being more likely is called *primary clustering*. The ideal hash function spreads the elements uniformly throughout the table—that is, does not exhibit primary clustering. In fact, we would really like a hash function that, given any z, chooses a random location in the table in which to store z; this would minimize primary clustering. This is, of course, impossible, since the function h cannot be probabilistic but must be deterministic, yielding the same location every time it is applied to the same element (otherwise, how would we ever find an element after it was inserted?!). The achievable ideal is to design hash functions that exhibit pseudorandom behavior—behavior that appears random but that is reproducible.

Unfortunately, there are no hard and fast rules for constructing hash functions. We will examine four basic techniques that can be used individually or in combination. The properties of any particular hash function are hard to determine because they depend so heavily on the set of elements that will be encountered in practice. Thus the construction of a good hash function from these basic techniques is more an art than anything amenable to analysis, but we will present general principles that usually prove successful, pointing out their pitfalls as well.

For convenience we will assume that an element to be hashed is encoded as a string of bits that can also be interpreted as an integer written in binary. The hash function has to take such a string of bits and produce an address from it. As a continuing example, we will use the 30 common English words in the trie of Figure 7.22. We will assume that each letter is encoded as a five-bit binary string, A = 00001, B = 00010, C = 00011, ..., Z = 11010. (This corresponds to the binary representation of $ord(c) - ord('A') + 1$ if the characters are represented in ASCII—see Section 2.2.3. In practice we would use ASCII directly.) Each word is thus a concatenation of such strings, so that, for example, THE would be represented as the fifteen-bit string

$$10100\ 01000\ 00101 = 20{,}741_{10}$$
$$\underbrace{\quad}_{T}\ \underbrace{\quad}_{H}\ \underbrace{\quad}_{E}$$

and OF would be represented as the ten-bit string

$$\underbrace{01111}_{O} \ \underbrace{00110}_{F} \ = 486_{10}$$

Extraction. The simplest hash functions are those that merely extract a few scattered bits from an element, putting those bits together to form an address. Suppose we want to store the eight words THE, OF, AND, TO, A, IN, THAT, and IS in a table. We could take the third bit from the left and the last two bits on the right as in Table 7.1. This works out neatly and is a perfect way to fit the eight words into $T[0..7]$. Of course, the same hash function would do rather poorly with the words THE, FROM, THEY, ONE, DRY, TEA, GLUM, and WE, each of which would give the result $(101)_2 = 5$.

Extraction is generally a poor way to do hashing except in ad hoc situations where the table contents are completely known in advance and the bits to be extracted can be carefully chosen to prevent primary clustering. The weakness of extraction as a technique for hashing is that the resulting location depends only on a small subset of the bits of an element. A first principle in the design of hash functions is thus that *the hash location should be a function of every bit of the element.*

Compression. A simple way to get a location from an element in such a way that every bit of the element participates is to compress the bits of the element into the number required for an address. We could, for example, break the bit string to be hashed into fixed-length segments and then add them up as binary numbers or take their exclusive-or. The function h_1 shown in Table 7.2 is just such a hash function, being formed by the exclusive-or of the bit strings of the letters in a word; thus $h_1(\text{THE}) = 10100 \ \textbf{xor} \ 01000 \ \textbf{xor} \ 00101 = 11001 = 25_{10}$. Exclusive-or may be

Word	Binary Form	Third bit ↓ ⌐ Last two bits
THE	10100 01000 00101	$(101)_2 = 5$
OF	01111 00110	$(110)_2 = 6$
AND	00001 01110 00100	$(000)_2 = 0$
TO	10100 01111	$(111)_2 = 7$
A	00001	$(001)_2 = 1$
IN	01001 01110	$(010)_2 = 2$
THAT	10100 01000 00001 10100	$(100)_2 = 4$
IS	01001 10011	$(011)_2 = 3$

Table 7.1
A simple hash function based on extraction.

z	$h_1(z)$	$h_2(z)$	$h_3(z)$
THE	25	2	23
OF	9	21	21
AND	11	19	4
TO	27	4	7
A	1	1	19
IN	7	23	30
THAT	9	18	17
IS	26	28	2
WAS	5	12	26
HE	13	13	27
FOR	27	8	16
IT	29	29	20
WITH	2	29	7
AS	18	20	8
HIS	18	5	30
ON	1	29	18
BE	7	7	8
AT	21	21	26
BY	27	27	16
I	9	9	16
THIS	6	25	23
HAD	13	13	30
NOT	21	18	21
ARE	22	24	4
BUT	3	12	11
FROM	22	21	3
OR	29	2	2
HAVE	26	5	26
AN	15	15	6
THEY	0	27	1

Table 7.2
Examples of the three major types of hash functions for the set of words used in
the trie of Figure 7.22. $h_1(z)$ = the **xor** of the characters; for example, h_1(THE)
= 10100 **xor** 01000 **xor** 00101 = 11001 = 25_{10}. $h_2(z)$ = value of z **mod** 31;
for example, h_2(THE) = 101000100000101_2 **mod** 31 = 20741_{10} **mod** 31 = 2_{10}.
$h_3(z)$ = 1 + $floor$(30 × $fraction$(0.6125423371 × value of z)); for example,
h_3(THE) = 1 + $floor$(30 × $fraction$(0.6125423371 × 20741)) = 1 + $floor$(30
× 0.74061) = 1 + 22 = 23. The ranges of these functions are $0 \leq h_1(z) \leq$
31, $0 \leq h_2(z) \leq 30$, and $1 \leq h_3(z) \leq 30$.

somewhat preferable to addition because there is no need to worry about arithmetic
overflow (also see Exercise 1).

One weakness of such a method of compression is that the operations of addition and exclusive-or are commutative, so that $a + b = b + a$ and a **xor** $b = b$
xor a. This means that in our example different words formed from the same letters

will hash to the same location: $h_1(\text{STEAL}) = h_1(\text{STALE}) = h_1(\text{TALES}) = h_1(\text{LEAST})$, and so on, suggesting another principle in the design of hash functions: *a hash function should break up naturally occurring clusters of elements.* In the case of h_1, this can be done by shifting different segments circularly by different amounts. Instead of the function h_1 of Table 7.2 we might therefore use $\hat{h}_1$, in which the first segment is left alone, the second is circularly shifted one position, the third two positions, and so on (Exercise 2).

In general, compression techniques are most useful for converting multi-word elements into a single word, making it easy to apply either the division- or multiplication-based hash functions that we now describe. These two classes of hash functions have proven to be extremely reliable in practice.

Division. Given a table $T[0..m-1]$, we can take

$$h(z) = z \bmod m$$

that is, $h(z)$ is the remainder when z is divided by m. The function h_2 in Table 7.2 is a hash function of this type with $m = 31$; therefore $h_2(\text{THE}) = 101000100000101_2$ **mod** $31 = 20{,}741_{10}$ **mod** $31 = 2$. Such a hash function satisfies a third design principle: *a hash function should be very quick and easy to compute.* Of course, to use such a division hash function we must choose the value of m carefully in order to satisfy our first two design principles, namely that the hash location depends on all the bits of the element and that naturally occurring clusters are broken up.

Suppose m is even. Then even elements will hash to even locations and odd elements will hash to odd locations. More generally, if d divides m, then $h(z) \equiv z$ (mod d), which would greatly increase collisions in the unfortunate event that the elements are not equally distributed across the equivalence classes modulo d. This strongly suggests that m be prime, or at least have no "small" prime factors.

Let r be the radix of the character set; in our example $r = 32$, because each letter is represented by a string of five bits, but r would more usually be 256 (on a binary computer with eight-bit bytes) or 100 (on a decimal computer). If $r \equiv 1$ (mod m), then $h(z)$ would degenerate into the sum of the individual characters modulo m (why?), so that all permutations of given letters have the same hash location. Exactly this occurs in h_2 of Table 7.1, where $r = 32$ and $m = 31$ (Exercise 4). Similarly, if $r^k \equiv 1$ (mod m) for some k, then $h(z)$ is a sum of blocks of k characters modulo m (again, why?). In general, $r^k \equiv \pm a$ (mod m) for "small" a results in combinations of individual characters or groups of characters that can be problematic. This suggests that in addition to being a prime number, m should *not* be of the form $r^k \pm a$ for small values of a. Getting back to our example of $r = 32$, we should choose as our value of m some prime *not* in the vicinity of 32, $32^2 = 1024$, or $32^3 = 32{,}768$.

Multiplication. Given a real number θ, $0 < \theta < 1$, we can construct a hash function as follows. To find $h(z)$ compute *fraction*$(z\theta)$—that is, the fractional part of $z\theta$. Multiplying this fractional part by m and taking the floor gives a value

$$h(z) = floor(m \times fraction(z\theta))$$

satisfying $0 \leq h(z) < m$. The function h_3 in Table 7.2 is such a function with $\theta = 0.6125423371$ and $m = 30$; 1 has been added so that h_3 can be used for later examples that require a hash function with a range $1 \leq h(z) \leq 30$.

Unlike the division hash function, we need not be concerned with the table size m, but we do need some guidelines in choosing θ. We do not want θ to be too close to 0 or 1, since this would cause small elements to cluster at the ends of the table. For instance, if $\theta = 0.99999$, all one- and two-letter words would hash to the last 1 percent of the table. Similarly, we do not want *fraction*$(r^k\theta)$ to be close to 0 or 1, where r is the radix of the character set, for then elements of the form $ar^k + b$ will cluster for small values of a. For example, if $\theta = 0.3066407$, then all three-letter words ending in AT will have hash locations of the form $m \times fraction((32^2a + 52)\theta)$ where $2 \leq a \leq 22$ (for example, BAT = 00010 00001 10100 = $32^2 \times 2 + 52$). But *fraction*$(32^2\theta) \approx 0.000077$, making the contribution of the initial letter of the word negligible, so that BAT, CAT, EAT, and so on will all hash to around $0.94m$.

Values approximately $i/(r-1)$, $1 \leq i < r-1$, are also problematic choices for θ, since *fraction* $(z\theta)$ will tend to cluster elements differing only by a permutation of characters. This occurs because

$$\frac{1}{r-1} = \frac{1}{r} + \frac{1}{r^2} + \frac{1}{r^3} + \cdots$$

written $(0.11 \ldots)_r$, and the product of z and such a θ will have base r digits that are essentially sums of base r digits of z—that is, sums of the individual characters of z. For example, consider $\theta = 6/31 \approx 0.193548387$ which, expressed as a decimal fraction, appears quite innocent. However, with our five-bit character encoding, EAT, TEA, ETA, and ATE all result in *fraction*$(z\theta)$ being approximately 0.032258. Such values of θ are obviously to be avoided. In a similar fashion, a value of θ close to $i/(r^2-1)$, $1 \leq i < r^2-1$, will tend to cluster elements that differ only by independent permutations of the first, third, fifth, ..., positions and the second, fourth, sixth, ... positions (why?). For example, with $\theta = 479/1023 \approx 0.468230694$, MATE, META, and TAME give *fraction*$(z\theta)$ as about 0.2610, while MEAT gives it as about 0.4731 and TEAM as about 0.0792. Generally, a value of θ close to $i/(r^k-1)$, $1 \leq i < r^k-1$, will exhibit a corresponding type of clustering, but in most cases we need only consider $k = 1$ or 2 [unless there is some special reason to suspect that the elements occurring in practice will differ from each other by independent permutations of the first, $(k + 1)$st, $(2k + 1)$st, ... positions, the second, $(k + 2)$nd, $(2k + 2)$nd, ... positions, the third, $(k + 3)$rd, $(2k + 3)$rd, ... positions, and so on, for some $k > 2$].

As a final comment on the choice of θ, various theoretical results suggest that $\theta = (\sqrt{5} - 1)/2 \approx 0.6180339887$ or $\theta = 1 - (\sqrt{5} - 1)/2 \approx 0.3819660113$ tend to spread values out most uniformly of all choices for θ. Care should be taken in using such a θ with $r = 100$, however, because the fractional part of $10^6 \times 0.3819660113$ is close to 0.

The computation of $h(z) = floor(m \times fraction(z\theta))$ can be simplified to a single-integer multiplication followed by the extraction of a block of bits from the product, if m is properly chosen. For simplicity, assume that we are working on a binary computer with w-bit words; the parallel case for a decimal computer is essentially identical. We write $\theta = q/2^w$ and choose a w-bit integer q so that the resulting θ does not exhibit primary clustering as outlined in the preceding paragraphs. Then the product of θ and a t-bit key z will have this form:

$$z\theta = zq/2^w = (\longleftarrow t \text{ bits} \longrightarrow) \times (\longleftarrow w \text{ bits} \longrightarrow)/2^w$$
$$= (\longleftarrow \qquad\qquad t \quad + \quad w \text{ bits} \longrightarrow)/2^w$$
$$= (\longleftarrow t \text{ bits} \longrightarrow \cdot \underbrace{\longleftarrow w \text{ bits} \longrightarrow})$$

radix — point $fraction(z\theta)$

Clearly, $floor(2^l \times fraction(z\theta))$ is just the leftmost l bits of the segment labeled $fraction(z\theta)$. Thus if we choose $m = 2^l$ then $floor(m \times fraction(z\theta))$ will be a block of l bits in the integer product zq:

$$zq = (\longleftarrow t + w \text{ bits} \longrightarrow)$$
$$\longleftarrow w \text{ bits} \longrightarrow$$
$$\underbrace{\longleftarrow l \text{ bits} \longrightarrow}$$
$$h(z)$$

Summary. There is no such thing as a general-purpose hash function! A good hash function should be efficient to compute, requiring only a few machine instructions, and it should minimize primary clustering. Both of these criteria depend heavily on the particular computer and application, so it is best to think carefully about the nature of the elements being hashed, looking for any nonuniformities of the machine encoding of characters and any naturally occurring clusters of elements. We must bear in mind, however, that even an excellent hash function for a given application will occasionally be defeated in its attempt to minimize primary clustering.

Exercises

1. Why should the operations of **and** and **or** not be considered for compression instead of **xor**?

2. Compute $\hat{h}_1$ for the words of Table 7.1 where $\hat{h}_1$ is like h_1 *except* that, as the **xor** of the characters is being accumulated, the accumulation is circularly right-shifted by one bit position before the next character is **xor**ed with it.

3. Under what conditions would compression hash functions be ill advised?

4. Verify that if two words differ from each other only by a permutation of letters, then h_2 of Table 7.2 maps them to the same location.

5. Under what conditions would a multiplicative hash function be ill advised?

6. In some applications elements tend to occur in arithmetic progressions (consider variable names *PARTA*, *PARTB*, *PARTC* or $T1$, $T2$, $T3$, for example). Which of the classes of hash functions described in the text avoid primary clustering in such a situation?

7. A hash function that has fallen into disrepute is the *middle-square* technique in which $h(z)$ is extracted from the middle bits (or digits) of z^2. This method is very similar to the multiplicative hash functions described, so we might think it acceptable or even desirable. Explain why it is definitely undesirable!

8. When might the hash function $h(z) = 0$ be useful?

7.4.2 Collision Resolution

Typically, the number of possible elements is so enormous compared to the relatively small number of table locations that no hash function, not even the most carefully designed, can prevent collisions from occurring in practice. A perfect illustration is the fact that the chances are better than fifty-fifty that among 23 people some two of them will have the same birthday. In terms of hashing, this means that if we have 365 table locations and only 23 elements to be stored in them, the chance of a collision is more than fifty-fifty. How much more likely, then, are collisions when we intend to fill the table to greater than $23/365 \approx 6.3$ percent of its capacity! In fact, the likelihood of collisions under even the most ideal circumstances (Exercise 1) suggests that the collision-resolution scheme is more critical to overall performance than the hash function, provided that at least minimum care is taken to avoid primary clustering.

When a collision occurs and the location $T[h(z)]$ is already filled at the time we try to insert z, we must have some method for specifying another location in the table where z can be placed. A *collision-resolution scheme* is a method of specifying a list of table locations $\alpha_0 = h(z)$, α_1, α_2, ..., α_{m-1} for an element z. To insert z, the locations are inspected in that order until an empty one is found. In parallel with the linear lists of Chapter 4, our two choices are to store pointers describing the sequence explicitly, or to specify the sequence implicitly by a fixed relationship between z, α_i, and i. Techniques for collision resolution based on these two possibilities are explored in this section. We assume throughout that an empty location has the value *emptykey*, which may be implemented as some specific value or as the setting of a bit in a flag field. We extend Declarations 7.1 with Declarations 7.5.

const
        m = "number of elements in hash table";
        mMinus1 = "$m - 1$";
        emptykey = "*KeyType* value indicating unoccupied entry";
type
        HashTable = **array** [0..*mMinus1*] **of** *KeyType*;
var
        T: *HashTable*;
        Next: **array** [0..*mMinus1*] **of** *integer*;   {used to chain elements of *T*}
function $h(z$: *KeyType*): *integer*; **begin**
        h := "function of z such that $0 \le h(z) < m$"
end;
function *hdelta*(z: *KeyType*): *integer*; **begin**
        hdelta := "function of z such that $1 \le hdelta(z) < m$"
end

Declarations 7.5

Chaining. In this scheme a sequence of pointers is built going from the hash location $h(z)$ to the location in which z is ultimately stored. As above, we will assume that the table consists of m locations $T[0..m-1]$. In *separate chaining* each table location $T[i]$ is a list header, pointing to a linked list of those elements z with $h(z) = i$. If the list is unordered, we insert z just after the list header $T[h(z)]$, before the first element on that list. A search for z in this case is done by applying Algorithm 7.1(b) to the list $T[h(z)]$. If the list is ordered, inserting z is done by applying Algorithm 4.1 to the list $T[h(z)]$; a search for z is done by applying Algorithm 7.2(b) to the list $T[h(z)]$. Figure 7.24 shows the 31-position hash table built when the 30 words of Table 7.2 are inserted by separate chaining with unordered lists using the hash function h_2.

Separate chaining is most efficient in cases where dynamic allocation can be used; space need not even be allocated for a key until it is encountered. If dynamic allocation is unavailable or undesirable, we can consider *coalesced chaining* in which the record for each table location $T[i]$ contains a field *Next*[i]. (For notational con-

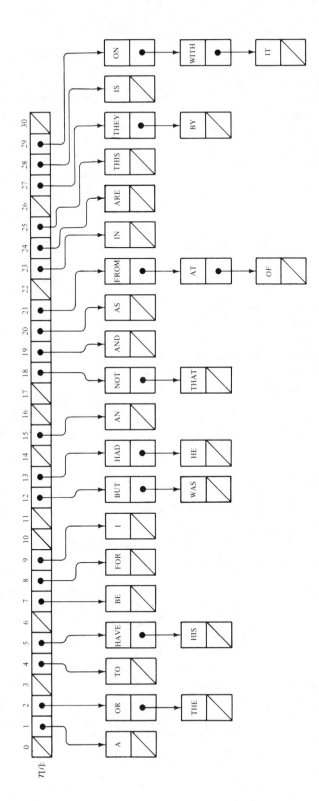

Figure 7.24

A hash table built by separate chaining with unordered lists and the hash function h_2 from Table 7.2. For an unsuccessful search requires an average of 1.40 "probes.," that is, comparisons of z against a table element. For an unsuccessful search in separate chaining probes are counted differently; see page 391. In this example an unsuccessful search requires an average of 1.32 probes.

venience we treat it as a parallel array.) When $T[h(z)]$ is found to contain another element on an attempted insertion of z, we follow the *Next* fields until we reach one that is null; then we take an empty table location $T[free]$, set that last null *Next* field to point to it, and store z in $T[free]$. The search for empty locations originally begins at $T[m-1]$ and goes backward in the table toward $T[0]$. Each time an empty location is needed, we continue backward from where we stopped on the previous occasion; to stop this search, we introduce a dummy element $T[-1]$ that is always empty. The table will overflow when all locations are full. The details of such a "search and insert" process for coalesced chaining are given in Algorithm 7.13; the global variable *fire* is initialized to m once, before the first insertion. Notice that the search portion of the algorithm can be easily separated from the insertion, if desired.

In separate chaining, elements with the same hash address stay in separate linked lists, hence the name. On the other hand, in coalesced chaining these lists can become intermingled, as an example will show.

Figure 7.25 shows how Algorithm 7.13 would behave when inserting the 30 words in the order shown in Table 7.2 into a 32-location table with h_1 as the hash function. The insertion of THE, OF, AND, TO, A, and IN results in no collisions, so in each case z is simply stored in $T[h_1(z)]$. On the insertion of THAT, however, a collision occurs, because $h_1(\text{THAT}) = h_1(\text{OF}) = 9$. So, we begin scanning the table backward from $T[31]$, looking for an empty location. We find one at $T[31]$ and then set $Next[9] := 31$ and $T[31] := \text{THAT}$, completing the insertion. Figure 7.25(a) shows the table at this point. Next, IS, WAS, and HE are inserted without collisions, but in the insertion of FOR we find $h_1(\text{FOR}) = 27$; $T[27]$ is filled already, so we scan backward looking for an empty location, this time from $T[30]$. We find $T[30]$ empty and store FOR in it, setting $Next[27] := 30$. The table is now as shown in Figure 7.25(b). Figures 7.25(c) and (d) show the condition of the table after more and more words have been inserted. We can see intermingling of lists here: TO, FOR, IT, BY, and OR are all on the same list although some hash to 27 and others to 29.

How well does chaining do in practice? In other words, how time-consuming are the search and insertion processes on the average? The answer, of course, depends on how good the hash function is at avoiding primary clustering. As is customary, we therefore discuss the behavior of this (and other) collision-resolution schemes as though the hash function were truly random—that is, as though given any element z, $h(z)$ were chosen as a uniformly distributed random value $0 \leq h(z) < m$. If our hash function has been carefully designed, it will exhibit pseudorandom behavior and this assumption will not be far from the truth. This assumption amounts to our completely ignoring the question of primary clustering when discussing a collision-resolution scheme.

function *CoalescedChaining*(*z*: *KeyType*; **var** *T*: *HashTable*): *integer*;
var
    loc, *i*, *previ*: *integer*;
    found: *boolean*;
begin
    loc := *h*(*z*);
    found := **false**;
    if *T*[*loc*] ≠ *emptykey* **then begin**
        {search linked list beginning at *T*[*loc*]}
        i := *loc*;
        while (*i* ≠ −1) **and not** *found* **do**
            {Assert: If *z* is in *T*, it is in chain starting at *i*. If *i* ≠ *h*(*z*), *Next*[*previ*] = *i*.}
            if *T*[*i*] = *z* **then** *found* := **true**
            else begin
                previ := *i*;
                i := *Next*[*i*]
            end
    end;
    if *found* **then** *CoalescedChaining* := *i*
    else begin {insert *z*}
        if *T*[*loc*] ≠ *emptykey* **then begin**
            {find place for insertion; note *free* is a global variable}
            repeat
                {Assert: Elements *T*[*free*..*m* − 1] are all occupied.}
                free := *free* − 1
            until *T*[*free*] = *emptykey*;
            if *free* = −1 **then** *Overflow*
            else begin {insert at *free*   Assert: *Next*[*previ*] = −1}
                loc := *free*;
                Next[*previ*] := *loc*
            end
        end;
        T[*loc*] := *z*;
        Next[*loc*] := −1;
        CoalescedChaining := *loc*
    end {insert *z*}
end

Algorithm 7.13
Search and insertion into a hash table with collisions resolved by coalesced chaining. The table consists of *T*[−1], *T*[0..*m* − 1] where *T*[−1] is a dummy location that is always empty. *free* is initialized to *m* once, before the first insertion. The value −1 signals the end of a linked list.

i:
$T[i]$:
$Next[i]$:

i	-1	0	1	2	3	4	5	6	7	8	9	10	11	12	13	14	15	16	17	18	19	20	21	22	23	24	25	26	27	28	29	30	31
$T[i]$			A						IN		OF		AND														THE		TO				THAT
$Next[i]$											31																						

(a) After the insertion of THE, OF, AND, TO, A, IN, and THAT. The table is 7/32 ≈ 22 percent full. A successful search requires an average of 1.14 probes and an unsuccessful search 1.03 probes.

i	-1	0	1	2	3	4	5	6	7	8	9	10	11	12	13	14	15	16	17	18	19	20	21	22	23	24	25	26	27	28	29	30	31
$T[i]$			A				WAS		IN		OF		AND		HE												THE	IS	TO			FOR	THAT
$Next[i]$									23		31				19														30				

(b) After the further insertion of IS, WAS, HE, and FOR. The table is 11/32 ≈ 34 percent full. A successful search requires an average of 1.18 probes and an unsuccessful search 1.06 probes.

i	-1	0	1	2	3	4	5	6	7	8	9	10	11	12	13	14	15	16	17	18	19	20	21	22	23	24	25	26	27	28	29	30	31
$T[i]$			A	WITH			WAS	THIS	IN		OF		AND		HE					AS	HAD	I	AT	BY	BE	ON	THE	IS	TO	HIS	IT	FOR	THAT
$Next[i]$			24						23		31				19					28								12	30				20

(c) After the further insertion of IT, WITH, AS, HIS, ON, BE, AT, BY, I, THIS and HAD. The table is 22/32 ≈ 69 percent full. A successful search requires an average of 1.45 probes and an unsuccessful search 1.31 probes.

i	-1	0	1	2	3	4	5	6	7	8	9	10	11	12	13	14	15	16	17	18	19	20	21	22	23	24	25	26	27	28	29	30	31
$T[i]$		THEY	A	WITH	BUT		WAS	THIS	IN		OF	AN	AND	HAVE	HE	OR	FROM	ARE	NOT	AS	HAD	I	AT	BY	BE	ON	THE	IS	TO	HIS	IT	FOR	THAT
$Next[i]$			24						23		31	15		19	19	10			28	28		17	16					12	30	14	22	20	20

(d) After the further insertion of NOT, ARE, BUT, FROM, OR, HAVE, AN, and THEY. The table is 30/32 ≈ 94 percent full. A successful search requires an average of 1.57 probes and an unsuccessful search 1.78 probes.

Figure 7.25
A hash table built by coalesced chaining (Algorithm 7.13) and the hash function h_1 from Table 7.2. Next values of −1 are shown as diagonal lines.

Examining Figure 7.25(a) we see that seven of the 32 table locations are filled, so the table $7/32 \approx 22$ percent full. On a successful search in which each of the seven elements present is equally likely, the average number of locations "probed" (examined) in the **while** loop of Algorithm 7.13 is 1.14, computed as follows: six of the seven elements are found on the first probe and one (THAT) is found on the second probe; the average number of probes is thus $8/7 \approx 1.14$. For an unsuccessful search we calculate the average number of probes by assuming that each of the 32 table locations is equally probable as the hash address. If that hash address is 0, 2 through 6, 8, 10, 12 through 24, 26, 28, 29, or 30, then a single probe suffices, since those locations are empty. Similarly for locations 1, 7, 11, 25, 27, and 31—since the *Next* fields are null, a single probe suffices. If the hash address is 9, however, two probes are required, first at $T[9]$ and then at $T[Next[9]]$. The average number of probes in an unsuccessful search is thus $33/32 \approx 1.03$. The computations are similar for Figures 7.25(b), (c), and (d).

In general, when collisions are resolved by coalesced chaining, the average number of probes in a successful search in a table of m locations containing n elements can be shown to be

$$S(\lambda) = 1 + \frac{1}{8} \frac{m}{n} \left[\left(1 + \frac{2}{m} \right)^n - 1 - \frac{2n}{m} \right] + \frac{1}{4} \frac{n-1}{m}$$
$$\approx 1 + \frac{1}{8\lambda} (e^{2\lambda} - 1 - 2\lambda) + \frac{1}{4} \lambda$$

and in an unsuccessful search

$$U(\lambda) = 1 + \frac{1}{4} \left[\left(1 + \frac{2}{m} \right)^n - 1 - \frac{2n}{m} \right] \approx 1 + \frac{1}{4} (e^{2\lambda} - 1 - 2\lambda)$$

where $\lambda = n/m$ is called the *load factor* of the table. It is customary to express the behavior of the collision-resolution scheme in terms of λ rather than n and m because the behavior of the algorithms is typically governed more by the fullness of the table in relative, rather than absolute terms.

The notion of a probe is somewhat different when separate chaining is used. On a successful search it is reasonable to consider each comparison made between the search object z and the entries in the table as a probe. For example, in Figure 7.24 we see that a successful search ends after 1 such probe (comparison) for 20 of the 30 words, in 2 probes for 8 of them, and in 3 probes for 2 of them. The average successful search in this example thus requires $(20 \times 1 + 8 \times 2 + 2 \times 3)/30 = 1.4$ probes. In general, the result is

$$S(\lambda) = 1 + \frac{n-1}{2m} \approx 1 + \frac{1}{2}\lambda$$

On an unsuccessful search this notion of "probe" is inadequate to measure the work involved since no comparison is made if $T[h(z)] = $ **nil**. So, to reflect more accurately the amount of work being done, we consider the number of probes on an unsuccessful search to be 1 if $T[h(z)] = $ **nil** and to be the number of comparisons made (as before) if $T[h(z)] \neq $ **nil**. In the table of Figure 7.24 we see that $T[i] = $ **nil** in 11 cases, points to a list of 1 element in 12 cases, to a list of 2 elements in 6 cases, and to a list of 3 elements in 2 cases; this gives $(11 \times 1 + 12 \times 1 + 6 \times 2 + 2 \times 3)/31 \approx 1.32$ probes on an average unsuccessful search. The general formula is

$$U(\lambda) = \left(1 - \frac{1}{m}\right)^n + \frac{n}{m} \approx e^{-\lambda} + \lambda$$

If the lists are kept in order, then the average number of probes for an unsuccessful search is decreased to

$$U(\lambda) = 1 + \frac{1}{2}\frac{n}{m} - \frac{m}{n+1}\left[1 - \left(1 - \frac{1}{m}\right)^{n+1}\right] + \left(1 - \frac{1}{m}\right)^n$$
$$\approx 1 + \frac{1}{2}\lambda - \frac{1}{\lambda}(1 - e^{-\lambda}) + e^{-\lambda}.$$

The top lines of Table 7.3 give some numerical values for all of these functions $U(\lambda)$ and $S(\lambda)$ for various values of λ. The remaining lines of the table give corresponding values for other collision-resolution schemes. A brief examination of Table 7.3 indicates that separate chaining is slightly superior to coalesced chaining which is, in turn, superior to other methods of collision resolution. In separate chaining we also have the advantage of ignoring the problem of the table overflowing its allocated storage since the usual *new* mechanism can be used to provide the actual storage for the table elements. This means that we can even have $n > m$, giving $\lambda > 1$; the formulas of Table 7.3 for separate chaining are also valid in this case. A further advantage of separate chaining is that it allows very easy deletion of elements, something difficult or impossible with other collision resolution schemes. The disadvantage of both chaining methods compared to the other schemes represented in Table 7.3 is that they require additional storage overhead for the *Next* fields (separate chaining requires even more storage than coalesced chaining); however, this may be partially offset in other schemes by the need to make m larger to be sure that λ does not get too close to 1.

Linear Probing. The simplest alternative to chaining that does not require the storage of *Next* fields is to resolve collisions by probing sequentially, one location at a time, starting from the hash address, until an empty location is found. This is called *open addressing with linear probing*, or simply *linear probing*. Algorithm 7.14 gives the details of such a procedure, and Figure 7.26 illustrates the use of this procedure

	$\lambda = n/m$					$\lambda = n/m$					Full Table
						0.25	0.5	0.75	0.9	0.95	($\lambda \to 1$)

Separate Chaining

$U(\lambda) = \left(1 - \frac{1}{m}\right)^n + \frac{n}{m}$ (unordered lists)   1.03   1.11   1.22   1.31   1.34   1.37

$\approx e^{-\lambda} + \lambda$

$U(\lambda) = 1 + \frac{n}{2m} - \frac{m}{n+1}\left[1 - \left(1 - \left(1 - \frac{1}{m}\right)^{n+1}\right)\right] + \left(1 - \frac{1}{m}\right)^n$ (ordered lists)

$\approx 1 + \frac{1}{2}\lambda - \frac{1}{\lambda}(1 - e^{-\lambda}) + e^{-\lambda}$ 1.02   1.07   1.14   1.20   1.22   1.24

$S(\lambda) = 1 + \frac{n-1}{2m} \approx 1 + \frac{1}{2}\lambda$ 1.12   1.25   1.38   1.45   1.48   1.50

Coalesced Chaining

$U(\lambda) = 1 + \frac{1}{4}\left[\left(\left(1 + \frac{2}{m}\right)^n - 1 - \frac{2n}{m}\right)\right]$

$\approx 1 + \frac{1}{4}(e^{2\lambda} - 1 - 2\lambda)$ 1.04   1.18   1.50   1.81   1.95   2.10

$S(\lambda) = 1 + \frac{1}{8}\frac{m}{n}\left[\left(1 + \frac{2}{m}\right)^n - 1 - \frac{2n}{m}\right] + \frac{1}{4}\frac{n-1}{m}$

$\approx 1 + \frac{1}{8\lambda}(e^{2\lambda} - 1 - 2\lambda) + \frac{1}{4}\lambda$ 1.14   1.30   1.52   1.68   1.74   1.80

Open addressing with linear probing	$U(\lambda) = \dfrac{1}{2}\left[1 + \sum_{k\geq 0}\dfrac{k+1}{m^k}\dfrac{n!}{(n-k)!}\right]$ $\approx \dfrac{1}{2}\left[1 + \dfrac{1}{(1-\lambda)^2}\right]$	1.39	2.50	8.50	50.50	200.50		$\dfrac{1}{2}m$
	$S(\lambda) = \dfrac{1}{2}\left[1 + \sum_{k\geq 0}\dfrac{1}{m^k}\dfrac{n!}{(n-k)!}\right]$ $\approx \dfrac{1}{2}\left(1 + \dfrac{1}{1-\lambda}\right)$	1.17	1.50	2.50	5.50	10.50		$\sqrt{\dfrac{\pi}{8}m}$
Open addressing with double hashing[a]	$U(\lambda) = \dfrac{m+1}{m+1-n} \approx \dfrac{1}{1-\lambda}$	1.33	2.00	4.00	10.00	20.00		$\dfrac{1}{2}m$
	$S(\lambda) = \dfrac{m+1}{n}\sum_{k=m+2-n}^{m+1}\dfrac{1}{k} \approx \dfrac{1}{\lambda}\ln\dfrac{1}{1-\lambda}$	1.15	1.39	1.85	2.56	3.15		$\ln m$
Open addressing with double hashing in ordered hash tables[a]	$U(\lambda) = \dfrac{m+1}{n+1}\sum_{k=m+2-n}^{m+1}\dfrac{1}{k} \approx \dfrac{1}{\lambda}\ln\dfrac{1}{1-\lambda}$	1.15	1.39	1.85	2.56	3.15		$\ln m$
	$S(\lambda) = \dfrac{m+1}{n}\sum_{k=m+2-n}^{m+1}\dfrac{1}{k} \approx \dfrac{1}{\lambda}\ln\dfrac{1}{1-\lambda}$	1.15	1.39	1.85	2.56	3.15		$\ln m$

[a]Based on the analysis of an idealization.

Table 7.3

Expected numbers of probes for successful (S) and unsuccessful (U) searches in hash tables with various collision-resolution schemes and various load factors $\lambda = n/m$. Other than for chaining, both $S(\lambda)$ and $U(\lambda)$ grow unboundedly with m as $\lambda \to 1$. For open addressing, the algorithms require $n \leq m - 1$, while coalesced chaining requires $n \leq m$. For separate chaining, the formulas are valid even for $n > m$ (that is, $\lambda > 1$).

(a) After the insertion of THE, OF, AND, TO, A, IN, and THAT. The table is $7/32 \approx 22$ percent full. A successful search requires an average of 1.14 probes and an unsuccessful search 1.31 probes.

i:	0	1	2	3	4	5	6	7	8	9	10	11	12	13	14	15	16	17	18	19	20	21	22	23	24	25	26	27	28	29	30	31
T[i]:		A						IN		OF	THAT	AND														THE		TO				

(b) After the further insertion of IS, WAS, HE, FOR, IT, WITH, AS, HIS, and ON. The table is $16/32 \approx 50$ percent full. A successful search requires an average of 1.31 probes and an unsuccessful search 2.03 probes.

i:	0	1	2	3	4	5	6	7	8	9	10	11	12	13	14	15	16	17	18	19	20	21	22	23	24	25	26	27	28	29	30	31
T[i]:		A	WITH	ON		WAS		IN		OF	THAT	AND		HE					AS	HIS						THE	IS	TO	FOR	IT		

(c) After the further insertion of BE, AT, BY, I, THIS, and HAD. The table is $22/32 \approx 69$ percent full. A successful search requires an average of 1.55 probes and an unsuccessful search 3.69 probes.

i:	0	1	2	3	4	5	6	7	8	9	10	11	12	13	14	15	16	17	18	19	20	21	22	23	24	25	26	27	28	29	30	31
T[i]:		A	WITH	ON		WAS	THIS	IN	BE	OF	THAT	AND	I	HE	HAD				AS	HIS		AT				THE	IS	TO	FOR	IT	BY	

(d) After the further insertion of NOT, ARE, BUT, FROM, OR, HAVE, AN, and THEY. The table is $30/32 \approx 94$ percent full. A successful search requires an average of 2.37 probes and an unsuccessful search 13.8 probes.

i:	0	1	2	3	4	5	6	7	8	9	10	11	12	13	14	15	16	17	18	19	20	21	22	23	24	25	26	27	28	29	30	31
T[i]:	HAVE	A	WITH	ON	BUT	WAS	THIS	IN	BE	OF	THAT	AND	I	HE	HAD	AN	THEY		AS	HIS		AT	NOT	ARE	FROM	THE	IS	TO	FOR	IT	BY	OR

Figure 7.26

A hash table built by linear probing (Algorithm 7.14) with $m = 32$ and the hash function h_1 from Table 7.2.

$i := h(z)$;
found := **false**;
while not *found* **and** $(T[i] \neq emptykey)$ **do**
      {Assert: z is not in $T[h(z)]$, $T[(h(z) + 1) \bmod m]$, ...,
      $T[(h(z) + i - 1) \bmod m]$, all of which are occupied.}
      if $T[i] = z$ **then**
          found := **true**
      else $i := (i + 1) \bmod m$;
{insert if needed}
if *found* **then**
    result := i
else begin
    if $n = m - 1$ **then**
        Overflow
    else begin
        $n := n + 1$;
        $T[i] := z$;
        result := i
    end
end

Algorithm 7.14
Search and insertion into a hash table in which collisions are resolved by linear probing. The table consists of $T[0..m-1]$. n is the number of elements currently in the table, initialized once to 0 before the first insertion. The table overflows on trying to insert the mth element; this guarantees that one location is always empty to stop the **while** loop.

in building a hash table with the 30 words and h_1 of Table 7.2 into a 32-location table; the words are added in the order given in Table 7.2.

The insertion of THE, OF, AND, TO, A and IN results in no collisions, so in each case z is stored in $T[h_1(z)]$. On the insertion of THAT a collision occurs, because $h_1(THAT) = h_1(OF) = 9$. So we begin scanning forward from $T[9]$, one location at a time, until we find an empty location. We find one immediately in $T[10]$, which is where THAT is stored, completing the insertion. The table now looks as shown in Figure 7.26(a). Figures 7.26(b), (c), and (d) show the table in various stages as the remaining words are inserted. Notice that in scanning forward to find an empty location we "wrap around" from $m - 1$ to 0; that is, the addition of one is computed modulo m, as shown in Algorithm 7.14.

Examining Figure 7.26(a), we see that seven of the table locations are filled, so the table is $7/32 \approx 22$ percent full. On a successful search in which each of the seven elements present is equally likely, the average number of locations probed in the **while** loop of Algorithm 7.14 is 1.14, computed as follows: six of the seven elements are found on the first probe and one (THAT) is found on the second probe; the average number is thus $8/7 \approx 1.14$. For an unsuccessful search for z, assuming each of the 32 locations is equally likely as $h(z)$, the average number of probes is 1.31, computed as follows. For the 25 empty locations a single probe suffices. For locations 1, 7, 11, 25, and 27 two probes are needed, for 10 three probes, and for 9 four probes for an average of $(25 \times 1 + 5 \times 2 + 1 \times 3 + 1 \times 4)/32 \approx 1.31$. The computations for Figures 7.26(b), (c), and (d) are similar.

The number of probes expected on the average with linear probing when a table has load factor $\lambda = n/m$ is

$$S(\lambda) \approx \frac{1}{2} \left(1 + \frac{1}{1 - \lambda} \right)$$

for successful searches and

$$U(\lambda) \approx \frac{1}{2} \left(1 + \frac{1}{(1 - \lambda)^2} \right)$$

for unsuccessful searches. The exact formulas for $S(\lambda)$ and $U(\lambda)$ in terms of n and m are given in Table 7.3, along with a tabulation of their values for various λ. We notice immediately that both $S(\lambda)$ and $U(\lambda)$ grow large as $\lambda \to 1$, that is, as the table occupancy increases and is filled to capacity. The values shown in Table 7.3 suggest that the behavior of linear probing is tolerable as long as the table is less than 3/4 full, but beyond that it deteriorates rapidly. Experience confirms this observation.

It is instructive to compare coalesced chaining and linear probing to see why linear probing behaves so poorly in comparison. In both schemes collisions result in lists of items that have collided, but comparing Figure 7.25(c) with Figure 7.26(c) we see that in Figure 7.25(c) the 22 elements comprise fourteen lists with an average length of just $22/14 \approx 1.6$, while in Figure 7.26(c) there are five lists with an average length of $22/5 = 4.4$. The comparatively poor behavior of linear probing stems from a tendency to have fewer (and hence longer) lists while coalesced chaining results in more (and hence shorter) lists. Such a tendency would indeed produce poor behavior, because the average successful search will have to examine about half the elements on a list and the average unsuccessful search will have to examine all the elements on a list (unless, of course, the first probe is to an empty table location; as the table becomes fuller this will happen more infrequently, but if the table is less than 75 percent full it happens often enough to lower the average number of probes significantly). It is easy to see why linear probing results in fewer, longer lists: the longer a list is, the higher the chances that it will get longer! This is true in coalesced chaining also and is just a consequence of the fact that the more elements in a list, the more likely a collision is to occur in that list, thus increasing the length of the list by one. The key difference between coalesced chaining and linear probing is that in linear probing two existing lists can become concatenated: in Figure 7.26(c), for example, $T[4]$ will be filled with z if $h(z)$ is any of the locations 1, 2, or 3. When that happens, the result is a single list of fourteen elements, $T[1]$, $T[2]$, ..., $T[14]$. The insertion of such a z increases the average list length to $23/4 \approx 5.8$, quite a jump from 4.4.

Double Hashing. Part of the problem with linear probing is the phenomenon of *secondary clustering*: the tendency of two elements that have collided to follow the same sequence of locations in the resolution of the collision. Clearly, such a tendency will aggravate the unavoidable fact that long lists are more likely to grow than short lists. This suggests that the sequence of locations followed in resolving a collision of z should be a function of the element z. This can be accomplished very easily by only a minor change to Algorithm 7.14: instead of incrementing i by 1 in the **while** loop, we increment it by an amount *del*, $1 \leq del < m$, where *del* is a function of z. In order to insure that every location in the table will be probed on a collision, we must have *del* and m relatively prime (what happens if an integer $d > 1$ divides both *del* and m?). Since we want *del* to have pseudorandom behavior, we can use another hash function *hdelta*(z), $1 \leq hdelta(z) < m$, as our value for *del*. This means that we will now have to compute two hash functions instead of one, but the resulting improvement in behavior will more than compensate for the extra calculation. As a practical matter, it is easiest to guarantee that *hdelta*(z) and m are relatively prime for all z by insisting that m be a prime number. Algorithm 7.15 gives the search portion of this modification of linear probing, appropriately called *double hashing*. Figure 7.27 shows the application of this algorithm to our example using a 31-location table with h_2 and h_3 from Table 7.2 as $h(z)$ and *hdelta*(z), respectively (see Exercise 5).

> $i := h(z)$;
> $del := hdelta(z)$;
> *found* $:=$ **false**;
> **while not** *found* **and** $(T[i] \neq emptykey)$ **do**
> > {Assert: z is not in $T[h(z)]$, $T[(h(z) + del) \bmod m]$, $T[(h(z) + 2 \times del) \bmod m]$, ..., $T[(h(z) + (i-1) \times del) \bmod m]$, all of which are occupied.}
> > **if** $T[i] = z$ **then**
> > > *found* $:=$ **true**
> > **else** $i := (i + del) \bmod m$
> {continue by testing *found* and inserting as in Algorithm 7.14}

Algorithm 7.15
Search in a hash table in which collisions are resolved by double hashing. The algorithm is identical to Algorithm 7.14 in all respects *except* that *del* = *hdelta*(z) is the increment in the **while** loop.

i: row is indexed 0 through 30; **T[i]:** gives the table contents.

(a) After the insertion of THE, OF, AND, TO, A, IN, and THAT. The table is $7/31 \approx 23$ percent full. A successful search requires exactly 1 probe.

i:	0	1	2	3	4	5	6	7	8	9	10	11	12	13	14	15	16	17	18	19	20	21	22	23	24	25	26	27	28	29	30
T[i]:		A			TO														THAT	AND		OF		IN							

(b) After the further insertion of IS, WAS, HE, FOR, IT, WITH, and AS. The table is $16/31 \approx 52$ percent full. A successful search requires an average of 1.25 probes.

i:	0	1	2	3	4	5	6	7	8	9	10	11	12	13	14	15	16	17	18	19	20	21	22	23	24	25	26	27	28	29	30
T[i]:		A	THE		TO	WITH			FOR	I	HAD		WAS	HE					THAT	AND	AS	OF		IN					IS	IT	

(c) After the further insertion of HIS, ON, BE, AT, BY, I, THIS, and HAD. The table is $22/31 \approx 71$ percent full. A successful search requires an average of 1.68 probes.

i:	0	1	2	3	4	5	6	7	8	9	10	11	12	13	14	15	16	17	18	19	20	21	22	23	24	25	26	27	28	29	30
T[i]:		A	THE	HIS	TO	WITH		BE	FOR	I	HAD	AT	WAS	HE			ON		THAT	AND	AS	OF		IN		THIS		BY	IS	IT	

(d) After the further insertion of NOT, ARE, BUT, FROM, OR, HAVE, AN, and THEY. The table is $30/31 \approx 97$ percent full. A successful search requires an average of 2.77 probes.

i:	0	1	2	3	4	5	6	7	8	9	10	11	12	13	14	15	16	17	18	19	20	21	22	23	24	25	26	27	28	29	30
T[i]:	HAVE	A	THE	HIS	TO	WITH	OR	BE	FOR	I	HAD	AT	WAS	HE	BUT	AN	ON	FROM	THAT	AND	AS	OF	THEY	IN	ARE	THIS		BY	IS	IT	NOT

Figure 7.27

A hash table built by double hashing (Algorithm 7.15) using h_2 and h_3 from Table 7.2 as $h(z)$ and $hdelta(z)$, respectively. The computation of the average number of probes on an unsuccessful search is omitted because of the complexity of its computation (Exercise 6).

A complete analysis of the average behavior of double hashing has not yet been made, but both empirical results and some fragmentary theoretical results indicate that it behaves approximately like an idealization of double hashing that we can analyze. We assume that the sequence of locations $\alpha_0 = h(z)$, α_1, α_2, ... used to insert an element z into the table has the property that each location α_i is equally likely to be any of 0, 1, 2, ..., $m-1$ *independently* of the other α_i's. In other words, we assume that the probe sequence $(\alpha_0, \alpha_1, ..., \alpha_{m-1})$ is equally likely to be any of the $m!$ permutations of $(0, 1, ..., m-1)$ [see Exercise 8(a)]. This assumption implies that each of the $\binom{m}{n}$ possible configurations of empty and full locations is equally likely to occur [Exercise 8(b)]; this does not fully hold for double hashing, but is close enough to the truth to give us a good approximation of the behavior of double hashing. In a table with load factor λ the probability of at least k probes being required in an unsuccessful search for z is

$$\text{Pr}(\textit{at least } k \text{ probes}) = \text{Pr}(T[\alpha_0], T[\alpha_1], ..., T[\alpha_{k-2}] \text{ are full})$$

Since the probability of any given location being full is $\binom{m-1}{n-1}/\binom{m}{n} = n/m = \lambda$

and of being empty is thus $1 - \lambda$, independently for all m locations, we have

$$\text{Pr}(\textit{at least } k \text{ probes}) = \lambda^{k-1}$$

The expected number of probes for an unsuccessful search for z in a table with load factor λ is thus

$$U(\lambda) = \sum_{k=1}^{\infty} k \, \text{Pr}(\textit{exactly } k \text{ probes})$$

$$= \sum_{k=1}^{\infty} \left[\sum_{i=k}^{\infty} \text{Pr} \, (\textit{exactly } i \text{ probes}) \right]$$

$$= \sum_{k=1}^{\infty} \text{Pr}(\textit{at least } k \text{ probes})$$

$$= \sum_{k=1}^{\infty} \lambda^{k-1}$$

$$= \frac{1}{1 - \lambda} \tag{7.20}$$

We can determine $S(\lambda)$, the expected number of probes for a successful search, by the following argument. In collision resolution by double hashing the number of probes needed to find z after it is in the table is the same as the number of probes used on the unsuccessful search when it is inserted. This observation is also true for linear probing as well as various other table organizations we have considered [see Exercise 2(e) of Section 7.2.2.]. If we consider the table as being constructed as elements are inserted one by one, the load factor increases in small discrete steps from 0 to its final value of λ. We approximate this situation by letting the load factor grow *continuously* from 0 to λ. $S(\lambda)$ is then the "average" value of $U(x)$ for x in the range $0 \leqslant x \leqslant \lambda$:

$$S(\lambda) = \frac{1}{\lambda} \int_0^\lambda U(x)\ dx,$$

a relation which also holds for the formulas given for linear probing. Substituting the value of $U(\lambda)$ from (7.20) gives

$$S(\lambda) = \frac{1}{\lambda} \int_0^\lambda \frac{dx}{1 - x}$$

$$= \frac{1}{\lambda} \ln \frac{1}{1 - \lambda}$$

These formulas for $S(\lambda)$ and $U(\lambda)$ for uniform hashing are only approximate; the exact formulas are

$$U(\lambda) = \frac{m + 1}{m + 1 - n}$$

$$S(\lambda) = \frac{m + 1}{n} \sum_{k = m + 2 - n}^{m + 1} \frac{1}{k}$$

whose derivation is left to Exercise 9. Examination of Table 7.3 indicates that double hashing (as approximated by uniform hashing) is much better than linear probing, performing reasonably well even for tables up to 90 percent full.

Ordered Hash Tables. In many, if not most, cases there is an ordering of the elements that may be useful in speeding up searches in hash tables just as it was for linear lists (Section 7.1). We will now investigate how such an ordering can be utilized in conjunction with a hashing scheme. The idea will be applicable to chaining, linear probing, or double hashing, but we will consider it only in the context of double hashing, because chaining is so efficient that it needs no improvement while linear probing is so inefficient we would probably never choose it over double hashing if economy were a factor.

If we had been extremely lucky in Algorithm 7.15 and the elements arrived in decreasing order to be inserted, then the search for an element in the table could be stopped as soon as a smaller element was encountered in the probe sequence (why?). Assuming that an empty table location had a value less than that of any element in the table (for instance, in our continuing example we might choose the empty string, which is lexicographically less than any sequence of characters), we could do a search by Algorithm 7.16(a). This algorithm stops a search as soon as it reaches an element less than the search object z.

$$i := h(z); \qquad \{0 \leq i < m\}$$
$$del := hdelta(z); \quad \{1 \leq del < m\}$$
while $T[i] > z$ **do**
> {Assert: z is less than $T[h(z)]$, $T[(h(z) + del) \bmod m]$, $T[(h(z) + 2 \times del) \bmod m]$, ..., $T[(h(z) + (i-1) \times del) \bmod m]$, all of which are occupied.}
> $i := (i + del) \bmod m;$
$found := (T[i] = z)$

Algorithm 7.16(a)
Search of an ordered hash table

Of course, we cannot count on the elements being inserted into the table in decreasing order, making Algorithm 7.16(a) useless unless we can somehow keep the hash table "ordered" no matter in what order the elements are inserted. Consideration of the insertion part of Algorithm 7.14 leads us to an insertion algorithm that maintains an ordered hash table. When an insertion is made and there is no collision or when the element being inserted is less than the elements it collides with, then the insertion scheme of Algorithm 7.14 works fine and the hash table remains ordered. When an insertion leads to a collision with a smaller element, the algorithm must react as though the smaller element were not in the table! In such a collision, then, the idea is to have the (larger) element being inserted "bump" the (smaller) resident element it collided with temporarily out of the table; the larger element takes the location formerly occupied by the smaller. To reinsert the displaced element into the table, we simply apply the insertion algorithm to it; if that leads to a collision with a smaller element, that smaller element is bumped from its location and then reinserted. Each element thus bumped is smaller than the previous one, so this process must end. The result of such an insertion is that the table is in the same order that would have resulted from inserting the elements in decreasing order (Exercise 10.)

An example to illustrate the method will make it more understandable. Suppose the hash table looks as shown in Figure 7.28, $hdelta(z) = h_3(z)$ from Table 7.2, and $h(HAVE) = 26$. The insertion of HAVE causes the following sequence of events: $T[26]$ contains AS and AS is bumped. $hdelta(AS) = 8$, so we try to insert AS into $26 + 8 = 34 \equiv 3$, but $T[3]$ contains FOR. Because AS is less than FOR, we

if $n = m - 1$ **then**
     Overflow
else begin
     $i := h(z);$
     $del := hdelta(z);$
     while $T[i] \neq emptykey$ **do begin**
     {Assert: Same condition as in Algorithm 7.15; though z may
     have changed from its original value.}
     if $T[i] < z$ **then begin**
                    $temp := T[i];$ {swap $T[i]$ and z}
                    $T[i] := z;$
                    $z := temp;$
                    $del := hdelta(z)$ {compute new *del*}
     end;
         $i := (i + del)$ **mod** m
     end;
     $T[i] := z;$
     $n := n + 1$
end

Algorithm 7.16(b)
Insertion of z into an ordered hash table

continue, probing at $3 + 8 = 11$. $T[11]$ contains AND, which is less than AS and therefore gets bumped. We now continue inserting AND; $hdelta(\text{AND}) = 4$, so we try to insert it at $11 + 4 = 15$, but $T[15]$ contains I, which is bigger than AND. We next probe at $15 + 4 = 19$ and, finding $T[19]$ empty, insert AND there. Notice that every time an element is bumped the increment function $hdelta$ must be recomputed. Algorithm 7.16(b) gives the details of the insertion of an element z into an ordered hash table. Algorithms 7.16(a) and (b) can be combined into a single search-and-insert algorithm in the style of Algorithms 7.13, 7.14, and 7.15.

We can give an approximate analysis of the number of probes needed on the average to search an ordered hash table; as in double hashing the analysis is based on the uniform hashing assumption: the sequence of locations $\alpha_0 = h(z)$, α_1, α_2, $\dots$ used to insert an element z into the table has the property that each α_i is equally likely to be 0, 1, $\dots$, or $m - 1$ independently of the other α's. In a table with load factor λ the probability of at least k probes in an unsuccessful search is λ^{k-1}/k, computed as follows:

$\lambda^{k-1} = $ probability that first $k - 1$ locations probed will be full,

$\quad 1/k = $ probability that of the $k - 1$ elements thus probed the
              search object will be smaller than all of them.

Figure 7.28
Insertion of HAVE into the ordered hash table shown, using Algorithm 7.16(b)

The former probability is just as we saw in double hashing. The latter should be understood as stating that it is equally likely for the search object to be larger than all $k-1$ elements probed, larger than only $k-2$ of them, ..., larger than only one of them, or smaller than all of them. Of these k equally likely possibilities, only in the last case will more than $k-1$ probes be needed. Assuming there is no significant correlation between $h(z)$ or $hdelta(z)$ and the size of z, the relative sizes of the elements probed will be independent of the distribution of elements within the table. The probability of at least k probes is thus the product $(1/k)\lambda^{k-1}$:

$$\Pr(at\ least\ k\ \text{probes}) = \frac{\lambda^{k-1}}{k}$$

The expected number of probes for an unsuccessful search in an ordered hash table can now be computed:

$$U(\lambda) = \sum_{k=1}^{\infty} k\ \Pr(exactly\ k\ \text{probes})$$

$$= \sum_{k=1}^{\infty} \left(\sum_{i=k}^{\infty} \Pr(exactly\ i\ \text{probes}) \right)$$

$$= \sum_{k=1}^{\infty} \Pr(at\ least\ k\ \text{probes})$$

$$= \sum_{k=1}^{\infty} \frac{\lambda^{k-1}}{k}$$

$$= \frac{1}{\lambda} \sum_{k=1}^{\infty} \frac{\lambda^k}{k}$$

This final summation is the Taylor series expansion for $\ln[1/(1-\lambda)]$ so that

$$U(\lambda) = \frac{1}{\lambda} \ln \frac{1}{1-\lambda}$$

For $S(\lambda)$, we argue that it is exactly as for double hashing. Since, as Exercise 10 shows, the ultimate contents of the table are as if the elements had been inserted in decreasing order by double hashing, we may assume that they *were* so inserted. In this case, the expected number of probes for a successful search is

$$(1/\lambda) \ln [1/(1-\lambda)]$$

from our previous discussion (that discussion was independent of the order of insertion of the elements).

In fact, the exact values of $S(\lambda)$ and $U(\lambda)$ can be shown to be

$$S(\lambda) = \frac{m + 1}{n} \sum_{k=m+2-n}^{m+1} \frac{1}{k}$$

and

$$U(\lambda) = \frac{m + 1}{n + 1} \sum_{k=m+2-n}^{m+1} \frac{1}{k}$$

(see Exercise 11).

Comparing this to double hashing, we see that successful searches are no different, but unsuccessful searches require many fewer probes on the average as the table fills up (see Table 7.3). Is the savings worthwhile, considering that Algorithm 7.16(b) requires extra work per insertion compared to Algorithm 7.15? To answer, we need to analyze the extra work done to keep the table ordered. Two quantities are of interest—the average number of times the comparison $T[i] < z$ is made (the number of probes on an insertion) and the average number of times that test is true so that *del* must be recalculated. The number of probes on an insertion can be seen to be about $1/(1 - \lambda)$ using the argument of Exercise 12. This means that the average insertion into an ordered hash table is no more expensive than the average insertion into a conventional hash table. As to the number of times the function *hdelta(z)* must be reevaluated, its analysis is somewhat involved, but it can be shown to be about $(1/\lambda)\ln[1/(1 - \lambda)] - 1$ per insertion.

In summary, ordered hash tables are to be recommended over conventional hash tables when unsuccessful searches are common and *hdelta(z)* can be computed without much expense.

Deletion and Rehashing. Except in separate chaining, deletion of an element from a hash table poses special problems. For example, consider Figure 7.26(c). The deletion of THAT by setting $T[10]$ to *emptykey* makes it impossible to find I in the table: $h(I) = 9$, so we would probe $T[9]$, finding that it was not what we wanted, then probe $T[10]$, and finding it empty we would abandon the search. It is clear that we cannot simply remove an element from the table, because such a removal will disrupt the probe sequence for elements that collided with the one to be deleted. Our only choice is to mark the table location as containing an element that has been deleted. Such a location acts like an empty location with respect to insertions, but like a full location with respect to searches. This causes two distinct problems. First, most obvious, and most serious, is that search times will *not* change for the better after a deletion; for example, if we fill a table to 90 percent of its capacity and then delete half the elements, the table still behaves like a table 90 percent full as far as searching is concerned. The second and more subtle problem is how the value of n should be treated in Algorithms 7.14, 7.15, and 7.16(b). Should n be decremented following such a deletion? If it is decremented, then further insertions can fill *all m* table locations, so that an unsuccessful search can go into an infinite loop. This is certainly not acceptable, but if n is not decremented, the table may signal an overflow when there is plenty of room. This second problem can be solved by not decrementing n and incrementing n only when inserting into a previously empty table location.

The only solution to the problem of degraded search times, however, is the ultimate reconstruction of the table by a process called *rehashing*. In rehashing, each table location is scanned in turn and its contents, if any, are relocated as necessary. That is also precisely what is required to reduce or increase the storage allocated for a hash table, so we will present the rehashing algorithm in this slightly more general context. We give the algorithm only for conventional hash tables in which collisions are resolved by linear probing or by double hashing, leaving rehashing algorithms for coalesced chaining and ordered hash tables to the exercises.

```
procedure Rehash(var T: HashTable; m, mNew: integer);
var
      max: integer;        {larger of m and mNew}
      numdone: integer;    {number of elements relocated}
      i, j, del: integer;
      temp: KeyType;
begin
      {mark every location as not yet containing an element from the new table}
      if m < mNew then max := mNew else max := m;
      for i := 0 to max − 1 do
          refilled[i] := false;
      for i := m to max − 1 do
          T[i] := emptykey;
      numdone := 0;
```

Algorithm 7.17, the rehashing algorithm, rehashes the table from locations $T[0..m-1]$ to locations $T[0..mNew-1]$. We can have $mNew > m$ for expanding the hash table, $mNew < m$ for shrinking it, or $mNew = m$ for simply eliminating deleted elements. If $mNew > m$, the new locations $T[m..mNew-1]$ are made to be empty. The hash functions $h(z)$ and $hdelta(z)$ used are for the new table size $mNew$, with $hdelta(z) = 1$ for linear probing. The algorithm uses a bit table *refilled*$[0..max(m-1, mNew-1)]$ to record whether or not the corresponding table position contains an element of the new table.

{relocate the elements}
for $i := 0$ **to** $m - 1$ **do**
    while not *refilled*[i] **and** ($T[i] \neq emptykey$) **do**
        {Assert: Each element of $T[1..i-1]$ and $T[m..max-1]$ is
        empty or refilled (but not both). $T[i]$ is not refilled and not
        empty. If an element of $T[i+1..m-1]$ is refilled its key is
        not empty or deleted.}
        if "$T[i]$ is deleted" **then**
            $T[i] := emptykey$
        else begin
            {relocate $T[i]$ to its new spot}
            if *numdone* $\geq mNew - 1$ **then**
                Overflow
        else begin
            numdone := *numdone* + 1;
            {follow new probe sequence for $T[i]$}
            $j := h(T[i])$;
            $del := hdelta(T[i])$;
            while *refilled*[j] **do**
                {Assert: j is on the search sequence for $T[i]$
                and all prior elements in the sequence are
                already refilled.}
                $j := (j + del)$ **mod** *mNew*;
            {bump current contents of $T[j]$}
            temp := $T[i]$;1
            if "$T[j]$ *is deleted*" **then**
                $T[i] := emptykey$
            else $T[i] := T[j]$;
            $T[j] := temp$;
            refilled[j] := **true**;
            {now the element that was at i is in $T[j]$}
        end
        end
end

Algorithm 7.17
Rehashing $T[0..m-1]$ to $T[0..mNew-1]$ and eliminating deleted elements

The rehashing algorithm is clearly very expensive since it requires time proportional to $max(m-1, mNew-1)$ in addition to the time required to insert all the elements into the new table. It should be used only when search times have deteriorated through many deletions, or when the size of the hash table must change.

Exercises

1. In a hash table with load factor λ, show that out of n elements inserted into the table, $\lambda(n-1)/2$ can be expected to have collided with a previously inserted element.

2. In some collision resolution schemes the number of probes used during an unsuccessful search followed by an insertion is the same number that will thereafter be required for a successful search for that element. Is that true of coalesced chaining? Is is true of ordered hash tables?

3. Suppose that in Algorithm 7.13 (coalesced chaining) we have *free* go forward from i, wrapping around from $m-1$ to 0 if needed, in searching for an empty table location. Does this improve or degrade the performance of the algorithm?

4. Explain why the poor performance of linear probing can be exacerbated by the use of division hashing if consecutive element values are likely to occur. Is this a problem with multiplicative hash functions?

5. What would be wrong with having a 32-location table using double hashing with $h(z) = h_1(z)$ and $hdelta(z) = h_3(z)$ of Table 7.2?

6. Explain how to compute the expected unsuccessful search time for the table configurations of Figure 7.27. Do the calculation for Figure 7.27(a).

7. Investigate the idea of using $hdelta(z) = f(h(z))$ in double hashing.

★ 8. (a) Prove that the assumption that each of the $m!$ possible probe sequences is equally likely could not possibly hold for double hashing.

   (b) Show that the assumption is stronger than the assumption that for all n, $0 \leq n \leq m$, each of the $\binom{m}{n}$ possible configurations of n full and $m - n$ empty locations is equally likely.

9. The object of this exercise is a more precise analysis of uniform hashing. As usual, let the table have m locations and n elements, assuming that the elements were inserted into random locations in the table so that each of the $\binom{m}{n}$ configurations of empty and nonempty locations is equally probable.

   (a) What is the probability that at least k probes are needed to insert the $(n+1)$st element?

   (b) Let U_n be the average number of probes on an unsuccessful search in such a table, so that $U_n = \sum_{k=1}^{m} k \Pr(exactly\ k$ probes are used$)$. Compute U_n using your result from (a). [*Hint*:

$$\sum_{k=1}^{m} \binom{m+1-k}{m-n} = \binom{m+1}{m-n+1}.]$$

(c) Let S_n be the average number of probes on a successful search in such a table. Prove that $S_n = (1/n)\Sigma_{k=0}^{n-1} U_k$ and use this to find S_n.

10. Prove that Algorithm 7.16(b), insertion into an ordered hash table, maintains the order of the elements in the table exactly as it would be if they were inserted in decreasing order. [*Hint*: Prove that the order of the elements in the table is unique by supposing that two different orderings were possible and arriving at a contradiction.]

11. Let $\hat{S}_n$ and $\hat{U}_n$ be, respectively, the analogs for ordered hash tables of S_n and U_n of Exercise 9.

    (a) Explain why $\hat{S}_n = (1/n)\Sigma_{k=0}^{n-1} U_k$. This means that $\hat{S}_n = S_n$.

    (b) Explain why $\hat{U}_n = \hat{S}_{n+1}$.

12. Let C_n be the average number of probes made during an insertion with Algorithm 7.16(b)—that is, the average number of times that the test of the **while** loop is made. Show that $\Sigma_{k=1}^{n} C_k = n\hat{S}_n$, where S_n is defined in the previous exercise. [*Hint*: Each time the loop is executed, the total number of probes to find one of the elements is increased by one.] Combine this result with the previous exercise to show that $C_n = U_{n-1}$.

13. When linear probing is used to resolve collisions, true deletions can be accommodated, because all the elements that may have collided with the deleted element are localized. Design an algorithm for deletion in such a hash table.

14. As in the previous exercise, deletions with coalesced chaining are not too bad. Explain how to delete elements in such a hash table.

15. Give a rehashing algorithm analogous to Algorithm 7.17 for hashing with coalesced chaining.

16. Give a rehashing algorithm analogous to Algorithm 7.17 for ordered hash tables.

17. Comment on the appropriateness of using a hash-table scheme for storing sparse matrices.

18. Suppose we split the n elements of a hash table into two tables, one of the $\lfloor \alpha n \rfloor$ high-frequency elements (to be searched first) that account for a fraction β of all searches and the other of the remaining elements that account for the remaining $1 - \beta$ of all searches. For what values of n, α, and β is this worthwhile?

19. Discuss the merits of the following technique for making unsuccessful searches faster. Maintain a bit table $B[0..m-1]$, all initially **false**. $B[j]$ is set to **true** during an insertion in such a way that in general $B[j]$ is **true** if and only if some successful search passes through $T[j]$. Thus if a search ever reaches a $T[i]$ with $B[i] = $ **false**, the search must be unsuccessful.

20. Design a data structure based on hashing so that the following operations can be done efficiently on the average:

Insert(a, b)	Adds the pair (a, b) to the table
Find(a, b)	Finds the pair (a, b) or indicates its absence
Find(a, $*$)	Returns a list of all pairs whose first element is a
Find($*$, b)	Returns a list of all pairs whose second element is b
Delete(a, b)	Deletes the pair (a, b) from the table
Delete(a, $*$)	Deletes all pairs whose first element is a
Delete($*$, b)	Deletes all pairs whose second element is b

21. Suppose we have a hash table in which collisions are resolved by coalesced chaining. Explain how the table locations can be shared by other linked data structures *without* degrading the performance of the search and insert algorithms for the hash table (in other words, table locations that are being used by some other data structure must have the effect of empty locations in the search and insert algorithms). Assume that in addition to the fields for the key and a *Next* for chaining, each table location has a two-bit *Tag* field. [*Hint*: Use the *Tag* field to distinguish four possible states of the table location—whether it is completely unused, part of another data structure, part of the hash table but not at the end of a chain, or part of the hash table and at the end of a chain. Describe some minor changes that will be needed in algorithms manipulating the *other* data structures sharing the space.]

22. We can improve the performance of Algorithm 7.13, collision resolution by coalesced chaining, by restricting the hash function so that $0 \le h(z) < \hat{m} \le m$. This means that elements *never* have home addresses in the last $m - \hat{m}$ table locations, called the *cellar*. Since Algorithm 7.13 is unchanged, these cellar locations are used *only* in the collision resolution phase. This technique delays, until collisions have filled the cellar, the tendency for long lists of collided elements to get longer. The factor $\hat{m}/m$ is called the *address factor*. By experiment or mathematical analysis, determine the optimal address factor as a function of the load factor. The value 0.86 has been proposed as a good compromise value for the address factor over a wide range of load factors; determine the range of load factors for which it is a good compromise.

7.4.3 Multiple Hash Functions

We conclude our discussion of hashing by examining an application that uses *none* of the collision resolution schemes. Instead, it uses multiple hash functions to reduce to an acceptably low level the probability of error caused by collisions.

The application is the maintenance of a spelling list for a word processing system. The development of a spelling checking program is a complicated affair involving many factors, but at the heart of any spelling checker is a list of acceptable words, typically containing about 25,000 entries and requiring about a million bits of storage when stored directly. Our goal is to store such a list in a compact form, without compromising its effectiveness or usefulness.

We need to examine exactly how the list will be used so that we can determine the effect of using a particular storage structure; thus we begin with a brief overview of one possible organization of a spelling checker. Assume that we have accumulated for the spelling list a large collection of words, names, and abbreviations. To save space we strip the affixes—prefixes and suffixes—from words and record only the stems. Care must be taken, however, to avoid accepting misspellings: consider "prefer", and "refer", and their derivatives. Blindly stripping the affixes pre- and re- and the suffix -er leaves the stem "f", which would then accept such erroneous words as "fing" and "pref". It turns out in this case to be better to store "refer" and "prefer" themselves as stems. (Even then we need an extra list of forbidden words to avoid accepting concoctions like "referment".) In general, the spelling checker must strip successive affixes and check each result for its presence in the spelling list.

Given a document to check, the spelling checker can reduce its work by sorting the words and eliminating duplicates. If the spelling list were stored in sorted order, the words and list could be scanned in parallel to determine which words are absent from the list. However, affix removal defeats this scheme because it spoils the alphabetical order of the list of words to be checked—we do not want to sort the words again after the affix removal. Thus the spelling list must allow efficient random access lookups. This suggests some form of hashing.

Before we continue our discussion, let us make a crucial observation: No spelling checker can be infallible. There will always be new words, unusual first or last names, technical jargon, foreign phrases, obscure geographical locations, and so forth. More importantly, there is no way to determine from a spelling list whether "fro" is a misspelling of "for" or "an" is a misspelling of "and". Since the spelling checker will not do its job perfectly no matter what we do, we have a margin of error that we can work with: If the spelling checker gets fooled into accepting a nonword once in 2000 misspelled words, and if we assume that most documents have about 20 misspellings, then the spelling checker makes a mistake about once in every 100 documents—an error rate that is negligible compared to the incidence of undetectable typographical errors in which one correct word is replaced by another.

Now for any word being looked up, we want only a one bit yes/no answer about its acceptability and we will tolerate an infrequent erroneous answer. We use hashing to accomplish this as follows. Suppose we have room in memory to devote m bits to the spelling list. We can think of these as m yes/no answers with a hash function h to map from a character string to a bit. If the bit corresponding to $h(word)$ is 1, then *word* is accepted as correct; otherwise it is rejected as a misspelling. Of course, collisions will cause errors so we want to minimize their likelihood.

We thus extend the idea by using k independent hash functions: all k bits probed must be 1 in order to accept a word as correct; if any one of the bits corresponding to $h_1(word)$, $h_2(word)$, ..., $h_k(word)$ is 0, we reject *word* as a misspelling. The bit table can be constructed from the spelling list by starting with all m bits set to 0. For each word in the spelling list, the k hash addresses are computed and those bits are set to 1.

Suppose we now discard the original spelling list and use only the bit table. By construction, all words on the spelling list will be accepted since all of the bits addressed by those words are 1. Words not on the spelling list will be rejected if they hash to a 0-bit for one (or more) of the k hash functions. Some words not on the spelling list will end up hashing to k bits all of which are 1—these nonwords will be accepted. We want this to occur no more than once in 2000 times and need to choose k appropriately, given a spelling list of n words and a hash table of m bits.

As we discussed in Section 2.4.2, the maximum amount of information is conveyed by a bit if it has an equal chance of being either 0 or 1 [because $p = \frac{1}{2}$ maximizes the entropy function $H(p) = -p \lg p - (1-p) \lg (1-p)$]. Thus after building the table we would like about half of the bits to be 0 and half to be 1. The probability that a given bit B is 0 after inserting n words is given by

$$
\begin{aligned}
\text{Pr(bit } B \text{ is 0 after construction)} = {} & \text{Pr(}word_1 \text{ does not set bit } B \text{ to 1)} \\
& \times \text{ Pr(}word_2 \text{ does not set bit } B \text{ to 1)} \\
& \times \cdots \times \text{ Pr(}word_n \text{ does not set bit } B \text{ to 1).}
\end{aligned}
$$

For any *word*,

$$
\begin{aligned}
\text{Pr(}word \text{ does not set bit } B \text{ to 1)} \\
= \text{Pr(}h_1(word) \neq B) \times \text{Pr(}h_2(word) \neq B) \times \cdots \times \text{Pr(}h_k(word) \neq B)
\end{aligned}
$$

but for each i, $i = 1, 2, ..., k$

$$
\text{Pr(}h_i(word) \neq B) = \frac{m-1}{m} = 1 - \frac{1}{m}
$$

since there are m bits, only one of which is bit B. Thus

$$
\text{Pr(}word \text{ does not set bit } B \text{ to 1)} = \left(1 - \frac{1}{m}\right)^k
$$

giving

$$
\begin{aligned}
\text{Pr (bit } B \text{ is 0 after construction)} &= \left[\left(1 - \frac{1}{m}\right)^k\right]^n \\
&= \left(1 - \frac{1}{m}\right)^{kn}
\end{aligned}
$$

It is this quantity that we want to be close to ½, so we set

$$\left(1 - \frac{1}{m}\right)^{kn} = \frac{1}{2}$$

and solve for k:

$$k = \frac{1}{n \lg \left(1 + \frac{1}{m - 1}\right)}$$

Using the series $\ln(1 + x) = x - x^2/2 + x^3/3 - \cdots$ gives us the approximation $\lg(1 + x) \approx x/\ln 2$ for small x so that

$$k \approx \frac{m \ln 2}{n}$$

In our case, $n = 25,000$ words on the spelling list and we will assume that we have about $m = 400,000$ bits (compared to the one million bits needed by the actual spelling list). We find

$$k \approx \frac{400,000 \ln 2}{25,000} \approx 11.09$$

Thus we take $k = 11$ and therefore set 11 bits to 1 for each word in the spelling list. The probability that a randomly chosen bit is 1 is then

$$1 - \left(1 - \frac{1}{m}\right)^{kn} = 1 - \left(1 - \frac{1}{400,000}\right)^{11 \times 25,000} \approx 0.4971688$$

This gives the probability that 11 randomly chosen bits will all be 1-bits as $0.4971688^{11} \approx 0.0004587$, an error rate of about one false acceptance out of every 2180 misspellings reported by the spelling checker—not bad, considering that this form of the spelling list requires only 40 percent of the space required by the original form.

Exercises

1. Discuss how to strip prefixes and suffixes from words in order to shorten the spelling list.

2. Is it true that the larger the spelling list is, the better the performance of the spelling checker will be?

3. Does the hash table as discussed in the text allow the deletion of words from the spelling list?

4. Suppose that instead of storing the bit table we store only the lengths of runs of 0-bits, that is, we store the distances between successive 1-bits. Can we save storage with this technique? How should these distances be represented? By how much is the look-up process affected? What would be the advantage of having an array of 512 pointers into this sequence of run lengths?

7.5 TABLES IN EXTERNAL STORAGE

The methods of table organization that have been presented so far in this chapter are geared to internal memory—that is, memory that can be accessed randomly at speeds matching the speed of the computer itself. For small or medium-sized temporary tables internal memory is fine, but for large or long-term tables, such as payroll, inventory, airline reservations, and so on, we must rely on (relatively) slow external memory devices such as magnetic tapes, disks, or drums. This section briefly examines some of the issues involved in searching tables stored on such external memory devices.

Magnetic Tapes. Magnetic tape is a sequential storage medium. This means that to examine the ith record on the tape it is necessary to have examined or moved past the first $i - 1$ records. Essentially, then, organizing a table on magnetic tape is the same as using a linked list. We have already examined such table organizations earlier in this chapter, and nothing need be said here except a brief recapitulation. Such a table must be searched in a linear fashion, and the only possible refinement is to order the records on the tape so as to minimize search time. The two relevant orders are (1) the natural order of the records (alphabetical, numerical, etc.) or (2) so that $p_1/L_1 \geqslant p_2/L_2 \geqslant \cdots \geqslant p_n/L_n$, where p_i is the probability that the ith record is the search object and L_i is its length—the cost of reading it into memory (see Exercise 4 of Section 7.1.1). In general, magnetic tapes are a poor choice for storing frequently accessed information unless that information will always be scanned in a linear fashion; the problem of sorting is an example of such an instance, and we will examine the use of magnetic tapes in sorting in Section 8.3.

Disks and Drums. Disks and drums do allow random access to all records stored, but the time required for such an access is very great compared to internal memory speeds. For purposes of this section we need not go into all the details of a disk drive or a drum. All we must know is that there is a high overhead in time to initiate an *access*—that is, a transfer of records from the disk or drum to internal memory. This overhead comes from the time required to position the reading mechanism at the proper location before reading the records into memory. Efficient organization of tables on disks and drums thus requires minimizing the number of times such an access is initiated and transferring large numbers of records on each access. We will now examine how this can be done within the framework of search trees and hash tables. For economy of style we will use the term "disk" exclusively, rather than "disk or drum."

7.5.1 Balanced Multiway Tree

The binary search tree techniques discussed in Section 7.2 could be used directly for organizing tables on disks; the *LEFT* and *RIGHT* pointers become addresses on the disk instead of addresses in internal memory. In this way the algorithms of Section 7.2 would require a disk access whenever a *LEFT* or *RIGHT* pointer was followed, essentially making one probe per disk access. Since disk accesses are costly compared to probes, it is preferable to make a number of probes for each disk access. We can do so if nodes in the tree contain m-way branches instead of two-way (binary) branches.

In analogy with binary trees, we define an *m-way tree*: such a tree T either is empty or consists of a distinguished node called the root and k subtrees $T_1, T_2, \ldots, T_k$, $2 \leq k \leq m$, each of which is an m-way tree. A node in an m-way tree specifies a k-way branch and thus contains $k-1$ elements, for some k, $2 \leq k \leq m$, as shown in Figure 7.29. In an *m-way search tree* we require additionally that $x_1 < x_2 < \cdots < x_{k-1}$ and that elements in subtree T_i be greater than x_{i-1} and less than x_i (with x_0 taken as $-\infty$ and x_k taken as ∞). Figure 7.30 shows a five-way search tree. Notice that we do not insist that every node of an m-way tree contain $m-1$ elements, for then the total number of elements stored in the tree would have to be a multiple of $m-1$; this would be an unreasonable restriction, so we merely insist that each node contains *at most* $m-1$ elements.

To search an m-way search tree for z we proceed similarly to the search of a binary search tree. Beginning at the root, we search for z among the elements $x_1, x_2, \ldots, x_{k-1}$. If we find z, the search ends; if not, we continue the search in the subtree T_i such that $x_{i-1} < z < x_i$. How should m be chosen? If we have a *complete m-way*

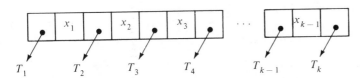

Figure 7.29
A degree-k node in an m-way tree, $k \leq m$.

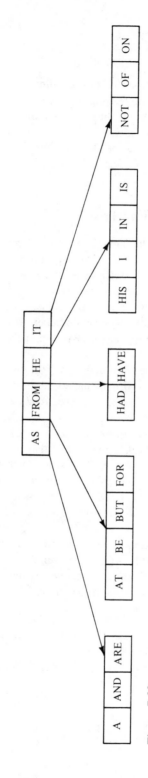

Figure 7.30
A five-way search tree

tree in which every node contains $m-1$ elements and is an m-way branch, then searching a table of n elements will require examining about $\log_m n$ tree nodes. The cost of examining a tree node is

$$I + Rm + S \lg m$$

where

$$I = \text{time to initiate the disk access,}$$
$$Rm = \text{time to read the } m\text{-way node from the disk,}$$
$$S \lg m = \text{time to do a binary search on the elements of the } m\text{-way node}$$

The total time for a search is thus

$$(\log_m n)(I + Rm + S \lg m)$$

and, since $\log_m n = \lg n / \lg m$, this becomes

$$\left(\frac{I + Rm}{\lg m} + S \right) \lg n$$

To minimize the search time we should choose m so that $(I + Rm)/\lg m$ is minimized. Differentiating this with respect to m and setting the derivative to zero, we find that the minimum occurs for m such that

$$\lg m = \frac{I/R}{m} + 1$$

The exact minimum depends on the value of I/R, but in most cases the cost of initiating a disk access is several thousand times the cost of reading a block of words, so that I/R will be something like 2000. The following table shows values of m for various values of I/R between 1000 and 3000.

I/R	1000	1500	2000	2500	3000
m	159	221	280	338	394

Thus we expect to be dealing with multiway trees with a branching factor of a couple hundred or so. The best choice depends on the precise physical characteristics of the storage device (access and transfer times), the size of the elements in the table, and the amount of internal memory available to store elements.

Have we saved on disk accesses? Yes! If we choose $m = 256$, for example, we will be able to search a table of over 16 million elements with no more than two disk accesses, provided that the root node of the tree is always kept in internal memory. Had we used a binary tree, such a table would have required 24 accesses. Since the accesses dominate the cost of a search, a search in the 256-way tree will be twelve times faster than in the binary tree.

Our analysis above assumed that the m-way search tree was perfectly balanced with every node containing $m-1$ elements. As we have seen with binary search trees, it is quite time-consuming to keep the tree perfectly balanced under insertions and deletions, so we need a compromise like that of height- or weight-balanced trees. A good compromise is the following: we insist that all paths from the root to an external node are of equal length and that each node except the root has at least $\lceil m/2 \rceil$ subtrees. (Exercise 9 considers the case in which each node has at least $\lceil (2m-1)/3 \rceil$ subtrees.) Thus we define a *balanced multiway tree of order m* or *B-tree* as an m-way tree in which

1. All external nodes are at the same level.

2. The root has anywhere from two to m subtrees.

3. Other internal nodes have anywhere from $\lceil m/2 \rceil$ to m subtrees.

Returning to Figure 7.30, we see that the tree it depicts is a B-tree of order 5 because all the external nodes (not shown) are two levels down from the root and the number of subtrees of each internal node falls within the prescribed limits. The case of $m = 3$ is of interest as an alternative to height- or weight-balanced trees (Exercise 3), and that of $m = 2$ is related to height-balanced trees (Exercise 4). For purposes of the organization of tables on disks, we will be interested primarily in m being around several hundred.

For B-trees to be useful, we need to verify that search times remain within bounds and that insertions and deletions can be accommodated. As to search times, suppose that there are n elements and $n + 1$ external nodes. The root has at least two subtrees and the remaining nodes have at least $\lceil m/2 \rceil$ subtrees. After l levels there are *at least* $2\lceil m/2 \rceil^{l-1}$ nodes. In a tree of height h there are at least $2\lceil m/2 \rceil^{h-1}$ external nodes, so that

$$n + 1 \geq 2\lceil m/2 \rceil^{h-1}$$

or

$$h \leq 1 + \log_{\lceil m/2 \rceil}\left(\frac{n + 1}{2}\right)$$

Thus in our example of a table with 16 million elements we need at most three disk accesses for a search if $m = 256$, so that such a search will be more than eight times faster than if we had used a height-balanced tree to organize the table (why?).

We now outline procedures to insert or delete elements in B-trees; the procedures require time comparable to that needed to search such a tree. To illustrate the process of insertion, consider inserting BY into the tree of Figure 7.30. We begin with an unsuccessful search for BY; as the search proceeds, a record is kept on a stack of the nodes visited—this lets us retrace the path up the tree. The search for BY fails at the bottom level of internal nodes in the tree. If the node at which it fails contains less than $m - 1$ elements, the new element is simply inserted into its proper place in that node (this would happen, for example, if we were inserting AN into the tree of Figure 7.30). BY cannot be so inserted because the node

AT	BE	BUT	FOR

already contains the maximum allowable number of elements. In such a case the m elements, consisting of $m - 1$ in the node and the new element, are split into two nodes containing the smallest $\lceil m/2 \rceil - 1$ elements and the largest $\lfloor m/2 \rfloor$ elements; the median element is pushed up into the parent node to be the separator element between the two halves. In our example, the split results in

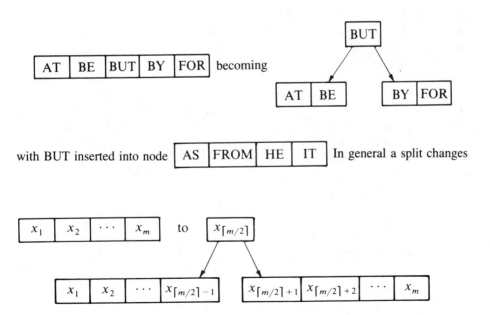

with BUT inserted into node | AS | FROM | HE | IT | In general a split changes with $x_{\lceil m/2 \rceil}$ inserted into the parent node. If the parent node contains $m - 2$ or fewer elements, the addition of the new element causes no problem and the insertion ends. If the parent node already contains $m - 1$ elements, as is the case of BUT inserted into

| AS | FROM | HE | IT |

then that node is split in turn; this process continues up the tree, as needed. When the root splits, a new node is created that becomes the root of the tree and the tree becomes one level taller. In our example,

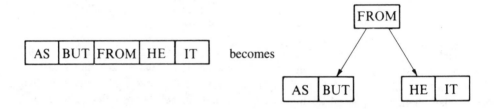

| AS | BUT | FROM | HE | IT | becomes

and the resulting tree is shown in Figure 7.31. The insertion process is remarkable in that trees grow taller by adding levels to the root, rather than to the leaves! This explains why we allow the root node a greater range of sizes than the other nodes in *B*-trees.

The deletion of an element is no harder than an insertion. We consider only the deletion of an element at the bottom level of the tree because, as in binary search trees, if an element is not at that level, its predecessor and successor are (Exercise 6). Suppose we want to delete HIS from the *B*-tree of Figure 7.31. Nothing could be simpler: we just delete HIS from its node in the tree; since that node has only empty subtrees and since it has enough elements, nothing else need be done. If we wanted to delete HAD, however, the deletion would leave the node

| HAD | HAVE |

insufficiently full. In this case we could take an element from the neighboring

| HIS | I | IN | IT |

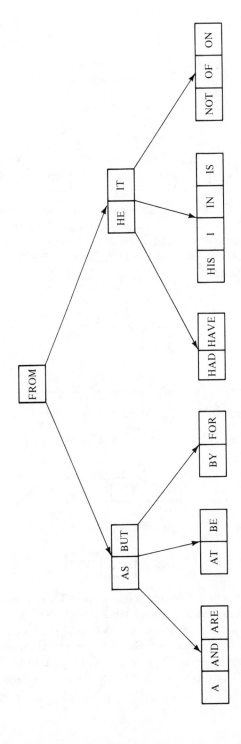

Figure 7.31
The *B*-tree that results from inserting BY into the *B*-tree of Figure 7.30

and use it to remake the tree into

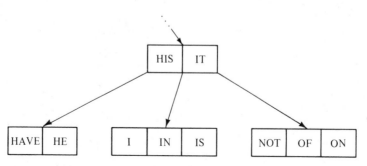

If we are deleting FOR, the neighboring node does not have an element to spare. In such a case of a minimally full node with a minimally full neighbor, the node, its neighbor, and the element that separates them in their parent node can be combined into an acceptably full node. Thus to delete FOR from the *B*-tree of Figure 7.31 we would replace the left subtree with

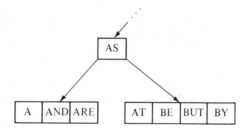

pushing the problem of the deletion up to the next higher level, where it is handled in precisely the same way: the neighbor

has insufficiently many elements to give one up, so

$$\boxed{\text{AS}} \quad \text{and} \quad \boxed{\text{HE} \mid \text{IT}}$$

and their separator are combined into a single node. The resulting *B*-tree is that shown in Figure 7.30, except BUT has been replaced with BY. Notice that as in an insertion, the height of the tree changes at the root, not at the leaves.

To close this section, a brief comment about storage utilization is in order. In the worst case, *B*-trees allow about 50 percent of their space to be wasted, since a minimally full node will have only $\lceil m/2 \rceil$ subtrees. On the average, however, the storage utilization can be shown to be about ln $2 \approx 69$ percent. The wasted space is the price we pay for fast search times involving few disk accesses, combined with the ability to make insertions and deletions.

Exercises

1. Give a declaration for a node in a B-tree of order m.

2. We have seen that the best value for m is so that lg $m = \lceil (I/R)/m \rceil + 1$. Verify that in general there is a fairly large *range* of values of m for which the value of $(I + Rm)/(\lg m)$ will be close to minimal.

3. A *3-2 tree* is a B-tree of order 3. Examine the possibility of using 3-2 trees as an alternative to height- or weight-balanced trees: What is the worst-case search time in a 3-2 tree of n elements? Can concatenation and splitting be done? Can 3-2 trees be maintained under insertions and deletions?

4. A *sibling tree* is a B-tree of order 2 with the additional property that if N is a unary node of the tree, then N must have a binary sibling. Prove that there is an exact correspondence between sibling trees and height-balanced trees.

5. Show the tree that results from successively inserting THE, TO, THAT, WAS, WITH, THIS, OR, and THEY into the B-tree of order 5 shown in Figure 7.31.

6. In parallel with the discussion given on page 340, prove that if an element is not at the lowest level of a B-tree, then its predecessor and successor are.

7. Show the tree that results from deleting BUT, HE, NOT, THE, WAS and OR from the tree that was the end result of Exercise 5.

8. Explain how the insertion and deletion processes (as outlined) would need to be modified if each level in the B-tree had its own limit on the number of elements in a node. What are the advantages and disadvantages of such a scheme?

9. Suppose we modify the definition of B-tree to (1) all leaves are at the same level, (2) the root has anywhere from 2 to $2\lfloor (2m-2)/3 \rfloor + 1$ subtrees, (3) other internal nodes have anywhere from $\lfloor (2m-1)/3 \rfloor$ to m subtrees.
   (a) What is the effect on the storage utilization?
   (b) Explain how insertions and deletions are done.

7.5.2   Bucket Hashing

We can adapt hashing schemes to disks by having the address computed by the hash function be a disk address. As in the previous section, we want to minimize the number of disk accesses needed on a search. There are two things we can do. First, we can enlarge the basic table component from a single element to a group of many elements. The elements would thus be grouped into *buckets* of b elements each; a hash address would specify the disk address of a bucket and a disk access would retrieve all b elements of the bucket. The elements in a bucket would then be searched one by one (the elements in a bucket would not ordinarily be kept in order). The second thing we can do is use a hash function that causes fewer collisions; even before, of course, we wanted a hash function with few collisions, but the cost of a collision is so enormous when disk accesses are at stake that it becomes worthwhile to spend much more time in computing the hash function so as to minimize collisions.

Because we are hashing to buckets rather than individual table locations, we expect collisions to be no problem, so we can use a relatively simple-minded scheme to resolve them. Every bucket will have a pointer that will be used to point to the $(b + 1)$st element that hashed to that bucket. That element has a pointer to the $(b + 2)$nd element, and so on. Thus the first b elements hashing to a given bucket are stored in that bucket; the remaining elements are formed into a linked list with the pointer to the start of the list kept in the bucket itself. All elements not in their proper bucket are kept in a special "overflow" area of the disk in which there are no buckets, only individual elements. If there are n elements and m buckets, we define the load factor as

$$\lambda = \frac{n}{mb}$$

(notice that this ignores the locations in the overflow area). The performance of such a hashing scheme is difficult to analyze, but it can be shown that for load factors λ up to 90 percent and bucket sizes b up to 50, an average of between one and two probes will be needed for either successful or unsuccessful searches. As λ increases past 90 percent, the performance degrades somewhat, with the average successful search requiring about 1.5 probes and the average unsuccessful search requiring about $\sqrt{b/2\pi} + 1$ probes.

Exercise

Explain why we might have a load factor $\lambda > 1$ in a hash table as described in this section.

7.6   REMARKS AND REFERENCES

In this very long chapter we have seen a diversity of table organizations, and we have only scratched the surface. Because of minor variations or combinations of table organizations, the possibilities are endless. The techniques of major importance have been presented, and many variations are covered in exercises. In choosing among the possible alternatives, some of the many things to ponder are

1. What are the elements? Are they simple keys, or complicated records of which the key is only a small part? Are the keys numerical? Alphabetical?

2. What kinds of operations are necessary? Is the table static or dynamic? Are the elements going to be needed in any special order? Is the table size known a priori, or must the table be expandable? Will we have to merge tables together? Will we have to split one into pieces?

3. What is the nature of a search? Will we want a yes-or-no answer, the closest element, or a range of elements? Will searches be mainly successful or unsuccessful? Will an unsuccessful search always be followed by an insertion?

4. Are we concerned about average time or worst-case time?

5. What is the nature of the storage medium?

Further details and complete analyses for most of the table organizations discussed here can be found in Chapter 6 of

Knuth, D. E., *The Art of Computer Programming*, Vol. 3, Sorting and Searching, Reading, Mass.: Addison-Wesley Publishing Co., 1972.

In two cases, more recent and/or detailed information can be found elsewhere. See

Gonnet, G. H., L. D. Rogers, and J. A. George, "An Algorithmic and Complexity Analysis of Interpolation Search," *Acta Informatica* **13** (1980), 39–52.

for an extended discussion of interpolation search along with an extensive bibliography. For hashing techniques see

Knott, G. D., "Hashing Functions," *Computer J.* **18** (1975), 265–278.
Amble, O., and D. E. Knuth, "Ordered Hash Tables," *Computer J.* **17** (1974), 135–142.
Guibas, L. J., and E. Szemeredi, "The Analysis of Double Hashing," *J. Comput. Syst. Sci.*, **16** (1978), 226–274.

The first of these three papers gives a comprehensive discussion of hash functions; the second gives, in great detail, the analysis of ordered hash tables; the third gives an analysis of double hashing.

The spelling checker example of Section 7.4.3 is drawn from

McIlroy, M. D., "Development of a Spelling List," *IEEE Trans. on Communications*, **30** (1982), 91–99.

This paper describes, in fascinating detail, how the UNIX spelling checker evolved. It is highly recommended reading as an example of how data structure techniques were combined with mathematical analysis to produce an extremely powerful applications program.

For an analysis of conditions under which various alternative *B*-tree strategies may be appropriate, see

Hansen, Wilfred J., "A Cost Model for the Internal Organization of B^+-Tree Nodes," *ACM Transactions on Programming Languages and Systems,* **3** (1981), 508–532.

Finally, for the reader interested in pursuing the examples used in this chapter on letter and word distributions in the English language, we recommend

Kahn, D., *The Codebreakers*. New York: The Macmillan Company, 1969.
Kučera, H., and W. N. Francis, *Computational Analysis of Present-Day American English*. Providence, R.I.: Brown University Press, 1967.

Chapter 8

Sorting

The old order changeth, yielding place to new.

The Passing of Arthur, Alfred Lord Tennyson

In this chapter we discuss methods for sorting a table of elements x_1, $x_2, \ldots, x_n$ into order, based on their arithmetic or lexicographic value. Section 8.1 discusses various methods, their strengths and their weaknesses, for the case in which all the x_i can fit into memory simultaneously for the sorting process. Section 8.2 discusses two problems closely related to sorting, that of selecting the kth largest among the unordered elements $x_1, x_2, \ldots, x_n$ and that of merging two ordered sequences of elements. Finally, in Section 8.3, we examine how sorting can be done when there are too many elements to be in memory together and it is possible only to examine the elements in piecemeal fashion, bringing them into memory in batches from an external storage device.

For most of the algorithms presented in this chapter, the locations holding the elements to be sorted are denoted $x_1, x_2, \ldots, x_n$ in exposition and $x[1], x[2], \ldots,$ $x[n]$ in Pascal. The type of x is *ElementArray* as given in Declarations 8.1. (In a few algorithms the x_i will instead be list elements or records in a file.) Loop invariant assertions in the procedures utilize the "$..$" notation to refer to a subsequence of x. Thus $x[a..b]$ is $x[a], x[a + 1], \ldots, x[b]$ and $x[t] \leq x[a..b]$ asserts that $x[t]$ is less than or equal to all elements of the subsequence. As in Chapter 7 we will write assignment and comparison as if *ElementType* were integer. More commonly the values would be records, and these operations rewritten appropriately.

8.1 INTERNAL SORTS

In this section we will examine about a half-dozen different strategies for rearranging $x_1, x_2, \ldots, x_n$ into order. Each of the algorithms we consider requires, more or less, direct access to all of the elements being sorted: this makes them suitable only as

```
const n = "number of elements to be sorted";
      nplusone = "n + 1";1
      MinusInfinity = "an ElementType value smaller than any other";
      PlusInfinity = "an ElementType value larger than any other";
type
      ElementType = "type for records to be sorted";
      ElementArray = array [0..nplusone] of ElementType;
      SubscriptRange = 0..nplusone;

procedure Swap(var x, y: ElementType);
var
      t: ElementType;
begin
      t := x;
      x := y;
      y := t
end
```

Declarations 8.1
Types used in describing sorting algorithms. The 0th and $(n+1)$st elements of an *ElementArray* are sometimes used to hold dummy values.

internal sorting methods; even though they could be used directly with tape or disk storage, the result would be incredibly inefficient. Additionally, the algorithms considered here are all *in-place* sorting algorithms. In other words, the rearrangement process must occur entirely within the sequence $x_1, x_2, \ldots, x_n$ along with one or two additional locations in which to store elements temporarily. This in-place restriction is based on the assumption that the number of elements to be sorted is too large to permit copying them into a different storage area as they are sorted. If sufficient storage is available to allow such copying, then some of the algorithms presented here can be speeded up considerably.

Just as there are many internal table organizations for searching, so there are many internal sorting methods. And, as is the case for searching, there is no universal answer to the question, "What is the best method?" The answer varies with the particular circumstances—the type of elements being sorted, the amount of storage available, the relative emphasis on good average performance versus good worst-case performance, the relative speeds of various computer instructions, and so on. For this reason we will examine a variety of algorithms, each having its own assets and liabilities.

8.1.1 Insertion Sort

The following simple idea leads to a sorting algorithm that is useful for small numbers of elements: repeatedly insert another element into the sequence of already sorted elements. Thus at stage i the ith element is inserted into its proper place among the previously sorted $i - 1$ elements. At stage 1, x_1 is inserted into place trivially, since there were no previously sorted elements; at stage 2, x_2 is inserted into place either before or after x_1; at stage 3, x_3 is inserted into place among the now sorted x_1 and x_2; and so on. Algorithm 8.1 describes this process precisely, with the jth stage inserting x_j among $x_1, x_2, \ldots, x_{j-1}$. This is done repeatedly, for $j = 2, 3 \ldots, n$. In each case the insertion is done by storing x_j temporarily in t and scanning the elements $x_{j-1}, x_{j-2}, \ldots, x_1$, comparing each with x_j and shifting it to the right if it is found to be greater than t. We thus have combined the finding of the spot where x_j will be inserted together with the process of making room at the spot for the insertion. For additional simplification, we have introduced a dummy element $x_0 = -\infty$ to stop the backward scan at the left end. Figure 8.1 illustrates this algorithm on five elements.

In this algorithm, as in most sorting algorithms, the performance depends on the number of element comparisons and the number of data moves made in the worst case, on the average (assuming that each of the $n!$ permutations of the elements is equally likely), and in the best case. The key to analyzing Algorithm 8.1 is the number of times the comparison $t < x[i]$ is made in the **while** loop, for once that number is known, the number of data moves $x[i+1] := x[i]$ can easily be deduced.

```
procedure InsertionSort(var x: ElementArray; n: SubscriptRange);
var
      i, j: SubscriptRange;
      t: ElementType;
begin
      x[0] := MinusInfinity;
      for j := 2 to n do begin
            {Assert: x[1..j-1] is sorted}
            {insert x[j] into place among x[1..j-1]}
            i := j - 1;
            t := x[j];          {make a "hole" at j}
            while t < x[i] do begin
                  {shift the hole one position left}
                  x[i + 1] := x[i];
                  i := i - 1
            end;
            x[i + 1] := t    {drop t into the hole}
      end
end
```

Algorithm 8.1
Insertion sort

j	x_0	x_1	x_2	x_3	x_4	x_5
2	$-\infty$	8	7	2	4	6
3	$-\infty$	7	8	2	4	6
4	$-\infty$	2	7	8	4	6
5	$-\infty$	2	4	7	8	6
	$-\infty$	2	4	6	7	8

Figure 8.1
The insertion sort, Algorithm 8.1, applied to $n = 5$ elements. The dashed vertical lines separate the already sorted part of the table $x[1..j-1]$ from the unsorted part $x[j..n]$.

The comparison $t < x[i]$ is made

$$\sum_{j=2}^{n} (1 + d_j) = n - 1 + \sum_{j=2}^{n} d_j$$

times, where d_j is the number of elements larger than x_j and to its left. We can understand this by observing that, for each j, the loop scanning backward from $j-1$ will make the comparison $t < x[i]$ until it finds an element $t \geq x_i$; it thus makes the comparison (and executes the contents of the loop) once for each element to the left of x_j that is larger than x_j and once more when it fails, finding an element less than or equal to x_j. The number of data moves is thus $(n - 1) + (n - 1) + \sum_{j=2}^{n} d_j$ because $t := x[j]$ and $x[i+1] := t$ are done $n-1$ times each, and $x[i+1] := x[i]$ is done $\sum_{j=2}^{n} d_j$ times.

It remains to analyze the quantity $\sum_{j=2}^{n} d_j$. In the best case, each $d_j = 0$; this occurs when the elements are already in sorted order. Clearly, the most number of elements to left of x_j and larger than it is $j - 1$, so the worst case is $d_j = j - 1$; this occurs when the elements are in *reverse* order. The average value of d_j, assuming that each of the $n!$ permutations of the x_i is equally likely, can be shown to be $(j-1)/2$ (Exercise 1). The time required by Algorithm 8.1 is thus summarized by the following table:

	Element Comparisons	Element Moves	Extra Storage
Best case	$n - 1$	$2n - 2$	One extra element (t) and integer variables i and j in all cases
Average case	$\dfrac{(n - 1)(n + 4)}{4}$	$\dfrac{(n - 1)(n + 8)}{4}$	
Worst case	$\dfrac{(n - 1)(n + 2)}{2}$	$\dfrac{(n - 1)(n + 4)}{2}$	

Notice that we have not taken into account the overhead for the loop controls and the incrementing and decrementing of the counters. We have ignored these because we cannot determine their expense relative to the cost of manipulating the elements being sorted. If the x_i are very long character strings, then what we have ignored is negligible. We have analyzed Algorithm 8.1 to the limit possible without knowledge of the elements being sorted or the machine instructions available.

Insertion sort has in its favor its elegant simplicity, which leads to very low overhead. Its disadvantage is that both on the average and in the worst case it requires time proportional to n^2, and we will find other sorting techniques that require only time proportional to $n \lg n$, a big improvement. Still, Algorithm 8.1 is the best choice for small numbers of elements (say, no more than fifteen to twenty) because of its low overhead, and it is the best choice when the elements are not in too much disarray, making $\Sigma_{j=2}^{n} d_j$ small.

Can the insertion sort be improved? We could do *binary insertion*, using binary search (Algorithm 7.3) and hence at most about $\lg j$ element comparisons to insert the jth element. A total of $\Sigma_{j=2}^{n} \lg j \approx n \lg n$ such comparisons would thus suffice. Unfortunately, after having found the spot in which to insert x_j, the in-place restriction causes the insertion itself to require moving $j/2$ names on the average, and the algorithm would still require proportional to n^2 operations. Alternatively, we could use a linked list for the sorted portion of the table, thereby making the insertion more efficient. Of course, in this case we could not use binary search to find the place at which x_j should be inserted, and we would be stuck with a sequential search. The number of operations required by the resulting sorting algorithm would again be proportional to n^2.

If we could combine the searching ease of a sequentially allocated list with the insertion ease of a linked list, we would be able to obtain an algorithm requiring $O(n \log n)$ time. This can be done by using the balanced tree schemes of Section 7.2.2, but the overhead involved makes such schemes prohibitive for sorting, since we will be able to achieve $O(n \log n)$ time with simpler methods. It *is* possible to use the insertion idea to obtain an $O(n(\log n)^2)$ time sorting algorithm; see Exercises 3 and 4.

Exercises

1. Given a permutation $\Pi = (\pi_1, \pi_2, \ldots, \pi_n)$ of $1, 2, \ldots, n$, let d_i, $1 \leq i \leq n$, be the number of elements in Π to the left of π_i and greater than it.

   (a) What is the possible range of values of each d_i?

   (b) Show that the permutation can be reconstructed from the d_i's, that is, that the d_i's uniquely determine the permutation.

   ★(c) Show that if each of the $n!$ permutations is equally likely, then each of the possible values of each d_i is equally likely and that the d_i's are independent of each other.

2. (a) Modify Algorithm 8.1 by adding a test $i > 0$ in the **while** loop so that the dummy element $x_0 = -\infty$ is not needed.

★(b) Analyze the modified algorithm. [*Hint*: The analysis is complicated by the fact that the number of times the comparison $t < x[i]$ is made is diminished by l, the number of times that $i = 0$, that is, the number of values j, $1 < j \leq n$, such that $x_j < x_i$ for all i, $1 \leq i < j$. Determine the minimum and maximum values of l. Show that the average value of l is $H_n - 1$, where $H_n = \Sigma_{i=1}^n 1/i$.]

3. Rewrite Algorithm 8.1 so that in a table $x_1, x_2, \ldots, x_n$ it sorts only the subtables $x_k, x_{k+\delta}, x_{k+2\delta}, \ldots$, for $1 \leq k \leq \delta$. Call this δ-*sorting* and show that, given any sequence of positive integers $\delta_t > \delta_{t-1} > \cdots > \delta_1 = 1$, successively δ_t-sorting, δ_{t-1}-sorting, $\ldots$, δ_1-sorting leaves the table correctly sorted. This sorting algorithm is known as the *diminishing-increment sort*. Why should we expect it to be better than Algorithm 8.1?

★4. (a) Show that, for any positive integers ε and δ, if a table is ε-sorted after being δ-sorted it remains δ-sorted.

(b) Show that if l and m are relatively prime positive integers, then the largest integer not representable in the form $ul + vm$, $u, v \geq 0$, is $(l - 1)(m - 1) - 1$.

(c) Let $t \geq s_2 > s_1 > s_0 \geq 1$. Use the results of parts (a) and (b) to show that if the values of δ_{s_2}, and δ_{s_1} in Exercise 3 are relatively prime, then the δ_{s_0}-sorting portion of the diminishing increment sort has running time $O(n\delta_{s_1}\delta_{s_2}/\delta_{s_0})$.

(d) Show that if the values of $\delta_t, \delta_{t-1}, \ldots$ in Exercise 3 are chosen as the set of all integers of the form $2^p3^q < n$, then the diminishing-increment sort described there requires time $O(n(\log n)^2)$. [*Hint*: How many inversions are there in a table that has been both 2-sorted and 3-sorted? How many integral points (p, q) are there in the triangular region $p \ln 2 + q \ln 3 < \ln n$, $p, q \geq 0$?]

5. When the elements being sorted consist of long records of which the key x_i is only a small part, the data moves in Algorithm 8.1 may be too costly. Develop a version of Algorithm 8.1 that eliminates the data moves by linking the elements being sorted with an extra pointer field in each record. The end result of your algorithm should be the linked list of the elements in sorted order.

6. Does Algorithm 8.1 disturb the relative order of equal elements? A sorting algorithm that does *not* is called *stable*. Why might it be necessary to know whether or not a sorting algorithm is stable?

★7. Find the necessary loop-invariants to prove that Algorithm 8.1 terminates and upon termination leaves the elements properly sorted. (See Section 1.3.)

8.1.2   Transposition Sorts

Sorting methods based on transpositions systematically interchange pairs of elements that are out of order until no such pairs exist. In fact, Algorithm 8.1 can be considered a transposition sort in which the element x_j is interchanged with its left-hand neighbor until it is in its correct place. In this section we discuss two transposition sorts: the well-known but inefficient bubble sort and quicksort, one of the best all-around internal sorting algorithms.

Bubble Sort (Pilloried). An obvious way to systematically interchange out-of-order pairs of elements is to scan adjacent pairs of elements from left to right repeatedly, interchanging those found to be out of order. This technique has come to be known as the *bubble sort*, since larger elements "bubble-up" to the top (that is, the right). Algorithm 8.2 shows how this simple idea is implemented with one slight improvement: there is no point in continuing the scan into the large elements (at the right end) that are known to be in their final positions. Algorithm 8.2 uses the variable k, whose value at the beginning of the **while** loop is the largest index t for which x_t is *not* known to be in its final position. Figure 8.2 illustrates how the algorithm works on $n = 8$ elements.

The analysis of the bubble sort depends on the number of passes (the number of times the body of the **while** loop is executed), the number of comparisons $x[j] > x[j + 1]$, and the number of interchanges $Swap(x[j], x[j + 1])$. The number of interchanges is $\sum_{j=2}^{n} d_j$ because each element must move past (be interchanged with) exactly those elements smaller and to the right. This is similar to the number of data moves in Algorithm 8.1, *except* that in the bubble sort we are counting interchanges—each interchange $Swap(x[j], x[j + 1])$ is shorthand for the three moves $temp := x[j]$, $x[j] := x[j+1]$, and $x[j+1] := temp$. The number of data moves in Algorithm 8.2 thus is $3\sum_{j=2}^{n} d_j$: 0 in the best case, $3n(n-1)/2$ in the worst case, and $3n(n - 1)/4$ on the average.

```
k := n;
while k ≠ 0 do begin
      t := 0;
      for j := 1 to k − 1 do
            if x[ j] > x[ j + 1] then begin
                  Swap(x[ j], x[ j + 1]);
                  t := j
            end;
      k := t
end
```

Algorithm 8.2
Bubble sort

	x_1 x_2 x_3 x_4 x_5 x_6 x_7 x_8	d_1 d_2 d_3 d_4 d_5 d_6 d_7 d_8
Pass 1	4 7 3 1 5 8 2 6	0 0 2 3 1 0 5 2
Pass 2	4 3 1 5 7 2 6 8	0 1 2 0 0 4 1 0
Pass 3	3 1 4 5 2 6 7 8	0 1 0 0 3 0 0 0
Pass 4	1 3 4 2 5 6 7 8	0 0 0 2 0 0 0 0
Pass 5	1 3 2 4 5 6 7 8	0 0 1 0 0 0 0 0
Pass 6	1 2 3 4 5 6 7 8	0 0 0 0 0 0 0 0
	1 2 3 4 5 6 7 8	0 0 0 0 0 0 0 0

Figure 8.2
The bubble sort (Algorithm 8.2) applied to $n = 8$ elements. Also shown are the d_i values: d_i is the number of elements larger than x_i and to its left.

Examination of the values of the d_i in Figure 8.2 suggests that each pass of the bubble sort, except the last, decreases by one each nonzero d_i; this is indeed the case (Exercise 1). Thus the number of passes is one plus the largest d_i: 1 in the best case and n in the worst case. The average number of passes can be shown to be $n - \sqrt{\pi n/2} + O(1)$. The number of comparisons $x[j] > x[j+1]$ can be shown to be $n - 1$ at best, $n(n - 1)/2$ at worst, and $[(n^2 - n \ln n)/2] + O(1)$ on the average. The following table summarizes the behavior of the bubble sort:

	Element Comparisons	Element Moves	Number of Passes	Extra Storage
Best case	$n - 1$	0	1	
Average case	$n(n - \ln n)/2 + O(n)$	$3n(n - 1)/4$	$n - \sqrt{\pi n/2} + O(1)$	In all cases, one extra element for the interchanges and integer variables k and j
Worst case	$n(n - 1)/2$	$3n(n - 1)/4$	n	

Comparison of this table with the corresponding table for Algorithm 8.1 makes it clear that *the bubble sort is inferior to the insertion sort in almost every regard*: the bubble sort requires many more element moves except under the luckiest circumstances when the elements are almost completely in order. It requires many more element comparisons on the average, the same number at best, and only slightly fewer at worst. Its extra storage requirements are the same. Furthermore, it is a more complex algorithm both in its technique and in its analysis. *Unless we are sorting elements that already are nearly in order, the bubble sort has nothing to recommend it as an internal sorting technique*! It is possible to improve the bubble sort slightly by alternating scans from left to right with scans in the opposite direction, but the improvement is not enough to make it competitive with other sorting algorithms.

In both the insertion sort and the bubble sort, a major source of inefficiency is the fact that the interchanges do very little work, since elements move only one position at a time. As Exercise 2 shows, such algorithms are doomed to require proportional to n^2 operations in both the average and the worst cases. Thus a promising improvement is to interchange elements that are far away from each other, which is why the diminishing-increment sort (Exercises 3 and 4 of Section 8.1.1) is asymptotically so efficient. Another way to make each interchange do more work is used in quicksort.

Quicksort. The idea in quicksort is to select one of the elements x_1, x_2, ..., x_n and to use it to partition the remaining elements into two groups—those less than and those greater than the selected element—which are then sorted by applying quicksort recursively. The partitioning can be implemented by simultaneously scanning the elements from right to left and from left to right, interchanging elements in the wrong parts of the table. The element used to partition the table is then placed between the two subtables and the two subtables are sorted recursively.

Algorithm 8.3 gives the details of this method for sorting the table $(x_f, x_{f+1}, ..., x_l)$, using x_f to partition the table into subtables. Figure 8.3 shows how Algorithm 8.3 uses the two pointers i and j to scan the table during partitioning. At the beginning of the third **while** loop i and j point, respectively, to the first and last elements known *not* to be in the correct parts of the table. When they cross, that is, when $i \geqslant j$, all elements are in the correct parts of the table, and x_f is placed between the two parts by interchanging it with x_j. In order to simplify the central mechanism of the loop, the algorithm assumes that x_{l+1} is defined and larger than or equal to x_f, x_{f+1}, ..., and x_l; as we will see, this can be easily arranged.

It is tempting to try to simplify the ungainly looking loop structure of Algorithm 8.3. For instance, could the loops be rewritten to eliminate the repetition of the scans in the initialization? Perhaps, but it is not clear how to do so. The problem is complex because the loops must work properly on the myriad of boundary conditions, including all combinations of equal elements, short subtables ($l - f \leq 2$), and $x[f]$ being the largest or smallest of $x[f..l]$. More than complex, the problem is also subtle: the partitioning must not introduce any bias into the order of the subtables that will be sorted recursively. If, for example, one of the subtables becomes more likely to have a small (or large) element as its first element, the subsequent partitioning of that subtable will be less likely to yield evenly divided subtables. Since, as we will show, the good performance of quicksort depends on the high probability of a roughly even split in the partitioning phase, such bias would result in degraded average performance. The reader is urged to *try* simplifying Algorithm 8.3 and to

procedure *SimpleQuickSort*(**var** *x*: *ElementArray*; *f*, *l*: *SubscriptRange*);
    {sort $x[f..l]$ assuming that $x[l + 1]$ exists and is greater than or equal to all the elements to be sorted}
var
    i, *j*: *SubscriptRange*;
begin
    if $f < l$ **then begin**
        {partition the elements into two subtables}
        $i := f + 1$;
        while $x[i] < x[f]$ **do** $i := i + 1$;
        $j := l$;
        while $x[j] > x[f]$ **do** $j := j - 1$;
        while $i < j$ **do begin**
            {Assert: $i < j$, $x[f..i-1] \leqslant x[f] \leqslant x[j+1..l]$,
            $x[i] \geqslant x[f] \geqslant x[j]$}
            Swap($x[i]$, $x[j]$);
            repeat $i := i + 1$ **until** $x[i] \geqslant x[f]$;
            repeat $j := j - 1$ **until** $x[j] \leqslant x[f]$
        end;
        {put $x[f]$ into place between the subtables}
        Swap($x[f]$, $x[j]$);
        {sort the subtables recursively}
        SimpleQuickSort(x, f, $j - 1$);
        SimpleQuickSort(x, $j + 1$, l)
    end
end

Algorithm 8.3
Recursive version of quicksort, using the first element to partition the remaining elements.

subject the resultant program to the rigors suggested in Exercise 4. Be warned, though: many erroneous or biased partitioning algorithms have been published!

    To analyze the total number of element comparisons, $x[\bullet]$ vs. $x[f]$, in Algorithm 8.3, notice that at the end of the loop **while** $i < j$ all the elements $x_{f+1}, \ldots,$ x_l have been compared once with x_f except the elements x_s and x_{s+1} (where the scans cross), which have been compared twice with x_f. Let $\overline{C}_n$ be the average number of element comparisons to sort a table of n distinct elements, assuming that each of the $n!$ permutations of the elements is equally likely. Obviously $\overline{C}_0 = \overline{C}_1 = 0$ and in general we have

	x_f	x_{f+1}	x_{f+2}									x_{l-1}	x_l
						...							
Start	27	99	0	8	13	64	86	16	7	10	88	25	90
		↑											↑
		i											j
First interchange	27	99	0	8	13	64	86	16	7	10	88	25	90
		↑										↑	
		i										j	
Second interchange	27	25	0	8	13	64	86	16	7	10	88	99	90
						↑			↑				
						i			j				
Third interchange	27	25	0	8	13	10	86	16	7	64	88	99	90
							↑		↑				
							i		j				
Scans cross	27	25	0	8	13	10	7	16	86	64	88	99	90
								↑	↑				
								j	i				
x_f put into place	27	25	0	8	13	10	7	16	86	64	88	99	90
								↑	↑				
								j	i				
Partitioned table	16	25	0	8	13	10	7	27	86	64	88	99	90

Figure 8.3
The partitioning phase of quicksort using the first element to partition the table. The value of $x[l+1]$, not shown, is assumed to be larger than or equal to the other values shown.

$$\overline{C}_n = \sum_{s=1}^{n} p_s(n + 1 + \overline{C}_{s-1} + \overline{C}_{n-s}), \qquad n \geqslant 2, \tag{8.1}$$

where

$$p_s = \Pr(x_f \text{ is the } s\text{th smallest element}) = \frac{1}{n}$$

since the two subtables produced by the partitioning are random—that is, since each of the $(s - 1)!$ permutations of the elements in the left subtable is equally likely and each of the $(n - s)!$ permutations of the elements in the right subtable is equally likely: the partitioning technique used in Algorithm 8.3 has been very carefully designed to insure this randomness in the two subtables.

The recurrence (8.1) simplifies to

$$\overline{C}_n = n + 1 + \frac{2}{n} \sum_{s=0}^{n-1} \overline{C}_s, \qquad n \geqslant 2.$$

This is an instance of the recurrence (7.9) of Section 7.2.2, the solution of which is given by Equation (7.14), page 339:

$$\overline{C}_n = 2(n + 1) \sum_{i=1}^{n} \frac{1}{i} - \frac{8}{3}n - \frac{2}{3}$$

$$\approx 1.386n \lg n \qquad\qquad (8.2)$$

In other words, on the average, quicksort requires a total amount of work proportional to $n \lg n$, since the amount of work done *per comparison* is constant (why?). This makes quicksort *asymptotically* better on the average than the other sorting algorithms so far considered. It turns out that, with various refinements, the quicksort idea gives better performance on the average in practice than other sorting algorithms.

The worst-case performance of quicksort is another matter, however. Let C_n be the number of element comparisons used by Algorithm 8.3 in the worst case on a table of n elements. We claim that

$$C_n = \frac{1}{2}n^2 + \frac{3}{2}n + O(1) \qquad\qquad (8.3)$$

making a quicksort's performance proportional to n^2 in the worst case—that is, no better than that of the insertion or bubble sorts. We verify (8.3) by showing an example on which quicksort requires $n^2/2 + 3n/2 - 2$ comparisons and then showing that no matter what, $C_n \leq n^2/2 + 3n/2$. First, consider what happens when quicksort is applied to an *already sorted table*: it makes $(n + 1) + n + \cdots + 3$ element comparisons, a total of $n^2/2 + 3n/2 - 2$. On the other hand, by inspection $C_0 = C_1 = 0$ and $C_2 = 3$. By induction, then, $C_n \leq n^2/2 + 3n/2$, for it holds when $n \leq 3$ and

$$C_n = n + 1 + \max_{1 \leq k \leq n} (C_{k-1} + C_{n-k})$$

$$\leq n + 1 + \max_{1 \leq k \leq n} [(k - 1)^2/2 + 3(k - 1)/2 + (n - k)^2/2 + 3(n - k)/2]$$

The maximum occurs at $k = 1$ or $k = n$ so that

$$C_n \leq n + 1 + (n - 1)^2/2 + 3(n - 1)/2 = n^2/2 + 3n/2$$

as desired. A slightly more careful analysis shows that in fact for $n \geq 1$, $C_n = n^2/2 + 3n/2 - 2$ (see Exercise 7).

Because $\overline{C}_n$ is $O(n \log n)$, the quadratic performance of the worst case would be extremely rare *on random tables*. In practice, however, the tables encountered are likely to be in rough order, or to have large segments that are in order; this makes the quadratic performance more probable, degrading the expected behavior. The difficulty is the choice of the element to partition the table; when the order of the elements is not random, the first element cannot be expected to split the table evenly, on the average. For this reason, we can improve quicksort for nonrandom tables by using a randomly chosen element to partition the table. This change is easily incorporated in Algorithm 8.3: add the statement $Swap(x[f], x[rand(f,l)])$ just before the statement $i := f + 1$, where $rand(f,l)$ gives a random integer r, $f \leq r \leq l$. The use of a randomly chosen partitioning element guarantees that the average indicated by Equation (8.2) will be the average in practice *regardless of the expected distribution of the permutations of the x_i.*

There is a disadvantage to the use of a random partitioning element, however: the generation of the required pseudo-random numbers is time-consuming if the numbers generated are to seem random (see Exercise 10). Moreover, the effect we want (that of keeping the partitioning element near the middle) can be achieved by a different method that also improves the average behavior. We choose as the partitioning element the median of a small sample of elements. The median of three elements turns out to be an excellent choice, since there is a process of diminishing returns when larger samples are used. To eliminate the possibility of nearly ordered tables causing poor performance, we choose as our sample the first element, the middle element, and the last element. We can implement this modification to Algorithm 8.3 by inserting the following statements just before the statement $i := f + 1$:

> $Swap(x[(f+l) \text{ div } 2], x[f+1]);$
> **if** $x[f+1] > x[l]$ **then** $Swap(x[f+1], x[l]);$
> **if** $x[f] > x[l]$ **then** $Swap(x[f], x[l]);$
> **if** $x[f+1] > x[f]$ **then** $Swap(x[f+1], x[f])$

This makes x_f the median of x_f, $x_{\lfloor(f+l)/2\rfloor}$, and x_l without introducing any bias in the expected distribution of the subtables. Furthermore, it leaves $x_{f+1} \leq x_f \leq x_l$ so that the initializations of i and j can be changed to $i := f + 2$ and $j := l - 1$, respectively. The complete partitioning part of the algorithm is thus as shown in Algorithm 8.4(a). With these changes, it can be shown that $\overline{C}_n \approx 1.188\, n \lg n$; of course, even in this case C_n is proportional to n^2, but such behavior is *extremely* unlikely, even on tables occurring in practice.

Unfortunately, the changes outlined above for using the median-of-three partitioning mean that the algorithm as written will no longer work properly for subtables of two elements; the point at which the recursion "bottoms out" must thus be changed. This is a wise idea in any case, because the overhead in Algorithm 8.3

{find the median of the first, middle and last elements}
$Swap(x[(f+l) \textbf{ div } 2], x[f+1])$;
if $x[f+1] > x[l]$ **then** $Swap(x[f+1], x[l])$;
if $x[f] > x[l]$ **then** $Swap(x[f], x[l])$;
if $x[f+1] > x[f]$ **then** $Swap(x[f+1], x[f])$;
$\{x[f]$ is now the desired median and $x[f+1] \leqslant x[f] \leqslant x[l]\}$
{partition using $x[f]$}
$i := f + 2$;
while $x[i] < x[f]$ **do** $i := i + 1$;
$j := l - 1$;
while $x[j] > x[f]$ **do** $j := j - 1$;
while $i < j$ **do begin**
      {Assert: $i < j$, $x[f..i-1] \leqslant x[f] \leqslant x[j+1..l]$,
      and $x[i] \geqslant x[f] \geqslant x[j]\}$
      $Swap(x[i], x[j])$;
      repeat $i := i + 1$ **until** $x[i] \geqslant x[f]$;
      repeat $j := j - 1$ **until** $x[j] \leqslant x[f]$
end;
{put $x[f]$ into place between the subtables}
$Swap(x[f], x[j])$

Algorithm 8.4(a)
Partitioning by the median-of-three method. See Exercise 3 for a performance improvement.

makes it less efficient than the insertion sort of Algorithm 8.1 for small numbers of elements. Depending on the particular instruction set of the computer, the optimum crossover point at which quicksort becomes worthwhile is between five and fifteen elements, with ten being typical. Thus we should select a crossover value m, $5 \leqslant m \leqslant 15$ (the exact optimum is *not* necessary), and change the **if** $f < l$ **then** at the beginning of Algorithm 8.3 to

      if $l - f + 1 < m$ **then**
            "apply InsertionSort to $x[f..l]$"
      else
            . . .

In fact, there is a better way to accomplish the same thing. Ignore subtables of size less than m during partitioning (that is, do not make a recursive call for such a subtable), leaving them unsorted; this is done in Algorithm 8.3 by simply changing the initial test from $f < l$ to $l - f + 1 \geqslant m$. Then, after all the partitioning has been finished, the table has all the elements used for partitioning in their final (sorted) locations with small groups of unsorted elements between them. A single application of Algorithm 8.1 completes the sorting of the table. The advantage of this approach to small subtables is seen as follows: it takes a single application of the insertion sort a bit longer to sort the entire table than it would have to apply it to each of the small subtables individually, but all the overhead of the multiple applications has been eliminated, more than making up the difference.

Algorithm 8.4(b) presents a version of quicksort that contains all the improvements outlined above, plus one more. In the worst case, the stack that is implicit in the recursion of Algorithm 8.3 can reach depth n, consequently requiring extra storage proportional to the size of the subtable being sorted. For large n this can be unacceptable, so we have written Algorithm 8.4(b) in an iterative manner, maintaining the stack explicitly (see Section 4.2). A stack entry is a pair (f, l); when it is on the stack, it means that the subtable $x[f..l]$ is to be sorted. Algorithm 8.4(b) puts the larger of the two subtables on the stack and applies the algorithm immediately to the smaller subtable. This reduces the worst-case stack depth to about $\lg n$ (Exercise 12).

The behavior of Algorithm 8.4(b) is summarized by the following table:

	Element Comparisons	Element Interchanges	Extra Storage
Best case	$n \lg n$	Between $\frac{1}{2}n \lg n$ and $n \lg n$	About $\lg n$ stack entries and several integer variables
Average case	$1.188\, n \lg n$		
Worst case	$n^2/2$		

Exercises

1. Prove that each pass of the bubble sort except the last decreases by one each nonzero d_i, where d_i is, as before, the number of elements larger than x_i and to its left.

★ 2. Let $\Pi = (\pi_1, \pi_2, \ldots, \pi_n)$ be a random permutation of $1, 2, \ldots, n$. What is the average value of

$$\frac{1}{n} \sum_{i=1}^{n} |\pi_i - i|$$

the expected distance that an element will travel during sorting? What can be concluded about sorting algorithms that perform only adjacent interchanges?

3. Access to an array element is more costly than to a simple variable. Rewrite Algorithm 8.4(a) to eliminate half the array accesses by moving one or two of the elements to simple variables.

procedure *QuickSort*(**var** *x*: *ElementArray*; *n*: *SubscriptRange*);
const
        m = 10; {this can be any value near the crossover point
                        between *QuickSort* and *InsertionSort*}
var
        f, *l*, *i*, *j*: *SubscriptRange*;
        S: *Stack*;
begin
        Empty(*S*);
        Push("(0,0)", *S*); {bottom stack entry, with values that will stop loop}
        f := 1;
        l := *n*;
        x[*n* + 1] := *PlusInfinity*; {to stop scan at the right end}
        x[0] := *MinusInfinity*;   {for the *InsertionSort* below}
        while *f* < *l* **do begin**
        {Assert: The regions remaining to be quicksorted are *x*[*f*..*l*] and those
        delimited by pairs on the stack above the (0,0). These regions are disjoint
        and each region on the stack is smaller than the one beneath it. No region
        has less than *m* elements. Elements not in any of the regions can be
        sorted by an insertion sort that never moves any element by more than *m*
        positions.}
                "partition as in Algorithm 8.4(a)";
                if *j* − *f* < *m* **then**
                        if *l* − *j* < *m* **then**   {ignore both small tables}
                                "(*f*, *l*)" := *Pop*(*S*)
                        else   {ignore small left subtable}
                                f := *j* + 1
                else
                        if *l* − *j* < *m* **then**   {ignore small right subtable}
                                l := *j* − 1
                        else   {neither subtable small, put larger on *S*}
                                if *j* − *f* > *l* − *j* **then begin**   {left subtable is larger}
                                        Push("(*f*, *j*−1)", *S*);
                                        f := *j* + 1
                                end
                                else begin   {right subtable is larger}
                                        Push("(*j* + 1, *l*)", *S*);
                                        l := *j* − 1
                                end
        end;
        InsertionSort(*x*, *n*)   {Algorithm 8.1}
end

Algorithm 8.4(b)
Improved quicksort

4. Using mathematical analysis and/or extensive sorting of random numbers, compare the efficiency of the following partitioning methods for quicksort with that of Algorithm 8.3. For each of the methods below, first verify that it correctly partitions the elements (especially for $l - f \leq 2$ and in the presence of equal elements). Assume that $x_{f-1} = -\infty$ and that $x_{l+1} = \infty$ as needed.

(a)
```
i := f;
  j := l + 1;
  v := x[f];
  while i < j do begin
         repeat j := j - 1 until x[j] ≥ v;
         if i ≥ j then j := i
         else begin
              Swap(x[i], x[j]);
              repeat i := i + 1 until x[i] ≥ v;
              if i < j then x[j] := x[i]
         end
  end;
  x[j] := v
```

(b)
```
i := f - 1;
  j := l + 1;
  p := (f + l) div 2;
  v := x[p];
  while i < j do begin
         repeat i := i + 1 until x[i] > v;
         repeat j := j - 1 until x[j] < v;
         if i < j then Swap(x[i], x[j])
  end;
  if i < p then begin
         Swap(x[i], x[p]);
         i := i + 1
  end;
  if j > p then begin
         Swap(x[p], x[j]);
         j := j - 1
  end
```

(c)
```
i := f - 1;
  j := l + 1;
  v := x[f];
```

```
    repeat
        repeat i := i + 1 until x[i] ≥ v;
        repeat j := j − 1 until x[j] ≤ v;
        Swap(x[i], x[j])
    until i ≥ j;
    Swap(x[j], x[i])   {undo extraneous exchange}
```

(d) $i := f$;
   $j := l$;
   $v := x[f]$;
   while $i < j$ **do begin**
       while $x[j] > v$ **do** $j := j − 1$;
       while $(i < j)$ **and** $(x[i] ≤ v)$ **do** $i := i + 1$;
       if $i < j$ **then** *Swap*(x[i], x[j]);
   end;
   $x[f] := x[j]$;
   $x[j] := v$

★ 5. Prove by induction that *SimpleQuickSort*(x, 1, n) using Algorithm 8.3 (and hence Algorithm 8.4) correctly sorts the table $x[1..n]$. [*Hint*: First prove by induction that the partitioning was done correctly.]

★ 6. Prove that the partitioning method of Algorithm 8.3 [and hence of Algorithm 8.4(a)] produces random subtables; that is, prove that if each of the *n*! permutations of the table is equally likely, then each of the permutations of the left and right subtables is equally likely.

7. Do a more careful analysis of C_n, the number of element comparisons used by Algorithm 8.3 in the worst case, to show that

$$C_n = \begin{cases} 0, & n = 0, \\ (n^2 + 3n − 4)/2, & n ≥ 1 \end{cases}$$

★ 8. Show that I_n, the average number of calls to *Swap* in Algorithm 8.3 called by *SimpleQuickSort*(x, 1, n), satisfies

$$\bar{I}_n = \sum_{s=1}^{n} p_s \left(1 + \sum_{t=0}^{s-1} q_{s,t} + \bar{I}_{s-1} + \bar{I}_{n-s} \right), \quad n ≥ 2$$

where p_s is the probability that $x[1]$ is the *s*th smallest element, $p_s = 1/n$, and $q_{s,t}$ is the probability that when $x[1]$ is the *s*th smallest element, then among $x[2..s]$ there will be *t* elements greater than $x[1]$,

$$q_{s,t} = \frac{\binom{s-1}{t}\binom{n-s}{t}}{\binom{n-1}{s-1}}$$

Establish the identity

$$\sum_{t=0}^{s-1} \binom{s-1}{t}\binom{n-s}{t}t = \binom{n-2}{s-2}(n-s)$$

and use it to show that for $n \geqslant 2$

$$\bar{I}_n = \frac{1}{6}n + \frac{2}{3} + \frac{2}{n}\sum_{i=0}^{n-1}\bar{I}_i$$

and thus that

$$\bar{I}_n = \frac{1}{3}(n+1)H_n - \frac{1}{9}n - \frac{5}{18}$$

where

$$H_n = \sum_{i=1}^{n}\frac{1}{i}$$

9. Show that I_n, the worst-case number of calls to *Swap* in Algorithm 8.3, is proportional to $n \lg n$.

10. Assuming that each of the $n!$ permutations of the elements in the table is equally likely, how many random numbers would be needed on the average to sort the elements with the random partitioning scheme described in the text?

11. Verify the claim in the text that, in the context of Algorithm 8.4, a single application of the insertion sort is, in total, more efficient than its application to the small subtables individually.

12. Analyze the worst-case stack depth required in Algorithm 8.4 as a function of n and m.

13. Is Algorithm 8.3 stable (see Exercise 6 of Section 8.1.1 for the definition of stability)? Is Algorithm 8.4?

14. Explain the effect of changing the stack in Algorithm 8.4 to a queue.

15. Devise and implement a sorting algorithm analogous to quicksort in which the partitioning is done on the basis of the most significant bit of the elements; if that bit is 1, the element goes into the right-hand part of the table; if that bit is 0, the element goes into the left-hand part of the table. Subsequent partitions are based on the less significant bits of the elements. This method is known as *radix exchange* sorting. Analyze the best and worst cases for

(a) The number of interchanges.

(b) The number of bit inspections.

(c) The maximum stack depth.

Analyze the average cases for (a), (b), and (c), assuming that the elements to be sorted are $0, 1, 2, \ldots, 2^t - 1$ in random order.

8.1.3 Selection Sorts

In a selection sort the basic idea is to go through stages $i = 1, 2, \ldots, n$, selecting the ith largest (smallest) element and putting it in place on the ith stage. The simplest form of selection sort is that of Algorithm 8.5: at the ith stage, the ith largest element is found in the obvious manner by scanning the remaining $n - i + 1$ elements. The number of element comparisons at the ith stage is $n - i$, leading to a total of $(n-1) + (n-2) + \cdots + 1 = n(n - 1)/2$, regardless of the input. This is clearly not a very good way to sort. Its behavior is summarized by the following table:

	Element Comparisons	Element Interchanges	Extra Storage
In all cases	$n(n - 1)/2$	$n - 1$	Integer variables i, j, k, and m

Despite the inefficiency of Algorithm 8.5, the idea of selection can lead to an efficient sorting algorithm. The trick is to find a more efficient method of determining the ith largest element, which can be done by using the mechanism of a *knockout tournament*. Make comparisons $x_1 : x_2, x_3 : x_4, x_5 : x_6, \ldots, x_{n-1} : x_n$ and then compare the winners (the larger elements) of those comparisons in a like manner, and so on, as illustrated for $n = 16$ in Figure 8.4. Notice that this process requires $n - 1$ element comparisons to determine the largest element (see Exercise 3); but, having determined the largest element, we possess a great deal of information about the second largest element: it must be one of those that lost to the largest. Thus the second largest can now be determined by replacing the largest with $-\infty$ and remaking all the comparisons in which the formerly largest element took part. This is illustrated in Figure 8.5 for the tree in Figure 8.4.

for $j := n$ **downto** 2 **do begin**
    {Assert: $x[j+1..n]$ is sorted and $x[j+1] \geqslant x[1..j]$}
    {stage $i = n-j+1$: find the ith largest (which is also the jth smallest);
    see Exercise 1}
    $m := 1$;
    for $k := 2$ **to** j **do**
        if $x[m] < x[k]$ **then**
            $m := k$;
    {put ith largest into place}
    $Swap(x[j], x[m])$
end

Algorithm 8.5
Simple selection sort

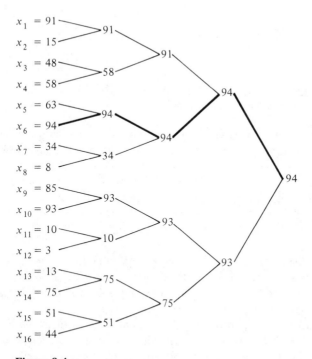

Figure 8.4
Using a knockout tournament to find the largest element. The path of the largest
element is shown by the darker lines.

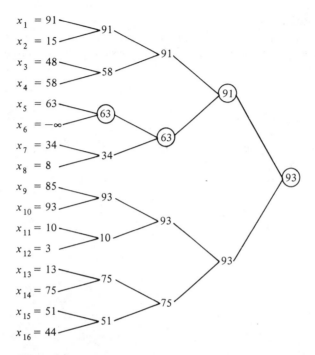

Figure 8.5
Finding the second largest element by replacing the largest with $-\infty$ and remaking the comparisons won by the largest element. Revised elements are circled.

Since the tree has height $\lceil \lg n \rceil$ (why?), we can find the second largest element by remaking $\lceil \lg n \rceil - 1$ comparisons instead of the $n - 2$ used in the simple selection algorithm. This process can obviously be continued. On finding the second largest element, we replace it by $-\infty$ and remake another $\lceil \lg n \rceil - 1$ comparisons to find the third largest element, and so on. Thus the entire process uses

$$n - 1 + (n - 1)(\lceil \lg n \rceil - 1) \approx n \lceil \lg n \rceil$$

element comparisons. This *may* yield a reasonable sorting method, provided that the movement of the elements can be handled in an efficient manner (recall that binary insertion, mentioned at the end of Section 8.1.1, uses only $n \lg n$ element comparisons but proportional to n^2 interchanges).

A tournament process as described above is essentially a *priority queue*, mentioned in Sections 4.2 and 7.2.2, except that in this case all the elements arrive before the deletions begin. Thus, an efficient data structure for priority queues will lead to a tournament-like selection sort with the potential for $n \log n$ worst-case behavior. In Section 7.2.2 we saw that balanced trees could be used to implement priority queues in which insertion, deletion, splitting and merging could all be done in logarithmic time. We hardly need such flexibility for a tournament sort, however, so we now introduce the *heap*, an efficient implementation for priority queues in which only insertions and deletions occur, not splittings or mergings.

A *heap* is a completely balanced binary tree of height h in which all leaves are at level h or $h - 1$ (see Section 5.3) and all descendants of a node are smaller than it; furthermore all leaves at level h are as far to the *left* as possible. Figure 8.6 shows a set of elements arranged into a heap. The advantage of a heap is that it can be stored compactly in an array, without the need for an explicit tree structure: the children of the element in the ith position of the array are the elements in positions $2i$ and $2i + 1$ (compare this with the ordering used in Figure 5.25). The heap of Figure 8.6 thus becomes

$$
\begin{array}{cccccccccccc}
i: & 1 & 2 & 3 & 4 & 5 & 6 & 7 & 8 & 9 & 10 & 11 & 12 \\
x: & 94 & 93 & 75 & 91 & 85 & 44 & 51 & 18 & 48 & 58 & 10 & 34
\end{array}
$$

We will leave the description of general algorithms for insertion and deletion in heaps to Exercises 9 and 10; these algorithms are needed in order to use heaps as priority queues. Our attention here will be restricted to the manipulation of heaps as required by sorting.

Notice that in a heap the largest element must be at the root and thus always in the first position of the array representing the heap. Interchanging the first element with the nth element places the largest element into its correct position, but it destroys the heap property of the first $n - 1$ elements. If we can initially build a heap and then restore it efficiently, we are finished, for we can sort as follows:

```
"build a heap from x[1..n]";
for i := n downto 2 do begin
    Swap(x[1], x[i]);
    "restore the heap in x[1..i - 1]"
end
```

This is an outline of *heapsort*.

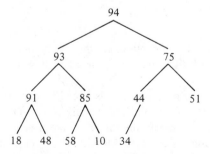

Figure 8.6
A heap containing twelve elements

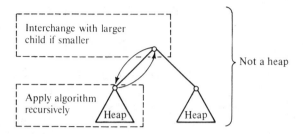

Figure 8.7
Recursive restoration of the heap. In this case the left child was larger.

Given a binary tree all of whose leaves are as far left as possible and both of
whose subtrees are heaps, how do we transform the whole thing into a heap? We
compare the root to the larger of the two children. If the root is larger, the tree is
already a heap; but if the root is smaller, we interchange it with the larger child and
apply the restoration algorithm recursively to the subtree whose root has been interchanged. (See Figure 8.7.) The procedure to restore $x[f..l]$ to a heap, assuming that
all the subtrees are heaps, is thus

```
procedure RestoreSketch(var x: ElementArray; f, l: SubscriptRange);
var
      child: SubscriptRange;
begin
      if "x[f] is not a leaf" then begin
            {Assert: x[2f..l] and x[2f+1..l] are heaps}
            child := "index of the larger of the children of x[f]";
            if x[child] > x[f] then begin
                  Swap(x[child], x[f]);
                  RestoreSketch(x, child, l)
            end
      end
end
```

Rewriting *RestoreSketch* in an iterative manner to eliminate the tail recursion and
filling in the details, we obtain Algorithm 8.6. Notice that x_j is a leaf if and only if
$j > \lfloor l/2 \rfloor$ (Exercise 6).

To build the heap initially, note that the heap property is already satisfied (vac-
uously) by each of the leaves $(x_i, \lfloor n/2 \rfloor < i \leq n)$ and that calling *Restore*(x, i, n)
successively for $i = \lfloor n/2 \rfloor, \lfloor n/2 \rfloor - 1, \ldots, 1$ transforms the table into a heap at all
higher levels. The heapsort procedure is thus as given in Algorithm 8.7: the first **for**
loop builds the heap and is known as the *creation phase*; the second **for** loop is
called the *sift-up phase*.

```
procedure Restore(var x: ElementArray; f, l: SubscriptRange);
var
      j, child: SubscriptRange;
begin
      j := f;
      while j ≤ l div 2 do begin
            {Assert: x[f..l] is a heap except x[j] may be smaller than one of its
            children}
            child := 2*j;
            if child < l then if x[child] < x[child + 1] then
                  child := child + 1;
            {x[child] is now the larger child of x[j]}
            if x[child] > x[j] then begin
                  Swap(x[child], x[j]);
                  j := child
            end
            else j := l {to terminate the loop}
      end
end
```

Algorithm 8.6
Restoration of the heap from a tree both of whose subtrees are heaps

The behavior of heapsort, on the average, is unknown, and so we consider only the worst case. We need to know the amount of work done during a call $Restore$ (x, f, l). In particular, if h is the height of the subtree (a single node having height 0) rooted at x_f, then $Restore$ will perform at most $2h$ element comparisons and at most h interchanges; thus we need to determine h. Notice that the left child of x_f is x_{2f}, whose left child is x_{4f}, and so on. The subtree has a height of h, where h is the

```
procedure HeapSort(var x: ElementArray; n: SubscriptRange);
var
      i: SubscriptRange;
begin
      for i := n div 2 downto 1 do
            Restore(x, i, n);
      for i := n downto 2 do begin
            Swap(x[1], x[i]);
            Restore(x, 1, i − 1)
      end
end
```

Algorithm 8.7
Heapsort

largest integer such that x has an element corresponding to subscript $2^h f$—that is, such that $2^h f \leq l$, which implies that $h = \lfloor \lg(l/f) \rfloor$.

The creation phase thus requires at most

$$\sum_{i=1}^{\lfloor n/2 \rfloor} \left\lfloor \lg \frac{n}{i} \right\rfloor \leq \sum_{i=1}^{\lfloor n/2 \rfloor} \lg \frac{n}{i} = \left\lfloor \frac{n}{2} \right\rfloor \lg n - \lg \left(\left\lfloor \frac{n}{2} \right\rfloor ! \right) = O(n)^*$$

element interchanges and hence also $O(n)$ element comparisons. Similarly, the sift-up phase requires at most

$$(n-1) + \sum_{i=2}^{n} \left\lfloor \lg \frac{i-1}{1} \right\rfloor = n \lg n + O(n)^*$$

element interchanges and hence $2n \lg n + O(n)$ element comparisons.

In summary we have

	Element Comparisons	Element Interchanges	Extra Storage
Worst case	$2n \lg n + O(n)$	$n \lg n$	Integer variables i, j, f, l, and *child*

Thus heapsort will require only proportional to $n \lg n$ operations for any table, in contrast to quicksort, which could occasionally require proportional to n^2 operations. Despite this fact, empirical evidence *strongly* suggests that quicksort is far superior to heapsort in practice (Exercise 8), unless worst-case performance is critical.

Exercises

1. Why is there no stage $i = n$ in Algorithm 8.5? In other words, why doesn't the outer loop go from n **downto** 1?

---

*This derivation requires the use of *Stirling's formula*, which states

$$n! = \sqrt{2\pi n} \left(\frac{n}{e} \right)^n \left(1 + \frac{1}{12n} + \frac{1}{288n^2} - \frac{139}{51,840n^3} - \frac{571}{2,488,320n^4} + \cdots \right)$$

so that

$$\ln n! = \left(n + \frac{1}{2} \right) \ln n - n + \ln \sqrt{2\pi} + \frac{1}{12n} - \frac{1}{360n^3} + \cdots$$

2. Is Algorithm 8.5 a stable sorting algorithm (see Exercise 6 of Section 8.1.1 for a definition of stability)?

3. Show that *any* method of determining the largest element in a table of n elements requires $n - 1$ element comparisons. [*Hint*: At most how many of the elements can be eliminated from consideration by any such comparison?]

4. Prove a result similar to that in the previous exercise for determining the smallest element.

5. Give a method using only $\lceil 3n/2 \rceil - 2$ element comparisons to determine both the largest and smallest elements in a table of n elements. Does this in any way contradict the results in the two previous exercises?

6. Show that a heap with n elements has $\lceil n/2 \rceil$ leaves and that they are $x_{\lceil (n+1)/2 \rceil}$, $x_{\lceil (n+1)/2 \rceil + 1}, \ldots, x_n$; the last nonleaf is $x_{\lfloor n/2 \rfloor}$.

7. Is heapsort stable (see Exercise 2)?

8. Perform experiments to support or refute the claim made that quicksort is superior to heapsort.

9. Design and analyze an algorithm for adding an arbitrary element to a heap of n elements to form a heap of $n + 1$ elements.

10. Design and analyze an algorithm for deleting a specified element x_i from a heap of n elements, leaving a heap of $n - 1$ elements.

11. Explore the idea of a ternary heap and a sorting algorithm based on it.

12. A *biparental heap* is like a heap except that most of the elements have two parents, instead of just one. Using an arrow to point from larger to smaller elements, the following is a biparental heap of ten elements:

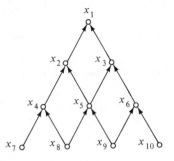

This can be neatly represented in a triangular array (see Exercise 4 of Section 3.3.1):

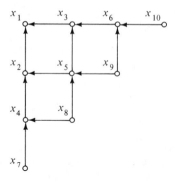

The elements of a biparental heap are thus regarded as being partitioned into *blocks*, the ith block consisting of the elements $x_{[i(i-1)/2]+1}$ through $x_{i(i+1)/2}$. The ordering imposed on the elements is that the kth element of the pth block is less than both the kth and $(k + 1)$st elements of the $(p + 1)$st block. In the triangular array representation shown above, a block is a southwest-northeast diagonal.

★(a) Using the result of Exercise 4 of Section 3.3.1, we can encode the above triangular array in a linear array by the addressing function

$$\text{loc}(A[i, j]) = \frac{(i + j - 2)^2 + i + 3j - 2}{2}$$

It is possible with this encoding to move along rows, columns, and diagonals without explicitly calculating the addressing function. Assuming that a one-dimensional array $x[1..m]$ is used to store a biparental heap of $n \leq m$ elements, find formulas (in terms of k) for the location in the array of the elements above, below, to the left, and to the right of $x[k]$.

(b) Design and analyze an algorithm to find the smallest element in a biparental heap.

(c) Design and analyze an algorithm to find the largest element in a biparental heap.

(d) Design and analyze an algorithm to insert a new element into a biparental heap.

(e) Design and analyze an algorithm to delete a specified element from a biparental heap.

8.1.4 Distributive Sorts

When faced with the real-life task of sorting a very large handful of index cards into alphabetical order, one might first attempt to make the task more manageable by dividing the cards into 26 piles—one of the a's, one of the b's, and so on, and then sorting each of the piles individually. This idea leads us to a class of sorting algorithms based on the distribution of the elements into "buckets."

In fact, quicksort can be viewed as a distributive sort in which there are two buckets, those elements below some chosen element and those above. Quicksort then recursively applies the same distribution idea to each of the two buckets. As we will see, the number of buckets and the way they are chosen is important to the efficiency of the resulting distribution sort, and in some cases we will be able to do much better than quicksort by choosing buckets based on the representation or the numerical distribution of the elements being sorted. This parallels the case in searching in which additional knowledge about the elements can allow us to use tries or interpolation search, methods not applicable to the general case. The benefit in the case of sorting is the possibility of sorting n elements in time proportional to n.

Radix Distribution. The sorting algorithm we are about to discuss differs from those considered so far in that it is based *not* on comparisons between elements, but on the *representation* of the elements. We assume that the elements $x_1, x_2, \ldots,$ x_n each have the form

$$x_i = (x_{i,p}, x_{i,p-1}, \ldots, x_{i,1})$$

and that they are to be sorted into increasing *lexicographic order*; that is,

$$x_i = (x_{i,p}, x_{i,p-1}, \ldots, x_{i,1}) < (x_{j,p}, x_{j,p-1}, \ldots, x_{j,1}) = x_j$$

if and only if, for some $t \le p$, we have $x_{i,l} = x_{j,l}$ for $l > t$ and $x_{i,t} > x_{j,t}$. For simplicity, we will assume that $0 \le x_{i,l} < r$, and so the elements can be viewed as integers represented in base r, each element having p r-ary digits. If the elements are of different lengths, the short elements are padded with zeros to make the lengths uniform. In the common example of alphabetic elements, we would take $r = 27$ (26 letters and the blank character), padding the short elements on the right with blanks.

In the *radix distribution* sort the buckets correspond to the r values of a base r digit. The sort is based on the observation that if the elements have been sorted with respect to the $p - 1$ low-order positions, they can be completely sorted by sorting them according to the pth (highest) order position, being careful not to disturb the relative order of elements having equal values in the pth position. In effect, this means sorting the elements according to the lowest-order position, then according to the next-lowest-order position, $\ldots$, and finally according to the highest-order position, never changing the relative order of equal values. This was the basis for old-fashioned mechanical card sorters: to sort cards on the field in, say, columns 76 through 80, the cards are sorted into increasing order on column 80, then on column 79, then on column 78, then on column 77, and finally on column 76. Each column sort is done by reading the column in each card and physically moving the card to the back of a pile (bucket) that corresponds to the digit punched in that column of

the card. Once all cards have been placed in the proper piles, the piles are stacked together (concatenated) in increasing order; the process is repeated for the next column
to the left. This procedure is illustrated in Figure 8.8 for three-digit decimal numbers.

Notice that both the buckets and the table itself are used in a first-in, first-out
manner, and so it is best to represent them as queues. In particular, assume that a
link field $Next_i$ is associated with each element x_i (perhaps as a parallel array); these
fields can then be used to build an input queue, $Qall$, by linking together all the table
elements. The $Next$ fields can also be used to link the elements together into the r
queues used to represent the buckets, $Q[0..r-1]$. After the elements have been distributed into the buckets, the queues representing those buckets are concatenated
together to rebuild the queue $Qall$. The broad outline of this sorting algorithm is
shown in Algorithm 8.8; the details of applying the techniques from Section 4.2.2 to
build the queues are left as Exercise 1. The result of the algorithm is that the queue
$Qall$ will contain the elements in increasing order; that is, the elements

```
function RadixDistribution(x: ElementArray; n: SubscriptRange): Queue;
const rminus1 = "r − 1";
var
      Qall: Queue;
      Q: array [0..rminus1] of Queue;
      j: 1..p;
      k: 0..rminus1;
      t: ElementType;
begin
      Qall := "queue formed by linking x[1..n] with the Next fields";
      for j := 1 to p do begin
            {Assert: Qall is sorted with respect to the j − 1 low order r-ary
                            digits in each element.}
            for k := 0 to rminus1 do Empty(Q[k]);
            while not IsEmpty(Qall) do begin
                  t := Pop(Qall);
                  k := "the jth r-ary digit of t";
                  Push(t, Q[k])
            end;
            Qall := "concatenation of queues Q[0], Q[1], ..., Q[r − 1]"
      end;
      {Queue Qall gives the elements of x ordered by following the Next links.}
      RadixDistribution := Qall
end
```

Algorithm 8.8
Radix distribution sort. The type $Queue$ is a pair of pointers, one to each end of
a list linked by $Next$ fields.

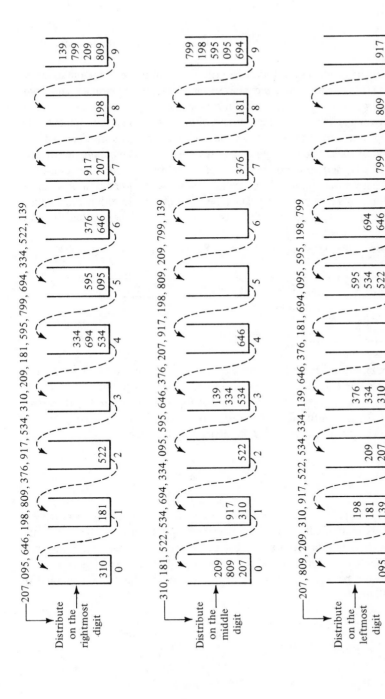

Figure 8.8
The radix distribution sort. The dashed arrows show how the buckets of elements are concatenated into a table.

will be linked in increasing order by the *Next* fields, starting with the front of the queue *Qall*.

The analysis of Algorithm 8.8 must be different from those of the other sorting algorithms, since we cannot count the number of element comparisons and interchanges. Instead we will count the total number of queue operations. There are always p passes over the table, and each pass requires removing each element from *Qall* and entering it on one of the Q_i. Hence there are a total of $2np$ insertion/deletion operations on the queues. Each pass also requires $r-1$ concatenations to produce *Qall* from $Q[0..r-1]$, and so there are a total of $(r-1)p$ queue concatenation operations. It is clear from Section 4.2.2 that an insertion/deletion operation or a concatenation operation can be done in constant time. Therefore Algorithm 8.8 requires time proportional to $np + rp$ to sort elements $x_1, x_2, \ldots, x_n$, where x_i has the form $(x_{i,p}, x_{i,p-1}, \ldots, x_{i,1})$ and $0 \le x_{t,l} < r$.

We summarize the behavior of Algorithm 8.8 with the following table:

	Queue Operations	Extra Storage
In all cases	np insertions np deletions $(r-1)p$ concatenations	n Next fields r queue header records

Value Distribution. If the elements $x_1, x_2, \ldots, x_n$ to be sorted are randomly distributed in the range (x_0, x_{n+1}) according to some known distribution, then we can base our choice of buckets on this range and distribution. For example, if the elements $x_1, x_2, \ldots, x_n$ are uniformly distributed over (x_0, x_{n+1}) and we have b buckets $B_1, B_2, \ldots, B_b$, we can let the bucket B_j be defined by the range

$$x_0 + \frac{x_{n+1} - x_0}{b}(j - 1) < x_i \le x_0 + \frac{x_{n-1} - x_0}{b} j$$

We can sort by making a pass over the x_i, distributing them into their proper buckets, sorting the buckets individually, and then concatenating the buckets together. If the sorting of the buckets is done recursively by the same method, then the number of buckets determines the performance of the technique. The following table summarizes the relationship between the number of buckets b and the average amount of work to sort n elements:

Number of Buckets b	Average Amount of Work to Sort n Elements
Constant	Proportional to $n \lg n$
Proportional to $\sqrt{n}$	Proportional to $n \lg \lg n$
Proportional to n	Proportional to n

The sorting technique outlined on page 458 is marred by the fact that at successive stages the numbers of elements in the buckets decrease to the point where the few elements in any bucket are better sorted by some more direct technique. Thus for the same reasons we made a hybrid of quicksort and the insertion sort, we should make a similar hybrid here: if there are m or fewer elements in a bucket, ignore it; otherwise distribute the elements into suitably chosen buckets, process each bucket recursively, and finally concatenate the buckets together. After returning to the top level of recursion, apply the insertion sort once to the entire set of elements (see Exercise 11 of Section 8.1.2). We leave the details of this hybrid to Exercise 7. This hybrid will work well, outperforming even quicksort, for even moderate numbers of elements, *provided that those elements really satisfy the assumed distribution* over the range (x_0, x_{n+1}).

Exercises

1. Using the techniques of Section 4.2.2 for implementing a queue with a linked list, fill in the details omitted from Algorithm 8.8 and implement it.

2. Use the bucket sort idea to sort *in place* an array of n records whose keys are a permutation of $1, 2, \ldots, n$. Show that your algorithm takes time proportional to n.

3. Devise a bucket sort to sort n elements of the form (i, j), $1 \leq i \leq m$, $1 \leq j \leq m$ according to the value

$$\phi[(i, j)] = \begin{cases} 2i, & j \geq i, \\ 2j, & 2j > i > j, \\ 2j + 1, & i \geq 2j. \end{cases}$$

Your algorithm should require only time proportional to $n + m$.

4. Examine the suitability of the following hybrid sorting scheme: use a radix distribution sort on the first few high-order positions and then apply the insertion sort. The purpose of the radix distribution on the high-order positions is to reduce the amount of disorder among the elements so that the insertion sort becomes efficient.

5. Are the two distributive sorts described in this section stable? (See Exercise 6 of Section 8.1.1 for a definition of stability.)

★6. Give a matrix $A = (a_{ij})$, suppose that each row is sorted into increasing order and then each column is sorted into increasing order. Do the rows remain sorted into increasing order? Prove your answer.

7. (a) Give a detailed algorithm for the value-distribution/insertion-sort hybrid described in this section.

(b) By analysis and/or extensive testing, determine the optimal crossover point m, below which it is more economical to sort by the insertion sort.

8.1.5 Lower Bounds

Now that we have examined various practical sorting algorithms, let us consider the problem of sorting from a theoretical point of view in order to get some idea of what kinds of improvements may (or may not) be possible. Except in Section 8.1.4 on distributive sorts, we measured the performance of the sorting algorithms by the number of element comparisons $x_i : x_j$. The algorithms based on distribution do not make comparisons of this type, since they are based on the representation or numerical distribution of the x_i; the other algorithms are all based on an abstract ordering among the x_i, and the only way to get information about that ordering is to make comparisons $x_i : x_j$. Of course, the number of comparisons is not the only determining factor in the performance of a sorting algorithm, but it usually does give a good indication of the amount of work being done. Consequently, the minimum possible number of element comparisons necessary to sort n elements is of interest because it will provide us with a benchmark against which to compare the performance of many sorting algorithms. In this section we derive some lower bounds that are meaningful in that context.

In order to eliminate from this discussion sorting algorithms other than those based on comparisons of the elements, we will consider only the algorithms that are based on the abstract linear ordering of the elements: between every pair x_i, x_j, $i \neq j$, either $x_i < x_j$ or $x_i > x_j$. (It is not difficult to extend this discussion to the case in which equal elements are allowed; see Exercise 2.) Any such sorting algorithm can be represented by an extended binary tree (see Section 5.3) in which each internal node represents an element comparison and each leaf (external node) represents an outcome of the algorithm. This tree can be viewed as a flowchart of the sorting algorithm in which all loops have been "unwound" and only the element comparisons are shown. The two children of a node thus represent the two possible outcomes of the comparison. For example, Figure 8.9 shows a binary tree for sorting three elements. In this section we will consider only sorting algorithms that can be written as such *decision trees*.

In any such decision tree each permutation of the input specifies a unique path from the root to a leaf. Since we are considering only algorithms that work correctly on all of the $n!$ permutations of the elements, the leaves corresponding to different permutations must be different. Clearly, then, there must be at least $n!$ leaves in a decision tree for sorting n elements.

Notice that the height of the decision tree is the number of comparisons required by the algorithm for its worst-case input. Let $S(n)$ denote the minimum number of comparisons required by any sorting algorithm in the worst case; that is,

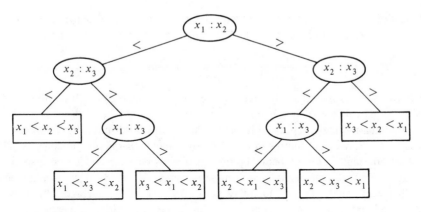

Figure 8.9
A binary decision tree for sorting three elements

$$S(n) = \min_{\substack{\text{sorting} \\ \text{algorithms}}} \left[\max_{\text{inputs}} \text{(number of comparisons)} \right]$$

Noticing that a binary tree of height h can have at most 2^h leaves, we conclude that

$$2^{S(n)} \geq n!$$

and so

$$S(n) \geq \lg n! \approx n \lg n$$

(See the footnote on page 452.) Thus *any* sorting algorithm based solely on comparisons of the elements being sorted will require at least $n \lg n$ such comparisons for its worst-case input.

We can also derive a lower bound for $\overline{S}(n)$, the minimum possible *average* number of element comparisons required by an algorithm that correctly sorts all the $n!$ permutations, assuming that each of these permutations is equally probable. That is,

$$\overline{S}(n) = \min_{\substack{\text{sorting} \\ \text{algorithms}}} \left[\frac{1}{n!} \sum_{\text{permutations}} \text{(number of comparisons)} \right]$$

The external path length (see Section 5.3) of the decision tree is the sum of all distances from the root to the leaves; dividing it by $n!$ gives the average number of comparisons for the corresponding sorting algorithm. Equation (5.10) from the end of Section 5.3 states that in an extended binary tree with N leaves the minimum possible external path length is $N \lg N + O(N)$; setting $N = n!$, we find that

$$\bar{S}(n) \geq \lg n! \approx n \lg n$$

Therefore *any* sorting algorithm based on element comparisons will require an average of at least $n \lg n$ such comparisons.

Comparing these results with the sorting algorithms discussed in Sections 8.1.1 through 8.1.3, we find that heapsort, requiring about $2n\lg n$ comparisons, is within a small constant factor of being optimal in the worst case and hence also on the average. Similarly quicksort, requiring an average of $1.188n\lg n$ comparisons is within a very small constant factor of being optimal on the average, although it is not in the worst case. The remaining algorithms, being quadratic in performance, are far from optimal for large n.

Exercises

1. Show the decision trees that arise for sorting x_1, x_2, x_3, and x_4 by
   (a) The insertion sort.
   (b) The bubble sort.
   (c) Quicksort.
   (d) The simple selection sort.
   (e) Heapsort.

2. Extend the argument given in this section to show that even if equal elements are allowed, at least $\lg n!$ element comparisons are needed in the worst and average cases for sorting n elements. (*Note*: Let o_n be the number of outcomes when n not necessarily distinct elements are sorted. The obvious extension would show only that $\log_3 o_n$ are needed, not $\lg n!$.)

3. (a) Suppose that all the elements are known to be zero or one. Prove that $n - 1$ element comparisons are necessary and sufficient in the worst case to sort n elements.

★(b) Prove that the minimum average number of element comparisons for such a sorting algorithm is $2n/3 + O(1)$.

8.2 RELATED PROBLEMS

In the previous section we studied the problem of completely ordering a set of elements, given no a priori information about the abstract ordering of the elements. In this section we consider two special cases of this problem: instead of requiring determination of the complete ordering, the *selection problem* asks only for the kth largest element. The *merging problem* is to completely sort a set of elements, starting from two sorted subsets. For both selection and merging, we will measure efficiency entirely in terms of element comparisons. As we have seen in the previous section, this is not because other operations are negligible, but rather because the number of element comparisons usually determines, to within a small constant factor, the overall performance of the algorithm.

8.2.1   Selection

Given the (unordered) elements $x_1, x_2, \ldots, x_n$, how can we find the kth largest element? The problem is obviously symmetrical: finding the $(n - k + 1)$st largest (the kth smallest) can be done by using an algorithm for finding the kth largest but reversing the actions taken for the $<$ and $>$ results of element comparisons. Thus finding the largest element $(k = 1)$ is equivalent to finding the smallest element $(k = n)$; finding the second largest $(k = 2)$ is equivalent to finding the second smallest $(k = n - 1)$, and so on. Of special interest is the problem of finding quantile values $(k = \lceil \alpha n \rceil, 0 < \alpha < 1)$ and especially the median $(\alpha = \frac{1}{2})$.

Of course, all these cases of the selection problem can be solved by using any of the methods of Section 8.1 to sort the elements completely and then trivially accessing the kth largest. As we have seen, this will require proportional to $n \log n$ element comparisons *regardless of the value of k*. But we would be computing far more information than we need, and so there should be better ways. There are: first we examine the application of various sorting algorithms to the selection problem and then we describe an algorithm that requires only $O(n)$ comparisons regardless of the value of k.

In using a sorting algorithm for selection, the most apparent choice would be one of the algorithms based on selection, either the simple selection sort (Algorithm 8.5) or heapsort (Algorithm 8.7). In each case, we can stop after the first k stages have been completed. For the simple selection sort, this means using

$$(n-1) + (n-2) + \cdots + (n-k) = kn - \frac{k(k+1)}{2}$$

element comparisons, and for heapsort it means using proportional to $n + k \lg n$ element comparisons. In both cases, we are computing more information than we need because we are completely determining the order of the largest k elements. This is not serious when k is a small constant, independent of n, since very little extra information is being computed; but when $k = \lceil \alpha n \rceil, 0 < \alpha \leq 1$, we are sorting a table of length αn and thus computing a great deal of unneeded information.

Although it does not seem so at first glance, the quicksort idea provides a reasonable method of selecting the kth largest element in $x_1, x_2, \ldots, x_n$. The table is partitioned into two subtables, those bigger than x_1, and those smaller than x_1, and then the appropriate subtable of the table is examined recursively. Assume that after partitioning, the original x_1 is in position $n - j + 1$ (that is, it is the jth largest element). If $k = j$, we are done; if $k < j$, we search for the kth largest element among $x_{n-j+2}, \ldots, x_n$; and if $k > j$, we search for the $(k - j)$th largest element among $x_1, \ldots, x_{n-j}$. (Compare this method with Algorithm 7.10.) It is straightforward to modify Algorithms 8.3 and 8.4 (*QuickSort*) so that they use this technique to find the kth largest element, and we leave that to the reader.

How efficient is this algorithm? If $\overline{C}_{n,k}$ is the number of element comparisons required on the average, we see that

$$\overline{C}_{n,k} = n + 1 + \frac{1}{n} \left(\sum_{j=1}^{k-1} \overline{C}_{n-j,k-j} + \sum_{j=k+1}^{n} \overline{C}_{j-1,k} \right)$$

and it is not difficult to show by induction that $\overline{C}_{n,k} = O(n)$ (see Exercise 1). Unfortunately, $C_{n,k}$, the number of element comparisons in the worst case, is proportional to n^2, and so, although good on the average, this algorithm can be *very* inefficient.

The inefficiency occurs because the element used to partition the table can be too close to either end of the table instead of close to the median, as we would like it (to split the table nearly in half). Thus the way to improve this algorithm is to discover a way of efficiently finding some element that is guaranteed to be near the median of the table and to use that element for partitioning the table into subtables. The following inductive technique shows how to do this. Assume that we have a selection algorithm that finds the kth largest of n elements in $28n$ comparisons. This is certainly true for $n \leq 50$, since $28n \geq n(n-1)/2$ element comparisons are sufficient to sort the elements completely, even using the bubble sort when $n \leq 50$. Suppose that $28t$ element comparisons are sufficient for $t < n$. First divide the table of n elements into $\lceil n/7 \rceil \approx n/7$ subtables of seven elements each, adding some dummy $-\infty$ elements if needed to complete the last subtable (that is, when n is not a multiple of 7). Then completely sort each of the $n/7$ subtables. Sorting a table with seven elements requires at most $7(7-1)/2 = 21$ element comparisons when using the bubble sort, and so sorting all these subtables requires at most $21(n/7) = 3n$ element comparisons in total. Next, apply the selection algorithm recursively to the $n/7$ *medians* of the $n/7$ sorted subtables to find the *median of the medians* in $28(n/7) = 4n$ element comparisons. At this point we have information about the elements as shown in Figure 8.10. (See Exercise 5.)

The elements in region A are known to be less than the median of the medians, and the elements in region B are known to be greater than the median of the medians; the remaining elements can be either less than or greater than the median of the medians. Clearly, there are about $2n/7$ elements in each of regions A and B. Therefore the median of the medians is guaranteed to be "near" the middle of the table, and we can use it to partition the table when applying the quicksort idea to selection. After partitioning the table, at least the elements in one of A or B will not need to be examined further.

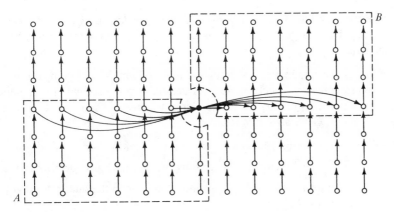

Figure 8.10
The information known about the elements after determining the median of the
$n/7$ medians. An arrow $\circ \rightarrow \circ$ means that the element at the arrow's head is *greater*
than the element at the arrow's tail. All elements are shown as $\circ$ except the
median of the medians, which is shown as $\bullet$.

How many element comparisons are needed in total? We used $3n$ to sort the
subtables, $4n$ to find the median of the medians, n to partition the table, and at most
$28(5n/7)$ to apply the selection algorithm recursively (since there can be as many as
$5n/7$ elements in the subtable to which the selection algorithm is recursively applied).
Thus at most $28n$ element comparisons are made; and since it is clear that the total
amount of work is proportional to the number of element comparisons, we have an
$O(n)$ selection algorithm. Of course, the algorithm is *not* as efficient as sorting by
heapsort unless $28n < 2n\lg n$, that is, $n > 2^{14} = 16{,}384$. But we were quite sloppy;
it is easy to bring the $28n$ down to $15n$ or less (Exercise 2), and, in fact, it can be
reduced still further to $391n/72 \approx 5.431n$, so that the algorithm becomes reasonable
for smaller values of n.

Exercises

1. Use mathematical induction to verify that, as stated, $\overline{C}_{n,k}$ is proportional to n for
   all k.

2. Show that the kth largest of n elements can be determined in at most $27n/2$ element comparisons. How large must n be for this to be more efficient than heapsort
   (in terms only of comparisons)? Try to lower the constant $27/2$ still further.

3. Is anything gained in quicksort if we use the $O(n)$ selection algorithm to determine
   the median of the table and use it to partition the table?

4. Suppose that instead of selecting the kth largest element, we are interested in determining the k largest elements but not their relative order. Can this be done in time $O(n)$?

5. Prove that at the termination of an algorithm based on element comparisons (that is, one represented by a decision tree) for determining the second largest element, there is enough information about the elements *already known* to determine the largest element. Generalize this result.

6. Use the previous exercise, together with Exercise 3 of Section 8.1.3 to prove that $n - k + \lceil \lg \binom{n}{k-1} \rceil$ element comparisons are necessary to determine the kth largest of n elements. [*Hint*: Use an argument similar to the one in Section 8.1.5 that shows that $S(n) \geq \lg n!$.]

7. Given sorted tables $x_1 \leq x_2 \leq \cdots \leq x_n$ and $y_1 \leq y_2 \leq \cdots \leq y_n$, how quickly can the nth smallest of the $2n$ elements in the combined sets be found? Does a lower bound (in the sense of Section 8.1.5) for this problem say anything about a lower bound for the problem of finding the median of a set of elements? Compare your result to that of the previous exercise.

8.2.2 Merging

The second sorting-related problem that we consider is that of merging two sorted tables $x_1 \leq x_2 \leq \cdots \leq x_n$ and $y_1 \leq y_2 \leq \cdots \leq y_m$ into a single sorted table $z_1 \leq z_2 \leq \cdots \leq z_{n+m}$. There is an obvious way to do this: scan the tables to be merged in parallel, at each stage selecting the smaller of the two elements and putting it into the output table. This process is simplified by adding dummy elements $x_{n+1} = y_{m+1} = \infty$, as in Algorithm 8.9. In this algorithm i and j point, respectively, to the last elements in the two input tables that have not yet been put into the output table.

The analysis of this algorithm is quite simple, for the comparison $x[i] < y[j]$ is made exactly once for each element placed in the output table—that is, $n + m$ times. This can be reduced to $n + m - 1$ times by slightly complicating the algorithm (Exercise 1).

When $n \approx m$, this method of merging is quite good; in fact, when $n = m$, it is possible to show that in the worst case at least $n + m - 1 = 2n - 1$ element comparisons are always necessary to do the merging (Exercise 3). However, when $m = 1$, we can merge far more efficiently by using binary search to find the place in which y_1 should be inserted. We would like a method of merging that combines the best aspects of both binary search and Algorithm 8.9.

Figure 8.11 shows the central idea of binary merging, a scheme that behaves like binary search when $m = 1$ but like straight merging when $m \approx n$. It also provides a good compromise for other values of m. Assume that $n \geq m$; the idea is

```
x[n + 1] := PlusInfinity;
y[m + 1] := PlusInfinity;
i := 1;
j := 1;
for k := 1 to n + m do
    {Assert: z[1..k − 1] is the result of merging elements
    x[1..i − 1] and y[1..j − 1]. k = i + j − 1}
    if x[i] < y[j] then begin
        z[k] := x[i]; i := i + 1
    end
    else begin
        z[k] := y[j]; j := j + 1
    end
```

Algorithm 8.9
Straight merging

to divide the larger table into $m + 1$ subtables. We then compare the rightmost (largest) element of the smaller table, y_m, with the largest element of the next to the rightmost subtable of the larger table, say x_k (see Figure 8.11). If $y_m < x_k$, then x_k and all the rightmost subtable of the larger table can be put into the output table. If $y_m \geq x_k$, then y_m is inserted into the rightmost subtable by using binary search; y_m and the x_i's in the subtable found to be greater than y_m can now be put into the output table, and the algorithm continues recursively. Recall, however, that binary search works most efficiently for tables of size $2^t - 1$ (why?) and so, instead of having the last subtable of the larger table contain about n/m elements, we do better if it has $2^{\lfloor \lg(n/m) \rfloor} - 1$ elements. Thus, for the case shown in Figure 8.11 we have $2^{\lfloor \lg(28/6) \rfloor} - 1 = 3$, and we would compare y_6 with x_{25}, as shown in Figure 8.12. If $x_{25} > y_6$, then x_{25}, x_{26}, x_{27}, and x_{28} can be put into the output table, and we continue merging $x_1, x_2, \ldots, x_{24}$ with $y_1, y_2, \ldots, y_6$. If $x_{25} < y_6$, we use binary search to find y_6's place among x_{26}, x_{27}, x_{28} in two element comparisons and put y_6 and the x_i's larger than it into the output table. Next, we continue by merging $x_1, x_2, \ldots, x_k$ with $y_1, y_2, \ldots, y_5$, where k is the largest integer such that $y_6 > x_k$.

Assuming that $n \geq m$, Algorithm 8.10(a) gives an outline of the procedure that

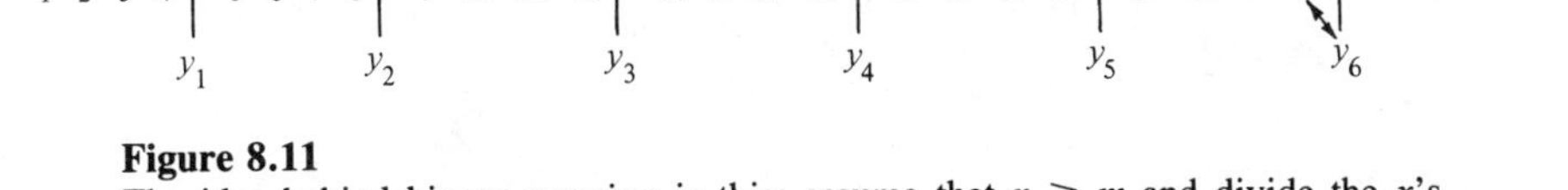

$$x_1 x_2 x_3 x_4 \mid x_5 x_6 x_7 x_8 \mid x_9 x_{10} x_{11} x_{12} \mid x_{13} x_{14} x_{15} x_{16} \mid x_{17} x_{18} x_{19} x_{20} \mid x_{21} x_{22} x_{23} x_{24} \mid x_{25} x_{26} x_{27} x_{28}$$

$$y_1 \qquad y_2 \qquad y_3 \qquad y_4 \qquad y_5 \qquad y_6$$

Figure 8.11
The idea behind binary merging is this: assume that $n \geq m$ and divide the x's into $m + 1$ subtables of $n/(m + 1)$ elements each. Then use binary search on the subtables. In this example, $n = 28$, $m = 6$, and $k = 24$.

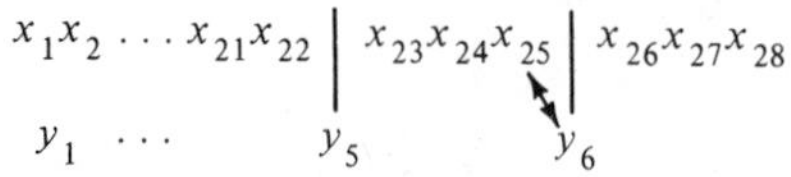

$$x_1 x_2 \cdots x_{21} x_{22} \mid x_{23} x_{24} x_{25} \mid x_{26} x_{27} x_{28}$$
$$y_1 \quad \cdots \qquad y_5 \qquad y_6$$

Figure 8.12
The first comparison in binary merging

performs the first stage of the binary merge as described above. By interchanging the parameters, Algorithm 8.10(b) applies Algorithm 8.10(a) properly to the general case, using it iteratively until the tables are completely merged. We leave the omitted details of Algorithms 8.10(a) and (b) for the reader to fill in (Exercise 5).

How many element comparisons are made? Let $C_{m,n}$ be the number of element

procedure *MergeStep(x*: *ElementArray*; **var** *n*: *SubscriptRange*;
                y: *ElementArray*; **var** *m*: *SubscriptRange*);
    {one step in binary merging to merge $x[1..n]$ and $y[1..m]$ when $n \geq m$;
    the parameters n and m are modified by the procedure as the tails of x
    and y are moved to the output table}
var
    t,   {number of compares in binary search}
    k,   {index of element in x to compare with $y[m]$
             and later, index of first element to output}
    j: {where to put $x[k]$ in output sequence}
    SubscriptRange;
begin
    $t := floor(lg(n/m))$;
    $k := n - (power(2,t) - 1)$;
    $j := m + k$; {Exercise 5}
    if $y[m] \geq x[k]$ **then begin**
             {For the next statement we use t element comparisons in a
             binary search over $x[k + 1..n]$}
             $k :=$ "largest value such that $x[k-1] < y[m] \leq x[k]$";
             $j := m + k$;
             "put $y[m]$ into the output table at $j-1$";
             $m := m - 1$
    end;
    "put $x[k..n]$ into the output table at j";
    $n := k - 1$
end

Algorithm 8.10(a)
An outline of the first stage of binary merging

while $(n \neq 0)$ **and** $(m \neq 0)$ **do**
      {Assert: Denoting the original values of n and m by $\hat{n}$ and $\hat{m}$, we
      now have $x[n+1..\hat{n}]$ and $y[m+1..\hat{m}]$ merged and stored in the
      output table at locations $[n+m+1..\hat{n}+\hat{m}].$}
      if $m \leq n$ **then**
              MergeStep(x, n, y, m)
      else *MergeStep*(y, m, x, n);
if $n = 0$ **then**
      "put $y[1..m]$ into the output table at 1"
else
      "put $x[1..n]$ into the output table at 1"

Algorithm 8.10(b)
Binary merging, using the *MergeStep* procedure of Algorithm 8.10(a) to do all
the work

comparisons made in the worst case by Algorithms 8.10(a) and (b) when merging
$x_1, \ldots, x_n$ and $y_1, \ldots, y_m$. It can be shown that

$$C_{m,n} = m + \left\lfloor \frac{n}{2^t} \right\rfloor - 1 + tm, \qquad \text{for } n \geq m, \, t = \left\lfloor \lg \frac{n}{m} \right\rfloor$$

(see Exercises 6, 7, and 8). When $m = n$, this gives

$$C_{n,n} = 2n - 1$$

and when $m = 1$, it gives

$$C_{1,n} = 1 + \lfloor \lg n \rfloor = \lceil \lg(n + 1) \rceil$$

These results mean that binary merging performs like straight merging at one extreme
and like binary search at the other. Furthermore, it is also reasonably efficient for
intermediate values of m (Exercise 9).

Exercises

1. Modify Algorithm 8.9 (straight merging) so that the dummy elements $x_{n+1} = y_{m+1} = \infty$ are not needed and thus give an algorithm that uses at most $n + m - 1$ element comparisons to merge $x_1 \leq x_2 \leq \cdots \leq x_n$ and $y_1 \leq y_2 \leq \cdots \leq y_m$.

2. (a) Give a version of your algorithm from the previous exercise for the case
   when the x's and y's are given as *linked lists*.

(b) Use this version of the algorithm as the basis of a sorting algorithm in which the list to be sorted is split in half, each half is sorted recursively, and then the two are merged together. Analyze the worst-case behavior of this algorithm. Is this algorithm stable?

3. Show that $2n - 1$ element comparisons are necessary and sufficient to merge $x_1 \leq x_2 \leq \cdots \leq x_n$ and $y_1 \leq y_2 \leq \cdots y_n$. [*Hint*: What if $x_i < y_j$ if $i < j$ and $x_i > y_j$ otherwise?]

4. Show the sequence of element comparisons made by binary merging [Algorithms 8.10(a) and (b)] when applied to merge the sorted tables

$$78 \leq 201 \leq 400 \leq 897$$

and

$$12 \leq 15 \leq 25 \leq 90 \leq 121 \leq 122 \leq 180 \leq 205 \leq 305 \leq 390 \leq 402$$

5. Fill in all the missing details in Algorithms 8.10(a) and (b). Explain why $m + k$ is the correct value for j.

6. Prove that in the worst case binary merging uses $C_{m,n} = n + m - 1$ element comparisons when $m \leq n < 2m$.

★ 7. Prove that for binary merging $C_{m,n} = C_{m,\lfloor n/2 \rfloor} + m$ for $2m \leq n$. [*Hint*: Prove by induction on m that $C_{m,n} \leq C_{m,n+1}$ for $n \geq m$ by observing that $C_{m,n} = \max(C_{m,n-2^t} + 1, C_{m-1,n} + t + 1)$, where $t = \lfloor \lg(n/m) \rfloor$.]

8. (a) By combining the results of the two previous exercises, show that $C_{m,n} = m + \lfloor n/2^t \rfloor - 1 + tm$ for $m \leq n$ where $t = \lfloor \lg(n/m) \rfloor$ as stated in the text.
   (b) Verify that this formula gives $C_{n,n} = 2n - 1$ and $C_{1,n} = 1 + \lfloor \lg n \rfloor$.

9. (a) In analogy with the discussion of $S(n)$ in Section 8.1.5, shows that there must be at least $\lceil \lg \binom{m+n}{n} \rceil$ element comparisons used in the worst case for merging $x_1 \leq x_2 \leq \ldots \leq x_n$ and $y_1 \leq y_2 \leq \ldots \leq y_m$.
   (b) Use the formula for $C_{m,n}$ to show that $C_{m,n} < \lceil \lg \binom{m+n}{n} \rceil + m, n \geq m$.
   [*Hint*: First prove that $m! \leq m^m/2^{m-1}$.]

10. Given the array $A[1..n+m]$ in which n of the elements are colored red and m of them are colored green, we want to unmerge them in place, keeping each color in its sorted order. That is, we want $A[1..n]$ to be the sorted block of red elements and $A[n+1..n+m]$ to be the sorted block of green elements. Develop and analyze an algorithm for such unmerging; it can be done in $O(n+m)$ time with only a constant amount of space outside of the array itself.

8.3 EXTERNAL SORTING

In the sorting methods discussed in Section 8.1 we assumed that the table fit in high-speed internal memory. This assumption is too strong for many real-life data processing problems. In this section we examine the sorting of very large tables that fit only on auxiliary storage devices such as magnetic tape, disks, or drums. In each case we will assume that we have a table of elements x_1, x_2, x_3, ..., x_n stored externally and that the internal memory can hold only $m \ll n$ elements, along with other data, programs, and so forth.

The general strategy in external sorting is to use the internal memory to sort the elements in a piecemeal fashion so as to produce *initial runs* of elements in increasing order. As they are produced, these runs are stored externally. Later they are merged together, again in piecemeal fashion, until finally all the elements are in order. In our discussion we examine these two phases separately. We describe first how to generate the initial runs (Section 8.3.1), then how to do the merging both for tapes (Section 8.3.2) and for disks and drums (Section 8.3.3).

8.3.1 Initial Runs

Assuming that there is room in internal memory for $m \ll n$ elements, together with whatever buffers and other program variables are needed, the obvious method to generate initial runs is simply to read in m elements, sort them in internal memory, and write them into external memory as a run, continuing in this fashion until all the n elements have been processed. The initial runs thus obtained all contain m elements (except perhaps for the last one). Since the number of initial runs ultimately determines the cost of the merging later, we would like to find some method of producing longer, and hence fewer, initial runs.

We can produce longer runs by organizing the m elements in internal memory into a priority queue that operates as follows. After initially being filled with the first m elements from the input file, the highest-priority element is deleted and put into the output file of the initial runs; the next element from the input file is then inserted in the priority queue. In this way the priority queue always contains m elements, except during its initialization and during the generation of the final run as it is being emptied. The priorities of the elements must be defined so that elements are deleted at the proper time and go into the proper run. Since each element selected from the priority queue to be added to the output is replaced by another element from the input, this method is called *replacement selection*.

To make certain that elements enter and leave the priority queue in the proper order, we will have the priority queue consist of ordered pairs (r, x), where r is the run number of the element x. A pair (r, x) has higher priority than $(\hat{r}, \hat{x})$ if $(r, x) <$ $(\hat{r}, \hat{x})$ lexicographically—that is, if $r < \hat{r}$ or if $r = \hat{r}$ and $x < \hat{x}$. After an element has been deleted from the priority queue and is being replaced by a new element x, we know the run number of x by the following reasoning: if x is smaller than the last element just added to the current run, then x must be in the *next* run; otherwise, x is in the *current* run.

An outline of the above described replacement selection is given in Algorithm 8.11, and we leave it to Exercise 2 to fill in the missing details. The major unspecified aspect of Algorithm 8.11 is the implementation of the priority queue. The easiest way to implement it is with a heap as described in Section 8.1.3, except that the pair (r, x) at the top of the heap is the *smallest* pair (lexicographically), not the largest, so the sense of the comparisons made in the *Restore* procedure (Algorithm 8.6) must be reversed. Furthermore, since the elements being sorted will in most cases be long records, there is no point in moving the actual elements around during the restoration of the heap—it is sufficient to maintain a heap of pairs (r, p), where r is the run number and p is a *pointer* to the actual element.

How long are the runs produced by replacement selection? Clearly it does at least as well as the obvious method of reading in m elements, sorting them, and writing them—all runs generated by replacement selection, except possibly the last, contain at least m elements (why)? In fact it can be shown that on the average, assuming that the elements are in random order, the expected length of the runs is $2m$, double the length of the runs with the obvious method (see Exercise 8). Furthermore, in cases where the elements are not too out of order the length of the runs will be very long; in fact in the best case we would end up with only one initial run— that is, a sorted table!

We can improve on replacement selection with the following idea. Note that the statement $Push(``(R + 1, eltIn)'', P)$ clutters the m locations in the priority queue with elements waiting to go into the next run. Suppose that instead of allowing this to happen we store such elements temporarily in external storage until, say, M of them are accumulated. At that point, we dump the remaining elements in the priority queue into the current run and use the accumulated M temporarily stored elements as the first part of the input for the next run. This leads to longer initial runs, but at the price of the extra input/output operations necessary to temporarily store the elements in external storage (see Exercise 9). The following table shows the expected initial run lengths with this technique; the size of M is given in terms of m. There is no improvement, and hence no point in the method, for $M \le 0.386m$.

M	Expected Run Length
$0.386m$	$2m$
m	$2.718m$
$2m$	$3.535m$
$3m$	$4.162m$
$4m$	$4.694m$
$5m$	$5.164m$

procedure *ReplacementSelection(m: integer)*;
var
      P: PairPriorityQueue; {priority queue with room for *m* elements}
      R: integer;   {current run number}
      rOut: integer;   {run number of element to write out}
      eltIn, eltOut: ElementType;
      i: integer;
begin
      Empty(P);
      {fill *P* with first *m* elements from input file}
      for *i* := 1 **to** *m* **do begin**
            eltIn := "next element from input file";
            Push("(1, eltIn)", P)
      end;
      R := 0;
      while not *IsEmpty(P)* **do begin**
            {Assert: All elements in *P* for run *R* are larger than all elements
            already output for run *R*.}
            {get next pair from priority queue, *P*}
            "(rOut, eltOut)" := *Pop(P)*;
            if *rOut* ≠ *R* **then begin**
                  {begin a new run}
                  "indicate beginning of new run in output";
                  R := *R* + 1
            end;
            "write *eltOut* as next element of current output run";
            {replace element removed from *P*, if possible}
            if "there are more elements in input file" **then begin**
                  eltIn := "next element from input file";
                  if *eltIn* ≥ *eltOut* **then**
                        {*eltIn* is part of current run}
                        Push("(R, eltIn)", P)
                  else
                        {*eltIn* is part of next run}
                        Push("(R + 1, eltIn)", P)
            end
      end
end

Algorithm 8.11
Replacement selection for generating inital runs

The fact that when $M = m$ the expected run length is em ($e \approx 2.71828$, the base of the natural logarithms) has caused this technique to be called "natural selection."

Exercises

1. Elements from how many different runs can be in the priority queue at the same time in Algorithm 8.11?

2. Fill in the details of the priority-queue maintenance in Algorithm 8.11 using a heap of pointers as suggested in the text.

★3. Given an infinite "random" sequence of elements $x_1, x_2, \ldots$, where random means that each of the $n!$ possible relative orderings of the first n elements is equally likely, compute the expected length of the first run in replacement selection.

4. Why would you expect the second run in replacement selection to be longer than the first?

5. Under what conditions will the last run in replacement selection be longer than m elements?

6. Under exactly what conditions will replacement selection result in a single run? [*Hint*: Examine the analysis of Algorithm 8.1.]

7. What is the "worst-case" input file for replacement selection?

★8. We can describe the behavior of replacement selection with the following physical model. A snowplow is going round and round a circular road, plowing snow that is falling continuously and uniformly. Once a snowflake is plowed off the road, it is hauled away in a truck. The snowplow corresponds to the replacement-selection algorithm and the snowflakes corresponds to the elements of the input file. Label the points on the road by real numbers x, $0 \le x \le 1$; a snowflake landing at x represents an element x from the input file. Assume the system is in a "steady state" in the sense that the speed of the snowplow is constant and the total amount of snow on the road is always m. Explain why the amount of snow removed by the plow on one revolution (the run length) is $2m$.

9. Under what conditions, if any, will natural selection put an element into the temporary external storage *twice*? Three times?

8.3.2 Tape Merge Patterns

After the initial runs have been generated, we have the problem of repeatedly merging them, piecemeal fashion, until we ultimately obtain the final, sorted table. The organization of this merging phase is heavily dependent on the type of external memory available. In this section we discuss merging the initial runs with tapes and in the next section we discuss the same problem with disks and drums. As pointed out at the beginning of Section 7.5, tapes are a completely sequential storage medium. Thus the entire problem of storing and merging the runs on tape is the organization of the tapes and the merges so that the runs are accessible on the tapes as they are needed.

We will assume that there are a total of $t + 1$ tapes; that is, initially we had t scratch tapes and an input tape containing the table to be sorted. The initial runs have been generated from the table as described in the previous section, so that the situation now is that there are r initial runs on one of the tapes and the remaining t tapes are empty.

To begin, let us consider a simple-minded merging scheme. Distribute the runs as evenly as possible onto t of the tapes and merge the runs together, one from each tape, to form longer runs on the $(t + 1)$st tape. The resulting (longer) runs are distributed onto the other t tapes and merged together to form yet longer runs. This process continues until there is only one run, the sorted table. In comparing the behavior of various merging strategies the dominant factor is the number of times the external storage medium is accessed; we can thus get a good idea of the relative performance of merging strategies by comparing the number of times each element of the table is "examined"—that is, read into internal memory and then written out again. In the case of our simple-minded t-way merging, each merging decreases the number of runs by a factor of $1/t$ (why?). Consequently, since there are r initial runs, $\lceil \log_t r \rceil$ mergings are required. Each of these mergings consists of first distributing the runs onto the t tapes and then merging the runs together. In other words, each of the elements is examined twice, and hence in total each element of the table is examined $2\lceil \log_t r \rceil$ times: we describe this situation by saying that there are $2\lceil \log_t r \rceil \approx (2/\lg t) \lg r$ *passes* over the elements.

Thus for $t + 1$ tapes (that is, t-way merging), the number of passes over the elements in this simple-minded merging strategy is approximately

$t + 1$	Number of Passes
3	2.000 lg r
4	1.262 lg r
5	1.000 lg r
6	0.861 lg r
7	0.774 lg r
8	0.712 lg r
9	0.667 lg r
10	0.631 lg r
20	0.471 lg r

Half the passes (the distribution passes) do nothing to reduce the number of runs; these passes are just copying the elements.

Polyphase Merge. The copy passes can be eliminated by being more clever. Suppose that 57 initial runs are distributed onto tapes 1, 2, 3, and 4 as shown in Figure 8.13. In this figure, $n \bullet i$ means n runs of order i, an ith-order run being the result of merging i initial runs together. The runs are merged as indicated by the arrows in the figure. The idea of this *polyphase merge* is to arrange the initial runs so that after each merge except the last there is exactly one empty tape—this tape will be the recipient on the next merge. Furthermore, we want the last merge to be merging only one run from each of t nonempty tapes. A distribution of initial runs with such properties is called a *perfect* distribution.

Suppose that we had $t + 1$ tapes instead of four tapes. The polyphase merge idea generalizes easily, and we want to compute the perfect distributions for this case. We do this by working backward. Let $a_{k,j}$ be the number of runs on the jth tape when k merge phases remain to be done. Moreover, we will assume that tape $t + 1$ is *always* the recipient of the merge and that tape 1 contains at least as many runs as tape 2, which contains at least as many runs as tape 3, and so on. This can

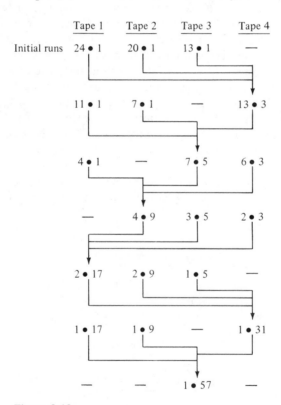

Figure 8.13

A merging pattern for 57 initial runs and four tapes. The notation $n \bullet i$ means n ith-order runs.

be done by using "logical" tape numbers and switching them around appropriately. Thus we have the distribution

$$j: \quad 1 \quad 2 \quad 3 \quad \cdots \quad t-1 \quad t \quad t+1$$
$$\text{Number of runs on tape } j: \quad 1 \quad 0 \quad 0 \quad \cdots \quad 0 \quad 0 \quad 0$$

when no more merge passes remain, that is, at the very end. If, when k merge passes remain, we have the distribution

$$j: \quad 1 \quad 2 \quad 3 \quad \cdots \quad t-1 \quad t \quad t+1$$
$$\text{Number of runs on tape } j: \quad a_{k,1} \quad a_{k,2} \quad a_{k,3} \quad \cdots \quad a_{k,t-1} \quad a_{k,t} \quad 0$$

then the next merge leaves the distribution

$$j: \quad 1 \quad 2 \quad \cdots \quad t-1 \quad t \quad t+1$$
$$\text{Number of runs on tape } j: \quad a_{k,1} - a_{k,t} \quad a_{k,2} - a_{k,t} \quad \cdots \quad a_{k,t-1} - a_{k,t} \quad 0 \quad a_{k,t}$$

It is easy to show that for $k \geq 1$, we have $2a_{k,t} \geq a_{k,1}$, and hence switching logical tape numbers so that the runs are in decreasing order gives us

$$j: \quad 1 \quad 2 \quad 3 \quad \cdots \quad t \quad t+1$$
$$\text{Number of runs on tape } j: \quad a_{k,t} \quad a_{k,1} - a_{k,t} \quad a_{k,2} - a_{k,t} \quad \cdots \quad a_{k,t-1} - a_{k,t} \quad 0$$

Therefore

$$a_{k-1,1} = a_{k,t}$$
$$a_{k-1,j} = a_{k,j-1} - a_{k,t}, \quad 2 \leq j \leq t,$$

or

$$a_{k+1,t} = a_{k,1}$$
$$a_{k+1,j} = a_{k,j+1} + a_{k,1}, \quad 1 \leq j < t,$$

Consequently, the perfect distributions for $t+1$ tapes are as shown in Table 8.1.

Of course, a perfect distribution for $t+1$ tapes is possible only when r, the number of initial runs, is of a special form. For example, in the case of four tapes shown in Figure 8.13, r must be one of 1, 3, 5, 9, 17, 31, 57, ... (What is the pattern here? See Exercise 2.) What do we do if we have, say, 40 runs, too few for the distribution (24, 20, 13) and too many for the distribution (13, 11, 7)? The easiest

Pass	Tape 1	Tape 2	Tape 3		Tape $t-2$	Tape $t-1$	Tape t	Tape $t+1$
$k = 0$	1	0	0	$\cdots$	0	0	0	0
$k = 1$	1	1	1	$\cdots$	1	1	1	0
$k = 2$	2	2	2	$\cdots$	2	2	1	0
$k = 3$	4	4	4	$\cdots$	4	3	2	0
$\vdots$								
k	$a_{k,1}$	$a_{k,2}$	$a_{k,3}$	$\cdots$	$a_{k,t-2}$	$a_{k,t-1}$	$a_{k,t}$	0
$k + 1$	$a_{k,2} + a_{k,1}$	$a_{k,3} + a_{k,1}$	$a_{k,4} + a_{k,1}$	$\cdots$	$a_{k,t-1} + a_{k,1}$	$a_{k,t} + a_{k,1}$	$a_{k,1}$	0

Table 8.1
Perfect distributions for the polyphase merge

way to handle such cases is to add enough "virtual" or "dummy" runs to fill out the distribution; if we had four tapes and 40 initial runs, we would add seventeen dummy runs to allow us to have the (24, 20, 13) distribution of Figure 8.13. These dummy runs are only a bookkeeping device: we do not actually have such runs on tape, we just keep track of how many there are and where they are. This can be done by having counters $d_1, d_2, \ldots, d_{t+1}$, where d_i is the number of dummy runs currently considered to be on tape i. In merging the runs together, it is easy to merge dummy runs! All we need do is change the values of the appropriate d_i.

How should these dummy runs be distributed on the tapes? Some distributions will lead to more economical merging than others because some of the initial runs will get handled more than others in the merging process, and we are better off if those initial runs are dummy runs, not real runs. Suppose we have seventeen initial runs and four tapes. The polyphase merge pattern is shown in Figure 8.14, with the location of every initial run shown. Counting the number of times each initial run is handled, we find the following results:

Run number: 1 2 3 4 5 6 7 8 9 10 11 12 13 14 15 16 17

Number of mergings
in which it participates: 4 3 3 2 3 2 2 4 3 3 2 3 2 4 3 3 2

Thus runs 1, 8, and 14 are handled more than the other runs, and so it would be wise to make them the dummy runs, if dummy runs are needed.

The optimal placement of the dummy runs is hard to determine, so instead we use the heuristic of distributing the dummy runs as evenly as possible on the various tapes. This heuristic produces excellent results in general, and its simplicity makes it inexpensive to implement. Algorithm 8.12(a) describes an implementation in detail. It works by computing the next perfect distribution (starting with the line $k = 0$ in Table 8.1), setting the d_i so that the differences between the new distribution and the previous one just attained are filled by dummy initial runs. As real initial runs are processed, they replace the dummy initial runs until there are no more dummy runs; at that point the new distributions has been attained and we go on to the next. At the

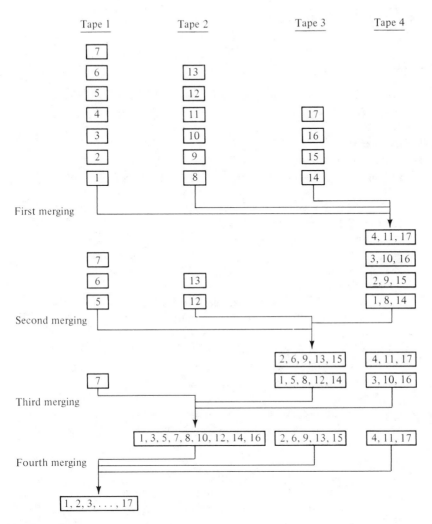

Figure 8.14
A four-tape polyphase merge of seventeen initial runs with the locations of each
initial run shown throughout

end, the distribution of dummy runs in the d_i is the heuristically chosen even distribution of dummy runs to be used to begin the Merge phase.

In the Algorithm: k is the number of passes, an index into Table 8.1; $tape[i]$ is the number of the physical tape corresponding to logical tape i; $d[i]$ is the number of dummy runs on logical tape i; $a[i]$ has the value of $a_{k,i}$ from Table 8.1—the perfect distribution we are working toward. The other variables are used only in local places.

procedure *PolyphaseMerge*;
const
    maxtapes = "$t + 1$, the number of tapes to use";
var
    k: *integer*;
    tape, *d*, *a*: **array** [1..*maxtapes*] **of** *integer*;
    i, j, t, Ta, $Ttape$, Td: *integer*;
begin
    $t := maxtapes - 1$;
{part 1. Initial distribution of runs to the tapes.}
    {initialize to start at line $k = 0$ of Table 8.1 of perfect distributions}
    $k := 0$; $j := 1$;
    $a[1] := 1$; $d[1] := 1$; $tape[1] := 1$;
    for $i := 2$ **to** *maxtapes* **do begin**
        $a[i] := 0$; $d[i] := 0$; $tape[i] := i$
    end;
    "rewind all tapes";
    while "there are more initial runs" **do begin**
        {Assert: The $a[i]$ specify the perfect distribution given by Table 8.1
        line k. For all i, $1 \leqslant i \leqslant t + 1$, $a[i] = d[i] +$ (number of real
        runs on tape i). $d[1] = d[2] = \cdots = d[j]$, $d[j] + 1 \geqslant d[j + 1]$
        $\geqslant d[j + 2] \geqslant \cdots \geqslant d[t + 1] = 0$}
        if $d[j] < d[j + 1]$ **then** $j := j + 1$
        else if $d[j] \neq 0$ **then** $j := 1$
        else begin
            {all $d[i]$ are zero so we have attained the distribution of line
            k of Table 8.1; we now go on to the next line}
            $k := k + 1$;
            $Ta := a[1]$;
            for $i := 1$ **to** t **do begin**
                {add dummy runs to take up the slack between the new
                distribution and the old}
                $d[i] := (Ta + a[i+1]) - a[i]$;   {new − old}
                $a[i] := (Ta + a[i+1])$ {set up new target distribution}
            end;
            $j := 1$
        end;
        "read an initial run and write it on $tape[j]$";
        $d[j] := d[j] - 1$ {the real run replaces a dummy run}
    end;   {**while** there are more initial runs}
    {At this point the $d[i]$ specify the initial distribution of dummy runs for the merge pha

Algorithm 8.12(a)
Even distribution of initial runs for the polyphase merge

{continue from Algorithm 8.12(a); k, $d[i]$ and $tape[i]$ retain their values}
{part 2. Merge the distributed runs}
    "rewind all tapes";
  while $k \neq 0$ **do begin**
        {at this point we have the distribution shown in line k of Table 8.1; the next loop empties $tape[t]$ and reduces all other tapes by the number of runs on $tape[t]$}
      while "$tape[t]$ has runs" **or** $(d[t] > 0)$ **do begin**
        if "we have $d[i] > 0$ for all i, $1 \leq i \leq t$" **then begin**
            {merge t dummy runs into new dummy on $tape[t+1]$}
            for $i := 1$ **to** t **do** $d[i] := d[i] - 1$;
            $d[t+1] := d[t+1] + 1$
        end
        else begin
            "merge together onto $tape[t+1]$
                one run from each tape with $d[i] = 0$";
            "**for** each $d[i] > 0$ **do**"
                $d[i] := d[i] - 1$
        end
      end;
      "rewind all tapes";
      $k := k - 1$;   {go up a level in Table 8.1}
      {renumber logical tape units}
      $Ttape := tape[t+1]$; $Td := d[t+1]$;
      for $i := t + 1$ **downto** 2 **do begin**
        $tape[i] := tape[i-1]$; $d[i] := d[i-1]$
      end;
      $tape[1] := Ttape$; $d[1] := Td$
  end
  {sorting is complete; $tape[1]$ contains the sorted file}
end {*PolyphaseMerge*}

Algorithm 8.12(b)
Polyphase merge after the distribution of initial runs by Algorithm 8.12(a)

Having distributed the initial runs, real and dummy, by Algorithm 8.12(a), we now face the problem of merging them according to the polyphase scheme as described above. The algorithm for doing this is given in Algorithm 8.12(b), which assumes that the values of variables left by Algorithm 8.12(a) are unchanged. The only subtle part of Algorithm 8.12(b) is that it proceeds by going up level by level in Table 8.1.

If there are r initial runs and dummy runs are added as needed to form a perfect distribution, it can be shown that the number of passes over the elements for $t + 1$ tapes is approximately

$t + 1$	Number of Passes
3	1.042 lg r
4	0.704 lg r
5	0.598 lg r
6	0.551 lg r
7	0.528 lg r
8	0.516 lg r
9	0.509 lg r
10	0.505 lg r
20	0.500 lg r

Comparing this table with the similar one given for the simple-minded merging strategy, we see that the polyphase merge is far superior for ten or fewer tapes, but diminishing returns cause little to be gained by going beyond eight tapes.

Cascade Merge. For $t + 1 \geq 6$ there is an even better way to do the merging; it is most easily explained by an example. Suppose we have 190 initial runs distributed on six tapes as shown at the top of Figure 8.15. The *cascade merge* merges in the pattern shown in that figure. First, one initial run from each tape is merged, the resulting run being written on the empty tape. Second, runs from the four tapes still containing initial runs are merged onto the newly emptied tape. Third, runs from the three tapes still containing initial runs are merged onto the empty tape. Finally, runs from the two tapes still containing initial runs are merged onto the empty tape. This completes the first phase of the merge, the remaining phases being similar, as shown. The final phase merges one run from each tape onto the empty tape. It is surprising that this merge pattern is a reasonable choice, compared to the polyphase merge, because it does first a t-way merge, then a $(t-1)$-way merge, ..., and finally a two-way merge, while the polyphase merge always does t-way merges. Nevertheless, mathematical analysis shows that the number of passes over the elements is as follows:

$t + 1$	Number of Passes
3	1.042 lg r
4	0.764 lg r
5	0.622 lg r
6	0.536 lg r
7	0.479 lg r
8	0.438 lg r
9	0.407 lg r
10	0.383 lg r
20	0.275 lg r

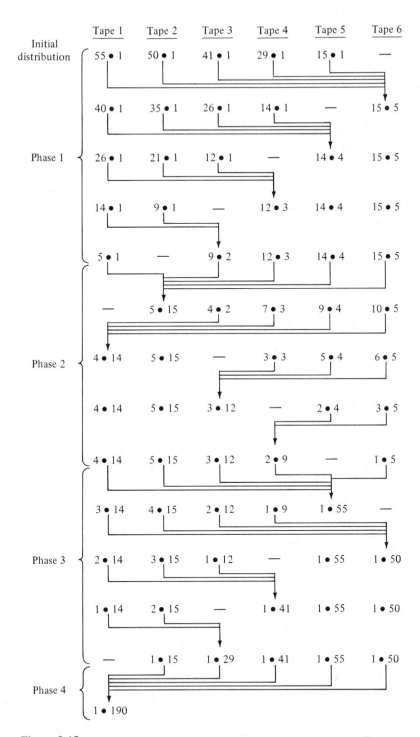

Figure 8.15
The cascade merge for 190 initial runs and six tapes

This is identical to the polyphase merge for $t + 1 = 3$ (Exercise 3), somewhat inferior to the polyphase merge for $t + 1 = 4$ or 5, and superior to the polyphase merge for $t + 1 \geq 6$.

An additional advantage of cascade merge is that less time is wasted waiting for tapes to rewind. A rewind of each tape can begin as soon as the last run is written to it. Since rewind is considerably faster than reading or writing (at least 3 to 10 times faster), the only waiting will be at the beginning of each phase for the one tape most recently written. In cascade merge, this most recent tape has the fewest runs. In Figure 8.15 the total rewind wait is for

$$9 \times 2 + 2 \times 9 + 1 \times 29 = 65$$

runs. In contrast the polyphase merge in Figure 8.13—which sorts fewer than half as many runs—would wait

$$1 \times 24 + 3 \times 13 + 7 \times 5 + 4 \times 9 + 2 \times 17 + 1 \times 31 = 199$$

runs. Thus cascade merge can be preferable even for $t + 1$ of 4 or 5.

The perfect distributions for the cascade merge are given in Table 8.2, derived by an analysis similar to the one given for the polyphase merge. The distribution of initial runs and dummy runs for the cascade merge is similar to Algorithm 8.12(a) and the merging itself is similar to Algorithm 8.12(b); we leave both of these algorithms to Exercise 4.

Buffering. In examining the various ways of utilizing $t + 1$ tapes for sorting, we have ignored an important aspect of the problem: how information is actually transferred from tape to memory and back again. Since the nature of tape sorting is

Phase	Tape 1	Tape 2	Tape 3		Tape $t-2$	Tape $t-1$	Tape t	Tape $t+1$
$k = 0$	1	0	0	$\cdots$	0	0	0	0
$k = 1$	1	1	1	$\cdots$	1	1	1	0
$k = 2$	t	$t-1$	$t-2$	$\cdots$	3	2	1	0
$k = 3$	$\dfrac{t(t+1)}{2}$	$\dfrac{t(t+1)}{2} - 1$	$\dfrac{t(t+1)}{2} - 3$	$\cdots$	$3t-3$	$2t-1$	t	0
$\vdots$								
k	$a_{k,1}$	$a_{k,2}$	$a_{k,3}$	$\cdots$	$a_{k,t-2}$	$a_{k,t-1}$	$a_{k,t}$	0
$k + 1$	$\displaystyle\sum_{i=1}^{t} a_{k,i}$	$\displaystyle\sum_{i=1}^{t-1} a_{k,i}$	$\displaystyle\sum_{i=1}^{t-2} a_{k,i}$	$\cdots$	$a_{k,1}+a_{k,2}+a_{k,3}$	$a_{k,1}+a_{k,2}$	$a_{k,1}$	0

Table 8.2
Perfect distributions for the cascade merge

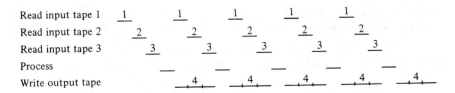

(a) Single buffering: Buffers 1, 2, 3, 4 for the three input tapes and the output tape, respectively, with the possible overlap of reading, processing, and writing.

```
Read input tape 1   1a       1b       1a       1b       1a
Read input tape 2       2a       2b       2a       2b       2a
Read input tape 3           3a       3b       3a       3b       3a
Process                         a        b        a        b        a
Write output tape                   4a      4b      4a      4b      4a
```

(b) Double buffering: Buffers 1a, 1b, 2a, 2b, 3a, 3b, 4a, 4b for the three input tapes and the output tape, respectively, with full overlap of reading, processing, and writing.

Figure 8.16
Time charts for single and double buffering with four tapes showing the overlap possible in both cases. The relevant buffer number is given above each time-line segment in which it is read or written.

reading-processing-writing, we can save a good deal of time by fully overlapping these operations, after some initialization. In order to accomplish this feat, we need to be able to initiate a read from the input tapes *before* we have completely processed the elements read previously. We can do this by *double buffering*, having two buffers for every tape. As we are processing elements from one of the input buffers, we fill the other; as we are putting elements into one of the output buffers, we write the other. A time-chart comparison of double buffering with single buffering is shown in Figure 8.16. Since the number of tapes is usually no more than ten, there is usually no problem in having enough internal memory to accommodate the extra buffers.

Figure 8.16 shows only one advantage of double buffering—the overlapping of not only read/write operations, but also the internal processing. Another significant improvement in Figure 8.16(b) compared to Figure 8.16(a) is that the writing operation need not stop as often. This is important, because one of the physical characteristics of tape is that once a read or write operation has finished and the tape is coasting to a stop, a good deal of time is saved if we can initiate the next read or write before the tape has slowed down too much. The time saved is that required by the tape to accelerate to its full reading or writing speed. When double buffering allows the writing to go on continuously, the savings in time can be much greater than Figure 8.16 suggests.

Exercises

1. What is the relationship between the Fibonacci numbers $F_0 = 0$, $F_1 = 1$, $F_{i+2} = F_{i+1} + F_i$ and the polyphase merge?

2. Let $p_k = \sum_{i=1}^{t} a_{k,i}$, where the $a_{k,i}$ are as defined in Table 8.1, so that the p_{k+t} are the numbers of runs in the perfect distribution on line k of Table 8.1.

    (a) Prove that the p_k satisfy the following recurrence relation:

    $$p_1 = p_2 = \cdots = p_t = 1,$$
    $$p_i = p_{i-1} + p_{i-2} + \cdots + p_{i-t}, \qquad i > t$$

★ (b) Determine the growth rate of p_i as a function of i. [*Answer*: $p_i \approx C\alpha^i$ for some constant C, where α is the dominant root of the equation $x^t - x^{t-1} - x^{t-2} - \cdots - x - 1 = 0$, $\alpha \approx 2 - 1/(2^t - 1)$.]

3. Why do both the polyphase and cascade merges require the same number of passes over the elements for $t + 1 = 3$?

4. Design algorithms comparable to Algorithms 8.12(a) and (b) for the cascade merge.

5. Investigate the advantages of the following compromise between the polyphase and cascade merges. Merge t tapes until one is empty, next merge $t - 1$ tapes (excluding the one just created), next merge $t - 2$ tapes, then $t - 3$, and so on, down to a $(t - r + 1)$-way merge. At that point, the cycle of t, $t - 1$, ..., $(t - r + 1)$-way merges is repeated. When $r = 1$, this is the polyphase merge, and when $r = t - 1$, this is the cascade merge.

6. To minimize tape start-stop time elements are written to tape in physical blocks of b elements each. Reading or writing a block needs only one start-stop time but demands a buffer big enough for b elements.

    (a) Suppose the memory available can hold M elements. Determine for a double buffered merge the maximum value of b in terms of M and $t + 1$.

    (b) Let b_{in} and b_{out} be the number of elements in each physical block read or written, respectively, during the generation of runs. Explain why b_{out} should be smaller than the value of b computed in part (a). Show how to compute the largest value of b_{out} that will give the smallest number of merge passes.

    (c) Describe how to adapt the merge phase to accommodate the difference between b in part (a) and b_{out} in part (b).

7. Suppose that the tapes can be read backward as well as forward. Show how this can be used to speed up the sorting process by doing mergings instead of rewinding the tapes. Be careful, because when merging runs while reading the tapes backward we get *descending* runs.

8. How should multireel tables of elements be sorted?

9. One way to describe a $t + 1$ tape merge pattern is by a t-way tree in which the leaves are initial runs and internal nodes represent merges. For example, the tree in Figure 8.17 represents the merge pattern corresponding to the polyphase merge of seventeen initial runs with $t + 1 = 4$ tapes shown in Figure 8.14. Each edge is labeled with the tape number on which the merged runs end up.

(a) What is the relationship between the external path length of such a tree and the merge?

(b) Draw the tree corresponding to the cascade merge of fifteen initial runs and $t + 1 = 6$ tapes.

(c) What trees correspond to $t + 1 = 3$ tapes for the polyphase and cascade merges?

(d) Where should dummy initial runs be placed in the tree to minimize sorting time? Why?

10. To use either the polyphase or cascade merging schemes in tape sorting, we need at least three tapes. Suppose that only two tapes are available: find a method for tape sorting. [*Hint*: Combine the ideas of bubble sort and replacement selection.]

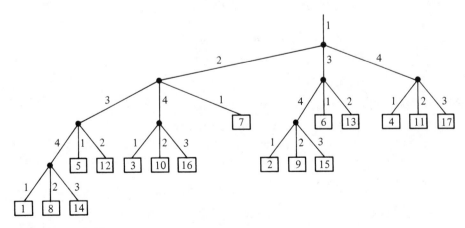

Figure 8.17
Exercise 9, the merge pattern tree corresponding to Figure 8.14

8.3.3 Disk Merge Techniques

As pointed out in Section 7.5, the key characteristic of disks (and drums) for external storage is direct access to anything on the disk, with a relatively high cost (in time) to initiate a transfer. When we do external sorting with tapes, after the generation of initial runs, all our energy goes into designing merge patterns so that runs are available as they are needed; this is necessitated by the sequential nature of access on tapes. The direct access to anything on a disk eliminates the need for such carefully arranged merge patterns—we can do any kind of merging we like! In particular, we can use the simple t-way merge because the copy phases, which are needed for tape sorting and which effectively double the input/output time, are not needed for disk merging because of the direct access.

With r initial runs and t-way merging, the number of passes over the elements with repeated t-way merging is $[\log_t r]$, so it is to our advantage to minimize r and to maximize t. In Section 8.3.1 we discussed the issue of minimizing r; the discussion there was independent of the external storage device, and it applies equally well to both tapes and disks. Maximizing t, however, is a new problem. For tape merging, t was limited by the number of tape units available; but for disk merging the only constraint on t is the amount of internal storage available for buffers. This is not typically a constraint for tape merging because, as pointed out in the previous section, the number of tapes is usually relatively small, with plenty of room even for the $2t + 2$ buffers needed for double buffering.

Suppose we have room for a total of M elements in internal memory for all the buffers. The more buffers we have, the smaller they are and the more often they must be filled or emptied. Each filling of an input buffer or emptying of an output buffer requires the initiation of a transfer with the disk, so the more buffers we have, the more time we spend filling and emptying them. If there are n elements and the buffers hold b elements each, each pass of the merge will require

$$2n/b \text{ read/write initiations,}$$

$$2n \text{ read/write transfers of elements}$$

If

$$I = \text{time to initiate an access,}$$

$$T = \text{time to transfer one element}$$

then the total time per pass is

$$\frac{2n}{b}I + 2nT$$

if there is no overlap of reading and writing (say, if we are sorting with only one disk—most disks do not permit simultaneous reading and writing) and

$$\frac{n}{b}I + nT$$

if there is full overlap of reading and writing. In either case, the total time *per element* over the entire sort is

$$C\left(\frac{I}{b} + T\right)\lceil\log_t r\rceil \tag{8.4}$$

for some constant C that also includes the internal processing time. The number of buffers would be $t + 1$ for single buffering and $2t + 2$ for double buffering, so that

$$b = \frac{M}{t + 1} \qquad \text{for single buffering,}$$

$$b = \frac{1}{2}\frac{M}{t + 1} \qquad \text{for double buffering}$$

Formula (8.4) is thus of the form

$$C\left(\frac{I}{M}k(t + 1) + T\right)\lceil\log_t r\rceil \tag{8.5}$$

where $k = 1$ for single buffering and $k = 2$ for double buffering.

We would like to choose t so as to minimize (8.5). This is difficult to do analytically, however, because of the ceiling function and the fact that t can assume only integer values. An example will illustrate, however, how the optimum t can be found by fairly simple calculations.

Suppose

$$M = 100 \text{ elements,}$$
$$I = 75 \text{ ms/initiation,}$$
$$T = 0.5 \text{ ms/element,}$$
$$r = 100 \text{ initial runs}$$

and we are doing single buffering. Without loss of generality, we can take $C = 1$ and compute the table on the following page:

t	Time per Element	Number of Passes
2	10.15	7
3	8.00	5
4	7.00	4
5	5.70	3
6	6.15	3
7	6.60	3
8	7.05	3
9	7.50	3
10	5.30	2
11	5.60	2
99	32.00	2
100	16.15	1

This minimum time occurs for $t = 10$-way merging. A similar table for $r = 60$ initial runs would have $t = 8$ as its optimum (Exercise 1), so we see that the number of initial runs has an effect on the optimum t.

Actually, we do not need to compute the entire table above to find the optimum t. Notice that the ceiling function in (8.4) causes five-way merging to be the most efficient way of finishing in three passes. There is no point in doing six-, seven-, eight-, or nine-way merging; they will be more costly than five-way merging, since the buffer size will be smaller, but the number of passes will be the same. Similarly, there is no point in considering eleven-, twelve-, . . . , or 99-way merging, since ten-way merging will require the same number of passes (only two), but with larger buffers. In general, for a fixed number of passes p, the most efficient t is the smallest one that requires exactly that many passes; that value is $t = \lceil r^{1/p} \rceil$ (why?). Of course, we will never require more passes than in two-way merging, $\lceil \lg r \rceil$. We can therefore find the optimum t by the following simple routine:

```
min := PlusInfinity;
for p := 1 to ceiling(lg(r)) do begin
        {compute smallest t using p passes}
        t := ceiling(exp(ln(r)/p));   {ceiling(r^{1/p})}
        cost := "value from formula (8.4)";
        if cost < min then begin
                min := cost;
                tOpt := t
        end
end
```

Since r will typically be at most a few thousand, the loop will be executed only about a dozen times, a trivial amount of time compared to what will be expended in the sorting itself.

Exercises

1. Compute the optimum t for $M = 1000$, $r = 60$, $I = 75$ ms, and $T = 0.5$ ms with single buffers.

2. Compute the optimum t for $M = 1000$, $r = 100$, $I = 75$ ms, and $T = 0.5$ ms with double buffering.

3. Suppose only a single disk is available for sorting. To prevent the irretrievable loss of data, it is wise to do a "read-back check" operation after writing. What is the effect of this on sorting time?

4. We have assumed that all buffers are the same size. Is there a way to reduce the number of disk initiations by using unequal buffer sizes?

8.4 REMARKS AND REFERENCES

Just about everything one might need to know about the sorting problems discussed in this chapter can be found in

> Knuth, D. E., *The Art of Computer Programming*, Vol. 3, *Sorting and Searching*. Reading, Mass.: Addison-Wesley Publishing Co., 1973.

This is an encyclopedic treatment of the entire subject. A lengthy bibliography of all the papers examined by Knuth in writing the section on sorting can be found in *Computing Reviews*, **13** (1972), 283–289. In addition, Section 5.5 of Knuth's book contains an excellent comparison of sorting methods and a short history of the subject of sorting.

A more complete treatment of quicksort and the variants of quicksort can be found in

> Sedgewick, R., "The Analysis of Quicksort Programs," *Acta Informatica* **7** (1977), 327–355.
>
> Sedgewick, R. "Implementing Quicksort Programs," *Comm. ACM* **21** (1978), 847–857.
>
> Sedgewick, R., "Quicksort with Equal Keys," *SIAM J. Comput.* **6** (1977), 240–267.

The linear time selection algorithm of Section 8.2.1 can be greatly improved. It is shown in

> Schönhage, A., M. S. Paterson, and N. Pippenger, "Finding the Median," *J. Comput. Sys. Sci.* **13** (1976), 184–199.

that the median of n elements can be found in $3n + O((n \log n)^{3/4})$ element comparisons; the kth largest can be found in a similar number of element comparisons.

Ohe, iam satis est, ohe, libelle,
Iam pervenimus usque ad umbilicos.
Tu procedere adhuc et ire quaeris,
Nec summa potes in schida teneri,
Sic tamquam tibi res peracta non sit,
Quae prima quoque pagina peracta est.
Iam lector queriturque deficitque,
Iam librarius hoc et ipse dicit
"Ohe, iam satis est, ohe, libelle."

Epigrams, IV, 89,   Martial

Appendix

Notation

Items with names marked (*) are not in standard Pascal.

Expression	Name	Description
i **div** j	integer division	the quotient from division of i by j
i **mod** j	modulus	the remainder from division of i by j
p **and** q	boolean AND	**true** when both p and q are **true**
p **or** q	boolean OR	**true** when at least one of p and q is **true**
p **xor** q	boolean XOR*	**true** when exactly one of p and q is **true**
not p	negation	**true** when p is not **true**

Table A.1
Operators used in text. i and j are integer expressions; p and q are boolean expressions.

Expression	Name	Description
$chr(i)$	character	ith standard character
$ord(c)$	ordinal position	index of c in the standard characters
$odd(i)$	odd	$abs\ (i\ \textbf{mod}\ 2) = 1$
$abs(x)$	absolute value	**if** $x < 0$ **then** $-x$ **else** x
$shift\_left(i,j)$	shift integer*	$i \times 2^j$ $(j < 0$ shifts to the right$)$
$sign(x)$	sign	**if** $x = 0$ **then** 0 **else** $x/abs(x)$
$trunc(x)$	truncate	$sign(x) \times i$, where $i \leq abs(x) \leq i + 1$
$floor(x)$	floor*	i such that $i \leq x < i + 1$; $\lfloor x \rfloor$
$ceiling(x)$	ceiling*	i such that $i - 1 < x \leq i$; $\lfloor x \rfloor$
$fraction(x)$	fractional part*	$x - floor(x)$
$power(x, i)$	raise to a power*	x^i
$sqrt(x)$	square root	the non-negative a such that $x = a^2$
$lg(x)$	base 2 logarithm*	a such that $x = 2^a$
$ln(x)$	natural logarithm	a such that $x = e^a$, $(e = 2.71828\ldots)$
$exp(x)$	exponential	e^x

Table A.2
Functions used in Pascal routines. x and a are expressions; i and j are integer expressions; and c is a character.

Expression	Name	Description
$\min(f,g)$	minimum	the smaller of f and g
$\max(f,g)$	maximum	the larger of f and g
$\min\limits_{\text{all } p(i)} f(i)$	minimum	The minimum value of $f(i)$ over all i for which $p(i)$ is true
$\max\limits_{1 \leq i \leq n} f(i)$	maximum	the largest value taken by $f(i)$ when i varies over the range $1 \leq i \leq n$
$\sum\limits_{i=1}^{n} f(i)$	summation	the sum of values of $f(i)$ when evaluated for each value of i in the range $1 \leq i \leq n$
$\prod\limits_{i=1}^{n} f(i)$	product	similar to Σ but takes the product instead of sum
$n!$	factorial	product of first n integers, $\prod\limits_{i=1}^{n} i$, $n \geq 1$; $0! = 1$
$\binom{n}{j}$	combinations	$\dfrac{n!}{j!(n-j)!}$; the number of combinations of n things taken j at a time
$\begin{cases} f, \text{ if } p \\ g, \text{ if } q \\ \cdots \\ h, \text{ otherwise} \end{cases}$	conditional	At most one of the boolean expressions is true. The value is: **if** p **then** f **else if** q **then** g $\ldots$ **else** h.
$|f|$	absolute value	$|f| = $ **if** $f < 0$ **then** $-f$ **else** f
$|S|$	set size	the number of elements in the set S
$f \approx g$	approximately	f is roughly equal to g
$f \ll g$	much less	f is very small compared to g
$f \gg g$	much greater	f is very large compared to g
$\log_b f$	logarithm	x such that $f = b^x$; $\log_b f = (\log_b c) \times \log_c f$
$\lg f, \log f, \ln f$	logarithms	logarithms to the base $b = 2$, 10, and e, resp.
e	2.718281828 . . .	base of the "natural logarithms"
$\infty, -\infty$	infinity	values larger and smaller than any others, resp.
$\lfloor f \rfloor$	floor	the largest integer not larger than f
$\lceil f \rceil$	ceiling	the smallest integer not less than f
F_i	Fibonacci series	$F_0 = 0, F_1 = 1, F_i = F_{i-1} + F_{i-2}$ for $i > 1$
H_n	harmonic series	$H_n = \sum\limits_{i=1}^{n} \dfrac{1}{i} \approx \ln n$
H	entropy	A measure of information content. For a set of probabilities p_i, the entropy is $H = -\Sigma_i p_i \lg p_i$. (p. 83)
$\Pr(p)$	probability	Probability that p is true. $\Pr(p \text{ and } q) = \Pr(p) \times \Pr(q)$. $\Pr(p \text{ or } q) = \Pr(p) + \Pr(q) - \Pr(p \text{ and } q)$.

Table A.3—Cont.

Expression	Name	Description
$A[l..h]$	subsequence	$A[l]$, $A[l+1]$, ..., $A[h]$ (p. 21)
ddd_{16}	hexadecimal	digit string ddd is an integer in base 16 (p. 42)
ddd_2	binary	digit string ddd is an integer is base 2 (p. 54)
$loc(v)$	location	the address where variable v is stored (p. 112)
ε	empty string	a string of length zero (p. 139)
$level(t)$	node level	Where t is a node in a tree: The level of the root node is zero; all other nodes have level one greater than their parent (p. 218).
$height(T)$	tree height	Where T is a tree: An empty tree has undefined height; the height of a nonempty tree is the largest level number for any of its nodes
$f(n) = O(g(n))$	"big-oh"	As n increases, $f(n)$ grows no faster than $g(n)$ (p. 309).
$f(n) = o(g(n))$	"little-oh"	As n increases, $f(n)$ grows more slowly than $g(n)$ (p. 309).

Table A.3

Mathematical Notation. In the examples, f, g, and h are expressions; i and n are integer variables. The ranges for $\sum$, Π, min and max can be specified in three ways: $\sum_{i=1}^{n}$, $\sum_{1 \leq i \leq n}$, $\sum_{all\ p(i)}$ where p is a predicate depending on i.

Index